For Samantha

Contents

Scent of a Woman (1992)

Carlito's Way (1993)

Two Bits (1995)

Heat (1995)

City Hall (1996)

Looking for Richard (1996)

Donnie Brasco (1997)

Devil's Advocate (1997)

The Insider (1999)

Any Given Sunday (1999)

Chinese Coffee (2000)

Insomnia (2002)

S1m0ne (2002)

People I Know (2002)

The Recruit (2003)

Gigli (2003)

Angels in America (2003)

The Merchant of Venice (2004)

Two for the Money (2005)

88 Minutes (2007)

Ocean's Thirteen (2007)

The early years of

Al Pacino

"My mom was a great influence on my life," Al Pacino recalled to TV host James Lipton during the legendary actor's appearance on the programme: *Inside the Actors Studio*.

The actor was born in East Harlem, New York on 25 April 1940 to Sicilian-American parents Salvatore and Rose Pacino. Alfredo James Pacino was an only child and was nicknamed "Sonny Boy" by his family after the 1928 Al Jolson song: "Sonny Boy". Pacino demonstrated an urge to perform early on in his life. Rose played Jolson records on their gramophone and young Pacino danced along while mimicking the words. At the age of two however, the actor's life was set to change forever. His father was drafted into the army during World War II and upon his return Salvatore decided he'd had enough of married life. He promptly left Rose and Alfredo for sunny California.

Faced with the prospect of being a single, working parent Rose moved in with her parents: James and Kate Gerardi. Consequently, she and her infant son came to live in the South Bronx area of New York City. Pacino's maternal grandparents had been born in Sicily, (specifically the town of Corleone) and immigrated to the United States of America in the early 1900s.

James and Kate became as influential in young Alfredo's life as his mother was. The relationship between Alfredo and James blossomed, as each day the grandfather regaled his grandson with tales of life in Corleone and also the adventures of immigrating to America. James was filling the void in Pacino's life, acting as a father. His mother, while not present during the day, would ensure she was always home in the evenings with little Alfredo. On many occasions, she took him to the movies after finishing work as an usherette at the Dover Theatre. There, they watched the latest offerings from Hollywood together. They were both fans of James Dean.

"My mother loved him, I loved him," Pacino has said.

At the tender age of five his mother took him to see *The Lost Weekend* starring Ray Milland. Too young to understand the harrowing storyline of a man trying to hide his alcoholism from those around him, Pacino latched on to Milland's stumbling and desperate performance and re-enacted it in front of his family and their friends. Rose, a big reader and lover of the arts, encouraged her son to act out scenes from the films they had been to see. It became a vehicle through which Pacino could express himself, as he had always been a quiet and shy child. When friends of the family came round to the Gerardi household they would often hear little Alfredo in another room mumbling to himself. Kate said to the visitors: "Al likes to talk to himself. He's doing OK." In an interview with Guy Flatley of *The Los Angeles Times* during 1973, Pacino said: "I was really all alone those first seven years of my life. In fact, I used to go steady with a broom, or maybe it was a mop."

To strangers, he was Rose's shy boy who wouldn't say a solitary word. To those who got to know him, he was a joker and an exhibitionist. One time he told his mother that he would like to join the circus and become a clown. Instead, Rose sent him to Herman Ridder Junior School in the Bronx. This was a daunting change for this somewhat introverted child and meant that he was allowed out of the house without adult supervision – on the understanding that he returned straight home each night after classes had finished. For a shy and withdrawn kid like Pacino, it was a difficult place to make friends. Instead, he had to contend with the bullies in the playground. To escape the constant, unwanted attention from both the boys and girls, he would make up stories about his life and where he was from. One time he told those listening he was originally from Texas or that he had a large number of man-eating dogs at home. It wasn't long before he got a reputation as someone who liked to tell stories and was dubbed: "The Actor."

Rose would constantly be called to school because of some mischief her son had taken part in, including ripping open his bottom lip on some barbed wire fencing and putting the teacher's glasses on her seat so she sat on them. His pranks started to earn him some popularity in school but these were not the types of buddies his family would approve of. They led him away from studying and into school rebellion. They also introduced him to cigarettes and alcohol. This disobedience eventually led to Pacino being reassigned to a class for emotionally disturbed children. He lasted two days with his new classmates before seeing the error of his ways and promising to behave so that he could return to his main class.

Struggling academically, a love of baseball was an outlet for the young Pacino. After squashing the idea of becoming a clown in the circus years earlier, he aspired to become a professional baseball player. While playing at school, Pacino not only wanted to win but also revelled in showing off to his teammates. "If I made a catch at third base, I'd do a double somersault and sprawl out on the ground," Pacino recalled when asked about his time playing. However, when the scouts for his beloved New York Yankees didn't knock down his door he started to wonder what his vocation in life should be.

At the age of thirteen Pacino appeared in the school's play, it was an adaptation of Craig Rice's mystery comedy *Home Sweet Homicide*. One scene called for his character to be sick and, showing the first signs of his love for method acting, Pacino became physically and emotionally nauseous during the production. Afterwards a teacher told Rose: "He's the next Brando."

To a packed school auditorium, he read passages from the bible with such enthusiasm that months later a letter was sent to Rose from drama teacher Blanche Rothstein that suggested his talents lay in acting. Sensing light at the end of the tunnel for a rudderless son, Rose encouraged him with his acting all through High School. Pacino starred in a school production of *The King And I* which required him to sing. His showmanship was clear for all to see; however, his school work was suffering and he dropped out of many classes. Eventually the only two classes Pacino could be found in were Drama and English.

When it came time to leave Herman Ridder Junior High School, Pacino decided he wanted to continue his acting studies but because of his low grades the only place that would accept him was The High School of Performing Arts. This meant leaving the familiar neighbourhood of the Bronx and venturing into New York City. A daunting thought for a teenage Pacino. Eventually though, he became accustomed to the hustle and bustle of the city. Occasionally, Rose saved enough money to take her son to see a couple of plays. A fifteen year-old Pacino, and his mother, went to see a travelling theatre production of Anton Chekhov's play *The Seagull* in a disused, vaudeville theatre called the Elsmere Theatre in the Bronx. It seated about three thousand people but that night only twenty seats were filled. "They probably weren't any good," Pacino later commented. "But I had never seen anything like it in my life. My life changed that day." Pacino was brought back down to Earth the next day when he walked into a coffee shop near The High School of Performing Arts and was served by one of the leads from the play. Pacino bumbled his way through complimenting the actor-cum-barista.

Pacino wanted to learn the craft of acting but struggled while at The High School of Performing Arts. There they taught the Stanislavski Method, a form of acting developed by Russian theatre practitioner Konstantin Stanislavski. The method encouraged actors to greater understand the art by going deeper than physical and vocal training. Actors were expected to feel out the character. This wasn't to Pacino's liking, he simply wanted to act; he didn't want to spend hours, days and weeks discovering who his character was. He started to grow disillusioned with the school and that was compounded by him taking Spanish classes only to realise the teacher taught it in Spanish "You've gotta be kidding?" he responded.

Aged sixteen, Pacino dropped out of the school. Partly because he had lost his enthusiasm but also because his mother had become seriously ill and he needed to supplement the family income. Rose had struggled with her health for a few years, at times coming home from work and going straight to her bedroom until the next morning. She had also taken against her son becoming an actor. Undiagnosed at the time, Rose struggled with depression and anaemia. She was in and out of hospital several times and then found she could work no longer. Never having been in the working world before, Pacino found jobs easy to get but hard to keep. He was a messenger, a toilet attendant, a supermarket cashier, a shoe-shiner, a furniture remover, a fruit picker and a newsboy all in quick succession. He became frustrated with the situation at home with his mother and opted to move out and live with a young woman he had met. He continued to send money home each month but would not be there to watch his mother gradually decline.

The desire to act still burned brightly in Pacino and he auditioned for a place at the Actors Studio. He was rejected but it didn't deter him. In between his many different jobs he continued to audition for roles. Work in the acting world continued to elude Pacino and he ended up with a job at *Company Magazine*, a monthly Jewish magazine in New York City. There, he would leap over desks to get to his own cubicle and distribute the post with boundless energy. With a steady pay cheque from *Company* coming in, Pacino managed to save enough money to attend the Herbert Berghof Studio which offered professional training in the performing arts. Here he met one of the great influences on his acting life: Charlie Laughton. This acting teacher saw a spark in Pacino and became his mentor both in and outside of the studio. They spent hours wandering the streets talking about acting and writing, and how it affected the craft of acting. Pacino became so obsessed with absorbing all of the knowledge Laughton was offering him that his job at *Commentary Magazine* fell by the way side. Without a steady income, Pacino was kicked out of his apartment and started to live rough on the streets. Occasionally he would crash at friend's house or sneak into the studio and sleep on the stage. It didn't matter where he slept just as long as he could continue his unofficial father/son relationship with Laughton.

Pacino's professional life was on the up but his personal life was delivered a devastating blow when his mother died of a heart attack in 1962. In the years since he moved out of the family home, Pacino had a very rocky relationship with his mother. She did not approve of his continued desire to be an actor and he took against her constant downbeat attitude towards him. Pacino fell apart when she died and the rest of the family were similarly traumatised by her death. Rose had struggled with depression for many years and a fatal heart attack at forty-three years old meant she would never get to see her "Sonny Boy" fulfil his acting ambition. Another blow struck the following year when Pacino's grandfather suddenly died. Devastated by the death of his long-time father figure, Pacino turned to Laughton for help during those dark times.

The "Eureka!" moment for Pacino came when he was cast in a production of August Strindberg's tragicomedy *Creditors* which was co-directed by Frank Bachimarso and Charlie Laughton. "It was a revelation to me," Pacino commented years later. "I could express myself in the play to such a point I couldn't do it in life." For the next four years Pacino would, under Laughton's tutelage, continue to study the craft of acting and appear in a couple of plays located in basements. Eventually, he was given another shot at auditioning for enrolment in the Actors Studio. As luck would have it on the day of Pacino's audition he got to perform in two scenes, as opposed to the standard one piece, that demanded two very different acting approaches. The Actors Studio accepted him, and he felt he was lucky to appear in two pieces that day because they would not have accepted him based on just the first performance. "It was an identity moment," said Pacino about being accepted.

After four years working with Laughton and living hand-to-mouth it was the moment Pacino had been dreaming of. From the outset, Pacino was nervous about attending the Actors Studio and at one point called Laughton to say he was done with it all. Laughton talked him down and told him to keep going. This was a smart move by his friend and surrogate father because not long after Pacino met Lee Strasberg, a teacher and one of the artistic directors of the studio. He would also become another father-like figure to Pacino. Strasberg had invented his own acting method, named after himself, that had been developed out of Stanislavsky's "system" method. The Strasberg Method encouraged actors to magnify and intensify their connection to the material by creating their characters' emotional experiences in their own lives. Pacino found much solace in Strasberg as a mentor and friend. Outside of classes they sat and listened to classical music, they also talked long into the night about acting and the world outside. During one workshop at the Actors Studio Pacino hadn't learnt his lines and thought he could blag his way through it. Strasberg put him right with one piece of advice: "Darling! Learn your lines!"

With his developed sense of confidence following his work with Laughton and Strasberg, Pacino ventured to Waterford, Connecticut to be part of a production of Israel Horovitz's one-act play: *The Indian Wants the Bronx*. Pacino was cast as Murph: one of the two punks who attacked the lead character, Gupta, as he arrives in New York City for the first time. A young actor called John Cazale played the other punk, Joey. The two struck up a close-knit friendship that would eventually see them on-screen together in the movies. Using his education at the Actor's Studio and the wisdom Strasberg bestowed on Pacino to "find the character", Pacino collaborated with Horovitz to enhance his performance before work on the text even began. The pair spent days walking the streets. They followed interesting-looking people, observing their movement and clothing and then translated that back into the performance of Murph.

After the run, Pacino returned to New York and the Actors Studio. During 1966, he was part of a New Theater Workshop production of John Wolfson's *The Peace Creeps*. The following year he appeared on stage in Boston, Massachusetts in two different productions: *Awake and Sing* by Clifford Odets and *America Hurrah* by Jean-Claude Van Itallie. While starring in *America Hurrah* Pacino became enamoured with his co-star Jill Clayburgh and they began a relationship that, upon their return to New York, would see the couple move in together. 1968 became a defining year for Pacino. He started the year back on stage at the Astor Place Theater in New York with another run of *The Indian Wants the Bronx*. Cazale also returned and it ran for over two hundred performances and earned Pacino an Obie Award (the off-Broadway equivalent of a Tony Award) for Best Actor. Cazale also picked up Best Supporting Actor and Horovitz won Best New Play.

During the production's run off-Broadway, the actor Faye Dunaway attended one of the performances and was so struck with the performance by Pacino that she recommended her manager Martin Bregman go see the play. Bregman was blown away by Pacino and offered to support him in any of his future projects. The young actor didn't exactly know what Bregman meant by supporting him. It was only days later in Bregman's office that Pacino understood what he meant. Bregman would act as a mediator between Pacino and the film studios. He would also be his financial advisor, and offer career advice. "Al still had no idea what I was going to do for him" recalled Bregman. In November an episode of the cop TV show *N.Y.P.D.* aired that featured Pacino and his real-life girlfriend Clayburgh. They played a couple and Pacino's character was suspected of being in the Ku Klux Klan, and bombing a church in the South. It was Pacino's on-screen debut.

The last year of the Sixties had its highs and lows for Pacino. He graduated to a Broadway stage in a production of Don Petersen's racially-charged drama *Does a Tiger Wear a Necktie?* It ran for forty-eight performances at the Belasco Theatre and at the Tony Awards ceremony Pacino won the Best Dramatic Actor in a Supporting Role for his performance as the psychotic junkie Bickham. Juxtaposing with that was a short-lived and poorly-received eight run performance of Heathcote Williams' play *The Local Stigmatic* at the end of the year.

By the early 1970s Pacino had finished at the Actors Studio, but continued to stay friends with Strasberg, and still concentrated on his stage acting, appearing in a Broadway revival of Tennessee Williams' *Camino Real?* at the Vivian Beaumont Theater inside the Lincoln Center, New York. This ensemble piece, in which Jessica Tandy also appeared, saw Pacino bellow his way through his scenes, stealing the thunder from the other actors. Bregman had started to receive the occasional call from film studios who wanted Pacino to star in their productions. Both the unofficial manager and the actor batted them all away except one.

Me, Natalie was a coming of age melodrama starring Patty Duke. Pacino was on screen for less than a minute. In that time his character, Tony grabs Natalie, Duke's character, and forces her to dance. He follows that up with the line: "You have a nice body, you know that?" and "Do you put out?" When Natalie responds in the negative, Tony replies "I don't know what I'm doing talking to you. Somebody like you should be asking me." Then he leaves her and grabs the next girl to dance with. It's a despicable, bold performance from a first-time film actor.

Another first for Pacino was directing. Travelling to Boston again he called the shots on Israel Horovitz's play *Rats* at the Charles Playhouse during March 1970 under the watchful eye of David Wheeler's Theatre

Company. Bregman became Pacino's official manager and it seemed wise for him to sign to a talent agency if he wanted to progress in feature films. He signed with Creative Management Associates who also represented, among others, James Coburn, Jackie Gleason and Judy Garland.

Movie offers soon started to fly in for Pacino and all offers were knocked back including roles in titles such as *Tell Me That You Love Me*, *Catch 22* and *Junie Moon*. He also turned down a lucrative Broadway production of *Zorba The Greek*. Laughton and Strasberg were on-hand if and when Pacino needed them, which proved to be most of the time. Unsure of his next move Pacino turned to Bregman for advice. His manager recommended he sign on to a small independent movie that was to be set in his old neighbourhood of the Bronx. A movie in which he would play out his first leading on-screen role as an actor.

The Panic in
Needle Park

Cast: Al Pacino (Bobby), Kitty Winn (Helen), Alan Vint (Hotch), Richard Bright (Hank), Kiel Martin (Chico), Michael McClanathan (Sonny), Warren Finney (Sammy), Marcia Jean Kurtz (Marcie), Raul Julia (Marco), Joe Stantos (DiBono). **Director:** Jerry Schatzberg.

Synopsis: Heroin addict Bobby introduces his clean cut girlfriend Helen to a new strung-out world filled with young derelicts who steal, love, cheat, befriend and betray.

Few actors make the jump from bit part to big break but that's exactly what happened to Al Pacino when he landed his first ever leading role in *The Panic in Needle Park*, Jerry Schatzberg's adaptation of the novel by James Mills. This haunting depiction of 70s drug-culture was released on 13 July 1971 in the U.S., and thereafter had a gradual release in other territories.

The Needle Park in question was located in Manhattan, between Broadway and Amsterdam Avenue. During the 1960s and 70s, it was an infamous drug-taking den. Growing up in the Bronx, Pacino would have been aware of the sleazier parts of New York and Sherman Square, the official name given to Needle Park, which was just 10 miles away from his childhood home. Where some of Pacino's acquaintances even died of heroin overdoses. In short, his first starring role was set in a world he was trying to escape.

It had taken several attempts to lure Pacino into making a full movie. He explained to author Lawrence Grobel: "I turned down eleven films before I made my first one. I knew it was time for me to get into movies. I didn't know what it would be. When *The Panic*...came along Marty Bregman [movie producer/personal manager] pushed and helped get it together." Bregman pitched *Panic* to the studio as Romeo and Juliet on junk.

Director Jerry Schatzberg had seen Pacino in the 1968 stage production of *Indian Wants the Bronx* at the Astor Place Theatre in New York. Based on that performance, he decided if he did venture into moviemaking, he wanted to work with Pacino. Schatzberg had previously turned *Panic* down but went back and re-read the script when he heard Pacino was interested in the project. Twentieth Century Fox told Schatzberg that Pacino was too young for the leading role. They didn't want Kitty Winn either; they were pushing for Mia Farrow. After a recommendation by producer Dominick Dunne, Schatzberg went to see Winn in a play and recognised in her the innocence and vulnerability required for the role of Helen. Eventually Fox relented and Schatzberg had his two lead actors.

Before the cameras started rolling, the trio (Pacino, Winn and Schatzberg) spent several weeks frequenting junkie hang-outs and attending seminars to gain insight into the characters Pacino and Winn were to play. At one point, a group of drug users thought Pacino and Winn were undercover police officers and set upon them. The pair made a swift exit. Filming on this picture lasted ten weeks in and around Manhattan using the filming technique called Cinema Verite, the technical term for using hand-held cameras on real locations, adding a raw, gritty edge to the situations and dialogue.

For the majority of the runtime, the movie is shown from Helen's point of view. Initially, Helen is a sweet, shy girl from the Midwest who has travelled to New York to experience bigger and better things. Her slide into the seedy underworld of drugs and prostitution, however, doesn't take long. This film is a harrowing tale of the unforgiving nature of the big city. How it can swallow you up without a care. The all-too-real battle for Helen is to stay strong; to resist temptation. Time and again however, she loses her mind, and body, to drug abuse. Her other tragic flaw is her attachment to Bobby. He is a drug unto himself to Helen, betraying further her addictive personality.

While Pacino went on to bigger and better movies, it's actually Kitty Winn who steals *Panic*. It's a demanding role, especially during the drug-induced scenes. Slumped and eyes rolled, Winn portrays Kitty as a woman who wants excitement and one who can only ultimately achieve this by shooting up. It's a bleak performance for any actor, and one that might traditionally be given to a man, but *Panic* shows addiction can bite either sex just as hard. Pacino's Bobby, while addicted to drugs, is functional without. He seems to operate two different lives through the film: the happy, upbeat twenty-something who enjoys playing stickball, and the drug fiend. The latter takes over increasingly as the film progresses. When not on drugs, his fast, electric patter is non-stop He is constantly on the move, looking for the next big rush like a firecracker waiting to explode. A particularly nasty scene in the movie sees Bobby learn that Helen has been selling her body to pay for their drugs. Pacino's now well-established tick of turning up the volume and punching out his dialogue is first seen here as he pummels Winn with blow upon blow. The scene ends with her retreating into the bathroom and locking the door as Pacino stands on the other side threatening to break in. Looking back on that scene now, it's clear this is where Pacino developed the bellowing attitude that would almost become his signature move.

Director Jerry Schatzberg opted to film the movie in a raw, almost docudrama, style. There is no music in this film, which adds to the realism. Moreover, an early scene depicts an unidentified man shooting up. The camera lingers long and hard on the method. In the background Bobby and Helen are caught up in their love for one another but the drug-taking is the focus of this scene. The camera never veers away from the injection; the slow insertion of the needle; the plunge of the solution into the body; the withdrawal, followed by a shuddering as the drugs take effect. Footage like this had never been so graphic in a movie before. Pacino noticed there were real-life dealers all around while filming one particular scene in which his character had to deal drugs on a street corner. He said in an interview with Lawrence Grobel "I looked at him, and he looked at me, and I got real confused." Chances are he is referring to the scene where Bobby tries to score drugs in front of the Museum of Natural History; a building located across from Central Park, which was itself a notorious crime den during the 1970s.

The Panic in Needle Park showcased the city within a city that New York had become. Movies such as *Manhattan*, *All That Jazz* and *Saturday Night*

Fever have glamorised the 70s era in New York. Films such as these portray the 70s as the disco culture decade, when drug-taking in places like The Loft, Paradise Garage and celeb nightclub Studio 54 was an accepted pastime. Nobody spoke about the dangers of getting hooked on heroin, cocaine or any other chic, fashionable drug.

The film's finale is open-ended, which is not unusual but does make the finish just as dark and disturbing as the rest of the runtime. Helen, post-abortion, is greeted by Bobby, fresh out of prison. He says two, simple words: "Come on," and they walk off together into an ambiguous future. Fans have speculated for years about whether the pair ever got clean. During the course of the film however, we never see them hit rock bottom; there is no awakening. Schatzberg has commented that: "I don't know what will happen to those two characters, whether they are going to go back to drugs or find a life." From the tone of the movie, one could assume they are set to revert to their old lives once again. That their addiction will become a life-long cycle.

The Panic in Needle Park was rated "R" in the U.S. upon release and Twentieth Century Fox took out newspaper adverts that played up the love and drama. When moviegoers went to see the film however, they witnessed something altogether very different. Consequently, Fox had to run another set of ads that explained: "If you see it now, it will sear your senses forever. And that's the truth." The movie was banned in the UK for three years due to its intentional depiction of drug use. Germany gave it the dreaded "X" certificate again because of its portrayal of drug addiction and violence.

Panic received mixed reviews. *The National Observer* said it was: "almost physically painful to watch." Pauline Kael described it as: "worthy, but a drag...it feels undramatic." *Saturday Review* magazine called it "A masterful accomplishment." Glossy homoerotic magazine *After Dark* exclaimed: "This is a film of horror and of pity and of love. It will knock you down without ever picking you back up." Many critics didn't like that a fashion photographer (Schatzberg) and a pair of literary novelists (Joan Didion and John Gregory Dunne) were responsible for such a frank piece of work. In a 2009 interview with IFC.com, Didion reflected on her work on the movie: "When we were shooting, I was overcome with what I had failed to do. Actually, when I saw it [again], I was struck by how much we *did* do." When asked what drew her to the project, she said: "The love story. Plain and simple. It was an interesting world that we hadn't seen on the screen in exactly that way, so I just felt as if it could work. We didn't really know about that life, so we did some research. We stayed at the Alamac Hotel for two or three weeks."

The Panic in Needle Park is a sobering romance film without a happy ending. Schatzberg tries to create compassion for the characters but ultimately they come across as unsympathetic losers who are the architects of their own downfall. The stark realism of the movie was too much for audiences at the time. With modern-day movies now keen to capture the true depths of drug abuse however, *The Panic in Needle Park* should be seen as a notable forerunner exploring the grim consequences for those who partake in substance abuse.

Kitty Winn went onto win Best Actress at the 1971 Cannes Film Festival for her portrayal of Helen. This said, she only made four more films after *Panic*, seemingly returning to her first love of stage work. Pacino however, had left his stage career behind and while he might not have been singled out for praise in his role as Bobby, something big just around the corner was about to announce him to the world.

Director Jerry Schatzberg on *The Panic in Needle Park*

You were an already established photographer, so why the jump into making films?

My first film was *Puzzle of a Downfall Child*. I had the story I wanted to tell about a model, about many models. One of my favourite models experienced this. Which is: when you get to a certain age or you've been used a certain amount all of a sudden the establishment just throws you away and you might only be twenty-five or thirty-five. You're still very young. In today's world they start at fifteen and by the time they are twenty they've had a career. They've been treated to first class everywhere in the world and all of a sudden they have to become a secretary somewhere. In those days the models were older and my model had had a couple of children and she was married and she did have financial problems because they live very high.

The story really affected me and I tried to think how I could do it. I thought I could do a photo-journalistic story in stills, but it just didn't work. Then I went to London, a couple of producers called me from Hollywood and asked me if I would be a technical advisor on a TV special they were doing called *The World's Most Beautiful Women*, and it took me about three or four seconds to say yes. When they came to New York I asked them who was directing it and they said they don't have a director yet and I said I had been fooling around with the film, would you look at it and see if it's possible? And they did and they showed it to the network and everybody said yes. So now I was the director.

When I went there [London] the first subject was Lady Antonio Fraser. I really liked doing it, it was really an exciting thing. I did that one segment and we were waiting for Queen Sirikit of Thailand to come. This was not just physical beauty but somebody who had a bit more brains and heart. My arrangement with them was if I had to go [back] to New York, I would [in order] to do my job and then come back again [to London].

I had to go back to New York and as luck would have it, the Queen [Sirikit] came in two days after I left and I couldn't come back right away, so the two producers did the next interview and they were a couple of guys who were always fighting with one another all the time, and again they started fighting and they confiscated one segment, the one that I shot and the one they shot, and they wouldn't give it to each other and the network cancelled them out. When I was flying back [to New York], I realised how much I liked that and that would be the best way to do my story and when I got back I talked to some friends of mine and they told me about different writers, and one of them had a friend that was a Frenchman who had written, in the 1940s. He did Gérard Phillippe's first film [*Les petites du quai aux fleurs*] and it was a period that was sort of dark cinema and mine was pretty dark I thought. So I hired him to do a screenplay for me. He didn't do a bad screenplay but he was so difficult to work with and he felt that a first-time director couldn't give him instructions or couldn't ask for rewrites. I felt it wasn't going to work so I stopped there and then went looking for a new writer.

By that time I had become friendly with Faye Dunaway and she became part of the project. I shot the film. Put it together. The lab had scratched the last six minutes of my negative and I was very upset and at that time my agency was looking for a director for *The Panic in Needle Park* because they represented the writers also. My agency said "Read this" and I read it and I turned it down because I was really upset about my situation. I went up to my manager's office and he said: "You know there is a good script out there" I said "What's It called?" and he said "*Panic in Needle Park*." I said: "I think I turned that down." He said: "I think it's a good script," and by now he was managing Pacino, so he said "Al is interested" and I had seen Al on stage about four years before I even thought about doing a film.

Marty [Bregman] was my manager then and I said: "If I ever do a film that's the guy I'd want to work with," and now here I was. So I went back and re-read the script thinking of Al as the character and I thought it would be great. I went back to the producers and apologised and told them how foolish I was and they probably agreed with me. We all made it work and we did *The Panic in Needle Park*.

You mentioned you saw Pacino on stage. What was it that you saw in him on stage that made you think: 'that's the guy I want in my movie?'

I was sitting in the audience and I couldn't turn away from him. He was so dynamic. Somebody exposing themselves so readily on stage was fascinating and I just thought he was a fantastic actor. He was just really dynamic.

When he was on set for the first time did you see nerves? Or was he as you saw him on stage?

On stage he wasn't nervous at all. He knew what he was doing. He had already won a couple of Obie Awards for theatre, he hadn't done any films yet. He was energetic. He knew what he was doing. He would knock you off your seat at times. It was just really exciting.

Watching the film, it's fair to say Kitty Winn steals the movie slightly. What directions did you give to her? Especially the scenes where she is shooting up and getting high.

We had the advantage of hanging out together – Kitty, Al and I. We hung out for about a month and half before we ever started rehearsals. Just going to places where drug addicts hung out. We went to hospital seminars, just sat in as part of the seminar. We did a lot of research at the time. I had some friends that were junkies, so I was able to contribute. I think Al knew people that were. Kitty didn't and then after the first couple of weeks of shooting I felt we had a problem because she wasn't opening up. I spoke to Dominick Dunne, the producer, and said: "maybe we've got a problem. We should think, since we are in the early stages, of replacing her." He was upset. I was upset and I said: "Listen let me talk to her." I called Kitty and I told her I just didn't think she.....she made every first choice rather than going deeper into the character and find the character, and using some of the stuff we researched. She was very upset and she cried. But she, by herself, went out to the places we used to go and she started researching more and it started to come to fruition.

You filmed in and around the Bronx, where you and Pacino are from. Do you think that helped you create a more authentic atmosphere in the movie?

That always has something to do with it. It's familiar to both of us in a way because you never forget your roots. Al and Kitty are both professionals. They know what they are doing. Kitty came from a repertoire company in San Francisco and she was well into it. Of course Al was on stage. This was a job and you always set it up. We had lots of discussions and it was easy to talk to both of them. I had a lot of former junkies on the set. I tried to make sure there weren't any users on the set and I didn't find out until after the film that there was one, but it didn't interfere with what we did. The former junkies were very helpful in telling us different things and the first one [in the film] that shoots up was a former junkie and he knows what it's like to shoot up, so he came off beautifully in what he did. In the factory when they are mixing the heroin we had two or three people that had actually worked in those factories. So we were able to make it really authentic, or as authentic as we could.

The movie is very raw in its depiction of drug use and I don't think that had been seen on screen before. Was it a conscious decision on your part to show all of it?

Yes. Yes. I felt unless you really knew their world you couldn't feel their world and I said: 'I do want to have them shooting up in the film.' I had never seen anybody really shoot up, they always turn away. I wanted people to cringe at it. I thought I was doing a film that would really deter people. I had some surprises along the way because we had a seminar once where students from the inner city came in and I was talking as if I had done a film that would stop everybody from doing drugs and one of the teachers got up and said: "You may think that but for these kids, what they saw in that film was a step up." It was a shock to me, but it was true.

When it comes to the finale of the film how do you view it? Do Bobby and Helen break their cycle and get clean? Or are they doomed to repeat?

I don't want to say how I see it. I like that everybody take[s] their own experience with that. Most of my films end like that. I think it's up to the individual. I think the audience is responsible for the film as much as anybody else. I don't want to tell them how to think completely because we don't know. My first film, I don't know if she is going to straighten herself out and get a life for herself. In the second one I don't know they are going to straighten out. Although I have known a lot of junkies that have and they go on and have a life. I think it's up to the audience. I, personally, am an optimist. I always leave a little optimism.

I had this funny situation with Harold Pinter, because he did one of my films [*Reunion*], we were in Germany looking at locations and he doesn't like to talk about work as much as he likes to talk about politics. We got into a conversation at dinner and he was talking about politics and was being very pessimistic about the world and I said: "I like to be a little optimistic. I don't want to say everything is going to turn out well." He said "Well I joined this organisation and that organisation." I said to him: "Harold, that's exactly why I'm a little optimistic." We laughed about it. I am a little optimist. So I like to think something good is going to happen. I know that it could go completely the other way.

There is no music in the film. What was the thinking behind that creative choice?

We had a score written. Every time I put music in it, it took it away from the reality that I was trying to get. Cue after cue I just took it out. Nobody complained. I feel the noise of the streets was enough for that. I'm not sorry we didn't have music. We tried but it just didn't seem to work in there. We could have gone other ways. I couldn't think of any music in there.

I'm not sure if you know this, the film was actually banned in Great Britain upon release. It was released three years later, cut. Then, when it was released on VHS it was cut by fifty seven seconds. It was finally released uncut in 2002. What is your reaction to hearing that your work has been cut?

I knew that it had been banned at first. I didn't know about the cutting. I go through my work pretty thoroughly so I don't like to see somebody else cut it. I would appreciate if they had talked to me about it. But I know that we are in a business and I know they are not really going to cater to some photographer's ego. I get very upset if people crop my pictures. But after I see it maybe I can agree with it. I don't know what they cut, if they cut the needles. If they did that's too bad. I did know that it was banned at first. *Man with the Golden Arm*, which never showed anything really, but talked about heroin addiction was banned when it first came out.

How would you describe *The Panic in Needle Park* in just a few words?

I thought it was a realistic drug adaption of, maybe, *Romeo & Juliet*. It's a love story that happens in all walks of life. I really like to get into some relationships with most of my films and I think that's what we all relate to. I'm not into special effects and that kind of film. I just think it's a realistic depiction of the drug world. Not taking into account that maybe it's a step up for some people, but for the people I showed that's what you could see. I remember walking the streets and looking in an alley way and seeing people shooting up. It was very much a thing then.

The Godfather

Cast: Marlon Brando (Don Vito Corleone), Al Pacino (Michael Corleone), James Caan (Sonny Corleone), Robert Duvall (Tom Hagen), Diane Keaton (Kay Adams), Talia Shire (Connie Corleone), John Cazale (Fredo Corleone), Richard S. Castellano (Clemenza), Richard Conte (Barzini), Al Lettieri (Sollozzo). **Director:** Francis Ford Coppola.

Synopsis: Ageing "Don" Vito Corleone is the head of one of New York's five families. After an assassination attempt on the Don goes wrong, his youngest son Michael reluctantly steps up to assume control of the family and to seek revenge on those who have gone against the family.

Mario Puzo's novel *The Godfather*, a look at the inner workings of a high-profile crime family, was released on 10 March 1969. It went on to sell 350,000 copies before the year was out. After two unprofitable novels, Puzo set out to write a book that would bring him the wealth he craved. He freely admitted *The Godfather* wasn't well-written. When talk show host Larry King asked Mario about the book, Puzo said: "If I'd have known so many people were going to read it, I'd have written it better." Within the first two years of printing, *The Godfather* had sold one million copies in hardback and eight million in paperback. Puzo had found his money-maker.

The option for the movie rights was secured long before the novel had even been published. Paramount Pictures were alerted to the novel in 1967 when a literary scout contacted Peter Bart, Vice President of Production at the studio, about Puzo's unfinished manuscript. The studio offered $12,500 for the work and a further $80,000 if it eventually made a movie. Paramount confirmed their intentions to make a film shortly after the novel had been released, setting an initial theatrical release date of Christmas Day 1971.

After approaching several other directors, including Sergio Leone, Peter Bogdanovich and Otto Preminger, the studio settled on Francis Ford Coppola. Confident he would work for a small wage and with a low budget. Paramount's Head of Production, Robert Evans, had further leverage over Coppola as his film company, American Zoetrope, owed Paramount money. That was thanks to George Lucas' movie *THX1138* going over budget. Coppola was officially announced as director of *The Godfather* on 28 September 1970 after which producer Albert S. Ruddy, writer Mario Puzo, casting director Fred Roos and director Coppola started auditions.

As patriarch of the family, the role of Don Vito Corleone required an actor who could dominate every scene. Coppola wrote a list of people he saw fit to play some of the main Corleone males in the movie. His list for Don Vito included such actors as Laurence Olivier, John Marley, Marlon Brando and, at one stage, Burt Lancaster. Puzo wanted Marlon Brando, the studio felt he was too much of a rebel and were pushing for Ernest Borgnine. Coppola was torn between Brando and Olivier. Paramount insisted it would be either Borgnine or Brando, but the latter would have to screen-test for the first time since 1953. Not wanting to offend Brando, Coppola tricked him into a screen-test by asking him to come in for camera and make-up tests. During these few hours, Brando created one of the most iconic characters in movie history. He swept his hair back; requested make-up that would age him twenty years and placed cotton wool balls in his mouth. When Paramount executives saw what a great job he had done, they relented and offered Brando the job. He was paid $50,000 for six weeks of work and an additional weekly expense of $1,000. It was further agreed he'd receive 5% of the film's gross but this was to be capped at $1.5 million. Coppola, Puzo and Paramount had their Vito Corleone but at a high price compared to the rest of the cast.

Numerous actors were considered for the role of eldest son, Santino 'Sonny' Corleone, including Peter Falk and John Saxon. Also on that list was James Caan. Robert Evans wanted him; Coppola had previously worked with him on *The Rain People*. Born in the Bronx, Caan had the Italian-American attitude that needed for Sonny and was thus brought onboard quickly. Like Caan, Robert Duvall, who would play lawyer Tom Hagen had worked with Coppola on *The Rain People*. He was the preferred choice over actors such as Peter Donat, Ben Piazza and John Cassavetes. Pacino's friend and roommate John Cazale was cast as the weak-willed and incompetent Frederico "Fredo" Corleone, the second son of Vito. Casting director Fred Roos saw him on stage in Israel Horovitz's play *Line*, opposite Richard Dreyfuss, and immediately brought him to the attention of Coppola. "There was no hesitation to cast him," Coppola said in the documentary *I Knew It Was You: Rediscovering John Cazale*.

Coppola gave small roles to members of his family but was reluctant to give the role of Constanzia 'Connie' Corleone to his sister Talia Shire. He thought she was too beautiful to play a homemaker. It was Robert Evans who signed Shire to play Connie. Coppola wasn't happy and told her: "The last thing you need when you are making a movie and your job is in jeopardy is your sister." Shire screen-tested and Coppola relented, not wanting to deny her the opportunity of a lifetime. Shire was paid $1,500 for her work which was considerably less than the rest of the main cast considering she had a lot of screen time (Duvall for example wangled the slightly larger sum of $36,000).

The role of Kay Adams, Michael's girlfriend and eventually his wife, went to Diane Keaton. Karen Black, Jill Clayburgh, Jennifer O'Neill and Cybill Shepherd had all previously auditioned for the role. Keaton was a relative unknown at the time; Coppola had seen her in the film *Lovers and Other Strangers* and thought: "maybe Diane could bring some eccentricity to it." Keaton had so many screen-tests with different actors auditioning for the role of Michael Corleone, she said: "I think they finally got tired of seeing me they said "Oh, for god's sake, just give her the part.""

Perhaps unsurprisingly, the toughest role to cast turned out to be one of the most important. Michael Corleone is the youngest son of Don Vito. A complex character who tries to steer away from the family business. On Coppola's casting list were names such as James Caan (before being cast as Sonny), Martin Sheen and Dustin Hoffman. The role almost went to Robert De Niro, but he pulled out after accepting the lead role in the film *The Gang That Couldn't Shoot*. Ironically, De Niro was taking the place of Al Pacino, the man who would eventually be cast as Michael Corleone. Coppola had seen Pacino on stage a few years earlier and wanted him from the start. Evans urged Coppola to consider Robert Redford or Ryan O'Neal. Other names mentioned were Warren Beatty and Jack Nicholson. But Coppola kept picturing Pacino in the scenes set in Sicily.

When reading Puzo's novel, Coppola could only picture Pacino in the role because he had a very Italian face. Coppola kept asking Keaton who he should cast as Michael and she looked at him and said: "You know, it should be Al." A mammoth effort was required to get Pacino into the movie. Coppola had to screen twelve minutes of *The Panic in Needle Park* before Mario Puzo agreed with him. But Pacino had problems during the first screen-test. He hadn't learnt his lines and started to improvise the scene. The studio felt this was sloppy and underlined why they didn't want him. A second screen-test was organised and the same problem happened again. Coppola had now dubbed him: "The self destructive bastard." A third and final screen-test was arranged a few weeks later. This time Pacino turned up having read and remembered his lines, and Robert Evans was suitably impressed with this "new" Pacino. Coppola screened *Panic...* for Evans as well. By this point Evans was on-board with the decision, but there were still some reluctant executives at Paramount. Through sheer determination Coppola got his wish and Pacino signed up for the role of Michael Corleone.

Filming began on 29 March 1971 and lasted for sixty-two days. Over forty locations were used for filming, the majority of them in and around New York. Further filming took place in Las Vegas and Los Angeles. Many scenes were also shot on location in Sicily.

Pacino's first week of filming was hard for him. He wasn't ready for a film like *The Godfather* which had such a huge scope. He was nervous around his co-stars, especially Brando. The first couple of day's dailies were sent back to Paramount head office. The executives still didn't like the way Pacino was acting. It wasn't until towards the end of the first week that things clicked. Filming the infamous restaurant scene where

Michael kills Police Captain McCluskey and Virgil "The Turk" Sollozzo, Pacino, on only his second take, offered a steely look that said everything Coppola and the Paramount executives wanted. It was the look of a man who has changed his destiny in two gun shots. A phenomenal shift for a young man who couldn't remember his lines two months previously. Pacino had always been a huge fan of Marlon Brando and it appeared Brando's method acting was rubbing off on his new protégé. Pacino withdrew from other cast members because he felt Michael was the outsider, and he wanted to stay in character throughout. Some of the cast found this difficult to understand, they wanted to help the young actor but he retreated into his own area of the set.

The mood on set was generally jovial. Brando kept writing little notes and sticking them to his head when the camera was focussed on the other actors. Brando, Caan and Duvall were constantly pulling down their trousers and baring their bums to the cast and crew. Marlon accomplished the ultimate "mooning" act when they filmed the wedding scene. At the end of filming he was given a belt buckle that said "Mighty Moon King." Pacino joined in with these antics as he told *Ladies Home Journal* magazine: "In a scene where I sit behind a desk, wardrobe made a big fuss about getting me a shirt with a smaller collar. So while everyone was looking at the shirt, I took off my pants. When I came out from behind the desk I got a laugh."

Unfortunately, this fun anecdote doesn't reflect Pacino's overall experience. He felt like the outsider because he had only made one movie unlike most of his other cast members. Furthermore, the threat of being fired loomed over him. Pacino had a hard time when filming in Sicily. He told *Esquire Magazine*: "It was so hot. If you haven't slept and you're not feeling well and its 120 degrees and you're dressed in all wool, well, you just want to go home. You start feeling, 'What am I doing? I'm just shooting this over and over and I don't know what this is anymore." Pacino couldn't speak Italian, so Coppola changed the script at the last minute. Michael spoke in English and Angelo, his bodyguard in Sciliy, translated. Coppola also had a tough time. At one point, Pacino found Coppola sat on a gravestone crying because the studio wouldn't give him the time or money to shoot an extra scene. He overheard crew members rubbishing both the film and him. He was constantly undermined by the studio heads.

Filming *The Godfather* had been a struggle for both Coppola and Pacino. Pacino learnt a lot about himself and the world of movie-making. He also finally understood his Italian heritage and what it had meant to those Italian-American's living in New York. He commented: "I felt like I could open up and cry for years. It was hard for me to liberate these feelings. But I spent too much time alienated and lonely". Pacino always felt like his work was being judged throughout the filming and that he "still had to win over these people [studio heads]."

Post-production wasn't much easier for Coppola. Towards the end of 1971 the film was ready to screen to studio executives. On the first screening, Paramount asked Coppola to trim down the runtime. He turned in a second cut of one hundred and thirty five minutes but Robert Evans hated the new cut and told him to restore it back to its near three hour length. There was further complication with the sound. Coppola worked with Maestro Nino Rota to create its iconic score. But Evans hated it and refused to release the film with that music. Coppola said the only way it would be changed is if they fired him and brought in another director. The stalemate lasted a few days. Then Coppola suggested they screen the film for the public with the Nino Rota score to see what they felt about it. Thirty or forty people sat through the first public screening with the Rota score and all agreed it was wonderful. Thus, the music stayed, but to show he still held power over everyone, Robert Evans insisted two music cues be changed.

Such was the demand to see Puzo's book come to life, the world premiere of *The Godfather* took place across five cinemas in New York on 14 March 1972. It was met with rapturous applause in each screen. There was however another screening Paramount didn't know about. Producer Al Ruddy had been holding secret talks with the Italian American Civil Rights League for several months. They objected to the film being made, arguing it would be disparaging to all Italian-Americans. Ruddy started these meetings after finding his car had been shot many times over. The script was changed to eliminate the words "Mafia" and "Cosa Nostra," replacing them with "the five families." The League suspended any picketing against the film after these demands were met. On the night of the premiere, however, one of the mobsters called Ruddy and complained the five cinemas wouldn't let them buy any tickets. Ruddy consequently snuck out a print of the film and gave a few hundred mobsters their own screening. Afterwards Ruddy received a phone call from the projectionist at the secret screening, who said: "Mr Ruddy, I've been a projectionist my whole life. No one ever gave me a thousand dollar tip."

The Godfather opened in New York on a Wednesday. It had already garnered $15 million in pre-rentals from movie theatres. The two Al's, Ruddy and Pacino, snuck into one of the first viewings in New York. They decided to leave early and come back towards the end of the film. Ruddy recalled to *Vanity Fair*: "The lights came on, and it was the eeriest feeling of all time: there was not one sound. No applause. The audience sat there, stunned."

Over the next twelve months, *The Godfather* had praise piled upon it. *The New York Times* called it one of the "most brutal and moving chronicles of American Life." *Chicago Sun Times'* critic Roger Ebert praised the film's ability to absorb the viewer over its three hour run time. *Variety* complimented Pacino's work: "It is Pacino who makes the smash impression here. Pacino matures under the trauma." By the time the film was withdrawn from cinemas it had grossed over $133 million and was to become the highest grossing movie of 1972 (Information courtesy of Box Office Mojo. Used with permission).

The Godfather was nominated in ten categories at the 1973 Academy Awards. It won three Oscars for Best Screenplay, Best Actor in a Leading Role and Best Picture. Producer Ruddy accepted the Best Picture award, he ran onto the stage accompanied by the sounds of Nino Rota's Love Theme from the movie and said: "Good audiences need good films as good films need good audiences. The American dream is represented, to me at least, by this (shakes the Oscar)." Not all of the speeches were positive however. Brando refused to attend because of the treatment of Native Americans within the film industry. Instead he sent

Sacheen Littlefeather, a small time actress but more importantly the president of the National Native American Affirmative Image Committee. She approached the podium and read a letter from Brando, explaining she was representing him and that: "he regretfully cannot accept this very generous award." She continued to read the speech with both boos and applause coming from the crowd. The speech lasted little over a minute but emphasized the passion Brando had for the cause. Consequently, while Brando's career was resurrected thanks to his turn as Don Vito Corleone, he still held dear that rebellious nature some of the Paramount executives were worried about when hiring him for the movie. Pacino, Duvall and Caan were all nominated in the same category – Best Actor in a Supporting Role. None of them came away winners. Pacino watched the ceremony from home and saw the Best Actor in a Supporting Role Oscar go to Joel Grey for his role as The M.C. in the musical *Cabaret*.

The Godfather provided a smorgasbord of complex characters. Possibly we aren't meant to love them. Still, something urges us to root for the Corleone family throughout the movie. Pacino's Michael begins the film as a naive army brat that doesn't subscribe to the family way but by the end he has lost his morals and fallen down the mafia rabbit hole. His steely stares become his trademark. Family and well-wishers talk to him but he gives no sign of emotion apart from the cold, calculating gaze. What is going on behind those eyes? What is the new Don Corleone thinking about? Michael has sunk so low that he's lying to his wife, Kay. The final shot of him closing the door on her, while he conducts business, is one of the most chilling moments in the trilogy. It shows the love Michael and Kay once had has been left behind in favour of something far more dangerous.

Producer Gray Frederickson on *The Godfather*

How did you become involved with making *The Godfather* feature film?

Al Ruddy and I had just made a movie for Paramount called *Little Fauss and Big Halsy* with Robert Redford and directed by Sidney Furie, and my background was low budget, guerrilla filmmaking out of Italy. We brought that film in for less than a million dollars, even back in 1969 it was pretty cheap for a Paramount movie, and they had just purchased the rights to Mario Puzo's book, *The Godfather* and they had a movie called *The Brotherhood* starring Kirk Douglas and Alex Cord about Mafia and organised crime and it died. They [Paramount] thought: "Oh my goodness we've got a book we paid money for and no one wants to go see Mafia movies. What are we going to do with this book?" They said: "Hire those guys – Al Ruddy and Gray Frederickson – as they made that movie starring Robert Redford very cheaply. So that was what the original plan was. As soon as Francis [Ford Coppola] came on board that changed and Francis said: "This book is a gem and I want to make it like the book." It was one long struggle from then on and every day we thought we were going to be fired.

What were the biggest issues you faced?

They [Paramount] hated the way it looked. They thought it was too dark. The first dailies of Marlon Brando in the office granting the wishes of the undertaker they said: "Wow! You spent all this money on this set. Ten thousand dollars on the desk. We can't see anything it's too dark." Marlon Brando was mumbling with a cat on his lap that was purring into the microphone so they couldn't hear him. They said: "This movie is going to be a disaster." And from then on they were sniping at us the whole time. We even found out they were grooming Francis's editor to come in and take over. I found that out and told Francis and he fired him. Every day Francis was joking: "We will start a new company called WU Productions. Washed Up Productions."

So you were in fear of being fired. So too was Francis. And the very famous story is that Al Pacino was almost fired as well. Did you hear who they would have replaced him with?

No. It was a struggle getting them to accept him. They didn't like Al. They thought he wasn't a movie star. Paramount was fighting for people like Ryan O'Neal because he had just come off of *Love Story*. They didn't like any of the cast in the very beginning. Francis had to fight for Brando; he had to fight for Pacino. There was lots going off during casting.

You were also the location scout for the film. Where did you look? And what places did you decline?

I did Little Italy in New York City. Everybody said: "No, no you can't come here." I looked in the windows and they all had the Italian-American Anti-Defamation League sign in the windows and we found out the anti-defamation league was run by the Colombo family. They were telling all those people that this [*The Godfather*] was anti-Italian-American. It would make you look bad. Don't cooperate with the filmmakers. So we even went to Kansas City and looked at Kansas City for possible locations. Finally Al Ruddy had a sit down with the Colombo family. Which was hilarious. They looked through the script and took out all the derogatory slurs that they thought were bad, anti-Italian, and then they signed off on it and said: "Yeah, now we are OK with it." It came out in the papers the next day that the producers of *The Godfather* had reached an agreement with the Colombo family, which was a crime family, and Charles Bluhdorn, who was chairman of Gulf+Western which owned Paramount, went crazy. He was going to fire us because it looked like Gulf+Western were in business with the Mafia. That was another incident where we thought we were finished [on *The Godfather*]. The whole thing was a disaster. Every day there was something. The scene I thought was really beautiful was with Jimmy

Caan and the undertaker, and Brando is there and he's looking down and he says: "Look what they done to my boy." Remember that scene?

Yes.

They sent it back and said: "you have to reshoot it. It's terrible. It doesn't work. Brando can't act. It's over the top." We kept saying we'll get through it. We never reshot it because we thought it was good. It was a rough experience.

How many cuts of the film did you see before the finished one was locked?

Well that's another story because Bob Evans, who became involved in post-production and he was in the editing room and he was fighting with Francis. Francis was fighting and trying to get his cut. There is a funny story – Evans said: "I'm the one who told Francis to let the movie be long, and it played better long." What actually happened was Evans went to Francis and said he had to cut about twenty minutes out of the movie which Francis did and when Evans saw the movie he went to Francis and said: "You're right. Put it back. Make it longer." So he gets credit for saying he told Francis to make it longer [*laughs*].

The Godfather **was released and went on to receive great acclaim. It was also a triumph at the box office. What is it like to be part of a film that receives so much praise?**

It's the gift that keeps on giving. In the beginning it was just another movie I had been working on and it was OK. It was nice. It was making money. Over the years it has become an icon. A classic. One of the greatest movies of all time. It seems like every year I become more of a celebrity because I was involved in that movie, which is weird.

Scarecrow

Cast: Gene Hackman (Max Millan), Al Pacino (Francis Lionel "Lion" Delbuchi), Eileen Brennan (Darlene), Dorothy Tristan (Coley), Ann Wedgeworth (Frenchy), Richard Lynch (Riley), Penelope Allen (Annie Gleason), Richard Hackman (Mickey Grenwood), Al Cingolani (Skipper). **Director:** Jerry Schatzberg.

Synopsis: Ex-con Max Millan and sailor Francis Lionel "Lion" Delbuchi form an unlikely friendship as they hitchhike from California to Pittsburgh. Once there, the pair plan to open up a car wash. Along the way Lion must stop off in Detroit to see the child he has never met and make amends with his wife who he walked out on.

Playwright Garry Michael White made the transition from writing plays to writing movies via "the back door" as he describes it. He wrote a play while studying at UCLA and the piece went on to win a Samuel Goldwyn award. This drew national attention to White's writing and he was featured in publications such as *Variety* and the *Hollywood Reporter*. He was then bombarded with offers of representation from numerous agents. Eventually, he signed with Hollywood agent Lee Rosenberg, who encouraged him to think about writing for film and to start work on his first script.

Drawing experience from his own life, White started to write a story about two hitchhikers who travel across America with a dream they hope will be realised at the end of their journey. Years previously, White actually hitchhiked from California to Pennsylvania and along the way he met a nomadic hitchhiker who he used as the basis for the character Max who appears in his script. In order to create a contrasting character to Max, White used his friendship with comedian Al Cingolani, who was known for his physical comedy, to create the character of Francis – a sweet and funny, yet wet behind the ears, man. White then developed the mutual dream and the secret that Francis was running away from. White titled his script *Scarecrow* because of the philosophy woven into this film that people enjoy life more if they spend their time making others laugh and smile rather than being aggressive towards them. This is illustrated in a scene in which Francis explains to Max that the birds are not frightened of the scarecrow because of his funny face and hat. It's so funny, he argues, that it makes the birds laugh and they won't bother the farmer's crops because of this.

United Artists entertainment studio purchased the rights to White's work. They then put it straight into turnaround and let it sit on the shelves for about eighteen months. The stalled project script managed to find its way onto Marty Bregman's desk, Pacino's manager. He, in turn, put it in front of his client.

Pacino was looking for a follow-up project after his work on *The Godfather*. After reading and being blown away by White's script, Pacino immediately decided he wanted play the role of Francis Lionel 'Lion' Delbuchi. Bregman engineered a script switch, moving the project from United Artists to Warner Bros Entertainment Inc. A contract between Warner Bros and Sanford Productions Inc was signed stating they (Sandford) would produce the film while Warner Bros would be responsible for finance and distribution.

Sanford Productions Inc was a small production company started in 1971 by directors Sydney Pollack and Mark Rydell. Initially, Rydell was attached to direct Scarecrow and called White into his office to say they were going to re-write the majority of the script, especially the ending. White had sold the script and had no power to stop them making these changes. Rydell flew out to Boston meet with Pacino, who was on stage performing Richard III, and outlined the new script they were working on. Pacino was unhappy with the new ideas as he loved the original script and by the time Rydell was back in Los Angeles he had been booted off the project. Bregman and Pacino wanted Jerry Schatzberg to direct given how well he and Pacino had worked together on *The Panic in Needle Park*. Schatzberg would only direct if he was given autonomy on whom to cast and Warner Bros agreed to this stipulation. Schatzberg commented "I was expecting them to want totally wrong actors, but I was told Gene Hackman and Al Pacino. They couldn't be more right for the picture."

Schatzberg brought in renowned Hungarian cinematographer Vilmos Zsigmond as his Director of Photography. Zsigmond had previous experience on successful productions such as *Deliverance*, *McCabe & Mrs. Miller* and *The Long Goodbye* and Schatzberg felt the DoP had just the right style for the lengthy scenes he planned on shooting.

Hackman had been given the script early on when he had told his agents that he was looking for something different: "an actor doesn't find all that many roles he is anxious to play," he commented. Describing *Scarecrow* as "a combination of *Of Mice and Men* and *Midnight Cowboy*," Hackman was transfixed by the script and agreed to play the part of Max Millan. Pacino was confirmed to play Francis and Schatzberg was ready to direct.

Warner Bros set a small budget of $800,000. Before filming began, Hackman and Pacino wanted to better understand their characters as neither had played this type of role before. To achieve this, they hitchhiked nearly three hundred miles from Bakersfield to San Francisco in character. They wore shabby clothes and allowed themselves to grow increasingly unkempt, eventually spending a week in San Francisco schlepping around the streets dressed as bums. They got away without being noticed until one day when Hackman asked a guy for directions to the Salvation Army. "He says: 'It's back two blocks down Market and in the middle of that block, and can I have your autograph?' Even with a beard and raggedy clothes, I couldn't get away with it."

Principal photography began in the fall of 1972 and unusually, the scenes were shot in chronological order. Both Hackman and Pacino appreciated this approach as it meant they could understand the relationship between their characters more thoroughly. The entire production team travelled in a cinemobile, a mobile cinema that was converted to hold the cast, crew and equipment. The crew consisted of director, cameraman, gaffer, key grip, soundman, dolly man and boom operator. It was a small crew that had everyone mucking in to do all sorts of jobs, even the bus driver was tasked to carry cables.

Filming began in Bakersfield, California on an open dusty road with a scene depicting the first meeting between Francis and Max. Soon after, production moved onto Reno, Nevada where further exteriors sequences were filmed. By the time the production rolled into Denver a frosty atmosphere had developed between Pacino and Hackman. They came from different schools of acting and this was causing tension when it came to preparing for each scene. Pacino pumped himself up by walking around acting like Francis. Hackman liked to sit and study the character. It was a clash of acting styles and years later Pacino would say: "It's the odd thing of not knowing who the other person is until after you've done the movie." Hackman and Pacino's relationship continued to stay at arms length throughout filming.

Production moved onto Colorado where it filmed exterior train track scenes at the American Gypsum Company in Gypsum. This was followed by a brief stop in Canon City where filming took place at the Colorado State Penitentiary and Main Street. Thereafter, the cinemobile bussed into the city of Denver where it spent several days filming at locations including a house on Elati Street and Turk's Supper Club on West 43rd Avenue. The cinemobile then faced an eighteen hour drive from Denver to Detroit which was the final filming destination. There, Pacino and Hackman were filmed walking Caniff Avenue and Lumpkin Street in the Hamtramck district, and also used the phone booth on the corner of the intersection. The Sweetest Heart of Mary Roman Catholic Church on Russell Street was used for an interior scene featuring Francis. The final filming location of the production was the James Scott Memorial Fountain on Casino Way. The scenes shot in this location were filmed in one day during bitingly cold winds. Pacino and Hackman had to get into the freezing waters of the fountain in order to film the scenes. Every time Schatzberg called "Cut!" the pair ran over to the trailer and stood under heated lamps to warm up.

Filming was completed by late afternoon and the production unit bundled their equipment into the cinemobile. By the next morning

Pacino had talked Schatzberg into re-shooting the finale in the fountain. Pacino had been troubled by his performance the day before and wanted to have another attempt at exposing Francis' inner demons. Schatzberg assembled a skeleton crew for a second day's shooting of the finale. Throughout filming, Pacino and Hackman improvised their dialogue together and the finale scene was no exception. The second day filming at James Scott Memorial Fountain proved to be a much more intense filming experience and this time Pacino was happy with his performance. At this point, Schatzberg announced a wrap on principal photography of *Scarecrow*.

Unfortunately, the production experienced problems on the run up to release as Warner Bros wanted to make cuts in order to squeeze in more showings per day at theatres. The majority of cuts made were to scenes White had carefully and painstakingly written to show the slow deterioration of Francis. White has recently spoken about the cuts: "I think it harmed the movie. I'm sorry that that happened and it's just about my only complaint about the film." Pacino also hated the way *Scarecrow* was treated and told Lawrence Grobel years later: "There were people involved in that who were really screwballs."

The cut version opened in U.S. theatres on 11 April 1973. Its box office return was slightly over $4 million, a respectable sum for a movie that cost less than $1 million. However, Warner Bros were banking on the star billing of Pacino and Hackman to drive ticket sales through the roof. This didn't happen because the general public saw the film as a small, art-house movie.

Critics could not come to a general consensus about the film. *New York Magazine* scathed: "The script is phoney from word one." Roger Ebert sat on the middle ground saying: "There are fine moments. And there are times of just rambling. Scarecrow somehow should have drifted out on a lower key." The *Los Angeles Times* enthused that it was: "One of the new year's best movies." Success may have eluded the movie in the U.S. but in Europe it played at the 1973 Cannes Film Festival and ended up winning the highest prize: The Palme d'Or – alongside the British movie *The Hireling*. Years later White praised the movie by saying: "I knew it

was a special piece of work and I knew that the actors were flawless."
Even with the awkward atmosphere between Hackman and Pacino on
set and the tepid response to the film, Hackman cites it as his favourite
work. When interviewed by Larry King on 7 July 2004 Hackman, when
asked what his favourite movie was, stated: "I always say this, that my
favourite was not a film that worked commercially. It was called
Scarecrow. I loved working on that." He also praised his co-star by saying:
"I love Al, I love his work. I just think he is one of our great, great
actors."

It's a shame that Hackman and Pacino didn't gel with each other during
the making of *Scarecrow* because they make a formidable duo. Their
connection on screen makes for some highly entertaining moments.
During the opening ten minutes of the movie, Max and Francis try to
outdo each other in hitching a ride while barely speaking. It takes twelve
minutes before they officially interact and by then the audience feels they
know them before they even get to know each other. Their love/hate
relationship is central to the whole film.

In a decade when the American dream was still very much alive, Max
and Francis know they will have to work together in order to achieve
that car-wash goal even if it means tolerating the idiosyncrasies of the
other. They are the perfect odd couple. For an hour and twenty minutes
Scarecrow is an entertaining and often humorous road trip movie.
However, Schatzberg hits the viewer with one of the most brutal and
painful finales to a movie ever. It's a deeply troubled ending that lays
bare the desolation felt by those with mental health issues.

Following his grandiose work on *The Godfather*, in this picture Pacino
plays Francis as a quiet, slightly goofy second lead. Occasionally he rises
up and takes command, normally when joking around and alleviating the
tension in some of the awkward situations Max puts them in. It is
evident throughout that Pacino is a decent comedic actor as he delivers
deadpan lines and slapstick humour with natural flair. His method acting
is also apparent in places, not least in the bleak finale in which Pacino
jerks and flails his whole body round in a moment that is difficult to
watch. Overall, Pacino seems most interested in making Francis an

entertaining, if slightly dysfunctional, character that we can all relate to. A character who simply wants to make things right while laughing and joking along the way.

The yin to Francis' yang is Max, a world weary exhibitionist. Max lets nothing stand in his way, and is equally prepared to perform a strip tease in a diner or fight his co-workers in a wash house. He is a grump of a character who barrels his way through life on sheer luck and determination. Hackman almost portrays Max as the bad guy of the film: a cigar chomping, ill-fitting, multi-layered clothes wearer with a tendency to kiss or punch first and ask questions later. It's difficult to figure out what is truly lurking under the surface of the character because he is so obnoxious. But that is part of the charm of the character: he is already broken and becoming friends with Francis fixes him. Max shows he cares about Francis when he accompanies him to the hospital. In Francis, he has finally found a reason to be happy. It may be too late for Francis, but Max has the opportunity to use that newfound, upbeat attitude to life and honour his pal.

Years later White said: "The theme of *Scarecrow* is really about a very hard man who becomes softened through friendship."

It's rare that the different elements of a movie fit together as flawlessly as they do in *Scarecrow*. This buddy road trip movie is sublimely executed thanks to Zsigmond's unique approach to capturing Dust Bowl America, adding a glimmering, golden sheen. Schatzberg's documentary-style direction compliments the two hilarious and emotional performances from Pacino and Hackman. In summary, *Scarecrow* is an underrated and often overlooked gem of a movie.

Director Jerry Schatzberg on *Scarecrow*

Scarecrow is a road trip movie. Is that the type of film you were looking to make at that stage in your career?

My first film was absolutely something I wanted to do. My second, I turned it down at first. I didn't think I would do another film after my first one. I was sent the script for Scarecrow and had known about it because Al was already involved in it and Al was working on it, and we would talk about it every once in a while. When it was sent to me by our agent, because we had the same agent, I thought Al was sending it to me to read and maybe give him some advice. I read it and I liked it. But I didn't think much of it. I didn't hear from Al but my agent called and said there is a problem because Al and Hackman didn't like the director that was assigned to it and they were looking for a director. My agent sent me out to L.A. to meet with Hackman to see if we could get along, because Al and I obviously got along, and we did get along. I came back and, I remember, Al and I would take walks and talk about the script and talk about scenes. At one point both of us got a sort of guilty tinge about axing another director. We decided we shouldn't do it and we called our agent and he was furious. He said: "Do you like this script?" and we said: "Yes" and he said: "Then you just leave the rest to me". They made some sort of arrangement with the other director and evidently he was happy, so we just carried on.

There are rumours that Hackman and Pacino did not get on with each other when they were filming. Is that right? Or were they good buddies on set?

They didn't really get on because they are two different type of actors. Al carries the character with him all the time and if he comes five minutes, ten minutes late to the set he doesn't care. Hackman is always on the set on time. Hackman knows everything that goes on on the set and when Gene puts on his costume he is the character, when he takes it off he is Hackman. Hackman is a tough guy on the set. In the second week of rehearsal, maybe the first week, he said: "You know I never get along with any directors I work with." I said: "Oh, that's great." He's pretty tough on the set and he sees everything on set and he's usually right. He hollers at somebody in the crew, which I don't appreciate and I had a discussion with him about that. They are two different guys. There were a couple of incidents and they didn't buddy together.

There is a buddy element to this film and some of the comedy is very much like Laurel & Hardy. Did this kind of comedy come easy to Pacino and Hackman?

Both of them are very funny in life when you talk to them. Scenes like the department store where Al goes running around, that comes from Al and I walking around the streets of New York and just coming up with that and we were hysterical thinking about it. The original screenplay had humour in it, Garry wrote it sort of like a high school prat fall comedy and that's not my idea of comedy, and I guess the others feel the same way. But they both have a great sense of humour. I hope I do too. We found the humour and made it work. I remember Garry, when he saw the film, he said: "It's a good film but it's not my film." Meaning it wasn't the prat fall and all that. Once the directors and the actors and the cameramen take over the film it becomes something that maybe the author didn't see. Although I believe that the most important thing in the film is the screenplay and the screenplay that Garry wrote had the basis for a good film and I think it came out a good film. We may have interpreted it differently to what he did.

Even though the film is comedic, the ending is very bleak. How careful did you have to be about ending a humorous film in this way?

I didn't think much of it. I was very touched by it and my first film deals with mental health. We all have to confront this sometime in life. I hope when I do something that somebody will... that a light will go on and say:

"ahhh, why am I doing that?" I didn't think of it as much of mental health as a home problem. He left his home. He left his wife. He left his child. He was guilty all the time. It was really the guilt that made him. He had to go back to Detroit to make an amends to Annie. When she tells him that the kid is dead, that really affects him. Obviously he comes from a religious background because I put that scene in where he goes into the church before he goes to see Annie. All of that guilt that the church puts on you. It all contributes to it. I don't say it – Bang! Bang! Bang! That's what it is. But it's there. It's in the film.

I read an interview with Pacino in which he referred to deleted scenes. Ones that had been filmed but the studio kept them out because they wanted to come in under budget. Do you know what scenes he was referring to?

Yes I do. But that's not quite what happened. I took them out. The studio didn't take them out. I took them out with the advice of the studio, maybe in some ways. One scene where I had him do an improv when he was going to be manager of the show, so I had him do an improv of a comic routine and we didn't have any ideas so I let him think up something. It came out very bad. It wasn't very good and it was long. The other scene was right after prison they go to a bar and Hackman has to go to the toilet and the way they have these locks inside the door and they had been drinking, so was a little drunk. Hackman lays down on the floor and goes under the door and reaches up and releases the lock and opens the door. As he's coming back out of getting up, Pacino is leaning up against the side of it and hits the door and it closes again. It's a funny scene and I love the scene, but it slowed the film down. At that point they are going to Detroit and I didn't need more funny scenes. I needed to go to Detroit. So I just took it out and it made the film move to where it had to go.

Al was unhappy about that. He also was influenced by his manager, our manager, who told him it wasn't his film. Which was a terrible thing to tell him and it's not true because fifty people come up to me and tell me Pacino is great in it and then fifty people come up and say Hackman was great, and they are both great. When it won the prize at Cannes, Ingrid

Bergman said: "With special mention to the two actors." Which they don't usually do because they give an acting award also. So everybody thought they were good and they were. But I didn't appreciate what the manager did and said. But then, Al thought that he would like to cut some things. I remember the first scene in the diner; I had two angles one a little bit to the right and one a little bit to the left. Hackman was sitting a little bit closer to the camera, not much though. They were so good that I didn't want to cut the scene at all. I didn't want to disturb it. Almost shooting straight on. Al thought I should have cut and put him closer to the camera. I tried it and it didn't work. He called the studio and said he thought it needed some editing. He spoke to John Calley and Calley said: "Did you speak to Jerry?" and he said: "Yes but he doesn't want to change it." Calley had already seen the film and he liked the film. He didn't think there was anything wrong with it. He said: "Well he is the director." Which is really unusual, especially at that time when Al had already done *The Godfather* and was in demand. I didn't want Al to feel bad, but Al did feel bad. In the end we are not there to satisfy individual personalities and egos. We are there to make a film and make the best film we possibly can. He didn't talk to me for a while but then we saw each other, and hugs and kisses and all that. We've been friends for forty/fifty years now.

You mentioned it winning at Cannes. Did you ever think it could win the Palme D'or?

I honestly thought maybe the actors would have a chance. There was a lot of competition. There was a lot of politics going on at the time. I was pleasantly surprised when we won.

It wasn't a huge success when it was released in theatres. What do you think that was down to?

I didn't think critics forgave me too much for being a photographer. My first film was probably ahead of its time and critics see something new and not everybody is into new stuff. They want to see something they are used to seeing. After that generation it started to catch on because my first three films are shown at film festivals all the time. They are films that last. But at the time, when you got bad reviews, it was the death of the film. If somebody like Vincent Canby gave it a bad review, and they did, it was pretty much the death of the film. But fortunately the French picked up on my first film and kept it alive. Through that the Cannes Film Festival wanted to see *The Panic in Needle Park* and then *Scarecrow*. *Panic* won a prize for Kitty [Winn]. That helped. But the films are still around, which is great.

I feel it didn't find its audience at the time of release because it showed the American dream turning sour, and people didn't want to see that. Would you agree with that?

Yes I would.

Scarecrow has found its audience over the past ten years. Why do you think that is?

I think that it's shown at festivals. I've just come back from Mexico. Thierry Frémaux, the creative director of the Cannes Film Festival, is a friend of mine for many years and he was down there presenting something. He asked if he could introduce the film. I said: "Oh it would be my honour." First thing he said to the audience was, how many of you have seen the film? And about three people raised their hands. So it's getting a new audience because the film hasn't been around. So somebody there is going to go out and tell somebody else who will tell somebody else. It's going to have a legend of its own, but it takes time.

You've spoken previously about working on a sequel to *Scarecrow*. Can you give an outline of where it would go for the two characters?

Oh yeah. It's thirty years later and they own a car wash. It's a very successful car wash. They are still two people who don't belong, in a certain respect. Lion, Pacino's character, has gone back to school because he was quite young and he has gone back to school to learn all about computers. So he's really taken on a new aspect to his character. Max, Hackman's character, is pretty much the same except he is married to Frenchy and they adopted a Chinese baby, she is now about twenty something years old and swears like he does, and she is just like him. They win awards for their car wash and Annie reads about it, and now her son is getting into trouble. He is a songwriter and the step-father keeps belittling him. He does have a job playing in a nightclub run by gangsters. He does little favours for them. Annie is worried and she wants the father to come back and do something about his son. So they set out on another journey to Detroit to save the son. We've got the character of the son in there and we have a couple of other nice characters. It's really good. The problem is Hackman has retired and he won't even read something. So I'm not sure what I'm going to do. I've got it. I don't know if it will ever get on.

Serpico

Cast: Al Pacino (Frank Serpico), John Randolph (Sidney Green), Jack Kehoe (Tom Keough), Biff McGuire (Captain McClain), Barbara Eda-Young (Laurie), Cornelia Sharpe (Leslie), Tony Roberts (Bob Blair), John Medici (Pasquale), Allan Rich (D.A. Tauber), Norman Ornellas (Rubello), Ed Grover (Lombardo). **Director:** Sidney Lumet.

Synopsis: Frank Serpico might be the best cop in New York, but he's unwilling to play dirty and give into the police corruption surrounding drugs, violence and kickbacks that his colleagues indulge in every day. When he decides to expose those around him, Frank finds himself a target – not just to the city's criminals, but to his own peers.

For his first three movies Al Pacino played characters that on the surface were normal guys. Underneath that façade however, lurked a dark side. A personality flaw that transformed them into a despised or diseased human being. Diversifying his screen presence, in *Serpico* Pacino became the good guy for once. This film was based on the book by Peter Maas which told the true life account of Frank Serpico: a plainclothes policeman who waged a one-man war against corruption within the New York Police Department.

Serpico had a swift yet rocky route to the big screen. Marty Bregman was then head of Artists Entertainment Complex. This newly-formed production company had just released *Kansas City Bomber*, a roller derby sports drama starring Raquel Welch. The film was a low budget B-movie went on to make a respectable return, putting AEC into the black on its first release. Bregman was scrambling around for a project for his former client Pacino, knowing there was only a few months gap between him finishing the promotional train for *Scarecrow* and the impending filming of *The Godfather Part II*. Bregman helped Maas pass his book around the Hollywood studios in exchange for being a producer. Several cop movies had already been released over the preceding twelve months however, including *Dirty Harry*, *The French Connection* and *Shaft* and consequently many a studio passed on the project. What happened next differs depending on who you talk to.

Bergman claims that he contacted Italian moviemaker Dino De Laurentiis, who agreed to take it on. De Laurentiis had a great working relationship with Charles Bluhdorn, an American industrialist who owned Gulf + Western – Paramount's parent company- and managed to get *Serpico* green-lit without too much trouble. According to De Laurentiis however, he spoke direct to Maas and bought the rights for $450,000 during a phone call that lasted no longer than thirty minutes. Whatever the real story, Bregman had his money and was ready to make his second movie for AEC; his first as a producer.

Bregman had already convinced Pacino to play Frank Serpico. Pacino, an avid method actor, met with Frank Serpico over a meal in New York. Bregman explained: "Within twenty minutes, Al was absorbing Serpico through his pores." Pacino and Serpico continued to hang out together for a few more weeks, going over many stories told in the book. At one point Pacino asked: "Why did you do it?" referring to the whistle-blowing of the corrupt officers, and Frank replied: "....If I didn't, who would I be when I listened to a piece of music?" After this reply, Pacino was more determined than ever to inject the character with all the traits of the real-life Frank Serpico.

While Serpico and Pacino were spending time together, Marty Bregman was looking for a director. De Laurentiis and Bregman settled on John G. Avildsen, a director who'd just had a critical and commercial success with his third film *Joe*. As pre-production progressed however, Avildsen continued to plague Bregman with threats of walking away from the project because he was not getting what he wanted. Avildsen called for a rewrite of the script, and after that was done he still threatened to leave. Bregman, under very tight time constraints and fearing his movie would never get made, took the decision to fire Avildsen before shooting began.

Bregman moved swiftly to find a new director before the start of filming. De Laurentiis and Bregman both agreed that the no-nonsense Sidney Lumet, a director with little commercial and critical success but known to be a consummate professional, would get the movie made in the small amount of time they had. Lumet agreed and *Serpico* was back on track.

Filming began right after the Fourth of July holiday of 1973. Sidney Lumet had not known pressure like it before. He commented in his book Making Movies that: "Six months of post production is a tight schedule. Three months is insane. But we had no choice." Lumet was known for his gritty and urban style, a style he wanted to use to the fullest in *Serpico*. Over one hundred New York City locations were used within the boroughs of Queens, Manhattan and Brooklyn, and parts of the film were also shot in Pacino's own birth place: the Bronx. The film was shot in reverse chronological order so that Pacino could start filming with the trademark beard and long hair, and then over the course of filming could slowly shave it off. This means the film starts with a clean-cut Serpico who gradually becomes less fresh-faced as the film progresses.

The pressure mounted on the cast and crew as the already announced release date of 6 December 1973 approached. Lumet filmed and then had his editor, Dede Allen, cut the footage right behind him as he shot the next take. It was a relentless schedule. Pacino found it tough but also liberating as the long, arduous filming meant his world-weary and bitter version of Frank Serpico came quite naturally.

Pacino championed method acting right until the end of the shoot. The time spent with the real Frank Serpico had enabled him to develop his mannerisms but he became so invested in being a police officer that he pulled over a truck one day while driving a blues and twos car in full police uniform. The truck was billowing smoke meaning other drivers on the freeway couldn't see much more than a few feet in front of their cars. Once pulled over Pacino shouted at the driver: "Why are you putting that crap in the street?" The driver asked: "Who the hell are you?" To which Pacino replied: "I'm a cop and you're under arrest." It was only after he said those words that he jolted out of his Frank Serpico persona and realised he had no powers to arrest anyone.

Most know Al Pacino for the way in which he bellows his dialogue. But Pacino didn't really develop that style until *Serpico*. It's the first time we really see him unleash the hairdryer treatment on numerous occasions. He lets fly at his girlfriend; at the Captain and at his fellow officers. Pacino completely goes for broke with his explosive shouting and then tops it off by throwing chairs around with such force that you feel sorry for the set designers and prop people. It's nothing short of entertainingly energetic mayhem. This is Pacino at his grandstanding, scene-chewing best.

The other element of Pacino's acting we get to see for the first time is his iconic running style. His pace is bullet fast but the flailing arms appear independent to the rest of his body. He's like a track star below the waist but above it's like he's waving a plane into position. Still, even while running, Pacino's intensity remains. In *The Godfather*, he became a household name but *Serpico* was the movie that would show the world his real acting talent. Cinematographer Arthur Ornitz said: "There's maybe 10 feet [of film] in the whole thing that he isn't in!....It's one of the great performances."

Director Sidney Lumet delivered the movie on time and within budget. It was released on 5 December 1973 in Los Angeles and New York (Receiving a U.S.-wide release in February 1974). It was a critical success, with the *New York Times* calling it: "A galvanizing and disquieting film." The *New York Daily News* saw *Serpico* as: "a triumph of intelligence, compassion and style" and believed Pacino gave "a masterful performance." These reviews proved to Pacino and to the world that he was a star: an actor who could play the main character without the need for a big name cast around him. Added proof came in the form of another Academy Award nomination for Pacino. This time in the Best Actor category: the award Pacino felt he should have been nominated for as Michael Corleone rather than being shunted into the Best Supporting Actor category. The Oscar, again, wasn't forthcoming for Pacino. He lost out to Jack Lemmon for his role as Harry Stoner in the drama *Save The Tiger*. This said, Pacino's numerous nominations meant Hollywood and the movie-going public could no longer think of Pacino as a one-hit wonder. Pacino was here to stay.

The actor attended a New York showing of *Serpico* during the opening weekend. Dressed in a pea-coloured coat and a pair of glasses, he stayed for the majority of the performance. As he left the cinema, Pacino put on his cap but was captured by a group of waiting photographers who had been tipped off that the star of the film was in the audience. Trapped in the doorway of the cinema, Pacino was rescued by a bouncer from a nearby bar who took him down a side alley and through a storeroom to escape. Pacino disliked this part of the industry. He wanted to act; he didn't want the after-hours attention.

Serpico became the ninth highest grossing film of 1974, raking in more than $14 million in North America (Information courtesy of Box Office Mojo. Used with permission). The film looks and feels almost like a biopic rather than a feverish look at the world of police corruption and Lumet's approach was to show Serpico at his most vulnerable. One of the challenges Lumet faced on this score is that he always felt ambivalent towards the character. He only fell in love with him because of Pacino's portrayal. It wasn't the scripted Serpico but the Pacino version of Serpico that captured the director's imagination. Lumet commented: "It's the way his eyes express an enormous rage, even in the tender moments, that enthrals me."

When Serpico lets out an emotional cry while his hospital bed, after being shot, you feel his pain. It's a pain of frustration. Frustration about corruption. Frustration with the system. Frustration with his fellow police officers and frustration with himself because he couldn't stop the unscrupulous behaviour. The realisation in this moment is that absolute power can, and most probably will, lead to corruption. Sidney Lumet best described *Serpico* as: "A real rebel with a cause."

Actor Tony Roberts on *Serpico*

Did you do any research for the role before filming began? Did you speak to any of the officers involved in the real case?

When I entered the rehearsal stage of things, Sidney Lumet famously rehearsed the entire film around a conference table for two weeks before we ever saw a camera, I was asked by Frank Serpico and David Dirk to listen to tape recordings they had each made of certain phone calls made between them that attempted to support their own scenarios of what had happened, to bring about the events depicted in the film.

Bob Blair is one of the few good cops. How do you think he survived in a corrupt precinct before he found a like-minded individual in Frank Serpico?

It is a story one can only speculate about from my vantage point. They were both obviously troubled by the illegality of what was going on around them. They bonded because it was unacceptable to each of them. I think they challenged each other to do something about it. After the Kerner Commission finished its investigation they each held differing views as to what they actually accomplished and who deserved the most credit for the results. Each of them had put themselves "on the line" as it were, and became vulnerable to those who wanted to maintain the status quo.

Do you think Bob and Frank could have cleaned up the department between them as they so wanted to?

To be honest about things, I was less interested in which of their views was accurate than I was in fulfilling Lumet's vision of what he wanted the film to be. We apparently had the liberty to create a commercially viable entertaining film about real events, which led to a fully fledged hearing of the issues involved.

What was it like acting opposite Pacino?

Acting with Al was a privilege, as far as I was concerned. He and I were both nominated for a Tony Award for our performances on Broadway during the same season. Al was in a dark play called: *Does a Tiger Wear a Necktie?* and I was in a light comedy by Woody Allen called: *Play It Again , Sam*. Al won. When we shot *Serpico* we rehearsed in a thoughtful way, but poked around with a few possible choices of how something should flow, but didn't plan anything too specific, beyond knowing where each of us needed to be in order for the camera to record the action.

There is a scene in the movie where you and Pacino go toe to toe shouting at each other. What was it like to shoot that?

There were two cameras rolling during the scene, each of them covering every move each of us made, Sidney thought that it would produce a more unbroken sense of the action because he could cut back and forth between us from the same "take". I think we only did two takes on that scene, and both Sidney, and the producer, Martin Bregman seemed satisfied with it.

What was the reaction like when the film opened?

When the film opened, I happened to run into Al at Elaine's [Restaurant] one night and he rushed to greet me with great enthusiasm. He was ecstatic about the reviews the film was getting and wanted to share his joy with me. He was genuinely surprised. I was thrilled that the film was so well-received and very proud to be a part of it. I can't deny that I also felt awkward about the dilemma I found myself in when promoting the film. Clearly Sgt. David Dirk, the character I played, whose name was altered for legal reasons was not happy with the way his role in the events of the film were portrayed. I found him to be affable and friendly, but frustrated by his lack of "input" into the final draft of the story. But he was still a hero in the story as I understood it from the script, and in the final film.

The Godfather Part II

Cast: Al Pacino (Michael Corleone), Robert Duvall (Tom Hagen), Diane Keaton (Kay Corleone), Robert De Niro (Vito Corleone), John Cazale (Fredo Corleone), Talia Shire (Connie Corleone), Lee Strasberg (Hyman Roth), Michael V. Gazzo (Frankie Pentangeli), Bruno Kirby (Young Clemenza). **Director:** Francis Ford Coppola.

Synopsis: In the early part of the 20th Century young Vito Corleone travels from his home in Sicily to America and begins a lucrative oil business in New York. Forty years later Vito's son Michael is the head of the family and plans to expand their criminal empire into Las Vegas, Florida and Cuba.

Francis Ford Coppola didn't want to do it. Al Pacino didn't want to do it. So how does a movie studio convince the two key architects of their biggest film in years to come back and make a sequel? Paramount had been dropping hints about a second film while the first film was still in cinemas. They even took out a trade paper ad during 1972 to say *The Godfather Part II* would be released in two years time. The big problem? Getting *The Godfather* mob back together.

Most had become big stars thanks to the success of the first film and were being courted by Hollywood studios who were throwing money at them. The prestige of having an actor from *The Godfather* in their movie was a prestige worth paying for. Word soon got around to the main cast that a sequel was being prepped. Duvall, Shire, Keaton and Cazale all felt a sense of obligation to return to the project. Coppola had taken a chance of them and they had become movie stars. It was time to repay the favour. As expected, due to the success of *The Godfather*, money became a big issue. Paramount knew they couldn't low ball these actors. A film without the main cast would not be a *Godfather* movie the public wanted to see. Bowing to financial demands, Paramount give respectable increases in salary to each actor compared to the meagre monies they received for the first movie. Pacino, now the big breakout star and the main character in *The Godfather Part II*, demanded a larger fee. In one meeting the actor was offered $1 million, but he turned it down explaining to the execs: "It doesn't mean anything – it's an abstraction." Pacino told his biographer Lawrence Grobel that he ended up apologising for not taking the million. He was given $600,000 and a 10% share of the U.S. box office receipts instead. It was the increase he wanted and deserved. Now he had to prove he could be a leading actor in a blockbuster movie. He had to, once again, prove to those Paramount executives that he wasn't a flash in the pan. *The Godfather Part II* rested on the shoulders of Pacino.

Novelist, and screenwriter, Mario Puzo was happy to continue his work and write the screenplay for a sequel. The first *Godfather* film had covered the time frame in his book but Puzo decided to expand on certain elements he felt were lacking from that film. The first finished script came from Puzo in the spring of 1972 but it took months for Paramount to finally convince Coppola to return and helm the sequel. At one point the director suggested hiring his friend and fellow American New Wave director Martin Scorsese. Paramount were having none of it. It was Coppola or nothing. Eventually after to-ing and fro-ing on contract negotiations, he relented. Coppola wanted to create an extension of the first movie rather than a direct sequel. To expand the Corleone universe. One of the stipulations Coppola insisted on was that he had total control. He didn't want to deal with any interfering studio heads, especially Robert Evans who he'd clashed with many times while making the first movie. Paramount agreed and allowed Coppola to be his own producer. He was given an initial payment of nearly $500,000 for producing, directing and co-writing *The Godfather Part II* and was also given a stake in the revenue share. This, at the time, was thought to be about 13% of the box office receipts.

The one cast member who was paid rather poorly was Robert De Niro. Coppola remembered his audition for the first movie and went back to that tape when looking for someone to play the young Vito Corleone. He also screened Martin Scorsese's *Mean Streets* which had De Niro in the lead role. Coppola recognised De Niro as an actor that could easily play the young Vito in the flashback scenes he was planning. These scenes would showcase a young Vito Andolini arriving in New York from Corleone. They would chart Vito's rise in the city during the early 1900s as he eventually became the head of one of the first mob families. De Niro was an Italian-American; he knew the style and eccentricities that would be needed for the role. Coppola needed an actor who could morph Vito into a warm and likeable character, the complete opposite to what Michael had become. Paramount executives were not hot on the idea of De Niro playing a young Brando but Coppola had complete freedom and decided De Niro was the only choice. De Niro was paid less than $30,000; a paltry figure compared to the other actors. This was however De Niro's first Godfather rodeo so there was no reason why he should be paid as much as those who had made the first movie such a monster, world-wide hit.

De Niro recognised he had to up his game considerably for the role of young Vito Corleone. This was a different Vito to the one Brando portrayed in *The Godfather*. While prepping for the start of filming, Coppola took De Niro to Italy in order to immerse him in the character. They toured the major cities and towns for several weeks, soaking up the atmosphere. Moreover, a Sicilian consultant was hired to tour with them in order to help De Niro learn more about the heritage of his character. The consultant – Romano Pianti – commented: "If you'd have asked me if it was possible for an actor to master a language like Sicilian in such a short time, I would have said "Never. Impossible." De Niro accomplished it.

Delays in shooting Michael's storyline meant De Niro was kept waiting a couple more months. Finally in the spring of '74 he became Don Vito on the newly-designed set built on New York's East 6th Street. The modern street was completely restructured to resemble Little Italy during the early part of the 1900s. Between his trip to Italy and numerous viewings of *The Godfather* (enabling him to mimic Brando's quirks), De Niro had developed his character. The majority of his lines were spoken in Sicilian tongue. His efforts to understand his character really paid off. De Niro gives one of the most nuanced performances ever seen on-screen. He portrays the boy who becomes a man and leader with such patience and guile. It's an incredibly restrained character delivery. The line between his Vito Corleone and Brando's is a natural one. Furthermore, appreciation is due over how likeable De Niro makes Vito even though he's a killer. When he takes revenge it's more mischief than maliciousness. Vito may have bumped off the local New York Don, but he doesn't rise into his new position with a bolshie attitude. Instead, he quietly carries on with his professional and personal life as if he's just part of the neighbourhood. Locals go to Vito for help and in a warm, caring way he makes sure they are taken care of. He's the type of person you could ask for a dollar to pay the rent and he'd give you two to make sure you could pay next month's as well.

Comparing the kindness of Don Vito to that of his son, Don Michael, some forty years later, it appears the apple has fallen a long way from the tree. Coppola's idea to contrast the rise of Vito with the downfall of Michael is a stroke of filmmaking genius. Pacino described Michael in Part II as "a desperately sad person." One scene in particular dominates *The Godfather Part II*. While in pre-revolutionary Cuba to conduct business, Michael spends an evening in the company of his brother Fredo and some American VIPs. At the nightclub, where they're watching a Superman show, Fredo lets slip he'd been told about the club by Johnny Ola (right-hand man to Florida gangster Hyman Roth). This implies Fredo had met Ola before, even though he told Michael no such meeting ever occurred. Michael interprets this as proof that Fredo conspired with another family for information on the Corleone business (this also resulted in an assassination attempt on Michael's life at his home). In this moment, Michael loses respect for his older brother. The one brother he always valued. Fredo may have been lost amongst the other sons but Michael always made sure he was looked after. That changed the instant Fredo unknowingly let slip about meeting Johnny Ola. It's a crushing scene, and even though Michael never lets his emotions show, he decides his only option is to kill his brother. This was one of Pacino's favourite scenes, he commented: "You see in that moment that Michael realizes his brother betrayed him. That's my favourite moment, but it's subtle." Later, as midnight is drawing in, Michael confronts Fredo with the classic line: "I know it was you Fredo, you broke my heart. You broke my heart." Fredo scuttles off in amongst the rebel takeover. Michael sends out an order to have him found and returned in one piece to the house at Lake Tahoe.

The scene between Michael and Fredo at Lake Tahoe is laden with eerie metaphor. As Michael gives the "You're nothing to me now" speech, Coppola frames the shot with Michael stood and Fredo almost lying flat out in a sun lounger. Is this a sign of his imminent demise? Also, two life buoys hang outside by the lake on Michael's side of the screen yet on Fredo's side there are none. Is this the second sign that Fredo will not be alive much longer? Leaves blow across the autumnal lawn of the house and we see Fredo going fishing with Al Neri, Michael's right-hand man. The camera pans in. We catch a glimpse of Michael pulling a gun. Fredo recites the Hail Mary. Cut back to Michael in the glass extension, looking out at the lake. A single gunshot rings out across the water and he bows his head in respect.

Michael's malevolence knows no bounds. He doesn't hesitate to kill even his own family, and the question must be raised: 'Was Michael ever capable of real love?' At the beginning of *The Godfather* he sits at a wedding table laughing and joking with his girlfriend Kay Adams. However, afterwards we never see them laugh as much as they did in that scene. By the end of *The Godfather* Michael has closed the door on Kay. His cold-heartedness comes to the forefront throughout *Part II*, especially as he starts to tighten his icy grip on the deals in America and Cuba. Michael never shows emotion and he never struggles with his own conscience. He has succeeded his father in every single facet of Corleone life, in business and in pleasure (assuming Michael knows what pleasure really is). Don Vito occasionally held back and thought about problems that happened within the family. Not so with Michael. So was Michael really a fighter and not a lover from the very beginning?

He would probably say he was not. That something snapped that day when he saw his father laid out in the hospital recovering from the assassination attempt. Yet, before that Michael was in the Marine Corps fighting in the Pacific during World War II. He'd been trained to fight and kill those who opposed America. This would have an adverse effect on anybody's mind but particularly someone from an organised crime family prone to violent dealings. A life ducking and diving from enemy fire during the war is traumatic but it's arguably worse to come home and find you have to watch your own back in near enough the same circumstances as being out in the Pacific. There is an argument to be made that Michael has not dealt with any post traumatic stress from his time fighting in the Marine Corp. He is too closed off. There is no way he'd allow these problems to surface in front of his family or friends. Instead he holds them deep inside and the only release he has is ordering the deaths of those opposing the Corleone business.

Michael's loneliness in the movie was something director Francis Ford Coppola could identify with. He had run himself into the ground during post production and only had a short window to finish it in time for entrance into the 47th Academy Awards. What would normally take weeks or even months took days as there wasn't enough time to analyse cuts, frames, shots, lighting etc. Coppola told *Time Magazine*: "If I had three more months on this one, I'd have a great film." Paramount initially set the budget at $8 million but the filming over-ran (Pacino became ill during filming in Santa Domingo and was rushed to hospital. He was suffering from exhaustion and was ordered to take three weeks off) and extended secondary units were required for filming and editing. The final cost totalled $15 million which was a staggering sum, even for a lavish sequel such as this. Paramount could not do anything about the escalating costs though as they'd conceded control to Coppola, who had now become a master of his own domain within the studio system. Still, there was the pressure of getting the movie released on time regardless of costs.

A preview screening took place in San Diego on 27 November 1974. Coppola and his crew, along with actor John Cazale, sat amongst the public. The general consensus in the packed theatre was enthusiasm. But Coppola wasn't happy. Friends remember him muttering into a small tape recorder throughout the screening. Notes included lengthening and shortening certain scenes, also the idea of an intermission was dropped. Before heading back to his home in San Francisco, Coppola held a meeting in San Diego's Butcher Shop steakhouse for the crew. He knew the final third was a mess. He had to re-cut it before the New York premiere, which was scheduled for 12 December 1974. There was also the issue that Paramount heads wanted to see the finished film before it played at the premiere or press screenings. They needed to know Coppola had fixed the issues that had plagued the last part of their tent pole film. Coppola and his three editors and several assistant editors worked around the clock to change the structure of the movie. Originally there were twenty-something shifts between time frames. That was reduced to eleven. This created longer and more substantial sections focusing on understanding the two lead characters in greater depth. Through all the hard work and very little sleep, Coppola managed to finish the new cut days before the screenings for distributors and film critics. It was a feat nothing short of incredible. He had pulled off one of the greatest editing jobs in cinema history.

The Godfather Part II was briefly screened in New York during the first week of December 1974. Though the studio stated the sequel was following the release path of the first Godfather movie, in reality it simply had to be screened during that month in order to be eligible for Academy Awards consideration. The official full U.S. release followed later in December. Reviews were, once again, very positive. Richard Schickel, writing for *Time Magazine*, called *The Godfather Part II:* "a worthy successor to its predecessor." *The Los Angeles Times* wrote: "Godfather II is more daring than the original...the risks were worth taking." *The Hollywood Reporter* called it: "...a grand historical epic." The three hour runtime meant theatres couldn't programme as many screenings as they could for shorter films. As such, this did have a slight impact on box office receipts. This said, *The Godfather Part II* still made a tidy $47 million in the U.S. alone (Information courtesy of Box Office Mojo. Used with permission). It didn't surpass the totals achieved by *The Godfather*, but was still seen as a critical and commercial success.

The masterstroke of holding those early New York screenings paid off handsomely come awards season. Nominated in nine Academy Award categories including Best Picture, Best Director, Best Actor, Best Supporting Actor and Best Supporting Actress, the film won in six of the nine categories (Best Picture, Best Director (Coppola), Best Actor in a

Supporting Role (De Niro), Best Writing (Coppola & Puzo), Best Music (Rota) and Best Art Direction (Tavoularis, Graham & Nelson). Pacino was nominated for Best Actor but lost out to Art Carney for his role as Harry Coombes in the road trip movie *Harry and Tonto*.

The Godfather Part II is a dark, complex movie. Much colder than *The Godfather*. A stark contrast of light versus dark. Good versus evil. Family versus business. Vito Corleone's early life is bright and bubbling with excitement as his immigrant family rise up in New York during the Italian-America revolution. Forty years later family values mean nothing to Michael Corleone. His life is one thing: business. And his business is a dangerous game. As Hyman Roth says to Michael: "This is the business we have chosen."

Producer Gray Frederickson on *The Godfather Part II*

How soon after the release of *The Godfather* did you discuss the possibility of making a sequel?

There were rumours about it but Francis was off doing *The Conversation* and I was off in France making another movie with Sidney Furie. When I came back from France and was in post production, Francis came and [said]. "Yeah, I finally need to make it. But I've given them a lot of... They couldn't have their people on the movie... They couldn't interfere..." He had total autonomy. So *The Godfather Part II* was a totally different experience. They totally left us alone on *The Godfather Part II*. Which was a very pleasant experience.

Because you had more freedom on Part II did you feel more pressure because it was just yourself and Francis?

No. We didn't feel pressure at all. We weren't worried at all. I guess we should have [*laughs*]. We were in Lake Tahoe in pre-production and Francis dropped in one day and said: "We got the crew here. We got the staff. Why don't we just start shooting?" So we shot for a couple of days. Two or three days we had been shooting the movie before they [Paramount] realised we had started shooting.

Was it difficult to incorporate the young Vito Corleone part of the story?

Well, it was very difficult. The editing went through a gruelling process. We looked at a lot of different versions. I was walking out of the theatre [after a private test screening] and Francis was sitting on the curb with his head in his hands. He got up and jumped on a plane, disappeared and went to Paris for a week. Then he came back and said: "I've figured out how to make it work." It was a hard thing to make it work.

There is a rumour that Pacino became depressed on-set because of the downward spiral his character was involved in. Did you hear or see anything to support that? Such as Pacino becoming quite introverted on-set?

[*Laughs*] Pacino is the most introverted person I've ever met in my life. He is very shy and very introverted and very quiet. What we used to marvel at, obviously we didn't shoot in continuity on the movie, and there were days when he was a totally different character. He was stoic and he was rough and tough, and in earlier scenes he was quiet. Later when we put the picture together he mastered it and what an arc he had. He was just a baby... how he knew what point in that arc he was at when he was shooting those scenes?! That's what we used to marvel at. We never knew he was depressed. We knew he was working hard at it. And it was quite the accomplishment to know where you are in that story. That's what amazed all of us.

Did you believe Part II would be better received than Part I?

No. We went to the Oscars and we were just happy to be there. It started winning and then I looked at Francis and said: "What happens if this wins Best Picture?" We were totally taken off guard with that one.

Dog Day Afternoon

Cast: Al Pacino (Sonny), John Cazale (Sal), James Broderick (Sheldon), Charles Durning (Moretti), Gary Springer (Stevie), Penelope Allen (Sylvia), Carol Kane (Jenny), Marcia Jean Kurtz (Miriam), Amy Levitt (Maria), Lance Henriksen (Murphy), Chris Sarandon (Leon). **Director:** Sidney Lumet.

Synopsis: Sonny, and his friend Sal, decide to rob a bank in order to pay for Sonny's boyfriend's sex change operation. However, the bank heist goes wrong and it becomes a hostage situation and a media circus.

"It was a hassle," that's what Al Pacino said about making movies after finishing *The Godfather Part II*. He was tired; strung out and feeling the after effects the illness he suffered while filming in Santa Domingo. His personal life was causing him more problems than he could deal with (women and drink). The last thing Pacino wanted was to make another movie. Regardless, his manager Marty Bregman was pushing him to make *Dog Day Afternoon*, the story of a botched bank robbery, based on real events, which explored sexual orientation as a sub-plot.

On 22 August 1972 John Stanley Wojtowicz, and two friends, walked into the Chase Manhattan Bank, Brooklyn, New York to get the money to pay for Elizabeth Eden's sex change operation (Eden was born Ernest Aron). Following a variety of slap-stick mishaps, Wojtowicz was arrested on the tarmac of John F. Kennedy Airport fourteen hours later. This daring daylight robbery caught the attention of the media and the general public. It also became the subject of a *Life Magazine* article by P.F. Kluge called: The Boys in The Bank.

Marty Bregman acquired the rights to the property, yet had a difficult time finding a studio willing to back the project. Bregman couldn't guarantee the interested studios that Pacino would be involved. The actor had said it was an interesting idea but wanted to revisit it at a later date. The *Life Magazine* article described Wojtowicz as: "a dark, thin fellow with the broken-faced good looks of an Al Pacino or Dustin Hoffman." With Pacino out, Hoffman was offered a chance to play the lead character, and finally Dick Shepherd, an executive at Warner Bros films, took a chance on *Dog Day Afternoon*. When the script was at last completed, Sidney Lumet agreed to direct (he had previously been unsure about the project, much like Pacino). Once Pacino heard Lumet was on board, he gave the newly-polished script another look and decided he could really do something with this character. This meant Pacino was back in and Hoffman was out. Pacino was pleased his long-time friend, and ex-flat mate, John Cazale had been cast in the second lead role, as Sal Naturale, after he'd recommended him to Lumet. At first sceptical as to how Cazale could play a character who was "good looking in an intense, boyish way," the director was won over within a matter of minutes after Cazale came in to read for him. The two buddies had always talked about being in a movie together; they got their wish with *The Godfather Parts I and II*. However, those were ensemble movies. This time it was just them, together, for the entire movie.

Names were changed for the film because the studio felt that the real surnames would be too difficult for audiences to understand and pronounce. Frank Pierson, the script writer, changed John Wojtowicz to Sonny Wortzik. Sonny was Wojtowicz's nickname and his surname was clipped for pronunciation. Three weeks of rehearsal moved swiftly. Pacino grew a moustache to replicate the look of the real life Wojtowicz. After the first day of filming, Lumet and Pacino watched the rushes and Pacino wasn't happy. He felt he'd not yet found the deepest core of Sonny's character. The actor stayed up through the night and re-examined the script and by the next morning he'd found the real Sonny. This guy was not a forward planner. He was a bit of a scatterbrain. He knew what he wanted but didn't focus on how to go about it. Pacino commented: "Sonny comes into the bank wearing glasses. And I said, no, hold it, he wouldn't be wearing glasses. Ordinarily he would, but on the day of the heist he would have forgotten them, because subconsciously he wanted to get caught."

With Pacino firmly in character, the crew sailed through filming without any problems. Lumet told his stylists he didn't want matching sets and costumes. In fact, most of the time the actors wore their own clothes. Also, for the first time in his directing career, Lumet permitted his actors to ad-lib some of the internal bank scenes. Mainly, when the characters were sat around waiting for phone calls from the police outside. The director felt this helped the realism of the movie. He said to them: "You're just temporarily borrowing the names of the people in the script. No characterizations. Only You." In the end about 60% of the movie was ad-libbed even though it was all spoken in line with what Frank Pierson originally wrote.

A scene that particularly challenged Lumet during filming was one in which Wortzik made two phone calls. They ran to fourteen minutes in total. Lumet didn't want to break the scene, knowing it would slow down filming and, more importantly, take Pacino out of the moment if he had to keep stopping and starting. Consequently, two cameras were mounted next to each other, each holding a thousand feet of film. On that amount of film they could record no more than eleven minutes. With the scene in full swing and Sonny making the emotional calls to his two wives Lumet waited until the first camera reel had used 850 feet of film and then started to roll the second camera which would capture the remaining few minutes of the scene. This made it seem as though there hadn't been a need for a camera change. Pacino had run through the scene with the gusto of a man possessed and felt he nailed it on the first take. Another take was called for by the director. The actor screamed at him: "What??! You're kidding." Lumet explained he needed to do it again. Pacino walked off set to compose himself and muster as much, if not more, emotion that he managed in the first take. By the end of the second take Pacino slumped over with exhaustion. He looked over at Lumet who had been crying at how intense and moving the acting was, which set Pacino off too.

Watching the phone call scene, Pacino's exhaustion is visible. He struggles to catch his breath when delivering his lines. The phone is held delicately but pushed right into his ear. Pacino, never-mind the character, can't take it anymore as he lets rip at Angie on the other end of the phone. A normally mild-mannered guy, he bellows down the phone; commanding his wife to shut up and listen to him. Even his swallowing is grandiose. The tight camera work makes a direct connection between Sonny and the audience. We should not feel sorry for him, he is robbing a bank after all, but this phone call draws us further into his world. Talking to his wife is his one last shot at redemption but he blows it by losing his temper with her. It's a heart-breaking moment; Sonny realises he is truly on his own.

Throughout *Dog Day Afternoon*, Sidney Lumet's filming style is fast and furious. The internal shots were all filmed in sequence on a purpose-built set, constructed in a warehouse around the corner from the site of the real robbery. Once filming had finished for the bank scenes, Lumet and the crew quickly moved a block away to a disused street; the shop fronts rebuilt to resemble how they would've looked in the 1970s. The bank frontage was so real that in the days before shooting members of the public tried to walk in and open accounts. Filming took place over seven weeks, including a week of night shoots in a local New York neighbourhood.

One of the key scenes in the movie, the one everybody remembers, is the "Attica! Attica!" moment outside the bank. During this scene, Pacino portrays a man experiencing his fifteen minutes of fame. He is on stage and the world is watching. Pacino waltzes up and down the sidewalk, making exaggerated gestures; his arms aloft; shouting at anyone who'll listen. He forces the police to stand back, ordinarily this wouldn't happen but this is a man on the edge. Pacino visibly revels in taking the character outside into the real world. He moves aggressively forward to one policeman and says: "He wants to kill me so bad that he can taste it." The crowd start to rile and he begins his repetitive blasts of: "Attica! Attica! Attica!" Fourteen times in rapid succession. The crowd understand he's referring to the Attica Prison riots in nearby Attica, New York. There, prisoners rose up against the correctional staff because of poor living conditions. The watching world saw those rioters as heroes rather than villains, and that's exactly what Sonny was looking for as well. He wanted to be the warrior who triumphed over the establishment. Lumet told Pacino: "It's his [Sonny's] day in the sun, with all those people out there."

Sonny might be the loud, brash leader in this heist but let's not forget his sidekick, Sal who utters few words apart from the unwelcome questions posed to an already stressed out Sonny. He knows not to push his buddy too far but at times he has to because he hasn't a clue what he should be doing next. He isn't the brains, he isn't even the brawn. He's willing to pull the trigger on the hostages far too quickly. He wants in and then out but gets stuck in the bank. His belief is that Sonny will see them right; he has always stuck up for him and will continue to do so. Cazale's ability to blend into the background for long periods is fitting for this painfully shy character, but the actor does manage to give Pacino a taste of his own medicine when he lets rip at him a couple of times.

Could Pacino and Cazale have changed roles? Absolutely. Cazale was more than capable of being the strung out Sonny who had backed himself into a corner. Yet Cazale is more suited for the second lead as it's a role that has a certain lamb to the slaughter quality about it. Sal is a nice guy but he doesn't know when to say 'No'. Sonny and Sal are like dog and owner. Sal looks up to his rather more aggressive counterpart and is too scared to say anything against him. One possible reason they stick together is their natural patter. At times, their chemistry is almost comedy duo calibre. The pair boast an element of circus clown buffoonery. No doubt Pacino and Cazale's previous living arrangements boosted the rapport between them; adding an extra dimension to not just the film but their scenes especially. *Dog Day Afternoon* may be remembered as Pacino's film but it's nothing without the comedic workings of John Cazale.

The rigorous intensity of the shooting schedule paid off as filming wrapped up three weeks ahead of schedule and under budget. Lumet and his editor Dede Allen had locked the first part of the movie down within a couple of weeks. However, something troubled Lumet. He'd chopped out four minutes because he felt the first half was too melodramatic. The bank robbery section had to be exhilarating and quick-paced yet the trimming of those four minutes slowed down what should have been the quickest part of the movie. After discussing it with Allen at length, the next day Lumet went and re-added two minutes from the chopped footage. The second half of the movie was already 'locked' and didn't need tinkering with. With the re-edited first half linking smoothly to the second half, Lumet was ready to send the film to Warner Bros. ready for distribution.

Dog Day Afternoon received its world premiere at the 1975 San Sebastian Film Festival in Spain on the 20 September. A day later it was released in the United States. The first reviews were hugely positive, the *New York Times* calling it: "Lumet's best film outside of *Long Day's Journey into Night*". *Variety* labelled it "an outstanding film." Roger Ebert described the film as: "a study of a fascinating character: Sonny." For a film about real life events the box office revenue was particularly good; it eventually raked in over $16 million domestically (Information courtesy of Box Office Mojo. Used with permission). Another triumph for Lumet and Pacino after their success with *Serpico*. Lumet said: "Pacino is incapable of doing a fake moment. He is a rare talent." That rare talent garnered another Academy Award nomination for his portrayal as Sonny Wortzik. The film was nominated in six categories (Best Picture, Best Director, Best Actor in a Leading Role, Best Actor in a Supporting Role, Best Film Editing and Best Original Screenplay) but it only managed to bag one Oscar, which was for Frank Pierson's screenplay.

The critics liked the gritty realism of *Dog Day Afternoon*. Lumet had always dealt with this kind of subject matter. Here however, realism was even more important to him as this film was based on a real-life event. *Dog Day Afternoon* is one of the films that predicted (unknowingly) the advent of the reality TV star. Sonny and Sal are watching themselves on TV from the news stations, all of which had cameras pointed into the foyer. From time to time they check to see how they are looking on camera. Even though they are criminals, they still want to look good for the viewing public. Moreover, after the pizza boy leaves the food, he turns to the cameras and shouts: "I'm a star." Even the getaway driver turns to Sonny and says: "Man! If you could see yourself."

Dog Day Afternoon was made at a time when homosexuality was not as accepted in mainstream society as it is today. The LGBT community endured terrible prejudices and hardships. Even after the Stonewall riots that took place in New York in the late 1960s, a story featuring homosexuals aimed at the mainstream movie-going public was a very tough sell. Director Sidney Lumet didn't see a story about a gay bank robbery though; he just saw a story about two ineffectual amateurs unable to pull off a daring heist. It was about human emotion, the type of human emotion that leads people to do idiotic things for those they love. Middle America might have seen these two gay bank robbers as Freaks. Lumet, Pacino and Cazale made them real. They made filmgoers connect with these characters simply because, as Lumet commented: "these are not the freaks we think they are." Further adding: "We are much more connected to the most outrageous behaviour than we know or admit." Sonny is a man who feels he has been wronged and sets out to seek retribution. The problem is he goes too far.

As a bizarre footnote, the real robbers John Wojtowicz, Bobby Westenberg and Salvatore Naturale went to see *The Godfather* at a Times Square theatre the night before the robbery. Their ransom note the next day had a line that said: "This is an offer you can't refuse." A riff on the line uttered by Brando and Pacino in the movie, which also starred John Cazale. Wojtowicz and Naturale could never have dreamed they would be played on-screen by two people they'd been in awe of the night before the big event. Life imitating art imitating life.

Actor Gary Springer on *Dog Day Afternoon*

Did you conduct any research into the real-life robbery when you signed on to play Stevie in the movie?

I was in Brooklyn driving past the street with the original robbery, so I saw all the hoop-la. I was actually visiting a friend who lived down in Ocean Parkway, and coming back I saw all this excitement and energy. I didn't stop but it turns out that it was the robbery two or three blocks away from where I was driving by. I really didn't do that much research. I had read newspaper articles about the robbery and the characters who were in it. But that was really about it.

When you were reading the script, what type of character did you perceive Stevie as?

He was kind of their buddy. He knew Sonny, he didn't really know Sal. He was a friend of Sonny's. He was just a kid hanging out on the streets more or less. Sonny said: "C'mon let's go to do this thing."

Stevie doesn't go through with the robbery at the last minute, which is a pivotal scene in the movie because it just leaves Sonny and Sal in there. Do you think he would ever have gone through with it?

I should have waited five more minutes then I couldn't have gotten out of the bank and I would have been in the whole movie. It would have been ideal [*laughs*]. Look, I was so nervous just working with Al and John and Sidney and that whole crew. It was only the second thing I ever did. I was ready to run out [*laughs*] and I'm sure Stevie was as well [*laughs*]. I think that if he was goaded into it he would have stayed. If Sonny had said: "Stevie we need you! C'mon" he would have stayed.

You mentioned working with Pacino. How was he to work with at that time? He had already enjoyed massive success with several movies.

It was one of the great experiences of my life. I knew who Al was very well. I had seen him in *The Godfather* and things before. It was a thrill working with Al and he was so intense and it just carried me through. His intensity and energy carried me through and I just thought it was great. A great experience.

He is very well known for his method acting. Did he give you any tips at all?

I don't remember. I just remember that when we were filming the car scene outside the bank I knew that we weren't mic'd for the sequence where I walk to the bank and then back to talk to them. I wasn't honestly sure what to do. He just said play the whole character, play it all. Which is what I did. Which made it easier.

What was it like to work with John Cazale? Because Pacino was a close friend of his and I think those two together are like a dynamic duo in the movie.

John was the nicest man who was around. I really, really liked John. Al was the intensity. Sidney was busy directing, and Sidney was wonderful. He was just so open and warm and funny. John actually kept me calm. I would ride home with John because he lived on 65th on the west side and I lived on 67th on the east side. He was such a calming influence on me while we were working.

As a new actor, how was it to be directed by the great Sidney Lumet?

He was very encouraging about what I was doing. Just watching him on the set and watching him deal with the actors and extras and the crew really enamoured me to the whole idea of movie-making.

What is your abiding memory of working on *Dog Day Afternoon?*

From day one it was a very tight little community. I actually stayed friendly with a lot of the people. I would see them all throughout the years. I've worked on other movies where you do it and you don't see anybody. But because we rehearsed for a couple of weeks with the entire crew... it was like a two week rehearsal at the, I believe, Ansonia hotel up on 72nd street, the whole thing was pretty much as focussed as they are. So it pretty much brought everybody together and I loved that. It made it almost like a family. It was very good and it was my second time out and it was so good having everybody there together and working together. It really was terrific. Sequence wise, probably the sequence where I walk over to the desk and stand next to Al. Because at that point Sidney had taken the wall out, so I walked up and stood next to him and then the camera just panned my whole walk then paused a little bit with Al and I and then continued right on down to John opening the briefcase with the gun. It was a brilliant shot. That sequence where I walk up to Al and say: "I can't do it. I can't do it." Was... I still remember how I felt to this day, forty-something years later.

You said you stayed friends with a lot of people from the production. You've acted with Pacino and represented him for a while. What does he bring to his roles and acting in general that makes him a unique presence?

It's because he is a unique presence. I don't know what he brings to the roles other than his focus and his intensity and his brilliance. Right after *Dog Day* I had time free, he and almost half the group from *Dog Day* went up to Boston to do *The Resistible Rise of Arturo Ui* and a friend of mine was working as a lighting assistant at the Charles Theatre. So I went up to stay with him and hung out with them all because we were all together on *Dog Day* and it was such a great experience.

Bobby Deerfield

Cast: Al Pacino (Bobby Deerfield), Marthe Keller (Lillian Morelli), Anny Duperey (Lydia), Romolo Valli (Uncle Luigi), Gérard Hernandez (Carlos Del Montanaro), Stephen Meldegg (Karl Holtzman), Monique Lejeune (Catherine Modave), Steve Gadler (Bertrand Modave), Norm Nielsen (The Magician). **Director:** Sydney Pollack.

Synopsis: Bobby Deerfield is a world-renowned race car driver. But when a colleague is killed in an explosive crash, Bobby's world is thrown into chaos; complicated by a beautiful woman who steals his heart and leads him on a roller coaster journey.

The career trajectory of Al Pacino had been accelerating at an unprecedented rate. *The Godfather* catapulted the star into the stratosphere of international fame and his popularity only grew with the back-to-back hits of *Scarecrow*, *Serpico*, *The Godfather Part II* and *Dog Day Afternoon*. The crest of the wave had to break at some point however, and 1977 was the year Pacino's hot streak finally came to an end.

Pacino hadn't made a move in two years. Instead, preferring to focus on his stage career. His star billing was still high, but he struggled to find his next film project. He explained to Lawrence Grobel: "I didn't know what to do next. I was very lost in my life." That was until he read the script for racing car drama, *Bobby Deerfield*. Pacino felt he could relate to the tale of the Formula 1 driver whose life was thrown into chaos on and off the track thanks to his love for a woman who is slowly dying. Loosely based on Erich Maria Remarque's novel, *Heaven Has No Favourites*. Remarque had previously written *All Quiet on the Western Front* before venturing into the world of sports drama.

Columbia Pictures purchased the rights to Remarque's novel while it was still being serialised in the German magazine *Kristall* during 1959, at the time it was called *Borrowed Life*. By the time the novel was released two years later, a feature-length film script had been written by Alvin Sargent. Some themes from the book had been kept; other themes were added to explore other sides to the characters.

Executives at Columbia wanted Laurence Harvey in the lead role. However he was busy making, on average, three movies a year. He did this throughout the 60s and early 70s. There was no time for him to fit in a romantic drama about a racing car driver. The project languished until Paul Newman's First Artist Productions came on board to produce. Columbia were now concerned about the commerciality of the movie, outside the racing fraternity. Consequently, First Artist Productions had to negotiate finance with both Columbia and Warner Bros to the tune of $5.6 million. Paul Newman's desire to play the lead helped in securing the finance. Newman was box office dynamite and the studios knew he would appeal to men and women. At one point, discussions with French actor Catherine Deneuve were ongoing for the lead female role of the terminally ill Lillian Morelli. However this fell apart about the same time Newman decided he could no longer commit to the picture.

French film director François Truffaut was first offered the job of directing *Bobby Deerfield*. He turned it down by saying it was the act of turning a steering wheel: "vroom vroom...too much!" He didn't like the idea of all the intense, blaring race car sounds. Sydney Pollack signed on soon after Truffaut declined the job, the attraction for Pollack was: "the idea of a man who has turned against his own past and therefore makes himself a totally isolated individual." Pollack was looking forward to working with Newman, until he had to drop off the project. This left the director in need of a new leading man. His search led him to Pacino. An actor he believed could display emotions just below the surface and still convey Bobby's outer stoicism. Looking for a new movie project, Pacino leapt at the chance to play a role that closely echoed his personal life. He stated: "Sometimes characters you play help you work things out in real life."

Pacino's manager Marty Bregman negotiated pay of $1.5 million for the picture. It was the first time Pacino had made over a million dollars for a movie. Pollack was looking forward to working with Pacino, he commented: "Once he starts on the track of a character, it's like a dog picking up a scent." Sydney signed Marthe Keller for the role of Lillian after seeing her in *Marathon Man* the previous year.

Bobby Deerfield began principal photography on 8 June 1976 in Leukerbad, Switzerland. The Swiss spa town served as the setting for the majority of the scenes involving the hospital Lillian was staying in. Also, the casual driving scenes between Lillian and Bobby were shot around the town and the higher peaks of the Valais Canton.

Shooting continued in Italy at the beautiful locations of Florence and Lake Como, before moving on to Billancourt Studios in Paris for the internal shots. Though this was a racing car movie, at this point no driving scenes had been shot because Pacino didn't have his driver's licence before the start of filming. He finally obtained it on a crash course and filming finished up at Le Mans race track where a whole host of famous F1 drivers showed up to shoot the racing scenes. British businessman Bernie Ecclestone owned Motor Racing Developments Ltd during the 1970s. He facilitated the production team on numerous levels and this is as acknowledged in the credits as: 'With special participation by' alongside his Alfa-Brabham Formula 1 Racing Team.

Five F1 drivers were used during the filming of the race track footage. They were: James Hunt, Mario Andretti, Patrick Depailler, Carlos Pace and Tom Pryce. Hunt drove the car with a camera attached to the bodywork and Pace doubled as Pacino during the F1 track scenes. He tore around the track on days with real, scheduled races so footage of the car in front of full grandstands could be captured. Before filming began, Pacino watched many hours of footage to understand how racing drivers had to get in and out of their cars, he said: "In this picture I've got to drive a couple of cars that you've got to be a contortionist to even get into."

For the first time in his life, Pacino followed a fitness regime. His character had to be physically fit and thus trainer Al Silvani, worked with Pacino throughout filming. This new regime bulked Pacino up, making him tough enough to endure the long, difficult filming schedule.

Filming finished in the September of '76, and Pollack returned to California to edit the movie. One issue that had bubbled to the surface during the seventy two days of filming, was an escalating tension between Pollack and Pacino. Initially they were the best of friends and were working from the same page. Soon tensions grew however, as they each had differing views on how the character should be played. Pacino was trying to find the other side of narcissism whereas Pollack hoped to portray someone true to their own morals. Artistic vision is everything in movies, but when an actor and director are not working from the same angle it can undermine the impact of the overall picture. Pacino commented to biographer Lawrence Grobel: "Maybe we would have been better off had I listened to him more. I didn't quite understand his point of view."

Two major clashes between actor and director led to the breakdown in their relationship. The first related to a scene which was ultimately cut from the finished movie. It depicted Bobby alone in his room at 7pm, not knowing what to do next. Pacino thought the indecision within the character was crystallized in that moment. Pollack thought otherwise. The second clash was regarding the film's finale. Pollack wasn't sure how to close it up and discussions centred on Bobby pulling the plug on Lillian's life support. This raised complications. Should Bobby be caught for enacting the illegal method of euthanasia? Both Pollack and Pacino knew this wouldn't work and needed an ending that fit with the emotional drama Bobby had been through. Pollack sent out a secondary crew to film some external tunnel footage, he pasted that together with a roughly prepared ending in which Bobby and Lillian, while on a stroll, have their photo taken by an American couple. The ending doesn't do justice to the magnitude of the problem the couple face, neither does it convey how lonely Bobby really is. Pollack believed it a suitable ending and kept it, much to the chagrin of Pacino.

Bobby Deerfield was released on 29 September 1977 in New York, and 5 October in Los Angeles. The majority of critics were not kind to the movie, with Pacino and Keller singled out for criticism. *The New York Times* said: "They succeed in creating not a single moment of genuine pathos." John Avant wrote: "People...won't believe how bad Al Pacino is in this movie." However, *Variety* and Roger Ebert gave the movie glowing reviews. *Variety* reporting that: "*Bobby Deerfield* is a brilliantly unusual love story" and Ebert commented that it is: "a big slick melodrama...with great craft." The viewing public were firmly in the first camp of critical reviews. The movie raked in a measly $9.3 million in the U.S. (Information courtesy of Box Office Mojo. Used with permission).

It's easy to see why the general public stayed away from *Bobby Deerfield*. This was not the Al Pacino they had come to know and adore. This was a quiet and subdued Pacino. For most of the film he talks to Lillian in hushed tones, whereas Lillian with her clipped German accent either barks depressive responses or conveys, merely through her expression, that she believes Bobby to be a pointless human being. There was no on-screen connection between the lovers (off-screen was where it appeared to be happening as Keller and Pacino embarked on a torrid love affair). Moreover, Lillian is a very cold person. It's understandable that she doesn't want to let Bobby too far into her life as there is very little of it left, but there needed to be a glimmer of warmth and love in this character in order for us to feel something.

This movie however, inspires no outpouring of grief from the audience. The characters are too shut off from the real world. Pollack never fully explains Lillian's terminal illness. It is alluded to several times and it appears she may have Leukaemia. For a melodrama such as this, never fully explaining the illness is a mistake. It leaves the viewer unable to connect with the suffering Lillian is going through. Without a name put to the disease all we see is a character in the second stage of the Kubler-Ross death model: Anger. Not something that should be sustained all the way through a romantic drama.

Bobby's professional career is juxtaposed with the melodramatic moments. The movie tries to emphasise that the exhilaration of racing is the opposite of what he feels around Lillian. The problem is, Bobby is rarely filmed actually driving his F1 car. There is no flamboyant racing. There are scenes that depict Deerfield during a race, but they never come across as fast-paced or heart-stopping the way a real F1 race would. The monotonous love story seems to bleed into the action sequences which rarely get past lap one. Even when a competing race driver dies, Bobby offers only a glazed, nonplussed reaction.

Some might say this is Pacino's method acting in full flow, however it was essential to display emotion in this moment to convey that the racers are all part of one group no matter what team they race for. Still, no tears flow, Bobby closes himself off further from those around him. Personally and professionally. Deerfield isn't seen as a big-time racing driver, there is something missing; the film fails to convey how successful he really is. He shoots Martini adverts with glamorous women, wears sharp suits and walks the streets in dark glasses in case he's mobbed. But it is never explained how successful Bobby is behind the wheel. Has he ever been a World Champion? Or is he just a middling F1 driver? Bobby might not be as good as the playboy racing driver James Hunt was on the track; but off it he craves the attention of the fans, and more importantly the women, much like Hunt did.

Bobby's brief back story goes someway to explaining why he is the way he is, yet it needed fleshing out more to fully understand why he would be captivated by a woman who is unobtainable for very different reasons to those he is used to. The one time there is a flicker of genuine human emotion is when he is trying to make a bed-ridden Lillian laugh by doing a terrible impersonation of sex queen Mae West. It shows that, behind the blank expressions, there beats in Deerfield the heart of a man who really is trying his damnedest to win the heart of this woman. Pacino doesn't prance around, instead opting to keep still and use his squawky voice to project the teasing of West's persona. This is the one point in the runtime when we get to see under the hood, so to speak, of Deerfield as a regular human being.

Director Sydney Pollack had a specific intent for *Bobby Deerfield* and how it should come across to the viewer. He did admit that: "Sometimes I lose track of black and white, and I find myself falling in love with the grey areas." Pollack made an American film with the style and look of a European art house movie. Sadly, it wastes the talents of its two lead performers on characters that are either unlikeable or aloof, in a movie that should more readily portray the pain of lovers caught in the pull of death. At one point, Lillian screams at Bobby for being dull. She should be aiming that insult at the entire movie, and all those involved.

Magician Norm Nielsen on *Bobby Deerfield*

How does a magician become involved in a film about a race car driver?

It's very bizarre. The acts that worked at the Crazy Horse [Cabaret club] would never go into the Crazy Horse during the day because the girls would have rehearsals and the boss didn't want the males there. So most of us abided by those rules. It wasn't a strict rule by any means but at that time I was expecting a contract to come from a German television show. So I thought I'll just run in quickly to the office and see if the mail had come. Sure enough it had. As I was leaving the Crazy Horse, walking away from it, the secretary came out calling my name. He said you have a phone call. I was startled as it's impossible for me to have a phone call at that time because I would never be there. I took the call and it was Sydney Pollack of all people, the director, and I was dumbfounded and he said he had been to the show the night before and that he was working on a movie called *Bobby Deerfield* and he would like to see me.

So I went to see him that day and it was very interesting because I knew nothing about that – to be in a movie with Al Pacino. [*Laughs*] I was blown away. It all worked out so well. It was very strange the way it happened but the way it came together and Sydney Pollack was a marvellous director. He made it so easy. He even set up a little change booth right next to where it was going to be. They were so helpful and cooperative. It worked out very, very nicely and meeting Al Pacino was a lot of fun [laughs]. But it was such a short part in the movie. Which was fine with me. I was just delighted to be there and do it.

What tricks did you perform in the film?

It was part of my act. I think some of the card moves that I was doing.

You have a couple of scenes with Al Pacino. Did you teach him any tricks?

There was one. They wanted me to walk into a bar scene where Al was sitting on a bar stool and then I was to take out a silver dollar and roll it up in my fingers and he wanted to see how to do it and that what's transpired.

How long did you spend teaching him that trick?

Just a few minutes. It was not a big deal. He couldn't do it anyway [*laughs*]. It was just something to do. Then I do it in the movie.

During the scene in the film, Pacino's character Bobby can't master the trick. So was that real? Or was it all fake?

Well to do that coin roll... it's not so easy to do. It's easy if you practise it for a while. He didn't have a chance to do that. I didn't imagine he could do it. So I just did the coin roll and that was it.

I'm not sure if you are aware of this. After *Bobby Deerfield*, Al Pacino went to make a film called *...and justice for all!* Where in between the takes he was showing off his magic tricks.

Oh really? I had never heard that before.

The whole cast were astounded that he did all these magic tricks. So did you teach him more?

I didn't. He must have got interested in it.

What was it like working for Sydney Pollack?

He was just so amazing. Watching him on the set... it was just astounding. You could almost see the wheels turning in his head. He would go from one thing to another so meticulously. Just marvellous. For me, it was such a treat. Just to be in the movie was such a surprise. Two days later I was going to Spain to work in a cabaret. Then the casting director called me in Paris to see if I could work as a Swiss soldier in another film. I said I couldn't because I was going to Spain on a contract. It was funny how that whole thing started. I wondered afterwards if I could have done it? Would that have led to something else and something else and something else? You never know.

When you finally saw the film, what did you think to it? And your performance?

[*Laughs*] Dumbfounded. Holy mackerel that's me! I don't believe it! It's surprising. The way the whole thing worked out. It was impossible that I went to the Crazy Horse when I did, during the day, because we never did that.

What was Pacino like on set?

He was very, very nice. It was very easy. I couldn't believe it. Just walking in to the bar where he was sitting and doing the coin roll. It was just so easy to do. Everybody on the film was nice to get along with. It was very, very nice.

...And Justice For All

Cast: Al Pacino (Arthur Kirkland), Jack Warden (Judge Francis Rayford), John Forsythe (Judge Henry T. Fleming), Lee Strasberg (Grandpa Sam), Jeffrey Tambor (Jay Porter), Christine Lahti (Gail Packer), Thomas G. Waites (Jeff McCullaugh), Craig T. Nelson (Frank Bowers), Dominic Chianese (Carl Travers). **Director:** Norman Jewison.

Synopsis: Arthur Kirkland is an honest, idealistic lawyer who is suddenly under pressure to defend a distinguished judge accused of raping and battering a young girl – and whom Arthur knows is guilty.

Pacino had played loners all the way up until the end of the 1970s. Those big characters he won acclaim for had one thing in common: they were all on the fringe of normalcy. The role of Arthur Kirkland in the courtroom comedy drama *...and justice for all* is by contrast a character who comes across as a regular Joe. This represented a dramatic change in Pacino's acting style and process. Alongside the everyman, the other yet-to-be-seen aspect of Pacino was the comedian. There are the occasional glimpses of his potential as a comic actor in *Dog Day Afternoon* - but we'd never seen him try his hand at full-on comedy even though Pacino had always wanted to do the slapstick comedy that he so admired from the likes of Buster Keaton. He told Lawrence Grobel: "I used to think of myself as a comedian." Also missing from Pacino's big screen outings thus far was his winning smile, the one that had won over many women in his personal life. *...and justice for all* rectified this and diversified Pacino's on-screen presence.

Screenwriter Barry Levinson had been working on an earlier draft of the movie in which Arthur Kirkland appeared as a secondary character. Soon however, Levinson became too engaged in Arthur's part in the proceedings. He collaborated with his wife Valerie Curtin, for the first time, to create a story that instead focussed on Kirkland as the lead. As research, Levinson and Curtin attended several judicial trials in Los

Angeles and Baltimore to understand the processes that lawyers have to go through.

When the first draft of the script was completed it was offered to Norman Jewison, a director/producer who already had a sizable body of work to his name, including *The Thomas Crown Affair, The Cincinnati Kid, Rollerball* and *In the Heat of the Night*. Jewison saw the script as a "terrifying comedy" about the U.S. legal system that required a charismatic actor to play the relentless lawyer Arthur Kirkland. Levinson mentioned to Jewison that when writing the script they pictured Pacino in the lead role. Pacino however, was, at the time, tied up trying to make the American war drama *Born on the Fourth of July*. After speaking with the director about the role he said: "Why don't I get some actors together and read it for you? Then I will see how I feel after I hear it." After the table read Pacino felt "It wasn't halfway bad   it had a nice structure to it." With Oliver Stone's *Born on the Fourth of July* delayed, Pacino left and signed onto *...and justice for all* during August 1978. Levinson, Curtin and Jewison had their Arthur Kirkland.

Jewison rounded out the main cast with actors old and new; Jack Warden and John Forsythe were cast as high-powered Judges Rayford and Fleming respectively. Christine Lahti was given her first movie role as Gail Packer, an ethics committee member who falls for the charms of Kirkland. Jeffrey Tambor was cast in his first movie role as Kirkland's work colleague Jay Porter. Craig T. Nelson was hired as Frank Bowers, a lawyer who would come to do battle with Kirkland in the courtroom. Pacino's acting teacher, and *The Godfather Part II* co-star, Lee Strasberg was cast as Kirkland's Alzheimer's-inflicted grandpa, Sam. Pacino insisted on being at every audition. He spent hours reading with those auditioning, claiming it was his responsibility to help them get the feel of the script.

Norman Jewison's *...and justice for all* wades through the murky waters of the U.S. courts system. Pacino's Kirkland chases justice for all his clients. He is intellectually honest in a world of dishonesty where lawyers value personal gain over moral triumphs. Kirkland openly criticizes his profession at every available opportunity. As he eloquently explains: "Being honest doesn't have much to do with being a lawyer."

The first time we encounter Arthur Kirkland, he's sitting on the floor of a police cell trying to avoid the steady trickle of urine emanating from the tramp next to him. Dishevelled and tired, for all his youthful years Kirkland looks like a man already at the end of his life. He lets out a fateful sigh as his name is called, signalling his release. No longer can he hide behind the bars, rather he has to face the bar once again. Kirkland is only trying to do his job, and the audience is made privy to several different clients he has chosen to represent that betray his desire to do good - most notably the case of a transgender client arrested for a petty crime. The focus of the movie's storyline, and Kirkland's caseload, is the alleged assault and rape of a young woman by Judge Fleming. Kirkland and Fleming did not see eye to eye before this trial (it was Fleming who put Kirkland in that cell at the beginning of the movie after Kirkland tried to punch him) and yet Fleming knows his only shot at upturning these allegations is to hire THE best lawyer in Baltimore. Kirkland has to deal with this high profile case alongside his other day-to-day cases, and also has to calm his work colleague Jay Porter after he has a meltdown in the halls of the courts. The only shining light in his depressing life is a romance with Gail Packer. Kirkland's problem is that he cares in a world where nobody else truly does. This is not the life Arthur Kirkland wanted, sadly it is the one he has found himself boxed into.

Barry Levinson had originally planned the script around the court houses of his home town of Baltimore. His hope was that the production crew would film there, which would make any script changes easier for him and his wife to cope with. In an article for *The Hollywood Reporter* dated 30 August 1978, it stated that Philadelphia, PA. was likely to be used for the shoot instead. However, the mayor's office in Baltimore had just set up an acquisitions panel designed to attract film crews to the Baltimore area and consequently Levinson got his wish. Jewison stated that the filming access to the Criminal Courts Building in Baltimore was one of the main reasons for returning to the city. He liked the aura of these buildings, especially the Baltimore Circuit Court which was built in 1896 and displayed a large collection of American art on the walls.

External filming began in the first week of November 1978 and lasted for four weeks. Production then moved to the sound stages of Culver City Studios in Los Angeles, CA. Principal photography was completed by the end of January 1979. According to the *Los Angeles Times*, Jewison had turned down the offer of advice from the American Bar Association. He wanted to avoid any possible disputes they might have over the manner in which some of the lawyers were depicted. Before filming began, Pacino, a loyal method actor, spent a couple of weeks with lawyers to better understand their workings. Much like his out-of-hours police arrest while making *Serpico*, Pacino become somewhat over-engrossed in the role of the lawyer. A close friend was complaining about a contract he was being cajoled to sign and Pacino grabbed it off him, thumbed through the finer points of it before realising that, once again, he wasn't a professional in that trade. If that wasn't enough, Pacino actually smashed the windscreen of a Cadillac with a briefcase, which is no easy feat considering the glass on a Cadillac was, at that time, over a half an inch thicker than standard windscreens.

Jewison compared Pacino to a Doberman Pinscher dog: "If you take him off the leash, forget it! The anger is incredible." That anger that Jewison so loved was particularly evident in the big, courtroom finale where Kirkland, defending Fleming in the rape trial, let's fly at his client in a string of typically vigorous Pacino shouts. He snorts, snivels, spits and cries throughout a six-minute monologue in which he verbally takes down Judge Fleming. At times he whispers to the jury then sucks in the air to launch into a merciless assault. By the time he shouts: "The man should go to jail" Pacino's head almost comes off his shoulders, such is the power of his aggression. Judge Rayford shouts at him that he is out of order which leads to the infamous and often mis-quoted line, "YOU'RE OUT OF ORDER. YOU'RE OUT OF ORDER. THE WHOLE TRIAL IS OUT OF ORDER." Pacino walks around the court room like an animal stalking its prey. Even while being dragged away by court room officials he continues to berate and abuse those he feels have wronged him along the way. Pacino practised the "You're out of order speech" over twenty times while sat on the ledge of the courthouse building. This was the Pacino that Jewison wanted, and needed, for the role of Arthur Kirkland. He became the character for the entire shoot. Jewison recalls going to dinner one night with Pacino and Strasberg only to find they were both still in their roles: "I found myself saying, "Grandpa, pass the salt" or "What did you think of the scene today, Arthur?" It was uncanny."

...and justice for all held its world premiere at Toronto's Festival of Festivals. It was the closing night's gala presentation on 15 September 1979. It was released in U.S. cinemas on 19 October 1979. The critics had mixed reactions to the film. Newsweek described it simply as "a mess." New York Magazine singled out the star of the film, stating: "Pacino's never been so unconvincing." Roger Ebert gave it three out of four stars, saying it was "an angry comedy crossed with an expose." He also described Pacino's performance as high-voltage and one "so sure of itself we hesitate to demur." The Hollywood Reporter gave a vaguely positive review of "One Terrific Movie." Sitting somewhere between the good and bad reviews was Stephen Farber writing for New West magazine who commented: "Pacino gives a showy, grandstanding performance. It's distressing to see him lapse into cuteness to win the audience's love." Though the budget was just $6 million, the film eventually took just over $33 million in the U.S. box office alone (Information courtesy of Box Office Mojo. Used with permission). Pacino was, once again, nominated for an Academy Award in the category of Best Actor in a Leading Role. Levinson and Curtin were also nominated for Best Original Screenplay. All three of them lost out on the night of the awards ceremony but box office success and numerous nominations are not a bad return for a court room drama that held little to interest the casual viewer outside of Pacino.

Pacino's co-star Lee Strasberg told the press: "This film is good for his sense of humour." And it was. This was a Pacino that the movie-going public had not seen. For two thirds of the film he is laughing and joking around. Playing the fool with his work mates, enjoying the romance of another colleague. Pacino was free to spread his comedic wings. Especially in the scene where the slightly unhinged Judge Rayford takes Kirkland for a ride in a helicopter. As the copter descends, Kirkland sinks lower and lower into his seat, gripping the seat belt. His eyes widen as he starts to think about his forthcoming death. Screaming: "Oh God! Oh God!" The copter drops out of the sky into the water. Next we see the main windscreen shatter and Kirkland almost pole axed in his seat with a dazed expression. While Judge Rayford passes it off as nothing more than a trivial matter, Kirkland breathes in the salty sea air as if it's a gift from God. As the Judge and Kirkland enjoy a coffee in the local air force base, Rayford says to Kirkland: "Why is everyone so pre-occupied with death?" A slow raise of the head from the flabbergasted Kirkland, he leans in and slowly says: "I'm not usually pre-occupied with it. But this certainly seems like a valid time."

At times, the comedy in this film borders on the slapstick humour of Laurel and Hardy but lacks that final pie on the face. That's not to say Pacino couldn't deliver it right in the eye, but rather the film doesn't stray that far into physical comedic territory. During a rather vigorous plate throwing scene inside the court house, Kirkland dodges crockery thrown by his work colleague Jay Porter. It's highly amusing to see a top-class lawyer dodging and dancing about. Jewison could have taken it further and allowed a plate or two to hit someone in attendance but instead he holds back just enough to keep it funny and true to life. Watching this film, there is a sense that Pacino felt Kirkland needed comedy to relieve stress, underlined by what happens when the jokes dry up and the pressure rises in the film's grand finale.

One other noteworthy point about this movie, which goes hand in hand with the comedy, is that Pacino successfully woos a female by being charming, funny and erudite. This was really the first time in his movie career, that the audience witnesses his big and bold smile. In this film, he goes all out to show his lady friend that he really is a sweet guy away from the stress and strain of the courts. Several times we see Kirkland and Porter in bed together, in a state of undress discussing the day's work. Though their sex life is not explored on-screen, the connection between the two is obvious, even if they do operate on opposite sides of the court.

The title of the movie ...*and justice for all* is almost entirely sarcastic. Officially it's a line from the United States Pledge of Allegiance. A proud expression of the possibilities of life in North America. However, the title use here is ironic. A cynical look at how contradictions in the U.S. legal system inhibit fair practice in a court of law. Jewison commented recently: "I think it's still difficult to find justice unless you're white and very wealthy." Commendably, the director has made a movie that strikes right to the heart of a flawed system. Unfortunately, the switch between light-hearted humour and the realism of the court room feels ill fitting. This dark and satirical courtroom comedy struggles to find an easy balance. ...and justice for all may have received respectable returns at the box office, but it's not a film that will be remembered for anything except Pacino's explosive "YOU'RE OUT OF ORDER!" speech. In fact, what it should be remembered for is the first glimpse of a cheery Al Pacino. One who acts the fool and flashes a winning smile. Arthur Kirkland may be a loner, but he is arguably more affable than any of the movie characters Pacino previously played.

Actor Thomas G. Waites on ...*and justice for all*

Your character, Jeff, is one of Arthur Kirkland's main clients. Did you know it was going to be such a key role?

Yeah. I did know it was going to be a key role. As a matter of fact, there was an additional theme that was cut. There is a scene in the movie where he comes to visit me in the hospital. So when I read the script I was like: "Wow! This is going to be a real opportunity for me." Back then the few people who were fortunate enough to get an audition knew that we were going to go in an audition with Al reading with us. That's an anomaly. It was so rare. So my agent called me and said: "You're not just meeting with Al, but reading with him." You have to understand that he was like my idol! When I was in high school I became Michael Corleone [*laughs*]. I walked around talking like him and walking like him. The guy is just a phenomenon.

The funny story I wanted to tell you was I get to Martin Bregman's office where the audition was being held and I see Pacino himself behind the desk talking to the secretary and he says: "Listen I have to go, I have a dentist appointment." So here I am, I'm like Mr. Nobody at twenty-three years old and I go: "Excuse Me! I was supposed to audition with you and you're leaving to go to a dentist appointment." [*Laughs*] I don't know where I got the audacity to say this and he looked at me and he was so sympathetic: "Jeez, I'm so sorry. Let's give this guy another appointment." So they gave me another appointment and I came back the next day and I went into the room and we got right into the scene. We auditioned with the big climactic scene in the movie and I kind of knew there that I was going to get it.

The big climactic scene is a tough moment to watch in the film. Was it tough to film as well?

Yes it was tough to film. I will tell you why. Because I was working with a method actor and I consider myself something of a method actor, not to the extent Al is but I try to get into the character, I stayed crouched down in that position that you… I stayed in that position the whole day. I wouldn't get up. So when I said: "Oh my legs are cramping" that was a real thing because I wanted to see the character… he was in so much fear… I wanted to try and recreate… it was amazing working on that movie. That was one of the highest points of my life because what happened was, I had to shoot the climactic scene the very first day I got there. I forget why. I was terrible.

They had the camera set up and I was just awful and Norman Jewison [the director] came up to me and said: "What's the matter kid?" I was like: "I dunno" and Al overheard us and was like: "Don't worry about it. Just relax." So Norman asked everyone to leave the room. Just the three of us, Al, Norman Jewison and myself sitting on the bed reading the script and Al said to me: "Just read it like you've never seen it before. Like you've never seen the words before." Because I was nervous and there is one of the greatest actors in the world sitting less than a foot away from you, and you're acting with him and he's got to be judging you right? [*Laughs*]. And sure enough after ten minutes in the room just the three of us, we knew that I was ready. We brought the crew back in and that's where I got the nickname One-Take Tommy because I did every angle in one take.

So what is it like acting directly opposite Pacino?

It's an interesting question. After I did *…and justice for all* I went on to do the play *American Buffalo* with him off-Broadway for almost a year. First I did it at the Long Wharf Theatre and then we brought it into New York. I really know what it's like to act opposite Al Pacino. What it's like to act opposite him is what it's like to stick your finger in an electric socket and get a spark. It's like being alive with electricity. There's never nothing going on. It is like a live wire. When he performs on stage it's like he is up on a veritable cross. He takes himself down from the cross at the end of the night. On film, the same thing. There is no difference. Same intensity. Same commitment. Same deep, deep emotionality. He's a guy who works a lot with the thing actors know as affective memory or emotional memory. So he's a deep guy. He's also a lot of fun. He doesn't really fool around on the set so much. He's a lot of fun to know as a person. We used to watch the baseball games together during the World Series. He's a regular guy.

You said he is fun and intense. In *...and justice for all* we see that because there is a comedic side to him as well. Is he a funny guy? Because he did class himself as a comedic actor growing up.

He appreciates humour in others and that's what makes him able to convey humour. He's always observing. His wisdom is derived from ability to observe and because he is always watching he really appreciates it when someone else is really funny. He's such a great actor that he gets inside every character. He's not like a 'Ha Ha' comedian. The humour is a result of the character. He creates a character from within. But he can be funny. We've had some laughs over the years. I haven't seen him in a while and it's a shame. I miss him. I always send him a Happy Birthday message and I always go to see him when he is in plays. But I don't like to bother him, you know.

You went to the Actors Studio after starring in *...and justice for all*. Was that a decision born out of working with Pacino and him discussing the studio with you?

No, to tell you the truth he never ...well I shouldn't say never mentioned it... No, I became aware of the Actor's Studio completely separate. Totally separate from Al and then I learned of his association later and then I auditioned....he didn't have anything to do with my audition. It's a very difficult place to gain entry to you know. I think Al auditioned six times before he got it, if the story I read is correct. I got in myself the first time. I was very fortunate. Arthur Penn and Ellen Burstyn were the judges for me. Then after I got in, I think Al was surprised I got in, he helped me to get a Broadway play. That was really, really nice of him. He's an icon. Every actor will tell you that there's Al, and then there's everybody else. He's a guy who always returns to the stage. He doesn't have to do that. Nobody else does that. What other American movie star returns to the stage almost every few years or so? It's tough work being on stage. It's a tough deal – seven, eight shows a week. But he does because of his enormous respect for the craft. He and I did Shakespeare together.

You did Richard III. He loves that play doesn't he?

He does. He was great in *The Merchant of Venice* too. Holy Fuck! He was fucking brilliant! I remember when I saw him, I said he was fantastic in it.

You're now running a very successful acting studio yourself – The Thomas G Waites Acting Studio. Do you teach method acting?

No I'm a Julliard-trained guy. So I was classically trained. Although my personal style is that I meld the two together. I start everybody off with Shakespeare to throw them in the deep end to teach them verse and what works to stress, almost formalistically. Then gradually, slowly, I put them into a contemporary scene and say: 'OK! Let's analyse and evaluate what is going on here from the inside out.' Which is the primary difference between the two. One is inside out, the other is outside in.

If you could choose just one Pacino film to play for your students to show them real method acting what would it be?

Dog Day Afternoon. There was the most incredibly brilliant acting. I thought they got a guy off the street. I knew it was Al Pacino but when the movie started I forgot completely about *The Godfather.* I thought: this isn't the same guy, they got some freak out of Attica [Prison]. He is the epitome of the anti-hero's hero.

Back to *...and justice for all.* Because of the incarceration theme in the movie, do you think it's becoming more and more relevant?

I do, yeah. Remember that was Barry Levinson's first movie. The great director, Barry Levinson. That was how he got into the movie. He wrote that script with his then wife. People forget that it was written by Barry Levinson. I remember Norman Jewison saying: "I saw this script on my desk and my assistant said: 'you have to read it.' I read it and I had to do the movie." Our prison is a disaster, our legal system is basically: if you're rich, you're OK everybody else forget it. Don't get in trouble with the law because you might get put in there and never come out. This movie... talk about prescient. This was 1978 long before they just busted everybody to Rikers Island. The criminality in the legal system is just awful. Barry Levinson and his then wife Valerie wrote the script that was so far ahead of its time. It didn't get good reviews and I remember Al was so upset. He picked me up to play a game of pick-up basketball and he said: "You know they shot us down kid. They shot us down." I said: "Yeah I know. I hear the reviews weren't good." He goes: "You know... some day they'll realise what a good film this is." And, of course, I was just thinking about myself. I was like Yep! But what about me? And he said: "Don't worry kid you got a beautiful talent. Don't worry. They'll find you." He was always very good to me. I miss him.

Cruising

Cast: Al Pacino (Steve Burns), Paul Sorvino (Captain Edelson), Karen Allen (Nancy), Richard Cox (Stuart Richards), Don Scardino (Ted Bailey), Joe Spinell (Patrolman DiSimone), Jay Acovone (Skip Lee), Randy Jurgensen (Detective Lefransky), Ed O'Neill (Detective Schreiber). **Director:** William Friedkin.

Synopsis: New York policeman Steve Burns infiltrates the underground S&M subculture to trap a serial killer preying on gay men.

Pacino had played characters operating on both sides of the law during the 1970s and, realising he couldn't play bad guys all the time, it seemed an obvious move to try and replicate the success he had with *Serpico* by taking on the lead role in *Cruising*.

In this picture, undercover New York policeman Steve Burns is plunged head-first into the city's homosexual nightlife, and the S&M subculture, as he tries to track down a serial killer preying on gay men. In some respects, *Cruising* could be thought of as an alternate version of *Serpico*. A cop trying to take down a bad guy while being hampered by his own colleagues is standard fare in police procedural dramas. However, *Cruising* ventures deeper and darker than most mainstream movies would ever dare to. Homosexuals had greater liberties by the end of the 1970s thanks to the Stonewall project, but mainstream society continued to view this social group as second-class citizens. There was still a stigma attached to being gay, a stigma this film sought to challenge.

George Romero had some success in this arena when he cast black actor Duane Jones in the lead role for *Night of the Living Dead* in 1968. The film was released just months after the assassination of Martin Luther King and the passing of the Civil Rights Act. White Americans were still unaccustomed to seeing black actors cast as the hero and there was some uproar over this element before the movie was released. When people finally went to view the film however they focussed largely on the horror of the movie, and both Jones and the film itself received a great deal of praise. The gay community needed their own Romero, so to speak. They needed a movie maker who wasn't afraid to push boundaries and represent their community in a mainstream production.

The film rights to Gerald Walker's novel of the same name were snapped up in 1970, the year the novel was published, by producer Philip D'Antoni. Flush with producer money after the success of *Bullitt*, *The French Connection* and *The Seven-Ups*, D'Antoni scrambled around for a couple of years trying to find a major studio for the project. None of them were interested in a film they felt could not be marketed to mainstream film-goers. It was seen as a niche, indie movie that would only to appeal to a certain demographic. D'Antoni had offered the directing job to his *French Connection* director William Friedkin, however when Friedkin finally read the book he didn't see much in there to make the type of movie he was looking to make. D'Antoni took the project to Steven Spielberg, who was interested in taking the reins. They continued to pitch the studios without success until Spielberg dropped out to make *1941* and start prep work on an adventure movie featuring a character called *Indiana Jones*. D'Antoni thus resigned himself to the idea that the movie was never going to be made and sold the rights to another Hollywood producer – the tenacious Jerry Weintraub.

Weintraub was in the process of helping Lorimar Productions, a TV studio known for such shows as *The Waltons*, *Dallas* and *Knots Landing*, branch out into major motion pictures. They'd experienced middling box office results with movies such as *The Tamarind Seed*, *The Choirboys* and *Twilight's Last Gleaming*. Weintraub kept pushing Friedkin to come back onboard and make the movie for Lorimer. Friedkin was still uninterested until a succession of events led to him reversing his decision. The director learned of a series of killings in the leather bars around New York which mirrored the storyline. Also, the first strains of what was to become the AIDS virus were first showing; homosexual men were dying without any knowledge of the disease they had contracted. Friedkin had further discovered that a bit-part actor from *The Exorcist* had been convicted of a couple of the murders in the bars. Via the prisoner's lawyer, Friedkin negotiated a visit to New York's Riker's Island Penitentiary and asked what happened. The convict explained that the police had offered him a deal if he admitted to more murders than he had been charged with. It turned out to be a harrowing tale of police brutality against homosexuals. These events all hit Friedkin hard, and he called Weintraub to say he was now convinced he knew what to do with the movie, and would be willing to direct.

Pacino had long been an admirer of William Friedkin's work. Initially they had been set to work together on *Born on the Fourth of July*. When it repeatedly hit stumbling blocks, both of them departed the project and it looked like they were never destined to work with each other. Pacino had been particularly enamoured with Friedkin's early work *The Birthday Party*, an adaptation of a Harold Pinter play. Pacino still felt much more of a stage actor than a movie star and very much enjoyed play adaptations that made it onto the big screen. Friedkin's *The Birthday Party* was not well received upon release, but it did show that, as a director, he was unafraid to tackle tough subjects. So was Pacino. Thus, this movie looked like the beginnings of a continuous working relationship that could've seen them work together more often.

Before filming had even begun Friedkin and Pacino conducted their own research into the gay bars of New York. Friedkin was friends with a former undercover Police Detective who gave them a tour of the local scene. This proved to be an invaluable experience; Friedkin found the sex clubs fascinating. It was in these dank and badly-lit rooms that he started to piece together the background for his movie. Separately, Pacino was taken on a tour of the same clubs by Friedkin's Police Detective friend. Dressed in the derigueur costumes needed for entry, Pacino wandered around in a leather jacket and tight jeans constantly worried he might be spotted and have to abandon his methodical research. However, nobody recognised that one of the world's biggest actors was in their bar. He made friends with several locals who helped him discover the ways of the underground homosexual movement, for example the meanings of the coloured hankies in the back pocket. Friedkin wanted to push boundaries. His previous screen-writing colleague Walton Green said Friedkin had "become obsessed with [Pier

Paolo] Pasolini's courage in using cinema to explore the most disturbing fringes of sadistic human behaviour." Friedkin had seen Pasolini's *Saló or The 120 Days of Sodom* at the New York Film Festival in 1977 and was ready to push the same boundaries with his own work.

Filming began in July 1979 and spanned ten weeks in and around New York's gay district in Greenwich Village. Friedkin felt that shooting the movie in the actual places the killings had taken place would add to the realism of the movie. Greenwich Village during the 70s, and after Stonewall, was a dirty and dark place to be. It may have been a hive for the arts, music and literature crowd, but the district looked more like a post-apocalyptic suburb. People wouldn't cross a street for fear putting their lives in jeopardy. Close by was the abandoned Pier 48, which was used as a rendezvous for casual sex. It was described by the painter Delmas Howe as "an arena for sexual theatre". This was exactly the type of cinematography Friedkin was looking for. However, when it came to filming the bar scenes he ran into a problem. Most of them were owned by the Mafia. Friedkin had to hold several meetings with the mobsters to convince them his movie was not going to raise questions about their lifestyle. Some of them ended up in the final movie as paid extras. If that was the only issue Friedkin had while making the movie then it would have been plain cruising. Sadly, a much larger and more volatile problem was already brewing.

Gay Rights activist and *Village Voice* newspaper columnist Arthur Bell had fired a rallying cry to the gay community encouraging them to picket the film. Bell had read an early draft of the script and deemed it an ugly portrayal of the gay lifestyle. This was true, however it was an early script and since then it had changed several times. Bell was further outraged when he requested a look at an updated script and was declined. Bell needn't have felt marginalised as most of the cast never got to see a full script either. Producer Jerry Weintraub tried to ease the tension by putting out a press release stating they were only using "selected characters and the title" for the movie, however this did not satisfy the gay community.

Organised meet-ups were staged and groups marched down to the sets to "mill within camera range, cause a barrage of noise via loud radios, block streets and remove no parking signs." There was even a large sit in around the bars during filming. About 800 people turned up that day to protest. Some of the bars due to be used for filming had to withdraw their offers after discovering they'd be boycotted by their gay clientele. Weintraub got in touch with the New York mayor's office to explain all the problems they were having on the streets of Greenwich Village. In response, Mayor Koch sent out the largest mounted police contingent they had to offer. Death threats were made to the bars owners, to Friedkin, to Weintraub and to Pacino. The leading actor's main concern was that he didn't want to upset anyone from the gay community over the movie and, especially, through his portrayal. "It makes me feel bad" he said, "It's actually hard for me to respond at all.... I'm coming from a straight point of view, and maybe I'm not sensitive enough in that area." Unbelievably, none of these problems physically delayed the filming of *Cruising*.

When the director retired to the editing suite to piece together his murder mystery movie however, trouble followed him. United Artists, the distribution company, were a member of the Motion Picture Association of America which required all movies to have a rating. Friedkin sent his cut off to the Classifications & Ratings Administration (CARA) for a movie age classification with the expectation that it would receive the dreaded "X" rating, usually reserved for pornography. It was worse. An X rating would be granted only if Friedkin cut three minutes from the movie. But Weintraub and Friedkin were not just going to cut into their movie, they wanted it released as they had made it – controversy or not. Both of them went to see the Chairman of CARA, Richard Heffner, at his house. They screened the movie for him and waited. By the end credits Weintraub asked Heffner for a response. "What do I think? Jerry, this is the worst film I've ever seen in my life. There are not enough X's in all the languages for this picture."

The censors had two major issues. Firstly, they objected to the brutal nature of the material, a killer plunging his knife into the victims was deemed far too grotesque. The editor Bud Smith had to go back and re-cut that sequence, removing an over the shoulder shot of the knife cutting down the victims' neck and also several shots of blood squirting from the gaping wound after the knife was pulled out. Friedkin, annoyed at the reduction of this sequence, inserted brief glimpses of hardcore anal sex within the knife sequences in an act of rebellion. These frames are not easily viewable when running the movie at the standard speed, slow it down however and they are clear to see. Though included in a fit of anger, this segment parallels the process of a knife entering and exiting the body and a penis entering and exiting the body. Drawing the audience's attention to the links between sex and death, a strand that has run though literature for thousands of years. Friedkin has kept quiet on this subject, so perhaps we will never know his true intentions.

The other problematic sequence for CARA was the notorious "precinct night" footage. All set in a damp, dirty underground bar where the entire attendance are wearing police uniforms in one form or another. The clothing wasn't the problem; it was the gratuitous nudity and sexual acts on display. They were not faked; these sexual acts were actually being filmed for inclusion in Friedkin's movie. He was trying to be as raw as Pasolini in his depiction of sex, but while Pasolini passed it off as Italian art house Friedkin had an Oscar-nominated actor in his movie. A movie that wasn't trying to represent homosexuals in a degrading manner, but was doing a good job of showing the degradation that some lived by. This almost-forty-minute "Precinct Night" sequence had to be cut from the movie.

This cut to the interior bar sequence didn't happen in one fell swoop however. Friedkin and Weintraub trimmed little bits and kept returning to CARA for a new assessment. The outcome was always the same – a rating denied. Consequently, they employed the founder of CARA, Dr Aaron Stein – who has since retired from the board, to help. They agreed to pay him $1,000 a day for his work. It ended up costing them $50,000 just to secure an "R" rating for *Cruising*. Ultimately, the footage that Friedkin cut was described as "pure pornography."

The controversy that surrounded *Cruising* doesn't end there. The largest theatre chain in America – General Cinema Theatres - had seen a rough cut of the movie and decided to pull it from being shown at the thirty-three screens it had scheduled for release day. Two weeks later, General Cinemas saw the finalised cut of the movie, and while some of the offending footage had been cut they still decided they would not screen the movie as planned. Other cinema chains did show the film but were still apprehensive about screening it as an "R" rated movie, and so it was given a special "X" sticker over the top of the original rating.

Released on the first weekend in February 1980, movie theatres in New York, Chicago, Los Angeles and San Francisco were picketed by gay rights activists, hoping to block potential movie-goers from seeing the film they so despised (but had not seen). The reality was that mainstream movie lovers were not interested in seeing Al Pacino play an undercover gay cop. He may be chasing down a killer on the loose but to witness him doing so in seedy gay bars was not what fans of Michael Corleone or Frank Serpico wanted. It may have been 1980 but mainstream society was still reluctant to explore the topic of homosexuality. There was confusion over the box office results for the first weekend of release. Initially a return of $1.6 million had come in from the 180 theatres showing the movie. However, nearly 400 theatres had not reported back by the time weekly box office numbers were due for publication. Once the final numbers did arrive at Lorimar's offices they stood at a less-than-healthy $8 million for the first week. Lorimer distributors put out a statement saying "as of now, the film is not knocking them dead." After six weeks in cinemas *Cruising* just about stumbled past the $13 million point in U.S. box office receipts (Information courtesy of Box Office Mojo. Used with permission). Critics had not been kind to the movie, the *New York Daily News* calling it "a depraved, mindless piece of garbage." The *Village Voice* newspaper said it was "hardcore homophobic." The *London Evening Standard* deemed it "a grotesque mess of a movie." *Cruising* was to suffer further indignation after it was screened at the Berlin Film Festival on 22 February and roundly boo-ed off screen.

Where had this mess of a movie come from? Viewing the film it's clear the blame cannot be laid on any one person. Friedkin saw source material that would serve him in his continuous fight to become an auteur. He wanted to be celebrated as a non-conventional director and *Cruising* certainly has all the hallmarks of a non-conventional film. Given the time it was made, this film could have established Friedkin as a champion of the homosexual community in the cinematic arena. However, somewhere along the line he appears to have lost his focus, the film veers off the main story about the killer and instead explores a world of sexual perversity. Friedkin seemed more content to film homosexuals engaging in hardcore sex acts than he was telling a murderous story. Gary Morris of *Bright Lights Film Journal* described *Cruising* as "the queer equivalent of [D.W. Griffith's] *Birth of a Nation*," explaining that the film was made by somebody outside the subculture portrayed in the film and offered a very negative depiction. Possibly that was the problem for Friedkin, he wasn't one to take advice from anyone within the community.

Pacino looks completely lost in *Cruising*. Even in the beginning he looks like a haunted man, his usual Italian dark skin and good looks are gone. Replaced by a pasty, wide-eyed actor who appears to have never been on a film set before. It's not that Pacino is bad in the film, far from it; it's more that he lacks the cutting edge that he usually brings to a role. Constantly looking uncomfortable whether he is shown in the basement of a club or having sex with his girlfriend. It's a stumbling performance from someone who held the world in his hand a few years prior. At one point, we see Pacino's Steve Burns being lured onto the dance floor of the underground club. Pacino's electric shock dancing is painful to watch. With no rhythm, or understanding of the movement, he appears to have his feet stuck to the floor while his torso lashes left to right. His arms move in rapid vigorous bursts up and down. Gifted with a bandana from his dance partner that is soaked in amyl nitrate, a substance that offers an instant high, his dancing catapults into spasmed shocks. It's a curious dance routine completely out of sync with those dancing around him.

There is meat to the character of Steve Burns, yet somehow the one actor who was relied upon to find the core of the character appeared lost. After seeing the finished film, Pacino commented to Lawrence Grobel: "I thought I had reached the bottom. But...it's really not so bad down here." Years later the film still rankled Pacino, saying "*Cruising* just wasn't a very good picture."

Cruising wasn't the picture everyone expected it to be. Cut to ribbons by a censor's board that was scared of permitting on-screen degradation. A director stuck between the two worlds of police procedural drama and homosexual exploitation movie. A lead actor so hidden within his shell that he had no idea how to escape. *Cruising* is a distasteful and rather reprehensible movie.

Author note: Pacino was so shocked and incensed by what he saw in the gay community while filming *Cruising* that after he received his pay check he put half a million dollars into a trust fund. The interest it accumulated went to many different charities including those searching for a cure for AIDS.

Former NYPD Detective turned writer/actor Randy Jurgensen on *Cruising*

During your time in the New York Police Department you became a consultant in the movie industry. How did that happen?

In the mid 1960s I was undercover. Narcotics, and I worked very much on the outside, not in the inner circle, on the Patsy Fuca case which became known as the French Connection. Robin Moore wrote a book called *The French Connection* and it morphed into a movie and while they were making the movie I was called, along with the other detectives, not only to consult but to take the actors and the director out in the streets to see how it was done. Jumping ahead, that's exactly what happened in *Cruising*. But that's how I came into the movie industry. I was so fascinated by it that I worked on other movies on the production side. I took a test and was welcomed in the Directors Guild of America. I went in as a second assistant director. I worked on a huge picture called *Annie*. From there I was promoted and I wound up as a production manager, a unit production manager and an associated producer on movies later on. That's basically how I got into the industry through a picture called *The French Connection*.

Returning to the subject of *Cruising*, you went undercover to investigate the murders committed against homosexuals in New York. This is the storyline of the film. However, the film is based on the book of the same name. Did you have any input into Gerald Walker's book? Or just William Friedkin's film?

I was working with William Friedkin on a movie that was going to be about a book... I think it was called *Love and Money*... I'm not sure... it was about this big socialite family in Texas and we were on our way to Texas, just Billy and myself, and he had optioned the book and we were on our way. The long story about that is that it did not work out. While we were returning back to New York from Texas, Billy said to me: "Randy you worked in the gay world." It was pretty well known throughout the Police department that yes, while in narcotics, I was taken out of narcotics and I was placed... from the Manhattan's district attorney office they suspected a salt and pepper assault team, one was white and one was black, and they thought they might have been cops.

So I went to work on that case. I was about seven months [undercover]. I ingratiated myself into, let's call it, that world. I made friends and I was tracking killers. I got lucky and I got them. It's a long story but I got them. That was long before Gerald Walker's book of *Cruising*. So while on the aeroplane coming back with Billy Friedkin, Billy said to me: "I'm going to do that story. I'm going to do that book and I only want to option that book for the title and Randy! Please don't read the book." Which I never did. We went to work on the screenplay. It took us months. Billy Friedkin drafted the screenplay and we worked on it. The next thing that I knew was that Richard Gere was definitely going to be the character loosely based on me. Frank Sinatra's name was mentioned along the line. He was going to be the Paul Sorvino character and the reason Frank Sinatra's name was mentioned was that the producer, Jerry Weintraub, was the manager of Frank Sinatra at the time. These were the things I heard straight from Billy. Then I was told that.. I believe it was 20th Century [Fox]... was going to pick up Al Pacino's salary and the rest of the picture below the line would come from wherever it would come from.

When I heard it was going to be Al Pacino, I knew Al and I knew him from *The Godfather*. I'm not going to say we were friends or that we socialised but I got fairly close to Al Pacino in the making of *The Godfather*. So when I met Al on *Cruising* one of the things he wanted to do was, he wanted to visit these clubs which I had gone through when I was undercover and before taking Al into the clubs I took Billy Friedkin into the clubs. I learned a long time ago, working a number of pictures with Billy Friedkin, he had to see it; he had to be aware of it.

Starting with the French Connection [real life drug smuggling case], when we made drug arrests Billy Friedkin was right there with us. So when I had gone into these clubs, I took Billy Friedkin with me. We actually danced, we dressed the part. I wasn't fooling anybody by this time. I wasn't fooling anybody as to why I was there and they knew we were going to make a film. I did the same thing with Al Pacino. We sat for hours learning, from me, the code... and there is a code. How you dress. Where you wear your hanky. My foray into that world was not about homosexuals working on Wall Street. Mine was a pretty violent world and it was the leather world. That's the world that I brought Al Pacino in to.

In the making of the picture there were a lot of firsts. Nobody had ever filmed in the medical examiner's office and I was able to get, through a medical examiner that I knew personally, I was able to get us into the morgue. That's the way Billy Friedkin makes the movie. Many of the locations in the film were where I actually worked. Those that were still operating. We were able to secure real homosexuals, we didn't have Screen Actors Guild people portraying homosexuals. The picture took on those that were for the picture and those that were very vociferous against the picture. There were times when we were out in the street filming and it was dangerous. The demonstrations against the movie... I, as a police officer, had a great concern for Al Pacino who showed up like a trooper and worked every night through it. There was a bottle thrown and it hit the film truck and Jerry Weintraub, who was also there every night standing alongside of Billy Friedkin, the bottle hit Jerry and required stitches in his hand. It was a very, very, very tough picture out in the street. We were out in the street of where it originally took place.

In the end, Al Pacino's portrayal was loosely based upon my exploits. To this day I could not answer whether the screenplay was based on Gerald Walker's *Cruising*. I sat with Billy virtually every night and said: "This is what I did. This is what happened. This is how I did this. This is how I gained entrance." Billy wrote it all out in long hand and adapted that to the screenplay. There is a scene in *Cruising* where Billy said to me: "I need to gain entrance to this apartment. Al Pacino needs to gain entrance to this apartment. How can I do it without a warrant?" I simply said: "Billy, at this stage we know exactly what the suspected killer is doing each day. I just go down there and climb up the fire escape." Which I did in broad daylight. Climbed up the fire escape with a newspaper, went in and stuffed the newspaper in the fan. Billy said to me: "What if a cop comes along?" I said: "I would say I'm on the job! I'm working! The cop would leave." That's how that scene got in there. I'm pretty sure that's not in Gerald Walker's book. I used that as an example, that what you see in *Cruising* is what I experienced up in Central Park, in the brambles. Also in the hotel, that scene actually took place when I was working on the case. I don't know the adaption from the screenplay to the book.

Did you find it strange that you were in a film based on your previous undercover exploits?

Actually no because by the time we got to *Cruising* we had made a number of movies throughout the seventies. They started making pictures on cases that I actually worked on. I never thought about it.

You sat with Pacino many times for him to understand what you had gone through. So what was it like to act with him?

I do have a couple of scenes in the movie with Al Pacino. Every day during shooting, while Al Pacino was in make-up... and he got made up in his own camper... we would sit there and he would ask a question and the conversation would go. Generally the conversation was one way because Al Pacino, like all other actors I have worked with, they are a sponge. They don't want to talk about their career. They want to talk about the character they are playing and I found that it is very, very helpful that the character, and this instance it was me, was sitting right in front of Al Pacino. There were times where he would say to me, just quietly lean over and say: "You're not fucking putting me on are you? You really did do this?" and I would say "Al, yeah I did. But the movie is enhancing it to make it entertaining. But yes I did." There were times I was afraid, I was very much afraid. One of the things I explained to Al was I was sort of losing my identity. He found that very interesting.

There are stories suggesting that Pacino was mentally affected by what he was filming. Did you see any of that?

Entering into that world, I will say personally for me, when I dressed like that and I was out in the street, and I am a policeman, and I would see a police car go by... I had fear. I was afraid. I would imagine, as an actor, taking on that... that's pretty foreign for an actor to become that character. First and foremost, what Al Pacino had to become was a cop. He had to become a cop, and we talked about that at length. We talked about a cop, how he would react, how would we do this and how would we approach it. There was no way I was going to catch these killers if I was not ingratiated into that life, and I feel that is exactly what Pacino would do.

When *Cruising* was released it was very badly received. Why do you think that was?

In my opinion because the gay press was very, very vociferous. Writing constantly about this is not the way we are. It was very controversial. There was no way, in my opinion, that any of the critics were going to come out...the picture, in my opinion, wasn't... it wasn't addressed as to how well it was filmed or acted. It was criticised for the subject matter and I don't think that is a fair review. When we went to the opening and Billy took questions, they were calling him "Liar!" and so on and I was in the theatre and I walked right down to the front of the theatre and I said: "Mr Friedkin filmed what I saw and what I lived." It sort of quieted them, but only for a few minutes. Then after that they continued to do the same thing. I think it was the world of the gay people, where the murders were taking place.. it was taking place in, what we called back then, the leather scene. It was very violent. It was very, very violent. Some of the scenes that took place, that I witnessed first-hand, they had Nazi night and they would dress up with swastikas and the Nazi flag, and that's what Billy filmed and that's the world that these killers operated in. That's what Billy filmed. That's what Al Pacino acted in.

Personally, what do you think to the film?

I'm certainly not going to criticise Al Pacino or Billy Friedkin or anybody who took place in the making of the film. Maybe... maybe... the film went too far to make its point. I don't know... I don't know. I do know what's in that film... happened.

Author! Author!

Cast: Al Pacino (Ivan Travalian), Dyan Cannon (Alice Detroit), Tuesday Weld (Gloria Travalian), Bob Dishy (Morris Finestein), Bob Elliott (Patrick Dicker), Ray Goulding (Jackie Dicker), Eric Gurry (Igor), Elva Josephson (Bonnie), Ari Meyers (Debbie), Alan King (Kreplich). **Director:** Arthur Hiller.

Synopsis: Life is getting complicated for Broadway playwright Ivan Travalian. His flaky wife Gloria is moving in with her lover, his director hates his new play and his leading lady is a terrified movie star who has never been on stage. With five children to look after (most of them Gloria's), a budding romance with his leading lady and a producer demanding a rewrite it's no wonder the emotionally and financially unstable Ivan starts to exhibit all kinds of irrational behaviour.

It is easy to see why Pacino took on the role of tortured playwright Ivan Travalian in *Author! Author!* He had grown up watching comedy, and had entertained family members with comedy skit routines from a very young age. There were slight touches of comedy in ...*and justice for all,* however that role never allowed Pacino free comedic rein.

Pacino had played the (anti) hero roles for over a decade. The thought of changing track and taking on a role that did not require any method research beforehand was appealing to him. Also *Author! Author!* was set in the world of stage productions. Pacino had been on stage before he was on screen; it was a world he knew all too well. Ivan Travalian could have been Pacino in a former life and, given the thematic scope of the film, it could even have been a semi-biopic conveying the struggles Pacino had in his early years, scratching around on stage off Broadway. Thus, the professional side of the movie appeared a natural fit for Pacino.

Some elements of Travalian's personal life were not so relatable to Pacino but others starkly mirrored the actor's experiences. Ivan Travalian is a working single parent to five children, most of them his ex-wife's, and leads a chaotic life. All of the children are at different developmental stages, each of them causing him different problems. Travalian has to navigate the bumpy road that is juggling a full time job with raising kids. A romance with his play's leading lady only heightens the non-stop anxiety for Travalian. Pacino might not have had any kids but he'd fallen for more than one of his co-stars since becoming a global star. The awkwardness of this picture was underscored further when it became clear he would be acting opposite his old girlfriend Tuesday Weld. It was to be art imitating life.

The seeds for *Author! Author!* were planted back in 1968 when Pacino appeared in *The Indian Wants the Bronx* at the Astor Place Theatre in New York. This off-Broadway production was a one-act play written by American director and playwright Israel Horovitz. The play ran for 177 performances and, during that time, Pacino became enamoured with Horvitz's work. After the play finished, and Pacino went off to make movies, the director and actor occasionally spoke about working together again, whether it be on stage or on film. Pacino directed several different productions of Horvitz's play *Rats,* fitting this alongside his filming schedule. When Horovitz wrote a loosely autobiographical piece about a playwright trying to stage his first Broadway play, Pacino jumped at the chance to work with Horovitz's material and show off his comedic chops. *Author! Author!* looked to be an engaging and fulfilling project for Pacino.

Arthur Hiller was recruited as the director based on his previous films which all had elements akin to *Author! Author!* Hiller was used to combining comedy and romance in a more personal setting; he had tasted box office success with *Love Story, The Out of Towners* and *The In-Laws. Author! Author!* seemed like a natural fit. The appeal for Hiller was what the movie "had to say about love and family relationships."

The director might have found his motivation early on but it was not so for the leading lady. With her long, curly, flowing hair and cheek bones to die for, actor Dyan Cannon had charmed audiences for more than twenty years. Initially offered the role of Gloria, Travalian's wife who runs off and leaves the kids, she turned it down saying: "I didn't like her. She's just bitchy, and I've played that kind of role." Cannon was then offered the role of Alice, the actor who is the star of the play and a lover to Travalian. Cannon told the *New York Post*: "Alice is terrific, and Ivan is adorable with her. They're friends who are lovers."

The role of Gloria eventually fell into the lap of Pacino's ex-partner, Tuesday Weld. The four-time wed Gloria, who falls-in-love-too-easily, is played as the villain of the piece. The audience are not encouraged to sympathise with her as she runs out on her kids yet again. At one point in the movie Gloria has to verbally abuse the leading man in the style that Pacino normally uses when he lets fly at other people. Could that be part of the reason Weld chose this project? Did she see it as an opportunity to extract some mighty ex-lovers revenge by bellowing in his face on camera? It's a theory.

Rounding off the main cast was Alan King as Travalian's Broadway producer Kreplich. King was known for his scathing wit and angry, yet humorous, rants (another cast member set to take on Pacino at his own shouting game).

Principal photography began on 2 November 1981 at Manhattan's Astoria Studios. Filming moved to outside locations during January 1982. The majority of external filming was in New York: Washington Square Park, The Plaza Hotel and Sardi's restaurant. Several scenes were also shot at Good Harbour Beach in Gloucester, Massachusetts. Principal photography was due to be completed by 1 February 1982 but a storm had been brewing, throughout filming, between the director and his leading actor. History was repeating itself as Pacino yet again fell out with his director. Echoing the parody seen in the movie itself, the *Author! Author!* script was constantly being re-written throughout filming and the newly written pieces were causing friction between Pacino and Hiller.

The initial strain of their relationship as actor and director became evident in the first few weeks of filming. Pacino was late on set several times, which Hiller found less than endearing. Hiller had been nicknamed by his crew as Arthur 'One More and We're Out' Hiller because of his continued use of that phrase even though it never was just 'one more.' Inevitably, the picture ran way over budget before "Cut" and "Print" was called. Pacino was used to doing several takes and then cutting out, he didn't like to have to keep going round in circles many many times.

Hillier ultimately found himself in a situation where he'd failed to get one of the big scenes in the movie in the can. The scene involved Travalian standing out the front of The Plaza Hotel by the fountain. When it was time to shoot there was a troublesome aspect with the script. So Hiller postponed the shoot until Horovitz had re-written it. A few days later the crew returned to set up the scene only to be caught in a torrential downpour that put the kybosh on filming. It rained for another entire day when it was rescheduled for a third time. Days later, the rain had stopped and filming was set to begin however it was noticed that the trees around the fountain had all shed their leaves which was no good for a movie supposedly set during autumn. Hillier stalked around the fountain trying to figure out how to shoot the scene without any further delays. A date in early January was set for the filming of the scene, by then the Christmas trees illuminating the background would also have been taken down. The miserable experience of trying to film one outdoor scene continued as the day in January selected for filming was deemed far too cold by the production manager. The next day a blizzard of snow completely covered New York, ending any hopes of actually filming the long-awaited scene.

While this filming disaster was playing out, the crew moved to Gloucester, Massachusetts. Pacino arrived ninety minutes late on the last day of filming. Hiller gave Pacino a very loud dressing down in front of the whole cast and crew. Pacino was told: "You have no respect for your fellow actors and crew." Not one to take a dressing down from a director he didn't respect, Pacino walked off set back to his trailer. It took several hours to coax him back onto the set to finish filming. The job of pulling Pacino out of his trailer was left to producer Irwin Winkler, who sat there for a few hours regaling their star with tales of working in the industry. Pacino eventually relented and returned to finish the scene. He did try to brush off the argument and his subsequent return to the set by saying: "I didn't know I was supposed to work that day. I remember being ready and wanting to work, but not being told." This temper tantrum cost production two more days of filming time. The tension between Hiller and Pacino didn't ease for the rest of shooting. Principal photography finally finished on 4 February 1982.

Despite this obvious tension, it wasn't a negative filming experience for the rest of the cast. Alan King had great fun playing a "producer that is a cross between Hall Price and Zero Mostel." Dyan Cannon had a delightful time on set and compared it to "being on a cruise." Pacino still bore a grudge though, and said "sometimes people who are not really meant to be together get together in this business for a short time. It's very unfortunate for all parties."

18 June 1982 was the day *Author! Author!* was released in the U.S. (Hiller and Reynolds had had to work non-stop to get it finished on time due to filming running over schedule). It garnered little fanfare from 20th Century Fox's PR machine. Instead the pieces of press it was picking up were from the scathing reviews. Roger Ebert commented that the movie "is never even able to establish consistent attitude toward its characters." *Newsweek* said: "There is nothing sadder than a movie that tries to be adorable and isn't." Pauline Kael of *The New Yorker* scolded the film by suggesting the movie had "some of the worst ideas and most doddering, bone-headed situations to be seen on the big screen in years." The lead actor was also singled out on occasion. Nigel Andrews of *The Financial Times* reported: "Pacino looks inert to shellshocked." Rex Reed felt: "Al Pacino hasn't much talent for comedy." Box office receipts were equally poor with the movie pulling in just over $2 million on its opening weekend. By the following weekend the movie was dropping like a stone, picking up receipts of only £1.7million. After *Author! Author!* had finished its theatrical run it had only drawn in $10.5 million domestically (Information courtesy of Box Office Mojo. Used with permission). While not a huge abomination of a movie, it certainly didn't help Pacino's reputation when he starred in yet another movie that failed to pull in the crowds.

Comedy is notoriously difficult to get right, and while Pacino had felt he always had the capabilities to be a comedic actor, his turn in *Author! Author!* shows his resemblance to a once-great comedy actor trying to find his old routines that worked so well. Pacino struggles with the comedy however appears at home with the playwright dialogue. This could be down to the fact that this part of the character resonated more with Pacino. After treading the boards for a couple of decades, he knew how the backstage politics worked. However, being flanked by several kids who veered between ditzy, cute and downright obnoxious was hardly going to help Pacino find his comedic timing. A lot of the problems with the movie do stem from how annoying the children are. It may be fun to see Travalian joke that he has forgotten to beat his kids today as they all scatter throughout the house, but when said kids start to offer life advice to Ivan there is a sense that these are pompous, know-it-all youngsters who really don't understand the world outside of their little, brownstone bubble.

One moment Pacino does get to shine in *Author! Author!* is when Travalian accidentally locks himself and his (step) kids up on their roof as they try and escape from the police. Stuck on top of their New York brownstone, with the police and many onlookers down on the street below, Travalian lets fly at them, explaining why he isn't willing to give up his kids. The scene recalls Pacino's work in *Dog Day Afternoon* when he exits the bank and plays up to police, crowd and movie cameras. It's farcically over the top, his arms wave and his voice is large and bellowing, however it feels like the method actor in Pacino is shining through. The movie has already fallen on its face by the time this scene rolls around, so whereas in previous movies it would be a real high point, here it feels completely detached from the rest of the storyline.

Travalian as an author deserves none of the recognition that we see in the movie. He is equally not at home with his kids or under the bright lights of Broadway. Sat waiting outside the theatre doors during the first performance of his play, he comments to his eldest child: "They didn't laugh. They aren't laughing."

These six words perfectly describe the viewer's experience of watching *Author! Author!* It's a TV movie with a better than average cast.

Writer Israel Horovitz on *Author! Author!*

Where did the story for *Author! Author!* originate?

I have no idea where the idea for *Author! Author!* came from initially. It's just ridiculous for a writer to try to explain where ideas come from. They come from a magic place. I sent him [Pacino] the script very early on and he agreed to do it. It was quite a departure for him to do a family comedy and I think he performed extremely well. I'm not sure his audience wanted to see him as a father of children particularly at that point in his career. I think they wanted to see him with a gun in his pocket.

Were you surprised that Pacino signed on for the role?

No, not at all. I think he has huge comedic skills and that's contributed to his success. In the plays of mine that he did, it was evident he was very, very funny and he could turn it on a dime. It was that he had done a bunch of films before that that were... let's say violent. So no, I wasn't surprised. It was completely within his skill set. I think it was something he wanted to try.

The film revolves around the male perspective of divorce, an idea that is not explored very much in movies. Were you concerned about how it would be received by the general public?

Not at all. I think it was not uncommon in America to... no, not all. That was what was unique about the film.

It is a persistently upbeat film. Even when Ivan is feeling down his kids rally round the character and pick him back up.

Yeah. In life he is a good father, and in the film he is a good father.

Ivan goes through many ups and downs trying to get his play made. Is that autobiographical?

I suppose it is for young playwrights [nowadays]. But it was absolutely typical, and I suppose it still is if you talk to a couple of young playwrights I'm sure you'll get the same story.

You knew Pacino from his time acting in your play *The Indian Wants the Bronx*. Did you spend much time with him when he was working on *Author! Author!*?

Yes. I was on the set every day.

Did you see any changes in attitude and style in this film when compared to his work in *The Indian Wants the Bronx*?

No, except he was doing a completely different character. His character in *Dog Day Afternoon* is extremely funny when it needs to be funny. I would say his performance in *The Indian Wants the Bronx* was very close, in a way, to his performance in *Dog Day Afternoon*. There are elements of comedic acting. Comedy doesn't preclude method acting. Truthful acting is truthful acting and Al was extremely truthful in *Author! Author!* He has a special skill of being extremely truthful but pushing the envelope, shall we say. He is a performer. He connects with the audience. He is never dull. It's always very alive.

What was Pacino like during his time working on *The Indian Wants the Bronx*? As it was before he had made the transition to filmmaking.

Yes it was the first play in which he was reviewed. During the run of that show Francis [Ford Coppola] saw him in the play and cast him in *The Godfather*. He was a very young guy. The play opened and the reviews were phenomenal. John Cazale was a very close friend of mine and he replaced an actor who wasn't very good. We needed a quick replacement. That's how John and Al met, in the play. They did the play for a year.

He likes to move between stage and screen. He is one of the few actors who continue to do that. That is quite a rarity nowadays.

Yes it is. The theatre is really his home.

What did you think to the finished film?

I loved it. The film changes quite significantly from the printed page to the screen. I loved it and I love watching it still.

What is the meaning of the phrase *Author! Author!?*

When a play is an enormous success on opening night very often audiences will call "Author! Author!" to the stage to take a bow. It is a very special honour.

Actor turned Entrepreneur & Investor Eric Gurry on *Author! Author!*

This was your first feature film. Do you remember what the audition process was like?

Indeed. It wasn't so different from hundreds of other auditions I did over the years (except, of course, that I got the part!). The auditions were held in a low-rise office building on 57th and 6th in Manhattan. I don't remember how many call backs there were, but I definitely was back to re-audition several times on several different days. They were reading for all the children's roles at the same time, so the waiting area was packed with boys and girls running lines. I remember one boy who would often read for the same roles as I did coming up to me after he read to tell me that the casting people really liked him. I replied: "Great!" to which he responded: "No, they REALLY liked me." That audition, like most, could easily become a pressure cooker if you let it get to you. Thankfully, I didn't.

Your character, Igor, is the sensible one in the household, and I include Ivan in that. Did you want to play the stable child-cum-adult or were you hoping for one of the other kid's roles?

Given the different ethnicities, ages and sexes of the characters, playing a different role was never a consideration. But it was generally more common at that point for me to be reading for the stable, logical, smarter-than-his-years characters than the alternatives.

Igor seems to be more in tune with Ivan than any of the other children. What was it like acting opposite Pacino?

That was a tremendous experience. I understand that Al can be a pretty reserved individual, and I witnessed that with some of his interactions on and off set, but with me he was open and friendly. He really took me in, partly due I'm sure to his method acting approach and his desire to build a relationship with his on-screen son. Even though I was young, I understood the magnitude of the writer, director, cast and crew with which I was surrounded and the amazing opportunity it represented.

This is the first comedic film Pacino had starred in, were you surprised to find he could do comedy?

Not at all. He lived in rarefied air to me, a character actor that could shape-shift to truly become his role. I assumed that if he wanted to take a part as the lead dancer in a film about the New York Ballet, he would nail it, no stunt-double required. So did I doubt his ability to do comedy? Never.

What was he like off camera?

Al really is a funny guy. He has a dry sense of humor that can veer into Vaudevillian at times. He usually retreated to his dressing room/trailer when not needed on set, but if you were hanging out with him there, the real Al came out. He always had great anecdotes about his formative years in New York, his training, his struggles to get his first role and the household names that he counted among his friends.

Did you get to spend much time with Dyan Cannon and/or Tuesday Weld?

My exposure to Dyan and Tuesday was more limited. We had time on-set and during read-throughs, of course, but not much beyond that.

The scenes in the house with all the kids running round are filled with chaotic energy. Was it difficult to remember placing in order to be on camera and deliver lines?

There certainly was a lot of energy on set! In hindsight, I think the ADs should have gotten some kind of medal for managing to control the chaos. But Arthur Hiller was a meticulous craftsman when it came to blocking scenes, and nothing was ever rushed. By the time you were ready to shoot a scene, it wasn't a challenge to remember where to be because the physical activity felt so natural and dovetailed so well with Israel's dialog.

The film is over thirty years old now. What is your opinion on it now?

Honestly, I think it has stood the test of time quite well. It was never destined to be an academy award-winner, but it still delivers an entertaining, cute and heart-warming look at interesting characters placed in emotionally challenging situations. The film, like the main characters that inhabit it and the man that penned it, doesn't take itself too seriously or harbour pretentions. I've often heard from people who want to discuss the role with me that they would like to see where all those characters end up thirty years later, and I feel the same way. Perhaps that is the best testament to the film: people remember it fondly and cared enough about the characters to wonder how their lives would have progressed.

Scarface

Cast: Al Pacino (Tony Montana), Steven Bauer (Manny Ribera), Michelle Pfeiffer (Elvira Hancock), Mary Elizabeth Mastrantonio (Gina Montana), Robert Loggia (Frank Lopez), Miriam Colon (Mama Montana), F. Murray Abraham (Omar Suarez), Paul Shenar (Alejandro Sosa). **Director:** Brian De Palma.

Synopsis: Tony Montana, a Cuban refugee truned small-time criminal, guns his way to the top of Miami's cocaine empire during the 1980s.

It was almost a decade since Pacino had had a box office smash hit. He had tried different roles and genres, but nothing was working for him or the film-going public. He made some poor decisions, famously turning down the role of Han Solo for *Star Wars IV: A New Hope* when offered it back in the late 1970s, and he needed a lead role that would grab the attention of those who had written him off.

One day, while driving through Los Angeles, he noticed the marquee of the Tiffany Theater read: "SCARFACE". This, Pacino decided, was the perfect character for him. He'd watched old 1930s movies during his time playing Arturo Ui on stage in the German play: *The Resistible Rise of Arturo Ui*. The play was a satirical allegory for the rise of Adolf Hitler and the Nazi Party before the events of World War II. Bertolt Brecht had written the play as a fictional 1930s American mobster production. Pacino learnt that Brecht had been interested in gangster films while writing the play, so to get into the mindset of Brecht's character Pacino started to screen some of the movies that the playwright had become so enamoured with.

One film he hadn't seen was *Scarface*, the 1932 movie directed by Howard Hawks and starring Paul Muni. Based on the 1929 novel by Armitage Trail, which in turn was loosely based on the life of American gangster Al Capone, Hawks' movie was difficult to find because it had run afoul of U.S. regional censor boards, which deemed it too violent for 1930s audiences. Alternate cuts were made of the film, but the new version still did not pass some censors boards. A year later than planned the first version of the movie was released and, much to the chagrin of the censors, it was a critical and commercial success. Over the decades it faded from view, apart from occasional showings at selected repertoire theatres. Pacino was lucky enough to catch one of these rare theatrical screenings. Dazzled by the performance of Paul Muni as Antonio "Tony" Camonte, Pacino felt the movie was ripe for a remake. He called his ex-manager and producer Marty Bregman and exclaimed: "I think we could do this thing. There's a remake here. I gotta be that Tony Montana guy. That's my license to live."

Having watched the film at Pacino's insistence, Bregman realizing that the actor could easily bring something to this role, so he set about trying to put together a remake of the notorious gangster movie. First, he approached Universal Pictures, who owned the rights to the original movie. The studio jumped at the chance to make a gangster movie with an actor who had previously created an iconic crime movie character in Michael Corleone. A budget of $18 million was set.

Bregman then had to find a writer and director. In very coincidental ways, both the writer and director of *Scarface* had previously been in touch with Pacino about other films. Oliver Stone had had success as a screenwriter with the films *Midnight Express* and *Conan the Barbarian*; his two directorial films which had not fared well and were considered outright failures. Stone had been talking to Pacino for a few years about making his passion project about the Vietnam War, a movie titled *Born on the Fourth of July*. But when Pacino bailed to make something else, Stone's war movie reversed back into development hell. Pacino still wanted to work with Stone but there were several obstacles on the road to finding the right director.

Initially, the job of directing the remake was offered to Brian De Palma, a director already known to Pacino. De Palma had chased him to play the lead role in his mystery thriller *Blow Out* but Pacino was caught up in another film at the time, so De Palma offered the role to John Travolta.

Both insisted, however, that they would work together on a future project. That was to be *Scarface* as De Palma jumped at the chance to do the remake. He started work on the screenplay in collaboration with playwright David Rabe. Originally, the film was going to be a straight remake set in the 1920s, and then when the story wasn't coming together they proposed an Italian remake. This idea was not well received by Bregman or Pacino. De Palma bowed out because he could not find the right style for the movie and he also finally had a movie green lit by Paramount. De Palma admitted: "We couldn't agree on what we were trying to do." This left the *Scarface* remake languishing without a director, so Bregman went to Sidney Lumet, the man who Pacino loved working for and whom he held in high esteem as a director.

It was Lumet who came up with the idea to set the remake in present day Miami so that Tony could be a Cuban refugee fresh off the Mariel boats. This idea was born out of the real-life events as Fidel Castro's Cuba was in a state of economic collapse. Cubans fled to neighbouring countries, including the United States. With greater and greater civil unrest, Castro was forced to open the previously closed port of Mariel, allowing anyone wishing to leave Cuba a safe passage through to Miami. Over 125,000 refugees travelled to Florida over the course of five months. The U.S. Government struggled to deal with the influx of Cubans. Castro had purged his country of undesirables and sent them to live in America. United States residents were concerned that many of these undesirables were criminals and were set to continue their crime wave in America.

The original *Scarface* film had an American taking down America; but times had changed and audiences were not used to seeing one of their own be the bad guy. It had to be an outsider. Bregman was excited by this new development. He had always believed that the true tale at the heart of *Scarface* was a metaphor for the American Dream and how anyone could succeed in the land of the free and the home of the brave. Now he needed a writer who could convey the angst and passion of refugees. The task fell to Oliver Stone.

By the time Stone signed on, De Palma had come and gone and Lumet was in. It seemed as if the new director had picked the perfect person to write the screenplay. Oliver Stone had previously undertaken research into the drug cartels and trafficking as he was developing a screenplay about the cocaine wars. He had travelled to Miami, Ecuador and Bolivia. He became friendly with some of the drug barons and almost lost his life when in Bimini he mentioned the name of a defence attorney who had previously helped with his research; Stone was unaware that the lawyer had helped jail one of the guys in the cartel. Stone decided to rent an apartment in the Iraqi Embassy in Paris, France to write the screenplay. There, Stone went cold turkey in order to kick his cocaine habit. This screenplay was his farewell to drugs; it became a cathartic experience for him as he let out his innermost fantasies. He said: "What better farewell than a guy falling into a big ton of cocaine."

Returning to Hollywood with a completed screenplay that both Bregman and Pacino loved, Stone was shocked to discover Sidney Lumet hated it. It wasn't political enough for Lumet, he wanted to tone down the violence and introduce a subplot which suggested the CIA were involved in the drug trade. Pacino and Bregman didn't like this idea. They felt the screenplay worked best as it was. Bregman secretly contacted Brian De Palma, now without a movie after Paramount did a U-turn on his project which he had left *Scarface* to make. De Palma loved the screenplay and the new take. He knew exactly how to make this picture now. So Lumet was cast out and De Palma was back in. Struggling with the budget Universal Pictures had initially agreed upon, De Palma and Bregman requested it be upped to $25 million because of the huge supporting cast and lavish sets required. The studio balked at the requested $7 million rise, eventually settling on a $5 million increase which made the budget $23 million.

Nearly every famous and non-famous actress auditioned for the role of Elvira Hancock, Tony Montana's trophy wife. Michelle Pfeiffer went for the role but had discovered that De Palma had seen her in Grease 2 and said that he could never use anyone from "that pink disaster." However, producer Marty Bregman flew her into L.A. for a special screen-test opposite Pacino. A small theatre was rented and they played out a scene set in restaurant where Elvira goes ballistic at Tony. At the end of the scene the crew came running over as Pacino was bleeding profusely. It turned out that during the smashing of some glasses by Pfeiffer, she had inadvertently cut Pacino. Pfeiffer believed this accidental bloodletting is what won her the role.

The inexperienced Mary Elizabeth Mastrantonio auditioned for the role of Tony Montana's younger sister, Gina; but her only acting experience had been in New York stage musicals. She had been in a revival of West Side Story and during the Scarface auditions she was featuring in Amadeus. Nevertheless, De Palma and Pacino both felt Mastrantonio had truly understood the character in the audition process, and there was a natural chemistry between her and Pacino. Signed onto the production soon after, Mastrantonio said she "went from panniers to machine guns!"

One person who got lucky in the audition process was the Cuban actor Steven Bauer. He was studying under Stella Adler (Marlon Brando's acting coach) in New York and got a call to meet the casting director. He walked in the room and was told by casting director Alixe Gordon: "Yeah. You're Manny." Bauer was then sent to see De Palma, and as soon as he walked in the room De Palma told him: "Yeah, you look like Manny." De Palma then called Bregman and told him he'd found Manny. Bauer was then sent to L.A. to meet Bregman face to face and the moment Bauer walked in Bregman said to him: "I'm going to tell you something. You're going to do this film. You're going to play Manny." Bauer had not even uttered one line of scripted dialogue before being cast.

Bauer was stunned when he was finally offered the role. He was the only genuinely Cuban actor in the main cast and he made the role his own by establishing a natural patter with Pacino when running lines. Pacino commented that: "Steven and I became very close friends and spent much, much time together." With the entire cast in place, De Palma insisted on four weeks of rehearsal time. He allowed the actors to play around with their characters "Al and the other actors would improvise scenes and find things to build into the scenes." The whole rehearsal process was so meticulous that it felt like a play rather than a movie to some of the cast.

Principal photography was set to begin in September 1982 around the city of Miami. However, the Cuban community of Florida took against the film, believing it would represent Cubans in a bad light. Led by former Miami City Commissioner Demetrio Perez Jr, the Cuban community ran the production out of town. De Palma and Bregman decided to relocate production to Los Angeles and New York for the twelve week shoot. Sets were built in and around L.A. The refugee camp was set between the junction of Santa Monica and Harbor freeways. Two large and spacious villas in Montecito were used for the homes of the Bolivian cartel. Little Tokyo doubled for Little Havana. The production units erected Spanish neon-glow signs over the original Japanese ones and the garish "The World Is Yours" blimp.

A disused warehouse in Compton was used as the outside of the Babylon Nightclub. F. Murray Abraham remembers some Japanese tourists trying to enter the club thinking it was a real venue: "They were set on getting in, no matter how many times we said no. And you should have seen the look on their faces when they finally got through the doors – there was nothing there apart from a great empty space." The interior of The Babylon Club had been erected on a Hollywood sound stage. This multi-level club was one of the biggest sets ever built at the time, incorporating an onyx dance floor, deep fluffy carpets, large Greek statues, fountains, neon lights and mirrored walls.

Despite all the promising elements the film had going for it, problems started to occur in the filming. Primarily incidents that involved Pacino. As Tony Montana was in almost every scene of the movie, Pacino was on set nearly every day. While filming the big finale, Pacino accidentally put his hand on an M-14 Machine Gun that had just finished off firing several rounds of blanks. The gun was burning hot and Pacino's hand was stuck to the barrel for a few moments. He was rushed off to Sherman Oaks Burn Centre where he was told he had second degree burns on his hand. Pacino was out of action for two weeks. Once back on set, he injured himself a second time by accidentally slamming his fingers in a phone booth door during a scene. Ever the method actor, Pacino finished the scene before looking at his fingers.

It wasn't just Pacino that was suffering however, even the locations took a battering. The wedding sequence between Tony and Elvira was set to be filmed in Santa Barbara County on one of their golden beaches but when a freak weather storm rumbled into the area, it shut down any hope of filming and caused millions of dollars of damage to the local area.

After all these setbacks, the shooting schedule went from twelve weeks to twenty-four and the Universal Studios bosses weren't happy. De Palma was called to a meeting with the Universal executives who lambasted him for being over schedule. They were specifically irate about Pacino's lateness on set. De Palma told them Pacino was working as hard as anybody on set and "if you've got a problem with what he's doing, his trailer is down the street from here." The executives went to speak to Pacino. De Palma remembers, "The[y] ended up having coffee with him and telling him how great he is." Production was completed early in the springtime of 1983; it was now down to De Palma to edit *Scarface* into the movie he'd visualised.

A U.S. theatrical release date of Christmas 1983 was pencilled in which gave De Palma and editor Gerald B. Greenberg plenty of time to whip *Scarface* into shape. Stone's screenplay ran for over one hundred and seventy pages and thus De Palma knew the runtime was going to be near three hours. The editing process was plain sailing compared to the shooting. Several rather lengthy scenes were edited out, including one that saw Manny sat in a Jacuzzi with three naked girls. Bauer remembers: "We shot it and I think I ended up dating one of them." There was also a scene cut from the beginning of the film where Tony and Manny are sat in the refugee camp watching *The Treasure of Sierra Madre*. By the time De Palma and Greenberg had finished their final cut *Scarface* ran for just over one hundred and sixty minutes. It was a flashy, over the top, bombastic movie that oozed glamour and wealth.

De Palma needed a soundtrack that would capture just that: "I thought it should have a very electric, disco sound." The man De Palma had in mind to create such a soundtrack was disco producer and soundtrack supremo Giorgio Moroder. Having won an Academy Award for his soundtrack to the movie *Midnight Express*, Moroder was hot property in the soundtrack milieu and De Palma liked his work. Moroder produced a soundtrack crammed with up-tempo, synth-heavy songs that perfectly accompanied the scenes in which they played. He also created incidental music for certain characters including Tony, Gina and Elvira. Moroder said that Tony's theme "had to reflect the character and personality of Al Pacino in the movie. It had to be dangerous, a little suspenseful, but a little deep too."

De Palma and Bregman had managed to pull everything together without any post production problems. The real fight began when *Scarface* was submitted to the Motion Picture Association of America (MPAA) for classification. In Stone's script the word "Fuck" was written around forty times. The final film had over two hundred uses of the word, mainly from Pacino. Also the graphic violence and excessive drug use would likely cause a problem for the censors. Nobody was surprised when the dreaded "X" certificate, meaning only adults could see it, was stamped across *Scarface*. De Palma re-cut it four more times and each time the censors returned a verdict of an "X" certificate. Bregman and De Palma appealed to the MPAA's Classifications and Rating Administration about their persistent "X" classification even after four different cuts were made in response to the notes given.

Film Critics Roger Ebert and Jay Cocks spoke in favour of the movie. Nick Navarro, a former narcotics officer who served as the film's technical adviser, also spoke of how the movie should be seen by young people as a warning sign to stay away from drugs. Even psychiatrists spoke to the MPAA and attested that children as young as thirteen would not be disturbed by *Scarface* because they have the capacity to distinguish "screen realism from real life." The appeal was successful and the classification was dropped to an "R" rating, allowing anyone under the age of seventeen to see the film as long as they were accompanied by an adult.

Scarface received its New York premiere on 1 December. Celebrities braved the winter weather to be among the first to see the new Al Pacino gangster film. However, there were walkouts after thirty minutes, the constant swearing and the obscene violence was too much for some people. The post premiere party was held at Sardi's Continental Restaurant in Manhattan. There, industry folk and celebrities mingled to discuss the film. Pacino appeared shortly before midnight and was greeted enthusiastically by Eddie Murphy, who loved the film. *Scarface* had its Los Angeles premiere the following night. Steven Bauer took his then wife, Melanie Griffith, and mother-in-law, Tippi Hedren, to the premiere. Hedren was not impressed, exclaiming: "it's too brutal." American director Martin Scorsese (who had previously tried to remake Scarface with Robert De Niro in the lead role) was sat in the row in front of Bauer. During the big finale montage he turned round to Bauer and said "Be prepared, they're going to hate you in Hollywood. You've made a movie about them."

Critical reviews were mostly scathing, Roger Ebert had already seen the movie and was very positive about it. However, the general consensus from U.S. movie critics was disapproving and *Scarface* was labelled: "an over blown B-movie", "Ultimately rather pointless" and "Much more a disaster than an outrage."

Scarface was released in North America on 9 December 1983. It was the second highest grossing movie of that weekend (behind *Sudden Impact*) taking $4.5 million from just under 1000 theatres. After dropping out of theatres in March 1984, Scarface's box office total was over $45 million in North America and a further $20 million internationally (Information courtesy of Box Office Mojo. Used with permission). Universal tried to put a good spin on the poor numbers by saying "the opening business has been bigger than anything else in the three hour class." *Scarface* wasn't considered a flop, but it wasn't the big blockbuster that Pacino, De Palma, Bregman and Stone were hoping for.

Scarface is a loud film. It's a bloody film. It's a brutal film. It's a sexy film. Most of all, *Scarface* is an angry film. The anger is mainly directed towards society. The type of society that won't let immigrants flourish. Tony Montana is an immigrant who, for a brief period, does flourish and believes the American Dream can be obtainable to anyone who enters America. That brief sojourn into wealth is brought about because of his anger and his refusal to play second fiddle to anyone. He sees a gap in the drug market and exploits it, strong-arming those who feel they are above a "Saltwater Nigger."

Anger courses through the veins of this movie and that anger comes from Pacino. Possibly feeling underappreciated because of recent movie flops, Pacino seethes from the off. Look at the way in which Pacino plays the opening scene. While being interrogated by US officials, Tony is a cocky, smart, loud mouth. Anybody being rescued from Cuba during that time would probably have been grateful to the US government. Not Tony. He barks and bites at every single question levelled at him. Pacino is Tony Montana from the very first scene; here is a guy who doesn't give a Fuck.

Pacino struggled to acclimatise to being off-set during the making of *Scarface*, and it's easy to see why. Fittingly, the only way a surge of acting energy that Pacino was portraying could ever end was in a blaze of glory. The finale is one of the most talked about, and quoted, endings in movie history. It's a huge blow out of an ending, the type De Palma always wanted and, eventually, delivered. Tony doesn't want to save his life. He just wants to save his cocaine supply. For a brief moment, before Tony climbs out of his gold and black throne there is a blank look on his face. Has he finally realised that his life, the life he dreamed of making, wasn't really worth everything he went through?

When all around him is crumbling down, this is one of only two moments in which we see Tony reflect on his actions. The first time we see Tony have any type of crisis of confidence is during the botched assassination of the UN official. Tony doesn't like what is taking place and breaks out into a spontaneous rage while driving. Ironically this moment, when Tony wants to do something right, is the start of his downfall.

Having Elvira on his arm isn't a winning masterstroke of romantic endeavour for Tony. Elvira eventually succumbs to Tony more because she feels it's a case of 'better the devil you know than the devil you don't.' There is no love there. She's just a trophy.

The finale shows Tony surrounded by his most treasured possessions – huge mounds of cocaine – and he realises the cocaine is the only trophy he has left.

Over the intervening years since *Scarface* was released, it has been reborn on VHS and DVD. Now, it's citied as one of the greatest movies ever made. On the surface it could be that those who now champion the film, hold the loud mouthed, gold chained, seriously wealthy Tony Montana up as an idol. Or perhaps they see their own early life struggles reflected in the young Tony Montana. He's a person trying to make something of his life, while all the time being told 'No.' The World Is Yours neon sign no doubt resonates with a lot of people, and flashes a different dream at everyone who takes the time to look at it.

Co-star Steven Bauer on *Scarface*

Based on the research conducted for this book, it sounds like you had a strange audition process for the role of Manny?

Yes, yes I did. What happened was: I was in New York with Melanie [Griffith], whom I had married, and I was in New York because we had both met Stella Adler [a teacher of acting] in a class in the summer in Los Angeles, and when she saw me on stage she said: "Young man you must come to New York. You are very, very good. You remind me of Marlon [Brando] and all my favourite men. You have to come to New York to study with me." So I said: "Yes, OK. Yes Ma'am." So we packed up and went to New York. We went and we studied and we did plays with her and we were in her classes but we also had no work. No paying acting work. I was very idealistic and I would refuse soap opera/daytime dramas. I wouldn't do that, so I couldn't make any money. So I got a job delivering furniture. What happens is at the end of our year there our agents in L.A., who think we are crazy; they convince Melanie to come home and get a job. She had an offer to do a television movie and so she does and I agreed to seek work in television. So she leaves and I stay in the apartment in New York City for three or four days and I get a call on the day I finally get a ticket back to L.A., I had no money I had just enough to get to the train station to get to the airport and get on the plane that afternoon, and they call me in the morning from L.A. and it's my manager she says: "Sit down. Just take a deep breath. They are casting a film with Al Pacino. It's called *Scarface* and it is a remake of an old film. The casting director hasn't opened her office yet but somebody has recommended you. Somebody has said you should go in for the role... the second role in the film is a tall, Cuban good-looking boy and they want to see you before you get on that aeroplane." I said: "OK." She said: "It's on the same avenue as where you live. It's on 8th Avenue.

It's in her apartment; the casting director is an old time New York casting director – Alixe Gordon." I said: "OK. Should I do it now?" She said: "Yes, go do it now and then you can make your plane."

So I walk right out of the door, up about ten blocks and I knocked on her door and she was vacuuming her apartment and I went in and she looked at me and she said: "WOW! YES! That's you. You are Manny. Come in, sit down and tell me what you have done and who you have studied with and do you really speak Spanish? And are you really Cuban?" I said: "Yes, I was born in Cuba and my parents brought me here when I was three years old." She goes "OH MY GOSH!" So she listens to me and then picks up the phone and calls Brian De Palma. She says to Brian: "Brian, I have this boy here and he is perfect for the role of Manny. He is perfect. He is Manny. He has to get on a plane in a little while so I'll send him over so you can see him." That was it. Literally that was it. I got on the subway and then got off and ran the last few blocks to Greenwich Village where Brian De Palma lived and I went into his house and he had an office there and... Brian is very aloof and he goes: "Yes, yes, Hello. Yes, you are perfect. You look right. Are you really Cuban?" and I say "Yes I'm really Cuban." He says "Let me do something. I know you got to get on a plane. Let me call Marty Bregman in L.A." He calls Marty Bregman and he says: "I've got this kid here and he is perfect. He is going to L.A. today. Alright, alright I'll tell him." BOOM! He hangs up the phone. He says "OK. Go to L.A. Go see Marty Bregman. Learn the script and in a couple of weeks we are going to have readings here. We will fly you back" and, those magical words in my ear [*Laughs*], "we will fly you", I just thought WOW! I haven't even auditioned and I'm in. It was incredible. When they saw me and they saw my type and my demeanour and they knew I had been studying and been on stage and I had done theatre and a lot of work already, they knew I could possibly be "the guy", the unknown guy that could get that role. There was other people... there was talk... because when Brian got the job he is best friends with John Travolta. So John is almost default, perfect choice to play Manny. And so is Eric Roberts who is very popular. Eric Estrada, the Latino from *CHiPS*... so there are all these guys that are just vying for this role before it was announced. John Travolta had the inside route because he is friends with Brian.

Then there is something else going on. On Brian's desk is a copy of *No One Here Gets Out Alive*. Which is the book by Danny Sugerman about Jim Morrison. Previously, for the last three years in L.A. I was Jim Morrison because I was very moved by Jim Morrison and I related to him. So I grew my hair long and I'm a musician first before I became an actor. So I can do Jim Morrison well... like really really well. My voice sounds like his and I can do all his stage nuances, all the stuff he would do and I looked a little bit like him. I didn't have the blue eyes but I looked enough like him. People in L.A. were saying: "when they do the movie it has got to be you. You have got to play Jim Morrison." So that was first and foremost in my mind. I knew Brian De Palma had gotten the rights to the book and he was going to do the movie *No One Here Gets Out Alive* with John Travolta as Jim Morrison. You imagine that?! [*Laughs*] So I'm in his office for the first meeting for this movie with Al Pacino and Brian says: "We will fly you back here in a few weeks." I say "Wow! OK, that's awesome. By the way, see that book? That movie? I'm playing Jim Morrison. Not John Travolta. I'm going to play Jim Morrison." And he says: "GET OUT OF HERE!" [*Laughs*]. And that is how that happened. I don't know why I had the confidence at the time where I felt like that was my destiny. I wasn't thinking about *Scarface*.

Later on I make my plane and I go to L.A. and the next day I go and see Marty Bregman and Marty says to me: "You really Cuban?" I say: "Yes" He says: "You are going to play Manny. You are going to do this movie. Just prepare yourself because there is a lot of people who want this role. You are going to play this role. I know it already." I was like Holy Shit! WOW! And then I told my agent and they said: "Why doesn't he give you a contract?" I said: "Well I gotta meet Al. I have to meet Al first but Al is not ready to meet anybody." "Why?" "Well because he is doing a play on Broadway called American Buffalo" and there is an actor in the play – Jimmy Hayden – who is a sweet sweet, sweet and wonderful actor and he was my friend and he was Al's friend and so when Al agreed to do *Scarface* and obviously there is a role for his best friend in the film, at least Al had to give him the opportunity to audition. But Jimmy had blue eyes and he was an Irish man. He wasn't the Manny type. But they had to wait... before he [Pacino] even saw me they had to give Jimmy the opportunity to audition for Manny. So I waited and waited and waited and I got another film offer. My first real film offer to play an American Indian who won the 1960 Olympics in *Track*. His name was Billy Mills and he was an American Indian from Oklahoma and the tribe that was financing the film, it was a Canadian director, and the tribe approved me and they were setting up to start the movie but it would conflict with *Scarface*... if I got *Scarface*. The problem was that the director would call me in the middle of the night and say: "Give up Scarface. Forget it. You are never going to get it. Just commit to our film. This is going to be a beautiful film about an American hero. Give up on *Scarface*. They are full of shit. Those arseholes. They are going to ruin your life" [*Laughs*].

In the middle of the night, we didn't have cell phones, he would call me at my home and berate me over the phone and say: "You are losing your chance... your opportunity at doing something beautiful. You are buying the word of a bullshit artist." I would say: "No, I need a little bit more time." And he said: "what do your agents say?" And I said: "My agents think I'm crazy. That I won't commit to this film," and he said: "Well you should pay attention to your agents. They are trying to steer you in the right direction. Those guys will fuck you over. John Travolta is going to play that part eventually. And you will miss out on a beautiful experience." Night after night I had to deal with it and I was in L.A. and we were still poor... completely broke. We had no money and I had this offer on the table to do this movie and it was a nice offer, it was a nice financial offer and it was a beautiful role. So I waited and waited. Eventually I would contact Marty Bregman and say: "Marty, the pressure is killing me." He would say "I'm sorry kid. We gotta wait for Al to be ready. We can't make an offer until Al's ready to meet someone else."

Finally, they fitted me for a wig for the little movie and then right about the time I was getting fitted to start that movie they finally made a decision. Marty Bregman called and said: "Al is finally ready to meet Steven." They flew me to New York and I went and met Al. It was love at first sight. Right away it was love at first sight. When you have chemistry with someone... right away. He says: "Why is your name Steve

Bauer if you are Cuban? Why do I keep hearing about this Bauer person who is supposed to be Cuban?" I said: "Because when I got to Hollywood with my Cuban name nobody wanted to hire me so I used my grandfather's German-Jewish name Bauer." He goes "Oooohhhh, so you are really, really Cuban?"

I said: "Yes, I'm really Cuban," and he goes: "Good because I'm going to need some help in this area. I'm playing a Cuban." I said: "I'm going to help you. I will teach you how to be Cuban," and that was it. Then there were auditions, real auditions but I was the first choice. I was all of them's first choice. They had other guys audition for the role of Manny and read with Al. But everybody knew I was going to play Manny because we had hit it off in our first meeting. Marty Bregman was already sold on me and Brian knew I was already Manny. So that was it. The only thing left to decide was who was going to play Gina.

Mary Elizabeth [Mastrantonio] was from Chicago and she had been on Broadway already. She is a singer and she is this beautiful girl. She could do the accent and she looked like a Cuban and the producer came out into the room, on the day of auditions, and said: "You two. You are it. You guys are it. Just come inside and read with Al. You guys are doing it. I love your chemistry." That was it. She got it, she got the role. There were thousands of incredible actresses, one of my best friends from college – Sandra Santiago, who became a very popular actress – also auditioned and she could have gotten the role. But Marty Bregman had a strong hand; he knew... he had very strong instincts about who should be in the film.

How did you work with Pacino on the relationship between Tony and Manny before filming commenced?

I was living in a little place on the Pacific coast highway with Melanie. We lived in a little apartment on the beach. Al, being a New Yorker, came to L.A. and took a house about ten blocks up the beach. A real house, a beautiful house that he rented and he moved in. Before rehearsals started he said: "Just come over for breakfast" and I would drive up the street and go in and we would have breakfast and we would sit outside and just start talking about our lives as the characters. Just getting to know each other and we did that for almost a month. People would come by... Martin Sheen would come by, Johnny Carson would walk on the beach and we would laugh and we would share our humour. It was all about having a sense of humour about oneself because you're an immigrant, and because you're an immigrant you are biding your time until you become part of society.

That's what we did; we created this repartee not even reading the script. Sometimes we would read a little bit of the script but most of the time we were improvising and talking to each other and sharing stories and thus he became my big brother basically. That's what he was... my big brother and my mentor. I was his loyal dog [*laughs*] and also his conscience to some degree. When he would listen. Every day we did that for almost a month and then we started rehearsals at Universal. Brian De Palma had the entire film storyboarded in stick figures in his office. The entire film. Scene by scene. Shot by shot by shot by shot. Which was amazing to me. It was like Hitchcock.

John Alonzo was his DP [Director of Photography] and John was right there and helped him create every shot. So when we were brought in to rehearse it like a play and we rehearsed it on a sound stage with marks and entrances and exits like a play. We would joke about it. The second week we were in rehearsals we said: "we could take this on the road and do it as a play because it's so right." Oliver Stone's dialogue... the screenplay of the film was so strong. It became an issue eventually because there were one or two scenes that Al and Brian weren't really in sync with. There were a couple of issues in the story, namely about the sister. There was also the beginning where the Universal people didn't really want to spend the money to put him on a boat going from Cuba to Miami. They really didn't want to spend that money. There is a scene in Cuba where he and I see each other and we are being rounded up and put on boats at Mariel Harbor and we've been let out of prison and we communicate. Oliver wrote it and it takes place in Mariel Harbor with guards and dogs biting people and the Cuban military rounding people up and forcing them on boats. That's the first scene in *Scarface*. Him and

I meeting and saying: "Hey you got out too?" "OK, what boat you on?" "I'm on this one" "OK, I'll see you in Miami."

There is a scene where he [Tony Montana] is on a boat and a kid falls overboard and Tony jumps into the water and saves him. It creates an... the audience already knows this guy is a good guy, he may be a criminal but he is a good person. He saves the kid and then we have the first few scenes in the camp. What happened was one of the heads of Universal Pictures decided that was too expensive to do so they cut the entire beginning. Oliver Stone went nuts. He went: "WHAT?! WHAT?! That establishes the character of Tony Montana." You know he is going to become a monster but it at least establishes that he's got a good heart. That happened in the first few months and the other thing that happened was that they were supposed to shoot in Miami the entire film but some local politician in Miami, a Cuban politician, decided based on a rumour about what the movie was about and that it was going to shoot in Miami he said: "No. No. We can't have a movie that makes Cubans all seem like criminals." So he threatened protests and Universal Pictures pulled out of Miami. They pulled out and suddenly we had to shoot in California and we had to create sound stages that would look like the locations. Eventually, they brokered a deal with that guy and we were able to shoot the location stuff in Miami Beach.

The drama that went on day to day on that film... and Oliver was mortified because he would come to the set and ask: "What are you shooting today? Are you shooting this scene yet?" and I'd say: "No they cut it" and he'd say: "WHAT?! WHAT?!" and he would go crazy. He would confront Brian De Palma and Brian was like: "You gotta stop this" and then they had a whole issue about the girl... about him and his sister. We had this whole issue about why she comes to him at the end and she is all fucked up and after he has killed Manny and he is all fucked up and he is sitting there doing coke and they says: "We got her." She is sedated and she comes into his office wearing this little robe and she has a gun and she says: "You can't stand another man to look at me or to be with me or to touch me. Is that because you want to fuck me?" There was an issue with the whole thing because Oliver wrote it with a certain underlying intention and Brian basically was on that side, he wanted it to seem as if there was something going on there. Al didn't. There was all this incredible drama about the intention of this scene and Al's response to it. The fact she raises the issue and they had to go with it and Oliver wrote it with the sense it is in her mind... in her very confused mind. It was really complicated, really complicated. That was an issue between Oliver and Al.

It appears to have been a difficult to shoot for everyone. Was it for you?

For me it wasn't. I just rolled with the punches and Al protected me, he really did. He was like a big brother. He protected me and kept everything very humorous. He would bring me into his trailer, I had a very tiny dressing room, and they would call for me. They would say: "Al wants you." So I went to his trailer and we would hang out and have fun and when it was time to go to work we would go to work. They come get us, he would get himself ready and I would get myself ready. We would put our game faces on and we would go to work.

The daily grind wasn't really apparent to me because he shouldered it somehow. He was dealing with it and then he found his play time with me. We played cards, we played imagination games, we would do impersonations of people or of each other and crack each other up all the time. We would do fake interviews about the future, about how people would respond to the movie. I bugged the shit out of him. I would bug the shit out of him all the time because we would do these scenes... these insane scenes and what is the audience going to think of this character that he is playing. He is such an asshole. He is such a monster. But he is so funny. I would say that after we finished the scene. We would do twenty, twenty-two takes of a scene and we would go back to his trailer and I couldn't contain myself. He would be satisfied with the scene and I would say: "what did we just do? And he would say "Do you think it was right? Do you think it was good?" and I'd say: "Yeah. It was insane. I can't imagine how the audience will respond to this. I can't imagine how they are going to see you. What about your fans? They've known you as Michael. How are they going to respond to this character that is such a fucking monster?" He would say: "I dunno. I guess they are either going to love it or hate it." I would say: "Wow! You are really walking on a wire. I can't believe you are so brave." He said: "I have to. I have to do this. This is what I do." It was an incredible experience for me because I saw someone that was so bold and so committed to going in a certain direction his instincts told him that was the way to go. He didn't care about the future. He didn't care about how the fans would respond. He told me every day "They are either going to hate it and we will be wiped off the Earth or they are going to love it. We are going to have to live with that. We have to commit." That was the most exciting thing for me. I was flying with him. I was on that high wire with him.

Upon release there was a huge outcry over the violence in _Scarface_ and a suggestion that it portrayed Cubans in a negative light. How did you react to those accusations at the time?

It was horrible. It was the worst thing that could have happened. It was the worst possible thing that could happen to two artists who are committed to something and when you think your heart is in the right place and your instincts and your experience tells you this is the way to go and you have to brave and then the response is completely negative... the response is completely negative. It was heartbreaking and... I can't even express how depressing and the degree of disillusionment. There was a moment right before the release where he said to me: "Here we go." He had seen it in different edits and I had not. We would talk every day and I remember one point when he said to me: "It's beautiful now" when he saw the cut he liked. There were different versions; different lengths and he said: "It's like an opera. It's operatic."

It's my first film so you have to understand I'm on pins and needles thinking I'm going to be in a great film and it's my debut next to him. Without being too vain, I thought Wow! This is going to be great for you but also great for me. Great for all of us and we are going to triumph with this thing and he said: "I think so. I think so. But there may be some people who still hate this film. I urge you not to read the reviews." He told me not to read the reviews because those are people with their own agenda and they're going to write what they feel will be noticed and what will bring them notice. If they have just a slight feeling of uncomfortableness they are going to write that and maybe they'll get noticed for that. I said: "Yeah but the reviews are important." He said: "No. No. Eventually people will determine, eventually history will say what the film is." That was it.

I was a big reader of film critics and film criticism. I've always been that way. I've always been a big literature and film and drama literature person. I've always read film critics and drama critics just to get a bearing on different points of view. But he said: "Do not read the reviews or it will hurt you. You'll take it personally. I know you." We went to the premiere in New York City and all our peers were there, great actors and actresses and directors and they loved the film and we had a gathering at Sardi's [restaurant]. People would line up to shake our hands. The next day the reviews were ninety-five percent negative in all the papers around the United States. I, of course, had to read them. I started gathering them and reading all the reviews. The ironic thing was most of the film critics treated me well. They killed him, they destroyed him and De Palma and Oliver Stone. They treated me well. It made me feel OK but it killed me that they hated the film so much because of the violence and because of the language.

Recently the film has had a huge revival and is now lauded as one of the greatest gangster films ever made. Why do you think it has finally found its audience?

We were in an era then that was so staged and people were very careful and very reactive to violence on film. There was a film out the same month – December '83 – there was a Clint Eastwood film, it was called *Sudden Impact*. It was released the same month and it had very manipulative violence in it where he follows a criminal down an alley and shoots him in the balls. It was a different kind of writing so it was a different kind of filmmaking. That was not what *Scarface* was. *Scarface* was just showing you this picture of this horrible moment in America and how violent these people were in the drug trade. *Scarface* was the first movie to put it on the big screen so the media responded so negatively to that. There was an old guard in Hollywood that said: this is too much, we cannot put out movies like this. It is not porn it is violence porn. So they crushed it. They destroyed it.

I would have auditions the following year and the following year after that, and it was known that I had done well in the film but the film was not beloved even in Hollywood, and I would go on appointments and meet with young executives and they would say: "You were fantastic in that piece of shit movie. You're the one bright spot in that stupid movie." I say: "What? What movie" and they would say: "*Scarface*. Everybody knows *Scarface* sucks and that Al Pacino was out of his mind in the movie." It was so weird to go through that for years and years and years. Then what happened was the rappers in America and all over the world saw that movie and they loved it right away and eventually they started bringing it into their art. They started to incorporate it because it was such a part of their mental state, which was get rich and die young. They started creating the iconic nature of *Scarface*. They would mention it everywhere.

Eventually Chris Berman, the voice of *ESPN*, saw *Scarface* at some point and I was watching *ESPN* at some point in the nineties when *Scarface* was all but forgotten and he would describe highlights of great sports plays of that day and if there was a home run he would say: "Say hello to my little friend!" and I was sitting at home thinking: holy shit, this guy saw *Scarface*. I can't believe he quoted Tony Montana. That's how it started coming back. The rappers started using it and then *MTV* started doing MTV Cribs which would go into rich rappers homes and all of them... all of them... the highlight would be their *Scarface* room. This is a movie that was a leper to society. Nobody wanted to fucking talk about it. Then society started to say: why are these guys so obsessed with *Scarface*? At the end of the 1980s they published a top 100 list of movies of the eighties and it was not there [*laughs*]. It didn't exist. It didn't exist. It was like a wave of disgust, a wave of negativity that lasted seven, eight, ten years well into the nineties. *Scarface* was released in '83 and from that point on until '95, '97, '99 nothing... nothing. *Scarface* was a leper. We couldn't even talk anymore. Al and I couldn't talk. We had to move on to other stuff.

There have been several commemorative screenings over the past decade where you and Pacino have been there to talk to the audience afterwards. What do you two reminisce about most when you are together?

What I remember, very strongly, is the scene at the Fountain Blue Hotel, and I do the tongue thing. Oliver came to me and said: "I have this idea." It wasn't improvised. He used to call me Manny. He said: "Manny, I saw this guy sticking his tongue out at a girl and she really didn't go for it. She was really disgusted. But he was really confident and I think that's what Manny would do. I wrote the scene." So he wrote the scene where I go: "No, that's not how you pick up girls. This is how you pick up girls" and I do the tongue thing and he [Pacino] says: "What the fuck is that? It looks like a lizard coming out of your mouth." Brian, who enjoyed moments like this, he would say: "OK do thing." So I would do the tongue thing and she would slap me. He would go: "No. That's not a real slap. Do it again." And we would do it again and she would slap me again and he would go: "No. Honey, no. You gotta really slap him." [*Laughs*] We did it twenty-two times. I remember that day in my hotel... and you know what else was incredible that day?! Brett Ratner was there. You know of Brett?

The director?

Yes. Brett was thirteen or fourteen and he was my little buddy. He was the son of one of the casting people in Miami. He used to say to me: "I'm going to be a big-time director one day," [*laughs*]. He'd say: "All these girls want to meet you. Which one do you want to meet?" He was like my little pimp [*laughs*]. He would say: "Hey this girl wants to meet you. She is really into you," [*laughs*]. Then he is in a scene. He is in a scene with one of the girls. He is in the pool when I get slapped. He is in the pool, on a float when I get slapped. You'll see Brett Ratner if you look at the film carefully. He was just a cool little guy who was really helpful. Now I'm just waiting for him and I to do a film together.

Do you have a favourite line in the film?

I have to say... One of the other scenes that I really really love is the scene that we did in L.A., that was meant to be in Miami, it is the first time we meet Omar... F. Murray Abraham. What happened was... I appreciated F. Murray as a person but at the time we didn't really appreciate him that much. Milos Forman was casting the lead for *Amadeus* other than Mozart, he was casting Salieri and I had seen *Amadeus* on stage and had seen the great British actor Ian McKellen as Salieri and we all thought it would be him or Anthony Hopkins. We were shooting *Scarface*, we had just started shooting *Scarface* and F. Murray Abraham was playing Omar and we hear he gets an audition and then suddenly Milos Forman decides he is going to play Salieri. So Al and I were like: holy shit, how did that happen? Omar's playing Salieri? How the fuck did that happen? So that night in L.A. we were shooting the scene outside the sandwich shop where I set up a meeting with Omar to get us a deal and it's him [Abrahams] and it was, unfortunately, November in L.A. and it was an incredibly cold night in downtown L.A. and we were wearing t-shirts and we are supposed to be sweating. We have to look like we are sweating but we are actually freezing and we go outside and we are dealing with Omar.

He pulls up with his friends and he says: "I've got something for you – Marijuana" That night I remember it specifically because we were cracking because we were thinking he got the lead in *Amadeus* [*laughs*]. How do you beat out Ian McKellen? Or Al Pacino even? Al could have played Salieri. They just cast it and this guy was just Omar, he was Omar. He is very fastidious in his acting. He does things very specifically. For some reason, to me because I was freezing and cold and trying to keep it together, it made me laugh. So every time we would cut and we would go back and they would throw blankets on us so we would be warm and I looked at Al and I said: "He's not making contact. He's so funny this guy." Al said "Don't look at him and don't look at me. Don't do it because I'll break up."

Al had told me in earlier years when he was on stage with the late John Cazale in *The Indian Wants the Bronx*, John would make him laugh on stage and it would break him up. It was a thing they would do, just break each other up and try and make each other laugh after they were into the run of the play. It's an old theatre thing where you try and make each other laugh. So I would look at Al in the middle of the scene with Omar [Abraham] and he would say: "You know anything about cocaine?" and I would look at Al [*laughs*] and would start laughing off camera. Al would look at me and he would start laughing. He said: "I have a terrible problem with this Steven. Don't do this to me. I can't stop laughing. Once I start laughing and a certain line is funny to me I can't stop." We would break up these takes with Murray and it was freezing and we were delirious basically, and Brian De Palma is getting impatient. "What's going on guys? Why are you laughing?" "Nothing [*laughs*] nothing [*laughs*] nothing [*laughs*]." We would go back and they would put blankets on us and I would look at Al and he said: "Don't look at me. Don't look at me during the scene or I will break." So he [De Palma] would go: "OK, ready? OK, rolling. Take the blankets off" and they would spritze us with water to make it look like we were sweating and we would go back out into the cold and go and face Omar, and Omar was... poor guy, F. Murray Abraham, had no knowledge of why we were laughing. We did like twenty-five takes of that scene because we were laughing in every shot. We kept breaking up and it was either me or him. I would look at him sometimes or he would look at me. That was one of the funniest and crazy nights. It was one of the first nights we shot in downtown L.A... I should tell Brian one day. He would probably be surprised to know why we couldn't get one full take of that scene [*laughs*].

Revolution

Cast: Al Pacino (Tom Dobb), Donald Sutherland (Sergeant Major Peasy), Nastassja Kinski (Daisy McConnahay), Joan Plowright (Mrs McConnahay), Steven Berkoff (Sergeant Jones), Dexter Fletcher (Ned Dobb), Sid Owen (Young Ned Dobb), Annie Lennox (Liberty Woman), Felicity Dean (Betsy). **Director:** Hugh Hudson.

Synopsis: Single father Tom Dobb is caught up in the violence of the American War of Independence after his only son Ned is drafted into the Army.

Kings Lynn, Norfolk, England. 1985. This setting doesn't exactly scream 1700s American Revolutionary War, yet British director Hugh Hudson believed it was the perfect filming location for his next movie. Having come off the tumultuous job of directing an adaptation of the Edgar Rice Burroughs' novel *Greystroke: The Legend Of Tarzan*, Hudson was looking for a straightforward directing job. Hudson was given the script by his agent and was informed it came from screenwriter Robert Dillon, who Hudson was, right then, working with on a different project.

The initial idea for *Revolution* came about because of American film producer Irwin Winkler's shock on learning his son knew nothing about the American War of Independence. He contacted Dillon, whose work on *The French Connection II* he respected, and asked him to write a script for a movie based on the American Revolution. When Dillon turned in his first draft, Winkler was so delighted with the story he immediately started to shop it to film studios. There was little interest. Revolutionary War pictures were few and far between. They didn't have the mainstream appeal Hollywood studios were looking for. Warner Bros initially picked it up, but soon put it in turnaround and allowed Winkler to pitch it to other studios.

Around this time Hugh Hudson came on board. He and Winkler had met and were both astounded to find they were of the same opinion about the direction of the film, it should be a story set during the Revolutionary War but with a father-son rebellion as the central focus. Hudson told Winkler to take the script to Goldcrest Films, a British movie studio. Even though money was tight at Goldcrest, with *Absolute Beginners* and *The Mission* in production, it was purchased. The budget was initially set at $10 million; however this didn't include payment for the director, producer or lead actor. An additional $800,000 was set aside for whoever was to be the headline actor. Negotiations had begun with Robert Duvall, Richard Gere and Sylvester Stallone. Each of these actors was commanding fees far in excess of the $800,000 set aside.

Hudson only ever had eyes for one man though. He had seen Al Pacino on stage during a production of *American Buffalo* in London's West End. The pair met and talked over the idea; Pacino was keen and liked the passion Hudson showed. The problem was Pacino wouldn't commit. Four months later, after many meetings and plenty of smooth-talking from Hudson, Pacino finally agreed to sign on. Hudson was the one to break the news to Goldcrest that they had their lead actor - good news: it's Al Pacino, bad news: we are paying him $3 million. Goldcrest didn't have that amount of additional money freely available, so had to go begging to other studios for it in exchange for distribution in different countries. Warner Bros, who had initially bought and then passed, put in $5.6 million in exchange for U.S. distribution rights. Norway's Viking Films added $4 million for the rights to Scandinavia. The budget was now set at $15 million.

The additional budget came in handy when the cast sheet became flooded with famous faces. The lead female role of Daisy McConnahay was given to Nastassja Kinski. Laurence Olivier's wife, Joan Plowright was cast as Daisy's mother. For the stern and brutal Sergeant Major Peasy, Donald Sutherland was cast. There were small but significant roles for playwright Steven Berkoff, Eurthymics singer Annie Lennox and *Rocky Horror Picture Show* creator Richard O'Brien. Also, because the film was to span several years, Hudson wanted two different actors for the role of Tom Dobb's son Ned. For young Ned, British actor Sid Owen was cast in his first major motion picture. For the teenage Ned another Brit was cast, this time it was Dexter Fletcher who already had films such as *Bugsy Malone*, *The Elephant Man* and *The Long Good Friday* on his resume. The cast was an intriguing mix of British and American talent.

Hudson had been on a location scouting trip to America "Only Williamsburg was suitable, but it's too much of a museum piece." He told *The Guardian* "King's Lynn had the right main street and light, so we combined shooting there with trips to Dartmoor for the battlegrounds." King's Lynn is a seaport and market town in Norfolk, East England. It's a small provincial town with a borough population of just under 50,000. Its cobbled streets and waterways buildings had the exact aesthetic Hudson was picturing for his movie. 1700s style building fascias were built in front of the giant 25,000 tonne storage capacity tanks that shadowed the port skyline. More fascias were added to the Custom House area of the port, which already resembled a docking area.

Before principal photography began, Pacino requested re-writes for his character Tom Dobb. Feeling he was too "ambivalent", it was requested that Dillon re-write Dobb as a tougher father and rebel. These re-writes plagued the production throughout as Pacino and Hudson struggled to find a middle ground as to the way Dobb should be portrayed.

Filming began on 18 March 1985 in King's Lynn's Kings Staithe Square, where Pacino sat and watched the first day's filming with Donald Sutherland playing Sgt Mjr Peasy, commanding his troops around the wet and muddy location. Pacino believed it to be one of the most authentic sets he had worked on. The streets were littered with horses and carts and old, wooden market stalls. Hundreds of locals, acting as extras, were dressed in Revolutionary clothing. Some got lucky and played military personnel, while the rest had to settle for being made to look like grubby peasants. The average wage for these extras was £25 a day. They were more than happy to be in a major Hollywood motion picture with international mega-stars such as Pacino, Sutherland and Kinski.

Though financed in the UK and Norway however, this was a Hollywood production and thus the crew couldn't anticipate the challenges caused by British winter weather. The streets of King's Lynn soon became mud baths as rain poured down. Hudson said: "I wanted the film to be wet and muddy; to show how tough it was for the soldiers, how squalid a beginning America had." Whether he wanted it as wet and cold as it had become was a different matter. Some of the crew complained that their hands were sticking to the metal of the scaffolding. Extras were quickly dropping out of production due to picking up colds and coughs after standing around, waiting to film, in the torturous weather. Kinski also became ill, suffering from chills. Sutherland slipped and cut his knee badly. Filming was not going according to Hudson's "easy movie-making" plan. Then it got worse as Pacino, who had been suffering with a cold from the start became quite ill and was diagnosed with low-level pneumonia. He was to be bed bound in his on-set tent until called to act. Then, having just dried off, he would suddenly rush out and film the scene. By the end of each stint in front of the camera he was soaked through all over again.

Pacino's attitude and energy was being sapped from all sides. Struggling with pneumonia, constantly having to rehearse new dialogue because of the re-writes, clashes with his director and, at one point, a big screaming outburst because his method acting wasn't understood. One scene called for Pacino and Kinski to be quite close together and several times Pacino's hand gravitated towards Kinski's breasts. A shout from one of the crew of "Get a load of randy Al," led to Pacino jolting up to his feet and declaring in a loud voice: "You don't understand me, I'm Al Pacino. My public expects me to react. How can I just lie there and take it?"

With filming complete in King's Lynn, the production moved thirty miles down the road to the city of Ely, which was used as a stand-in for Philadelphia. With only a few scenes to be filmed in Ely, photography didn't last long in the city. The same extras used in Kings Lynn were bussed over every day, all wearing their customary wartime outfits. Once filming was complete in Norfolk production was taken down to Burrator Reservoir in the South West of England. Surrounded by woodland, and with a huge expanse of water, Dartmoor's Burrator Reservoir was the film's stand-in for the Hudson River. The dam was covered in thick branches to disguise it. A large wooden fort was built on Challaborough Bay. These two areas would be the setting of the large-scale battle. The weather continued to hamper production with thick, driving rain hitting England's south coast. One of the cranes used for large scale panning shots had not been stabilised properly and the next morning was found at the bottom of a very large cliff, broken into pieces. Production had to be halted for a few days while a new crane was brought in at additional cost. There was also a fire in the catering tent due to a fault gas cylinder.

Bad karma seemed to be following Hudson across England. Maybe the trip to Norway for the last stint of principal photography would cast out those demons. Norway was used for some of the forest scenes and shots of waterfalls. Part of the deal with Viking Films included a clause about parts of the movie being shot there. Norway would double as upstate New York. For once, filming was not hampered by bad weather or ill actors. However, with all the problems faced in England the production, which was meant to finish in June, had rumbled on until the end of August. This put the final budget up to $26 million.

If Hudson thought he had experienced the worst that *Revolution* could throw at him then he would be proved very wrong. Warner Bros initially wanted Sutherland's character Sgt Mjr Peasy to die at the end of the film. Hudson fought, and won, to keep Peasy alive for the duration of the movie. The other part of the storyline that Warner Bros vigorously insisted upon was that Daisy, although killed off in the movie, should be reconciled with Tom Dobb at the end. With filming now finished and no such ending in the can (Daisy died. Why would they shoot an alternate ending that didn't make sense?), Hudson had to request a day's worth of re-shoots back in King's Lynn between Pacino and Kinski. When it was time to film, Pacino was ready but there was no sign of Kinski. She had hopped a train to Rome without telling anyone, only to return two days later without an apology.

With the alternate ending now filmed, Hudson and his editor Stuart Baird set about piecing together his historical movie. Goldcrest were insistent that the film be ready for December 1985 as it could then be entered into the Academy Awards. This meant there was little time for the movie to be put together in the way Hudson wanted. Also, it turned out that Goldcrest had overextended on budgets for their two other big films – *The Mission* and *Absolute Beginners* – which were way behind schedule. *Revolution* was the film they were banking on to bring them back into the black and to help them regain some much-needed credibility. Hudson still wasn't sure that the film flowed right by the time he was screening it for Warner Bros and Goldcrest: "They made me rush *Revolution* out before it was finished. I'd taken it to my friend Lindsay Anderson [British film and theatre director], who said it needed a voice-over narration, but we didn't have time."

Released on 25 December 1985 in North America, *Revolution* was savagely mauled by the critics. *The New York Times* called it: "England's answer to *Heaven's Gate* [The Michael Cimino film that bankrupt an entire studio]." *Variety* magazine said it was: "a little like visiting a museum – it looks good without really being alive." *The New York Post* described it as "idiotic". The reviews weren't just bad, they were vitriolic. *Revolution* lasted four weeks in North American cinemas before being pulled off the circuit. Its total domestic box office receipts amounted to $358,574 (Information courtesy of Box Office Mojo. Used with permission). It was an unmitigated disaster. Years later, Hudson told *The Guardian* newspaper: "The scorn heaped on my film was painful but perhaps right – it was incomplete and that has rankled with me and Pacino ever since."

The glaringly obvious problem with *Revolution* is that it lacks emotion. Dobb talks to his son without empathy; instead it appears he is more into directing orders to his son. Those lines are either delivered in hushed, clipped tones or the usual bawling shout. Pacino researched the way dialect would have been spoken around that time and proceeded to use it in the movie. When hearing the accents its clear why nobody ever did this before in movies as it doesn't sound clear or even close. It's nothing more than a rather muffled twang. We are meant to root for Dobb and his son as the American Revolution plays out around them. Dobb fights to keep his son out of a war that he accidentally enrolled into. They are anti-heroes of sorts but they give the audience very little to identify with, which itself is a major battle lost for a movie.

Very little care was taken to portray a meaningful relationship, be it romantic or platonic, between Tom and Daisy. This could be due to the constant re-writing of the script or at the wishy washy nature of the directing of these two central adult characters. They become ships that pass in the night, spouting the latest news on the war. There is no real aiding or loving of each other. Why have a character that one minute appears to be significant in the life of the protagonist and then the next banished to a secondary role of insignificance? This is what happens to Daisy and it is one of the most problematic elements of the movie.

The identity of the movie was also uncertain. Hudson envisioned *Revolution* as a lavish epic that recounted a sordid time in American history whereas Pacino saw it as a quieter, gentler movie which brought together beautiful cinematography and intimate acting. Consequently, it's a real shambles of a movie that confuses viewer with different plots and characterisations that never come to fruition. With all of these problems, it's no wonder *Revolution* brought Goldcrest to its knees, pushed Hudson to breaking point and caused Pacino to go into hiding. Pacino told his biographer Lawrence Grobel: "It was that single film that took the rug out from under me." *Revolution* put Pacino's entire career into jeopardy.

In 2008 Hudson finally got the chance to do what he had wanted to do since the calamitous release of *Revolution*. He received the go ahead from Warner Bros to release a Director's Cut of the movie. "I went to New York and sat with Pacino for five days as we laid down this new track." With a new voice over that explained some of the missing information from the original movie, this re-release went some way to rectifying the problems that the original version had. Hudson also trimmed the movie by ten minutes and, finally, we get to understand the reasons behind Tom and Daisy's love/hate relationship.

This new version *Revolution: The Director's Cut* was praised by *The Observer's* film critic, the late Philip French, as: "profound, poetic and original.

Hudson's film should take its place among the great movies about history."

Director Hugh Hudson on *Revolution*

How much did you know about the American Revolution when you agreed to direct the film?

I knew quite a bit about it and did a lot of research before. I liked the script. I liked the simplicity of the script. It wasn't much appreciated when it came out for many reasons. It was the simplicity, literally the simplicity about one poor guy who was reluctant to fight and he got forced into war because of his son being enlisted against the father's will. I liked that he wanted to avoid conflict and just wanted to get on with his job of hunting and making a living.

He was a poor ordinary guy from the back streets or the back country, if you like, of upstate New York. I just liked the simplicity. I didn't want to do a history lesson and that is what everybody complained about when it came out. They didn't get that. Twenty or so years later it has been reappraised by the top critics. So to answer your question I knew enough about George III, the colonies and the make-up of the British Colony in America. The strong British people and the people who wanted to get away from the hegemony. I've always been somebody who likes to deal with innocent characters in my films. I seem to have done that all the time. He was an innocent – the character, Tom Dobb was an innocent – in every sense. He was a fairly simple man but he grows during the course of the story to realise he has got to be part of the cause. The innocence is something that attracted me very much. Not only the innocence of the character but the way Pacino was able to do that.

Why the decision to film in King's Lynn and Dartmoor?

We looked right through America to find something that would work - old buildings in a Georgian style – and there was only one availability and that was in Williamsburg, and Williamsburg is a museum and they didn't want us to come in and dirty it up because we had to dirty it. We couldn't shoot it pure pristine, it was a living city therefore it needed all that aspect to it.

I've seen photos of you showing Pacino around King's Lynn. What was his reaction upon first arriving in the town?

Do you mean King's Lynn dressed for the film?

Yes

Well he was amazed that this kind of thing existed. These towns exist all through England in all states of period and King's Lynn is one of the best and it had a wonderful street and wharf area. We adjusted it and it could have been part of the New York waterfront.

What was it like to direct Pacino?

Well, you have to get on with them and he's a very straight forward guy actually. We got on very, very well. Quite strange really because we had different backgrounds. I came from upper/middle class background and Pacino came from the complete opposite. But sometimes opposites attract. He came from the Bronx and a very, very divided, broken family background and I'm from the opposite. I appreciated him very much as a character. I get on very well with him now. I see him a lot still as a result of the experience of *Revolution*.

He had just come off Scarface. What was he like to work with at that time?

He was at the top of his game. He was at the top of his popularity. You couldn't get a bigger star and he just understood it. He got what I was trying to do and I spent two weeks with him in New York, every day talking about it. He is a simple man. He's not a pretentious man. He doesn't stand on his position. He never did that. He was a star so he was treated with all the necessary requirements a star gets. However, he doesn't play that game. He is not in any way a prima donna. We got on really well from the get-go.

It sounds as if the filming was plagued with problems. How bad did it get?

It was very, very cold that year. We were building scaffolding and doing the buildings in King's Lynn absolutely well below freezing. They just found it very difficult to build. The builders' hands were being frozen to their scaffolding. Then it got very wet. A lot of problems. We went into production very fast. Once we got the cast together – Pacino, Donald and Nastassja – we went into a very fast production. The biggest problem was being forced to release it too early. This was a major film. A major, major undertaking and there wasn't any CGI in those days. CGI was just barely developing properly so everything is real in the film. So we had to do it for real. Many hundreds of extras. That requires time and lots of coordination and energy in winter conditions. That was a big problem – the weather – Pacino getting very wet and very cold. Everything done outside in those appalling weather conditions. Things got extended. Money was short. We always had to have more money because of the delays in filming.

Is it correct Goldcrest took money away from *Revolution* to put towards a couple of other big films they were making at the time?

I don't think that's quite fair to say but they had three big productions going at the same time. So they were short. We all went into production together I think, if I'm right in saying. I can't say they took it away and gave it to *The Mission*. Or gave it to *Absolute Beginners*. But they divided themselves into three. All of us were up against it. My job as a director is to get the upmost out of my film; I don't care about anybody else's. It's not my responsibility. It was the responsibility of the head of Goldcrest to raise more money. Once they put De Niro in one film and Pacino in another. De Niro and Jeremy Irons and Pacino and Donald Sutherland. This is top casting and they loved that but they didn't realise or they didn't anticipate that those kinds of people in films automatically increase your overhead.

They made you rush release the film

That was an outrageous thing to do. It was a killer. We had written a narration, but not the final narration, and doing a narration is very hard. It takes a long time to get the tone of the narration right. You can't just do it over night and say "Oh that's it." You have to go again and again and again to make it fit and work. I asked for another two months and they said "No. You can't have two months. We are short of money and we need income." I was forced to abandon the narration. Which did major damage to the final product of the film. People were slightly confused by the story because the narration, eventually we went back and did twenty five years later with Pacino, was a sort of inner voice going on from the character saying what he understood and didn't because he was an ordinary soldier so he never understood the overall scheme of things. It was an essential part of the story to have this inner voice narration and then them in their infinite wisdom said: "Oh no, you don't need that. You've got to get it out." I tried to persuade Warner Brothers, they were on my side actually, but Goldcrest overruled.

When it was released it was crucified by the critics. How badly were you affected by it?

We weren't quite sure what was going to happen. We were furious we had to come out... we needed another two months and we would have come out in February or March. We probably would have gone to Cannes [Film Festival]. I think it would have done very well in Cannes. But that wasn't to be. The other films at Goldcrest were allowed to continue. They weren't pushed out. *The Mission* was allowed to drift. It went to Cannes and, of course, won Cannes. Well good for them and good for Goldcrest for choosing that one. It was persuaded by David Puttnam, who was on the board of Goldcrest as well as the producer of *The Mission*, to allow his film to have more time but I needed more time and I was sacrificed, I believe.

Why do that? Why not let a film have its natural course? We started shooting in March. We were still shooting in August and we had to bring it out by Christmas. Very tough. I needed those extra two or three months and it did enormous damage for all of us. We got a very bad attack on us. Nobody understood the film, in a way they are probably right because it should have had the narration blending it and sticking it together and it was always intended like that. It was how it was written. We were attacked on every level – Donald Sutherland's voice, Pacino's accent... it was devastating for him. Pretty devastating for me too.

You released a director's cut a few years back that included the voice over from Pacino's character. How did that come about?

We had wanted to do it for many years. Warner Brothers put up some money for it. It is expensive to do – open up the film and re-do it. Pacino persuaded them because he would do some work on DVD's, DVD commentaries for other films of his, he said he wouldn't do them unless they allowed us to do *Revolution*. He persuaded them and they did, they put the money up very generously. They weren't obliged to, they did it. Then the BFI [British Film Institute] got involved and the BFI have produced a very nice, very handsome... they always liked the film did the BFI, they were very supportive. A nice DVD called: *The Director's Cut*. It wasn't actually; it was the original concept of the film. So I suppose they call it director's cut. It was a director's re-cut. It was how the film originally should have been, how it was written. I showed it to a few people, including Phillip French who is sadly no longer with us, and he loved the film then. He reassessed it. We were vindicated in a way but it was too late as you can't go back.

Is the new version as close to your original vision as you could get it to be?

Pretty well was how the script is. It was faithful to the script. Obviously in hindsight after twenty years it [the voice over] is written slightly differently. First of all his voice is twenty years older. So it has a strange time adjustment. So he seems slightly older. It's almost as if he is thinking back of his experience. But it's not actually written like that but it's almost as if because his voice has changed and that gives it a strange quality. We would never have had that thirty years earlier. I have to say we put in things that we would probably have not have put in if we had been allowed to include the narration. It wasn't quite the same narration as written in the script. The narration in the script is much sparser than the one we finally did because we felt... well we got the opportunity and we shortened the film slightly, we took some things out of it we didn't like that we were forced to put in. We eliminated certain things. We shortened it by ten minutes I think, which improves it. We put the narration in.

What was Pacino's reaction to the new version?

He loves it. He's finally been vindicated and he's finally happy. He finally thinks the film, which was a wonderful film, is even better now. It's a very strange thing that happens when you work on a film and you have a big disaster you become more attached to those things. It took us a long time to get what we wanted and we can put it to bed now and it can exist as we wanted it.

Has it given you closure?

Totally. Yes I'm closed on it. Absolute closure and Pacino has got closure, which is very satisfying.

Sea of Love

Cast: Al Pacino (Det. Frank Keller), Ellen Barkin (Helen Cruger), John Goodman (Det. Sherman Touhey), Michael Rooker (Terry), William Hickey (Frank Keller Sr.), Richard Jenkins (Gruber), Paul Calderon (Serafino), Gene Canfield (Struk). **Director:** Harold Becker.

Synopsis: Veteran New York City Police detective Frank Keller is a workaholic living on the edge. Joining forces with Detective Sherman Touhey to track down a bizarre serial killer, he encounters a beautiful suspect. Convinced of her innocence, Keller enters into a passionate affair despite hard evidence linking her to the murders.

A four year absence from the silver screen would cause any actor's stock to drop. When it is somebody of Pacino's prominence it often sparks debate about whether they are finished with movies entirely. Pacino hadn't appeared in an out and out box office hit since *The Godfather Part II* in 1974, and this was a huge concern. After the disaster that was *Revolution*, Pacino needed a big hit to re-establish himself as a bankable actor.

Pacino was initially drawn to working with director/producer Harold Becker on *Johnny Handsome*. A film that follows a criminal who had plastic surgery, exploring how it affected him. However when Pacino and Becker tried to create a decent script they hit a brick wall and eventually put it to one side. The other work Pacino had in hand was *Sea of Love*, a script from the pen of acclaimed novelist Richard Price. Price had his first screenwriting experience writing for Martin Scorsese on the sports drama *The Color of Money* but his new work would be very different to that; Price was looking at the world through a policeman's eyes. It was an angst-ridden story about a cop on the hunt for a killer. During his search the cop finds Miss Right but comes to believe she might be the suspect he is looking for.

The script for *Sea of Love* had been doing the rounds in different guises for a few years, in one incarnation it was a close adaptation of Price's own 1979 novel *Ladies Man*, but eventually Universal Pictures took a chance on it. The decision was made just six hours after the studio heard Dustin Hoffman was going to play the lead role of Frank Keller, the mopey cop. When the script was finally completed Hoffman was already working on *Rain Man*. Price became the writer on *Rain Man* so he could keep working with Hoffman but after six weeks Price quit, and Hoffman decided not to do *Sea of Love*.

Throughout Pacino and Hoffman's careers they had been offered the same roles time and again, and *Sea of Love* was no exception. Price contacted Pacino and handed him the script directly. The script was then passed to Marty Bregman who felt it was incomplete as a cop thriller and told Pacino as much. The project was passed on. Six months later, Tom Pollock, an executive at Universal Pictures, asked Bregman to take another look at the script. In the initial script, the female love interest didn't enter the action until around fifteen minutes from the end of the movie. For a film that relied on the sexual dynamism between the two lead characters, this seemed odd. Bregman convinced Price to bring her in earlier: "So I says, 'All Right, but not from page one. How about if I bring her in at 30?' They said okay – finally – but even then they were kind of hinky about it."

This film was to be Pacino's big return; the script had to be as tight and powerful as it could be. Sydney Pollack was initially approached by Pacino and Bregman to direct *Sea of Love* but was heavily into pre-production on *Havana*. Next, they went to another director who had helped establish Pacino as a big-time actor: Sidney Lumet. Lumet couldn't understand why Keller would exploit the sexual nature of the murders, so he declined the offer. With a director still yet to be attached, Bregman called Harold Becker. A director who had previously made crime movies such as *The Ragman's Daughter*, *The Onion Fields* and *The Black Marble*. He jumped at the chance to work with Pacino, an actor he had long admired. Pacino, Bregman and Becker were all ready to start a new stage in their careers – this was to be a comeback movie.

When casting took place, the unknown John Goodman came in to read for the part of Frank Keller's cop partner Detective Sherman Touhey. Bregman had seen Goodman in theatre many years before and believed there would be great chemistry between Goodman and Pacino on set. While signing on for *Sea of Love*, Goodman had been cast in a new TV sitcom called *Roseanne*. He had it written into his contract that he could leave filming at a certain date, regardless of whether *Sea of Love* had finished filming or not, in order to start work on *Roseanne*. Michael Rooker was cast as Terry after Harold Becker saw his portrayal of Henry Lee Lucas in the true crime drama *Henry: Portrait of a Serial Killer*. He had the build Becker wanted for the nefarious character of Terry. For the role of the love interest/possible killer, Becker needed an actor who "could take charge of the eroticism of the moment. A woman who could give as good as she gets. Or I should say a woman who gives as good as she takes." Blonde bombshell Ellen Barkin was his only choice. He had previously seen her in *The Big Easy*, a romantic crime drama. *Sea of Love* would be the first time she'd played "an object of desire", a woman that women wanted to be and men wanted to be with. Barkin instantly signed on based on one factor – Pacino. She said: "I would have said yes even if I never got to read the script." It was a dream comes true for the native New Yorker, who grew up not far from where Pacino used to live. They had also both studied method acting at the famed Actor's Studio. Becker believed that having two actors on set dedicated to their craft was perfect casting.

Filming began in May 1988 and in order to save money on the budget a lot of the interior shots were filmed on sound stages in Toronto's Kleinberg Studios. A disused Toronto police station was remodelled for filming the internal police station scenes. A total of eight weeks were spent filming in Toronto. Eleven weeks were spent filming on and around the streets of New York, mainly in the city's Upper West Side. The lonely hearts date scenes were all filmed on a sound stage, but the set up had to exactly match that of the real restaurant - O'Neill's restaurant at 44 West 63rd Street and Columbus Avenue (Now called P.J.'s) – otherwise the external and internal shots would not match when edited.

Becker found the New York night shoots physically demanding "There was never a moment to relax." Filming on live streets during the day time was not without its problems either. Towards the end of the film, when Keller is trying to win back Cruger out on the streets of New York, Pacino is knocked into by a passer-by. This was by accident. Pacino, being the method actor he is, continued with the scene until cut was called. Becker liked the take so much he left it in the film. Also during that scene there are members of the general public who realise that a movie featuring Al Pacino is being shot. A man and two women can clearly be seen following in the background throughout most of the scene. Also a teenager, wearing a white shirt and carrying a brown envelope, continuously comes into shot grinning at the camera. Whether these takes were left in for authenticity or the director didn't notice is up for debate. It had been a long and arduous nineteen weeks of filming when principal photography finished in September 1988.

Becker and his editor David Bretherton spent nine months getting the film in shape. Test screenings had come back with overwhelmingly positive comments. A preview screening happened in Sherman Oaks, almost a year to the day since principal photography finished in New York, where Pacino turned up in disguise to hear the reactions of the audience. Nobody spotted him.

Sea of Love opened on 15 September 1989 in North America. Critical reviews were entirely positive. *The Washington Post* proclaimed it "leagues deeper than the average buddy movie." *The Observer* called it "A first rate, genuinely adult thriller." *At The Movies* described it as "the most erotic, heart-pounding thriller since *Fatal Attraction*, but better." The majority of praise went to Pacino. "Pacino is amazing," commented *The Village Voice*. *Variety* also dished out praise: "A superlative performance by Al Pacino." *People Magazine* called it "Pacino's first good movie in fourteen years." Roger Ebert felt there were others to credit besides Pacino: "what impressed me most in the film was the personal chemistry between Pacino and Barkin." The critics were seeing a new Pacino, one the general public wanted to see as well.

Within its first weekend the picture had made $10 million. Not bad for an "R" rated, erotic crime thriller. *Sea of Love* continued to do brisk business right up to the end of 1989 when its box office takings totalled over $56 million (Information courtesy of Box Office Mojo. Used with permission). Pacino was nominated for Best Actor in a Motion Picture Drama at the 47th Golden Globe Awards for his performance as Frank Keller. He lost out to Tom Cruise for his portrayal of the Vietnam Veteran Ron Kovic in Oliver Stone's biopic *Born on the Fourth of July*, a role Pacino had been close to taking on years before. Not winning a Golden Globe aside, *Sea of Love* had re-established Pacino as an actor worth watching.

Sea of Love could be seen as a 'some years later' version of Pacino's other cop undercover thriller *Cruising*. It plays to the same cop on the edge tropes and both feature heavy, steamy sex scenes. What makes *Sea of Love* stand out is the engaging performance from Pacino. Gone are his dream boy looks and in place are the early signs of his hangdog expression. This didn't matter though, it gave the character of Frank Keller a lived-in look. A vibe that he had been there, done that and was world weary and underneath all this was the transfixing Pacino who had wowed audiences years before.

It is in this film that Pacino unleashes his trademark bellow for the first time, a tick he would become well-known for. He had occasionally done it in previous films but here it is much more developed and biting. During one howling scene Pacino scared Barkin so much that she visibly shook, and the rings on her fingers were making loud clanking sounds.

His professional efforts may have been focussed on the character, but Pacino also made time for mischievous antics on set with Barkin. Before the filming of one love scene, Pacino drank lots of coffee and ate muffins, so when Barkin went to kiss him he would have smelly breath and crumbs lined around his mouth. During the filming of another sex scene, Barkin stripped naked ready to act and Pacino stood there wearing a raincoat. The leading man was clearly enjoying his return to movie acting.

Would Sea *of Love* have been a box office hit if Pacino had been acting opposite anybody else apart from Barkin? It's an important question. Barkin wasn't just there to sizzle up the screen; she was the perfect match for Pacino. Tight fitting clothes and a wiggling walk is what most will remember about her in this film, yet she was much more than simple eye candy: her character was spunky and full of attitude. The first time Barkin appears on screen she lets a wry smile creep over the right side of her mouth, she fixes a gaze that could be sexual or murderous. It had both a heat and a coolness to it. Through their scenes the audience witnesses the start of a tumultuous and destructive relationship where the lovers want to stay together forever because they can't bear to be apart, even though they know it will eventually kill one, or both, of them. Pacino and Barkin's sexual chemistry permeates the entire film. The sex scenes are as lurid and steamy as anything seen in other Eighties movies such as *Fatal Attraction* or *Wild Orchid*.

In terms of the couple's respective personalities, Keller is a loner. He struggles with his own thoughts. He is on the edge, almost slipping through the cracks of life. Cruger could be classed in the same category yet she stays strong because of her loving family. She has become a nocturnal creature who lives and breathes the intensity of the New York nightlife. Unlike Keller, Cruger's life isn't slipping away, more passing her by. Keller and Cruger are two wrongs trying to make a right.

Context is everything in this film. The main storyline about a lonely hearts killer echoes other sub-plots about broken romances. How many people, by the end of movie, have been cheated on? Personal betrayal is rife within *Sea of Love* and it has caused hurt and harm to all. Neurotic characters seek out equally neurotic characters. In one scene Keller asks: "What does anybody see in anybody?" Could this be a way for Keller to deny the feelings he has started to develop towards Cruger beyond their dangerous liaisons? Or could it be that he truly has given up on love and life? It is easy to say both. Dig a little deeper and it is possibly that Keller has finally found someone who is his equal in life and love in Cruger. She is smart, sexy and down on life. All the things Keller is but doesn't want to admit.

The setting of New York City injects another layer of context into the movie. The city was at its lowest ebb after Black Monday two years prior, there were more people walking the night time, neon-hazed streets looking for work than striding through the morning rush hour in their suits. New York had become a midnight city and *Sea of Love* reflected that by not only employing the usual horror movie trope of a killer stalking and slashing during the early hours, but also through the way Keller and Cruger become more comfortable conducting their business during the witching hours. This grittier edge even extended to make-up and costumes. Look at the way Cruger presents herself – bright red lipstick, nails teamed with a leather jacket. Red, a colour associated with love and danger hints at Cruger's inner femme fatale.

Sea of Love was Pacino's comeback movie, proving he still had the X factor, so to speak. The film made stars out of Ellen Barkin and John Goodman. Talk of Harold Becker and most will associate him with directing this film. It's also, arguably, Richard Price's most successful turn at movie screenwriting. *Sea of Love*'s electrically charged eroticism combines impressively with the melancholy of the central characters. This neo-noir thriller single-handedly re-invented Pacino for the new era.

Actor Paul Calderon on *Sea of Love*

What did you think of the script for this film when you first read it?

I thought it an awesome script. [A] very nitty gritty, New York crime drama. It was a very different script; more of a personal odyssey of a New York City Detective whose loneliness is explored outside the precinct. After we started shooting (originally a ten week shoot in Toronto) *Fatal Attraction* opened and the producers decided to change the script to make it a sort of *Fatal Attraction*, and the ten weeks that we had already shot was swept to the side and we started shooting the revised script to fit into the *Fatal Attraction* mode. It went from a great script by Richard Price to, in my opinion, something much less.

There is a scene at a Policeman's ball where John Goodman is singing "Sea of Love", is that him actually singing it? How many times did he do that scene?

He has a great voice and that was him singing, and he nailed it in a couple of takes.

Pacino had been out of film making for four years when he made *Sea of Love*. Did you see a different edge to him?

He was very relaxed on the set. I knew him from the Actors Studio where we're both members, and we would hang out on the set and talk baseball and boxing. He was fun to work with. Not the ultra-intense clique method actor I had heard so much about.

There is a scene where you, Pacino, Goodman and a couple of others are trying to think up rhymes to put in the newspaper to lure

the killer. It's a very funny scene. Did you improvise much during the filming?

The dialogue was all Richard Price. A great, great writer who captures New York cadences very well.

***Sea of Love* has such a phenomenal cast. Did you pick up any acting tips from some of your colleagues that you still use to this day?**

I remember one day Michael Bregman (one of the producers, son of Marty Bregman) grabbed me on the set and said: "Check this out," and led me to where Pacino was doing [an] interior scene, just sitting and listening and responding. Michael whispered: "Watch. He isn't gonna do anything and the $##%^ comes out looking fantastic." And I stood near the camera (back then directors didn't have monitors) and watched and I saw that he indeed was doing "something". He was allowing his thoughts to drive the silences in the scene. It was very powerful. Yet extremely simple.

You've featured in some fantastic films and TV shows over the years. Where does *Sea of Love* rank?

It was my first big film and I have wonderful memories. Pacino, Goodman and the rest of the cast were a treat to work with and it sort of spoiled me for a bit, thinking that this was what every set, production would be like. Maybe a handful of productions since then have lived up to that expectation.

The Local Stigmatic

Cast: Al Pacino (Graham), Paul Guilfoyle (Ray), Joseph Maher (David), Michael Higgins (Drunk Man), Brian Mallon (News Vendor), James Bulleit (Theatre Manager). **Director:** David F. Wheeler.

Synopsis: Graham is a bitter East-End Londoner who has an almost mesmerizing hold on his more timid roommate Ray, who he asks to perform increasingly deviant acts.

The process of filming in England had not been kind to Pacino. *Revolution* was an absolute nightmare, personally and professionally. The one thing that kept him going was being on stage in the West End with the play *American Buffalo*.

Pacino preferred being on stage to being on camera and one of his earliest stage roles was portraying one of the nihilists – Graham – in the play *The Local Stigmatic*. A story about two British symbiotic sociopaths who play mind games with each other and engage in acts of violence against the innocent. This one-act monologue play came from the pen of Heathcote Williams, an Englishman who is described as an anarchist and poet. The play was first staged in 1966 at London's Royal Court Theatre in a double bill performance with Harold Pinter's *The Dwarfs*. Williams' play has been interpreted in many different ways over the years. The playwright believed it to be a study of envy. Pacino on the other hand interpreted the text as an analysis of the nature of fame and how it can be perceived by those on the outside of that circle.

The play was taken to America in the early 1960s by director David Wheeler, who had been recommended it by Harold Pinter. It was to feature in amongst seven of Pinter's one-act plays in an off-Broadway production in 1969. Pacino was first introduced to *The Local Stigmatic* by a small workshop project at the Actors Studio the year before, he commented: "It took a few readings for all of us to realize we were reading something special." When the full production, featuring Pacino, opened off-Broadway it was panned heavily by critics and the cast were informed it would be closing after just one night. Actor Jon Voight enjoyed the play and stumped up the money to keep the production running for a week. It may have only run for eight performances, but Pacino formed a personal connection with *The Local Stigmatic*.

While performing *American Buffalo* in London, Pacino began to play around with the idea of making *The Local Stigmatic* into a film, or, as he envisioned it, a play captured on camera. The only footage actually filmed in England was the external dog track scenes, which took place at Walthamstow stadium in 1984. Upon returning to America, Pacino put filming on hiatus. He did however enlist actor, and friend, Paul Guilfoyle to play the part of the other nihilist Ray. They both worked on the dialogue and staging for a couple of years, whenever their schedules would allow them to meet, before finally re-starting the shoot in 1989. More footage was filmed in New York, specifically the SoHo District and the Cedar Tavern in Manhattan. The last bit of footage the crew needed in the can was of the two lead characters coming out of a cinema. Back in New York, Pacino couldn't find a cinema that resembled those in England. Travelling to Atlanta on other business, Pacino stumbled across The Rhodes Theatre which perfectly fitted the aesthetic he needed to evoke England on-screen. Across the road from the cinema was Rhodes Hall: a turn of the century built Memorial Hall that had run into disrepair. Further filming took place there; it acted as stand-in for British architecture. Save for the aforementioned scenes filmed in 1984, the entire play was shot during 1989 in just seventeen days.

The Local Stigmatic was Pacino's pet project; he was financing it completely and had already sunk thousands of dollars into the production. His obsession with the picture became its downfall as he edited, re-edited and then edited again. It was a never ending cycle of Pacino tinkering and toying with the way the film should play out. At times he would give the film to the other actors and ask them to re-edit it. Creating one finalised edit was proving difficult. He told director Bette Gordon: "When you don't know something, you don't know what you're doing wrong, but you also don't know the rules. So you come up with things that might be different." Deciding to screen it for friends and family on occasions proved fruitless. After one such screening Diane Keaton was overheard telling Pacino: "I'm glad these flash-forwards are gone now. But it still needs something, don't you think?" *The Local Stigmatic* became Pacino's own *Cleopatra*. It was whittling down his confidence, and his bank balance, quicker than he ever expected.

The Internet Movie Database (IMDb.com) lists *The Local Stigmatic* as a film made in 1990. The source of this date is a mystery but could be the date it was first shown to a viewing public. Pacino screened a version of *The Local Stigmatic* at Harvard University. This was in part due to the director of the film being on the faculty of Harvard. A further screening took place during March 1990 at The Museum of Modern Art in New York. A copy of the movie was given to the museum and it could only be played under the expressed permission of Pacino himself. For the decade that followed the film almost disappeared from view. Pacino set-up occasional showings to friends and family and at teaching establishments such as Harvard and The Actors Studio.

Its absence from view gave the film an air of mysticism. It was the Holy Grail of Pacino films, it could take years to seek out a means of seeing it and when a person finally completed their quest, they became part of a small and exclusive club. Pacino did consider releasing it officially during 1994 when Quentin Tarantino's *Pulp Fiction* exploded the box office. Pacino felt the nihilists in *The Local Stigmatic* were very much in-line with those in Pulp Fiction and his movie could be the perfect companion piece to Tarantino's. It never transpired and, once again, *The Local Stigmatic* disappeared from view with Pacino calling it "an experimentation. An interesting way of learning more about making movies."

Then, in early 2006, a mysterious DVD box set listing appeared on several retail websites in the U.S. entitled: *"Pacino: An Actor's Vision."* There were no notes or suggestions as to what would be included in the box set. As the original release date approached, the date was pushed back to November 2006. By October the date was, once again, pushed into 2007. A release date of June 2007 was given and as the date grew closer, finally technical details were updated. This enigmatic box set would include a documentary called *Babbelonia*, the part documentary/part feature film *Looking for Richard* and two unreleased movies called *Chinese Coffee* and *The Local Stigmatic*. Finally, Pacino had made a deal with 20th Century Fox studios to release *The Local Stigmatic*. Pacino had finally let go of the tinkering and allowed his baby to be born into the world.

The only major outlet that reviewed the box set was *Time Out New York*, who said: "though far from perfect, the films are revealing, because they suggest that Pacino, who started out on the New York stage, is still a theatre artist at heart." The box set was for die-hard Pacino fans only; an example of Pacino giving something personal and unique to his legions of fans. The added bonus was that Pacino had recorded a commentary for *The Local Stigmatic* DVD release. Also included were a prologue and epilogue between Pacino, director David Wheeler and film professor Richard Brown. Not content with just throwing it out in a box set, Pacino wanted to educate the viewers as to why he took on the project, what caused the delay and also what his thoughts were on the project finally being released.

For fans, the pleasure of finally getting to appreciate *The Local Stigmatic* feels like a small triumph after years of hearing about it but thinking it would never be commercially available. It's pretty clear that Pacino returned to his roots for this film and wanted to make something on the fly that appealed to him, and also had some resonance. The film is rough around the edges. The camera is unsteady at times and the colour saturation leaves the viewer wondering if there is a problem with the television. As Pacino wanted, the film does feel more like a play than a motion picture.

Pacino and Guilfoyle make a dislikeable duo. Their narcissistic tendencies play out very much like those of the droogs from *A Clockwork Orange*. They spit out long monologues about life that look and feel passionate but become increasingly difficult to understand. The banter between them is infused with dark humour and subtext. It's as Williams would have intended his play to be produced, a positive for those very familiar with the text. The outrage over the original play largely stemmed from the violence towards the celebrity character. In this scene, the fear in the film is rooted in the choice of camera angle as Pacino and Guilfoyle bear down, snarling soliloquies about fame and its profound effect on society. The sequence is brutal and unflinching, even though the beating is never shown.

Arguably, this is the only time that the film finds it feet. Those viewing *The Local Stigmatic* for the first (or second) time will likely find its pretentious nature jarring. In some moments, it almost feels like a joke at the viewer's expense as they are left dangling; unable to understand the dialogue and/or characters. It's not an easy film to watch. Fifty six minutes can feel like a lifetime in the company of characters such as these and the British accents concocted by Pacino and Guilfoyle are very poor. Guilfoyle initially projects a posh, upper class Brit and manages to make it sound semi-respectable. Sadly with time, that accent wilts into a soft mockney accent that purrs and whistles through his tight lips. Pacino's cockney is worse than Guilfoyle's. Apparently from the East End of London, Pacino's Graham sounds like he's never been anywhere near a postcode starting with the letter E. The words tumble out of his mouth accompanied by the sound of sucking saliva. Pacino's natural New York accent breaks through time and again causing a riptide of rolled consonants that are neither cockney nor British. Guilfoyle and Pacino's failure to perform cockney accents makes a mockery of everything else they went through in order to establish their characters. It is completely distracting to the audience and as such they produced some of the worst British accents seen on-screen since Dick Van Dyke in *Mary Poppins*.

As Pacino's first personal, home-grown film *The Local Stigmatic* doesn't showcase him at his best. Making the film was a bold move and he may have enjoyed the idea of being immersed in the grotty character of Graham but it simply doesn't transfer into an engaging piece about the pursuit of fame and fortune. It may have struck a chord with Pacino's own life, but for the viewer it's like watching two classic actors constantly shoving you out of the in-joke. It's a production only interested in serving viewers who know the text and understand its meanings. In summary, this film succeeds only as a work to be shown to study groups who are dramatizing the play; Pacino has created a strong text book study piece. For any other purpose however, *The Local Stigmatic* is not a movie anybody would choose to watch of their own accord.

Actor Brian Mallon on *The Local Stigmatic*

The source material for this picture is quite unique. Were you aware of it beforehand?

I had never heard of Heathcote Williams. I had heard the title before but if anybody quizzed me on it, I wouldn't have known what it was.

How did you become involved in the film?

I was told, at the time, that I had been recommended by the Actor's Studio. Ellen Burstyn gave my name and there was someone else, who I didn't know, knew David Wheeler and had seen my work and just recommended me for it.

How long were you at the Actor's Studio before being cast in the film?

At that point not really that long. I was fairly new around there then, but I've been a life member since 1984 and this would have been about 1980. I guess I was an observer at the time. I had been up working a few times and there was, let's say, interest. But it surprised me. It hit me out of the blue when I heard this was Al's project and he wanted me on it. It was great.

Do you remember when you started filming? How long you were filming for?

I was only there for one day. I think this was around 1980 or 1981. It was an early morning on a Sunday because they didn't want traffic. It was down in Madison Square, around 17th Street. It was a news vendor's stand that they had refitted to make it look British. I think they kept things tight because there is no way New York looks like London. I couldn't think of a single spot in it that would resemble it.

What direction were you given from David Wheeler and Al? Were they both giving you directions?

Not really. I didn't really get much direction. It always came from David. Al didn't say anything. He was amazing to work with. It's exciting and fun to be with someone like that and he is so intense. I've always been a fan of his, especially *Dog Day Afternoon*. He zeroes in on you. He wants to get to know you in a New York minute, but in a very friendly way. I talked to him a lot off-camera that day. We were both in this room and there was nobody else in the room and he didn't acknowledge my presence. We were strangers and he didn't acknowledge me in anyway. Eyes never met. Then David Wheeler came in and he introduced me to him as an actor in the film. At which point he became very friendly and he was full of chat. The funny part was that it had to all be in his cockney accent [*laughs*], being the method. So I had to oblige in the same way and he wanted to know all about my acting experience but it all had to be in this cockney accent. So I'm telling him all about my time at the Irish Arts Centre. It was slightly ironic and certainly comical. Great fun.

What do you think to his cockney accent in the film?

I would say he did as much as was appropriate, say for his American base. His fans want to see Pacino doing that performance in a certain way. At the same time he was going at it with great dedication and I think he was shooting for something, perhaps, beyond that. I think that he acquitted himself fairly well.

It was filmed over a number of years. Did you wonder what had happened to the film? Or did you hear little bits and pieces because you were still at the Actor's Studio?

I was hearing things. I saw a fairly early cut that I was really delighted with and I kept hearing reports around the studio. Sully Boyar, he was the bank manager in *Dog Day Afternoon*, he was telling me that Al was very excited about my work in the film. So I was getting all this stuff and then when I ran into Al in the office. He said: "Oh you're terrific in the film. Harold Pinter wanted to know all about you and where I found you." So I was very excited about it. He said that they were still editing it. When I saw the first cut I thought it looked pretty good. Lots of close-ups [*laughs*]. I knew that it was only an hour long, so when I knew that I wasn't sure how it was going to emerge for the public. It went on and on and I was in L.A. and somebody introduced me to Diane Keaton, who was going out with him at the time, and she said: "Oh he just loved that scene but he's still tinkering with it. He won't put it down and he keeps going at it." I knew it was a personal project of his and you just had to wait until he was ready to release it. It was a mystery alright.

How long was it between seeing that first cut to the film's release?

I just don't know. I'd seen it and I was delighted. I didn't really keep dates on it. Finally, I got an invitation in the mail to a screening at Joe Papp's Public Theater [in New York]. It was a big night and I saw Arthur Miller towering over the crowd nearby and I was very star struck. When my scene came up, as an actor I was a bit disappointed because my close-ups had been cut out [*laughs*] and some of my lines that I had were now off-camera. So small became smaller, and any actor is going to feel that way. Overall I enjoyed the film. It's a peculiar animal in a way. When Al first fell in love with Heathcote Williams' play he was very young. The two main characters are, supposedly, corner boys in their late teens and, at this point, Al and Paul [Guilfoyle] were in their late forties. It gave it a very strange and new dimension. Sort of dark and sexually askew with these two women-less men that are living together, going out and bullying people. Something strange about it. Having said that it was charged and compelling at the same time, in a different way to the play. I thought it was a wonderful Pacino performance, and a film I was proud to be part of.

Dick Tracy

Cast: Warren Beatty (Dick Tracy), Charlie Korsmo (Kid), Glenne Headly (Tess Trueheart), Al Pacino (Big Boy Caprice), Dustin Hoffman (Mumbles), Madonna (Breathless Mahoney), William Forsythe (Flattop), Ed O'Ross (Itchy), Paul Sorvino (Lips Manlis), Kathy Bates (Mrs. Green). **Director:** Warren Beatty.

Synopsis: Dick Tracy is a hard-nosed, soft-hearted detective who takes on the responsibility of looking after a streetwise kid. Together they fight to clean up the crime-ridden streets of the city... but standing in their way is a mob of the most colourful gangsters ever assembled, led by the sinister Big Boy Caprice.

Obtaining the rights to make a motion picture of an already established work can be very tricky. Especially if the work to be adapted has been in circulation for forty something years in comic book form and has a legion of followers. Consequently, if actor/director/producer Warren Beatty thought bringing comic book crime detective *Dick Tracy* to the big screen would be an easy task then he had not done his homework. Even before Beatty purchased the film rights to the comic strip character, there had been numerous attempts to produce a new *Dick Tracy* picture.

The first time creator Chester Gould saw his police detective on the big screen was in 1937, only six years after his comic strip debuted. The stories spanned a fifteen-chapter movie serial produced by Republic Pictures lasting for two years. The legendary American film company RKO Radio Pictures released four *Dick Tracy* feature films between 1945 and 1947. This was the last time Tracy was seen on the big screen. A couple of live action TV and animated shows appeared between 1950 and 1971 with modest success.

A brief news article on 23 November 1977 in *Variety* magazine announced that *Dick Tracy* would be returning to the big screen.

Paramount Pictures had agreed to distribute the film. The director, Floyd Mutrux, had purchased the theatrical rights for $25,000. It was expected to be the first in a series of *Dick Tracy* films, and the first two movies were to be shot back to back. Filming was due to commence in the summer of 1978 with a budget of $7 million. Harrison Ford was mentioned as a possible Dick Tracy but it never happened.

The next time the yellow fedora detective was mentioned in the Hollywood press was in 1981 when there was some discussion about the movie rights moving from Paramount to Polygram. John Landis was onboard to write and direct and Clint Eastwood contacted Landis to play the role of the infamous detective. By 1983 the project was still waiting to be given the green light. The rights reverted back to Paramount in 1983. Landis was out and Walter Hill was bought in as director. Principal photography was due to begin in October 1983. The budget was set at $25 million.

This is when, officially, Warren Beatty first came into the *Dick Tracy* picture. He was being tapped up to play the chiselled-jaw detective but the studio baulked at his salary demands ($5 million upfront and fifteen percent of the film's gross). Walter Hill left the project to prep for his new film *Streets of Fire*.

Beatty now had the upper hand in negotiations to a film that he had wanted to make for over a decade. He had grown up on reading the comic strip and when he started to see the project fall apart, it was obvious to him that he should be the man to step in and make a film that honoured his childhood hero. The film rights to *Dick Tracy* reverted back to their original owners Tribune Media Services. Beatty knew this company all too well as he had previously had a concept for a *Dick Tracy* film in 1975, which he pitched to the then rights owner Michael Laughlin. The problem was Laughlin couldn't get a "Yes" from any of the Hollywood studios. So he let the rights return to Tribune before Floyd Mutrux picked them up two years later.

Beatty wasn't quick enough, and didn't have the money to buy the *Dick Tracy* film rights at that time. By 1985, Beatty had become a very wealthy man thanks to his share of the profits from his two previous movies: *Heaven Can Wait* and *Reds* where Beatty had directed, produced, acted and written the screenplay. Leaping at the chance to acquire the rights and be able to make the film he wanted to make, Beatty purchased the *Dick Tracy* rights from Tribune Media for an undisclosed fee. Now firmly in the driving seat, Beatty set about assembling a team that he thought could do justice to his vision of *Dick Tracy*.

The script was already in place as Beatty decided to use the Jim Cash and Jack Epps Jr script that was originally commissioned by Floyd Mutrux. Beatty and screenwriter Bo Goldman worked on re-writing some of the dialogue though. Martin Scorsese was hired as director and set about looking at ways to make this new version of *Dick Tracy* much more serious. However, disagreements with Beatty over final cut led to Scorsese leaving the project not twelve months since signing on to it. Beatty, at first, didn't want to direct. He offered the job to a number of other directors including The Coen Brothers, Sam Raimi, Hal Ashby, Bob Fosse and Brian De Palma. All of them turned him down. Eventually Beatty decided he should direct the movie, he owned the rights so why not make it in his own style?

By summer 1986, Paramount had put the production in turnaround citing the bloated budget of $25 million. Taking the project to Walt Disney Pictures, Beatty was given the green light from his old friend and ex-Paramount executive Michael Eisner alongside Jeffrey Katzenberg. Soon both execs found contacting Beatty about finalising the deal very difficult. Bo Goldman said: "Katzenberg would call every day. Every once in a while, Beatty would give him a glimpse of the World According to Warren." Retreating into his mansion to re-write the script and start casting, Beatty alienated himself from the company that was going to finance his long-gestated project. The deal was completed in the summer of 1988. Disney would release the film under their Touchstone Pictures studio with a budget of $36.8 million. That figure included $9.5 million to Beatty alone for writing, directing and starring in the film. On top of that was his fifteen percent of gross box office returns. It was a gamble for Disney, but they had faith in Beatty. Now it was down to Beatty to return it.

Casting proved nearly as tricky as finding a director. Beatty was looking for an actor with the square jaw features of *Dick Tracy*. The problem was he couldn't find one. Eventually he decided the role of the detective should go to him. It was his project after all. Not having the natural resemblance to *Dick Tracy*, Beatty tried different prosthetics including different shaped noses and also sharper jaw lines. None of it worked and Beatty came to realisation that the prosthetics would be a distraction. Tracy was the hero; he didn't need look like him he just had to act like him. Beatty quickly hired some of his friends and acquaintances for some of the secondary roles.

Pick of the bunch was Academy Award winner Dustin Hoffman as Mumbles, a sloppily-spoken, heavy-lidded criminal from master villain Al 'Big Boy' Caprice's gang. Initially Beatty had wanted Gene Hackman to play Al 'Big Boy' Caprice. They had worked together briefly on *Reds*. Hackman didn't like that his on-screen time was cut down to two brief scenes and that it took over fifty takes for Beatty to be satisfied with one of those scenes. Hackman told Beatty: "I love you Warren, but I just can't do it." Still in the throes of trying to convince Hackman, Beatty was having lunch in a restaurant in Burbank, California when he spotted Al Pacino at another table. Beatty went over to say hello and ended up pouring out his troubles to Pacino. During the conversation Beatty asked Pacino who he would cast, Pacino was unsure and said he would think about it.

The next day Beatty received a phone from Pacino asking: "Are you serious about wanting me to play this part?" He replied with: "Well, I am now!" Beatty convinced Pacino by telling him that he should use the same character style as when he worked on stage playing Arturo Ui in Bertolt Brecht's gangster play: *The Resistible Rise of Arturo Ui*. "I want you to take that character and bring it to Dick Tracy." Initially, Beatty was worried that the casting of Pacino would take the budget over the agreed figure. However, in the end, Beatty believed that it was imperative Pacino be cast regardless of cost. He explained the additional cost away by saying: "Al is one of those centrifugal people that cause good acting around them."

As his character was not one that recurred in the comic strips, Pacino set about unravelling who Big Boy Caprice truly was: "Could he be a man who dresses like a boy, sucks lollipops? Partly, it was a visual thing; the character had a deformity" Pacino commented before filming started. With the villain cast, Beatty turned his attention to the role of Breathless Mahoney, a slender blonde seductress.

Kim Basinger, Michelle Pfeiffer, Kathleen Turner and Melanie Griffith were all considered for the role. The pop star Madonna also bombarded Beatty with pleas to be cast in the role. Her film career had yet to take off so she organised for Beatty to take her out on a dinner date to the Ivy Restaurant in Los Angeles. Knowing full well that this would be an audition of sorts, Madonna dressed exactly as Breathless Mahoney would – a tight, black leather jumpsuit zipped down just enough to show some of what she was made off. Beatty enjoyed her humour, this wasn't just a casting audition it was an actual romantic date. Beatty offered her the role on the spot and then got to kiss her goodnight. With the budget already rocketing past the agreed $36.8 million, Beatty asked Madonna to work for Screen Actors Guild scale wages. This amounted to $1,440 per week. Desperate to be part of the movie, and to please her new boyfriend, Madonna agreed to the low pay. In a rather cunning move she negotiated a percentage of the box office gross and also had eyes on releasing an entire album related to her role in the movie. Madonna was playing the long game with both *Dick Tracy* and Beatty.

Dick Tracy's principal photography began on 27 February 1989 with scenes shot on the Universal backlot acting as the unnamed city's downtown district (later in the film the deed to the night club owned by Big Boy Caprice indicates the city is called Homeville). Beatty decided to create the *Dick Tracy* world using only primary colours. Beatty was inspired by the work of cartoonist Herb Gardner, who drew cartoons that associated a number to each primary colour. Cinematographer Vittorio Storaro commented: "These are not the kind of colours the audience is used to seeing. These are much more dramatic in strength, in saturation."

Costumes set and production designs had to be made with "undistinguishable simplicity." Beatty wanted it to have the air of the *Dick Tracy* time period without actually presenting anything that had a physical time stamp on it. The automobiles used were stripped of any designs and branding so as to all appear in keeping with the "undistinguishable simplicity" of the film. Alongside using the Universal Studios, California backlot and sound stages, some of the interior scenes were filmed at Warner Bros Studios in Burbank. It wasn't just the cars that had to be stripped of branding, the actors had to as well. For a cast that features many recognisable faces, Beatty was determined to cover up the majority of them under facial prosthetics. Make-Up artists John Caglione Jr and Doug Drexler spent hours assembling the weird and wonderful prosthetics for each individual actor. William Forsythe spent up to four hours each day having his prosthetics attached. His character Flattop had fourteen individual pieces to be applied. R.G. Armstrong, who played Pruneface, would fall asleep in the make-up chair because he was there for so long. Beatty had offered the role of Pruneface to President Ronald Reagan, but was turned down. So as a little in-joke Beatty made sure the facial construction looked like Reagan. Pacino was the only actor who was allowed to work on his own facial prosthetics. Very little was added to the face. Instead it was more about the size of Big Boy Caprice. Pacino opted for a fat suit that made the character hunch over and have a penguin-style waddle. It was the over the top, zany comedy Pacino had always wanted to bring to the movies.

Only a week into filming Beatty had a problem. He had hired Sean Young to play Dick Tracy's girlfriend Tess Trueheart. In the script, Trueheart and Tracy look after a street urchin known as The Kid. When looking back on the first week's dailies, where Tracy and Trueheart first meet The Kid, Beatty felt she was wooden in her delivery. When he told screenwriter Bo Goldman his fears, Goldman replied: "I never liked her. I think she's a creepy creature." Beatty fired Young. Young retaliated by saying she was fired for refuting Beatty's sexual advances. She also asserted that Beatty withheld the script changes until the last minute so that the actors struggled to learn their lines. Beatty denied all of these accusations. He realised he had got the casting wrong and told Goldman:

"I fucked up." Young was replaced by Glenne Headly. Beatty's difficulties continued well beyond the first week of filming as an acting battle between his now-girlfriend Madonna and his close friend Pacino ensued.

Shooting a scene in Big Boy's nightclub, Beatty wanted perfection and that meant many, many takes before he felt the actors had got it right. Part of this particular scene sees Breathless perform a song and dance routine. During this moment, Big Boy walks around her shouting instructions into her ear, slapping her stomach and generally showing her up. It's a bullying scene that has strong parallels with what real cabaret stars used to have to go through in order to succeed. Having spent several hours on the same scene and with the whole crew tired and frustrated, Beatty finally allowed Pacino to improvise. Madonna was already struggling with the attitude Pacino was giving her in that heated moment of filming. It was dialled up even further when he was given the go ahead by his director to improvise.

His Big Boy went ballistic at Breathless. It was the classic shouty style, brimming with bravado, that Pacino was so known for. Beatty called "cut" when he realised Madonna had stopped acting and had broken down in tears. Beatty gave her a hug and calmed her down. But she never forgot that moment and for the rest of filming was on edge whenever a scene between Breathless and Big Boy was scheduled. Recounting the episode, Madonna said: "Al kept slapping me in the stomach, being really rude. He made me cry, and Warren never really stopped him." Pacino may not have been Madonna's favourite person on set, but he was Beatty's. Having been friends for years previously, they were enjoying working together. At one point, Beatty asked his co-star to call: "Action!" whenever he was on-set. It was a way of giving back to his friend. Someone who had been through some rough years in film, much like Beatty, and had come out the other side a stronger and more intelligent actor.

Dick Tracy completed filming on 28 June 1989. The shoot lasted for eighty-seven days. Beatty locked himself away in his editing suite, even ignoring pleas from Madonna to come and join her on a couple of dates of her Blond Ambition World Tour (which included music from her own *Dick Tracy* album: *I'm Breathless*). Beatty refused. At one point he requested screenwriter Bo Goldman help with the editing as well. Goldman knew better: "I purposefully went to Taos to write a picture, lived in the Holiday Inn, trying to get far away from him." Disney marketed the film heavily. Novels, graphic novels, audio books, soundtracks, figures, plush toys, walkie-talkies, wristwatches, backpacks, lunch boxes, McDonald's Happy Meals, Quaker Oats promotional boxes, shower curtains, yellow fedoras and black lingerie. All promotional avenues were explored. At a final count, over six hundred individual products were made with *Dick Tracy* the movie branding on them. $54 million was spent on promotion for the movie. Disney were banking on *Dick Tracy* being as big a release as they had a year previously with Tim Burton's *Batman*.

In honour of *Dick Tracy's* creator Chester Gould, the movie had its premiere in Gould's old hometown of Woodstock, Illinois on 13 June 1990. A day later there was another premiere, this time in Orlando, Florida. That was followed by the U.S. theatrical release at 00:01am on 15 June. Those in attendance for the midnight screenings were given a t-shirt beforehand which served as their ticket. Critical reviews were mainly positive. *The New York Times* called it: "a great uninterrupted grin." *Newsweek* said: "a class act." Roger Ebert said: "It is one of the most original and visionary fantasies I've seen on a screen." Out of all the actors involved however, only Pacino received acclaim across the board. *New York Daily News* commented: "Al Pacino will simply kill you with his gleefully comical performance." Roger Ebert also picked out Pacino, saying: "He really steals the show." Joel Siegel on the *Good Morning America* TV show believed his performance: "worthy of an Oscar nomination."

Dick Tracy grossed $22.5 million on its opening weekend in the U.S. box office. Rising to $34.7 million for its first week. It wasn't doing the numbers *Batman* had the year before, but *Dick Tracy* was still strong. It was the biggest opening Disney had ever had after ten days on release with returns of $50.3 million. After eight weeks on general release it brought in a respectable return for Beatty and Disney: $103 million

(Information courtesy of Box Office Mojo. Used with permission). It wasn't the financial windfall that Disney expected it to be but it did receive seven nominations at the 63rd Academy Awards. Pacino was nominated once again, this time in Best Supporting role. There were also nominations for Best Original Song, Best Sound, Best Art Direction, Best Cinematography, Best Make-Up and Best Costume Design. It won in three categories – Best Art Design, Best Make-Up and Best Original Song.

This film is sadly overlooked during discussions about impressive comic book movie adaptations. *Dick Tracy* has visual style and storytelling panache that is still rooted in the original Chester Gould mould. Beatty had a vision for his *Dick Tracy* movie. It was to be a film version of the comic books that he had so loved as a kid. He had big production values; a star ensemble cast and complete control. Yet if Beatty thought *Dick Tracy* would be another star vehicle for himself then he didn't bank on being out manoeuvred by two of his closest allies. The sultry, sexual seduction of Madonna's Breathless Mahoney sizzled the screen. It was her attempt at taking the blonde bombshell mantle from the actress she so admired: Marilyn Monroe. Was Madonna acting? Or was that really her on screen? Beatty knew it was one and the same and putting her in the film was a masterstroke. But even he couldn't have predicted that the "pop singer" would turn out to be the attention grabber. And if Madonna made it OK to steam up the movie then Pacino made it OK to chew up the scenery. It was a role that required him to be over the top in every single scene. A zany, slobbering, spitting bulk of a character that enjoys taunting and teasing. Pacino knew there was no bounds to the character and ran wild with it. It was a performance that allowed him to explore, and enjoy, his comedic acting. This was Pacino as the ultimate pantomime villain.

Co-Star Charlie Korsmo on *Dick Tracy*

***Dick Tracy* was only your second acting role. How did it come about?**

I had done one other movie. I lived in Minneapolis at the time. It's pretty far from Hollywood. I sort of got lucky at a cattle call audition to do a movie called *Men Don't Leave*. Which was with Jessica Lange and it was Chris O'Donnell's first movie. It didn't do well at the box office but it was well-regarded with reviews. So I started getting lots of calls for other auditions and *Dick Tracy* was one of them. I think I was in Los Angeles doing post-production on *Men Don't Leave* when I got a call to come to Warren Beatty's house to audition for this movie. So it went from there.

What was it like auditioning at Warren Beatty's house in front of him?

He had me staying there the rest of the day so I would say I was pretty sure I had the part then and there. I ended up spending the day with him and he called up Madonna to come over and meet me. It was an interesting day for me and my mother [*laughs*].

What direction did Beatty give you?

It's a little hard for me to remember. It's been twenty-seven years at this point. I don't remember him giving me any direction out of the gate when I first got the role. He just said: "It's a street kid that is used to being on his own and is suspicious of everybody else and has a bit of a hot temper."

So you were on your own?

Yes, more or less. Once we made the movie, as you may have heard, he is a bit of a perfectionist so he ended up doing fifty or sixty takes of each scene. You end up trying it a bunch of different ways for each scene.

The day-glow sets are fantastic. What was it like filming on them?

It was interesting. We did it on the back lot of Universal Studios. On the classic New York street they have there. Although I think it burnt down about fifteen years ago, but it was where every movie since the 1940s that had New York street settings has been filmed. They were filming *Back to the Future II* at the same time right on the next street. You had this very bizarre, futuristic set on one side of the street and this bizarre, 1930s comic book set right next to it.

The film has a huge ensemble cast. Who did you enjoy working with the most?

Frankly, Warren and I got along really well. My mother always takes credit for him settling down and having kids [*laughs*] because of his time working with me. I don't know if I would take that credit though [*laughs*]. It was long shoot. It was almost six months long. So we spent a lot of time together. We had a good relationship.

There are two people I wanted to ask you about in greater detail. One of them is Madonna. What was she like as an actor?

I didn't have a lot of scenes with her. I had a couple of scenes with her and I don't remember anything unusual about that. This is one of the advantages of being a ten year old; you are not overawed by working with these rich and famous people. The first time I met her was auditioning and we made popcorn [*laughs*]. That's about as exciting as it was. I think she was a little unsure of how to behave around kids and my mother [*laughs*]. In that her usual persona is this outrageous person but I think she knew not to really behave that way around kids. She was quite respectable around me.

Didn't she sign a scrapbook of yours with a naughty note?

Well not that naughty I wouldn't say. I'm trying to think what she exactly said. I think she said "Someday you'll appreciate me." I think I know what she meant [*laughs*].

Of course, the other person I want to ask you about is Al Pacino. How was it working with him?

He was great. Very low key, cool guy. Again, as a ten year old, I certainly didn't place him on a pedestal and think: 'boy, I'm working with the great Al Pacino!' I don't think I'd seen *The Godfather* or *Serpico* or *Dog Day Afternoon* when I was nine years old [*laughs*].

He just seemed like a cool guy to me. In fact I remember we had dinner one night at Warren Beatty's house. It was just a bunch of people working on the movie and I was with my chaperone, my parents weren't in town for that, and my father was asking me: "what was it like? What did you do?" and I said: "I dunno. I mainly talked with Al most of the time." "You mean Al Pacino?" "Yeah that's his name." It wasn't a big deal to me.

They were actually trying to hide that he was Big Boy Caprice in the movie, so he was under a code name on all the call sheets. I think it was Guido Friscadai that was his code name. So that was what everybody called him on the set. I think by the end they had given up as everybody knew who he was. I guess it was because he was in a comeback stage of his career. He hadn't done much in the late 1980s, and *Sea of Love* and *Dick Tracy* were comeback movies for him. He was wearing a lot of make-up in the movie, he was almost unrecognisable, but for whatever reason they wanted to keep it a secret he was working on this movie.

What was it like seeing him in all that make-up?

Frankly, it was a bit scary in real life. Him and some of his sidekicks... Bill Forsythe... he played Flattop in the movie, and was kind of an intimidating guy even out of his make-up. But in the make-up they really were kind of monstrous. So I would say it did really put some distance between the actors playing the bad guys and me. The scene I remember most filming with Al was one where Dick Tracy is tied to the chair with the boiler about to explode, and I come in and cut him out. We do dozens of takes of these things and he was quite frightening in that scene [*laughs*].

You only acted for eight years. Is *Dick Tracy* your favourite film that you starred in?

I would say it's the one that I would watch now and think that's a real movie. I would hope people still find it interesting fifty years from now. *Dick Tracy* is a classy movie.

The Godfather Part III

Cast: Al Pacino (Don Michael Corleone), Diane Keaton (Kay Adams Michelson), Talia Shire (Connie Corleone Rizzi), Andy Garcia (Vincent Mancini), Eli Wallach (Don Altobello), Joe Mantegna (Joey Zasa), George Hamilton (B.J. Harrison), Bridget Fonda (Grace Hamilton), Sofia Coppola (Mary Corleone). **Director:** Francis Ford Coppola.

Synopsis: The ageing Don Michael Corleone seeks to legitimize the family interests and remove himself from all Mafia connections. He aims to purchase a large stake in the Vatican run International Immobiliare real estate company while also donating over $100 million to the Catholic Church. Don Michael takes under his wing Vincent Mancini, the illegitimate son of his dead brother Sonny. Mancini soon starts to cause problems with Joey Zasa, the boss of all Corleone-owned crime operations, leading to repercussions that force Don Michael to take a stand.

"Just when I thought I was out.....They pull me back in."

The most famous quote from *The Godfather Part III* was spoken by Michael Corleone as he describes his attempt to escape his former criminal activities. This line also chimes with director Francis Ford Coppola's return to *The Godfather* franchise.

For over a decade he steadfastly refused to talk about making another film about the Corleone family. The only time he would engage with the idea was when he joked it would be a slapstick comedy: something akin to Abbot and Costello meet The Godfather. Coppola ultimately found himself facing bankruptcy however. He hadn't had a hit movie since 1983's *The Outsiders* so this and the collapse of his Zoetrope film studio possibly forced his hand to return to a franchise he knew well.

The first outlines of *The Godfather Part III* were drawn up in 1977 by the head of Paramount Studios at that time, Michael Eisner. He envisioned a story about a new Mafia family which offered to help the CIA with an assassination attempt in return for drug trafficking support. Several screenplays were written, all of them focussing on the next generation of the Corleone family. The co-writer of *The French Connection*, Alexander Jacobs, wrote a screenplay focussing on Michael's son, Anthony, trying to legalize the family business. In 1978 author of *The Godfather* Mario Puzo and *Dirty Harry* screenwriter Dean Riesner wrote a draft of *The Godfather Part III*. This script also centred on Michael's son, Anthony: a naval officer working for the CIA. The screenplay also included a story about the Corleone family's involvement in a plot to assassinate a Central American dictator.

By the end of the 1970s, fifteen treatments had been written by at least nine different writers. Further treatments saw Michael killed off, cause the implosion of his own family or permitting an illegitimate son to take over the family business. Paramount CEO Frank Mancuso who felt the story needed to focus solely on the Corleone family relationship, was simultaneously struggling to convince Francis Ford Coppola to return as the director. Coppola was still recovering from his ordeal filming *Apocalypse Now*. "He never said, No" Mancuso said. "He always had some reason why he couldn't do it now."

For some people at Paramount this wasn't the worst news. Ned Tanen, Paramount production chief, didn't want Coppola back. There was bad blood between them that stemmed from the making of *The Godfather Part II*. By 1985 Mancuso had, unofficially, started to offer out the project to other directors. Rumours suggest it was first offered to Russian director Andrei Konchalovsky, director of Runaway Train starring Jon Voight. Other directors approached included: Martin Scorsese, Michael Mann, Richard Brooks, Dan Curtis and Sidney Lumet. All declined the offer. The one person who did show interest in making the movie and that Paramount entertained as a possible director was Sylvester Stallone. Following the success of his *Rocky* and *Rambo* movies, Stallone was already hard at work for Paramount, directing his friend John Travolta in the *Saturday Night Fever* sequel *Staying Alive*.

Stallone knew how to bring a film in under budget and ahead of schedule. The studio wanted to cut down on the lavish expense of a crime movie without the final product looking like it had a smaller budget. Stallone told *People* magazine that he planned to direct *The Godfather Part III*, and he would be starring in it alongside his buddy John Travolta. There was even talk of Eddie Murphy signing on to play one of the lead actors.

In 1987, Puzo delivered a screenplay featuring flashbacks that showed Vito Corleone continuing to build his empire. These were interspersed with contemporary scenes of Michael's struggles. This idea was based on a treatment by Nicholas Gage, a former *New York Times* Reporter. Mancuso was making it his top priority to finally put *The Godfather Part III* into production by any means necessary and that meant getting this Puzo/Gage script into the hands of Coppola through his sister Talia Shire. A meeting was arranged between Coppola and Mancuso where Coppola ripped apart the screenplay he was given. Afterward, he explained what was wrong with it. Coppola then proceeded to make his vision clear on what the story should be. Mancuso said to him: "If you think that's what it should be, why don't you do it?" *The Godfather*'s esteemed director didn't want to direct a second sequel, but he also didn't want to see the Corleone family taken in a direction that wasn't suitable.

Coppola was also desperate for money. Having lost $27 million on making the box office bomb *One from the Heart*, bankruptcy edged closer every day. Mancuso agreed to pay Coppola $3 million to direct, $2 million to produce and a further $1 million to write. As with the writing for the previous two Godfather films, Coppola and Puzo split writing duties, each writing a segment and then passing it to the other for them to look over and alter as necessary. This time they set up a writing camp at the Peppermill Hotel Casino in Reno during the February of 1989. If they felt they had cracked a major plot point, the reward would be an hour spent downstairs on the gambling tables. The first draft was completed within eight weeks and ran for 133 pages.

Pacino once mentioned during a press junket for *The Godfather* that he would be open to sequels: "I'd like to age. I'd like to go to about sixty-five if I could." Coppola and Puzo wrote this idea into their script. Set during 1979, Michael, now an elder statesman, is looking to make his business interests legitimate. He is also seeking forgiveness from his children and ex-wife. Some of the earlier scripts saw Michael die early on but Coppola understood that Michael needed to be front and centre throughout. Pacino wanted $7 million for the part. Coppola declined. Pacino held steadfast. Coppola re-wrote the script to start with the funeral of Michael, therefore not needing Pacino. An offer was made of $5 million which Pacino agreed to. Diane Keaton accepted $2 million to reprise her role as Kay Corleone. Coppola's sister Talia Shire would also return as Connie Corleone. The other central character Coppola wanted back was Tom Hagen, played by Robert Duvall. Questioning the amount Pacino was to be paid compared to himself, Duvall wanted $1.5 million to reprise the role of Michael's attorney and adopted brother. Paramount turned him down flat. The studio felt $1 million was too high a price to pay. Duvall never signed on and as such Coppola and Puzo had to rewrite the script again so as to not include Tom Hagen (in the film it is mentioned that Hagen has died, but nothing more is forthcoming about his death). New cast members signed on included Andy Garcia as Vincent Mancini, Eli Wallach as Don Altobello, Joe Mantegna as Joey Zasa, Bridget Fonda as Grace Hamilton, George Hamilton as B.J. Harrison, Franc D'Ambrosio as Anthony Corleone and Winona Ryder as Mary Corleone.

By the time principal photography started on 27 November 1989, Coppola and Puzo had written seven scripts with lengths ranging from 113 to 145 pages. One of the first signs of a difficult shoot was that the director continued to re-write the script while he was filming. In total, Coppola gave out nine different scripts throughout shooting. He issued a new script page three times in one day. Filming started at Italy's Cinecittá Studios and lasted for six weeks. The crew had built sets on four separate sound stages, including Michael's penthouse apartment and the Atlantic City suite that was used in the scene in which several Mafia bosses are gunned down.

Moving on to film in Rome, the crew were initially denied entrance to the Vatican when it turned out nobody had contacted the papalcy to request filming access. Eventually, access was granted to the required areas including Rome's Palazzo di Giustizia, the Santa Maria della Quercia church, and a farm. Shortly after Christmas the filming resumed but the production was to have its biggest setback. Winona Ryder flew into Rome directly from finishing on the set of *Mermaids*. Her then-boyfriend Johnny Depp was concerned about her health and requested a doctor attend to her the first night she was in Rome. Diagnosed with a nervous collapse and exhaustion, Ryder had to drop out of making the picture. This happened only a few days before Ryder's first scenes as Mary Corleone were due to be filmed and created a difficult problem for Coppola.

Actresses such as Madeleine Stowe, Laura San Giacomo, Linda Fiorentino, Julia Roberts and Madonna had at one time or another been in the running to play Mary. The director chose to cast his daughter Sofia in the role instead. Having acted in only a small number of roles (including some uncredited work on the previous *Godfather* movies) Sofia was a bizarre choice to all but her father. He knew her well, but the rest of the cast had troubled feelings about bringing in a novice actor at this late stage in the proceedings, and for such a key role. Further delays occurred when Pacino's grandmother died while he was in Italy. Pacino and Keaton (who were in an on-again off-again relationship during filming) flew back to New York to be at the funeral.

With filming now three weeks behind schedule, the cast and crew moved to Sicily during March 1990 to shoot the exterior scenes of the finale which takes place during an opera at the Teatro Massimo. Further filming took place in Palermo, amd Taormina, with many of the locals trying to catch a glimpse of Pacino. By May, the cast and crew had relocated back to New York for the remainder of the shoot. Scenes were shot in Little Italy and within Manhattan borough including the Lower East Side and Park Avenue. Mancuso was pushing Coppola to have the film ready for the original release date of Thanksgiving 1990 but after all the delays there was no way Coppola could meet that deadline. He was still filming the last portion of the movie during September. Eventually principal photography was completed in early October and Mancuso hired a group of editors to help Coppola cut the film into shape. The budget had ballooned from the $44 million originally agreed upon at the start up to $54 million. This additional cost came from all the delays Coppola had suffered while in Italy. Mancuso and Paramount were willing to swallow the costs if it meant *The Godfather Part III* was going to be delivered to theatres by 25 December. The studio needed a holiday release and *The Godfather Part III* was what they were banking on.

A press screening took place on 12 December in New York. Critics could not understand a lot of Sofia Coppola's dialogue. Called back in to re-loop about 20% of her work, the continued challenge for the director was to now re-dub the new audio over the existing footage. Eventually finished a few days later, Coppola's final part of the *Godfather* saga ran at two hours and forty-two minutes. And in case anybody was counting: the final shooting script ran for 120 pages. The premiere of *The Godfather Part III* took place at The Academy Theatre, Beverly Hills in Los Angeles on the 20 December 1990 with many of the cast in attendance. Mancuso, Puzo and Coppola had pulled off the unimaginable and managed to get the movie into U.S. theatres on 25 December 1990.

It pulled in $14 million within its first three days. A healthy amount that probably had Paramount seeing dollar signs again. Footfall soon dropped off though, through less than favourable word of mouth and critical reviews. Consequently, the film returned $22million in its first full week. A respectable amount for any film, but this wasn't just any film. It was the third of an epic saga. The following two weeks saw its box office returns drop to $11 and $5 million respectively. By the end of its U.S. theatrical run it had pulled in $66 million (Information courtesy of Box Office Mojo. Used with permission). Paramount had covered their costs for making the film, but the return wasn't anywhere near as high as they expected it to be.

Critical reviews were middling on the whole. *Rolling Stone* said: "*The Godfather Part III* feels as if it were written and directed by Michael Corleone." *New York Times* called it "a valid and deeply moving continuation of the Corleone family saga." *The Washington Post* were not so enamoured with the film, suggesting it "isn't just a disappointment, it's a failure of heartbreaking proportions." The majority of criticism was directed at Sofia Coppola. *Time* Magazine believed "her gosling gracelessness comes close to wrecking the movie." *The New York Post* were equally scathing by saying "Coppola has virtually ruined his movie by casting [her]." Andrew Sarris of *The New Yorker* really hit Coppola hard: "Sofia just doesn't hack it as an actress or as someone with screen charisma." Throughout all of the reviews, Pacino was only singled out for praise a couple of times. *Variety's* Todd McCarthy said: "I believe Pacino is magnificent." and Alexander Walker, of the *London Evening Standard* saw "Pacino...at his peak." At the 63rd Academy Awards *The Godfather Part III* was nominated in seven categories: Best Picture, Best Director, Best Actor in a Supporting Role, Best Original Song, Best Art Direction, Best Cinematography and Best Film Editing.

It failed to win anything.

The Godfather Part III suffers from a range of problems. Pacino's overacting in some scenes is excruciating. He made Michael into an over the top character rather than the cold, calculating Mafia boss from the previous movies. Michael's diabetic storyline feels like an afterthought. It's alluded to in the previous films by Michael drinking a lot of water, but here it is fully forced into the movie in order to help a secondary story gain more traction. There is the tragic waste of Diane Keaton. The blink and you'll miss it storyline for Bridget Fonda's character. The creepy incestual cousins-in-love storyline. The poor acting and singing of Franc D'Ambrosio (who played Anthony Corleone). The heavy-handed editing. The lack of the classic Godfather cinematography in terms of style and tone (even though original Godfather cinematographer Gordon Willis had been hired). A screenplay that has so many different strands, it never feels like it all comes together to any satisfactory level. The Pope assassination plot is never fully realised. The convoluted International Immobiliare real estate storyline. Coppola's direction is missing the cutting edge he had during the 1970s; here it feels like he is on auto pilot. In an early scene between father and son, Anthony Corleone tells his father: "I won't fail." And Michael's response is: "Men always believe that." Unknowingly, in that one moment, Coppola had written about himself and his relationship with *The Godfather Part III*. The director might not have failed financially with his return to the Corleone family - it did respectable business at the box office and garnered several award nominations - but for the movie-going public it was not the film they were expecting.

Though the bloodshed and Mafia family values remained, there was an attempt to redeem the character of Michael Corleone. Who wants to see a movie about one of the biggest Mafia Don's turn his life around and become a good guy? Redemption doesn't work for a character like Michael Corleone. His entire focus is on being a calculating and methodical killer who only cares about what's right for the family business, even if it means killing family members. Burning in the fires of Hell is too good for Michael Corleone. Thus to have him absolved of all his previous indiscretions under the eyes of God is not palatable to the audience.

Pacino believed that was the fundamental problem with the movie: "Nobody wants to see Michael have retribution and feel guilty. That's not who he was." People loved him for what he wasn't and hated him for what he was. Why set about changing that? Michael, as a character, rises through the ranks in *The Godfather*, we see him cement his power in *The Godfather Part II*, yet in *Part III* he does nothing. His character arc comes to a complete standstill. It is little wonder people lost their emotional connection with him in *Part III*. Possibly the biggest problem in the movie however is the absence of Tom Hagan (previously played by Robert Duvall). He was Michael's right-hand man, his confidant, his best friend and his enforcer. To suddenly take away that character without any replacement doesn't work. Pacino wasn't happy about it either, commenting to his biographer Lawrence Grobel: "The third one didn't seem so focussed as the other two; it seemed unfinished. We missed the Duvall character strongly."

For all its misfires though, *The Godfather Part III* does boast some enjoyable moments. Andy Garcia plays Vincent Mancini with such guile and bravado that he feels like the only true mobster who would still be able to kill with his bare hands. Joe Mantegna's slimy Joey Zasa is the perfect old time-y Mafia boss that isn't afraid to ruffle a few feathers. The Catholic Church storyline shows the frightening and very real power that they hold throughout the world (this element was based on the real-life Papal banking scandal of the early 1980s). Talia Shire does a brilliant job of moving Connie, once the beaten wife of the Corleone family, into a position where she is the matriarch of the family. Sofia Coppola, for many years the butt of jokes about why *The Godfather Part III* was so bad, isn't as terrible as most believe.

Thrown into an impossible situation at the last minute, Coppola portrays a moody self absorbed, love-sick teenager. It's not the greatest performance, yet there is enough in the character to make you feel her pains in love and family conflicts. Pacino delivers occasional humorous lines that naturally role off his sharp-witted tongue. His wardrobe is also of note: he is dressed somewhere between an upper class English gent, thanks to his sharp suit and cravat, and Roy Orbison, because of his near constant insistence on wearing sunglasses. Pacino had created a different Michael. One that, guilt aside, is finally comfortable in his own skin.

The Godfather Part III is not the terrible film that some have made it out to be. It was never going to live up to the hype. If *The Godfather Part III* was called something different and had no association with the previous two films, then it would be spoken about as a respectable crime movie. Instead it's now seen as an unfortunate footnote to the franchise; Coppola described *Part III* as an epilogue and that is possibly the best way to view the movie.

Producer Gray Frederickson on *The Godfather Part III*

How much pressure were Francis and yourself under to make a third film?

Francis was very stressed. He said: "I can make a science fiction film. I just can't screw up a *Godfather* movie. That's my heritage. That's what I'm remembered for." So, he said: "It's got to be as good as the others." He felt tremendous pressure, and because of him being under such pressure I was under pressure. He was more agitated, a little bit more difficult to work with and it was a little less pleasant, the experience. Then when we lost Winona Ryder we were going to put it on hold and then he [Coppola] pushed for his daughter to be in it and that upset a lot of people. He said: "I had my daughter in mind when writing the script and that's how it's going to be." I don't know to this day if it would have been any better without her. It was supposed to be a hot, torrid love affair between Andy Garcia and Winona Ryder, and instead it was Francis' daughter and she said: "How can I do this?" Her dad was right there watching. It was very intimidating. I don't know if that harmed the movie or not.

Did you find it difficult to bring new characters into *Part III*?

A bit. George Hamilton instead of Robert Duvall because Duvall wanted the same fee that Pacino got. Francis fought very hard for Bobby and he got it down to where he only had to work a week and he said: "I work fifteen minutes, I want the same amount of money as Pacino." He didn't do it so we got George Hamilton. It probably would have been better if we had Winona Ryder and Robert Duvall, but we changed casting in Part II and that didn't seem to bother people. George kept us all laughing and had poker games. George was a wonderful addition because he kept everything light.

In the film it is mentioned that Duvall's character – Tom Hagen – has died. But it is never elaborated on. Were you ever told how it happened?

No. No. He just had to say he died. I know Francis, in his mind, knew why he died but he never said how he died.

There are rumours that one of the initial scripts for *Part III* killed off Michael Corleone. Is that true?

I never heard that. Well they did kill him off at the end of *Part III*.

I think it was referring to killing off Michael earlier on in the film.

I never heard that. Not in any of the scripts I read. When he dies at the end it was an afterthought by Francis. It wasn't in any of the original scripts.

So it was an off-the-cuff moment from Francis?

Francis said: "I don't want them to get me to make another *Godfather* film. I'm ending it right here with this." [*Laughs*].

When *The Godfather Part III* was released it wasn't as universally loved as Parts I and II. Why do you think that was?

Everybody says that but it did over one hundred million dollars. Yes... it wasn't the success of Parts I and II. But again I think maybe it's because of the relationship between the Ryder and Garcia characters. I think that was meant to be a dark and sexy affair right underneath the Godfather's nose that could have been... I love Sofia, I think she is a sweetheart and she didn't want to do that part. I don't know. Who knows what makes these things work and what makes these things not work.

Do you think part of the reason people took against it is because they didn't want to see Michael achieve redemption? That fans of Michael didn't want to see him become a good guy?

I didn't see him redeeming himself. I don't know... I hadn't thought about that in a long time.

Do you have a favourite of the three films?

Part II

Which one do you have the best memories of working on?

Part I and *II*. *Part I* because it was the first big movie I was ever on and it was exciting. We were in New York and we were dealing with a big studio. It was fun for me. And working with Marlon Brando, *Part II* was also fun because we were travelling everywhere. It was easier and not as stressful. But I guess *Part I* was the most rewarding to pull off.

Frankie and Johnny

Cast: Al Pacino (Johnny), Michelle Pfeiffer (Frankie), Hector Elizondo (Nick), Nathan Lane (Tim), Kate Nelligan (Cora), Jane Morris (Nedda), Ele Keats (Artemis), Glen Plummer (Peter), Tim Hopper (Lester), Sean O'Bryan (Bobby). **Director:** Garry Marshall.

Synopsis: Outgoing ex-convict Johnny is hired as a short order cook in a New York City diner. He's head-over-heels crazy for Frankie the waitress. But to Frankie, they're as different as scrambled and hard-boiled eggs, and she isn't looking for a new man in her life. Johnny is determined their romance can blossom if she just gave him a chance.

"Love. A home. Marriage. Screw that shit."

A line from director Garry Marshall's romantic comedy drama that, over the course of the narrative, insinuates true love can find even the unlikeliest of souls.

Following up the huge worldwide success of *Pretty Woman*, Marshall's new project was less opposites attract, focussing squarely on two lovers from the same broken branches of the relationship tree. Adapting American playwright Terrence McNally's two-character play *Frankie and Johnny in the Clair de Lune* into a big budget movie seemed like a natural fit for someone of Marshall's directorial calibre, and it was a genre he had operated in previously.

McNally wrote the play after he had an image of Frankie and Johnny appear to him without knowing where it came from. "Maybe it has something to do with getting older, my feeling how fragile life is and how terribly important relationships are." The play opened Off-Broadway on 2 June 1987 with the two lead roles filled by Kathy Bates and F. Murray Abraham. It ran for two weeks and then closed. It re-opened on 14 October and Abraham was replaced by Kenneth Welsh.

This time it was a smash hit. Bates was nominated for an Obie Award during the '87-88 season. The play eventually closed on 12 March 1989. Marshall had expressed interest in making a film version of the play very soon after its stage debut. His producer Scott Rudin looked into setting it up as a project for both of them at 20th Century Fox. However, they found themselves outbid by Paramount Pictures. Director Mike Nichols was initially assigned to make the film by the studio. Two years later the film was still languishing in development hell and Nichols dropped out. This cleared the way for Rudin and Marshall to take over. When Paramount first bought the rights they contacted McNally about producing a film version of his play and also asked him to write the screenplay. This was a brave move from the studio as McNally had not produced a screenplay since 1976 for *The Ritz*. McNally said: "I didn't want to be tempted to use my favourite lines" and locked away his physical copy of the play, starting all over again.

This time around McNally knew he had to open out the story beyond the two main leads and include a visual back-story alongside other orbiting characters, characters that are only alluded to in the play.

The movie was eventually green-lit in the fall of 1990. When Paramount asked Marshall to direct he was looking forward to making a small, intricate low-budget movie with only Frankie and Johnny on screen. "But then Terrence rewrote it, and it blossomed from a two character, one-set play to a $29 million production with superstars," he explained to *New York Magazine*. McNally felt Marshall was the right choice as director. The playwright was addicted to *The Flamingo Kid*, a movie Marshall made in 1984. Having received rave reviews for her performance in the play, Kathy Bates lobbied for the role of the physically and emotionally wounded Frankie in the film. Marshall explained however, that the version of Frankie in the film would be vastly different to the one played on stage. Bates was passed over in favour of Michelle Pfeiffer for the lead role. The decision to cast a younger actress caused snorts of derision and snippy gossip from the theatre community such as *Newsday* Theatre Critic Linda Winer who wrote: "Either this is the funniest casting since Dustin Hoffman was Sean Connery's son in *Family Business*, or director Garry Marshall has rethought the concept." Signing on for a reported $3 million, Pfeiffer read the script while on a flight to Canada and instantly knew she wanted to do it. As soon as she landed Pfeiffer called Marshall and committed to the project.

The casting of Johnny proved slightly easier. Having previously met with Marshall to discuss the lead role in *Pretty Woman* (which he turned down), Al Pacino was deemed the perfect fit for the slightly kooky, romantic ex-con trying to win Frankie's heart. The role meant a $6 million pay day for Pacino and another opportunity to work with his *Scarface* co-star, Pfeiffer.

During the filming of *Scarface*, Pfeiffer and Pacino had very little to say to each other offset. Marshall wanted to get them better acquainted and invited them both over to his house for an informal read through. The night started with Pfeiffer firing questions at Pacino so she could better understand him and in turn the character he would be portraying. She asked him: "What's your favourite colour? Your favourite food? Your favourite time of year?" Suddenly, Pacino responded with: "What are you trying to be Michelle, a talk show host?" It was the ultimate ice breaker and from then on throughout filming Pacino, Pfeiffer and Marshall stayed as a tight knit trio.

Filming began on 29 January 1991 on the lot at Paramount Studios in Los Angeles. Several exterior shots were filmed there including those set in subway entrances and crowded streets surrounding the diner. Most of the interior locations were shot on the lot including Frankie's apartment, the New York Flower Mart, and the Apollo Diner where Frankie and Johnny work. The diner was built from scratch and was given the look over several times by the director's friend and esteemed restaurateur Steve Restivo. Having spent a few weeks following short order cooks around at a real diner, Pacino was then taught the intricacies of how to chop, dice and slice by Restivo. He continued to practise flipping cardboard eggs in his on-set trailer throughout filming.

Not to be outdone by her co-star, Pfeiffer spent long hours sat in a diner with Marshall observing the female workers. She also had three local waitresses acting as technical advisers on the set. The film version of McNally's play was much more dialogue heavy than the stage version. This meant Pacino and Pfeiffer would have to meet every Saturday. It was the only time both they and the director could meet to work on the next week's dialogue. Mainly, they would congregate around Pacino's house as he employed a personal chef and thus served the best food. While on set, they would retreat to Pacino's trailer because he had the most yoghurt in his fridge and six different toppings to choose from. The decision to move the production from L.A. to New York was on a knife edge for a long time because of studios boycotting filming in the Big Apple. The International Alliance of Theatrical Stage Employees (IATSE) and Moving Picture Machine Operators had rejected a proposed 30 percent pay cut, effectively putting an end to any productions that wanted to film in many U.S. cities, including New York, which hired skilled workers from the two companies.

With this continued delay, alongside the fact the production had made a commitment to shoot in New York, Marshall decided to over-run with the filming in California by two weeks and extend the entire production into the month of May. By the time they had run out of schedule on the West Coast, the IATSE had settled their argument and filming could commence in New York. The majority of scenes were filmed between Manhattan and Brooklyn and locations included such recognisable landmarks as the Port Authority Bus Terminal, Brooklyn Heights Promenade and East Broadway Station. Sidewalks and entire streets were cornered off over the five days of shooting. One day, during the filming of an exterior scene outside an apartment block, just as Marshall called action for the two lead actors to begin the scene a buzzer would sound in the background. This happened several times. It turned out that it was a protest from one of the residents living the apartment block they were filming outside. She was not happy about all the noise and kept pressing their door buzzer at precisely the right moment to interrupt the scene. Some very delicate talking to the resident from the production crew resulted in them being able to continue filming without the BZZT BZZT BZZT of the buzzer disrupting them further. Principal photography finished at the end of May, and in total it had lasted twelve weeks.

Frankie and Johnny received its U.S. premiere at the Academy Theatre in Beverly Hills, Los Angeles on 8 October 1991. It opened in North America three days later. Critical reviews were varied. *The New York Times* suggested: "Mr Marshall, Mr McNally and their superb leading actors are able to retain the intimacy of their material." *Entertainment Weekly* said it "does what any true romantic movie should: It makes the mysterious push-and-pull alchemy of love seem, once again, worth the effort." *The Chicago Reader* hit comparatively hard by saying: "This is more than just an irritating movie; it's a disappointing one." Within its first three days on release it had returned nearly $5 million from 1,150 theatres, making it to number three on the U.S. Box Office. The following week saw it jump up to number two but with slightly diminished returns of $3.5 million. By the time it had finished its theatrical run at the end of 1991, *Frankie and Johnny* had grossed nearly $23 million domestically (Information courtesy of Box Office Mojo. Used with permission).

Pacino's idea of making Johnny "physically anonymous" works perfectly in the context of the character and the entire movie. For it is not he who we, the viewer, should be hoping falls in love. It's Frankie, the oh-so-badly-in-need-of-real-love waitress who is wracked with self doubt. Johnny may be forceful at times with his undying love, but essentially he is a character that 99% of the people would easily walk by and never give a second glance. Outside work he is Mr Invisible to everyone except Frankie. Some could accuse Johnny of being too heavy-handed, even forceful, of his pursuit of love yet when Pacino strokes his full head of swishy hair and produces his winning smile it's easy to see why all of that could be forgiven in favour of falling into his arms. It's an uncomplicated performance. He is only after one thing (love) with one person (Frankie). For once Pacino doesn't chew up the scenery, instead that's left to Nathan Lane as Frankie's fabulously sarcastic gay neighbour Tim. Any time Lane pops up the movie bristles with riotous comedy. The exchange between Pacino and Lane about Johnny's cousin being gay is teeth clenchingly awkward and side-splittingly funny at the same time.

Tim is the perfect foil for Frankie. He makes her laugh and is also her shoulder to cry on if need be.

This is probably Pfeiffer's most captivating role. She creates this broken shell of a woman that is standoff-ish to everything, even when love is right there staring her in the face. Always on the defensive and ever looking for the negative. Yet over time she slowly starts to open up and dares to crack a smile. It's a hugely understated role, especially against a restrained but detectably goofy Pacino. At one point Frankie buys a VCR for her apartment. However even with the help of her neighbour Tim and his boyfriend, she can't seem to get it plugged in and working. The unworkable VCR player and the unlovable Frankie have something in common: both need that delicate touch in order to operate properly.

Regardless of whether Pacino and Pfeiffer are too good looking for the roles (as was suggested from some quarters) they still convincingly convey the heartbreak and it pours out of the screen. There is also a lot of fun to this script thanks to the banter between Frankie and Johnny. It's as if the outside world doesn't matter to them and the only thing surrounding them is a heart shaped-frame filled with strains of Debussy's classical piece of music Clair de Lune. Marshall's direction allows Pacino and Pfeiffer to partake in natural boy-meets-girl exchanges and as such, we the viewer, are treated to a very genuine second shot at love and relationships.

Frankie and Johnny is continually overlooked. It is one of the better rom-com movies in the genre. Pacino's playful persona is perfectly juxtaposed with Pfeiffer's determined and flouncy female. It may have rom-com clichés, but the underlying suggestion that there is 'someone out there for everyone' is a positive message for even the most dedicated of pessimists. Marshall delicately handles the domestic abuse strand to this story. It is always lurking in the background for Frankie but never overtakes the film, allowing the director to convey an ultimate message of hope. A hope that those who are abused can move on and find real love. A hope that is wrapped up in this wonderfully captivating and sweet movie.

Director Garry Marshall on *Frankie and Johnny*

What prompted you to adapt Terrence McNally's off-Broadway play *Frankie and Johnny in the Clair de Lune* for the big screen?

I have always been a big fan of the playwright Terrence McNally. When I met with him to talk about the script, he said he wanted to adapt it into a movie but he didn't know how to write a screenplay. I told him: "No problem. I'll teach you how to write a screenplay and you teach me how to write a play." And that's how we worked together – teaching each other the form of writing we didn't know. In addition to working with Terrence, I also love the plot of *Frankie and Johnny*. I had already made my movie *Pretty Woman* which was basically a fairy tale. *Frankie and Johnny* represented the opposite side of a fairy tale. It was a movie written for women who had decided that Prince Charming got hit by a truck and wasn't coming, and the guys who were sure Cinderella was still locked away, out of their reach. I liked the idea of a movie dedicated to those people who had given up on romance only to see it sparkle again.

This was the second time Pacino and Pfeiffer worked together. Was it a conscious decision to get them back together?

Our agents put us all together. But, of course, I knew they had worked together on *Scarface*. So the first day I took Michelle aside and said: "So how did you and Al get along on *Scarface*? Without missing a beat she said: "I never met him." I said: "WHAT?!" It turns out when the cameras were not rolling they barely said two words to each other. He was a famous actor, and she was just a young actress new to the business. So with *Frankie and Johnny* I started from the beginning: "Michelle this is Al. Al this is Michelle. Let's get to know each other."

She started interviewing him like a talk show host, which made him feel a little uncomfortable. But over time they got along great.

You incorporated personal aspects of Pacino and Pfeiffer's lives into the film (Pfeiffer's love of bowling and Pacino's enjoyment of handball). Why did you include these details?

When Al and Michelle first got to know each other on the movie, I overheard her telling him that she thought her hands were *too big*. She hated her big hands. I love that kind of detail. It is not only a great thing for an actor to play, but also comes naturally when the actor really feels that way. So throughout the movie I had people handing Michelle big jars to open with her capable hands. The same came naturally when I had Michelle in the bowling alley, and had Al play handball. Building a good character can come from the script or it can come from the actors themselves. Both roads work.

The domestic abuse element in this film makes it a lot darker than your previous works. Was that a challenge when filming? And how did you ensure it was handled sensitively?

I'm the guy who did *Happy Days* and *Laverne & Shirley*. I created those shows. I enjoyed them and I think I did a good job. As a producer and director you can stay with what you know, or you can venture elsewhere. I decided to try something new when I directed *The Flamingo Kid*. It was a comedy but also had dramatic elements. The more I directed, the more I wanted to explore different angles of a story. When I first got the script for *Pretty Woman*, the prostitute ended up dead in the gutter in the last scene. Then the businessman walked away and said: "Bye bye, Baby." That was a little too dark for me. When I saw Terrence's play *Frankie and Johnny* on stage for the first time, I was intrigued by the challenge of taking a story that existed in a single room on stage, and opening it up on the big screen. Michelle and Al and I worked hard to make sure the darker elements of the story line felt true and authentic. I later directed a movie called *Georgia Rule* with Jane Fonda that also addressed abuse.

Some of the most entertaining scenes in the movie are in the diner. Are there any fun anecdotes?

Al is a very intense actor to work with. He can ask for up to fifteen takes to get a scene right. He is a brilliant actor but the crew can get tired after fifteen takes. Al can get tired too. One day he came into a scene and was distracted by seeing his own reflection in a small mirror on the set. "Grrrrr.... Garry. I can see myself in that mirror!" he screamed angrily. Trying to ease his tension I said: "So, how'd you look?" He snapped back, "No. No. It distracts me. Get rid of it. Start the scene again." He went offstage to wait for his order to be followed. I turned around and told the crew to take down the small mirror, and replace it with the biggest mirror they could find. A few minutes later Al came bursting into the scene, saw the super sized mirror and cracked up laughing. He took the joke well and we were able to move on. Sometimes the best way to deal with movie stars is to kid them. It reduces the tension.

Your friend and restaurateur Steve Restivo gave cooking tips to Pacino. Did you ever let Pacino cook for you and the cast/crew?

Steve used to own my favourite Italian restaurant called Vitello's in the Valley. They used to have a special dish for me on the menu called Arroz Con Pollo Garry Marshall. When I found out I was doing a movie about a restaurant I asked Steve if I could bring Al over. He put on a chef's uniform and went with Steve into the kitchen. Steve taught him how to use some knives to chop food fast. As you can imagine, the other waiters and chefs in the kitchen and even the customers were pretty surprised to see Michael Corleone across the cooktop from them. But no, to answer your question, Al never cooked for me. But I'm a man who has dozens of allergies to many foods and condiments, so I'm not an easy man to cook for. I like basic things like tomato soup and grilled cheese.

Pacino looks like he is having an absolute blast in the film. Was he as energetic when cameras weren't rolling?

Al gives 110 per cent with whatever he does. However, movie audiences are used to him screaming things like: "Attica! Attica! Attica!" or "This whole trial is outta order" or "You wanna play rough? Say hello to my little friend." People are not used to seeing him in a playful and romantic light. One of my favourite moments in the movie is when Al and Michelle kiss at the flower mart just as a delivery truck pulls up to unload. Behind their kiss is a gorgeous array of blooms. It's not every day you see Al kissing a girl amid a sea of flowers. It was a special moment, and an unusual moment for Al and Michelle and it worked well.

Is it true you arranged for William Shatner and Leonard Nimoy to be on set one day?

We were shooting a scene one night and it was after midnight. The actors and the crew were beyond tired but we had to finish the scene. So, during a break, I went next door to another sound stage where they were filming the movie *Star Trek* [VI: The Undiscovered Country]. I asked William Shatner and Leonard Nimoy and a couple of other guys if they could come over in their costumes for a few minutes to surprise Al. So a half hour later Al bursts into his scene – which he had done so many times that night - but this time he found the room filled with characters from *Star Trek*. It woke him right up, and he was able to finish the scene so we could all go to bed. Sometimes pranks get you through a hard night.

Do you have one stand out memory of making *Frankie and Johnny*?

My favourite memory is that I got to direct the movie at all. I got a call one day from producer Scott Rudin and he said: "I want you to come to New York to have breakfast with Terrence McNally and talk about directing *Frankie and Johnny*." I said: "great." I started making my plane flights and packing my bags. Then, Rudin calls again. "Your trip is cancelled. Mike Nichols is going to direct *Frankie and Johnny*." I was disappointed but the business can be cruel sometimes. So a year later

Paramount calls again. "Mike Nichols dropped out. When can you come to New York to meet Terrence?" I said: "Do I get breakfast, too?" So, I went to New York, and I did get to meet Terrence and have a nice breakfast. Sometimes things work out. Some people have criticized the movie saying that Al and Michelle were "too pretty" to play the leads in the film. I think they both did an excellent job, and I was happy to be a part of the film.

Authors note: The interview was conducted on 17th February 2016.

Glengarry Glen Ross

Cast: Al Pacino (Ricky Roma), Jack Lemmon (Shelley Levene), Alec Baldwin (Blake), Alan Arkin (George Aaronow), Ed Harris (Dave Moss), Kevin Spacey (John Williamson), Jonathan Pryce (James Lingk), Bruce Altman (Larry Spannel). **Director:** James Foley.

Synopsis: A group of real-estate salesmen-cum-con artists live on the edge. Life is good for the one on a roll, for the rest life hangs in the balance. There is no room for losers. A-B-C Always Be Closing. Sell or go under is the salesman mantra. So begins a rainy night of cut-throat business and shattered lives.

Much like when comedian Ricky Gervais created his award-winning faux-docu TV show *The Office*, playwright David Mamet used his experience as a real estate agent in Vermont at the end of the 1960s for the basis of his play about the patriarchal world of salesmen in America. *Glengarry Glen Ross*, so titled because of two of the real estate properties mentioned in the work: Glengarry Highlands and Glen Ross Farms, received its World Premiere in London's National Theatre during the autumn of 1983. It then transferred to Mamet's hometown, and the real-life setting of the play, Chicago in the February of 1984. March saw another transfer, this time it hit Broadway at the John Golden Theatre. It ran for almost a year and completed 378 shows in that time. It garnered four Tony Award nominations and won the Pulitzer Prize for Mamet in the category of drama. Sitting in the audience during one of those Broadway productions was movie producer Jerry Tokofsky. Having just worked on Abel Ferrara's *Fear City* and a sci-fi adventure movie called *Dreamscape*. Tokofsky was looking for his next project. He had previously read the play at the suggestion of director Irvin Kershner who wanted to make it as his next movie after his work on the official, yet unofficial, James Bond movie *Never Say Never Again* with Sean Connery.

The day after Tokofsky saw the play on Broadway he called Mamet to discuss a movie adaptation. The playwright's asking price was $500,000 to purchase the rights and a further $500,000 for him to write the adaptation. Tokofsky agreed to both. Pacino had wanted to be in the stage production, however he was tied up in London during 1995 performing one of Mamet's other stage works; *American Buffalo,* and also shooting *Revolution.* When Tokofsky contacted him about the adaptation Pacino agreed immediately. Jack Lemmon also committed to the project around the same time and there was interest from Robert De Niro and Alec Baldwin as well.

Tokofsky brought in Stanley R. Zupnik, a movie producer he had previously worked with on *Fear City* and *Dreamscape.* Zupnik had seen the play and been confused by it. He knew in order to make it a sellable option to movie studios they needed the big names. Yet even with names such as Pacino, Lemmon and Baldwin attached it was shunned when Tokofsky and Zupnik pitched it.

Without heavy financing the project started to fall apart and Kershner left. Tokofsky acted quickly and offered the project to up-and-coming director James Foley. However, he couldn't see how the movie could be anything more than filmed theatre, so dropped out of the project. Followed closely by Pacino and Lemmon. Baldwin left when it transpired that he was not guaranteed to be paid by a certain date, whether the movie started filming or not. For the next five years Zupnik and Tokofsky tried to raise financing one way or another, but without a director or cast it was proving impossible. Then in March 1991, Baldwin called Tokofsky and said: "I've read 25 scripts and nothing is as good as this. OK. If you make it, I'll do it." Baldwin was back in, closely followed by Lemmon and Foley. Pacino made a similar call as Baldwin to Tokofsky to say that the script was "obsessing him" and he wanted back in as the cool and suave salesman Ricky Roma.

Around this time Jake Bloom, a lawyer for Tokofsky, called the Creative Artists Agency to ask if they may be able to send over any currently out-of-work actors to read through the script alongside Lemmon, Baldwin and Foley. CAA were not interested in sending big names to a project that had little to gain for their clients. Eventually Ed Harris and Kevin Spacey were sent over. Pacino and Foley had seen Spacey onstage in a play called "*Lost in Yonkers*" and felt he was right for the role of John Williamson, the office manager for the sales team. Having turned it down twice before, Alan Arkin eventually relented when his wife, agent and manager pushed him into taking on the role of the unlikeable and stupid George Aaronow. Arkin created a back story that allowed him change the character from a weak-willed individual to an innocent man who was led astray. The acting stars had finally aligned for Zupnik and Tokofsky.

Foley went to see Mamet at his home in Cambridge, Massachusetts to discuss the script before filming began. The playwright had to extend a portion of the play by including additional scenes such as Levine's many phone calls to clients and also his house visit to Larry Spannel. One extended scene, and one of the best moments in the film, featured a Head Office boss speaking to the salesmen. That character became Blake, played by Alec Baldwin, who was created to inject additional tension to the sales story and also make it visible how much pressure the salesmen were under. Foley said: "The play's ultimate reality includes Alec's scene." Baldwin finally signed his contract when Pacino thought he might have to drop out of playing Ricky Roma. His terms were that if Pacino could no longer play Roma, he would step into that role and they would have to find a new actor to play Blake. Pacino ultimately didn't drop out and Baldwin picked up $250,000 for a day's worth of filming and half a day of rehearsal beforehand. Pacino cut his usually high salary demands down to $1.5 million in order to ensure the film got made. Lemmon was paid $1 million. The budget was set at $12.5 million.

Tokofsky and Zupnik financed the movie through methods that would have made Mamet's salesmen proud. The producers begged and borrowed money from far-ranging sources including cable and video companies, a German Television station, an Australian movie theatre chain, several banks and also New Line Film Productions Inc, who offered to pay their costs over a period of four years.

The actors had the rare luxury of rehearsing together for a three week period before filming began in order to understand and adapt to the flow of Mamet's writing. Foley had the actors act out scenes that were not going to be on camera, just so they could get used to the ebb and flow of each other's movements.

Principal photography began in August 1991. Exterior scenes were filmed at Sheepshead Bay, Brooklyn, including the China Bowl Restaurant on Sheepshead Bay Road and East 16th Street, alongside the empty office across the road. That empty office used to belong to an existing real estate company; however it was vacated several months before filming began. As the real estate agency still owned the property they permitted filming in exchange for the hoardings, canopies and office doors to be left up and featured in the film. Production then moved to the Kaufman Astoria studios, where the interior scenes were shot.

Most scenes were shot in long takes so as to not interrupt the flow of the actors. Harris remembers shooting five and six page scenes all at once: "It was more like doing a play at times when you'd get the continuity going. All of us felt we really wanted to do it word for word." The director allowed additional time for Pacino to prepare for, what was deemed, the "crazy take". This meant the method actor could take Roma in any direction and style while filming, and Foley would continue filming. A lot of those "crazy takes" ended up in the finished film. It was such a tight knit group of actors that on their days off they would appear on set just to watch the others act. The actors started to call the movie: "Death of a Fucking Salesman" because of the amount of profanity within the dialogue (the word "fuck" is said 137 times and "shit" is used 50 times). Ed Harris spoke about the incessant swearing: "The language is a direct result of their inability to think of other words to describe their frustration." As the end of filming approached, Pacino addressed the cast and crew to say that this had been the best work experience of his life. He tried to continue to talk but started to tear up. The same happened to Jack Lemmon on his last day as he spoke to the cast and crew. Away from the set, the two producers (Tokofsky and Zupnik) had a major falling out over what credit they should each be given on the film. Neither spoke to each other for the rest of filming and their animosity only got uglier. Principal photography finished at the end of October.

Glengarry Glen Ross received its world premiere at the 49th Venice Film Festival, where Jack Lemmon won the Volpi Cup for Best Actor. There was also an out-of-competition screening at the Montreal Film Festival. Its North American premiere was at the Toronto International Film Festival. This was followed by a smaller screening at the Directors Guild of America, Los Angeles on 29 September 1992. It also had a benefit premiere at the DC Film Society, Washington in honour of the one-time real estate agent now movie producer Stanley Zupnik.

The film opened in North America on 2 October to non-stop critical praise. *Rolling Stone* magazine said; "This brilliant black comedy doesn't just dazzle, it stings." *The New York Times* felt that: "People will be reviving and discussing it in 10, 20, 30 years time." Roger Ebert complimented Mamet's dialogue: "There is a great energy to it. You can see the joy with which these actors get their teeth into these great lines." Critics couldn't pick a favourite standout performance. There was praise for all of the actors, even Baldwin's ten minute cameo.

Sadly its box office release was at odds to the critical lauding it received. Its first week on release only returned $2.8 million in box office receipts. The following four weeks saw it drop to takings of $1 million and by the time of its fifth week in theatres the movie was effectively dead in the water. In total it pulled in slightly over $10 million (Information courtesy of Box Office Mojo. Used with permission). Given the budget was $12.5 million topped off by another $12 million on publicity, the movie needed to make $25 million to break even. It was a disappointing release considering the star power on display.

To further complicate matters the bad blood between Zupnik and Tokofsky didn't abate after the film's release, as Tokofsky launched a legal case to have Zupnik removed as a producer including his credit and shares of the returns. Zupnik countersued, claiming he personally put up $2 million of his own money to make sure the production got started.

He also claimed that Tokofsky was fired during the fall of 1991 for embezzlement. Eventually both suits were settled out of court and both men remained as producers on the film. It wasn't all bad for Tokofsky though, as he did receive a delightful letter from Mamet that read: "Dear Jerry. Glengarry is magnificent. I am thrilled and delighted and honoured. I'm proud to have my name on it." Pacino was nominated for Best Supporting Actor at The Golden Globes and The Academy Awards. He was unsuccessful on both counts.

Glengarry Glen Ross is a movie about individual performances. Pacino's Roma is an independent man of the world. He doesn't need to hear about the fine intricacies of "how to sell" from some corporate stooge sent down from head office. This is a man who wears the finest suits, has the perfectly coiffed hair and lashes out some of the finest bullshit lines a salesman can ever speak. He is a winner, and Pacino plays the role as such. He chews gum with a brand of sarcasm that makes you want to punch him in the face for being such a cocky bastard. His usual grandstanding is evident, especially when he realises Williamson has screwed up his winning of $6,000 and a Cadillac, yet just as he is about to go full throttle with his shouting Pacino holds back, almost whispering his disparaging comments delicately into the ear of Spacey.

With repressed aggression, Pacino opts to place emphasis on each derogatory word in his speech. It's a marvellous scene, and one that shows how an actor can convey aggression without resorting to shouting and swearing. Pacino spent time with real-life salesmen before filming began and here he demonstrates a natural rhythm and patter. The scene in which Roma spouts a long monologue to the weak-willed target James Lingk is one of the finest cases of an actor expertly delivering his lines. It's a transfixing scene that shows Pacino understands well when to reign himself in.

Pacino might be the leading name on the film, but he is arguably eclipsed by Alec Baldwin and Jack Lemmon. Baldwin's Blake bowls into the office like a force ten hurricane. As he fires out consistently foul yet quotable lines of dialogue, he is the one who awakens the salesmen. They now know who and what they are dealing with, a man with brass balls who isn't afraid to say: "You're fired!" in front of everyone else. It's a vindictive role and Baldwin plays it brilliantly. On the opposite end of the spectrum is the tired and dejected salesman Shelley "The Machine" Levene. A man living not day-to-day but hour to hour, a man constantly chasing his own tail. Lemmon's hanged demeanour and twitchy attitude contribute to a frighteningly realistic take on a man who used to be the top salesman and is now being forced to feed off weak leads. Levene's hunched posture coupled with the manner in which he is constantly pushed around makes for upsetting viewing. His desperately sad attitude makes us connect with him more as we root for the guy to find a way back to the top. Lemmon runs through a gamut of emotions, creating a timeless interpretation of an old man struggling in a new world. Lemmon had a phenomenal acting career, yet it took until his final decade to produce a performance as captivating and enthralling as he does with Shelley "The Machine" Levene.

Foley's movie, and in turn Mamet's play, is a depressing look at strung-out and stressed men in an oppressive, prison-like room. The writing, direction and the incredible acting from an all star cast elevate the movie into a fascinating character study of men who lie for a living. Mamet's scathing look at competitive capitalism hasn't dated and is very unlikely to, especially in an age in which only the rich seem to get any richer.

Actor Bruce Altman on *Glengarry Glen Ross*

How did you approach Mamet's work?

I know that there is a sense of How-To-Do David Mamet, but I found
that the writing was so strong and, at least the part that I played, the
character Larry Spannel was so clearly written that there was no Mamet
technique. It was basically working on who the character was, and there
were many clues in there, and then understanding the circumstances. I
don't believe there is a Mamet style. I think maybe when he directs there
is. He has very strong ideas. He has written wonderful non-fiction books
that I love. I just see it as he is a great writer.

**Glengarry Glen Ross is a very claustrophobic movie because it
involves a small number of actors in an even smaller number of
locations. Did you feel that while filming?**

It was a small house that we shot in. I agree with you about the
claustrophobia. I thought one of the great things about Foley as a
director was adding all that rain. I thought the rain added so much
weight and a sense of claustrophobia. It was like being overwhelmed to
the entire milieu of their lives. Certainly my character wanted to get Jack
Lemmon out of my house. That was very clear, in my mind, that this
guy... my wife had such a difficult time with him that I wanted him out.

**It is a very powerful scene, especially when he tries to give you the
hard sell. So many of us can relate to that scenario. Was it difficult
to convey those frustrations?**

Jack Lemmon was such a sweet guy and I had never met him before. It
was only my second movie and it was really exciting to meet him. He was
just so down to earth and nice to me. He was just really focussed on his

part. There is a certain pathos... this is Shelley 'The Machine' Levine! And 'The Machine' could at one point sell ice to an Eskimo. My character immediately sees that he's inept at what he does now. It's like 'The Machine' with Alzheimer's. I think that was very sad, and the sadness of that scene and the rain. But perhaps there is something a little funny too.

Did you go through a lot of takes to get that scene just right?

We did. That one scene...they picked me up early in the morning, I got there and they did my hair & make-up and we shot all day. I remember Jack was not a kid then and he had most of the lines in the scene, he was so energetic. We did a lot of takes and I remember we ate lunch and he was very animated and then he shot all afternoon. I don't think we filmed for a full twelve hours, most shooting they give you a twelve hour day, but we may not have. But I remember we did a lot of takes.

Did you do any improvisation?

For me – none. I felt that Mamet was like Shakespeare. Every word I wanted it to be exact and even the No's, I wanted it to be exact. I think James [Foley] wanted me to improvise just a little bit. I had certain ideas I wanted to convey with the character that I had such a clear idea of who he was that improvising wasn't something that I wanted to do much of. I love to improvise but in that one I had to say no.

***Glengarry Glen Ross* is a look at the American Dream. Why do you think a film about Real Estate agents showcased it at its most brutal and dishonest?**

I think David Mamet worked in a real estate office when he was younger. He has such a queer ear. He's got such a remarkable ear and his genius is to understand these circumstances. He studied with Sanford Meisner when he was younger, I understand. The idea of not only the emotion but really focussing in on the understanding to the true dynamics of what is going on. I don't know how he did it. I think that movie is spectacular. The performances are phenomenal in it. If you saw it from maybe a sociological point of view, these little pathetic guys... it's a Greek tragedy. How did he do that? I don't know. Amazing!

What was your reaction on seeing the film for the first time?

I was amazed by the addition of the rain and the performances... oh my God! I love all the performances in the film. Really, top to bottom, I think it's incredible. You talk about a Mamet style and you think more of William Macey. The way Bill Macey approaches Mamet is remarkable. Then I think people try to do a take on Bill Macey because he is such a genius. He can do that. I think certain great artists can do their own take on great writers. That doesn't mean that that is the way to do it. He fulfils it. You think about Pacino. I felt like his performance was circular. It worked brilliantly. I think [it's] one of his greatest performances... of many.

Was there one main character you identified more with?

I was shocked because I had seen a production with it on stage and the way the actor played Aaronow on stage was as a pathetic, kind of dumb guy. But this is where again, Mamet's great writing, and Arkin's such a great actor that I felt he didn't play Aaronow dumb. I thought he played him broken. It's like the business had worn him down. He didn't have the strength to say no. He was afraid to disagree. Not because it was stupid but just because he was broken. I was so moved by that. That was remarkable. But everybody... I have to say I thought every performance... wonderful.

Alec Baldwin is only in the film for about twenty minutes, but what a sequence to feature in.

Mamet wrote the screenplay, and obviously Mamet wrote the play, and the screenplay really follows the play. It's a great adaptation and a very truthful adaptation. But there are two characters that are alluded to in the play but are not in the play. Mine and the guy from Mitch & Murray – Alec Baldwin. I thought those two scenes were wonderful and they are not in the play. He just created these incredible characters and Alec Baldwin... people talking about that scene all the time when they talk about the movie. Absolutely amazing the thing with the balls and coffee is for closers [*laughs*]. The lines in it are incredible.

Do you have a favourite line?

Well I think "Coffee's for closers" and "ABC – Always be Closing." I say it all the time. I think "Always Be Closing" is my favourite just because it really is such a deep and meaningful line.

Scent of a Woman

Cast: Al Pacino (Lieutenant Colonel Frank Slade), Chris O'Donnell (Charlie Simms), James Rebhorn (Mr. Trask), Gabrielle Anwar (Donna), Philip Seymour Hoffman (George Willis, Jr.) Bradley Whitford (Randy) Gene Canfield (Manny), Frances Conroy (Christine Downes). **Director:** Martin Brest.

Synopsis: Retired Lieutenant Colonel Frank Slade is blind and overbearing. Prep School student Charlie Sims is hired to assist him for a weekend. Little does Charlie know that Slade has booked a wild weekend in New York City. It will be a trip that changes the lives of both men forever.

There are some in Hollywood who feel that the Academy only awarded Pacino his Best Actor Oscar for *Scent of a Woman* because they dropped the ball a couple of decades earlier when he should have won for *The Godfather* or *Serpico* or *The Godfather Part II* or *Dog Day Afternoon*. There is no doubting that those movies are incredible and, yes, Pacino did deserve to win for any/all of those. Yet to dismiss his performance in *Scent of a Woman* would be a mistake. This film showcases the actor's finest method acting. Pacino uses his approach to elevate his performance and create a character with depth.

Scent of a Woman's origins stem from the 1974 Italian movie *Profumo di Donna*, which in turn was based on a story by Italian writer/journalist Giovanni Arpino called *Il buio e il miele* (The Darkness and the Honey). *Profumo di Donna* won two David di Donatello Awards at the L'Accademia del Cinema Italiano. One for Best Director (Dino Risi) and the other for Best Actor (Vittorio Gassman). It went on to be nominated for two Academy Awards in 1976 for Best Foreign Film and Best Writing/Screenplay Adapted from Other Material. Though it was a successful film in its native country it was met with negativity in America. *The New York Times* review read: "The journey is funny, acid and intriguing. The destination is mawkish, melodramatic and interminable."

By the time director Martin Brest viewed the movie in the early nineties it was a long-forgotten piece of Italian cinema. Screenwriter Bo Goldman, who had worked on *Dick Tracy*, received a call from Brest to visit him at his home in Los Angeles and watch a movie he was thinking of remaking. Brest's company City Lights Film (named after a 1931 Charlie Chaplin film because Brest was a Chaplin fan) had acquired the rights to *Profumo di Donna* in the late 1980s. The director was friendly with Casey Silver, the Vice President of Production at Universal Pictures, and so a deal was struck between City Lights and Universal for the production of Brest's next film.

Goldman remembers what drew him to the project: "I looked at the movie, and this character [Slade] struck me as being exactly like my brother. The character was crossed with my first sergeant in the army, who was the second man I've ever really been afraid of, and the first man I was afraid of – my father. So this character became a hybrid of all these people."

Pacino had missed out on playing the role of a disabled Vietnam vet when the long-gestating *Born on the Fourth of July* movie was put into production without him. As Lieutenant Colonel Frank Slade in *Scent of a Woman* he could use the research and method acting he had undertaken for *Born on the Fourth of July* and channel it into a character that was slightly older but with similar physical and mental wartime scars. There was talk that Jack Nicholson had previously turned down the role after he saw the script. Officially only Pacino was offered and accepted the role of Lt. Col. Frank Slade even though he had to be forced into taking the role from his agent. The casting of prep school student cum babysitter Charlie Simms proved to be slightly more difficult. Actors such as Ben Affleck, Matt Damon, Brendan Fraser, Leonardo DiCaprio, Cole Hauser, Christopher Serrone, Stephen Dorff and Anthony Rapp all auditioned for Brest. Comedian Chris Rock wanted to read for the role but was turned down before he even got through the door. Eventually the role went to fresh-faced, twenty-year-old actor Chris O'Donnell. It was a nerve wracking audition for him, even after preparing diligently O'Donnell was awestruck by Pacino: "Al is such an intimidating presence and the character is supposed to be intimidated by him. I was able to play on that natural nervousness that I had around him in the audition process that helped me to win the role."

Another key role to be cast was that of Donna: a lonesome woman who Simms spots and comments to Slade about. Eventually they end up dancing in the legendary tango scene. British actress Gabrielle Anwar had previously studied ballet during her formative years in high school. She also performed cabaret at a nightclub in her home village of Laleham, Surrey. Having sent a pre-recorded VHS tape to the producers she was then whisked to New York to meet Pacino. After the meeting Anwar was told she didn't get the part because she wasn't quite right. Then out of the blue, she was contacted again to say she did have the part and was asked to come to New York immediately. "It was kind of a surprise. It was lovely," she commented.

Other recognisable faces in the secondary cast included James Rebhorn and Frances Conroy who signed on to play teachers at the prep school. Young and inexperienced actors Todd Louiso, Nicholas Sadler, Matt Smith and Philip Seymour Hoffman were brought in to play Charlie's prep school friends and bullies. All of them had been in previous movies as an extra or bit part player; this was their first big collective acting break. Hoffman had been stacking shelves at a deli in Manhattan while auditioning five times for the movie. When he signed on to play one of the antagonists of the piece he quickly departed his old line of work.

While Brest was casting, Pacino had set about "finding" the character of Lt. Col. Frank Slade. He started by asking his very young daughter Julie how she would play a blind person "She was spot on. She was just perfect," he told Larry King. "I said, Bam, no work, no preparation, no nothing. I did a variation on that theme." Actually Pacino spent months researching blindness. He continuously visited two assistance organizations for the blind – Associated Blind and LightHouse. During his time at the Associated Blind he met with many people who had lost their sight because of trauma. "They traced the entire progression for him, from the moment they knew they would never see again to the depression – the "why me?" period – and on through acceptance and adjustment," said Jean Azzato, the film's resource planning and development manager.

Pacino's time at Lighthouse was much more geared towards how to function when blind. He was shown how to use a cane to be able to walk independently and how a blind person would walk with a sighted person as a guide. He was also schooled in how a blind person would locate numbers on a telephone pad, how to find a chair and sit down, pour liquor from a bottle and even how to light a cigar. Spending time with both organizations enabled Pacino to greater understand who Lt. Col. Frank Slade had become since the accident that robbed him of his sight. The immersive research for Pacino continued as he spent time with an ex-lieutenant colonel from the army as he trained to assemble and disassemble a .45-caliber gun. Being as the character was blind, Pacino had to learn how to do it blindfolded and also in the dark. Finally when he managed to complete the complication puzzle in under forty five seconds for the first time, the lieutenant colonel shouted "HOO-AH!" Asking what it meant, Pacino was told it was military slang referring to "anything and everything except 'no'." It was a phrase used by soldiers in the U.S. Army and over the years it had come to mean different things depending on enlisted time and regiment. The majority of Army officer's used it as an affirmative to whatever question their drill sergeant asked them. Pacino liked this bellowing phrase and started to incorporate it into his practice, eventually making its way into the script and the finished film. Continuing his deep methodical research into the character, Pacino spent every afternoon for eight weeks with the professional ballroom dancer and instructor Paul Pellicoro at his New York studio DanceSport in order to learn how to tango correctly. They would tango for twenty minutes and then take a fifteen minute break. "I like breaks," Pacino commented when asked how the dancing was going. Being taught the basic principles of the tango before filming began ensured that Pacino at least knew the right steps and posture. He would stand there watching and then imitate his dance instructors. Before cameras had even started rolling, Pacino had spent over half a year developing Lt. Col. Frank Slade.

Principal photography began on 10 December 1991. The cast and crew spent two weeks filming in Troy, New York at the Emma Willard School. This grand old female boarding school was used mainly for exterior shots for the scenes set at Baird College. As the filming took place during term time, some of the classes had to be moved to other locations to accommodate the crew's movements. Following completion of filming at "Emma" cast and crew moved on to filming in the New York City area.

Many of the street scenes were filmed in Manhattan, mainly around 5th Avenue and also Park Avenue. The Plaza Hotel is located on 5th Avenue, a luxury 20 storey hotel which is a century old and contains the wood-panelled The Oak Room. A restaurant used for a dinner scene between Charlie and Frank. The European style hotel The Pierre, also on 5th Avenue houses the Cotillion Ballroom, which was used for filming the infamous tango scene. Another hotel used was the world famous Waldorf-Astoria situated at 301 Park Avenue. Exterior and lobby scenes were filmed on site. The scenes inside the hotel suite that Charlie and Frank stay in were not filmed at The Waldorf-Astoria; instead they were shot on a sound stage at the Kaufman Astoria Studios in Queens.

The scene in which Slade drives the Ferrari was filmed along Plymouth Street, Brooklyn between the Manhattan Bridge and the Brooklyn Bridge. Exterior scenes were also shot in Prince's Bay, Staten Island and the Guggenheim Estate, Long Island. Hempstead House, located in the Guggenheim Estate, was used for several Baird College exterior shots. Rockefeller College, part of Princeton University, and its Holder Courtyard were also used for establishing shots of Baird College.

Pacino continued to train at DanceSport while filming was in progress, yet this was a different Pacino than the one his dance instructors had been teaching beforehand. He was now in character as Slade and refused to attend his practises, instead insisting that the editors of the movie would make it work. And this was not the only sign of Pacino's swiftly-altering attitude as he immersed himself in his character.

One day during a coffee break he exclaimed that his hot drink was stone cold. Three times it was changed but to no avail as he continued to shout and scream about it being freezing. Eventually he took a wad of dollar bills from his pocket and threw them on the floor dictating: "There's a hundred dollars in it for anyone who can get me a hot cup of coffee." It was something the instructors in the class had never seen before – a method actor. Shortly before an exterior scene was about to be shot, Pacino fell into a bush on Park Avenue. He was always in character, which meant he never focussed his eyes when walking and he stumbled into the bush. A piece of shrubbery stabbed his eye and became lodged in his cornea. This caused an infection and a ruptured blood vessel; it meant Pacino physically couldn't see out of one eye for several days. Though an accident, this added to his method acting for the part.

The tango scene took four days to film. During that time Pacino entertained the extras by playfully dancing around the room and cracking jokes. Years later Anwar recalled that Pacino's dancing wasn't as on point as it could have been: "It was a bit dodgy. It was interesting... it's Al Pacino, God's sake: I couldn't exactly complain. I was afraid... He was incredibly nice to me." Speaking to Lawrence Grobel, Pacino discussed learning to tango: "To have learned to tango would have taken me years, but we just limited it to the steps in the scene and learned that. The freedom comes once you've learned the steps, then you're free to enjoy the music."

When it came to editing the movie Brest butted heads with Universal Pictures. The studio constantly requested it be trimmed down from its two and half hour length. Screenwriter Goldman recalls: "The studio was hammering at us to try to cut the movie because it was two hours twenty five minutes and, just practically speaking, that meant one less show a day. One less show a day meant I don't know how many millions of dollars less in the grosses worldwide." The first cut shown to Universal ran for one hundred and sixty minutes. However Universal requested a much shorter cut to be shown at preview screenings. The feedback received was that the one hundred and thirty minute version didn't play as well as the original, and longer, version they had previously seen. Brest stuck by his finalized cut and Universal eventually backed down. The studio did, however, have the last laugh as when the film was shown on aeroplanes and TV, as the runtime was heavily chopped. Brest was unhappy at this decision and asked for his name to be removed from these versions and replaced with the pseudonym "Alan Smithee".

Scent of a Woman had its premiere on 8 December 1992 at the Coronet Theatre, New York City. Critical reviews were somewhat middling. *The New York Times* suggested it was "a glorified father-son buddy film with a needlessly sensitive title." Malcolm Johnson of the *Hartford Courant* commented: "This rambling account of a bitter blind Pangloss and his prep school Candide offers assorted pleasures without ever becoming believable." Roger Ebert gave the film a glowing review: "By the end of *Scent of a Woman*, we have arrived at the usual conclusion of the coming of age movie, and the usual conclusion of the prep school movie. But rarely have we been taken there with so much intelligence and skill." Ebert praised Pacino by saying it's "one of his best and riskiest performances."

Opening to the movie-going public on 23 December, the box office returns did not produce the type of numbers Universal craved. In its first week of release it pulled in a return of just $122,828 from twenty screens. However it must be remembered that it was two days before Christmas when the movie opened, which is possibly not the best time for a new release to open. It didn't hit the million dollar mark at the box office until the third week of release when it made nearly $9 million. It continued to make steady million dollar returns each week through to the third week in April. By the time the film was removed from theatres it had amassed $63 million and spent thirty-three weeks in the box office top twenty (Information courtesy of Box Office Mojo. Used with permission).

It wasn't the big box office winner that Universal had hoped for but it did last eight months in theatres. This extended run might possibly be accounted for by the awarding of a little gold statuette. The 65th

Academy Awards took place on 29 March 1993. Pacino had been nominated for his performance as Lt. Col. Frank Slade in the Best Actor category. He was up against unfamiliar opposition in the shape of Robert Downey Jr. (for *Chaplin*), Clint Eastwood (for *Unforgiven*), Stephen Rea (for *The Crying Game*) and Denzel Washington (for *Malcolm X*). It was a tough category but the big noises out of Hollywood were that this year was Pacino's year. Actress Jodie Foster opened the white envelope and read out the winner: "And the Oscar goes to... Al Pacino in *Scent of a Woman*". The camera focussed on Pacino as he flung his head back in delight. Facial beard and full mane of hair, Pacino reached the podium and smiled. The whole of the Dorothy Candler Pavilion stood and applauded. Always the comedian, Pacino opened with a joke: "You broke my streak," referring to his being nominated several times but never actually winning. After a three and half minute speech, Pacino walked off clutching an Academy Award. The thing he had been denied for far too long.

The Oscar story wasn't to end there for Pacino though. He was in the middle of filming *Carlito's Way* and so was rushed outside to a waiting car to get back to filming. While in a full elevator on his way out, Pacino was clutching his Oscar statuette. In front of him was a well-known actress who had started to move about a little bit as if trying to get out of the way of something or someone. Suddenly, Pacino realised that the head of his Oscar is touching her buttocks. He pulls the Oscar back up to his chest, then leans into her and said: "Oh pardon me, that wasn't me that was my Oscar."

Scent of a Woman belongs to Pacino. It's his movie. There is nobody else. O'Donnell, Anwar, Rebhorn, Hoffman et al give fine performances. But it does feel they are mostly there to support Pacino's performance and the journey his character goes on. O'Donnell's son-looking-for-a-father-figure character is the perfect opposites attract for Pacino's crotchet-y bastard. O'Donnell spends the majority of his screen time acting like a rabbit in headlights, constantly on the back foot never really understanding how far his babysitting responsibilities will be stretched. There is growth in the character and we see that in the third act as he starts to answer Slade back with vigour and determination.

Pacino, on the other hand, bellows and grandstands his way through much of the film and, at times, it can feel a little bit overcooked. At times it's funny to watch; at others his character can feel quite spiteful. One thing is for sure, is that it's Pacino at his most rousing and entertaining. Pacino's quieter more serene moments are the moments in which his acting talent truly comes to the fore. When he is contemplating the existence of females with Simms during his aeroplane ride to New York, or when he's enjoying a glass of Jack Daniels. Or the powerful moment where he is in bed, not wanting to get up except to commit suicide. These are Pacino's shining achievements. Pacino showcases his fun and playful side when dancing the tango and driving a Ferrari around empty streets. And yet it's the acerbic Slade that the audience perhaps relishes most. The one who spits out derogatory lines regardless of the consequences and who will turn up, unannounced, at his family's Thanksgiving meal and ruin it for all.

Still, we laugh as he rips apart human beings who mean little or nothing to him. Maybe it's because, much like Simon Cowell when judging X Factor contestants, he says whatever he wants without fear of holding back, and we wish we could do that. Or maybe it's because we want to see behind the façade, into the real Lt. Col. Frank Slade. The man who is desperately unhappy, the man who will never recover or adapt to losing his sight. Is Slade a deeply complex character? Highly doubtful. He just wants to be loved. Fully loved and appreciated by someone who deeply cares for him, whether it be a family member or a friend.

By the end of the film he finds that friend in Simms. When Slade is ready to commit suicide in the hotel room, Simms goes to stop him only to be thrown onto some furniture. As Slade grabs him, Simms shows the courage and determination to say: "You fucked up, all right? So what?" Depicting a father-son relationship in which both parties tolerate the other's faults because they know deep down inside their loved one has a heart of gold. Sometimes it takes a big life event for this to bubble to the surface. That event comes at the end of the film when Slade goes to aid Simms in his schoolboy snitching battle against the posh, upper class twits that profess to be Simms' friends yet are ready to hang him out to dry. Pacino's commanding charisma in the school pseudo-courtroom is mesmerizing. It's like watching a car slowly change up through its gears before hitting full speed. These ten minutes of runtime capture Pacino at full thrust and volume, and at this pivotal point the actor doesn't flinch one iota away from the building emotion. He knows what it takes to win over not just the staff at the school but also the audience viewing the film. This is his redemption moment. He may have been a tyrant for two hours but this is his moment to shine as the sweet and caring father willing to defend his son's honour.

Scent of a Woman is an outstanding film about surrogate father/son relationships. The characters have an impressive intellectual depth and demonstrate that love and friendship can conquer all.

Actor Gene Canfield on *Scent of a Woman*

Originally you were in the New Jersey City Police Department, why the change to acting?

I started in 1976. I started doing theatre. I did theatre for ten years and I got a part with Al in *Sea Of Love*, which was made a couple of years previous to *Scent of a Woman*. It was always a part time thing for me. It was better than doing off-duty armed security.

How did the role of Manny in *Scent of a Woman* come about?

I got called in by, and I read for, Marty Brest, he directed it. There is a part in *Scent of a Woman* that a cop pulls him over in Red Hook, Brooklyn when he has the Ferrari. I read for that and he said: "Would you read for this other one?" So I read for it and they brought me back with Al and Chris O'Donnell, and I got cast.

I think Manny is the only person Slade trusts implicitly, and I include Charlie in that. Would you agree with that?

Yeah. Yeah. He was obviously providing a necessary service for that whole jaunt and showed up on time, kept his mouth shut and did his job.

What was it like working with Pacino?

Oh great! We got along on a personal basis too. The guy is Al Pacino. He was there all the time and it was kind of neat with the Slade character because when the cameras were rolling he was blind. But most of the time the cameras aren't rolling, and to see how seamlessly he went in and out, and then to see how it translated to film was really something.

What was it like seeing him change into that character?

There wasn't a big transition in doing the work during the filming because he didn't look at you. He was always a bubble off of staring into your eyes. So that's what you got when you were doing it. How it translated into the final product was really, really something. I just took it as dealing with a blind guy. I have a very good friend of mine who has been blind since birth, so I got it. I knew how the blind just never really get a focus on you, even directionally they are always a little bit off and it's orientated towards the ear because that's what they depend on and he [Pacino] got it.

You were in the room when Slade gave that massive speech in the school to defend Charlie. What was that like to watch?

Magnificent. I got to see every single take and it was always just a little bit different. If they did it once they did it thirty times. Each time he did it there was a different nuance in place. Each and every time it was magnificent. I think that's pretty much what nailed it for him as far as the Academy Award went.

Clint Eastwood, Robert Downey Jr, Stephen Rea and Denzel Washington were all up for Best Actor that year. It was a tough category. Did you think Al Pacino would win?

I thought he put in an Academy Award calibre performance. He also put in an Academy Award performance during *The Godfather Part II* and he didn't get it. I would say yes I believe he could have won the Academy Award but I wasn't sure if the politics were going to lean his way.

You spoke about reading and working for Marty Brest. He has now become a virtual recluse. I'm interested to know from someone who has worked with him what he is like as a director?

He is a very nurturing guy. Very patient. He took the time to establish a language with me. So I'm sure he did that with the other actors. I always had a sense of what he needed and he was very supportive so you wanted to give that back to him. Best guy I ever worked with.

You've been involved in some big films including *Goodfellas*, *Riding in Cars with Boys*, *Bullets over Broadway* and many more. Where does *Scent of a Woman* rank in your filmography?

It's the one I get noticed for. Anybody knows that I did that, it's the first thing that comes up. So I have to say that and *Sea of Love* would be one and two. I wouldn't commit to saying which was first or second. It's certainly a big event in my life.

You've worked with Pacino three times – *Sea of Love*, *Scent of a Woman* and *Carlito's Way* – so what makes him continue to be one of the greatest actors?

He's certainly one of the great talents of his generation. I think what makes him Al Pacino is his dynamic as a human being. He is just a powerhouse of a human being when he is acting. He can play the entire eighty eight notes. He can play small, he can play large. I've seen him on stage a couple of times and he just does it all. Al might just be the best stage actor out there in America. He covers all the bases which a lot of the other actors nowadays don't.

Carlito's Way

Cast: Al Pacino (Carlito Brigante), Penelope Ann Miller (Gail), Sean Penn (Kleinfeld), John Leguizamo (Benny Blanco), Ingrid Rogers (Steffie), Luis Guzmán (Pachanga), James Rebhorn (Norwalk), Joseph Siravo (Vinnie Taglialucci), Viggo Mortensen (Lalin), Jorge Porcel (Saso). **Director:** Brian De Palma.

Synopsis: Former drug kingpin Carlito Brigante is sprung from prison early on a legal technicality thanks to his cocaine-addled attorney Kleinfeld. Vowing to go straight Carlito takes a job managing a glitzy nightclub. He also rekindles his romance with old flame Gail. But Carlito's dream of going legitimate is undermined at every turn by murderous former cronies and even deadlier young thugs out to make a name for themselves.

The origins of *Carlito's Way* can be traced back to the point when Pacino began his research for *Serpico*. As always with his method acting, Pacino paid meticulous attention to those he was shadowing. At one point he came into contact with Edwin Torres, a Puerto Rican New York state court judge. During their discussions, Torres told Pacino he was writing a book about a Puerto Rican gangster who is released from prison and tries to go straight. His knowledge of the criminal underworld and the justice system, having worked many times as criminal defense attorney, put him in the perfect position to write a fictional book that was steeped in real life. Pacino went off to make *Serpico* and Torres finally released his first novel - *Carlito's Way* - in 1975. A second book called *After Hours* was published four years after that. However, it would take a lawsuit and a reteaming of the director and the lead actor of *Scarface* to bring worldwide attention to Torres' work, and also for Pacino to become associated with the judge once more.

Legendary American film producer Elliott Kastner, whose previous work included *Where Eagles Dare*, *The Nightcomers* and *Angel Heart*, had slapped a lawsuit on Pacino just before filming of *The Godfather Part III*. Kastner claimed he had entered into an agreement in April 1988 with Pacino, an agreement for him to produce and star in a movie based on Torres' first novel: *Carlito's Way*. The actor was to receive $4 million and a box office percentage from the deal. According to Kastner, he and Pacino had worked on selecting writers and a director for the project. Also it had been confirmed that Marlon Brando was to be cast in one of the lead roles for the movie. Shortly before the movie was to launch into full pre-production Kastner claimed Pacino reneged on their deal, leaving him in a position of having to release "a unique and extremely valuable opportunity to produce a film starring Marlon Brando." The lawsuit came to an end several months later when it was completely dropped by Kastner. Yet hints were dropped that the film would still be made, this time by Pacino's long-time friend and producer Marty Bregman. The option to make the film transferred from Kastner to Bregman, but there were many others who tried to put Torres' work on the big screen. He had resold the development rights ten times before *Carlito's Way* was finally put into full production under Bregman.

Early on in pre-production Torres took Pacino around East Harlem so that the lead actor could learn the attitudes, accents and styles of the Latino community. Originally Pacino had wanted to grow a ponytail for the role, upon walking around East Harlem he noticed that wasn't the style Puerto Ricans favoured and ditched that idea. Sticking with his flowing hair and full beard.

Director Brian De Palma didn't want anything to do with making *Carlito's Way* when asked. He was given Torres' second novel *After Hours* (The film was to be renamed to *Carlito's Way* because Martin Scorsese had made a film called *After Hours* the decade before and the producers didn't want to confuse the audience) and refused it straight away: "I didn't even want to read it. I didn't want to return to this terrain again." The search for a director became a huge task for Bregman. Fortunately a script writer had already been commissioned; it was *The Shadow*'s screenwriter David Koepp.

Continuously writing and re-writing the screenplay through numerous drafts, Koepp developed the script while the producer tried to find a director. John Mackenzie and Abel Ferrara were spoken to, yet neither was interested in making the film. Bregman asked De Palma to read the newly completed script, and at first feeling like he would be making *Scarface* all over again because of the Spanish speaking characters, De Palma read it and found an unexpected edge to the story. There was a sense of crime noir to it that De Palma liked so much that he signed on to direct. The role of Carlito's coke-fiend friend and lawyer, David Kleinfeld went to Sean Penn. Not before Charlie Sheen had been sounded out about taking on the role however. This was the part Brando would have played if the Kastner production had ever taken off, but by the time of filming Brando had long-since lost interest.

De Palma offered the role of Carlito's girlfriend Gail to Alison Doody. She turned it down because she didn't feel comfortable doing the nude dance scenes. Michelle Johnson screen-tested for the role but it was Penelope Ann Miller who, thanks in part to a direct request from Pacino to De Palma and Bregman, won the leading female role. John Leguizamo turned down the role of Benny Blanco, an up and coming gangster from the Bronx, four times. Eventually he relented when De Palma promised he could improvise most of his lines. One strange piece of casting was Jorge Porcel. Bregman had seen the comedian on Spanish TV and felt him perfect for the role of club owner Saso. However, Porcel spoke no English, a fact which would cause problems during filming.

Principal photography began on 22 March 1993. The first shooting scene was meant to be the climatic running gun battle through New York's subway ending at the World Trade Center. However, Pacino had turned up a few days before on crutches after breaking his foot. This meant changing the shooting schedule dramatically. The first few days of filming instead became a bar scene featuring a gun battle. A few days after finishing the scene, a note came back from the studio to say the scene needed to be shortened. Going against their wishes, De Palma actually extended the scene without the executives knowing, injecting tension-building moments such as Carlito setting up his trick shot. The newly extended scene was sent to the studio, a note returned saying: "much better shorter."

Aside from flying out to Florida to shoot the poster sequence of Gail dancing on a beach, the rest of the movie was filmed around New York. Locations included: The New York County Supreme Court, Joffrey Ballet School and the Copacabana Nightclub, all in the borough of Manhattan. The crew then spread themselves all over the city; Greenwich Village, Brooklyn and Rikers Island. The filming at Rikers Island ended with Penn screaming at De Palma that he wanted another take. The director felt they had the shot and moved on. On the way back into the city, Penn continued to verbally abuse De Palma. He continued this later in the evening, calling his director and screaming the same vitriol at him. This was the only time they fell out throughout filming.

The same cannot be said for Leguizamo and Miller however, who did not get on with each other at all. In his autobiography, Leguizamo says: "You really have to know Penelope Ann Miller. She's the kind of girl who would flirt with anyone in the world as long as people are watching." His, and the crew's, hatred towards Miller manifested itself in the form of tighter clothes. The wardrobe department continued to take her clothes in an inch at a time. Leguizamo writes: "Every day her outfits are getting a little tighter. She goes on a starvation diet, you'll see she gets thinner and thinner." One person who didn't have a problem with Miller was Pacino as they were having an on-set affair at the time. This became public knowledge and the press hounded Miller during filming.

The problems for Pacino on-set stemmed from Bregman's insistence on hiring Jorge Porcel to play Saso. The Spanish comedian couldn't speak a word of English; his lines had to be phonetically spoken to him. He was cued into his lines by learning the last few words of Pacino's dialogue so he knew when to start. This caused problems for Pacino as he liked to bounce off the other actors and couldn't with Porcel. During one scene in the finished film, Carlito's reflection is in the mirror while he talks to Saso in the nightclub. You can see Pacino mouth Porcel's lines to him.

The gorgeous neon-vis, art deco El Paraiso was built at the Kaufman Astoria Studios. This two-storey set was designed by Richard Sylbert in the style of a 1930s Ocean liner. In order to cast extras for the interior club scenes, some of the film crew were sent out to clubs around Manhattan asking clubbers if they wanted to be in the film. Vans were filled with real revellers and returned to the studio in Queens for shooting.

The rescue of Tony T from the East River after he escaped Riker's Island Prison proved to be a problematic shoot. The waters were too dangerous to film on location. So an empty section of the Navy ship yard in Brooklyn was used. River water was pumped in for authenticity. Smoke machines and tall metal structures with spotlight on them were installed in order to give it the look of the Rikers floating prison at night. The big finale chase sequence proved to be a shooting nightmare as well. De Palma was going to end the film at the World Trade Center, yet because of a bombing in the February of that year, he had to relocate to Grand Central Station. Something he wasn't particularly happy about as De Palma's movie *The Untouchables* also ended in a New York train station (Union Station).

The foot chase was filmed over several months "We started the chase in the winter and finished it in the middle of summer" said De Palma. It proved to be an epic shooting schedule. It started at Brooklyn's Smith and Ninth Street station (which was standing in for Broadway and Seventh Avenue) and continued through to the escalators of the Grand Central Station. Subway trains were constantly re-rooted and re-timed in order for the crew to film Carlito and his would-be killers darting between cars and carriages. With all the running around during the summer months in the sweltering heat of New York's subway system, Carlito's thick, black leather coat began to irritate Pacino. As De Palma was in another carriage with the monitoring screen, Pacino often shouted through to ask: "What are you doing?" becoming more and more impatient. One day he just took the train back to where his trailer was because he was so annoyed at having to wait around in the sweltering subway car, while wearing the big leather coat.

The inclusion of one long tracking shot through Grand Central station is in keeping with De Palma's masterful eye of space and camera movement. However, it was fudged at the last minute by a miscommunication between the first AD and the steadicam operator, meaning the camera panned to Pacino before he was ready. Because of the time it takes to set up a tracking shot of that magnitude, that was their only attempt. The issue would have to be fixed in the editing suite.

Principal photography was completed in July 1993. Editor Bill Pankow had worked with De Palma on *The Untouchables*, *Scarface* and *Dressed To Kill*. His editing began in early March. Being on such a tight schedule and wanting to be able to show De Palma a rough cut asap, Pankow brought in a second editor, Kristina Boden, to work on the footage leading up to the Grand Central entrance. It was then passed to Pankow to complete and also cover up the mistimed end of the steadicam shot: "It was kind of fun to do that" he said in an interview with *Film Comment* magazine. The scene was saved by a cut away to another character and then the camera moved back to Pacino.

Carlito's Way had its New York premiere on 7 November 1993 at the Ziegfeld Theater. An awkward moment ensued when Pacino, having had an affair with Miller during filming, turned up to the premiere with his girlfriend Lyndall Hobbs, prompting the one-time lovers to ignore each other for the entire evening. A Los Angeles premiere took place on 11 November. With a U.S. wide release the following day.

Critical reviews varied. Roger Ebert praised the film, especially picking out De Palma's direction saying: "here he paints a gallery of colourful gangsters and lowlifes." *The New York Times* also praised the director: "Mr De Palma ends his film with a sequence Hitchcock might have envied." *Rolling Stone* magazine were not so enthralled by it, with comments such as: "too many of the 144 minutes are wasted on this dud romance," and "...what might have been if *Carlito's Way* had forged new ground and not gone down smokin' in the shadow of Scarface." *The Chicago Reader* absolutely hammered the film and especially the director: "If Brian De Palma has made a duller movie than this 144-minute snoozefest, I count myself fortunate to have missed it."

At the box office it raked in slightly over $9 million in its debut weekend on release. At the end of its first full week in theatres, De Palma's crime movie had pulled in $12 million. By the end of its U.S. theatrical run in December the grand total of ticket sales amounted to $32 million (Information courtesy of Box Office Mojo. Used with permission). Both Sean Penn and Penelope Ann Miller were nominated for Best Supporting Actor and Actress, respectively, at the 1994 Golden Globes. Losing out to Tommy Lee Jones, for *The Fugitive*, and Winona Ryder, for *The Age of Innocence* respectively. Not even a month before the Golden Globes however, the movie suffered yet another problem. In late '93 American lawyer Alan Dershowitz threatened to sue De Palma, Penn and Universal Studios as he felt Kleinfeld was based on him. The case was never brought before a court.

When it comes to the film itself, framing is everything in *Carlito's Way*. De Palma frames Pacino perfectly, focusing on the centre of his face so the viewer's eyes is directly drawn to Carlito's eyes. There is a heavy emphasis on eye movement throughout the film and because of that the viewer is instantly transfixed by Pacino's piercing eyes. The first time we see Carlito, he is grandstanding in a courtroom as he is released from prison. He's giving a lecture on his rehabilitation to the judge. Yet by the end of the movie he is almost a ghost. A man who only wants to be seen by his one-time love, the outside world means nothing to him anymore.

A moment in the movie that perfectly captures the ideal of a man in love is when Carlito heads to a rooftop to watch Gail perform ballet. It's a dark and blustery night, and Carlito holds a trash can lid over his head to shield from the rain. In that moment, given the way De Palma shoots it, it feels like nothing else matters to Carlito. The camera slowly pans to him and his face softens as he becomes enthralled in the movement of the ballet, and specifically Gail. The camera focuses on Carlito's wet yet love-stricken face, the space around him blurs slightly to further focus our gaze on Pacino. Then the soulful voice of Carlito, which is based on novelist's Torres' own Puerto Rican-cum-New York tones, comes oozing through. It's enjoyable to watch Pacino play a gangster who is so subdued. It is the complete opposite to Antony Montana. Rather than slowly building up to the shouting and bravado, instead here he starts as a large presence and slowly dissolves into a person who wants to become invisible.

The aggression we see in the other crime movies Pacino has made is left to Penn's Kleinfeld. This is a man who wants to be Carlito, a man so hell bent on being a gangster that he will stop at nothing to achieve it. Some might say that lawyers are little more than legitimized gangsters anyway. Kleinfeld knows that and still wants to operate on both sides of the law. Penn's performance has two separate prongs: he is upbeat and energetic in some scenes and is scared and panicked in others. During a five minute scene where Kleinfeld visits mobster boss Tony Taglialucci, we see both edges to the character. As Kleinfeld enters the scene De Palma uses a long shot, via helicopter, of the character walking down the caged walkway with his head held high, arms swinging wildly and a giant smile on his face. Several moments later, after being told that he is to orchestrate a breakout for Tony T otherwise Taglialucci will 'snap his neck like a breadstick,' Kleinfeld walks out of the floating prison hunched over, eyes looking at the floor in a total state of shock. He then falls into the wire fence and proceeds to be sick into his hand. It's a dramatic turnaround and one that shows how swiftly the character can break down. Penn absolutely nails the role; he understands that a slimy, conniving weasel like Kleinfeld would have to be unlikeable from the very beginning. His haunting eyes peering through those John Lennon-style glasses as he looks you up and down before saying anything. Considering Penn only took the role to fund his movie production of *The Crossing Guard*, he does a fine job of playing a sadistic and lecherous sleaze of a man.

This might be an unpopular opinion: *Carlito's Way* is a better movie than *Scarface*. The previous De Palma/Pacino team up was loud and sweary. *Carlito's Way* is a much more intelligent piece. One that looks at the struggles of those trying to adapt to their life after being in prison. For all the gangster rigmarole that goes on in *Carlito's Way*, essentially this is a movie about love. Everything pales into the background when the movie latches onto the relationship between Carlito and Gail. This is their second shot at love and they won't make the same stupid mistakes that they had previously, before Brigante was incarcerated. They are teenagers-in-love all over again. There is true heart and fire between them, Pacino and Miller are electric together (perhaps due to their dalliance during filming). The scene in which Carlito breaks down Gail's door as she sexually teases him is the absolute epitome of their relationship: she keeps him at arm's length but offers just enough provocation to keep him interested. It's wonderful to watch a movie that features a storyline about having a second chance of love. Sadly, this angle is overlooked by many who discuss *Carlito's Way* even though it is the whole crux of the film. A once big-time mobster seeks a better life for himself and his woman. But gangsters cannot simply walk off into the sunset; it all too often ends in tragedy. This time it's not in a hail of gun fire (á la *Scarface*) but a lovers' tiff.

This is a subdued yet sophisticated movie about the recollections of a gangster who grew a heart.

Actor Ingrid Rogers on *Carlito's Way*

This was your first film role, were you nervous?

I was nervous because I didn't know what I was doing. I was so green. I wasn't nervous about the prestige of meeting Pacino, Penn or De Palma. I was nervous about fucking up.

What was your first day on the set like?

It was very exciting. Overall it was such a fun shoot. The club set was amazing and the music was fun, fun, fun. I do remember feeling very constrained on one of the first shots because it was so tight that if I breathed deeply I'd be out of frame. I was coming from the freedom of a three camera soap opera and theatre in acting school so the restraints of the close-up in film was new and very different.

How would you describe your character, Steffie?

An around the way girl. Always up for a good time and the good things in life.

Steffie is the main reason behind the war between Carlito and Benny, were you pleased to see your character so deeply involved?

Sure. It made her more integral to the story and that's always a good thing.

What was it like filming with Pacino and Penn?

Iconic, since they arguably rank among the best actors of all time. I was so inexperienced and they were very welcoming and supportive and encouraging.

How was Brian De Palma to work for? And what direction did he give you for your character?

He was great. He pretty much left me alone. I remember during the scene in the club when Benny Blanco comes to the table to get me from Dave, Brian asked me to be more nervous about the circumstances. That's really the only direction I remember him giving me. A couple of times I didn't feel great about a take and Brian let me do it again. He was very accommodating.

As an actor, what did you take away from working on Carlito's Way?

That making movies is super-fun. That you come together with creative people and make something together and then you move on. If you're lucky you get to make something else with some of those people down the road. In retrospect, I can say that I did good work as an actor. I was so critical of myself back then. Time and experience has taught me to do my work and keep moving without the judgement.

Two Bits

Cast: Al Pacino (Grandpa), Mary Elizabeth Mastrantonio (Luisa Spirito), Jerry Barone (Gennaro), Patrick Borriello (Tullio), Andy Romano (Dr. Bruna), Donna Mitchell (Mrs. Bruna), Mary Lou Rosato (Aunt Carmela), Joe Grifasi (Uncle Joe), Geoff Pierson (Dr. Wilson). **Director:** James Foley.

Synopsis: A hot day in South Philadelphia during the summer of 1933 and twelve year old Gennaro is hoping his Grandpa will give him his last quarter so he can buy a ticket for the new movie theatre that has opened up. However, before Grandpa will relinquish the quarter he asks Gennaro to visit a woman from his past that still lives in the city.

The shower scene in Alfred Hitchcock's *Psycho* is arguably one of the most memorable in movie history and it was penned, alongside the rest of the movie, by Joseph Stefano. Stefano was a veteran screenwriter who had previously worked on TV shows such as *The Outer Limits*, *Star Trek: The Next Generation* and *Swamp Thing*. A native of South Philadelphia, Stefano had been writing TV movies of the week during the 1970s. The next decade saw him struggle with depression. While psychoanalysing himself, he commented: "I began to deal with a lot of things I had suppressed in order to be happy."

During regular visits to a therapist to discover the root of his long-gestated rage issues, the writer revisited his childhood on a near daily basis. After finishing therapy and understanding more about himself, Stefano dusted off a screenplay he had partially written in the 1960s called *Two Bits*. Feeling he had a deeper understanding of his life, Stefano decided it was time to complete his unfinished screenplay which was also an "analytic journey" about his own life.

The completed manuscript found its way to Swiss-born film producer Arthur Cohn. Having previously produced Academy Award winning movies *The Garden of the Finzi-Continis*, *Black and White in Color*, *The Yellow Star* and *American Dream*, Cohn loved Stefano's American depression-era story and optioned the rights to it, on the basis that it echoed his beliefs: "We are driven by dreams. Whether or not a dream is possible is irrelevant." *Two Bits* was to be Cohn's first American feature film production. He set about finding the right director for his new project. This task alone would last five years. During 1991 - the second year of option - a bid by the Pittsburgh Film Office to make the movie in the city was accepted. They undercut all competitors. Stefano wanted the movie to be made in his hometown, but the Philadelphia Film Office was badly underfunded and could not afford to have films shot in the city at that time. Fortunately, production failed to start in Pittsburgh as Cohn was still scratching around for a director.

Nearly two years later, the screenplay was handed to director James Foley who found himself in floods of tears by the final pages. Coming off the back of the highly acclaimed *Glengarry Glen Ross*, Foley was struck by "how two men, a boy and his grandfather, make a really meaningful impact on each other's lives." He saw *Two Bits* as a companion piece to *Glengarry Glen Ross* "Both are about being a man." The aim for Stefano, Cohn and Foley was to make this film a small, independent movie. They were looking at unknown actors for the role of the Grandpa. It was only when Foley mentioned this particular role to his friend and *Glengarry Glen Ross* actor Al Pacino that a big name came suddenly knocking on their door.

Pacino loved working with Foley on *Glengarry Glen Ross* and decided to take on the role as a favour. Raised by his maternal grandparents and Mother, Pacino liked the script because he felt it projected part of his own life where his grandfather was one of the most influential people: "I felt a kind of warmth toward the character." Despite adding Pacino to the cast list Foley staged open casting calls in key cities around the U.S., determined to stick as much as possible with unknown actors. In Chicago, over seven hundred and thirty boys turned up to read for the central character, a 12 year-old, Italian-American Gennaro Spirito. On his third call back Jerry Barone, a kid from Chicago who had been urged to audition by one of his school teachers, had made it through the selection process into the final two. Pacino was called to act out the same scene with both boys before he and the director made their final decision. Despite having never acted professionally before, Foley and Pacino noticed Barone had the natural tongue of a Philadelphian: "He just had exactly what we were looking for." Foley said: "The most important quality he had was that he wasn't intimidated by Al or by the movie-making process."

Another native Chicagoan was brought onto the production. This time it was experienced actress Mary Elizabeth Mastrantonio, who had signed on to play Luisa, a grieving widow, Gennaro's mother and Grandpa's daughter. Having previously played opposite Pacino in *Scarface*, Mastrantonio joked: "First I am his sister, then I'm his daughter. I don't know what it takes to actually be the romantic figure in his life... perhaps I have to be blonde. It could happen."

During the casting process, Cohn managed to strike a deal with newly revitalised Greater Philadelphia Film Office for production to commence in South Philadelphia in the summer of 1993. Stefano had brought Foley over to Philadelphia in the March to show him around the old neighbourhood: "I wanted *Two Bits* to be a tribute to the streets I grew up in, the streets that had formed me." Foley liked the idea that the city was very much an existing standing set. They also met with the Greater Philadelphia Film Office, whom they found much more helpful than in 1991. "I was thrilled," commented Stefano about his own screenplay being filmed in his hometown.

Principal photography began in July 1993. At first locals were excited to see a film production visiting the city, especially one starring Pacino. Soon their enjoyment turned to resentment however as the crew shut down streets for filming. Durfor Street is a very narrow one-way road that was used for exterior filming. Residents on that street complained that crews would set up heavy equipment and large lighting fixtures around 5:30am, disturbing the peaceful street. Filming on that street would also, on occasion, last into the early hours of the next day. During one of the hottest weeks of the summer, the crew had to remove all air-conditioners from the houses which faced onto the cameras in order to maintain the authentic 1933 era setting – not a popular request. The conflict continued to escalate and on one particularly early morning, a major confrontation occurred between a production worker and several of the neighbours due to a 10,000-watt light shining into their houses.

Days later a petition signed by all the residents on Durfor Street and surrounding areas. It was delivered to Two Bits Production Inc. requesting all homes be given $500 compensation. Ted Albert, the publicist for Two Bits Production, said an investigation into the complaints would take place. He did also emphasise that members of the on-site production crew had been helping residents whenever they could, including driving them to and from their cars and also taking one woman to the grocery store and back because she had missed her bus. "Truthfully, I can't wait till it's over," commented one Durfor Street resident.

Despite these problems, the main filming schedule ran smoothly. Barone and his family had moved from Chicago to Philadelphia during shooting. Stefano made sure he was on set every single day: "I feel that somehow protects my movie more than if I directed it." Seven weeks of filming were completed in South Philadelphia and then the production uprooted to New York for three weeks of filming at Astoria Studios. The majority of scenes filmed there comprised of Grandpa and Gennaro talking to each other in the garden under the burning sunshine. Some of the scenes set in the house interior were also shot there. Principal photography was completed in less than eleven weeks. To tie the film together, a voice-over narration from the now-adult Gennaro was required. This part of the film was to encompass the analytical elements of Stefano's screenplay. The adult, now looking back at his childhood, sees how this period formed his later years. For this task, Foley immediately went to Alec Baldwin, another of his cast members from *Glengarry Glen Ross*: "Alec just has the most incredible voice which I think allows people to see beyond Gennaro as a little kid." This was to be the reassuring part of the story that conveyed what Gennaro took away from his time with Grandpa had turned him into a man.

A short article appeared in *Variety* during the second week of January 1994 that announced Miramax Films had purchased the North American rights to *Two Bits*. It marked the largest acquisition by the company and a final budget of $21.8 million was equated against the production. It was due to receive its world premiere at the 30th Annual Chicago International Film Festival with Pacino and Mastrantonio present to walk the red carpet, greet fans and talk about the film. However, at short notice Miramax pulled the screening because of the title. Festival founder and director Michael Kutza explained the decision: "They didn't like *Two Bits* because it didn't make any sense translated into foreign languages. Most foreign moviegoers have no idea what Two Bits means." Eventually the film played at the festival on 12 October under the new title of *A Day to Remember*.

Critics sat on the fence with their reviews. *The San Francisco Chronicle* said: "It's pleasant and worthy, but as big-screen entertainment, it feels more like an appetizer than an entree." *Variety* called it "just too slight to stand up as a viable theatrical B.O. [Box Office] entry." *The L.A. Times* found it to be a "slight but earnestly told tale." It opened in two U.S. theatres on 22 November; earning a pathetic $26,282 during its three week run (Information courtesy of Box Office Mojo. Used with permission). It sank faster than the Titanic.

If you've ever wanted to see a film that features Pacino doing nothing other than sitting in a chair then this movie is for you. Actually that's a slight overstatement as Grandpa manages to make it a few feet from his chair before falling into a flowerbed. He is then put back in his chair. And later in the film we see him slowly dying while laid on the grass of his backyard. The character does not walk more than ten steps the entire movie, making it a less than demanding role. Pacino whispers and rasps his dialogue. All of it punctuated with large gasps of air to convey Grandpa is approaching death's door. Towards the end, Grandpa and Gennaro have a profound discussion about life and their wants and needs. The problem is that the discussion never quite reaches its full potential. The profound message that could be discussed here actually comes at the end of the film: the message that through death happiness can arrive. Even if it means happiness to you is finally gaining entrance to the newly opened film theatre.

Pacino's presence both hinders and helps the film. It helps because he is a recognisable name in a leading role, yet he hinders the picture with his limited performance that never once moves out of first gear. Even his method acting appears to be missing here. Pacino commented to his biographer Lawrence Grobel about *Two Bits* missing its target: "I don't know quite what it was. You just don't know. I was happy with my performance in it. I enjoyed playing the character." For once, in this movie, Pacino is not the stand-out actor. That accolade is left to first-time actor Jerry Barone. His portrayal of Gennaro is the glue that keeps the entire film together. It's not an emotional or moving performance but it is one that keeps the viewer interested. His heart-warming love for his family, especially Grandpa, is at odds with him just wanting to be a kid. His character is a boy finally breaking free of his family yet still wanting to cling to them through their trying times. Barone manages to make the performance feel nostalgic and forward-looking all at once. Especially with his reactions to the way adults continue to talk down to him even though he appears to be the only one willing to find the answers to the questions life is throwing at his depressed family. It's surprising to find that this was Barone's only film role because there is a twinkle in the eye that could have lead to bigger and better roles. Certainly any child out-performing Pacino should have been offered more film roles.

Two Bits attempts to be a nostalgic family drama but never fully hits the right notes. Rather beautifully filmed in a sepia tone, the acting is not of the highest order (Barone not withstanding). Made in the same year as Steven Soderbergh's wonderful adaptation of A.E. Hotchner's depression memoir *King of the Hill*, *Two Bits* lacks the drama, subtlety and emotion impact of Soderbergh's movie. Ultimately, the film is a rather benign attempt at a veiled autobiography that will only truly appeal to those who were children during the depression. Is it worth paying two bits for? Just about.

Actor Mary Lou Rosato on *Two Bits*

Two Bits **was a small film for Pacino as there was so much happening at that point in his career. It was sandwiched between** *Carlito's Way* **and** *Heat*. **Were you surprised to see him in the film?**

Yeah, I think it was a labour of love for the writer [Joseph Stefano] as I recall on this set. He was so excited about that, it was getting made and it was very important to him. It had a real familiar feel to it. It was done rather quickly. I think the narration was added at a later date.

They asked Alec Baldwin to come in at a later stage and act out the voiceover narration. I'm not sure if the film would work without the voiceover. It plays so much better with it included.

It does. It adds a whole dimension and it ties it together. When I saw it, I was pleased with the whole feel of it. It felt very wistful and very soulful.

How did you become involved in *Two Bits*?

I auditioned for it. The director [James Foley] had me audition for several of the roles and I kept coming back and I was really fried. I think he thought I somehow fitted into the family and I felt very much that I did too. I was thrilled to death. It was a huge opportunity for me and I loved getting the chance to do it.

You play Aunt Carmela, who appears to be the only voice of reason in the family. Would you agree with that?

I know that she is practical. Her system... her way of life comes from a tradition. From a sensibility of decency and what is done is done. She is a very... I want to say old-fashioned girl. The scenes she had with the young boy where she is aghast that he is singing in the street, you simply don't do things like that.

Do you think she is the opposite of her sister? Or are Carmela and Luisa, underneath it all, the same person?

That's a hard one because I think they have different struggles. Luisa has got a hard road home-raising the baby, raising the son by herself. There is a sensitivity in Luisa, the privateness that Carmela doesn't allow out of herself. But they both have deep feelings, really deep feelings. That ties them together. They have a really strong emotional life.

What about the relationship between Carmela and Grandpa?

[*Laughs*] Well I don't know exactly... there is not a lot to go on. I always sensed because of the strong feelings between Luisa and the Grandpa that there is sometimes that Carmela might feel a little not as involved, because she is not there.

Your character has an emotional scene with Grandpa. Was it difficult to film?

Oh my gosh yes! Oh my gosh. I remember it well. It was horrible. It was a very hard scene for both of us and it took many takes to film it. I think it was tough on everyone. It was an emotional climax.

Grandpa is played by Pacino. What was it like to work with him?

His demeanour is always so concentrated and so in the world of what he is doing and it was so wonderful. Actors need to give each other space and the concentration in that particular scene was very respectful. I was so lucky to watch him because I could see how strong his craft was and how connected he was to the character. It was beautiful. The whole thing was beautiful. He wants you to enter into the same world that he is in. He makes it easy for you to live in that space with him by the commitment he brings to it, which is a thousand percent.

Did you spend much time with him off-camera?

No. I think because of the way those scenes were we kept it very low key. We kept working through and it was like a play in that respect. To break the concentration, to fall out of it would be... I think it was one of the most atmospheric and focussed I've ever encountered. It felt like I was in church, it had that sanctity to it.

It is a very quiet performance from Pacino. Were you surprised by that?

Well yes because he did such a beautiful job – delicate. He was very delicate.

You've directed a stage production of Richard III and Pacino has been looking for Richard II for decades now. What is about Shakespeare that draws American actors such as yourself and Pacino to the Bard's work?

When you work on Shakespeare for a long time you start to see the possibilities are endless. The emotional life of the characters is open ended. They have size, there is a depth, there is a breath to them that is an endless search. For me, every time I work on Shakespeare it's almost as if the vista opens before me and you begin that search... that journey. I'm not surprised that he is consumed by that search. It is well worth your time because it will fulfil you. The discoveries along the way are astonishing. I found such joy in it and it is something that will always be with me.

Have you seen Pacino's *Looking for Richard* documentary?

I have seen parts of *Looking for Richard*. I have never sat and watched the whole thing straight through [*laughs*]. One of these days I must sit and watch it.

You have been an acting coach for many years. Which of Pacino's films would you show to your students to help them explore the craft of acting?

Oh my gosh! Maybe *Dog Day Afternoon*. I think that might have been one of the most extraordinary performances anybody can give on film. There are bits and pieces of all those films, watching his work... even in *The Godfather* there is such compelling scenes of his intensity, of his ability to bring that ferocious intensity onto the screen. As a young actress, I remember watching him on stage in *Does a Tiger Wear a Necktie?* And even back then, watching him live, nobody gets the pleasure to do that much these days... he can fill a space like nobody's business. I was astonished. I was mesmerized. I think that was one of the things that started him off, as I recall. I think I sat there in my chair with my mouth open watching him work. I keep coming back to the word intensity.

Heat

Cast: Al Pacino (Lieutenant Vincent Hanna), Robert De Niro (Neil McCauley), Val Kilmer (Chris Shiherlis), Jon Voight (Nate), Tom Sizemore (Michael Cheritto), Mykelti Williamson (Sergeant Drucker), Wes Studi (Casals), Ted Levine (Bosko), Diane Venora (Justine), Amy Brenneman (Eady). **Director:** Michael Mann.

Synopsis: The personal lives of brilliant thief Neil McCauley and obsessive L.A. cop Vincent Hanna intertwine – and quickly unravel – as the bank robber and his gang plan one final heist. Hanna and his team put the heat on the criminals, hoping they will make one vital mistake rather than disappearing forever.

By the time sunshine and crime TV show *Miami Vice* had begun to air on the NBC network in 1984, Chuck Adamson, an ex-Chicago detective, had been friends with director/producer Michael Mann for a number of years. Adamson moved to Los Angeles during the 1970s to be a screenwriter, and met Mann when the director was conducting research for his episodes of *Starsky and Hutch*. Mann enjoyed listening to Adamson's stories of his time in the Chicago police force and used some of them as the basis for episodes of *Miami Vice*. He also hired Adamson as a technical consultant for the show. Believing Adamson was a source of pretty limitless material, Mann asked him to help create a new crime TV show for NBC.

Working alongside investment banker turned screenwriter Gustave Reininger, Adamson created *Crime Story*, a TV show about the major crimes division in Chicago during the early 1960s. It ran for two seasons between September 1986 and May 1988 before being cancelled. Back in the late 1970s, during the early days of Mann and Adamson's friendship, the former had written a one hundred and eighty page treatment based on a story Adamson had told him about a real-life incident he had been involved in. Criminal Neil McCauley was responsible for several bank robberies and murders in Chicago during the 1950s and 60s and Adamson, alongside his major crimes team, was heavily invested in taking down McCauley at all costs. One day in 1963, Adamson saw McCauley go into a diner and followed him. Sitting at a table opposite each other, Adamson explained that if he saw McCauley involved in illegal activities he would stop him no matter the cost. The career criminal sipped his drink and replied: "Well, look at the other side of the coin. I might have to eliminate you." A year later and one of them had fulfilled their promise to the other. Adamson was called to an armed robbery of a supermarket. Arriving just in time to see McCauley escaping, Adamson chased on foot. As he rounded a corner, McCauley was there pointing his gun, he pulled the trigger but it misfired. Without hesitation, Adamson shot him six times. As the detective looked down on the body of the deceased, the mutual admiration and respect that had developed between the two of them that day in the diner came flooding back.

By 1983, Mann had edited his one hundred and eighty page screenplay down into a shooting script. It was titled *Heat*, and when asked if he would direct it Mann replied that he would only be a producer on it. The directing job was offered to Walter Hill but he declined it. The more Mann tried to tweak the ending the more he felt something wasn't quite right. Mann told *Rolling Stone* magazine: "When something's not ready, it's like *not ready*." Eventually he put it back in his desk draw and went off to make the horror film *The Keep* followed by an adaptation of the Thomas Harris crime novel *Manhunter*. Neither film was a huge box office smash; in fact *The Keep* was ripped away from him by the studio. Mann found television much more compatible with his style of directing/producing. *Miami Vice* was *the* hot TV show of the mid to late eighties. *Crime Story*, though short lived, drew respectable critical reviews. However by the end of the decade *Miami Vice*'s plug had been pulled and Mann was without a TV show or film to produce or direct. Reopening his desk draw and plucking out his script for *Heat*, Mann thought he could make it as a TV movie for NBC. That would then be the precursor to a new TV show called *Hanna*, which would follow the life of one of the central detectives in *Heat*. Ripping one hundred and ten pages out of the original *Heat* script, Mann filmed a ninety minute pilot episode over the course of two weeks. The central character of Sgt Vincent Hanna was played by Scott Plank, an actor mainly known for his work on *Miami Vice* and *Melrose Place*. NBC executives did not like Plank in the lead role and told Mann they would only pick up the series if they replaced Plank. Mann refused and NBC decided not to go ahead with the TV show *Hanna*. The pilot did eventually air on NBC on 27 August 1989 as a standalone TV movie called *L.A. Takedown*. It was poorly received by critics and viewers alike. *Empire* magazine called it: "A bit of a dud." A disappointed Mann turned his back on the crime genre, after a decade working in that arena, and went off to make the historical action/adventure drama; *The Last of the Mohicans*.

After the near universal acclaim for *The Last of the Mohicans*, Mann signed on to direct a biopic of the deceased actor James Dean. He selected Leonardo DiCaprio for the leading role, however when Mann wanted to wait an extra year for DiCaprio's age more to be in tune with Dean's, Warner Bros studios declined the year hiatus. Mann dropped out and so too did DiCaprio. Though this was frustrating, Mann wasn't fully invested in the project because he had been working on his original *Heat* script again.

By late 1993, Mann had completed a revised draft of *Heat* that included additional characters. He gave the completed work to his friend and producer Art Linson to have a read through and see if he liked it. If Linson was happy with it then Mann planned to produce the project alongside Linson and the pair agreed to find a director between them. The next day Linson met with Mann and told him: "You're out of your fucking mind. You've *got* to direct this." Mann at last understood that he should be the one in the director's chair; he had after all been working on this script for over a decade. On a whim he mailed it directly to the two actors he wanted as his central cop and robber: Al Pacino and Robert De Niro.

Miraculously the script found its way directly into De Niro's hands, who was taken by the prospect of playing Neil McCauley. He called up Pacino and told him about the script he had received and that it would pit them against each other for the first time ever on-screen. The pair had appeared in *The Godfather Part II* together, but were never on-screen at the same time and Pacino liked the idea of facing off against his buddy. Once De Niro signed on, so too did Pacino - who was set to play Sergeant Vincent Hanna. Both actors asked for slight alterations to their characters, and thus Mann continuously worked on the script throughout 1994.

At the same time, Linson and Mann set about casting other roles for the movie. On the side fighting for good, Mann and Linson hired talented actors such as Mykelti Williamson as Sergeant Drucker, Wes Studi as Lieutenant Casals and Jerry Trimble as Detective Schwartz. Ted Levine was offered the role of criminal and prostitute-killer Waingro until Levine told Mann he was done playing scumbags and would rather play the role of homicide forensic tech: Mike Bosko. Mann agreed to the role change. These characters were to form the core group of the Major Crimes Unit alongside Hanna. Madeleine Stowe was offered the role of Hanna's wife Justine, but turned it down. Chinese actor Li Gong also turned it down because the script was not translated into Mandarin for her. It was offered to stage and screen actor Diane Venora, who accepted amidst puzzlement as it said in the script that Justine was a redhead with thick thighs. Venora had neither of these.

Mann's script bulged with bad guys, so finding the perfect actors to play every last one of them proved quite tricky. Mann contacted veteran actor Jon Voight about playing McCauley's crime jobs facilitator, Nate. Voight turned it down twice, making it clear that he didn't want to go through the hassle of sitting through make-up, prosthetics and a wig-fitting each time he was due to film. Eventually he relented because "Michael was a friend of mine, and I knew Bobby and Al well, and they were insistent." Mann based Nate on the life of career criminal Edward Bunker, previously one of the FBI's most wanted men. For the role of Michael Cheritto, a brutal, no-nonsense criminal of McCauley's gang, Mann initially discussed bringing in his old *Miami Vice* star Don Johnson. When that fizzled out, Jean Claude Van Damme's name was mentioned several times. Ultimately, Mann signed up Michael Madsen instead.

When it came to the casting of McCauley's right-hand man, Chris Shiherlis, Keanu Reeves was first approached for the role. He eventually turned it down to go to Winnipeg and perform Hamlet on stage. Mann also talked with Carsten Norgaard, Jean Reno and Johnny Depp. All of them lost out when it became known that Val Kilmer was interested and could film *Heat* in-between his shooting schedule for *Batman Forever*. TV-turned-movie actress Ashley Judd was signed up for the role of Charlene Shiherlis, Chris's long-suffering wife. Caught up in a love affair with McCauley is a woman called Eady. In the script she was, originally, of Chinese origin. However, Mann sought out Amy Brenneman for the role. She turned it down because she felt the work had a lack of morality. Mann explained that this was exactly the type of attitude Eady would have, and consequently Brenneman signed on.

Several weeks into casting an unexpected acting change occurred. Michael Madsen was pushed out, for unknown reasons, and replaced by Tom Sizemore. Mann wasn't going to let one casting decision derail his long-awaited passion project and thus carried on regardless. Further casting occurred for smaller, yet important, roles including Dennis Haysbert as Donald Breedan an ex-parolee turned getaway driver. William Fichtner as Roger Van Zant, an off-shore drug money launderer. Natalie Portman as Hanna's depressed stepdaughter Lauren Gustafson. Hank Azaria as Charlene Shiherlis' lover, Alan Marciano. Xander Berkeley played Waingro in the TV movie *L.A. Takedown* and this time he was offered the small role of Justine's lover Ralph. Mann further diversified his cast by selecting two musicians in minor roles. Tone Loc played Richard Torena, a confidential informant to Hanna and Henry Rollins was cast as Hugh Benny, a bodyguard for Roger Van Zant. The production now bulged with big names. Fortunately Mann had already agreed the sizeable budget of $60 million with Warner Bros Studios.

The final script was completed by Mann in December 1993 and ran for one hundred and fifty four pages. Before filming began, Mann brought in ex-SAS soldiers Andy McNab and Mick Gould to instruct the actors on how to fire the different types of guns. They set out a rigorous training regime at a gun range in Orange County, California that the actors were obliged to follow. The range was so large that Mann and his crew were able to build wooden structures exactly the same as the real locations he was planning to use in the picture. The training was conducted differently depending on whether the actors were playing criminals or cops. Live ammunition was used every day. Kilmer became so good at changing magazine clips on his weapon that years later the footage of him doing it quickly and correctly was used in training instruction videos for new recruits to the Special Forces.

Sizemore was actively encouraged to stake out a real bank as if he were planning on robbing it. He pretended to apply for a loan and got to talk to some of the bank's executives. He later explained: "It was a trip how much knowledge we got, and they didn't know what was going on."

De Niro, Sizemore, Kilmer and Mann visited Folsom State Prison, California to talk with prisoners about their crimes. De Niro was given memoirs and poetry from some of the inmates to take home and study. The movie script was also passed to convicted members of the Aryan Brotherhood to validate details on jailhouse tattoos, prison behaviour and language. Judd spent time with females whose partners were imprisoned, to discover what it was like for women to be associated with high-powered criminals. An unnamed, downtown Los Angeles restaurant played host to weekly dinners for cops and criminals on separate days. Mann planted his actors in the restaurant on their respective nights and this is when Venora discovered that women married to policemen "were not that important. I felt pretty much second class." To round off the character study, De Niro and Mann sat together for hours one night that January discussing what made McCauley tick. The entire conversation was transcribed for De Niro so he could flesh out his character in greater detail. One week before filming, Mann sent De Niro a memo about McCauley. At the end of it he wrote: "Neil and Hanna are the smartest men in the movie."

Pre-filming training wasn't limited to just the cast. Mann rode alongside L.A.P.D. commander Tom Elfmont randomly taking police calls: "That's how I learned about L.A." Mann staged interrogation scenes with real-life police for his cast to study. The director took some of his most immediate crew on a three hour helicopter ride around L.A. so they could get a closer look at the various locations used in the movie. They also walked around the city taking photos of random objects or unique vistas, anything that contributed to Mann's vision of Los Angeles, which in the film is a character in its own right. The second unit director, and Mann's daughter, Ami Canaan Mann is described as telling the crew to: "Talk to the most extreme people you can talk to. Get as much information as you can."

Principal photography began in late February 1996. No sets were built. Mann used only real locations in and around Los Angeles including Redondo Beach Metro rail station, St. Mary's Medical Centre, Johnie's Broiler restaurant (now called Bob's Big Boy Broiler), Hennessey + Ingalls bookstore, Broadway Deli on Santa Monica Promenade, Bob's Big Boy restaurant, The Oxford Center shopping precinct, Centinela Drive-In cinema, Ivy At The Shore restaurant, El Cielito Restaurant, The Los Angeles Smoking & Curing Company, Hotel Angeleno, Hilton Hotel at Los Angeles airport, Quinn Shepherd Machinery rental company, Zero Zero Japanese restaurant and The Blue Room bar in Burbank. The Los Angeles Harbor Docks (on the John S. Gibson Boulevard side) was used for the filming of McCauley's fake set-up in which he trails Hanna. On the west side of the Harbor freeway is an oil refinery that was used when McCauley's team were spying on the detectives. The white storage tank used in the movie was numbered 120002.

The pit-bull fighting area/chop shop was an actual cock fighting arena located on Terminal Island, situated behind the Balfour Beatty Rail, between the 103 freeway and the Leeward Bay Marina. The interior shots for the final bank robbery were filmed at the Far East Bank at 350 South Grand Avenue in downtown L.A. Private residential premises were used as homes for a selection of the characters. These houses were located on Speedway and Navy Street, Palisades Park and several houses were situated on Dodds Circle. A private, beach-front residence on Colony Drive, Malibu was used as McCauley's sparse living space. Mann wanted a location that would homage Alex Colville's 'Pacific' painting of a solitary man looking out to sea while a pistol sits on a table in the foreground. The production team stuck blue filters across the sliding doors from the floor to ceiling, using natural sunlight instead of setting up lighting rigs. A small coffee table was brought in and positioned close to the camera so only the corner of it could be seen. Mann called action, De Niro walked in, placed the gun on the table and proceeds to the glass door. Next, he put his arm up on the frame and looked out to sea. The final moment of this shot is an almost exact replica of Colville's painting.

The opening scene of the film was to involve an armoured car robbery. This was filmed beneath the Santa Monica freeway, where the streets of Venice Boulevard and Georgia meet. Mann staged the scene so the truck would run from a gated road, located underneath the spiralling Freeway on-ramps and behind the Los Angeles Convention Centre. The armoured truck was rigged with devices so it would flip onto its side when the large pick-up truck hit it. Mann used real-life police officers and paramedics for the aftermath scene to inject added authenticity. The ambulance that McCauley and his team escaped in, and subsequently abandoned, was blown up above the Harbor freeway on South Figueroa Street and West 22nd Street. On 25 April, Hank Azaria turned up on set to film his first scene. It was also his birthday. As action was called Azaria sat in a chair in his character's office ready to deliver his lines, and he received a rude awakening. In the scene, Marciano replies tersely to Hanna's questions about his affair with Charlene Shiherlis, and at that moment Pacino let rip at Azaria. Bellowing into his face: "I BET SHE GOT....A GREAT ASS.......AND YOU GOT YOUR HEAD ALL THE WAY UP IT!" Azaria wasn't prepared for that style of response from Pacino. He sat there open mouthed before uttering "Jesus" under his breath. Mann used that take in the finished film as he felt it was the most natural. Another off-script sequence happened during the filming between Hanna and Van Zant's bodyguard Hugh Benny, played by Henry Rollins. The scene called for Hanna to slap Benny around the face during a rough interrogation in his apartment. After a few takes, Rollins told Pacino not to hold back. "So the next take he grabs me by my hair so hard I almost started crying and he hauls off and whacks me across the face to where I could feel it in my toes. My face went numb."

In mid-June, Mann was ready to shoot the first ever on-screen meeting of Pacino and De Niro. Pacino had wanted to rehearse the scene for several weeks, however De Niro kept telling him "No." He wanted to keep it as fresh as possible, without it being over-rehearsed. The location for this iconic scene was to be the Kate Mantilini restaurant in Beverly Hills. Chosen because of its minimalistic decor and furniture, Mann wanted the focus to be exclusively on his two stars: "I did not want anything to take away from what was happening on Al's face and Bob's face." Director of photography Dante Spinotti was tasked, by Mann, to run two cameras simultaneously over the shoulders of Pacino and De Niro as Mann wanted to capture the unity of the performance. Spinotti also set up cameras in other positions including one looking down on them both and one camera to capture them both in profile. By take five, Pacino and De Niro were so engrossed in the scene that they started to mirror each other's movements - a tilt of the head, a lick of the lips or a darting of the eyes. The scene was acted out nearly twenty times on camera. "I could not wait to film that scene," said Mann. The extras in the background of the scene were all workers from the Kate Mantilini restaurant and upon completion of filming there, Mann gave each of them membership to the Actors Equity Association of the United States.

The large scale bank robbery caused problems for production as it had to be filmed over a series of weekends. The city of L.A. would only grant complete shutdown of the streets on Saturdays and Sundays. For several weeks during production the cast and crew's working week changed to Wednesday through Sunday in order to accommodate filming over the weekends. The exterior bank robbery footage of McCauley's gang leaving the bank was shot outside a forty-eight storey office block, called 444 Building, located at 444 South Flower Street in downtown L.A. This location was chosen because the exterior looked very much like the Far East Bank, the building used for interior shots.

Leading towards the on-ramp for Harbor freeway, the top end of South Flower Street was the filming location for the climactic shootout. During the training regime at the gun range in Orange County, several LAPD cars were driven in and the actors practised shooting at them with real bullets. These were moved into positions on Figueroa Street. The bullet holes were filled in with timed explosives and then covered over with putty. When the time came, the explosives detonated and exposed the bullet holes. As a nod to the involvement of McNab and Gould, Mann inserted a busted up car for Shiherlis to hide behind which had the registration plate '2LUP382'. British Army terminology for lying in the face up position is 'LUP'. This car was the second LUP for Shiherlis, hence the 2LUP in the plate.

Busted up post boxes, bus stops and telephone boxes were also brought onto the street for further continuity. In keeping with their gun training, each actor was given a specific gun for the downtown street shootout. Kilmer and De Niro used Colt Model 733s, while Pacino had a semi-automatic FNC 223 Sporter. Each take consumed between eight hundred to a thousand blank rounds of ammunition. Filming on South Flower Street should have finished by 7th May, however it fell behind a week. On the following weekend, which happened to be Mothering Sunday (May 14), the newly opened Cafe Pinot on Flower Street had pre-organised a huge Mother's Day buffet for families. Unable to go outside, those in the restaurant got to eat their meals while watching the huge gun battle being shot right outside. Additional filming of the robbery gone wrong was shot ten miles away on Figueroa Street, outside the Union Bank Plaza. Here Mann used the entire width of the street to shoot McCauley dragging the injured Shiherlis between abandoned cars. The corner of 4th Street and Figueroa, known as Union Bank Square, was used for the escape and subsequent kill of Cheritto. Mann stationed cameras at opposite ends of the square in order to film the death scene.

The final chase sequence in the movie, between Hanna and McCauley, was filmed on wasteland off Aviation Boulevard and West 104th Street, across from Runway 25R at Los Angeles International Airport (LAX). Production spent months trying to organise access to the wasteland with LAX. The film's art department spent three weeks measuring the distances between the giant containers in order to set them up in such a manner that the flight path floodlights would light the boxes for the scene. Production was permitted to set up additional spotlights also. The sequence took several nights to complete. Principal photography was completed by mid-July. In total, one hundred and sixty real L.A. locations were used.

Because of the quick turnaround with filming, Warner Bros asked Mann if it would be possible to release the movie earlier than planned. Mann told them that he wanted to get the post-production mix perfect, he didn't want to rush it. So an earlier than scheduled release would not be possible. Working with the original release date of the end of 1995 still left Mann and his editing team working to an unrelenting schedule. Mann organised a team of four editors to work around the clock on the movie, as one would check out another would take his place. The majority of editing time was spent on the large scale bank robbery. When Mann viewed a rough edit of that sequence, he was horrified to discover the editors had overdubbed the sound of the on-street gunfire with standard audio clips of gunshots. Mann commented that: "Nothing artificial could come close to delivering the fear of the sound of the automatic weapons and the way the sound ricochet off the walls of an empty downtown. You couldn't manufacture the sound." Thus, all of the pre-dubbed gunshot audio was stripped from the mix, leaving only the deafening sounds recorded on location.

When it came to editing the iconic diner scene, Mann and his team opened with an establishing shot of Pacino and De Niro sitting at the table together. However, when they viewed the full scene Mann was unhappy with the early profile shot because "It's so intensely personal that as soon as you go to the objective [shot] instead of the subjective [shot] you stop being internalised as to what is going on." The decision was made to only use the two over the shoulder view points. Mann used the majority of take eleven with a couple of quick seconds from take thirteen to make up the complete scene.

Mann chose Elliot Goldenthal as the composer for the movie. Goldenthal, who had previously worked on movies such as *Alien 3*, *Demolition Man* and *Pet Sematary*, wanted to experiment with percussions, guitar textures and homemade instruments. When it came to finally scoring the film, Goldenthal used the tapes from his musical experimentation and combined those into the musical elements of the score. One piece Goldenthal had written was to be used over the final scene between Hanna and McCauley. When Mann viewed it with that particular musical cue, he felt it didn't fit with the mood of the scene.

Electronic music artist Moby had allowed two of his works to appear in the film – a cover of Joy Division's "New Dawn Fades" and his own composition called "God Moving Over the Face of the Waters." Initially Mann wanted "New Dawn Fades" to play out over the end credits and "God Moving Over the Face of the Waters" playing out as Hanna chases McCauley on the freeway. When Mann decided to switch them around he found that "God Moving" played much better over the final scene and into the credits because it was such a cathartic piece.

Mann, Pacino, De Niro and the rest of the cast walked the red carpet at the world premiere on 6 December at the Warner Bros Studios in Burbank, California. Critical reviews were overwhelmingly positive. Roger Ebert described *Heat* as: "not just an action picture. Above all, the dialogue is complex enough to allow the characters to say what they're thinking: They are eloquent, insightful, fanciful, poetic when necessary." *Variety* was blown away by the film describing it as: "stunningly made and incisively acted." *The Los Angeles Times* was equally pleased with it, lauding it as: "A sleek, accomplished piece of work." There were a couple of outlets that didn't quite see things the same way. *The New York Times* called it: "fundamentally hollow and its characters haven't much to say." *Salon.com* scathed: "a 3 hour fusillade of clichés." For a film with such star power, *Heat* spluttered at the box office. Opening exactly one week before Christmas 1995 in North America, it pulled in $12.6 million in its first week. This wasn't enough to see it claim the top spot in the box office chart. It went in at number three behind *Jumanji* and *Toy Story*. The following week it raked in $13.5 million yet sunk to sixth position. *Heat* eventually bowed out of North American theatres during the first week of February 1996. Its total theatrical haul amounted to $67.4 million, making it the twenty-fifth highest grossing film of 1995 (Information courtesy of Box Office Mojo. Used with permission).

It had to happen. It was inevitable. Two acting titans of the silver screen coming face to face – Pacino vs. De Niro. Their characters, Hanna and McCauley, are cut from the same cloth; in fact they are the same person just on opposite sides of the law. Both of them understand that their lives revolve around each other and neither is willing to back down. They are prepared to take a bullet if it means the other won't get back up again. As they sit down together in that diner, they are simply two men being honest with each other. Two men who have never met but know about each other's lives in great detail. Pacino and De Niro's first ever scene together is not about which character comes out on top. It's a scene that lays bare the repercussions they've had on each other's lives. They talk like two old friends who haven't seen each other in years. Neither is afraid of the other, in fact throughout the conversation both of them scan the diner rather than keeping their eyes set across the table. Both know that this moment is not how it will end. It is simply a precursor for what is to come. McCauley and Hanna's lives intertwine throughout the film, as one is on the way up the other is coming down and vice versa. That final cross over point occurs when they come face to face in the wasteland of Los Angeles International Airport.

Pacino plays Hanna as a fast and loose detective. One that is happy to bark and bite. He hams it up with big blasts of hilarious dialogue such as "GREAT ASS!", "DON'T WASTE MY MOTHERFUCKING TIME!" and "GET KILLED WALKING YOUR DOGGY!" He gives a wide-eyed rendition of Glen Campbell's song: "When I get To Phoenix." There is also footage of him laughing, dancing and having sex with his wife early on in the film. Soon however, the screw turns and Hanna becomes obsessive as he hunts McCauley. His dark, brooding attitude just about destroys all of the happiness he had previously known. It's a descent into madness that he knows he is never coming back from. At one point Hanna tells his wife: "It's like you said 'All I have is what I'm going after.'"

Hanna does boast some of the familiar detective clichés often seen in police procedural films and TV shows, yet in the hands of Pacino there is a deeper level of pain attached to them. It's a main character that could have been portrayed in a quite lightweight style (see Plank's Hanna in *L.A. Takedown*) but Pacino creates a wild, brash, unhinged and self-destructive detective. On the opposite end of the emotional scale is De Niro's McCauley. A man who blends into the surroundings without drawing attention to himself (notice how many extras also wear grey suits in scenes with McCauley, enabling him to easily drift in and out.) De Niro makes himself a silent menace; a character who is much more willing to let you talk while he listens. Everything is happening behind those eyes; he doesn't need or want to say anything.

Watch the scene in the diner in which McCauley meets Eady. She is the chatty one while De Niro merely regards her in silent scorn. He also surveys the room to make sure nobody is watching him talk to a complete stranger. He then snaps: "what business is it of yours?" It's a brutal rebuttal which stops Eady dead in her tracks. Eventually, however, McCauley loosens up and develops a relationship with her, allowing himself that moment of pleasure and a smile (McCauley only smiles five times in the film). It's an out of character moment for the robber, but one that fits in with the man who finally comes to understand that there is more to life than self-discipline. Still, he cannot escape the feeling that this could all be fleeting. McCauley is a methodical master criminal and he could never lose sight of who he is. Both Hanna and McCauley share this attitude; they can never change. During the infamous diner meeting they discuss changing their jobs. Hanna says: "I don't know how to do anything else." McCauley replies: "Neither do I." "I don't much want to either" says Hanna. To which McCauley retorts "Neither do I." At this they both break into sly smiles.

Of course, this is not a film solely about McCauley and Hanna. There is a whole host of characters that though peripheral are an integral part of the script's proceedings. The care and attention that has gone into making each of them well-rounded characters is deeply impressive. From Dennis Haysbert's getaway driver to Azaria's cheating sleazebag and Kilmer's troubled yet accomplished thief, all of them are unique individuals with their own agendas.

For a film that is nearly three hours long, Mann makes every single minute count. He rarely uses establishing shots, trusting the viewer is intelligent enough to recognise the locations and situations on-screen. The blue neo-noir visual look that Mann uses in his films is present in *Heat*. There is coldness to it and yet like a cold pool on a hot day, the tone is appealing. His action set pieces are terrifyingly relentless as he positions the camera in the eye of every storm, so that the viewer can relish the sensation of being caught up in the action. The final bank heist is one of the most thrilling action set pieces in the history of cinema. Shiherlis fires off round after round at the cops. The noise is like a cacophony of fireworks being let off in a steel barrel, one which happens to be strapped to your head. Mann doesn't use loud, bombastic music to accompany these set pieces, instead he opts for a single, drawn out, ear-piercing note.

Mann directs the final reel of the film with huge intensity. As McCauley runs away Mann stills the camera and films him in long distance with wide angles. In contrast, Hanna is filmed up close and personal with a shaky camera but in both instances the camera is doing a great deal of the work. It is quite possible this is Mann's way of conveying that even in the end neither character has changed. McCauley is cool and calm, whereas Hanna is chaotic and volatile.

The final shot of McCauley and Hanna holding hands shows not just one life disappearing but both. Now McCauley is dead, where does that leave Hanna? His life has been consumed by McCauley. *Heat* doesn't revolutionise the crime movie, but it does elevate its common tropes. Mann's respect and discipline for the genre turned *Heat* into a triumph of realism.

Co-star Wes Studi on *Heat*

You had worked with Michael Mann on *The Last of the Mohicans*. Did he mention what his next project might be? Or that he might possibly cast you?

No, not all. *The Last of the Mohicans* was, as far as I knew at the time, a one shot thing with Michael. I'll tell you how it all sort of began, at least from my viewpoint, was one day I saw notices in the *Hollywood Reporter* or *Variety*, it was one of the two, about his plans for the picture. I can't remember if it was called *Heat* at the time but it referred to Al Pacino and Robert De Niro which was an historical first in terms of those two actors working together. I happened to have his production office phone number so I gave it a call and it surprised me when he jumped on the call and said: "Hi, how you doing?" So we exchanged pleasantries for a bit then I said: "Michael I hear you are going to do a new film with Al and De Niro and myself." He chuckled a bit [*laughs*] and said: "Let me get back to you on that." About two weeks later my agent got a call. That's how it all started out.

Did you audition?

I don't think I did. I think we might have had a meeting or something like that, and then off we went.

Before filming began did you spend time with real police officers? Or were you involved in police training?

Oh yes. We didn't do any formal training, but we did training with some of the weapons. We went out and had ride alongs with the Los Angeles county police and we went out several times on night patrol. One of the interesting things that happened on one of those was an escalation of killings by gangs in the Rampart area of Los Angeles. What happened was a young man in a wheelchair was gunned down by supposed rival gang members, and he was killed on the street. The police we were riding with went to investigate and we saw the man being carried away in the ambulance. They started their investigation and found, within thirty to forty five minutes, a retaliation had happened by the supposed rival gang and then that happened at least two more times. So there was a body mass of four people who got killed, only to find out that the very first person killed was not even a gang member. The gang had made a mistake because the guy was in a wheelchair and looked like the guy they actually wanted to bump off. That happened all in the process of, maybe, eight hours within that particular district. We learned a lot about what the police have to deal with there in terms of gang violence.

Around the time of release you gave an interview where you described working on *Heat* as fun. What was fun about it?

Well what happens is a person gets to play out fantasies in his own mind and build character and be in pretend situations, that are extremely intense and dangerous if they were for real, and you are able to walk away from it without any injuries as if it were the real thing. It was fun to pretend to be a person involved in such activities – gun fights and arrests and physical violence. In that context it can be fun to do those things.

One thing that comes across in the film is the sense of camaraderie between the group of detectives. Is that something you worked on off-camera?

To a certain extent. Most of the police surrounding Pacino were from Los Angeles and because everyone lived there, everyone had their own lives. There were times when we were able to get together after shooting. We did a bonding of sorts between actors. Mykelti and Levine and myself and others would sometimes have the opportunity to have a beer, play a little pool or do something like that afterwards. Essentially everyone lives there so the business is you work and then you go home. It's not like being on location.

Casals, your character, works very closely with Hanna. What was it like working that closely with Pacino?

Pacino is an out and out pro. He's someone that you tend to pick up a few tips just from watching him. You don't say: "How would you do this?" or: "How would you do that?" You don't talk acting. He's a very giving kind of a person. Very socially adept. I think, very good to work with and when you work with somebody that is of such a calibre in the acting world your performance can only be enlightened by someone you consider better at it. Someone who is so accomplished in the acting world. Hopefully your performance is lifted by... you have to step up to the mark and do your best.

Did you constantly have to be on your toes, so to speak, in case he changed any of his dialogue which in turn affected yours?

I think he may have been pushed into changing and/or adding to a scene mainly because a lot of the times, when Michael would roll camera, we would do a scene and in our own minds we would think we are going to hear cut in a minute but no he would keep the camera on Al just to see what he would do at that point on knowing that scene hadn't been cut. I think it was an experiment on Michael's part just to see what Al would do [*laughs*]. To either extend the scene or make more of it. So yes we did have to stay on our toes until the time we did hear 'Cut!' or 'Roll Out!'

Does Michael allow room for improvisation?

I think he is open to it. Not to the extent some people do but I think Michael has a certain stick-to-the-script idea on shooting the scene, but he is also open to what might happen.

In *Heat* we see many comedy moments from Pacino including the line: "She's got a great ass! And you've got your head all the way up it." Is it difficult to keep a straight face when he is bellowing these funny lines?

[*Laughs*] Well if it was difficult I would never tell you it was [*laughs*].

Did you notice him making the most of his comedic capabilities during filming?

I think Al is known to be such a dramatic actor that a lot of the times people might miss those things. It takes a cinematic eye to catch these things. An actor always has to be open to what might happen from scenes in front of the camera, or on stage you always have to be on top of what's going on.

What is the one thing you are most proud of about your time working on *Heat*?

I suppose that I could add to my resume that I worked with Al Pacino and Robert De Niro in their first time meeting on film.

When you watch the film now, what is the one moment you are most proud of?

There was one part in the shoot out when I got to shoot Val Kilmer [*laughs*].

City Hall

Cast: Al Pacino (Mayor John Pappas), John Cusack (Deputy Mayor Kevin Calhoun), Bridget Fonda (Marybeth Cogan), Danny Aiello (Frank Anselmo), Martin Landau (Judge Walter Stern), Anthony Franciosa (Paul Zapatti), Richard Schiff (Larry Schwartz), Nestor Serrano (Detective Eddie Santos). **Director:** Harold Becker.

Synopsis: Deputy Mayor Kevin Calhoun is caught up in a trail of subversion and cover-ups after a young boy is accidentally shot dead in New York City. Calhoun's findings begin to loop back to the man he serves and reveres, Mayor John Pappas.

Pacino can usually be found to be "sticking it to the man" in his film roles. *City Hall* is one of the few films where he would find himself playing "The Man" as he portrays one of the biggest political figureheads in America – the mayor of New York City – in a tale that comes direct from the pen of a man who lived it.

Ken Lipper went to Harvard Law School and followed that up with a stint at the University of Paris, France. There, he specialised in Law and Economics. Upon his return to New York he spent a year at a Wall Street law firm before moving to Washington D.C. to serve as a director of industry policy for the Office of Foreign Direct Investment. He was a partner at the now infamous investment bank Lehman Brothers Holdings Inc. between 1969 and 1975. After that he moved into being a partner at another investment bank, Salomon Brothers, until 1982. Then came the call from the mayor of New York, Ed Koch, who requested he become the deputy mayor in charge of the budget, taxation and economic development for the city. Lipper had become a man of power, vast net worth and an even greater status... so why would he decide to write a screenplay for a movie?

Lipper wrote a story based on a scandal in New York that saw Donald Manes, the democratic politician from Queens, embroiled in corruption during the mid-1980s. Lipper had been writing his story every free weekend he had. When it was finished he contacted his old childhood friend, Al Pacino. The pair had grown up in the Bronx and stayed in touch from time to time over the intervening years. Lipper felt the Bronx-born actor was perfect for the role of the mayor of New York City. Pacino was given the script and liked it, but never took it any further. In the meantime the story Lipper had written was then passed to *Taxi Driver* screenwriter Paul Schrader and *Goodfellas* author Nicholas Pileggi to be written into a screenplay.

Schrader wanted to direct the film but couldn't get a big enough star to entice any of the major studios that he had been hawking it around to. Eventually, Schrader took it to New York film director Harold Becker who agreed to make it. With a new director onboard, Castle Rock Entertainment snapped up the option to make the film. Schrader was paid a kill fee in-order to not direct the film now that the studio had found a bigger director.

Having read through the Schrader/Pileggi screenplay Becker didn't want to make their movie so brought in his own screenwriter Bo Goldman, who had just finished work on the *Scent of a Woman* screenplay. Becker requested the script be completely rewritten. Lipper guaranteed Goldman and Becker access to a lot of the people caught up in the Manes scandal. They spent four months speaking to these people and after that Goldman went off to write his, and Becker's, version of the movie.

Castle Rock Entertainment wanted a big star for the role of Mayor John Pappas. The director contacted Pacino, who he had previously worked with on *Sea of Love*. Becker believed Pacino was perfect for the role of the mayor as Pappas was "a good man. Somebody who loved the city and there was nobody better than Pacino to convey that." Pacino had not been available when Schrader had enquired as he was prepping to appear as Manuel Noriega in Oliver Stone's biopic of the Panamanian dictator. When that was cancelled because of complications with the script and financing, it freed Pacino to film *City Hall*. However, he had also received another offer from New Line Cinema to play the ageing detective William Somerset in a psychological thriller called *Seven*. Pacino mulled over both films while Becker set about casting the deputy mayor. There are rumours that Tom Cruise, Alec Baldwin and Brad Pitt all passed on playing Kevin Calhoun. The role went to John Cusack, a quirky and likeable actor previously known for such 80s teen films as: *Sixteen Candles*, *Stand by Me* and *Say Anything*, who was by this time making more off-beat movies such as: *The Grifters*, *True Colors* and *Bullets Over Broadway*. Becker believed that Cusack and Pacino would perfectly contrast on-screen.

The female lead in the movie is a strong-willed lawyer called Marybeth Cogan. An actor from the Fonda family dynasty – Bridget - was cast in the role. Having had success with *Singles*, *Single White Female* and *It Could Happen To You*, Fonda was hot property. She had also previously had an almost blink-and-you'll-miss-it role in *The Godfather Part III*.

By this time, Pacino had now turned his back on *Seven* and was fully committed to *City Hall*. Thanks to Lipper's connections, Pacino met with former New York City mayors Ed Koch and David Dinkins on several occasions to grill them about life as mayor. The New York mayor Rudolph "Rudy" Giuliani allowed Pacino unprecedented and complete access into his world for two full working days. "I'm indebted to all three of them. I was surprised at their willingness to open up and share with me so many things of value," Pacino recalled. For the role of Brooklyn-politician-with-organized-crime-links Frank Anselmo, Becker spoke to Marlon Brando. For a couple of months Becker and Brando batted back and forth ideas for the character. Anselmo loves going to the opera with his wife, he also enjoys Rogers and Hammerstein musicals. Brando wanted to include that in his portrayal. He also wanted to make Anselmo a Mexican-American who loved to play the banjo and/or bongos. Becker felt this wasn't the right way to go, so while still trying to find compromise with Brando, contact was made with New York actor Danny Aiello. Six months after making initial contact with Aiello's agent, Becker called him back in to discuss the role. Aiello had always wanted to work with Pacino: "I was excited to say the least." Becker offered him the role and Aiello said yes. The last part of casting was complete and the next day Becker called a production meeting with the entire cast. Castle Rock Entertainment set the budget at $40 million.

Principal photography began in the summer of 1995. The Booth Theatre on West 45th Street and 7th Avenue was used for the opera scenes. Gracie Mansion, the official residence of the New York City Mayor, was also used. The New York City Hall, Manhattan was used for extensive exterior and interior shots. Movie productions companies had found it very difficult to gain permits to film inside the real City Hall. Thanks to Lipper's connections and Pacino's involvement, they were granted instant access. Filming in City Hall didn't take place in the main wing, where the real mayor presides. Instead it was shot in the city councilmen's chamber, which had almost identical architecture and layout as the real mayor's office. "We were lucky that way," recalls Becker. Production then transferred across the Verrazano-Narrows Bridge, Brooklyn for shooting on the Shore Parkway.

While filming in New Jersey, the production unit moved to Lehrer-Gibilisco funeral home, Rahway. There, they repainted the entire funeral home and made some non-permanent changes to the front of the building. It was the middle of summer in eighty degree weather, that two winter-y snow covered scenes had to be shot in New Jersey. One at the Wayne Route 23 Transit Center, Wayne, and the other at the legendary Tunnel Diner in Jersey City. Fake snow covered the ground and was pumped out from an overhead snow machine as Cusack and Fonda, dressed in thick winter clothes, filmed their scenes. Additional interior scenes of the mayor's office were shot inside a private mansion in Teaneck, Bergen County.

Screenwriter Bo Goldman continued to re-write scenes throughout filming. The Sept/Oct 1995 edition of the Motion Picture Editors Guild newsletter included an interview with Goldman, where he commented about still working on the script: "We're redoing some of the ending on *City Hall*. I come in and he [the editor – Bob Jones] shows me the footage and I'm trying to write stuff around it."

Castle Rock set a U.S. Theatrical release date of 16 February, 1996. The word from critics should have troubled the top brass at Castle Rock even before a general release to the public. *The New York Times* were not overly receptive to it: "This knotty investigative thriller has trouble achieving the rock-solid credibility to hold an audience in thrall." *The Washington Post* was scathing in their assessment: "The ultimate verdict on *City Hall* is easy: It's no good." Roger Ebert felt that: "*City Hall* covers so much material that at times it feels uncomfortably episodic." The average-to-poor reviews were reflected in the box office takings. In its first weekend it opened in fourth place, behind *Muppets Treasure Island*, with a haul of just $8 million. By the end of its second weekend its box office takings were down by half to $4 million. It lasted five weeks in U.S. theatres before being dropped. Total box office returns amounted to a poor $20 million, half of what it cost to make the film (Information courtesy of Box Office Mojo. Used with permission). Cusack blamed the poor takings on the weather: "There was a huge snow storm along the East Coast. If people hadn't been snowed in, the movie would really have played to that New York crowd."

Filmed with his usual gritty cinematography, Becker shows that the seedy underbelly of New York calls to anyone who is given even the slightest of opportunities. The city lives and breathes as a separate entity through most of the scenes. The filthy atmosphere of the city breeds on-screen, from the corrupt mayor downwards. The real-life scandals portrayed still rock the city to this day.

"We come out fighting" is a line Mayor Pappas says towards the end of the film, and that line directly correlates with Pacino's performance. Always on the front foot, always delivering the lines with zeal, he hoots and holler's his way through the entire movie. Pacino's top billing on the movie's tag is at odds to his actual screen time, which is less than forty minutes. Pacino more than makes up for this though thanks to the usual grandstanding which comes so naturally to him in roles that afford his character strong lines of dialogue that demand powerful delivery. "I thought some of *City Hall* had good words in it." Pacino told his biographer Lawrence Grobel. The film keeps hammering home a message about the bonding of honour between two men (Pappas and

Calhoun). The term menschkeit is mentioned so regularly that it almost becomes an unofficial motto for Pappas – the use of this Yiddish expression and all that is associated with it, was likely unfamiliar to quite a few audience members.

A true failing of the film, given that it is shown from the view point of the deputy mayor, is the miscasting of Cusack. The actor mumbles his way through most of his lines and is left flailing his way through the couple of action scenes he has to perform. Cusack seems too content to rest on his laurels, making no effort to push the character into a brave or powerful space. This idealistic, wanna-be mayor doesn't fit Cusack's acting style. While Cusack cannot get to grips with the material, Fonda is barely allowed to touch it. Relegated to a role that requires her to question everything while never receiving an answer, she is pushed to one side for the majority of proceedings. She is eventually trotted out only when the scriptwriters attempt, and fail, to force the flirtatious storyline between Calhoun and Cogan into the proceedings. Fonda does amicably well with what she is given, but it's evident she could easily have handled a meatier storyline. This potentially interesting female character is largely ignored for no real reason.

City Hall is a middling affair. Entertaining performances from Pacino and Aiello are in stark contrast with Cusack and Fonda who look lost. Maybe that is to do with having four different writers working on the material. It's never sure if it wants to be a film about political whistle-blowers or a damning indictment on political greed or a corruption drama, or a straight up crime film. Sometimes too much talent can lead to everyone cancelling one another out and that appears to have been the case with *City Hall*.

Actor Nestor Serrano on *City Hall*

The death of your character acts as a catalyst in this film. Did the director say anything to you beforehand about how important your character would be to the story?

I knew going into it that it was a character that was central to the story and the plot. He didn't give me much. The interesting thing I can tell you about Harold Becker is that he really, really liked me a lot. There were three guys in the scene, and I happen to know the other two guys as well, and Harold treated one of the guys neutrally, he treated me like his long lost son, and he treated the other guy miserably during the shooting of the scenes. I couldn't understand why he chose that guy to be the runt of the litter and why he chose me... at the end of the film I got a beautiful bouquet of flowers in my trailer with a big bottle of champagne and the other two didn't get it. I had to find out through the underground channels because I certainly wasn't going to walk over to them and go: "Hey! Look what I got!" [*laughs*]. That's the thing I remember most about working on *City Hall*.

How long were you on set?

I don't remember now. It was probably a week.

When the film came out did you get to see it in the theatre? And what did you think to it?

I thought it was a good movie. I was really uncomfortable because I was dating a woman for ten years, and she was an actress. She had never worked in the few years that we were together. When my manager called me, she said: "I have good news and bad news." I said: "Well what's the good news?" she said: "They want to cast you in this movie." I said:

"OK, but what's the bad news?" And she said: "Lauren Vélez, the girl you just broke up with is playing your wife," [*laughs*]. We had to do all kinds of pictures, acting all love-y dove-y so they could keep them in the background. So, my new girlfriend at the time did not want to meet Lauren Vélez. So I just wanted to get out of the theatre [*laughs*]. I enjoyed the movie. It was a good movie. And I enjoyed meeting Tony Franciosa, who I was a big fan of when I was younger.

Was he nice to you?

He was very nice. In fact, Tony Franciosa, Danny Aiello, Al Pacino and myself were talking and we were all having a really nice conversation about politics, so he [Franciosa] said: "By the way I haven't introduced myself. I'm Tony Franciosa" I hadn't seen him in twenty years and I'd only seen him on television, so I say: "Oh my God! You're Tony Franciosa." And he goes: "Am I that old-looking, really?" He was really sweet and I enjoyed my time with him.

How was Pacino?

In this particular setting it was a table read and a kind of meet and greet, and I think he was just trying to be a team player. He came out and was just very accessible and charming. I should say also that growing up –Al Pacino to me – he was the supreme actor. He was my idol. I wanted to be Al Pacino. The first play I ever did in college was *Does a Tiger Wear a Necktie?* Which was, I think, a play he won an Obie for [Pacino won a Tony Award for *Does a Tiger Wear a Necktie?*]. Although I didn't play his role, I was so excited to be in that play only because it was a play you could associate with Al Pacino. So I was so excited when we were sat at that table read and just chatting with this guy. It was something out of this world for me.

Looking for Richard

Cast: Al Pacino (Himself/Richard III), Kevin Spacey (Himself/Earl of Buckingham), Alec Baldwin (Himself/Duke of Clarence), Kevin Conway (Himself/Hastings), Winona Ryder (Herself/Lady Anne), Aidan Quinn (Himself/Richmond). **Director:** Al Pacino.

Synopsis: *Richard III*, Shakespeare's play about a deformed & devious man whose lust for power knows no bounds, is transferred to the screen in *Looking for Richard*, the directorial debut of Al Pacino. The camera follows cast and crew throughout rehearsals, eavesdropping on the behind-the-scenes process of creating characters and mounting a production.

The Actors Studio was the breeding ground for Pacino's obsession with Shakespeare's *Richard III* play. There, he performed the first half hour of the play at the tail end of the 1960s and this stoked his desire to showcase the play in public. His first public attempt at portraying Shakespeare's Machiavellian King was in December 1972 at the Loeb Drama Center, Cambridge, Massachusetts. The following month the production moved seventeen miles down the road to Boston's First Presbyterian Church on Franklin Street. In February it continued its unofficial Boston tour at the Church of the Covenant, Newbury Street. The *Boston Globe* called the portrayal: "a Richard of quick, relentless energy and bone-chilling power." It was a production that had Pacino physically punching walls and banging his head on a table because it was driving him crazy as he inhabited the character to a deeper level with each passing performance. This David Wheeler-directed production of *Richard III* closed in the first week of March 1973.

It was six years before Pacino donned the crown again. This time it was in New York, at the Off-Broadway Cort Theatre. Official opening date was 10 June 1979. There had already been 25 preview performances starting on 10 May. The majority of the cast struggled to get to grips with their characters. The critics gave the production a mauling. *New York Magazine* scathed: "What Pacino seems to be playing most of the time is Rumpelstiltskin, the mean, foot-stamping dwarf." *Variety* picked on Pacino's height declaring him "too small for his hump." *People Magazine* sarcastically remarked: "Attempting *Richard III* has made Al Pacino the toast of Broadway. Burnt toast, that is." This ill-fated *Richard III* production closed on 15 July. Pacino acknowledged that it wasn't his greatest work: "My performance was controversial. I learned from it. Let's say I'm certainly going to perform *Richard III* again."

That return would be fourteen years in the making. Pacino's continued quest to not only fully understand and appreciate Shakespeare's work, but also bring it to the masses sparked a film-making idea: "I had a real desire to do it. Because I wanted to impart some of the difficulty and mystery we have with Shakespeare." Having previously viewed Lawrence Olivier's 1955 movie and realising he could not better that version, Pacino had a vision of making a documentary. "I didn't want to do the entire play: I wanted to do a taste," he explained. Much like with making *The Local Stigmatic* previously, Pacino stumped up his own money in order to make *Looking for Richard*. There was no studio backing him "There's something liberating about that, because you don't have anyone to answer to."

Being such a high-profile actor and having many contacts in the right places, Pacino recruited all the real actors himself. Having missed out on working with Winona Ryder on *The Godfather Part III*, Pacino brought her in as Lady Anne. While on the set of *Glengarry Glen Ross*, Pacino talked Alec Baldwin and Kevin Spacey into appearing in his soon-to-be filmed Shakespeare movie as the Duke of Clarence and Earl of Buckingham respectively. Penelope Allen, a friend of Pacino's and one of the original performers during the doomed 1979 Off-Broadway production, was also brought on board as Queen Elizabeth. Lord Hastings was to be played by Kevin Conway, one of the few American actors who regularly appeared in Shakespeare plays. Considering how in demand actor Aidan Quinn was during the late 80s and early 90s, it was another classic coup by Pacino to have him sign on to play Richard's nemesis: Henry, Earl of Richmond. Each actor worked for scale rate (an average of $40 a day) and Spacey returned his weekly pay back into the production costs. When asked how he managed to cast so many big-name actors in the production, Pacino replied with a laugh that it was a case of "knowing the right people."

There was no official start date for principal photography as the majority of filming took place in-between Pacino's hectic 90s movie work. The voiceover narration and the to-camera pieces from Pacino create a sense of place for the majority of scenes. There was also a process of time-stamping when each segment was filmed. During his walk around New York with Frederic Kimball, Pacino has the beard and floppy hair, the style he was using during the filming of *Carlito's Way*. That footage was shot around 1992. The bearded Pacino plays up to the camera as he re-enacts the death of Richard on the steps of a New York City building. Continued exterior filming took place at The Cloisters museum, Upper Manhattan where Kimball and Pacino continue to stage scenes from the play. During one moment as Pacino is moving furniture he ushers out sightseers as he tells them: "we are filming a scene in here."

Additional outdoor filming in New York saw scenes filmed at the Cathedral of Saint John the Divine, in Central Park (mainly the Delacorte amphitheatre, which is used for staging plays by Shakespeare) and outside the Metropolitan Museum of Art, Manhattan where Pacino, walking towards the camera, ventures down the large paved steps re-enacting Richard's stumped walk and hanging arm.

The rehearsal scenes shot inside CHAL Productions office (a company formed by acting coach Charlie Laughton and Pacino) has Pacino sans-beard but with longer hair. This dates the footage to some time after completion of filming on *Carlito's Way* (1993) yet before *Heat* (1995) or *City Hall* (1996). Here he sits amongst the rest of the cast and crew as they read lines and tries to evaluate everything that has been said. In this segment, he also merrily walks around the streets of New York wearing backwards baseball cap that is inscribed with the logo from *Scent of a Woman* (a metaphorical nod to Richard's crown / Pacino's crowning glory).

During a walk and talk between Pacino and Kimball the actor/director stops to watch a horse-drawn carriage pass by which Kimball is blind to having continued walking without his conversational partner. During this same shooting period, as Pacino still has his floppy hair, the production hops the Atlantic Ocean over to London. A visit to the under-construction Globe Theatre on the Southbank is followed by a trip to Stratford-Upon-Avon, Shakespeare's birth place, and the actual chamber in which he was born. A moment of inspiration for Pacino and Kimball soon turns into an amusing escapade as the fire alarm is set off, ensuring a visit from the fire brigade. Making a quick escape, the director/actor and producer ruminate on the Bard's early life and his inspirations.

Back in London the crew filmed footage in the Victoria Tower Gardens and Pacino interviewed members of the general public on the streets of the capital, inviting them to discuss their relationship with Shakespeare's work.

All of these interviews and pilgrimages are juxtaposed with key scenes from *Richard III* and the final, climactic battle was filmed towards the end of Pacino's work on *Heat*. Director Michael Mann was struggling to decide how to complete *Heat* and loaned Pacino a small crew for one day in order to shoot the full dialogue and costumed ending. The lush green battlefield appears to have been filmed in England's green and pleasant lands but in fact was shot in the Simi Valley, California. That final footage concluded a project that was four years in the making, during which time Pacino had made three other films and starred in two different plays. In total, the filming of *Looking for Richard* had amassed over eighty hours of footage. Pacino remarked that it was the: "culmination of a personal journey."

Pacino's next challenge was that he had no idea how to formulate the mounds and mounds of footage he had accumulated into an actual movie. It was left to *Sea of Love*'s director Harold Becker to tell Pacino how to make it into a movie. "Make the film four acts" he suggested. Pacino liked that idea and set about editing his picture. With so much footage to tear through, it became too big of a job for the director/actor alone and consequently a team of editors were hired to knock it down to a respectable theatrical runtime. "I had wonderful help from the editors to construct the story I had in my head" Pacino commented upon release. The editors had to work from two different film stocks, as Pacino had used 16mm and Super 16mm during the filming as he could not decide on what look he wanted for the final movie.

Over eight different cuts of the movie were shown to family and friends throughout the editing period. Miramax chairman Harvey Weinstein was at one of those screenings and spoke to Pacino about snapping up the distribution rights. It was suggested that Miramax would market it as a Non-Fiction movie, which Pacino was not sure about. One other studio executive who had shown a keen interest was Tom Rothman, who was head of Fox Searchlight Pictures (a distribution company within the 20th Century Fox studios). Rothman had been friends with Pacino for over thirty years and had continued to unofficially oversee the project until he was officially announced as head of Fox Searchlight. Rothman stated: "It was the very best movie I had ever seen about the process of acting." Pacino opted to go with Rothman's Fox Searchlight as his distributor. The final cut of the docu-drama was locked in at one hundred and twelve minutes.

Looking For Richard received its world premiere at the 1996 Sundance Film Festival. The founder of the festival, Robert Redford, introduced Pacino to the theatre audience before the screening and congratulated him on making a film that was a risky project rather than just resting on his laurels. The film screened Out of Competition and was met with a buzz of critical praise. The *New York Times* felt it was: "sharp, funny and illuminating." *Variety* commented that *"Looking for Richard* is a master class in Shakespeare and acting conducted by an uncommonly passionate and delightful teacher." Pete Travers of *Rolling Stone* magazine enthused: "Pacino makes *Looking for Richard* a great adventure and outrageous fun." Roger Ebert was equally as pleased "a delightful inspiration," he called it. *Looking for Richard* was entered into the Un Certain Regard section of the 1996 Cannes Film Festival. Its first full country release came in Finland where it opened on 5 July. Elsewhere it continued its tour of film festivals. Playing at the Toronto International Film Festival on 8 September and the following month at the Chicago International Film

Festival. Its North American release came on 11 October 1996. Opening on only two screens during that first weekend, the film made a return of $33,843. After the limited opening week, Fox Searchlight did expand it further, eventually playing on 81 screens throughout the U.S. It closed with a return of $1,408,575 (Information courtesy of Box Office Mojo. Used with permission). Possibly not the greatest of returns, but the allure of a Pacino-directed film, albeit about Shakespeare, was still a draw to discerning U.S. theatre goers. Reward came at the 1996 Directors Guild Awards where the trophy for Outstanding Achievement in Documentary was presented to Pacino for his directorial debut.

Pacino has made a "two for the price of one" with *Looking for Richard*. Through the film, he expresses concern about Shakespeare's work effectively alienating most in the modern era, and he is proven correct. The ingenious idea to show the inner workings of the text through modern means is a brilliant one. The staged and costumed scenes, while interesting and beautifully shot, can drag on for too long if you are a viewer who is less-interested in Shakespeare. The greatest sight throughout the movie is Pacino, in full Richard III regalia, limping down a grass covered hill while reciting the most famous lines from the play before eventually being shot by two arrows. He is then brutally pierced by a sword. Spoiler alert. This docu-drama seems to have been immense fun for everyone involved, and this fact shines through the footage.

The camera is never far away from Pacino, understandable given that he is the star and the director. Occasionally he mugs up to the camera, other times he playfully jokes around with the cast and crew. When in London's Globe Theatre (the spiritual home of Shakespeare's plays) Pacino delivers lines of dialogue while throwing himself on the floor like a kid caught in a tantrum, however this is not him getting in touch with his inner diva, but rather an actor who just can't help himself when it comes to method acting. In moments like these, we see how much fun this type of project is to an actor like Pacino. As the rest of the cast sit around for a table read they all laugh and joke in-between reading lines. It's clear there is an instant rapport between all of them, especially Conway, Spacey and Allen, who are all seen to be engaging deeply with Pacino. Friend, and fountain of Shakespeare knowledge, Kimball is a non-stop ball of energy around his director. Constantly goading him on and trying to find ways to explain the inner workings of *Richard III*. A couple of times he oversteps the mark and receives a deadpan, slightly sarcastic rebuttal from his friend. There is a clearly a mutual love between them for the work and it does, at times, become a little bit too much to bear. But maybe this level of passion is what is required when trying to extend a work of Shakespeare to the masses. Even a worldwide acting superstar like Pacino struggles throughout the documentary. At one point he delivers the classic line of "A horse, a horse! My kingdom for a horse!" to a room full of bemused teenagers. He asks them if anyone knows what it means. No one answers. The footage quickly cuts to the back of the room where a couple are heavily kissing oblivious to anything around them. One of the great actors of our time discussing Shakespeare is clearly not enough for some to cease with their teenage tongue action. Admittedly, there are times when the docu-drama does go too deep for mainstream appeal, especially the discussions and dissections on the iambic pentameter. Coupled with the slight dragging of the cast re-created scenes, this leaves the viewer in the precise mindset that Pacino is trying to avoid: bored with Shakespeare.

All actors have their passion projects and *Looking for Richard* is Pacino's. Yet it extends beyond a self-serving example of docu-drama and becomes an educational text about one of Shakespeare's most performed plays. If this type of work became the "way in" to understanding and appreciating the Bard then there would be many, many more people lauding his work. *Looking for Richard* is regularly screened in high schools and colleges nowadays, with many accompanying educational resources available to those studying it, and in turn *Richard III*. Praise has to go to Pacino for creating an alternate way to digest Shakespeare's work, essentially breaking it down and fusing together elements of education and entertainment.

Co-star Kevin Conway on *Looking for Richard*

How did you become involved in this project? Was it a normal audition process or were you contacted directly by Pacino?

I was contacted directly by him. We are roughly the same age and this was back in the early seventies he was doing *The Indian Wants The Bronx* as a play in New York and I think I was doing *Cuckoo's Nest* and we just met around the scene. So we've known each other for quite a while. He invited me...he made an early film, the name escapes me, it was a short film by a British playwright and he made a movie out of it [*The Local Stigmatic*]. He invited me to see that and I was very impressed with his directing of it. I direct here and there but I prefer to be an actor rather than a director and when *Looking for Richard* came up it started out as a table reading. As you can see in the movie, discussing the play and discussing Shakespeare kind of stuff. The opportunities to do Shakespeare are limited here for American actors. But he asked me to get involved and that's how I wound up doing it. It stretched out over time because it wasn't a job of any kind, it was just reading through scripts. I would say it was a year and a half in the making – maybe more. Some of us would go away, do jobs and come back. So that's how I wound up in it. It was such a great idea to take Shakespeare and break it down the way he did – to discuss it and then do it for real – and I just thought it's a wonderful tool for theatre departments all over the country to show a film like that. I wish he had done a couple more.

It's a very unique way of showcasing Shakespeare's work. There are scenes from the actual play and then afterwards you are talking about what you have just done, all while being filmed. As an actor how do you approach that type of set up?

I kind of loved it because you get a chance to sit around with people, your peers, and discuss it and you learn a lot. It was a stellar group of people he put together. It was kind of stimulating even sitting around the table for a couple of hours just talking about it. Then a month or two would go by and I'd get a call from him and he'd say: "We are going up to The Cloisters." We would shoot actual scenes up there. A couple of more months would go by and we would do another piece somewhere else, the St John the Devine Church for example. So it was kind of fun to do because it wasn't a 'job job' it was something we had a passion to do.

How many times were you called back?

Probably half a dozen times.

So how long do you think you spent working on the project in real-time?

Between the discussions and the actual shooting of certain scenes, and even shooting rehearsals, I would think it would be about a couple of weeks. A lot of it was made up. Pacino would get an idea and we would shoot something else and he was very much in control of it. He had a pre-screening, before Fox picked it up, where it was a longer version and he elicited a little commentary from me and some other people about whether it was too long. We discussed it and he went ahead and cut it down to the film that you saw.

How much longer was it?

I think about another twenty minutes. I don't remember exactly what it was. Some of it was just more verbiage. I think most of the scenes that he actually shot are still in the film. But when you got actors like Spacey and Alec Baldwin and people like that...and me, we work a lot so it was always a time thing – have you got a day? Or an afternoon to come up and shoot this, that or the other thing. If you look at the film you'll see our appearances are slightly different. The hair's a little bit longer, shorter, beards, no beards and it's because we were doing other things and so we had to adapt to what we were doing. But it didn't matter in the way the film was put together, the street people walking on the street, going to England, going to the old Globe – I thought that was terrific. Also to have terrific British actors weighing in on the play and the meaning of it and the importance of it, I think it was a great idea. I have to say a word about him [Pacino]; I don't have to tell anyone what a really consummate and fabulous actor he is. I think sometimes he didn't know how good he was. But he is a very good director. He knows what he wants and he knows how to convey that too.

Was there a difference between Pacino the actor and Pacino the director?

Yes, I would say so. He was more interesting in the directing than in his own performance, although he did very well with that, it was a thing of passion for him. An idea that he had and an idea to kind of spread around his love of Shakespeare to get it out there because he has done Richard a couple of times and he really has that passion for Shakespeare. He imbued that. I think the thing on the set that I got the most was that everybody got passionate about doing it and I think it showed in the movie. I was very proud to be in that movie.

In the film you play Lord Hastings, who is central to the play, were you happy with the way that Pacino directed you and your character?

I would say I was. From my reading of it, that was pretty much what I wanted to get across and the betrayal and someone with the sense of entitlement that he was untouchable in a way. When you are dealing with Richard nobody is untouchable. In the short, individual scenes we tried to have a camaraderie with Richard and yet with the feeling that I was still smarter than he was somehow or more entrenched in the political system. I was reasonably happy; I'm never 100% happy with my work.

There are some great actors in the movie. Besides Pacino, who else did you enjoy working with?

Most of it was with Al. I've known Kevin Spacey for a while and Alec Baldwin I know quite well. I've worked with Alec a couple of times in movies including one that Alec was the producer. There were a whole bunch of others that I had known from being around Pacino, like Penny Allen and people that were close friends of his. I certainly knew most of them. So it was fun to work with people like that. We all knew each other and it was kind of a tight group in terms of if we were actually good friends then we all at least knew each other, respected each other's work.

It's a very unique way of putting Shakespeare's work on the big screen. Do you think it works?

Yeah I do and I would really love to see more of this kind of taking it and showing scenes of some length so you can see what it would look like as a dramatic piece. But just intellectually as a tool in high school and colleges, I think the same dissection of the play and dramatisation would work with Hamlet and with Lear and certainly in The Scottish play [Macbeth]. I'd love to see that. If anybody asked me to do it I would love to be involved.

Donnie Brasco

Cast: Al Pacino (Benjamin "Lefty" Ruggiero), Johnny Depp (Joseph Pistone/Donnie Brasco), Michael Madsen (Dominick "Sonny Black" Napolitano), Bruno Kirby (Nicky Santora), Anne Heche (Maggie Pistone), James Russo ("Paulie" Cersani), Zeljko Ivanek (Tim Curley). **Director:** Mike Newell.

Synopsis: FBI undercover agent Donnie Brasco infiltrates a New York City mob family. Donnie becomes friends with an ageing hit-man Lefty Ruggiero, who trusts Donnie and vouches for him to the mob. As Donnie goes deeper into the mob he realises that he is not only crossing the line between federal agent and criminal but is also leading his friend Lefty to an almost certain death sentence.

The 1997 film *Donnie Brasco* was Pacino's sixth crime picture of that decade. The previous five being: *The Local Stigmatic* (even though it wasn't released at that time), *Dick Tracy*, *The Godfather Part III*, *Carlito's Way* and *Heat*. There could be an argument to include *City Hall* in that list too as that project also features strong crime elements.

Though Pacino had a lot of experience starring in crime films, not just in the nineties but in earlier decades, this time was different. Pacino saw something in the story and his character that resonated more deeply with him: "I think there are things in this guy's struggle that, hopefully, people who are civilians outside of the underworld will relate to. There's aspects of this human being, that when we pay attention to it, are in ourselves." It's an interesting quote as a few years prior Pacino had passed over making *Donnie Brasco*. By '97 he appreciated that the story was "a little bit more in the distance. The fact that it was in 1979, I sort of appreciated that aspect. That made it a little more interesting for me and that's why I did it."

FBI Agent Joseph D. Pistone's autobiography *Donnie Brasco: My Undercover Life in the Mafia* was released in 1988. He had collaborated with writer Richard Woodley and casting director/film producer Louis DiGiaimo in order to complete the book. DiGiaimo had been a casting director since 1972, working on films such as: *The Godfather*, *The Exorcist* and *Cruising*. The first time he became a producer was for *Donnie Brasco* and he commented: "It took me five years to get *Donnie Brasco* together. I first found the book and then a screenwriter to adapt it. Barry Levinson and Mark Johnson helped me develop it." DiGiaimo had worked as a casting director for Levinson on *Rain Man*, *Good Morning Vietnam* and the TV show *Homicide: Life on the Streets*.

After pitching Pistone's book to Levinson, who snapped it up for his production company Baltimore Pictures, DiGiaimo set about finding his lead actor and director. Levinson would have made the film but was stuck in Los Angeles due to domestic reasons. So DiGiaimo met with British director Stephen Frears in Los Angeles. In that meeting he offered a worldwide megastar to play Brasco and another big, yet younger, movie star to play Lefty. Frears felt that the actor who wanted to play Donnie would be better suited as Lefty. He explains: "I said....he would be great as Lefty, and that all he had to do was sit around, make jokes and break people's hearts – what more did he want?" A mighty tug-o-war between several agents began over the roles and attempts to beef up their own client's parts in the script. After a month of darting between the actors and agents interested in making the movie, and trying to appease all of their demands, Frears dropped out: "I have told the producers to go ahead and cast the film. If the combination makes sense to me, I'll direct it."

Around the time DiGiaimo was trying to get *Donnie Brasco* off the ground, a glut of realistic gangster movies were released including: *The Godfather Part III*, *Goodfellas* and *Bugsy*. Sensing that this would be seen as a cash-in, DiGiaimo and Levinson postponed production for a couple of years. During February 1995, *Variety* reported that *Donnie Brasco* was likely to go into production with Al Pacino and John Travolta playing the roles of Brasco and Lefty respectively. The article also stated the director was yet to be confirmed and announced. In the following October, *The*

Hollywood Reporter announced that a deal had been struck between TriStar Pictures and Mandalay Entertainment to produce, finance and distribute *Donnie Brasco*, a film starring Al Pacino and Johnny Depp. When Pacino insisted on playing the mobster "Lefty" Ruggiero instead of accepting the part of Brasco, he recommended Depp for the role of undercover FBI agent Joseph Pistone.

At the time, the producers were looking at actors such as Tom Cruise, John Cusack and Nicolas Cage. They were unsure about casting Depp as he was known for his less mature roles in films like *Cry-Baby*, *Edward Scissorhands* and *Benny & Joon*. Screenwriter Paul Attanasio suggested that Depp's arrest for trashing a hotel room in 1994 is ultimately what won him the role. After this incident, he was seen as "dark and dangerous."

Around the same time Depp was getting arrested, English director Mike Newell was travelling around the world on a press junket for his smash-hit British rom-com *Four Weddings and a Funeral*. Levinson and DiGiaimo approached Newell about helming their mobster movie. Eager to break into making big-budget Hollywood movies, Newell agreed to direct. "I really wanted to do something tough, about men," Newell commented. The script had been through multiple incarnations at the hand of Attanasio, however Newell felt the first version was the one he could best work with. Having never been involved with crime movies or in the company of gangsters before, Newell spent time in Brooklyn social clubs talking and drinking with real-life mobsters. In one of the clubs the jukebox was filled solely with Sinatra records. There was also a handwritten note warning patrons the payphone was bugged. Newell explained: "They didn't trust me. I talked funny. I looked funny."

DiGiaimo, Levinson and Newell rounded out the immediate cast with Michael Madsen as "made man" and boss, Dominick 'Sonny Black' Napolitano. Bruno Kirby and James Russo were cast as mob soldiers Nicky Santora and Paulie Cersani respectively. The real-life Joe Pistone was hired as a consultant on the film, helping Depp get into character several months before filming began.

TriStar Pictures, Mandalay Entertainment and Baltimore Pictures set a budget of $35 million. Principal photography began in the autumn of 1996. The majority of the movie was filmed in Manhattan. Locations included Mare Chiaro restaurant (also known as the Mulberry Street Bar), Katz Delicatessen (previously used in *When Harry Met Sally* for the infamous "orgasm" scene), Kenmare Street and the Queensboro Bridge. The narrow thoroughfare of Mott Street, that runs north to south through Manhattan, was fully closed to traffic and pedestrians for several days. The Brooklyn Docks were used for several scenes and is also the place where Depp and Pacino broke the ice with each other. Depp recalls: "He was sitting there, just staring out. I was standing there smoking a cigarette and I couldn't take it anymore, so I said "Here's the funny thing, Al. The one thing that I never could have expected or imagined is that you're certifiably insane." I felt good for saying it. He gave probably one of the most perfect, comedic responses. He just looks at me and he went: "Oh, yeah! Oh, yeah! Oh, yeah! You didn't know that?" I said: "No I didn't actually." And then, with the most perfect execution timing he went "You know something? You're pretty fucking strange yourself."

Filming moved down to Broward County, Florida to make use of the Convention Centre which would double as an airport entrance. Some of the "Miami" scenes were also shot at this location. During downtime in Florida, Madsen took his girlfriend DeAnna to Jamaica and married her. Madsen explained: "She had a gold bikini on, I had my *Donnie Brasco* wardrobe. It wasn't planned at all, I had no idea." Further Florida filming locations included an abandoned steakhouse doubling as the mobsters' hangout: The King's Court Lounge. The production returned to New York to shoot the final scenes. This is when Anne Heche at last joined the cast. Her scenes with Depp, playing Pistone's wife Maggie, were filmed last. By the time filming commenced, Depp was exhausted. Fortunately this worked in favour of the movie because Maggie constantly has to confront a weary Joe about his undercover work taking him away from his family.

On the evening of 24 February 1997, a shaven-headed Depp arrived at the *Donnie Brasco* premiere with his supermodel girlfriend Kate Moss.

Depp, Pacino, Heche and Madsen all posed for paparazzi photos and signed autographs for the fans waiting behind the barriers at the Cineplex in Century City, California. The film opened in U.S. theatres four days later. On its first weekend it raked in $11 million. At the end of its first full theatrical week it had made over $15 million, claiming the number two spot on the U.S. Box Office chart. It was beaten to the top spot by the special updated edition of *The Empire Strikes Back*. The film finished its U.S. theatrical run with over $41 million in box office takings but actually fared much better internationally where it received returns of $83 million (Information courtesy of Box Office Mojo. Used with permission). It was also a hit with critics, as *The New York Times* proclaimed it: "The best crime movie in a long while." *Rolling Stone* magazine commented: "the movie blends the intensity of a docudrama with the intimacy of a character study." Roger Ebert described the story as: "two men who grow to love each other, within the framework of a teach-student relationship. It's not about sex. It's about need."

Critics weren't the only ones who had something to say about the movie. The Bonanno crime family member John "Boobie" Cerasani filed a libel suit against TriStar Pictures. He'd had real-life dealings with Joe Pistone aka Donnie Brasco but was acquitted of racketeering charges from the Brasco investigation and claimed the movie defamed him. His case was thrown out of court with Manhattan Federal Judge Denny Chin calling it "nonsense" then going on to list all the crimes Cerasani had been convicted for during a ten year period. Actor Zeljko Ivanek, who played FBI agent Tim Curley, was reminded of his time on *Donnie Brasco* a decade later when he was filming a new movie: "I was given a wardrobe – some suit – and I put my hand in my pocket and pulled out a notecard I'd used in *Donnie Brasco*. I was wearing the same suit some ten years earlier, and the notecard – which was a prop – was still in the pocket after having been sitting in some costume shop for all that time."

Pacino conveys an incredible amount through Lefty's eye contact. When in the presence of Depp, for the majority of the film, Pacino never directly lays his eyes on him. Not until Lefty can fully trust Brasco. His eyes are focussed slightly off to one side, as if to say: "I'm still sizing you up". Yet when Lefty meets with Sonny Black he is constantly eyeballing him. This is a sign of respect; Lefty respects Black and feels he can make direct eye contact. Pacino perfectly captures the character of Lefty through this fluctuation in his eye contact. He's never going to fully let his guard down unless the person in question has done right by him time and again.

Pacino also plays with the New York accent that Lefty has by dropping hard thudding consonants. His F's and R's are deep and low, almost consumed by the expelling of air before he even gets to the peak of the letter. At times it's difficult to follow as the accent is so thick and deep, you do have to really concentrate on Lefty's dialogue. Pacino, a native New Yorker, changes his own accent enough to make it feel as if he has studied an entirely new phonetic language for this role. Newell had to reign in Pacino sometimes: "If I didn't yell cut, Al would walk on as Lefty until he fell off the edge of the world."

However, let's not forget that Depp is equally fantastic in the movie. Any fears of him using the quirky man-child acting style of previous films are long forgotten when he utters: "It's a fugazi." It's an astute performance as we see him, as a character and an actor, grow throughout the film. We see the loving and sweet side of Pistone when with his family; the light side of his persona. This is in deep contrast to the way in which Depp's face darkly contorts when he turns into a nasty, deceitful, and aggressive wanna-be mobster. It's a dual personality role that Depp conveys with ease. Bouncing off Pacino, Depp is given the opportunity to spread his acting wings and share leading status with Pacino. The entire movie hinges on the relationship between the two lead characters. The viewer cares about both of them equally, regardless of who is deemed good or bad. Even Joe Pistone was impressed with how close Newell's movie was to the real thing: "It portrayed the mob the way it is."

Newell's quiet and unassuming movie shows that you don't need endless gun battles, explosions and filthy language to make a crime film that is a near masterpiece.

Co-star James Russo on *Donnie Brasco*

***Donnie Brasco* is based on real events and real people. Did you meet any of the people it was based on?**

There were a lot of them hanging around and it was almost as if they were like ghosts. They came and went and left into the night. They were definitely hovering around the film set. We were filming right in the ground zero, right where the story took place.

When you were reading the script, where did you see Paulie's role within the group?

Here's an interesting point, the character that I'd played was originally called Boobie and he was still alive. Half way through filming...or maybe after filming...he had a lawsuit or a pending lawsuit against TriStar. So they changed the name of Boobie to Paulie. So if you watch the film carefully it was ADR'ed [Automated Dialog Replacement]. Which to my dislike they also cut out a lot of scenes of mine because of that.

Could Paulie have ever been a Made man?

No. I don't think so.

What was stopping him?

I don't think he had the capability to do it. I think he was just a hired hand for the most part.

You share many scenes with Pacino, what was he like to work with?

I have to tell you, honestly... I never had so much fun on a movie. Al, Johnny, Bruno, Madsen... we would just laugh all the time. So there was a lot of laughing and joking around and then all of a sudden when action was called it seemed we just snapped out of it. I think that helped. We had a two week period of reading that script every day. So prior to filming we sat down at a table and went over that script from beginning to end every day and whatever changes were needed. We sat in that room with Mike Newell and the writer and the actors and we went from beginning to end for almost two weeks. During that course we would go to various restaurants and places where they [mobsters] hung out – social clubs, restaurants in Queens, restaurants in Manhattan. So for two weeks it was like a history lesson on that atmosphere.

What was it like when you were on set with them?

Very friendly. Very connected. There was no star shit. Al was very accessible to everyone and I think that's why the movie looks the way it does...because of that. It wasn't like you started work on Wednesday and you met the actor and you didn't talk to him till you worked with him on Friday. No, we hung out... we laughed. All I remember was there was a lot of laughter. Actually at some point it agitated Newell because we were fooling around so much.

What were you doing to annoy him?

Just jokes... and laughing. It's hard to remember. I just remember it was fun. Usually, I like to stay by myself and come out when I have to and then leave. I developed a good friendship with Johnny. I still see Al now and then. Bruno died. I don't see Madsen much.

Al is known for being a method actor. Did he stay in character after cameras had stopped rolling?

It didn't seem that way. The most amazing thing was I had read the book and the way Al was playing Lefty it wasn't [the impression] I had of Lefty. So, watching him... Al didn't go off in a corner, torture himself before a scene... he was right there. Hanging out with you, talking...and then all of a sudden: "Action!" and it almost seemed effortless. I really didn't understand what he was doing with the hat and the schlepping along. I just didn't get it. I didn't get it. What the hell is he doing? And then watching the dailies and finally seeing the movie...Wow! That was the most amazing thing because connecting with him and having this friendly relationship and having fun and laughing... I didn't see what was actually going on. That's the magic of Pacino. A lot of directors I talk to don't see it or they see a bit of it and then they see it on-screen and it's like: Wow! It's one of his better performances.

It's an understated performance.

Maybe that's why I didn't see it. Maybe I was expecting *Scarface*. It wasn't that. It was almost buffoon-ish in a subtle way with the hat and trying to break open the parking meter.

You've worked with Johnny Depp on a couple of other crime movies since. Do you think *Donnie Brasco* is his best work in that genre?

It's hard to say. I look at actors' careers as one big painting. They are all connecting. A body of work, to me, is like a large canvas.

When you were on set and everyone was in character, who did you find the most terrifying?

Myself [*laughs*]. I really didn't have much to do in that movie. Here is an interesting fact: I was interested in the Madsen role [Sonny], I didn't want... I thought the Boobie role was too small. So, when I went in and met with Louis DiGiaimo [Producer] and Mike Newell, I thought they were going to look at me for the Madsen role and I left and Louis calls me and says: "I've got some good news and some bad news." I go: "What's the bad news?" He says: "You're not going to get the Sonny role. But they want you to play Boobie." And I said "Boobie??? It's a nothing role. He's sitting in the back of the car for the most part."

But the money was crazy and I was promised that the role would be fleshed out and broadened, and it was. However, a lot of the stuff was taken out later on. Then about four weeks afterwards... or maybe longer, I can't remember... Louis called me and said "Look Russo, we got a problem. I don't know if it's going to work out with Madsen. Mike

Newell is coming out to California. Can you sit with him? He wants you to read" It's not like it's an Elizabethan drama and he needs to hear my English accent. I read the entire script in the Sonny role in his hotel room...just me and him. So there was a point where I almost got that role.

My portrayal would have been very different. I think Michael played it very cool. Mine would have been far more maniacal and that was a problem for me in the film. That fear factor wasn't there. But people come up to me and they say they love that scene in the back of the car when we kill the guys in the basement. We shot that at three o'clock in the morning and originally the dialogue was: "I'm on to you and know what you are up to and I don't trust you." I had all this dialogue and I felt that by saying that dialogue it gave things away...it was too... it killed the suspense of that moment. So I didn't want to say anything and I remember getting into a big argument with Newell. He said: "You gotta say something." I said: "No, I don't," and he goes: "You just going to sit there and not say anything?" I say: "Yeah" and he goes: "You can't do that." I say: "Well that's what I want to do." I remember Johnny backing me with "That sounds right," and Newell, just exhausted, walked away. We shot that scene and a days later he [Newell] came up to me and said: "You're absolutely right about that moment." Which I felt was terrifying being sat in the car and not saying a word. A lot of people love that scene.

I'd describe *Donnie Brasco* as a family movie. As in you five guys are a family, not so much a mobster family but just a family looking out for each other.

Yeah. To me, Brian De Palma or Scorsese or Abel Ferrara or someone like that, someone who knew that environment, I think should have directed. I think the fact that he was British [Newell], it was [a] different take on it. It was an outside look on that environment. I think it shows in the movie. One thing I hate about the movie is that horrible montage when we are in Florida. It's like a different movie. But the performances in it... I think Al and Johnny are the best things in the movie... and their relationship. That's the core of the movie – the relationship between Al and Johnny.

Former NYPD Detective turned writer/actor Randy Jurgensen on *Donnie Brasco*

You had previously worked with Pacino on *The Godfather* and *Cruising*. What was he like to work with many years later on *Donnie Brasco*?

By the time we got to *Donnie Brasco*, it seemed to me that our careers were paralleling each other [*laughs*]. Guess who I took to see the real mob people? I took Al Pacino. It took me days to set that up and to make sure there was going to be safety and it was secure.

I told Joe Pistone, you know... Donnie Brasco, who in real life is the Godfather to my daughter. Joe Pistone and I have forty years... when he was an FBI agent I worked for him etcetera, etcetera. So by the time I took Al Pacino... I knew exactly what Al wanted. I knew what he wanted to see. Everybody that was involved was very, very respectful. Then after, I took Al Pacino then the director wanted to go.

I took the director and said: "This is the last time. I'm not taking anybody else." I did absolutely nothing in *The Godfather* except I was the machine gunner that killed James Caan at the tollbooth. When I met Al Pacino on *The Godfather* he was coming off of a picture called *The Panic in Needle Park*, and boy that portrayal... that was it. I am an admirer of Al Pacino in a different way than a fan. I'm an admirer of Al Pacino as to how deep... how deep that he goes into the work that he is going to portray on-screen.

Devil's Advocate

Cast: Keanu Reeves (Kevin Lomax), Al Pacino (John Milton), Charlize Theron (Mary Ann Lomax), Jeffrey Jones (Eddie Barzoon), Judith Ivey (Mrs Alice Lomax), Connie Nielsen (Christabella Andreoli), Craig T. Nelson (Alexander Cullen), Debra Monk (Pam Garrety), Pamela Gray (Mrs Diana Barzoon). **Director:** Taylor Hackford

Synopsis: Hotshot attorney Kevin Lomax has never lost a case. A tempting offer is received from an elite New York firm run by the charismatic John Milton. But when Lomax accepts the job he soon discovers the firm and its employees are not all what they seem.

The Devil's first, official on-screen appearance was in the 1914 Danish movie *Den mystiske Fremmede* (*A Deal with the Devil*). In that picture, the Prince of Darkness went by the name of Mefisto. When thinking about the best interpretations of that character, the mind normally wanders to such works as Robert De Niro in *Angel Heart*, Harvey Stephens in *The Omen* and Tim Curry in *Legend*. Memorable female representations have included Rosalinda Celentano in *The Passion of the Christ*, Jennifer Love Hewitt in *Shortcut to Happiness* and Elizabeth Hurley in the *Bedazzled* remake. There have been versions of Lucifer that subvert the traditional characterizations including Harvey Keitel in *Little Nicky*, Ned Flanders in *The Simpsons'* Halloween episodes of Treehouse of Horror and the openly gay Satan from the *South Park* cartoon TV show and movie. With all of these many versions of Satan, how does an actor make their own portrayal stand out above all others? This was the question Al Pacino faced when he decided to take on the role for the movie *Devil's Advocate*.

The film was adapted from the book of the same name by novelist Andrew Neiderman. Neiderman had had previous books adapted, including the horror movie *Pin* and the thriller *Playmates* (renamed *The Maddening* for the film). Before becoming a novelist Neiderman taught film studies at a high school. Here he learnt the importance of writing with a visual style: "My books lend themselves to other medium[s]." Released in 1990, Neiderman's novel *The Devil's Advocate* sold around 180,000 copies and was immediately snapped up for film rights by Warner Bros. Even though Neiderman had taught screenplay writing, the author didn't take up the option to write the screenplay for his own material.

Warner Bros thus farmed it out to screenwriter Jonathan Lemkin. Known primarily for his work on *Hill Street Blues* and *21 Jump Street*, this was the second book-to-screen adaptation Lemkin worked on. He had previously worked on the flop buddy cop-actioner *Showdown in Little Tokyo* without being given official credit. Lemkin's screenplay found its way to Pacino very early. He turned it down and later commented: "It was more of a special effects movie with a monster in it and satirical overtones. It really didn't have an idea in its head." The Lemkin script was continually kicked around Hollywood and at one point was offered to Keanu Reeves, who also turned it down. He was already signed up to a barrage of films (Reeves made nine films in three years during the mid-90s).

Eventually the script came to the attention of Taylor Hackford who is chiefly known for directing *An Officer and a Gentleman*. Hackford was initially drawn to the good versus evil element of the script: "I liked the premise Jonathan set up and the events in the story, but there were certain aspects of it that I wanted to develop even further." The director had just finished work on an adaptation of Stephen King's novel *Dolores Claiborne*, during which he worked on the screenplay with novice screenwriter Tony Gilroy and enjoyed it. The pair discussed working together on *Devil's Advocate*. Discussing how they might expand the idea of evil in a modern-day environment. Hackford commented: "The people in this story who get into trouble are people who have made certain choices. Tony and I don't believe in blaming the Devil for these terrible events." Gilroy and Hackford re-wrote Lemkin's screenplay from page one turning it into a righteous satire that made Lucifer "a Nietzschean Devil". Soon after, a budget of $57 million was agreed by Warner Bros Studios.

With a new and improved script completed, Hackford went to Pacino and explained this was a completely revamped screenplay that included "more Faustian, more humour, more temptation." There was continued hesitation on the part of Pacino as he had seen the other actors who had played the Devil, such as Jack Nicholson in *The Witches of Eastwick* and Robert De Niro in *Angel Heart*, and felt those portrayals were better than what he could create. Ultimately however, Pacino realised that the best devilish portrayals continued to be accepted as marvellous works of acting and signed on to play the role of John Milton/Satan. "The Devil is a wide-open part. Who can turn it down when someone offers you that kind of a classic character?" He mused.

Hailing from the Actors Studio and being a method actor meant that Pacino couldn't just play the character, he had to find it first. This meant reading books like *Paradise Lost* and *Dante's Inferno* and watching classic on-screen portrayals of the Devil in films such as *The Witches of Eastwick*, *Angel Heart* and *Angel on My Shoulder*. "But the one that gave me wings was Walter Huston's performance in *The Devil and Daniel Webster*. He was brilliant. He didn't have to do anything, yet you felt his power," Pacino commented to his biographer.

As Hackford's lead actor immersed himself in finding his inner Devil, the search for his co-stars had begun and was quite straightforward. Having previously passed on the project, Keanu Reeves was impressed with the new version and signed on for the other central character: a lawyer called Kevin Lomax. "I was attracted to it because it was artistic and the script writing was different – it was storytelling." Following the blockbuster hit *Speed*, Reeves was hot property in Hollywood. He was paid $10 million for *Speed* but took a pay cut of $2 million to star in the *Devil's Advocate*.

The other main character to be cast was Kevin's wife, Mary Ann Lomax. Hackford auditioned a large group of already established actresses for the part. One of those who read lines was newcomer Charlize Theron, who had just received rave reviews for her performance in the comedy crime thriller: *2 Days in the Valley*. She tested four times for the role of Mary Ann and Hackford really liked her but was worried about one aspect: "She is so beautiful, I was afraid audiences wouldn't be able to empathize with her. In the end, Charlize's talent and perceptiveness convinced me that she was the right woman for the role." Secondary cast members included Craig T. Nelson as Alexander Cullen, Jeffrey Jones as Eddie Barzoon, Connie Nielsen as Christabella Andreoli, Ruben Santiago-Hudson as Leamon Heath and Judith Ivey as Alice Lomax, Kevin's mother.

Principal photography began on 28 October 1996 and much of the production was centred in and around New York City. Two working courtrooms were used for interior and exterior shots. They were the Surrogate Court Building and Foley Square Jury Court, both in Manhattan. Further filming in the Manhattan district took place in Chambers Street subway station entrance, numerous streets around Chinatown including Mott and Baxter, Central Park West, Madison Avenue and Park Avenue. The top two floors of the Continental Club were transformed into Milton, Chadwick and Waters law offices. While the rooftop of the Continental Plaza was reconstructed to become the rooftop garden for Milton's office, only the walkways existed which Pacino and Reeves had to navigate in blustery February winds, fifty storys up. The infinity water pools were to be added in post-production.

5th Avenue at 94th Street, one of Manhattan's most prestigious addresses, was also used as a location. So too was Donald Trump's gold interior apartment in Trump Tower, 5th Avenue. East 57th Street between 2nd and Park Avenue was closed to through traffic early one morning for a single shot which saw Reeves' Lomax walking down the empty street with no motor vehicles or pedestrians in sight. Exteriors of the Central Presbyterian Church on Park Avenue and 64th Street were used; however the interior shots were filmed at the Most Holy Redeemer Church on 173 East 3rd Street. The interior of the Church of the Heavenly Rest on 5th Avenue also featured in the picture.

Reeves developed a loud buzzing in his ear the night before the filming of the first meeting between Lomax and Milton. Reeves struggled with his lines that day and it resulted in an ear-bashing from Pacino. From then on the two actors worked in harmony together. "We work in totally different ways but our relationship was, for me anyway, fantastic. I had some of the best times of my life with him." Reeves commented upon completion of filming.

Keanu Reeves and Charlize Theron also had an excellent working relationship which made some of the more challenging aspects of the script easier to handle. A highly passionate and aggressive love-making scene in the movie was scheduled to be shot early on. It was only Theron's second sex scene and her first for a major studio blockbuster so she was, understandably, nervous. Reeves soon soothed her worries: "At one point he was standing there completely naked and joked 'This is what I do for a living. I'm just gonna call my mum right now and tell her how my day went.' Keanu was wonderful."

With filming complete in New York, the production moved south to Gainesville, Florida to capture establishing shots of Lomax's hometown. The Swamp, known locally as the flagship restaurant of Gainesville, was used for a bar scene. The Tower Road Baptist Church located on the west side of the town also featured. Mark Berman of *Gainesville.com* comments that when "Lomax yells out "I'm not going back to Gainesville!" according to my brother (who saw the film upon its release in 1997 in a Gainesville Theater), the audience burst into applause at the line."

Production finished up on a sound stage in Los Angeles, which had been built especially for the scenes inside Milton's penthouse apartment. Production designer Bruno Rubeo had been working on the set for months and had a clear idea about how he wanted it to look. "We wanted Milton's apartment to be very loose and very sexy. This particular set was designed in order to fully capture the mystery of John Milton."

Principal photography concluded on 12 February 1997. During post-production, visual effects specialists Richard Greenberg and Stephanie Powell worked on the digital side of the special effects, creating quick glimpses of devilish transformation. Hackford wanted to take an original approach to depicting evil: "Things appear and disappear in a moment sometimes they seem real and sometimes they seem like a bad dream" the director commented. The climax of the movie saw Milton regress in age and then turn into Lomax. To accomplish this, Reeves had a mask made of his face by Oscar-winning makeup effects specialist Rick Baker. A young Pacino mask, made while filming *The Godfather*, was obtained from Dick Smith the special make-up effects artist. Hackford then helped Baker to make the transformation by using "all three to transform Al from a mature face to a youthful face to a blend of his own and Keanu's youthful face, and finally into an angel, which is, of course, what Lucifer was before he was cast out of Heaven."

Devil's Advocate had its U.S. and Canadian theatrical release on 17 October 1997. Four days prior to general release, it received its premiere at the Mann Village Theatre in Westwood, California. Critical reviews were middling at best. *Entertainment Weekly* called it: "a shlock-religioso legal thriller and it's at once silly, overwrought, and almost embarrassingly entertaining." *The Washington Post* commented: "If *Devil's Advocate* won't save any souls, its great entertainment on the road to hell." Roger Ebert was visually impressed but not thoroughly entertained: "If the whole film were as good as its production design, we'd really have something here." *Christian Spotlight* were highly scathing: "*Devil's Advocate* is very offensive. This movie, by any measuring stick, deserves the lowest possible rating for Christian content."

The indifferent reviews were not enough to put filmgoers off seeing the movie upon its release. The film took $12 million in its opening weekend and by the end of its first week it had taken $16.4 million in receipts. Lasting a healthy seventeen weeks at the U.S. Box Office, by its close in February 1998 the film had raked in a respectable $60.9 million (Information courtesy of Box Office Mojo. Used with permission). It was an impressive return for a film that was equal parts horror and family drama. The bad news for Warner Bros and Time-Warner came in the form of a lawsuit filed 4 December 1997, alleging that they had copied a sculpture that depicted the Bible's creation story and distorted its meaning to make it appear demonic. Frederick Hart's "Ex Nihilo" sculpture looms in the entrance to the Episcopal National Cathedral in Washington D.C. The Cathedral and Hart contested that Warner Bros and Time-Warner had violated Federal copyright law by "copying, grotesque distortion and unauthorized use of a profound and beautiful religious sculpture, 'Ex Nihilo,' for commercial gain."

An out-of-court settlement was reached on 15 February 1998, when a Federal judge from Virginia ruled that Hart and the Episcopal National Cathedral would likely succeed should the lawsuit go to a full trial. The deal allowed 475,000 home entertainment rental copies to be distributed without cuts. But nearly twenty minutes of edits would have to be made before the film could be released for VHS sale. Moreover, any TV station broadcasting the motion picture would have to make the necessary cuts. Later, home entertainment releases included a disclaimer on the reverse of the case that read: "The large white sculpture of human forms on the wall of John Milton's penthouse in "Devil's Advocate" is not connected in anyway and was not endorsed by the sculptor Frederick Hart or the Washington National Cathedral, joint owners of the Cathedral sculpture "Ex Nihilo" in Washington, D.C."

Devil's Advocate succeeds in large part through its representation of Satan. Milton's slow rise from surrogate father to all out evil makes for an entertaining piece of cinema. Pacino plays it for fun throughout. Miming along to Frank Sinatra's *It Happened in Monterey*. Wining and dining and playfully toying with Mary Ann's hair during the early stages of their relationship. But by the final act of the movie Pacino is in full on scene-chewing mode. There is fire, brimstone, women stripping off, walls moving and souls crying out in anguish as Pacino shows his inner demon. The scene in which the apartment starts to burn around him recalls classic Gothic movies, such as *The Fall of the House of Usher*, that end with the antagonist going down in flames with their mansion. This thrilling climax is the perfect fit for this neo-Gothic movie.

When a script gives Pacino something meaty to sink his teeth into and go full tilt crazy it makes for riveting viewing. His bellowing, frothing and spitting out witty lines is all hugely entertaining. At the centre of it all however, is the father/son relationship between Milton and Lomax in which one seeks to rain chaos while the other seeks acceptance. It's a toxic family tug-o-war that only gets nastier and more depraved with each passing New York minute. Reeves' portrayal of a small town American's descent into hell is a slow-burn transformation. Lomax is the proverbial rabbit caught in headlights as he is seduced by the bright lights of the big city and what riches can afford him.

But is Lomax really changing or is it Milton altering his perception of reality? At times it does feel like Reeves is out of his depth in the movie but he comes back stronger in later scenes, especially those towards the end where he goes toe-to-toe with Pacino in the gut-busting bellowing. Reeves holds back, opening up his performance a little too late in the proceedings. There is an interesting character there but the storyline of his downward spiral is never fully realised.

The more dramatic descent into madness is reserved for Mary Ann. She struggles to adapt right from the very first day in New York City. Theron is heartbreakingly engaging throughout as she is pulled apart before our eyes in the most devious of ways. The sorrow she experiences is instantly recognisable to anyone who has been homesick. There is the desolation of not fitting in; the sense that this new environment could never be 'home' and the isolation from your nearest and dearest. That isolation is developed early on when Mary Ann is left at a party, thrown by Milton, while her husband is talking business several storeys up. Nobody is there for her and her self-esteem diminishes from then on. It's a harrowing performance from Theron that culminates in precisely the way we all truly hope it doesn't.

Featuring three entirely contrasting central performances each culminating in their own personal journey into the fiery pits of Hell, *Devil's Advocate* depicts dreams turning into nightmares. It's a modern-day Faustian bargain story that speaks about vanity, ego, greed, jealousy, lust and the loss of innocence. It may have its schlocky, camp moments but it's all the more entertaining because of it. Pacino had no need to be concerned about his version of the Devil. It's one of the most sardonic, coquettish, flamboyant and humorous portrayals, and is now considered one of the greatest screen representations of Satan.

Actor Pamela Gray on *Devil's Advocate*

Before you started filming did you do any research into the devil and the dark arts?

Yes. In fact I was meant to become a demon later on [in the film]. There was a scene in a car, where I was in a car pulling away from Charlize and she sees my face turn into a demon as I'm pulling away. But I don't think we even shot it, I think it was cut even before we shot it. I think they changed their minds about having us both turn. You know how Tamara [Tunie]'s face turns into a demon in the dressing room? They had my face turn as well while pulling away sort of like looking out the back window of a car. But they didn't end up doing that. It was significant to the demon research because I didn't know what images she would be seeing.

In the film there is a cauldron of evil between your character, Pacino's, Tamara's and Connie Nielsen's. Was it fun to play bad with those actors?

Very. It was ten weeks of it. It was extremely fun. The way the film was directed made us all slim and slinky, we were all physically the same type in terms of being long, thin women. I remember the church scene in particular and Al is walking me down the aisle as Jeffrey Jones' character – Eddie Barzoon – has died, I remember that being a particularly ominous feeling on that day. They have this old church... Anybody who has ever been to church... having this embodiment of evil, even for play, it brings out an ominous energy. It's a little scary. That was a very palpable feeling in that room. What we were trying to do in that church on that day. There's a moment when Al puts his finger in the water and it boils... I was hanging out with him a long time that day because they kept shooting the procession up the aisle... he was in character pretty much the entire day. I was very young when I did this, in my twenties and I said something idiotic to him... something actor school-y... trying to shoot the shit with Al Pacino [*laughs*] and I'll never forget the way he turned to me and looked at me and it was so... without being unkind, he sorted of flashed me where he was with his work that day. In complete concentration and beyond, far beyond my observation.

You have other scenes in the film with Pacino. What was it like to act in such close quarters with him?

It's incredible. It's incredible. He's the master. Every single take is different but completely inside of the circumstances and inside the character. Every moment... it's like being in a warm bubble of imaginary truth. The circumstances for him are very real or he makes you feel as if the circumstances are very real. But he is not one of these actors that is not going to be available as a human to everyone on the set. I think he must have known Taylor [Hackford] before. Their relationship seemed so mutually respectful. It was fun. It was inviting. He was welcoming and then highly, highly, highly committed in the imaginary circumstances and professional at the same time. I honestly cannot say enough nice things about Al Pacino. I've auditioned for him since. Not for years, but the years following that film on a couple of projects and he was always incredibly gracious to me. Incredibly respectful and incredibly fun to act with. I remember when I first got to set and said to the make-up guy "I want you to make me look as though everything is made of plastic." I wanted to look like I'd had tons of plastic surgery. Al was sitting in the trailer and he said: "Then they should make a study of me," [*laughs*]. He was very funny. He was always joking around.

How would you describe his acting technique?

There is no effort to transform once the camera is on. It's the fluid ability to take exactly where you are, to take exactly where he is physically and energetically and tunnel it into the imaginary circumstances. Play the scene. There is no effort visible. It's not like: "And now I'm turning on this guy. And now I'm turning off this guy." It's rooted in organic person. So it's rooted in the truth. From my observations, he is always in a focussed place. It's without imposing a heavy mantle of character. It comes through him and it is perfectly organic. He is a very technically proficient actor. But he is not a result orientated actor. I think a good actor can organically become anybody if it's rooted in the truth and if they know the characters.

What did you think to the finished film?

I can't be totally objective about it because I was there a lot of weeks - we were all, a long time. It was a very ensemble feeling. I think it's really good. I think at that time nothing had really been done quite that way because it's a thriller completely rooted in a dramatic text without tricks or gimmicks. But there are some supernatural broad strokes that happen without it going into another genre. I think it's executed really well and really imaginatively. That one shot of the street in New York that is entirely empty in the morning... I don't remember why I was there that day... I was probably waiting in the trailer to do another shot. That would be done with a digital image now. But they actually did that and the result is so beautiful. I feel like there is so much detail on Taylor's part and Al's part that went into the construction of those images and the storytelling.

There is some fabulous scene chewing from Pacino at the end isn't there?

Yeah, in his office with the paintings that come to life [*laughs*]. Al Pacino is sometimes thought of that scene-chewing guy and, as I said, it's an evolution out of the truth and the organic work he does. It's not rooted in falseness. You don't get the feeling he made a decision to let loose. It erupts out of the truth.

What is your favourite memory of working on *Devil's Advocate*?

I really have a lot of wonderful memories. I would guess that day when I was with Al hanging out all day long at the church. We didn't speak very much but it was just the two of us and we had to hold hands and we locked arms and we shot that so many times. We exchanged a few lines... we had more exchanges at other times but that day was so beautiful.

Whatever bubble was around us I just have such lovely, warm feelings about the silence of that day and the presence of his energy. It is really one of my favourite days as an actor.

The Insider

Cast: Al Pacino (Lowell Bergman), Russell Crowe (Jeffrey Wigand), Christopher Plummer (Mike Wallace), Diane Venora (Liane Wigand), Philip Baker Hall (Don Hewitt), Lindsay Crouse (Sharon Tiller), Debi Mazar (Debbie De Luca), Stephen Tobolowsky (Eric Kluster). **Director:** Michael Mann.

Synopsis: After seeking the expertise of former "Big Tobacco" executive Jeffrey Wigand, seasoned TV producer Lowell Bergman suspects a story lies behind Wigand's reluctance to speak. As Bergman persuades Wigand to share his knowledge of industry secrets, the two must contend with the courts and the corporations that stand between them and exposing the truth. All the while, Wigand must struggle to maintain his family life amidst lawsuits and death threats.

Since its debut on the CBS network in 1968 the American investigation television programme 60 Minutes has broken some deeply shocking stories, including the CIA's involvement in drug smuggling, the accusations of rape at a University Lacrosse team party and the killing of Iraqi civilians by U.S. Marines. Arguably one of its most controversial segments was an interview with a whistleblower in the tobacco industry. Jeffrey Wigand was a former Vice President for Research and Development at the American tobacco company Brown & Williamson. Wigand was fired in 1993 after a disagreement with B&W, when he discovered they had been adding an addictive chemical into their nicotine and wound up taking a job at the ABC television company. He worked there as a technical advisor in their $10 million lawsuit against the tobacco giant Philip Morris.

60 Minutes producer Lowell Bergman contacted Wigand and asked for an interview so that the show could lay bare the full extent of what he had witnessed at B&W. As Bergman started to conduct research into the allegations, he was opposed by CBS lawyers, who were concerned about

the possibility of a court case with B&W. By agreeing to the interview, Wigand was breaking a non-disclosure agreement he had signed upon his departure from the company. There was also concern that airing the segment would jeopardise the sale of CBS to the Westinghouse Electric Corporation due to the scandal it would cause. It further transpired that Andrew Tisch, the son of CBS president Laurence Tisch, became caught up in the Justice Department's perjury cases against CEOs of eight big tobacco companies for suggesting that nicotine was not addictive. At the time, Andrew Tisch was CEO at Lorillard Tobacco Company and these numerous factors made the airing of this interview problematic at best.

Due to the prolonged waiting period, 60 Minutes lost out on breaking the story to an article in *The Wall Street Journal* on 18 October 1995. Eventually, in November 1995, 60 Minutes did run Wigand's interview but in a heavily censored format, removing the majority of his most substantial claims. The full unedited interview did not air until 4 February 1996. Then in May 1996, *Vanity Fair* published an article by journalist Marie Brenner called 'The Man Who Knew Too Much'. The article featured an in-depth interview with Wigand in which he vented about everything he had been through over the past couple of years.

One person who read that article was film director/producer Michael Mann.

Mann had been friends with Bergman for several years and the pair had first talked about working together in 1989. Mann relished Bergman's stories about the experiences he'd had on 60 Minutes. One project they hoped to collaborate on was about an arms dealer in Marbella, Spain that Bergman had become friendly with. When that venture failed to make it off the ground, Mann went off to make the crime film *Heat*. While Mann was working on post-production for *Heat*, Bergman was battling with the issues surrounding the Wigand interview.

Mann watched both segments of the Wigand story on 60 Minutes. After the airing of the censored cut, Mann started to piece together an idea for a film based on the accusations against the tobacco industry. Then Mann read the *Vanity Fair* article and decided to make a film about the real-life events surrounding this story according to Wigand, Bergman, 60 Minutes and CBS. "I thought it would be interesting to do something that was totally situational drama. What drew me to the characters was the degree in which they are multifaceted," Mann explained.

After reading a very early draft of *The Good Shepherd* by Eric Roth, a fictional story based on the birth of the Central Intelligence Agency, Mann hired Roth to work on the script for his movie. Once they had the first completed script, Roth met Wigand at the Broadway Deli, Santa Monica in a bid to seek more insight and enrich the screenplay. As much as Roth pushed for more information however, Wigand was still bound by the non-disclosure agreement he had signed with Brown & Williamson.

Roth continued to tweak the script and Mann set about casting the film. Mann and Pacino worked together in *Heat*, and enjoyed the experience. Consequently, Mann contacted Pacino to see if he was interested in playing 60 Minutes producer Lowell Bergman. Mann felt this opportunity demanded a reserve from Pacino that audiences had never seen before. Pacino jumped at the chance to work with Mann again and immediately signed on.

For the role of Jeffrey Wigand, Mann initially considered casting another actor from *Heat*, Val Kilmer but Pieter Jan Brugge suggested Australian actor Russell Crowe to the director, after seeing him in *L.A. Confidential*. A script was sent to Crowe who loved it but had been given no indication about which part he would be playing. When the actor met the director, Crowe didn't understand why Mann wanted him to play Wigand, a person much older and bigger than he was. During their four-hour meeting, Crowe suggested hiring an out-of-work, middle-aged actor instead. It wasn't until Mann leaned into Crowe, tapped the heart area on his chest and said: "I'm not talking to you because of your age. I'm talking to you because of what you have in here." With that, Crowe accepted the role.

The final leading role was that of veteran 60 Minutes correspondent Mike Wallace. Casting this part was a tough process because Wallace was incredibly well known not just through 60 Minutes, but also for his game show hosting and acting. Pacino suggested Canadian actor Christopher Plummer for the part after being wowed by his performance in the movie *Stage Struck*. Plummer accepted the role of Wallace, saying: "He has created a great monster of a character in himself, which is a delight to play."

Before filming started, Pacino and Crowe wanted to meet their real-life counterparts. Pacino spent time with Bergman discussing the case and also went along to ABC News and *Time Magazine* to interact with the journalists there. When Crowe met with Wigand, he discovered that the scientist still could not talk about the case because of the non-disclosure agreement. They chatted for a couple of hours before Crowe left and has since commented: "I have respect for him, for what he did, and he understands how serious I am about my job."

Crowe had to put on over thirty-five pounds of excess weight, proving his dedication to the part. He binged daily on cheeseburgers and bourbon. He also had to shave back his hairline, have his hair thinned out and bleached, and have daily treatment injected into his skin to achieve wrinkles and liver spots. Two months before filming began, Mann and Crowe spent days discussing the details of Wigand's a character in great depth. Crowe was given access to all of Wigand's video interviews and also to a six hour audio recording that he listened to over and over again to pick up Wigand's nuances. Shortly before filming was due to commence, Crowe drove to a meeting scheduled with his director. When he parked his car, he had to rock back and forth several times in order to get enough momentum to lift himself out of the car. Crowe had surpassed the requirement of gaining thirty-five pounds of additional weight and was now carrying an extra forty-eight pounds.

Mann and Roth's final script included some requests from the real Wigand. He requested that the names of his daughters be changed, that one of the health issues he suffered from be altered and he insisted that smoking was not to be glamorized at any point in the film. All three requests were granted. A budget of $68 million was agreed between Disney's Touchstone Pictures, Spyglass Entertainment and Mann's own production company Forward Pass. The film would be distributed by Buena Vista Pictures Distribution, part of the Walt Disney Company.

Principal photography began in the spring of 1998 in Louisville, Kentucky. During the first couple of days of shooting Mann made Crowe re-take a scene in which he simply walked through a door seventeen times. Eventually Crowe bellowed at Mann: "Michael, don't spend the first ten takes looking at the fucking shadow on the wall. Don't even call me until you've worked out where the fucking shadow is. Don't waste this stuff because I'm working from take one. I don't care who you've worked with before, mate. I don't need a warm-up. I'm ready. And if we go into double figures, then someone's gonna have to fucking die!" Mann replied by comparing Crowe's acting to owning a Ferrari sports car: "Are you going to leave it in the garage? Or are you going to get in and drive it?" A metaphor directed at Crowe that he should use his anger and aggression in front of the camera rather than keep it locked away and released after the scene had been shot. Crowe took Mann's advice and from that moment on the pair got along perfectly.

Filming locations in Louisville included the historic Seelbach Hotel, The DuPont Manual High School and a local bank office. Production moved out into the suburbs to Seneca Park to film exterior shots of Wigand's home then on to Los Angeles to shoot several scenes at the Long Beach Polytechnic High School. During the final day of filming, students included in the scene watched as Crowe ripped off his grey wig and screamed. Most didn't realise it was a joke until the actor and crew started to laugh. Following this, the crew relocated to the San Bernardino National Forest, primarily the Big Bear Lake, Big Bear Valley. This area was to double as Montana during the winter. As it was early July however, fifteen tons of biodegradable artificial snow had to be shipped over from a UK company called Snow Business to create the desired weather conditions for the scene. Two days were spent covering a corner of the Big Bear Lake with fake snow before filming took place.

The production then returned to California, shooting in Berkeley, Santa Ana and in San Francisco before returning to Louisville where they hired out a disused studio at one of the local TV station affiliates. The studio was redesigned to film the 'live' news studio segments. After Louisville, the next stop was the Jackson County courtroom in Pascagoula, Mississippi where the real-life Wigand was giving his pre-trial deposition in November 1995. Mississippi Attorney General Michael Moore was asked by Mann to play himself during filming in the courtroom, he commented: "I guess it does add a dose of reality. It was the most important thing I'll ever do as a lawyer." Mann and his set designers recreated the courtroom exactly as it was during the real-life hearing. Moore further recalled: "There were about fifty or sixty tobacco lawyers piled up [in the far side of the courtroom]. They were the most arrogant bunch I've ever seen. But when we finally got word that Jeffrey would give his deposition, I walked in and gave the signal, and these guys went nuts."

While in Pascagoula, production also filmed on Beach Boulevard, a road bordered by the Gulf of Mexico. Real-life prominent trial lawyer Richard Scruggs allowed his home overlooking the Gulf of Mexico to be used in the scene in which Wigand decides he will testify. Once again art was imitating life as this was the house where the real Wigand made that decision. Following Pascagoula, production uprooted to Mobile, Alabama for night shoots which were to double for a scene set in New Orleans. A handful of the cast and crew flew to Abaco Island in the Bahamas for a couple of days to film scenes involving Bergman's forced vacation from 60 Minutes. Full production then moved to New York for exterior filming and to capture interior shots of the CBS offices. Their final stop was Baka El Garbia and Umm El Fahm in Israel. These two cities were used for the opening scenes set in Lebanon. Upon completion of principal photography, Crowe gave Pacino a personalised Louisville slugger baseball bat. "It cost about $40 and it was no big deal. So, I just left it in his trailer. I didn't know Al Pacino was the world's biggest baseball fans. He thought it was the greatest thing since sliced bread and he's like "'How did you know?'" When Crowe returned home to Los Angeles, he discovered Pacino had sent him a baseball pitching machine and accessories.

The Insider held its premiere at the Academy Theater, Beverly Hills on 28 October 1999. Critics praised the film highly. *Rolling Stone* said: "The Insider will pin you to your seat." *Vogue magazine* called it: "one of the most breathlessly entertaining pictures of the year." Leonard Maltin, writing for *Playboy Magazine*, suggested: "Pacino and Crowe ought to be Oscar contenders." Released on Friday 5 November 1999 in North America, *The Insider*'s first weekend in theatre's returned $6.7 million. By the end of its first full week it had pulled in $9 million. *The Insider* finally left theatres after twenty-two weeks on release and generated a return of $28.7 million theatrically in North America. This was not the massive return Disney Pictures were hoping for. Disney Chairman Joe Roth commented that: "Everyone is really proud of the movie. But it's one of those rare times when adults loved a movie, yet they couldn't convince their friends to go see it any more than we could convince people in marketing the film." Internationally, the movie played much better with a theatrical return of $31.2 million (Information courtesy of Box Office Mojo. Used with permission).

Leonard Maltin's suggestion that Pacino and Crowe should be Oscar contenders was a fairly astute one. At the 72nd Academy Awards, *The Insider* was nominated in seven categories including Best Picture, Best Director and Best Actor (for Crowe). However, it failed to win in any of the categories. Though this was disappointing, the film's cast and crew also had to endure the severe battering the picture received from those associated with the real story. A day before the film was to be theatrically released a judge in Miami, Florida presiding over a case about against the tobacco industry ordered his jurors not to watch the movie, saying the fictionalized account could prejudice the panel. Brown & Williamson issued a statement before the film had been released to say they would "reserve comment until after we've seen the movie." However, their press release did state: "Brown & Williamson Tobacco Corporation said today that a previously sealed FBI investigation uncovered by the news media has now exposed the truth behind the soon-to-be-released film *The Insider* and shows that the government's key witness lied to federal agents and fabricated death threats. The question now is how can Disney continue to promote a film based on fabrications and lies?"

CBS network also issued a statement: "It's important to point out that the producers of the movie *The Insider* have admitted, in a disclaimer, to adding, for dramatic effect 'fictionalized events' to its Hollywood version. So it's obvious that the film is not true to the real-life events surrounding the 60 Minutes tobacco piece that was broadcast on February 4th, 1996." A Disney spokesman responded: "The film itself never suggests who might have been behind the threats." Allegedly, 60 Minutes correspondent Mike Wallace was furious with the movie's depiction of him as not standing up for Wigand. He told Fox News: "I resent being used in a dishonest way to create fictional drama." Also 60 Minutes founder Don Hewitt started to speak out against the film and Bergman in particular, by saying: "When a journalist who professes to be dedicated to the truth, the whole truth and nothing but the truth conspires with a screenwriter to concoct a movie about himself that portrays him, by name, saying things he never said and doing things he never did, that is not a journalist I would allow within a hundred miles of a newsroom." Bergman fired back at Wallace and Hewitt: "These are people who are used to being in control. They don't like it when the cameras or the microphones or the pens are pointed at them. Ultimately, *The Insider* shows what can happen when the target you're after is just as big as your employer and may have several economic links to your employer." When asked what he thought to the movie Wigand, who was still under a confidentiality agreement, said: "As a film, I believe *The Insider* captured powerfully and accurately the tone and terror of what I was experiencing on a daily basis during that period."

Much like *Heat*, *The Insider* is a huge ensemble movie that boils down to two men sitting down together and talking. It is talk that will change the lives of both parties. The first hour of the film builds up to an explosive moment, and that comes when Wigand, on camera, finally breaks the NDA and explains how Brown & Williamson knew they were adding an addictive substance into their cigarettes. That moment is like a volcano finally erupting. You can see and hear it in Wigand. His eyes flutter, he stutters slightly and slaps his lips together, he knows what he is about to say will have far reaching repercussions and he hesitates, then finally lets it all out in a wave of emotion. It's almost too much as the viewer sees him begin to tear up before the shot cuts away to allow him and the viewer that moment of recover from what we have just witnessed.

Mann's fluid direction style continues throughout the film. He never cuts a scene too early or allows it to run too long. It's like he is painting a picture and each brush stroke adds a new layer to the drama. That signature blue hue is in every frame of the picture. Even when Bergman is banished to the beach by the crisp blue sea, Mann still uses a deep blue filter that makes it feels cold and uninviting, the way in which this tone is established is a credit to Mann and, more importantly, cinematographer Dante Spinotti.

When Wigand is introduced into the film, Mann films his opening sequence via point-of-view angles. The camera follows Wigand as he is fired from his job, he walks down the hallway and out to his car. All of the time, the camera is hovering slightly above his right shoulder with his right ear and the view through the corner of his varifocal glasses in shot. In this scene, Mann connects the viewer and Wigand. He is the protagonist. He is the one we should have an emotional link with, be it positive or negative.

Crowe's performance as Wigand is stunning. It truly is the best performance in the film and one that should have won him the Oscar. Not only is it a physical transformation, but it's also a psychological one. This isn't the Crowe we are used to seeing on screen; normally he is an aggressive powerhouse. Here he is afraid at every turn. He is the proverbial deer caught in headlights with nowhere to run. His lumbering frame makes him an everyman, regardless of his high-powered job and his qualifications as a doctor of science, he is an average Joe. A guy you would say 'Hi' to at the supermarket check-out and not remember him the next time you were in line together. Crowe makes him that man; his performance is impeccably reserved considering he is the lead character.

Pacino also delivers a reserved performance. His usually loud demeanour gives way to a quiet authority. He doesn't need to produce bellows, screams or grand gestures (although that does occur twice towards the end of the film). Instead his portrayal is all about intelligence and how to outsmart the other players. It's a highly engaging performance, one that has just as much power in the non-verbal moments – a look of the eyes, a flick of the head, a telling scowl – as it does in the dialogue. There is so much subtle nuance in the performance that it's difficult to fully appreciate it on first viewing. The character's layers are peeled away as the situation surrounding the censorship of the interview intensifies. Even though Bergman has the weight of the world on his shoulders, Pacino doesn't make the performance depressive. It's easy to side with him even if he isn't warm and loving because he is making a decisive move towards empowerment and taking on greedy corporations. The first moment we see Bergman smile is when he is stood outside on the grass looking out into the sea after Wigand's deposition. Wigand pats him on the shoulder, the two look at each other and a smile of relief and triumph flits across both of their faces. It's a beautifully tender moment, the moment they stopped being individuals and became friends.

The Insider should always be spoken of in the same breath as *All the President's Men* when discussing whistleblower films. The subject matter is just as high profile as Carl Bernstein and Bob Woodward's and yet *The Insider* seems to be routinely overlooked. The phenomenal powerhouse performances of Pacino and Crowe, alongside Mann's direction, serve to create a suspenseful contemporary thriller that centres on doing the right thing in the face of corruption.

Investigative reporter and producer Lowell Bergman on *The Insider*

When did you first hear about *The Insider* being made?

Michael Mann expressed interest after the New York Times story of 11/95. There wasn't a commitment until at least a year later and even then there wasn't a screenwriter. "Being made?" Maybe nine months after that?

What do you think to Pacino's portrayal of yourself?

Hard for me to articulate. He was great. Was it me? I didn't, don't yell so that was a bit hard for me to see and experience. Overall, understanding it was a dramatization, I was honoured.

Were there differences in the way Pacino and Crowe played the relationship compared to Wigand and yourself?

Sure. It captured in so many ways that we were different, from different life experiences. That is so often true in the reporter-source relationship. Crowe did a great job with Jeff's geeky side and naïveté or should I say Eric [Roth]'s dialogue.

Hollywood has a tendency of glamorizing certain aspects of true stories. In *The Insider* how much is real and how much is Hollywood?

Not sure there was much glamorizing. Hewitt got off easy compared to actual behaviour. Mike slipped in an interview once and described Don as lacking a moral compass. Alas, it was true. Jeff had a side that was definitely difficult for others to abide. And I was a lot more freaked out, as was my wife, who reminds me how tough those times were, than what was portrayed. But what makes the film work is the nuance, the honesty and, I think, the fact that it did not really go after CBS as hard as Michael could have. Wallace and Hewitt were not self aware. CBS never confronted the reality that the film never told the audience that the Seven Dwarfs included James Tisch, son of Larry, the owner. The Tisch family's biggest cash cow was their privately held Lorillard Tobacco.

At my first meeting with Al in Michael's office he turned to me and asked: "After 14 years with Wallace for you to go off the reservation, this couldn't have been the first time this, [killing a story] this happened?" I replied: "Yes. You're right !" As I tried to describe an earlier episode that involved Hewitt killing a story that had been advertised, lawyered and scheduled for air, Michael interjected: "This is not a documentary!" Al's observation that: "it must have happened before," instantly impressed me. And in various encounters afterward his intelligence, his savvy was so evident, so impressive that I always felt I was blessed by his willingness to be in the movie!

Mike Wallace spoke out against the film quite venomously. Were you surprised by his comments?

No. I expected him and Hewitt to try and destroy me. They marched into the newsroom of the New York Times and harangued Joe Lelyveld and the managing editor Bill Keller, and demanded I be fired! I had seen them destroy others, so I was prepared. By the time they went on the warpath I had three other jobs to slide into. Mike eventually softened, but he revealed his willingness to confabulate to preserve the image that he never waivered. Hewitt, as you may know, denounced me before 1000 journalists! That was his biggest mistake. More on that in my memoir.

How do you feel when you see films like *The Insider*, *All the President's Men*, *Spotlight* and others winning critical acclaim, but not having huge box office returns?

Box office isn't the point. Real reporting is a Public Good. You do it because you are compelled to. Fame and fortune can make life a bit easier, but recognition for trying to do the right thing is rare. You know that ATPM created the line: "Follow the money?" *The Insider* has a great scene where the context of the story is laid out in a lunchroom scene. It's brilliant. And *Spotlight* shows a bunch of ink stained wretches facing down immensely arrogant private power. That's what counts!

Actor Nestor Serrano on *The Insider*

Do you remember when the story on which this film is based became international news in late 1995?

No, I didn't remember it at the time. After I became involved in the movie I did do some research into it.

Did you audition? Or were you picked directly by Michael Mann.

Michael Mann called me and asked me to come down to Kentucky. I think he had begun shooting, and he asked me if I would be interested in doing it. I said 'yes'.

Mann likes to sit with each of his actors and explain the character they are portraying in great detail. Did that happen to you?

That's exactly right. I went into his office at the hotel and we talked for probably about thirty minutes. And he asked me a lot about me and he asked if I knew about the original story and I told him I didn't, which I felt pretty bad about [*laughs*]. But it turned out he felt sorry for me and gave me the job anyway [*laughs*].

What was filming like?

My time on this movie was pretty limited. I would fly in, do my day or two and... I was never there more than a few days.

There are some beautiful locations in the film. Please say you got to go and film at the Gulf of Mexico?

[*Laughs*] No. I was on set and they would put a hole in the wall and doll it up so it looked like I was somewhere else and then they would put me back on a plane and send me back home.

Did you get to meet Pacino?

Yeah. Here's my story: I was going to shoot a phone conversation with Al Pacino and so I've been in the business long enough to know this is the way it usually works – you are speaking with the first AD who is pretending to be Al Pacino or, even worse, the script supervisor, and they deliver the lines and pretend they are sounding natural. I was prepared for that because that's the way it works and then three months later Al Pacino will do his version.

So I'm getting ready to go in... oh, first I should say that I went into my office and it was the first day anybody had seen my office and they had spent two weeks setting up my imaginary office on set, and I was there and I sit down and all of a sudden Michael Mann comes over and leans in and says: "Nestor I'm really sorry but this is just not going to work." I thought: Oh my God! I'm getting fired and I've not even opened my mouth yet. But what he was talking about was the way they had decorated the office. He scrapped the entire thing and sent me home for the weekend and then I came back on the Monday and shot it.

So we go back on set and I'm waiting to hear who... maybe I can rehearse with the script supervisor and then the first AD says to me: "Nestor we are ready to rehearse with you and Michael and Al," and I said: "well, that's odd." But immediately I thought that because Al is such a method actor perhaps he wanted to hear what I sounded like so he could replicate that down the road.

I was very pleased to sit in a room with Michael Mann and Al Pacino – my hero. We sat and did the scene and after a couple of tries they said: "OK great" and everybody walked away and I went back to my desk and the first AD says to me: "OK so this is your phone and this is the other phone where you will speak with Al and let him know that we are ready to go." I say: "OK" but [was] very confused. I went along with it. So, he said: "Pick up the phone and call Al downstairs." I go: "Wait! What is going on?" He said: "Well, what is going on is we are going to shoot the scenes concurrently." I'm going to be upstairs and they are filming me and Al Pacino is going to be downstairs and they are going to shoot that at the same time. I had never done anything like that before but Michael Mann wanted the interaction to be included. Typically, when you are doing a scene you have to stop talking so they can overlap the other person's dialogue and it will help the editing process.

Now we are doing the scene and I pick up the phone and go: "Al are you ready?" and he says: "yeah sure." So I call him on the practical phone – the real phone – and proceed to do the scene. So the scene is heated... it gets heated... he is accusing me of possible corruption and all sorts of things. After the third or fourth take I forgot what my next line [is] and I say: "Oh sorry I lost my place," and Al starts yelling at me and he's going: "FINISH YOUR THOUGHT! FINISH YOUR THOUGHT!" and I'm thinking: I guess he means find it. I find it and we do the scene. Immediately thereafter I pick up the non-practical phone "Al are you ready? Let's go. OK!" So he picks up the phone and we begin the scene and he forgets his first line and goes "Arghhhhhh Fuck!" and he hangs up, and I go: "What happened to finish your thought?." [*Laughs*].

Were you excited to see the completed film even though your role was quite small?

When I did the movie, the last scene I did, Michael Mann said to me: "Well, you can be proud that you did a great job in a small role in, what we hope, will be a wonderful movie." So I knew going in that it was going to be a tiny little bit. But I was very proud of that movie and very proud to have been in it. For many, many years people would ask: "what is the one work you are most proud of?" and I would say: "I'm not necessarily proud of the work, but the film I'm most proud to be a part of is *The Insider.*"

Any Given Sunday

Cast: Al Pacino (Tony D'Amato), Cameron Diaz (Christina Pagniacci), Dennis Quaid (Jack "Cap" Rooney), James Woods (Dr. Harvey Mandrake), Jamie Foxx (Willie Beamen), LL Cool J (Julian Washington), Matthew Modine (Dr. Ollie Powers), Aaron Eckhart (Nick Crozier). **Director:** Oliver Stone.

Synopsis: Tony D'Amato is the coach of the Miami Sharks American football team. Off the field he is battling against a new team owner, an injured quarterback, a flashy bull-headed backup Quarterback, a slithery team doctor and a running back with an incentive-laden contract. On the field, he must stop the consecutive losing streak, falling attendances and the very real possibility of not making the playoffs.

The seeds of *Any Given Sunday* were planted way back in the early 1980s when American screenwriter/producer/director Oliver Stone wrote a treatment for a movie about an ageing linebacker, to be played by Charles Bronson. Soon after, however, Stone became interested in other projects (notably *Scarface*) and thus never pursued the idea in a serious fashion. It wasn't until the late nineties that Stone returned to his outline of an American football movie.

Stone was burnt by the failure of his 1995 *Nixon* biopic (which had a budget of $44 million and box office return of $13 million), and so discussed his next movie idea with journalist Richard Weiner who was in the process of ghost-writing for Joe Montana, a four-time Super Bowl champion for the San Francisco 49ers. Stone was an ardent 49ers fan and liked the idea of making a film about them. Weiner started work on a script with ex-49ers tight end Jamie Williams called *Monday Night*. Their production would focus around a black quarterback called Stuart Polaris and his struggles within the game, primarily his experience of constant racism. "I told Oliver: 'Look at what you did with Platoon.' People had a John Wayne perspective to war and you pulled the curtain back and showed war in such a different way. You're doing the same thing with football."

At the same time as Weiner and Williams were working on their treatment, Stone purchased a speculative football screenplay from playwright-turned-screenwriter John Logan and followed that up by buying *Playing Hurt*, a script by experienced TV and film screenwriter Daniel Pyne. Stone immersed himself in re-writes that would incorporate ideas from all three treatments. A deal was agreed in principal with Turner Pictures to produce the movie. Then in the summer of 1995, Turner Pictures announced it would be merging into Time Warner, the world's largest communications company. Stone's movie hit the skids as he learnt that Warners were already working on a football film based on the book *You're OK – It's Just a Bruise*, written by former Los Angeles Raiders team physician Robert Huizenga. The Time Warner treatment was being handled by Richard and Lauren Donner via their production house – The Donners Company - but when the merger was completed in early 1996 a deal was struck to combine both productions. As part of the deal, the project had to be handed over to Stone for completion.

Costs for the production began to rise even before casting had happened. Initial reports speculated that the proposed casting of Robert De Niro would sky rocket the budget to $55 million. Stone, sensing he needed more money to make his big, lavish football movie, took the job of directing crime thriller *U Turn* starring Sean Penn and Jennifer Lopez. Script re-writes continued while Stone was off filming in the Arizona desert. *U Turn* turned out to be a spectacular flop and Stone was in need of a box office smash more than ever. Upon returning to the treatment in early 1998, Stone discovered that locations had changed and an additional set of characters had appeared. Also despite his previous upbeat correspondence with the National Football League he was now being treated as a persona non grata. The NFL had heard rumours that the film depicted the unhealthier side of American Football and decided to renege on any help they had previously offered. "The NFL didn't want people to see that these football players are just like the rest of society. These are guys that do too many drugs or spend their money unwisely, but then go out on Sunday and are gladiators," said Williams.

Further complicating matters, the NFL issued memos to all teams encouraging them not to participate. Due to these problems and continued script re-writes (Stone and the writers could not get the "black vernacular and all the football jargon right") pushed the start of production from April 1998 to December 1998. Warner Bros agreed to a budget of $55 million. Big product placement contracts were signed in order to additionally fund the production, the biggest chunk of the sponsorship money came from MET-Rx – a bodybuilding supplement company.

The delays caused by script re-writes caused further problems with casting. Ving Rhames and David Duchovny were both forced to drop out before a finished script had been completed. So too did Tom Arnold and Edward Burns. Cuba Gooding Jr met with Stone about playing Willie Beamen, the star quarterback; however, he was turned down because having played a pro footballer in the rom-com Jerry Maguire two years previously it was felt that with Gooding Jr in the role it could have been seen as a sort of prequel or sequel to the Tom Cruise/Renee Zellweger film rather than its own entity. Comedian Chris Tucker also turned down the role. Eventually, the part ended up in the hands of rapper/actor Sean "P. Diddy" Combs. This was to be Combs' first film acting role. Only Robert De Niro and Al Pacino were offered the role of Tony D'Amato. Pacino had seen an early draft of Logan's screenplay and was interested as it was completely different to the usual cop and gangster parts he was offered. By the time De Niro had rejected the offer, Pacino had already signed on.

Since her striking debut in *The Mask*, Cameron Diaz had been making romantic and comedic movies and Stone believed her the ideal person to play the greedy, conniving American football team owner Christina Pagniacci. The cast of supporting footballers included rapper/actor LL Cool J as Julian Washington and Dennis Quaid as Jack 'Cap' Rooney. Real-life active and ex-ballers were hired for substantial roles, including Jim Brown as Montezuma Monroe and Lawrence Taylor as Luther 'Shark' Lavay. Stone also called in two actors he had previously worked with for key characters in his sports drama. John C McGinley was cast as the mouthy, cigar-smoking sports journalist Jack Rose and James Woods signed on to play the Sharks' dodgy team doctor Harvey Mandrake. There was also room to squeeze in Matthew Modine as the team's by-the-book doctor, Ollie Powers.

Stone's second unit director, and a veteran of making American football movies, Allan Graf recruited pro footballers to be extras in the movie: "We started recruiting football players in September 1998 with a national manhunt and invited the best of them down to Miami. We held a week-long combine where we chose and cut them down to about 50." Their time in Miami coincided with Stone holding a training camp for both pro ballers and actors alike. "We ran it like an NFL Camp," said Graf. Over one hundred different American football plays [set pieces] were given to the cast to learn, then Graf would evaluate at the end of each day.

Combs began his first day at camp by practising how to receive the ball from the formation pre snap. In the afternoon instructions were for him to practise his throwing. By the end of the day Combs was tossed out of the film. In an interview with *XXL Magazine* years later, Combs said it was because he was being asked to push back his European tour in order to accommodate filming: "They were pushing it back and pushing it back and it got to the point that I was losing so much money. I was like: 'I can't wait'. The director was like 'Your tour doesn't matter'. But it does matter. I waited a year." A different side to the story surfaced from many who witnessed his antics at the training camp. Actor Andrew Bryniarski explained it brutally: "Puff Daddy threw like a girl so they put him on a plane." Producer Eric Hamburg was more diplomatic: "Puffy couldn't throw a football properly and he came on set with a big entourage. Al Pacino was there, the ultimate pro, and he was offended. So was Oliver." Fortunately, Stone had a substitute waiting on the bench for the part of quarterback Willie Beamen.

Comedian Jamie Foxx previously auditioned for the role of Julian Washington (a part that eventually went to LL Cool J). At the end of the second audition Stone told Foxx he didn't like his audition for Washington however that the main character was still to be cast and that he could read for that. An audition tape was made and sent to the execs at Warner Bros, who didn't like the idea of a comedian taking the lead in a serious sports drama. Stone told Foxx to make a tape of him throwing ball, but make it different. "I got my guys together and we made like a training camp video. The music blaring, I got my Deion Sanders jersey on. And I came up with the chant: "My name is Willie, Willie Beamen, I keep the ladies screamin'." We mix all this on the tape, turn it in – and that's how it started off."

Principal photography began at the tail-end of January 1999 in Florida. The interior studio work was filmed at Harbor Beach, Fort Lauderdale and Greenwich Studios, Miami. The majority of the production was filmed in around the city of Miami. The Villa Vizcaya, a huge Italian Renaissance style building in Coconut Grove, was used for a decadent party scene. Another party was shot at the Cardozo Hotel on Ocean Drive. Miami Dolphins star quarterback Dan Marino gave permission for his 10-bedroom, 12-bathroom lakefront house on the Windmill Ranch Estates to be used as the home of Sharks veteran quarterback 'Cap' Rooney. The Homestead Sports Complex, primarily a baseball training facility, was used for scenes set in the training facility for the Miami Sharks.

The production managed to circumnavigate the unofficial blacklisting by the NFL by creating their own football league called the Association of Football Franchises of America (AFFA). It was a struggle to find a stadium that would allow filming but college football team, the Miami Hurricanes finally gave consent to the cast and crew to film three games at their Orange Bowl stadium. Locals were invited along to watch filming and act as extras. Black and White clothing was dished out by production staff to attendees to make it seem as though they were Sharks fans. Each of the three filming days at the stadium lasted around nine hours in the intense Miami heat. Following the filming of those games, production moved to the Pro Player Stadium, home to the Miami Dolphins. Clearly The Fins didn't care for the NFL's heavy handed approach to blacklisting, if only unofficially, Stone's movie as it was used as the home ground of the Los Angeles Crusaders.

With the intense heat and long, physically gruelling schedule, tensions boiled over one day when LL Cool J's character and Foxx's were meant to clash because of a fumbled ball. In the heat of the moment, LL improvised and punched Foxx. The rapper was afterwards told not to do it again, but did it once more when filming restarted. A brawl quickly ensued involving most of the cast and crew while Pacino, caught in the middle, tried to split them apart. The local police were called to the set. No assault charges were filed but both actors received a severe ticking off. Foxx told the *New York Daily News* that "The incident was settled to my liking. It's done, it's over." Years later, LL explained that tempers flared because of improvising: "I had to defend myself and in defending myself somehow his helmet got snatched off and he got hit in the temple."

Once filming was completed in Miami, production moved to Dallas, Texas. The final game featured in the movie was shot at the Texas Stadium, home to the Dallas Cowboys. Before filming started in the stadium and on the field, Stone's director of photography, Salvatore Totino and key rigging grip Scott Howell hung two lighting grids, measuring 120 feet by 100 feet, above the field. This meant they could control subtle changes in the lighting according to the time of day. They used remote-controlled cranes within the stadium that could swing around and pick up shots of the crowd before swooping down onto the field of play. In addition to that, Stone implemented two in-your-face camera styles. The first, which became known as the "ratcam", was the use of small, portable cameras strapped to the chests of key actors. This captured the intensity of the action up close and personal. The second camera style was the "image shaker." Stone had screened award-winning war movie *Saving Private Ryan* for his crew and demanded camera work much like the opening of Spielberg's movie. These "explosive" shots were used for aggressive formation pre-snaps and thundering in-play tackles. Stone proclaimed: "I don't think I've ever worked harder over a whole film over a period of time as I did here." Principal photography was completed within sixty-five days. In that time however, the budget had risen to $65 million.

Stars of the film walked the red carpet at the premiere on 16 December 1999 at the Mann Village Theatre, Westwood, California. An after-party took place in the courtyard of the Armand Hammer Museum, Wiltshire

Boulevard. Critics did find some merit in the movie even if they didn't view it as the blockbuster Stone intended to make. The *New York Times* felt: "In the end the movie cops out. Although the story presents many opportunities for tragedy, '*Any Given Sunday*' turns ludicrously upbeat as it hastily ties all its strands together." Roger Ebert had slight reservations, saying: "Oliver Stone's '*Any Given Sunday*' is a smart sports movie almost swamped by production overkill. It's a miracle the underlying story survives, but it does." *Empire Magazine* gave high praise: "There can be no argument that this is one of the most visually exciting experiences you will have this year." *Any Given Sunday* received its U.S. theatrical release three days before Christmas 1999. By the end of its first full week on release it had only returned $7 million, however part of that release covered the holiday period. By the end of its second week the takings had made a significant jump to $27 million. By the end of its U.S. theatrical run, *Any Given Sunday* had spent fourteen weeks in theatres and pulled in a tidy sum of $75.5 million (Information courtesy of Box Office Mojo. Used with permission). When the film was distributed on home entertainment formats on 1 September 2000, it was labelled: "Director's Cut." It was not an extended version, rather a trimmed edit. The theatrical version ran at one hundred and sixty-two minutes and the home entertainment version played for one hundred and fifty-six minutes. Stone removed twelve minutes from the theatrical version, including shortening the game footage and trimming a drunken speech at the bar from D'Amato. Stone then re-added six minutes of previously unseen footage back in. The original theatrical version was finally released on DVD/Blu ray to coincide with the film's 15th anniversary in 2014.

Testosterone doesn't just ooze from the pores of *Any Given Sunday*, it forcefully and consistently pummels you in the face. These are modern-day gladiators who care not for the weak and feeble. They only truly feel alive on the field of play every Sunday. That is their moment to shine, to become almost god-like. It's a sports movie that is set in a man's man's man's world where females fear to tread. The treatment of women in this film is nothing short of typical sports sexism, it looks down on them as subjects who should obey their masters regardless of the request. It has no qualms about depicting them as pieces of meat to be used and abused.

The one female character who transcends all that is Diaz's Pagniacci. A brute force of a woman who is equally at home telling the players to "not stiffen up on me" as she is screaming obscenities at fellow businessman. She is a powerful woman in a bright red pants suit who isn't willing to take shit from anyone; this is her club and her rules stand. This is a woman to look up to, she may have her faults but she isn't willing to bow down to anyone. It's a lively role that Diaz more than makes her own. She prowls like a lioness ready to pounce on anyone willing to argue back. There is no nonsense from her. For all the crap the other females are subjected to in the movie, Pagniacci is a full-blown feminist role model that should be taken seriously.

Diaz is without doubt equal to her co-star Pacino throughout. Pacino delivers his lines either whisperingly drunk or bellowing at full blast. It's a role that perfectly befits his trademark, roaring persona. Perhaps not all real-life coaches are as animated but Pacino brings to life an unenviable, thankless job and makes it appear as if it is the coolest job in the world regardless of all the pressure. His 'Inch By Inch' speech has now gone down in history as one of the greatest speeches delivered, not only in movies but also in football. His character is constantly cited by real coaches in various sports-related and motivational seminars.

Pacino's performance as D'Amato is based on a combination of many different American football coaches through the decades. The actor drew on small elements from a range of characters to create his fictional coach. The closest comparison to D'Amato would be English football's Brian Clough, a man who took a lowly second division team and made them world champions. One scene in particular is inspired by the Clough coaching book. Towards the end of the final playoff game D'Amato pulls Beamen to the touchline and rather than talk to him about plays he asks about what Beamen thought to his Jambalaya. It's a classic strategy designed to relax the star player during one of the most intense moments of the game by taking his mind off what is to come. Clough used this technique with his team all the time and its success rate was impressive.

D'Amato is Clough in a different sport and time. Beamen on the other hand, is a character straight out of the modern era of money-orientated sports. His rags to riches story echoes that of most male sports superstars. They suddenly make it big and experience an influx of more money, power and women than they know what to do with. It sends them into a spiral. They begin to believe their own publicity. Bank notes are tossed around like Monopoly money. Women are discarded like yesterday's newspaper and their celebrity power allows them access to virtually anything they want. It's only when they are tossed out the other side that they realise it was all for nothing and their game has suffered because of it.

Foxx conveys this story arc perfectly. His is a central role, and he manages to capture it with intensity. Forget Pacino's speech, Foxx's performance is the one that sports stars should be watching. It's a warning, a cautionary tale for them. The only time Foxx allows a bit of humour to seep into his representation of an American footballer is when he is shooting a music video, but that likely came naturally to him due to his background in music. For the rest of the movie he creates a character the audience are hoping to see succeed in that rags to riches fairy-tale, while also hoping he resists giving in to egotism. That doesn't happen, yet by the time he has been chewed up and spit out by the fame game, the audience are back on his side willing him to make that crucial touchdown.

The film wants to, and does, make him a winner. He embarks on a physical and psychological journey and comes to understand what he truly wants and needs in life. Part of that journey is the father son relationship that he establishes with D'Amato. As with most player/coach relationships, there are ups and downs but overall it shows how inspirational an experienced role model can be for a youngster. Here, Pacino once again takes a role that has a father element to it and Foxx reciprocates by portraying Beamen as a son who wants to do well in the eyes of his "father." Sadly, this part of the storyline gets overlooked time and again in favour of the pummelling powerhouse of visuals created by Stone.

This said, the director does seem to have granted the actors a certain freedom with their performances. The acting doesn't feel micro-managed and Stone clearly has faith in his cast to deliver what he needs. Stone's stamp on the movie is definitely made through its visual impact. It's shot in the style of an art-house movie and edited like an EDM music video – beautiful yet in-your-face relentless. Stone opts for bright, almost translucent colours that pop off the screen and at one point a beautiful time lapse shot of fluffy clouds is sharply cut to a shot of blood streaming out of a Sharks player's mouth. Shifting from the glorious to the gory within seconds. The actual games are so bone-crunchingly blood thirsty that at times it almost feels as though Stone is remaking Platoon for a different demographic: the sports fan. With blood, sweat, tears and vomit pouring from these on-the-field soldiers, Stone seeks to use American football as a metaphor for war and power. After previously using Nietzschean subtext within *Scarface* and *Wall Street*, similar philosophies continue here because of the power struggle happening at every level of the organisation. Pagniacci struggles for power in the boardroom, D'Amato struggles for power in the locker room, Beamen struggles for power on the pitch. It's a layered power struggle set within the world of American football.

Four editors worked on the movie but at times it feels like there were dozens more. Almost as if the filmmakers were trying out each new button on their editing console while working on the film. Virtually every available editing graphic or frame style is used, meaning the movie has so many tonal shifts and not one of them truly feels like a fit with the aesthetic of the film. Thankfully the main storyline does at least reel the viewer in.

Regardless of your feelings about American football, there is no denying that *Any Given Sunday* is hugely entertaining and at times exhilarating. It never holds back, jolts forward in fifth gear going a mile a minute. Dazzling you with spectacle after spectacle. Most people identify with the central struggle: being so close to achieving greatness while simultaneously battling with uncertainty. That's what happens throughout *Any Given Sunday*. As D'Amato's speech professes: "the inches we need are everywhere around us," and this film is about taking that chance, taking that shot, saying those words just at the right time to make you a winner.

On the surface *Any Given Sunday* may be concerned with football but at a deeper level it discusses life and how we play it. Additionally, Stone includes a sub-plot about high powered women within the sports industry allowing him to convey the outlandish behaviour they are subjected to because they aren't in "the boys' gang" and thus aren't given the same respect as their contemporaries. It's disgustingly sexist yet is pulled direct from real-life. Stone's narrative pushes the idea that women not only could, but should, be involved at all levels in the sports industry.

Any Given Sunday is every bit as thrilling as it should be. It's a movie that enthrals and exhilarates for every minute it plays out. One hundred and fifty-one minutes of American football doesn't sound like the ideal movie for those uninterested by sports. But it offers interesting perspectives on life, love and happiness. Exploring how each of us should strive to be the best we can be no matter what obstacles are put in front of us. This is a film about taking chances and never being afraid of them. How going that extra yard can be the difference between winning and losing.

American football player Lawrence Taylor on *Any Given Sunday*

Given your pro-athlete background, were you actively sought out by the casting director for this film?

It was a crazy time in my life. I was actually just coming out of rehab and Oliver's people reached out to my agent to arrange an audition. I'll never forget it. I remember walking into the Tribeca Film Centre, and Oliver Stone walking out of a room to greet me...the rest is history.

Is it difficult to keep the intensity of real-life games going when you're filming the same scene over a number of days?

It's certainly not the same as an NFL game but there was plenty of intensity on the set. If you think about that cast, there was a lot of very talented individuals. Let me tell ya, there was also a lot of testosterone from all the dudes during the football scenes.

It's a huge ensemble movie, who did you enjoy acting with the most?

Ah, shit. Listen, I enjoyed working with everyone. Jim Brown and I have been friends for a lot of years. A lot of the cast played golf together. Again, for me, I was coming out of a dark period in my life so I was a little more toned down in general.

Your character Luther "Shark" Lavay gives a very passionate speech to Jamie Foxx's Willy Beamen about being proud of what he has achieved. How did you prepare for that scene? and were you given any direction by Oliver Stone?

Man, that was a bitch to do. It took me numerous takes. I was nervous as shit and yes, Oliver coached me up quite a bit.

What was it like to be part of the scene where Pacino delivers his "inches" speech?

So many NFL players have told me over the years, how their coaches have used Al's speech as a motivational tool on Saturday night's before games. I still get chills....

How many takes did it take to get that scene in the can? Were any of the other takes vastly different to what was in the film?

I can't remember what I had for lunch today so I definitely can't recall that stuff.

As a film about American football, how close to the truth is *Any Given Sunday*?

Like everything about Hollywood, there are some parts that were somewhat real, and others that were stretched.

Scarecrow – Al Pacino and Gene Hackman receive direction from Jerry Schatzberg.

Author! Author! – Igor (Eric Gurry) talks to his father Ivan (Al Pacino) while the rest of the children listen on.

Scarface - Al Pacino and Stephen Bauer during filming.

Scent of a Woman – Lt Col Slade (Al Pacino) returns home accompanied by Charlie (Chris O'Donnell) and Manny (Gene Canfield).

Heat – L.A. Police detectives including Casals (Wes Studi) and Hanna (Al Pacino) survey the aftermath of an armoured car heist.

Looking for Richard – Julie Moret and Kevin Conway receive direction from Al Pacino.

Donnie Brasco – Al Pacino, James Russo, Bruno Kirby, Michael Madsen and Johnny Depp on set.

Devils Advocate – Mary Ann (Charlie Theron), Diana (Pamela Gray) and Jackie (Tamara Tunie) are caught in John Milton's (Al Pacino) clutches.

The Insider – Russell Crowe and Al Pacino meet the real Jeffrey Wigand (far left) and Lowell Bergman (far right).

Stand Up Guys – Courtney Galiano and Al Pacino on the set.

Phil Spector – Linda Kenney Baden (Dame Helen Mirren) and Nick Stavros (John Pirruccello) defend Phil Spector (Al Pacino) in court.

Salome & Wilde Salome – Jessica Chastain and Al Pacino attend the BFI Southbank for the UK Premiere.

Chinese Coffee

Cast: Al Pacino (Harry Levine), Jerry Orbach (Jake Manheim), Susan Floyd (Joanna), Ellen McElduff (Mavis), Joel Eidelsberg (Harry's brother), Christopher Evan Welch (Hamlet actor), Neal Jones (Eteocles/Actor in play, Maria Gentile (Sarah/Bellydancer), Libby Langdon (Julie/L.A. Golden Girl). **Director:** Al Pacino.

Synopsis: Struggling author Harry Levine wants his best friend Jake's feedback on the manuscript for his new book. At first denying that he has read it, Jake eventually admits he has, and denounces the piece as the ultimate betrayal of their friendship, forcing Harry to question everything he stands for.

By the time American playwright Ira Lewis Metsky died on 4 April 2015, his best-known work was a one act play called *Chinese Coffee*. Originally written in 1982, Pacino saw a production of it during 1983 at the Actors Studio in New York. But it wasn't until Pacino decided to stage the play at the Circle in the Square Theatre in the spring of 1992 that Lewis's play received wider acclaim. Pacino and actor Charles Cioffi completed 24 shows before it closed on 1 August 1992. Almost eighteen months later Pacino performed the play with Ben Gazzara in Stamford, Connecticut. Much like his previous directorial movie *Looking for Richard*, Pacino wanted to make a film version. "I like to make records of things I do. I'm closer to a filmmaker than a director," he said years later at the Venice Film Festival.

In 1997 Pacino was virtually forced into taking on the role of director for *Chinese Coffee* as "there just wasn't anyone around to do it. And I had Jerry Orbach just for a couple of weeks." Orbach, a veteran of stage and screen, was known for playing Jake Houseman in *Dirty Dancing* and Detective Lennie Briscoe in the long running U.S. TV show *Law & Order*. Pacino commented: "I always wanted Jerry Orbach to play Jake. Jerry is really a wonderful actor who really knows how to just get in there." Orbach had three weeks to learn the material before principal photography commenced in New York's Greenwich Village during the summer. Holed up together in a small apartment, Pacino and his co-star tore through filming eighty-four pages of non-stop dialogue in twelve days. These one-room scenes comprised almost the entire movie. The two remaining days were used for filming exterior scenes around Greenwich Village with Orbach and Pacino. They were accompanied by Susan Floyd and Ellen McElduff who played Joanna and Mavis respectively, the one-time girlfriends of Harry and Jake.

Come September 1999, more than two years since filming wrapped, Pacino was still editing *Chinese Coffee*. He gave an interview to *The New York Times* where he stated: "We're heading into three years on *Chinese Coffee*. If I'd shot it right in the first place, we might be done already." *Looking for Richard*, *The Local Stigmatic* and *Chinese Coffee* all betray Pacino's constant desire to edit, re-edit and re-re-edit his directorial work. Clearly a perfectionist, his reluctance to complete these movies no doubt winds up feeling like a weight around his neck. Even the score for *Chinese Coffee* was re-recorded. Initially Howard Shore composed the music for this movie but Pacino rejected that work and hired Elmer Bernstein as a replacement in 2000. When asked what it's about, Bernstein replied: "It's an interesting film about artistic endeavour." When grilled about a potential release date he further explained: "I don't think Al intends for it to be released. It was fun doing the work. I thought we had it made."

Originally, the three films mentioned above were never destined for release. Pacino planned on showing all three at various film festivals and one off events throughout his lifetime, and to leave the negatives to his children. Ultimately, *Chinese Coffee* received its World Premiere at the 27th Telluride Film Festival in 2000. From there it featured at the Toronto International Film Festival in the same year. Before its World Premiere in 2000 it was announced that Fox Searchlight Pictures had acquired the rights to *Chinese Coffee*, negating Pacino's original plan of passing the movies onto his children after death. The only other screening of *Chinese Coffee* happened at the Tribeca Film Festival in 2003. After this, it disappeared from view. Resurfacing in 2007 as one of the films included in the *Pacino: An Actor's Vision* DVD boxset, alongside *Looking for Richard* and *The Local Stigmatic*. Essentially a boxset of Pacino's long-gestating projects. There was little fanfare for the release of the boxset but *Chinese Coffee* did get a review in *Variety*. Chief film critic Todd McCarthy said it was: "Overacted, overwritten and overly elaborated for what it is, wearing out its welcome even before it approaches the heart of the matter."

Pacino was heavily financially invested in the movie as he was funding the entire production. This is likely one of the many reasons it took so long to be released, as Pacino had to keep making other films in order to fund this passion project. Working on films such as *Any Given Sunday*, *The Insider* and *S1m0ne* enabled Pacino to further tinker with his movie but of course also side-tracked him from finishing the project.

Chinese Coffee is a two-hander movie, a story in which there are two characters of almost equal importance, that isn't the easiest to digest. Pacino's Harry is a yuppie writer who whines and whinges. The type of guy who can pick up any woman he chooses thanks to his way with words. The problem however, is that he isn't a man who easily gets along with others once they get to know him. He is a writer after all and aren't they all closed off, self indulgent narcissists?! Harry constantly and desperately scratches around trying to find ways of rebutting Jake's mean-spirited put downs. By the time we discover that Harry and Jake's friendship is false, Pacino and Orbach have the audience's undivided attention. Captured through their monologues on jealousy and regret. The rapid, quick-fire dialogue however can sometimes feel as if it's used to alienate all those that are not full immersed in the language of the movie/play. It can be difficult to connect with the movie & the characters when the heavy and constant dialogue doesn't have an easy entry point for those not familiar with Lewis's work.

While Pacino is his usual energetic self in the film it's also a pleasure to see Orbach let out equally venomous roars in the face of Pacino's aggressive performance. Here, Orbach stalks the room. Constantly pouncing on even the slightest pause to extol the virtues of living the life of an almost bankrupt photographer. It's not the most uplifting of characters, yet Orbach conveys the character with more to offer besides the depressing commentary he is hell-bent on reciting. His interaction with the women in the piece show that Orbach's Jake still has a twinkle in his eye and he can find enjoyment in his life.

The two leads are magical together as they bounce off each other with perfect aplomb and to watch this movie is to understand where Pacino came from, and why he continuously returns to the stage. He paints a portrait of a struggling artist trying to find his own rhythm and career path in a business that is fraught with back-biting and passive aggressive friendships.

Chinese Coffee is not a movie, it's a play caught on camera with added, exterior vignettes to make the scope and scale of the production feel broader. As an everyday motion picture it can be quite a tiresome watch as the two actors act within the confines of one room. For actors watching this picture in a bid to develop their craft however, there is possibly no finer example of how to play the full range of emotions while juggling consistently heavy dialogue.

Actor Meira Moet Shapiro on *Chinese Coffee*

How did you come to be in *Chinese Coffee*? I don't believe there was an open casting call for the film.

In my younger days I had a track record of work that casting directors who had hired me knew my work and some of them would just call me. On resumes, it has a list of special skills and on my resume it had belly dancing because I was studying belly dancing at a local New York City school and at the time it was my main hobby. The casting director knew that and they knew I was somebody honest and they said: "would you like to work tomorrow on a movie with Al Pacino?" I had the costume because the teacher sold it to me. So I said: "Yeah, sure" and just showed up.

Was it a day of filming or were you there longer?

I think it was maybe two days at the most.

***Chinese Coffee* is based on an Ira Lewis play. Were you aware of that beforehand?**

Oh no, they told me nothing. They just say: "You'll be belly dancing and it's an Al Pacino movie" and then they say what time to be there. They don't give you the back story. They just tell you this is what you are going to do "Al Pacino is sitting over there and you are going to walk across the room and you are going to belly dance." They give you instructions and you follow them. I was an extra on *Carlito's Way* and that was my first time working with Al Pacino and I remember the director [Brian De Palma] had announced that Al Pacino doesn't like to be spoken to at all on set unless you are in the scene. So I tried to make little eye contact with him or little conversations because I didn't want to disrespect what I heard from another director. It was just another day in the life.

Pacino directed and starred in *Chinese Coffee*. What was he like as a director?

In *Chinese Coffee* I was belly dancing. He was in the scene with me, if you look at the shot he is in the shot. So he tells the assistant director what he wants and how he wants it and then the assistant director yells "Action!" If he is in the scene he doesn't call his own shot or tell the people what to do.

What was he like to work for?

During that time it was a very close knit community of independent filmmakers, even the higher budget films were... it was like a little private club of actors working in New York City. It was almost like they used the same girls in over twenty different scenes and they used the same men. It was a small knit of people that were on speed dial of the casting director. Even though he [Pacino] was a celebrity, you didn't feel that. You were not on the set going: "Ooooh there is Al Pacino!" It was almost like he was one of us. It wasn't like he was: "AL PACINO", you gave him space because he was Al Pacino but he didn't act any different. He just acted like a regular guy. He was very humble and it just wasn't a big deal. He would sit around like everybody else on set. He would smirk a little and look at other cast members and smile. He didn't talk very much. It was just another day.

It is a little oddity of a film. Pacino directed and starred in it. Yet he spent years and years tinkering with the editing. Did you wonder what had happened to it?

It was years before it got finished editing. It basically went into oblivion. It was right around the *Carlito's Way* period. I remember when we filmed it, it was a low budget film and after the shooting they usually update you with: "oh, it's in the editing room it will be out next year." But they kept saying "We don't know. We are not sure if we are going to put the movie out. We don't know when we are going to finish editing it." It was kind of on hold. So I put it out of my mind and years later I googled it and saw they had finished the movie.

Have you finally seen the DVD that was released several years ago?

I saw my scene online but I didn't bother to watch the whole movie [*laughs*]. I don't stalk myself and I don't watch every film I've been in. It's not like I have a big enough role in the whole film to watch it from start to finish. *Any Given Sunday* I'll watch from start to finish. I'm sure it's a great film.

You worked on *Carlito's Way* and *Any Given Sunday*. Did you notice a difference in Pacino between those big budget films and the small indie of *Chinese Coffee*?

Any Given Sunday was such a large budget so he has more space to go off on his own and you see him less. There are more trailers; there are bigger holding sections so you're not on top of each other waiting to film. *Any Given Sunday* was really all about Oliver Stone. He was really the star of the day. All the attention was on Oliver Stone. All the stars Oliver had were paying attention to him. He was the star of the room. He was the main focal point. There were so many stars in *Any Given Sunday* that Al Pacino just blended right in. On *Carlito's Way* I was much younger and that was really more dramatic. When he walked into the scene – it was a club scene – and there was a lot of women in that scene, attractive women, and every woman in the room was quiet and every woman in the room was staring at him. At the time it was a really big deal to have him in the room and everybody watched every move because at the time it was his show, *Carlito's Way* was all about Al Pacino.

When you look back at your time on *Chinese Coffee* what is your favourite memory?

It just felt like the acting... his acting and the whole scene was so, so good and deep that when I was there I actually lost the sense of time and space and I was there in the moment. I was not only acting but in the moment. I felt like I was there. Time stood still. That is what it felt like. I was not who I am, I was the girl in the scene. Al Pacino and everybody was so in the zone.

Insomnia

Cast: Al Pacino (Will Dormer), Robin Williams (Walter Finch), Hilary Swank (Ellie Burr), Maura Tierney (Rachel Clement), Martin Donovan (Hap Eckhart), Nicky Katt (Fred Duggar), Paul Dooley (Chief Nyback), Katharine Isabelle (Tanya Francke), Jonathan Jackson (Randy Stetz). **Director:** Christopher Nolan.

Synopsis: Veteran LAPD detectives Will Dormer and Hap Eckhart are sent to a remote Alaskan town to aid in the investigation of a horrific murder. As they close in on the murderer, Dormer's partner is killed, and the jaded cop is compromised by the calculated mind games of the primary suspect – reclusive writer, Walter Finch.

How does a nobody become a somebody in Hollywood? How does an actor, a writer, a producer or a director get their foot in the door at a big-name studio? That was the question British writer/director Christopher Nolan was struggling to answer at the tail-end of the nineties.

Nolan had spent over a year on the festival circuit with his feature film debut *Following*, which was shot at weekends in London, over the course of a year using his own money (£3,000 in total). The film had won over audiences and critics alike, and garnered several awards. As the festival run for *Following* continued, Nolan was looking towards his next project and had earmarked an English-language remake of the Norwegian crime thriller *Insomnia*. His plan was to write & direct and cast Stellan Skarsgård in the lead role. Warner Bros Studios owned the rights to the 1997 film which meant Nolan had to convince the executives at the studio to allow him, an unknown, to tackle a Hollywood remake. Warner Bros executives agreed a meeting with the director, but as he laid out his plans for *Insomnia* he was informed they had already begun working on a script for the remake with Hillary Seitz, a new scriptwriter. Nolan left Warner Bros despondent and continued on the festival circuit with *Following*.

On a road trip from Chicago to Los Angeles, Nolan and his younger brother Jonathan discussed a film idea that would centre on a man with anterograde amnesia who used tattoos and post-it-notes to hunt down his wife's killer. Jonathan wrote the short story for *Memento Mori* and sent it to his brother, who worked on fleshing it out into a feature film screenplay. A couple of months later, Nolan hit on the idea to tell the story backwards and shortened the title to *Memento*. The completed screenplay made its way to Newmarket Films via Nolan's girlfriend, British film producer Emma Thomas. It was immediately optioned for production with a budget of $4.5 million. Once again Nolan took *Memento* on the festival circuit during 2000 where it received both standing ovations and awards. In the time it took to find an American distributor for *Memento* (it was over six months before Miramax signed it) producer/director Steven Soderbergh, who was prepping *Ocean's Eleven* for Warner Bros, championed the film and also suggested to the studio that Nolan would be the perfect director for their upcoming remake of *Insomnia*. "I talked to Warner Bros and told them Chris Nolan is really interested in doing this [*Insomnia*] and has an interesting take on it, and I think you would be well served to see his film *Memento* and then let him come in and talk to you," said Soderbergh.

The studio had previously made contact with *The Silence of the Lambs* director Jonathan Demme to direct *Insomnia* but he passed on the project almost immediately. Nolan loved the original Norwegian *Insomnia* and felt it was "unimprovable"; he did, however, see a way of transforming it for the remake: "What I was interested in was the plot turns, the situation, if you recast it in a different idiom." Nolan's changes very closely resembled the work Seitz had done in her screenplay without either of them knowing the intentions of the other. Seitz had spent over a year working on her draft. One of her drafts found its way to Alcon Entertainment who were wowed enough to get involved in financing the production. American TV producer Paul Junger Witt and film producer Ed McDonnell, working under the Witt/Thomas production banner, were equally impressed and also offered further funding. Soderbergh, having championed Nolan, also put up part of the financing for the film after Warner Bros took his advice and offered the directing job to Nolan.

Nolan accepted, a budget of $46 million was set and Warner Bros agreed to distribute the film globally.

Nolan had made a couple of passes through Seitz's original draft while still working closely with her. Nolan was keen to remove the coldness that was a feature of the characters in the original film. He also wanted to make it clearer as to why Detective Dormer was struggling with his insomnia. In addition to these changes, the film's location switched from Norway to Alaska.

The director and producers only had one name in mind for the role of Dormer, and that was Al Pacino. Before Nolan was brought in to direct, there was a brief flirtation with Harrison Ford but it was a fleeting dalliance. Nolan wanted Pacino and arranged to meet the Oscar-winning actor to discuss the role. Pacino had been sent a copy of *Memento* to watch beforehand and when Nolan arrived the two discussed the vision they each had for *Insomnia:* "He didn't sign right away, he had some reservations about the script, and so did I. But we kept talking until we worked it out," said Nolan. The alterations to Pacino's character included changing where Dormer was from (Oregon changed to L.A.) and the addition of a back-story in which his character had previously put an innocent man in prison by planting evidence. Dormer was to be called to Alaska because the details of that previous case matched those of the one on which he was about to work.

While Nolan made those changes in his final draft, he was also hiring actors for other roles. Hilary Swank had just won an Oscar for her performance in *Boys Don't Cry* when Nolan acquired her for the role of Ellie Burr, the young local detective in charge of the murder investigation. Maura Tierney, one of the stars of the hit NBC medical drama *ER*, signed on to play Rachel Clement, the owner of the local lodge. Jonathan Jackson, from TV's *General Hospital*, filled the role of Randy Stetz - the boyfriend of the murdered teen. The part of Tanya Francke, school friend to the deceased teen, was taken by Katharine Isabelle. TV and film star Martin Donovan came in to play Dormer's police partner Hap Eckhart. The role that Nolan and his producers were struggling to cast was that of killer Walter Finch. And then Robin

Williams was mentioned. "I forget who exactly it came from, our side or their side first, but I hadn't really dared hope he would play something so different than he had done in the past, as it turned out he was looking for that kind of challenge right now," commented Nolan.

Williams was attracted to the idea of discovering how being placed under intense stress in an unfamiliar location affected people mentally. He also liked the idea of playing against his comedic acting type: "It's exciting to play a character as despicable as Walter Finch. You're free to explore darker things like the seductiveness of evil – or the banality of it." Nolan was pleased that Williams saw the character in the same light he did: "When I met him, it was very clear that he got the character the way I did. The character is a very unexceptional human being. I really don't think he's ever played anybody like that." Pacino was equally happy to be playing opposite the comedian turned dramatic actor: "Have you seen what he does onstage? This is a guy who just pays attention to everything. It's great to act with somebody like that, but also it makes a movie shoot in Alaska more enjoyable. It makes those long days go faster."

Principal photography kicked off on 16 April 2001. The majority of filming took place in British Columbia, Canada. The city of Port Alberni was used as a double for the fictional town of Unkumuit in the film. Here, production staged the chase sequence between Pacino and Williams that culminated in the pair running across moving logs. This death-defying sequence took place on the Alberni inlet directly outside the Port Alberni pulp and paper mill (operated by Catalyst Paper). While in Port Alberni, filming also took place at locations along Argyle Street at the Somass Hotel and the former Arrowview Hotel. During this time Williams, draped in a royal blue rain coat, often wandered off to speak to onlookers and have his picture taken with them. One particular night, Williams went to the Steamers Cafe and regaled customers with his stories and jokes.

In the town of Squamish the How Sound Secondary School and The Rock Church are located next to each other and were used as the location of the local police headquarters in the film. The real-life

Squamish police station on Finch Drive was also used for filming. Many Squamish streets were used for exterior footage to represent the town of Nightmute in the film and further filming took place outside the local hospital where Williams, on a break from shooting, sauntered around the building posing for photos and making both patients and employees laugh. The same thing happened next door to the hospital at the Hilltop House residential care facility when it was used as a location. The local hunting lodge was also used for exterior shots as a double for the hotel that Dormer and Eckhart stay in (the interior scenes were shot on a sound stage in Hollywood).

Just outside Squamish is a small area of land known as "The Spit." It's mainly used for wind surfing and overlooked by "The Chief" vertical rock face. No doubt thanks to its dramatic aesthetic, filming took place there for a funeral scene. The crew laid large amounts of grass, trees and built several walls over the sandy area to make it resemble a cemetery. Britannia Beech, located outside Squamish town, was the filming location for one of the on-the-water wooden huts that Dormer uses to track Finch. Filming then moved to an inlet called Indian Arm. It is surrounded by huge mountains on three sides, which often have landslides running from them, and a bleak expanse of cold water on the fourth side. Though it looks spectacular, the remote location caused problems for the production crew. Eventually it was decided that all production trucks and trailers would have to be unpacked and all equipment taken onto a series of large floating barges. That way, production had everything they needed close by and no longer needed to scale jagged rocks if they required anything that wasn't at hand. The barges were a great solution to the challenges posed by filming in an area such as this however once filming wrapped for the day a complex tugboat marathon ensued to bring them all back to land.

The wooden hut in the inlet had a semi-functioning interior that was used for entrance scenes (the full interior scenes were shot on the sound stage). Large fog machines were installed in the inlet and a small speed boat with a mobile fog machine on-board was brought in to create a mile of thick mist. The fog surrounded the cabin and because of its almost soup-like consistency, Nolan had to walk behind the camera directing rather than sitting and watching via a bank of monitors. Production also brought in fifteen Styrofoam rocks that the actors used to hold onto during the chase sequences. The fake rocks had originally been created for 1979's *Star Trek: The Motion Picture.*

If filming at Indian Arm was challenging then the location at Bear Glacier near the tiny hamlet town of Stewart, British Columbia was an even bigger adventure. This location was selected as the lakefront home and nearby boathouse that Finch was hiding out in. There were no lakehouses at the location so production had to build one directly on the lake. This was further complicated because chunks could break off the glacier at any time and drop into the water, creating foot high waves. It also meant that some of the harder ground became softer thanks to the waves pounding the terrain. As such, production built the lakehouse on stilts and added a protective barrier of log booms on all four sides to shield against the icebergs and any subsequent waves.

Another big problem for the cast and crew was trying to find somewhere in Stewart where the six hundred strong team could stay every night. In a hamlet with a population of just under two hundred this proved tricky. Some of the local residents offered to house people but it still wasn't enough. Consequently, it was decided that the principal actors, make-up, hair and wardrobe crew would be housed on three yachts on the lake. Twice during their time at Stewart the Bear Glacier roared and an avalanche cascaded down towards the town, and the production trucks. Fortunately the avalanche petered out just before it hit anything.

After filming was complete in Stewart production dismantled the lakehouse they had built and then hopped over the border to Alaska using the Prince of Wales-Outer Ketchikan Census area in Hyder (now called the Prince of Wales-Hyder Census Area, Alaska) as an exterior location. Production moved on to the town of Valdez, situated at the top of the Gulf of Alaska. Along the way, scenes were shot on the long, picturesque AK-4 N road from Valdez to Delta Junction, also known as the Richardson Highway. If you watch the film closely, you'll notice the Bridal Veil Falls in one scene. Valdez was used in the opening shots of the film which depicts Dormer and Eckhart in a small plane flying into

Alaska. It was shot at the Columbia Glacier close to Valdez (the remaining part of that scene, with the seaplane landing on water, was previously filmed at the north end of the Howe Sound fjord close to Squamish). It was the last footage shot and filming completed on 30 June.

It was almost a year before *Insomnia* was first screened for the public. It received its world premiere on 11 May 2002 at the Tribeca Film Festival in New York City. Pacino, with blonde hair, walked the red carpet. As too did Williams and his wife. Also in attendance that night was Robert De Niro, Sofia Coppola, Edward Norton and Kristin Davis, who had all turned out to see the film at the Tribeca Performing Arts Center. Todd McCarthy at *Variety* was one of the first critics to see the film and he was full of praise for it and its director: "*Insomnia* is a gripping, highly dramatic thriller that more than confirms the distinctive talents of young Brit helmer Christopher Nolan." Roger Ebert praised the film too, calling it "a strong, atmospheric, dread-heavy film," and he also praised the two leads: "Pacino and Williams are very good together."

The few negative reviews tended to focus primarily on the idea that Nolan's remake was inferior to the Norwegian original. *The Wall Street Journal* called it: "a flawed remake." However, Alan Jones at *The Radio Times* rebutted those accusations by saying: "This skilfully-directed psychodrama from Christopher Nolan proves that hit European movies can be remade successfully."

Warner Bros held a special Los Angeles premiere of *Insomnia* on 22 May. It was a benefit for the St. Jude's Children's Research Hospital. The main cast, bar Pacino, were in attendance and so too were other actors including Colin Farrell, Jeff Bridges, Ming-Na Wen and Alyson Hannigan. Two days later the film arrived in American theatres. Warner Bros ensured a wide release for the film, dropping it into nearly three thousand theatres in the first week of release. By the end of that week it had pulled in $31.6 million in box office returns. The second full week of release saw it rake in over $14 million. Insomnia spent eighteen weeks in U.S. theatres with a total box office haul of $67 million. A staggered release around the world saw it struggle to hit a $1 million in most territories. In Bulgaria it was released two years after the U.S. release and returned just $43,940. However, in the United Kingdom and Japan it passed the $7 million mark in both territories. By the time it had finished playing in theatres around the world *Insomnia*'s haul was a respectable $113.7 million (Information courtesy of Box Office Mojo. Used with Permission). Soderbergh was eventually vindicated for championing Nolan to Warner Bros. The film made back its budget and an additional $50 million in profit, which must have impressed the studios, the producers, the crew and the cast. Another person who was happy with *Insomnia* was the director of the original film Erik Skjoldbjærg, who commented: "I felt lucky that it's such a well-crafted, smart film and that it had a really good director handling it, because as a remake I think it did really well and it doesn't hurt any original if a remake is well done."

After a decade of huffing, puffing and bellowing in his films Pacino's first theatrical release of the noughties saw him play against that style to portray Detective Dormer. Pacino's hangdog expression worked wonders for the character alongside a slouching shuffle and his heavy eyes, caused by the insomnia. Dormer is a character that Pacino has played many times before – a cop gone rogue. Yet this performance is more reserved, more delicate and much more discombobulated than any cop performance before. There is something to this detective, something that doesn't quite fit. From the moment he walks into the local police office and he snaps out orders. He is a man with power but also a man with something to hide. What is he overcompensating for? Pacino's woozy portrayal indicates a man at the mercy of both inner and outer demons. His performance is, at times, similar to that produced for Vincent Hanna in *Heat*. There's a sharpness that shines through in both. They also both believe operating in the grey area of the law to catch whoever they think is the killer: "The end justifying the means," as Dormer explains in the film. This is a good guy turned bad, and that in turn raises the question: should the viewer still like, respect and want this man to succeed, if he isn't following the law to the letter?

The *Heat* comparisons continue as Dormer and Finch sit together on the transport boat, recalling the scene in *Heat* between Hanna and McCauley at the diner. This time Pacino doesn't come out on top and is outwitted by the smirking Williams who knows his character has had the upper hand from the beginning. In previous films Pacino might have bellowed the line: "You're about as mysterious to me as a blocked toilet is to a fucking plumber." Instead he moves in close and whispers it into Williams' ear. It's a powerful line for the character but delivered in such a way that it feels as if it's an on-the-back-foot response, like a boxer trying to fight his way off the ropes before being knocked out.

The interplay between Pacino and Williams is thrilling to watch. A comedian versus a serious method actor. Yet underneath the layers of seriousness lies that comedian from Pacino's youth. So although the dialogue is dramatic, Pacino and Williams bounce it between them as might a comedic double act. They visibly tune in to each other's style to create a dynamic partnership. Who would have guessed Pacino would share such on-screen intensity with a larger-than-life comedian playing a dramatic role?! Pacino and Williams make for a superlative double act.

Nolan, undaunted by the tenfold rise in the budget compared to his last film, directs with unapologetic vigour to create a slow sense of impending dread. Though he reverts to a standard linear storyline after *Memento*, Nolan's *Insomnia* still has as many twists, turns and surprises as the director's previous film. There is no lull in proceedings as the story shifts up through the gears, culminating in a final third that is a psychological test for two men who are more similar than either of them know.

Nolan's subtly infused action re-invigorates Pacino. No longer is he stood on the sidelines barking out instructions instead he is on the field going head first into the rough and tumble. Especially during the big action set piece when Dormer chases Finch across a log-filled lake. It is a tense few minutes not so much because the audience are questioning whether Dormer can catch the killer but because they are asking if Dormer can actually survive the chase and subsequent fall into the water only to be trapped under moving logs? This is a man struggling with guilt and getting trapped under the logs could be his way out of everything – the guilt, the job, and the life... his life. Nolan goes on to examine similar moral quandaries in subsequent films.

Insomnia boasts all of the hallmarks of the sub genre Film Noir from the 1940s and 1950s – the twisting investigation, the world-weary detectives, the flashbacks, the voiceovers and the colourful secondary characters. While the film misses a classic femme fatale, it could be argued that Williams is the substitute for that part. His character torments Dormer and continually forces him into dangerous situations, recalling the actions of a "fatal woman." Not content with simply making a film noir, Nolan subverts the sub-genre and creates a film blanc (for want of a better term). It still uses the recognised tropes of a film noir, but instead of the characters operating during the night, under the street lights and in the shadows, *Insomnia* plays out during the twenty four-hour daylight of the barren landscape of Alaska. There is nothing to hide behind or within. The two main characters dive head-first into their inner darkness, while surrounded by the light.

Despite having never before directed a big-budget movie, with *Insomnia* Nolan would be able to fool anyone into believing that he'd been directing Hollywood movies for years. *Insomnia* is a riveting modern-day film noir that features one of the top ten box-office grossing performances of Pacino's career.

Actor Katharine Isabelle on *Insomnia*

Director Christopher Nolan likes to give his actors only their pages of dialogue rather than the full script. Was that the case with *Insomnia*?

I think we got the scripts. I don't think it had the sort of secrecy his projects do now.

Had you seen the original Norwegian film beforehand?

I did know about it but I didn't watch it.

Is it true that the first scene you shot with Pacino involved him shouting maniacally at you by a garbage dump?

That was the first time I met him...well I went to his birthday dinner but I sat at the opposite end of the table. Then yeah, the second half of the first scene I had with him was me on the beach and we shot that first. I had gotten food poisoning the night before from scallops in a shitty motel and was barfing my guts out and they were like "Al's ready" and I was like "OK hang on BBBBLLLUUEEERRGHH" [*laughs*].

For a first day of shooting that must have been quite intense.

It was definitely intense. Parking, dropping him off, screamed at me on a beach and then left. I was like "What just happened?!"

What was it like to act opposite Pacino?

The first day was so brief and so bizarre that I didn't know what to think. But the next day we shot the car scene that leads up to the garbage dump and I was basically locked in a car with him for eight hours. I didn't know if he was cool or not. I didn't know if I was allowed to speak to him [*laughs*] or if he was a total asshole [*laughs*] I didn't know. I thought it would be safe to ask about his kids. So I said "Mr Pacino, Congratulations. I hear you've just had twins. What did you name them?" Then he said "Al and Al after me," and looked away.

I almost started to cry...this was right at the beginning and I was like, great I have nine hours with this total asshole and then he burst out laughing and said: "I'm just kidding. They are Anthony and Olivia" and then he became like my best friend [*laughs*]. He started talking about theatre and how I should do theatre because it's the greatest thing an actor could do and talked about poker because he loves to play poker. He said: "if I set up a poker game would you go?" I lied to him and said I could play poker and then I had to prove it.

Is it true that you beat Pacino and other cast and crew members at Poker one night?

Yeah. I got invited to Al Pacino's poker game and I called the office and said: "how many people will be at this poker game?" and she said: "Oh you know, twenty or so." So I can just show up, have a drink, say thank you very much Mr Pacino and leave. I got there and it was Al, myself and six producers from L.A. and they had a table and the metal snapping case that has all the chips in it. It was a for real poker game and I lost my mind. I had no idea what I was doing and I bluffed my way through the whole thing and I won [*laughs*].

How much did you win?

I think I went in with fifty dollars and came out with about a hundred. We played for pretty cheap because they were playing with me – the poor Canadian kid.

Were they annoyed with you?

No. At the end I fessed up. When we sat down he said: "OK, now we are going to play Texas Hold 'Em" and I said: "OK" but I already don't know how to play poker and I especially don't know what Texas Hold 'Em is and he started to explain the game but referring to me to make sure he was right because one of the producers didn't understand. He was like: "You do this, right Katharine?" and I said: "Yeah totally. That's how you do it." [*Laughs*]. At the end I fessed up and they were: "Oh she took all our money and she has never played. She probably does this all the time."

Was it an enjoyable filming experience for you?

I only had the two scenes. I was so terrified when he screamed at me on the beach and then the next day we... I guess I had a nine hour road trip with Al Pacino and I was chain-smoking a cigarette the whole time. It was really fun because after he scared the shit out of me, he became super-friendly and really encouraging. I was only there for those two days, I can't attest to what the rest of the shoot was like but my stuff was fun. I was basically on a road trip with Pacino [*laughs*].

Did he give you any guidance on how he was going to play the scene with you?

No, no, no. Not for what we were doing. I think that's his thing – he acts so well that your reacting is elevated a whole bunch that you don't even notice, you don't even know it's happening. He did carry on and tell me I should do theatre. I actually did end up doing theatre quite soon after that just because he yelled at me that one time in the car [*laughs*].

So his advice worked then?

Yeah. Absolutely. The way he interacts with you in the scene elevates your performance and then in-between the scenes he would yell at me to do theatre, and then I did [*laughs*].

What did you think to the finished film?

I loved it. I loved it. I loved seeing Robin Williams as a bad guy. I loved how dark and moody it was. I like how you really did get the sense of sleep deprivation by watching it. I think they did a really good job with that.

S1m0ne

Cast: Al Pacino (Viktor Taransky), Catherine Keener (Elaine Christian), Jay Mohr (Hal Sinclair), Evan Rachel Wood (Lainey Christian Taransky), Winona Ryder (Nicola Anders), Pruitt Taylor Vince (Max Sayer), Jason Schwartzman (Milton), Rachel Roberts (Simone) **Director:** Andrew Niccol.

Synopsis: Director Viktor Taransky has just lost his lead actor after she walked off the set of his latest movie. Hank, a computer genius who is dying, comes to Viktor's rescue and bequeaths him a piece of software called Simulation One. With just a few key strokes an overnight sensation is born: S1m0ne. Suddenly, Viktor has a taste of the success he always craved and the world's most beloved, beautiful and sexy star under his thumb.

After the phenomenal success of comedy-drama *The Truman Show* at the tail end of 1998, director Andrew Niccol started work on his next project. The script was called *The Hollywood Project*, a comedy-drama that examined the film industry and how films were made, and offered an added sci-fi twist: the main actor would be computer generated without the knowledge of the general public. This film was envisioned as almost an expose of the Hollywood, myth-making machine: "We are entering an interesting time where we don't know what's fake and what's real anymore," Niccol told the L.A. Times.

The script was written without anyone specifically in mind for the role of Hollywood producer/director Viktor Taransky. It appeared on Al Pacino's desk at the start of 2000. "Its relationship to success was at once interesting and ironic. It was also amusing and had a light touch and in having that light touch it expressed a deeper, more profound ideas," the actor commented. Pacino signed on, much to the delight of Niccol: "I thought it would be both subversive and funnier if one of the world's most respected actors is saying: 'Who needs actors?'"

Casting for the role of Simone, the AI actress created by Taransky, proved trickier. Niccol had cut out hundreds of photos of from fashion magazines and advertisements looking for the right model; the right face. Some had been retouched and others were natural. Niccol wanted a look that was both human and slightly digitized. An audition process of unknown models and actors proved unsuccessful. Then in the summer of 2000, *The Hollywood Reporter* announced that Niccol was to completely digitize the role; Simone would be completely computer-animated. Shortly after, this idea was challenged by the Screen Actors Guild who were worried that if film studios could replace one actor, then all actors could be replaced by computer-generated characters. Niccol backed down and re-started the audition process for his leading lady.

Rachel Roberts, a Canadian model, caught the director's eye as a possible Simone and was offered the role, but it came with conditions. She had to sign a confidentiality agreement that would not permit her to talk about working on the film with anybody, not even friends and family. She would have to operate under a pseudonym during filming in case the information that she was a real person leaked - Niccol wanted to keep her identity a secret during filming and beyond. Roberts, or Anna Green as she became known, signed on. Further cast members were added including Winona Ryder as the diva actor Nicola Anders, Jay Mohr as the slightly dim actor Hal Sinclair, Catherine Keener as Viktor's ex-wife Elaine and child actor Evan Rachel Wood as Viktor's daughter Lainey. New Line Film Productions Inc. (part of the Warner Bros studio) sanctioned a budget of just $10 million.

By the time filming began, the movie had gone through two name changes. Originally called *The Hollywood Project* it was changed to *Simone* and lastly to *S1m0ne*. Changing the letters to numbers was a reference to computer binary code.

Principal photography for *S1m0ne* began in late 2000. The entire production was shot solely in California, mainly in and around Los Angeles. As New Line Cinema were part of the Warner Bros family of studios it meant the backlot of Warner Bros Burbank Studios was made available to the production for the on-the-lot, exterior studio scenes.

Indoor sound stages were erected at the Sunset Gower Studios and also Paramount Pictures. While on the lot at Paramount Pictures, production renovated the front gate to serve as the entrance to the fictitious film company: Amalgamated Film Studios. "Even Paramount were surprised at how it transformed the look," said production designer Jan Roelfs. One scene shot on the Paramount Studios sound stage involved an uncredited appearance by Rebecca Romijn-Stamos. Her character was to act as a stand-in for Simone to lure the paparazzi away. The scene called for her character to get passionate with Pacino. Romijn-Stamos had a bad cold and while rehearsing the scene she was straddling Pacino when a massive drop of mucus fell from her nose right onto Pacino's face. "I was shouting for Kleenex... I was mortified. Pacino was very sweet about it [he said] 'Don't be silly. I loved it!'"

Exterior L.A. filming took in locations such as the mansion at Greystone Park, the Los Angeles memorial Coliseum, Pasadena's City Hall, the Clark Family Mausoleum at the Hollywood Forever Cemetery, the Huntington Library and Botanical Gardens and the Sepulveda Dam. The physical filming was straight forward for Niccol and his crew. It was the digital work after principal photography had finished that took up a large portion of the crew's time.

BlackBox Digital, BUF and Gray Matter FX were tasked with making Roberts look like a computer generated image. There were nine versions of Simone before Niccol was happy to sign off on using that one style throughout the film. BlackBox scanned Roberts using three-dimensional lasers and sent the scans to Gray Matter who matched it frame by frame with Roberts' performance. BUF were assigned to create a full digital head and body to be utilized in the film when Taransky flicked through different styles while creating his actor. Gray Matter were charged with making the hologram of Simone that appeared in the concert sequence. They filmed Roberts on stage at the Coliseum and then shot the same sequence on a sound stage against a black screen, rather than green, because of her reflective outfit. Gray Matter used empty background footage from the Coliseum, the footage of Roberts at the Coliseum and from the sound stage shoot and then digitally combined all of those along with a dissolve, scan lines and an exaggerated light beam.

For the scenes during Simone's concert at the Los Angeles Memorial Coliseum, Niccol shot close-ups of the main actors stood amongst a group of extras making it look like they were in the stadium. When it came to fill the stadium for the wide shots Niccol favoured digital trickery once again and used stock footage from other live music events. Most of the footage came from the concerts held by UK pop star Robbie Williams at London's Wembley Stadium. BlackBox had to digitally insert the scenes of Simone on-screen, mimicking Taransky's movements. Pacino and Roberts shot the scenes at the same time however there was still a time lag between the movements of the two actors as they were in different studios viewing each other on monitors. BlackBox took the shots of Roberts that most resembled Pacino's movements and tightened up the time lag so they occur simultaneously and then superimposed them onto the green screen monitors in the scene.

Roberts' natural features had to be toned down with a matt finish for the entire film. With the special effects completed and the final cut of the film signed off by Niccol and New Line, a release date of 12 October 2001 was set. Then the studio balked at the amount of films being released at the time (including *Hardball*, *Glitter*, *Don't Say a Word*, *Zoolander*, *Joy Ride*, *Serendipity*, *Training Day* and *Bandits*) and pulled *S1m0ne* from its 2001 release schedule. Months later a new date was announced of 16 August 2002. As the date edged closer New Line pushed it back a further week to 23 August so it wouldn't clash with *The Adventures of Pluto Nash*, a comedy starring Eddie Murphy. New Line Cinema did go heavy on the marketing. It created multiple fake websites that professed to be associated with Taransky and his movie studio. All publicity material listed Simone as herself as they wanted to keep the identity of the actor under wraps until the DVD release if possible. This sent internet speculation as to who Simone really was into overdrive. The public were falling for the studio's line, assuming she was a digital creation. It was only days from release that the truth was uncovered – Simone was a Canadian model called Rachel Roberts.

S1m0ne didn't make a positive impression on either critics or audiences. *The Washington Post* said: "You don't so much admire the movie as feel bludgeoned by its attitudes." *The Hollywood Reporter* suggested it: "never fully establishes the credibility of its premise nor does the satire have much sting." Roger Ebert struggled with the film, saying *"It's fitfully funny but never really takes off."* Ebert's ex-colleague Richard Roeper found a glimmer of hope: "Though at times the satire is over the top, Simone raises some interesting and troubling questions about the future of cinema." Its first full week in U.S. theatres pulled in $5million. The film limped into the box office top ten at number nine. By the second week it had dropped out of the top ten and the following four weeks saw it plummet like a wounded bird. Only six weeks into its U.S. release and it was finished in theatres. Its total domestic box office takings stood at $9.6 million. Foreign sales followed the U.S. returns with a total haul of $9.8 million. *S1m0ne*'s worldwide box office gross was $19.5 million (Information courtesy of Box Office Mojo. Used with permission). Could it be classed as a flop? No, because it made back its budget with a tiny bit extra, but it wasn't the digital revolution breakout hit New Line Cinema were hoping for.

Though the film didn't achieve commercial and critical success, this is possibly one of Pacino's most underrated roles. His dry wit and sarcasm really stand out here. It showcases Pacino the comedian brilliantly throughout. When Viktor makes Simone we see the playful, energetic and humorous side to Pacino. The first third of the film is a delight to watch as Pacino larks about, digitally playing Simone. He opts for subtlety rather than slapstick and this style of comedy suits Pacino best. He can be witty and very deadpan and this approach to comedy blends perfectly with his more serious acting. It is fun to watch this side of his acting talent, but his desire to get back to the serious parts of the storyline is almost visible on-screen. The madness takes hold of Taransky as the plot progresses but Pacino doesn't resort to his trademark shouting and instead opts to play those scenes in a brow-beaten and submissive style. That familiar Pacino hangdog expression comes into play because he knows he can't win against his own creation and it is all his own fault (the film plays heavily on Mary Shelley's Frankenstein – right down to the Victor/Viktor naming of the central character).

As Pacino reins in his performance, it makes for a much more realistic portrayal of a director working within the Hollywood studio system. Taransky's annoyance at being unable to make his own films his way instead having to make a picture under the rule of the studio, is something that we can all identify with. When our hard work is taken away from us and given to someone who doesn't understand what it is really all about is both frustrating and annoying. This problem, depicted brilliantly here, is further complicated when everybody wants a piece of the film pie and it truly becomes the studio's movie rather than the director's.

This isn't a make-believe storyline, it happens to every single big budget movie. It is a dark storyline that exposes the studio system to be a treacherous place. It is a brave move by Niccol to do that, not many have satirised the system they currently operate in and still been able to make big studio movies afterwards. It's impressive that Niccol managed to make a black comedy about the studio system that was paid for by the studio system. The story itself is highly-entertaining and Pacino is on fine form, along with the rest of the cast, so the question has to be asked: why didn't the film find an audience? *S1m0ne* was simply too far ahead of the movie game for its own good. The offering of holographic actors before they become media mainstream (thanks to the likes of Tupac Shakur and Michael Jackson who used holograms at music concerts) was always going to be a tough sell. Riffing on the idea of a star being born and challenging it with the idea that a star is not born but created was possibly too blatant for a lot of movie goers, it was happy to acknowledge it wasn't an actor (when really it was). To start a film saying that one of the lead actors would be made from a binary code was exposing the truth too early. If *S1m0ne* had held back and continued to perpetuate the lie that Simone was real (following the path of the film's actual storyline) and then pulled an M Night Shyamalan style twist by exposing the truth at the same time as Taransky breaks down to his family then audiences would possibly have been more receptive to it as it fitted the thriller genre format that was being pushed in the movie's trailers. But it was asking the audience to be in on the lie from the start, a lie that possibly they were not comfortable with as they did not know the full extent of what the technology could achieve at that time. This was before the revolution of green screen acting and computer wizardry with films such as *The Lord of the Rings*, *Life of Pi* and the majority of superhero movies that programmed film fans to appreciate rather than feel cheated by computer generated imagery. It was also incorrectly sold to the general public. The trailers pitch it as a drama/thriller, when they should have been cut to show the amount of humour in it. Audiences thus badly mis-judged the tone of the film and stayed away and Niccol's biting satire on the Hollywood studios and the acting fame game went overlooked.

It is time to re-evaluate *S1m0ne*. Peeking behind the curtain of how movies are made is no longer a taboo subject. It has now been embraced by filmmakers and fans alike; look at the hours of extras on new Blu-ray and DVD releases. *S1m0ne* showcases both sides of the "making a film" coin so there is no reason why this movie shouldn't have a second lease of life now, because moviegoers will always be interested in discovering how films are produced (behind the scenes featurettes in magazines and on websites will never go out of fashion), and *S1m0ne* exposes the green screen digital technology within the movie's narrative. The film also plays with the idea that Hollywood is a major influence on how we view reality and the manipulation that occurs because of this. It could be seen as a cautionary tale for the modern internet age, warning that anything can be faked by the press of a button. These two angles work thanks to the explosion of social media, giving rise to citizen journalism and opening up a forum to directly question corporations.

The movie even touches on philosophy and the meaning of life as Simone is asked in an interview: "Who are you really?" and she responds with: "That's a good question" followed by a quote from Nietzsche. With an ever greater number of people trying to find the answer to that question through spiritual, philosophical or religious meditations, it feels more relevant with each passing day. The biting satire is possibly what most viewers will enjoy about the film as it is a huge middle finger up to the film industry, especially to actors who believe they hold all the power on a movie production. Niccol's 'a star is created' story is much more relevant than ever before because of the multi-dimensional nature of the film.

S1m0ne has finally ripened into a thought-provoking movie about the movie industry.

Co-Star Jay Mohr on *S1m0ne*

The concept of *S1m0ne* is very interesting. How was it pitched to you?

The concept of the film is so intriguing that the result of the film is more puzzling. It's such a great concept, that you create a fictional lady in Hollywood where everything is fictional anyway. People step off the aeroplanes to reinvent themselves, you could be a waiter in Charlotte, North Carolina but here at L.A.X. "Ahhhh! I'm an actor." "What have you been in?" "Don't worry about it." Everyone's walking around telling themselves these things.

The script is, I'm actually going to create a lady on a computer to act in films and she just keeps getting more and more press and notoriety and eventually she wins an Oscar. I don't know how that didn't land as well as it should have landed.

Do you think it was ahead of its time?

No. Never. They said that about the TV show I did – *Action*. Everyone said *Action* the TV show was ahead of its time. They said it was too inside... well, not really because everybody loves show business and nobody wants to be in hospital but there are five hospital shows on at all times no matter what year it is. The show didn't work because it was on opposite *Friends* and the counterprogramming was wrestling. So there was really no audience for it and they should have moved it to another night perhaps. But I don't know if anything is ahead of its time other than stand-up comedy. Gary Shandling was ahead of his time. Andy Kaufman doing Mighty Mouse on *Saturday Night Live* was ahead of its time. But it also has to be palatable enough to be digested and taken in real time. That concept [of *S1m0ne*] is not ahead of its time and, if it is, it is interesting enough that it should draw a big audience. I'm going to create a fictional person and put them in films and they will be lauded and win awards. I could have told you that in 1950. You have to take computers out of it and figure it out down the line, but I think the studios would say: "That sounds great."

Hal Sinclair, your character, desperately craves attention from the invisible co-star. Did you base him on anybody you know or had worked with?

No. That was the first time I had not. Every character I have ever done or played... I don't know how good an actor I am, but I know I'm a good impressionist. So I create a human being to behave the way this person is written and then I jump over the entire film doing an impersonation of that person I have created. But they are never anybody real, like in my life. It's just a guy.

What would Bob Sugar be like? You've met one in every meeting with agents... there has to be just one guy that is the alpha, even if he is the shortest guy in the room. I just picked that up and improvised and did an imitation of that guy. With Hal Sinclair I didn't base him on anyone, and I knew he was desperate and I wanted to play desperation and wanted to play a leading actor so you can't be that desperate. So, it was really fun to create that person and in the end I'm an old David Mamet... I go by everything he writes acting wise. It's on the page, if you say these words correctly. And there is no backstory and it was written really well and my scenes were with Al Pacino. So if there is any ambiguity in the scene it would flush out pretty quick because Al doesn't deal with ambiguity.

What is Pacino like to act with?

First of all, when you meet a guy like Al Pacino there is such... I've worked with a lot of Academy Award winners and nominees and there is presence, and there is presence to certain athletes, and when Al... the presence he enters the room with, it takes you back because the presence is humility.

You think: it's AL PACINO! "Hey Al Pacino. Oh my God, I'm so nervous." Then he walks into the room and he is this beautiful, kind, gentle, altruistic, soft spoken, incredibly passionate for all the right reasons, man and then that giant, giant, giant aura that you were nervous about... you are drawn to it now because you want to be like that. He doesn't big time you. He walks down the street of New York City and people go: "Hey Al" and he goes: "Hey how are you?" and I always gravitate... my wife has a rule to never meet your heroes... I have the opposite rule of oh no we are going back to say 'Hi.' You are either coming with me to see Better Midler or not, I'm going.

When I went up to Al and began speaking with him and breaking his chops a bit of a wall came down because I don't think anybody ever talks to Al Pacino like 'a guy on a set'. But when a comic goes up and says: "Is that what you are wearing? Whatever man, good luck," and then walks away, he then an hour later comes up to me and goes: "You know your clothes... I wouldn't be too proud of what you're wearing. Look at this... you call that a necktie?"

Now he is in on it.

We went to his house once; my wife made him cupcakes on his birthday. You would have thought my wife had delivered him his first born son and some treasure from Atlantis. Cupcakes! Twelve cupcakes! And he just kept marvelling, he was astonished, gobsmacked. "You made me cupcakes?"
"Yes. It's your birthday."
"Cupcakes?"
He'd look at me. "Your wife made cupcakes? She made them last night?"
"This morning."
"This morning?"

He couldn't process that and then it became sort of sad because of how kind he is. He could have cupcakes every day. Talk to Al and treat Al like 'a guy' and I think that's what someone like him, a New Yorker, someone who has scraped and fought [wants]. A seeker, he is still trying to figure out Richard III. No role is ever finished. "Let's do it again" and it's not self-indulgence... you are watching a man truly trying to find perfection. It doesn't exist but he will kill himself trying. He will not stop. I've worked with actors where you think: 'can we go home? Is this guy serious?'

And Al is just a guy. Humble, sweet, kind and quiet.

You've been doing comedy from a very young age. Pacino saw himself as a comedic actor in his early years. In *S1m0ne* he has several very funny lines. So, from what you saw, did comedic timing come easy to him?

Very. When he knew that I was a comic and when he knew that I just wanted to talk to him and not take anything away from the relationship apart from: we are here together for two months let's have a nice time, he opened up to me [with] these facts [about] and him and his childhood that nobody knows. They are the most fascinating facts about Al Pacino.

He was in a comedy troupe with his brother and they used to do improv. I thought he was putting me on and then he starts explaining one of the sketches and it's so detailed and funny, and then he tells me another one and then this guy got kicked out of the troupe because he couldn't be there on time. I realise: Oh! He actually did comedy. He told me about a sketch when you go to the shooting gallery at a carnival and you shoot those weird targets – a jug of whiskey, you knock that over and you get a point or there is a piano player and [when] you hit [him] in the butt, he plays piano.

In the sketch that him and his brothers did as kids, that they wrote as kids, they shoot the bear and keep shooting the bear and then the bear gets up and starts walking towards them as if he has had enough and he follows them home. This is hilarious. I was on *Saturday Night Live* for two years and I never even approached anything remotely [that] funny.

Al Pacino at eleven has the sketches down.

Do you think he could have had a career in stand-up?

I don't know if anyone can do stand-up unless you're born with it. You cannot do stand-up unless you are a stand-up. It's not a learned trade. You can be funny. Bill Murray – nobody is funnier. Chris Farley – nobody can touch ever, he is an immortal. But as far as doing comedy movies... that's the missing piece of the puzzle for Al. I don't know why they don't come across his desk. Maybe he's not shown the one's he could be doing comedically. But he absolutely could for the next twenty years only do Will Ferrell movies and at first... it would be like this incredible resurgence but he's always had it in him. So I'll take stand-up off the table and just say as far as doing movies such as *Step Brothers* or *What About Bob?* Or things like that... Yes! Of course he could.

I'd love to see him in a movie like *What About Bob.*

Picture Al Pacino with those finger puppets talking to his daughter: "Look at me Emma! Emma, I'm talking to you. Remember what Dr Freud said... express your anger Emma! Look at the puppets." He would kill it. It would be amazing.

He is a method actor. So seeing him use the Strasberg method in his comedy would be fantastic to watch. Did you take away any tips from working with him?

What I took away from working with Al Pacino, for acting purposes, was there are several oceans between myself and Al Pacino. When I cross several of them, there will be several more. I realised that [he] is in a complete separate galaxy from what I can comprehend as an actor. The application of the words. You can't wrap your mind around what you are seeing, and I'll give you an example.

In the scene when Simone wins the Oscar and he is sitting there pleased in the audience and she gives her speech, and I remember because I had a scene earlier that day and I just watched but I watched on the monitors, and his daughter says: "She didn't mention you." The whole movie is for him to create because he doesn't feel appreciated. So now his actress won Best Actress and the whole movie is leading up to a woman saying: "and if it wasn't for Viktor Taransky, I wouldn't be this great of an actress because he is the single greatest director that has ever lived." That is the validation that he is working towards and he forgets to put it into the speech and his daughter tells him. He says to his daughter: "Yes she did" and she says: "No" and Elaine goes: "No she didn't."

I watched on the monitor twenty seconds of Al Pacino's face and I cried because without speaking I saw a man who didn't pull a face, he didn't look around all uncomfortable, and it was just him staring straight ahead. I've never seen anything like that before... ever! That's the same guy that an hour ago walked into Long Beach auditorium, and knew my parents were visiting, and said "Is that moron Jay Mohr still on the film? He is terrible." [*Laughs*]. Now I'm watching him do this scene without words and he comes undone. I've seen him do it. I've seen Meryl Streep do it. It's a very tiny group of people that can pull that off because actors are selfish. He didn't have any of that in him. I don't know how you can be a method actor at all. I can't even process that.

So now, I'm just going to watch and pick up some pointers and then what he did let me know: there are no pointers here. It's like... I'm pretty good at soccer, let me play against David Beckham in his prime. Then you realise I'm not good at soccer at all. These guys are in another dimension.

What does it feel like for an actor to be part of something like this production?

It makes you feel fantastic because you are with him and... There is an old expression: tell me who you are with and I'll tell you who you are. If you are in a movie with Al Pacino and Catherine Keener and Winona Ryder and then the movie doesn't do so well, that's not a failure at all. I spent time with these people and I got to say words and share an experience and I got to have a scene or two or three or four, and play make believe with people that are fantastic. So I take away from it gratitude and from Al I took away friendship. I was not sure that he truly wanted to be my friend and then you realise when he does, you are filled with... I don't know how someone can fill you with compassion by accepting your friendship. But that's how beautiful a person he is.

He is very private, and people don't know that. If you make him cupcakes that's of import and to spend time with the kids that's of import. Oh... one of the kids knocked over a drink at a table when we were eating and my wife picked up paper towels and started wiping water off the floor. Al looked at me and went: "She's good." My wife just popped up cleaning for him and he couldn't quite believe someone would do that for him. I don't think he expects a lot from humanity because he goes off into his own world to create these characters, and that's why we get the performances we get from Al. In real life it is completely different, not movie star, sweet man. You just call him and he answers. There is no goofy stuff. I took more away from the human side than the acting side. Acting, I realised, he is just as great as I thought he was. Even better actually. The kindness and humility and gentility, I never saw that coming and that's what put me on my heels and that's what I take with me after leaving his company.

You've worked with a lot of big actors and comedians. Where does working on *S1m0ne* rate for you?

Automatically it goes to the top of the heap because it's with Al, and *Jerry Maguire* is with Tom, and *Playing by Heart* all my scenes are with Ellen Burstyn. So there are many different ways of shuffling the deck for your own ranking system. As an actor, especially as a comedian who is acting, all you care about is how you are in your scene and then you fast forward through everyone else, and then you end up watching the whole movie. So A) I was happy I was with Al Pacino. B) I thought my roles... that's how I wanted them done. Then when I watched the whole movie I thought this is a brilliant idea, something is not clicking, and I'm not sure what it is. It's not him and I think it's not me. Everybody is good. Nobody in the movie is poor. Nobody in the movie is below average. When I was done watching the film I thought: how did this not work?

People I Know

Cast: Al Pacino (Eli Wurman), Kim Basinger (Victoria Gray), Ryan O'Neal (Cary Launer), Téa Leoni (Jilli Hopper), Richard Schiff (Elliot Sharansky), Bill Nunn (Rev. Lyle Blunt), Robert Klein (Dr. Sandy Napier), Mark Webber (Ross). **Director:** Dan Algrant.

Synopsis: Throughout his career, highly-connected press agent Eli Wurman has successfully and smoothly managed the public lives of the rich and famous. Then one night, away from the glittering lights of Manhattan, a sizzling scandal turns into murder and innocent lives will be traded or sold. And the man who's made it his business to know everything, suddenly realises he knows too much.

Being a celebrity - whether they are an actor, musician or sports star - normally requires employing professionals to work on their behalf. At any given time a celebrity will at least be employing an agent, a publicist, a manager and an attorney. These are the core group of people who ensure the star is getting the best deals in every career choice they make. Someone as endurably famous as Al Pacino will encounter and employ hundreds, maybe even thousands, of professionals over his career. Pacino's intimate knowledge of such professionals might well be the reason he chose to sign on for the lead role of press agent Eli Wurman in *People I Know*.

People I Know was written by American playwright Jon Robin Baitz and was his second feature film screenplay. Known better for his plays, Baitz had experienced minimal success on the silver screen. He co-scripted a 1993 episode of the *Fallen Angels* TV series called *The Frightening Frammis*, directed by actor Tom Cruise. In 1996, Baitz adapted his own play *The Substance of Fire* for the big screen. It starred Sarah Jessica Parker and Ron Rifkin, both of whom had appeared in the off-Broadway production five years earlier. By the tail end of the year 2000, Baitz had written the screenplay for *People I Know* and it had been picked up for production by

Myriad Pictures and Robert Redford's South Fork Pictures. A distribution deal was struck with Harvey and Bob Weinstein's successful entertainment company Miramax for U.S. theatrical release towards the end of 2001.

Pacino had read an early draft of the script and signed on to the project almost immediately. Baitz continued to edit the screenplay throughout pre-production, making changes to the style of the film. One of the biggest edits was Baitz's choice to move the crime element into the background while bringing out Wurman's personality. "The culture now depends so heavily on spin, puffery and exultation of personalities. These guys [press agents] are the disseminators, dealing in a strange currency," said Baitz. One press agent/publicist that the character of Wurman closely resembles is that of New Yorker Bobby Zarem, the man credited with creating the "I Love New York" campaign. Wurman and Zarem were both brought up in the American South, both attended Yale, both lived on the East Side of New York and both regularly visited Elaine's bar & restaurant on 2nd Avenue. Zarem insisted that the work was not based on his life, especially the death and drugs element of the script. Knowing Zarem for many years did help Pacino find the character however and he managed to mine little nuggets from the publicist to further enrich his portrayal of Wurman. Acting alongside Pacino, several famous faces can be seen slumming it in this small indie production, including Ryan O'Neal who plays Wurman's last big client: Cary Launer, Richard Schiff as Jewish civic leader: Elliot Sharansky, Bill Nunn as the Reverend Lyle Blunt, Mark Webber as Wurman's assistant Ross, Téa Leoni as the troubled actor: Jilli Hopper, sex siren Kim Basinger as Wurman's brother's widow: Victoria Gray and comedian Robert Klein as Sandy Napier, Wurman's go-to doctor.

The task of directing *People I Know* fell to New Yorker Daniel Algrant. Known mainly for directing three episodes of the hit HBO show *Sex and the City*, Algrant had also written and directed the romantic comedy *Naked in New York* starring Mary-Louise Parker, Tony Curtis and Timothy Dalton. It is fair to say Algrant knew his way around New York and was a good choice for a film about the inhabitants of The Big Apple. Reports put the budget by Myriad Pictures and South Fork Pictures in the region of $20 million. Pacino commented to film critic Roger Ebert: "When we were getting ready to make the movie, I said it had to be made cheaply. It's that kind of film. Close to the bone."

Principal photography began on 6 February 2001 in New York City. The majority of filming took place in Manhattan. Exterior and interior filming took place at the One Liberty Plaza skyscraper on Broadway. Further exterior filming took place on Park Avenue and East 50th Street. Pacino and Basinger were caught by the paparazzi shooting a kissing scene outside the Towers of the Waldorf - Astoria. Central Park was used as a backdrop for a scene featuring Pacino and Sophie Dahl, the granddaughter of children's author Roald Dahl, and American Actor Patricia Neal. Several exterior scenes were shot on the streets leading up to the World Trade Center, and Algrant made sure he filmed the twin towers from all angles for stock footage as it was to be a central figure throughout the film.

The exterior shots at Wurman's apartment were filmed at 11 5th Avenue and West 8th Street in Manhattan's Greenwich Village. Production required an apartment that had a hallway leading straight into a bathroom that was fitted with a 1950s-style interior. Letters were pushed through doors of one Greenwich Village apartment block to request permission to film. The quickest reply came from Mildred Grossfeld, the mother of Pulitzer Prize winning photographer and writer Stan Grossfeld. Production quickly accepted Mrs Grossfeld's open invitation to use her apartment. Days later, with the apartment ready for filming, Pacino arrived to shoot his scenes. One included him peeing into the toilet with the camera located behind him, catching the stream of urine. However, it wasn't urine that was used but rather a hot water bottle filled with cranberry juice stuffed in Pacino's pants. The red stream was to indicate that Wurman had blood in his urine.

At the end of the scene Pacino forgot to close off the valve to the hot water bottle and cranberry juice spilled onto Mrs Grossfeld's Oriental rug. Pacino noticed it and turned to the crew and joked: "Why do I have the feeling that the woman who owns the apartment is going to sue me?" Grossfeld's daughter Sandy assured them that she wouldn't. With the scene in the can, Pacino retired to his trailer out on the street while production moved cameras and lighting around for the afternoon's filming. A short while later, Pacino actually needed to use the bathroom. Without one in his trailer and unable to use the one in Mrs Grossfeld's apartment, her son Stan knocked on a couple of doors to see if anyone might be willing to let an Oscar winning actor use their toilet. A neighbour called Helen, unsure if Stan was playing a trick, asked "where is he?" to which a voice boomed out "I'm a-comin' Helen." Pacino walked around the corner dressed in a green bathrobe and slippers. Helen's face lit up as Pacino said to her: "I'm so sorry we have to meet under such unusual circumstances." Pacino continued to charm the two generations of the Grossfeld family who watched filming take place and at the end of the day he made sure they had all had a photo taken with the actor. "Let's make a family picture," he said.

Production moved on to film inside the legendary Palm Restaurant at 250 West 50th Street and Broadway. The American steakhouse has played host to celebrities and the general public alike since 1926. The walls are lined with caricatures of the famous faces who have eaten at the Palm over the years. It is a regular haunt for customers wanting a meal before they catch a Broadway show. One week towards the end of March 2001 however, it closed its doors for five days to all paying customers in order for filming to take place. The layout of the tables and the hanging pictures all stayed exactly where they were to keep the ambience of the restaurant as authentic as possible. Production even kept Pacino's caricature on the wall, but stuck a piece of paper over his real name and replaced it with J. Eli Wurman. Principal photography wrapped in the early summer of 2001.

Algrant showed Miramax reps and a carefully-selected audience an early cut of *People I Know* at the start of September. The word that came out of that screening was that Pacino's portrayal of publicist Wurman might see him nominated for another Oscar. A release date was pencilled in for quarter four of 2001. Several days after the screening however a cataclysmic event took place. Terrorist attacks saw The World Trade Center's twin towers stuck by two airplanes and collapse into the streets below. In just a few minutes the whole world had changed.

Algrant, the director, lived five blocks from the World Trade Center. His apartment was off limits. So too was the cutting room he was using in downtown New York. As the days and weeks passed people tried to come to terms with the atrocities they had witnessed on September 11th, but in light of what had happened the producers had to make a tough call to Algrant. They insisted that he remove all references to and shots of the twin towers from the movie, especially the ending which showed the twin towers filmed upright and then slowly turned sideways, with a fade to Wurman waking up from a night of booze and pills. "It is an abstract, highly stylish shot that is completely inappropriate and will be removed from the film," said producer Leslie Urdang.

Miramax pushed the U.S. release date back to an unconfirmed date sometime in 2002. With the film sidelined for an unspecified time in its native country, Miramax saw to it that the film would still be released in foreign territories. Taking its first bow in Italy on 11 October 2002, where it pulled in $682,000 from 274 screens in its first weekend. A month later the film was released in Peru and that was followed by a straight-to-DVD release in Australia during December.

Its first U.S. screening took place at the 2003 Sundance Film Festival on 17 January, where it was screened in competition (making it awards eligible at the festival). A packed Eccles Theatre not only watched the film but was also treated to a brief talk about the movie from Algrant, Baitz and Pacino. Shortly afterwards Miramax finally confirmed a U.S. theatrical release. It would have a limited release in New York and Los Angeles on 25 April followed by a nationwide release in May. Opening in only five theatres on the last weekend of April, the movie pulled in a limp $34,211. Its nationwide release two weeks later didn't help its cause as only three more theatres opted to show the film. By the third week of May it had dropped out of U.S. theatres with a measly return of $126,793. The film's biggest box office returns came from two foreign territories – Spain and Italy, with cumulative figures of $1.6 million and $1.5 million respectively (Information courtesy of Box Office Mojo. Used with permission). Due to the low-key nature of the release, very few critics were able to review the film. Roger Ebert didn't get to write a review as it never opened in Chicago (he did screen it later at Ebertfest).

The New York Post had more opportunity to catch the film and called it: "Nasty but compulsively watchable." *Variety* praised the film and the star: "Compelling 24 hour odyssey into the life of a world-weary Gotham publicist, driven by a vivid performance by Al Pacino." *The Wall Street Journal*'s review was scathing "Not a pretty sight, any of it." *TV Guide Magazine* suggested: "Pacino's no-holds-barred performance is either the reason to see this tepid thriller or the reason to avoid it." Had the almost two year release delay hindered the film finding an audience? Or could it be that the general public were not interested in seeing a movie about 'the man behind the man'? Or maybe they were confused by the woozy darkness of the trailer? Whatever the case may be, *People I Know* found only the smallest of audiences.

Eli Wurman is a character type that audiences haven't seen Pacino play before. This character is a person who is happy to be in the shadows while simply making things happen for his clients. He likes the association with the glitterati, but doesn't want the tiresome restrictions that go with being famous. He knows he sold himself out in his previous job in L.A. as he says: "I sucked cocks in Hollywood." Explaining his figurative journey to acquiring the power he needed to be this legendary publicist. This film picks up years later in New York, when the sad decline of a once-great man is nearing its end.

Pacino's smooth face and confident demeanour is completely replaced by a hangdog expression, heavy bags under his eyes and a hunch. His hair is a fountain spray that doesn't look like it has been styled in years. He wears little, beady-eye glasses and is dressed head-to-toe in drab, grey clothes. He is a world-weary guy who looks like he could die standing up, and people would still just pass by him.

Pacino dials his entire performance back to almost a sighed whisper. He only unleashes his famous bellows once. The most delicate scenes come from Pacino and Basinger in a hotel room discussing their downtrodden lives and how they yearn to be back in Georgia enjoying the peace and quiet of the farm. There is real emotion between them and a genuine belief that they are perfectly suited for each other. Even without the bright lights and oodles of make-up, Basinger radiates beauty. Her high cheekbones and soft lips are the aesthetic opposite of Pacino's face. This is why their storyline works so well. There is a sense that he needs her to feel complete, to take him away from the job that is killing him. If the movie had solely been a rom-com about Gray and Wurman's so-near-yet-so-far romance then it might have become one of the classic New York City romance movies. Instead this sub plot makes up just one strand of the movie.

Another subplot, and one that meant the movie was held back two years, revolved around the criticism of the mayor of New York City and his treatment of immigrants. An issue that feels increasingly relevant with each passing year. It isn't tackled head-on as much as it should be; however there are enough echoes of racism reverberating throughout the film for it to be seen as passing comment on the matter.

The finale in the Palms Restaurant shows how far away Rev Blunt is, politically and financially, from the rest of the room that is mainly made up of rich, white people. Even the mayor won't entertain Blunt on a professional level unless demands are met. It is a searing subplot that plays out like spin-off from Pacino's earlier work: *City Hall*.

The constant prescription pill-popping throughout the film is indicative of North America's reliance on pharmaceuticals to numb out the problems they are having. Dr Napier thinks nothing of telling Wurman to take more drugs, even though all the publicist truly needs is a good night's sleep without the constant interference from clients and the buzz of the city. The over-reliance on pills worsens his condition with each swallow. Nobody, except Gray, offers to tell him that he should just stop and let his body heal naturally. Instead Dr Napier and others see it as a way to keep Wurman under their control. To ensure he keeps throwing money at them for the next fashionable drug that will supposedly help. The original ending featuring a woozy camera twist/fade from the twin towers to a drugged out Pacino sprawled on his bed could have been a very powerful closing shot.

From the trailer, *People I Know* looks like a rather drab affair. However the movie is anything but drab. This multi-strand, murder mystery takes shots at the mayor of New York City, racism, the entertainment industry and pharmaceutical practises. A powder keg of explosive issues for a small indie movie to light a fire under. Sadly, due to the handling of the release by the distributors, most will have missed this fiery political conspiracy thriller that features one of Pacino's most understated performances.

Comedian Robert Klein on *People I Know*

Is it correct that you knew Pacino before you began filming *People I Know*?

I knew him a bit socially before I did the movie with him. We had mutual friends – Theodore Mann who ran the Circle in the Square theatre in New York for years. Then I wound up in this movie, I play his doctor.

How did you become involved?

I guess the agent thought I would be good for it. I didn't have to read for it. They gave me the part. My overwhelming memory of the production... well first of all there was a lot of beefing and bitching about Harvey Weinstein not putting enough resources into advertising it, which is typical in the movie business. It is one of his more obscure movies.

The film wasn't released in the UK until 2004 and when it was it seemed to be pretty much thrown out on DVD. I find this bizarre considering the big names in the cast.

Wonderful cast and a wonderful, very interesting screenplay by Jon Robin Baitz – who is a well known playwright here. The thing about working with Al is, every take he did differently. The same scene, he never did the same take twice. In fact the very first scene I shot with him, we were in this medical office in Brooklyn, and we were doing the scene and I missed my cue because I was so fascinated watching him [*laughs*].

Also, I know that he walked around for a good month and half like that character. He wore a tattered overcoat, he didn't shave regularly, he tried to get into the idea of this character. There was a PR guy that it was supposed to be named after, but that PR guy in New York was not a drug addict... Bobby Zarem! Bobby Zarem was who it was modelled on, the kind of guy that knows everyone in New York. We had two rehearsals in his [Pacino's] apartment and I remember the apartment was stocked with tuna fish and stuff but it didn't look like it was very lived in and we are going to rehearse and he opens a can of sardines, cuts a piece of onion, grabs a piece of bread and devours it.

Then [he was] ready to rehearse.

He was eternally polite, wonderful to get along with. The director was inexperienced. Anything between the two was always off to the side, private, nothing to show him up or anything like that. I noticed that. These little indications of civility and courtesy. Each time he said: "Let's do it once more. Once more." And he would give it a different way so the director had at least seven different choices. He showed he knows what he is doing.

The scene you feature in with Pacino is quite close and confined because you are in a very small room. What was it like to act with him in such circumstances?

It was a wonderful experience because it was easy, smooth and, obviously, prepared. It's always a pain in the neck when an actor is ill-prepared or temperamental or unhappy or something. My feeling about Al is, he is married to his profession. He is so devoted to it that he can't stop it; he can't stop working at it. I've been in six Broadway shows and I wouldn't want to be in another one. I'm seventy-four years old, I'm still working as a comedian and an actor but I wouldn't want to have to show up eight times a week. How he has the energy... and after that performance in *The Merchant of Venice* he was physically exhausted... I mean just wiped. The part was so physical. He is one of the greatest actors I've ever seen, and I've worked with a lot of good ones.

He doesn't mail anything in. Nothing is mailed in. He is aware that any shot could wind up in the movie and his consistency is amazing. I think a long time ago he stopped drinking and pretty much takes care of himself.

He seems a man of modest habits. Maybe had a wild youth around the time of... what was the heroin movie again?

The Panic in Needle Park

That's the first time we saw him and it was amazing. He has a wonderful sense of humour too. I can make him laugh. I used to imitate him in parts of *The Godfather* and kid him about it. He is a pretty good guy. He doesn't stand on ceremony. He is gracious. That is my experience. I bumped into him not long around and we chatted for a while. He had seen one of my HBO specials and told me how interesting it was and how funny.

You are a comedian first and foremost. Pacino always wanted to be a comedic actor. Do you think he has got the natural talent?

I don't know. The closest was the Israel Horowitz piece. The one with the kids...

Author! Author!

Isn't that the lightest thing he has ever done?! I'm not sure...

He did a comedy called *Jack & Jill* with Adam Sandler where he was playing himself rather than a character...

Right. It's funny because I did a film with Adam Sandler. The only serious work he ever did. One of his better efforts and it fell on its face; it was called *Reign Over Me*. It's a very good film. Getting back to your question about Al, I don't really know. All of his work has been pretty much drama except for *Author ! Author!* It's an interesting question. I think he could do anything. He knows his lines and knows the nuance of what the author is trying to say so I imagine he could. He is a good laugher. It is just his work usually involves dead serious stuff.

Going back to *People I Know*. The film was suppressed for two years. This was around the time of 9/11. Do you think it was the right decision to hold off on the release?

I have no idea why... there was questions... there is a shot of the twin towers because the criminal machinations are supposedly done in the World Trade Center and there was some talk in the editing of removing the long shot because it's too heartbreaking. I don't think they did. What do you mean about the mayor? Was that the reason for the controversy?

Apparently they held it back because it was critical of the fictional New York mayor in the movie.

It's all fictional. I can't imagine why... but it wasn't repressed here in the States. It came out. I don't think it was held two years. Here you mean?

Yes. From my research it was two years before it was officially released. It was shown at a couple of festivals but the full release was two years later because of it being critical towards the mayor.

I just don't remember. I remember we had a little party... a very little party after the premiere. I made the tremendous faux pas... I used to do a show on the A&E network and on my staff was a young lady named Eve who was married to Harvey Weinstein. I hadn't seen her in a long time and Harvey was there [at the party] and I said: "Harvey how's Eve?" Suddenly everyone froze and then Harvey starts to laugh and says: "She's fine." He was in a terrible divorce.

I remember it was at the party for the movie that Al and the director and, I guess the producer, were kind of grumbling about Harvey not giving them the proper resources to advertise the movie.

I did not remember it was held back. It was pure fiction... it's no more offensive than a Batman movie with a crooked mayor or something. It was a made up story about a secret power structure that doesn't really exist. That's very interesting. I had no idea. It just got lost and I think that it's a very interesting film. It's one of his best performances and not enough people saw it.

When you finally saw the movie, what did you think to it?

I liked it. It was dark and I thought it held together nicely. I liked it. I liked the movie and I liked myself in it. I thought Al was terrific. Like any actor, he is in bad movies too. Actors have to make a living and a lot of them are misses. This may have been a miss commercially but I think it was a well put together, original type of film. I liked it very much. Interesting side note: I was doing something in California at Warner Bros I think… and a man with dyed black hair and a moustache and he tells me he is Al Pacino's father. He was working as an extra. At that time when we were rehearsing in Al's apartment I told him: "I bumped into your father."

What did Pacino say when you told him?

He gave an ironic smile and said: "yeah, where was he when I needed him?"

He has mainly spoken about his mother and grandparents in interviews.

This guy kind of looked like him. As I recall he wore some sort of gold ring. I reported to Al "I bumped into your father" and it was like: "Some father" you know! I think they have been in some contact. My memory of it is that he had never not seen him in forty-five years or something like that. It sounded more like the father showed up when he became a big star and they became friends again. It didn't sound like they had much of a relationship. I do know that we talked about… many many years ago I thought I was drinking too much and I was talking to Al and he said he doesn't drink anymore and he gave me a pep talk without it being a pep talk and after our conversation I laid off the sauce for a while. I've only known him to be sober as a judge and completely in charge of his performances and a totally disciplined actor. He has a sense of what things are going to look like. Has he directed anything?

He has directed a handful of films. A couple of films he didn't release for many years because he continued to tinker with them.

So he kept on editing and editing? Sounds like him. He is a perfectionist. He can't let it go.

The Recruit

Cast: Al Pacino (Walter Burke), Colin Farrell (James Clayton), Bridget Moynahan (Layla Moore), Gabriel Macht (Zack), Kenneth Mitchell (Alan), Mike Realba (Ronnie Gibson), Eugene Lipinski (Husky Man). **Director:** Roger Donaldson.

Synopsis: James Clayton, one of the smartest college graduates in the country, is just the person Walter Burke wants in the CIA. James quickly rises through the ranks and falls for Layla, one of his fellow recruits. But just when he starts to question his role and his cat and mouse relationship with his mentor, Burke taps him to root out a mole.

Though many films have been made about the American Central Intelligence Agency, the CIA had never actively reached out to filmmakers or studios to discuss working in unison on films and/or TV shows. That was until CIA officer Chase Brandon was given that very assignment by the agency. Brandon had worked in intelligence for over twenty-five years, mainly working undercover as a covert operations officer carrying out foreign assignments. His mission when he moved to the position of public affairs spokesman in 1996 was to open channels between the CIA and the entertainment industry.

Briefed with helping the general public better understand what goes on within the CIA, without infringing on classified information, by February 1997, Brandon was linking up with screenwriter Roger Towne for a second time. The pair had previously worked on the action thriller *In the Company of Spies* and this time around they teamed up to write an outline for a movie about CIA training facility, The Farm.

The story was pitched to Tom Reed at The Walt Disney Company but didn't yield a response. Four months later, Brandon tweaked Towne's original story to simplify it, continued to work on the screenplay and even started to write long dialogue pieces, and several story arcs for the characters. Brandon and Towne's original screenplay, called *The Farm*, saw a CIA instructor unmasked as a Soviet Spy and his partner would be instrumental in uncovering his betrayal.

In the pre-9/11 world assigning a Russian identity to the antagonist was a common trope of Hollywood movies but studios remained uninterested. Jeff Apple, a movie producer who co-founded his own production company, Apple Production, came onboard as a producer following his success with the secret service movie *In the Line of Fire* and the extra-terrestrial comedy *Evolution*. Still, *The Farm* languished in development hell for a few years. After the events of 9/11, the CIA received heavy criticism and needed to show that it was doing everything it could to protect the country and that it had the ability to thwart modern terrorist tactics. Ultimately, it became clear that Brandon and Towne's script had become outdated and needed a post-9/11 rewrite. Thus, it was given to writer Kurt Wimmer, who wrote the screenplay for the remake of *The Thomas Crown Affair*, and Mitch Glazer, who wrote the screenplay for Alfonso Cuarón's adaptation of Charles Dickens *Great Expectations*.

During this time, film producers Roger Birnbaum and Gary Barber joined the team of producers on this project. The pair founded Spyglass Entertainment, a film production company, in 1988. Given Spyglass Entertainment's strong track record, this was good news for *The Farm*. Two of Spyglass' first three films turned out to be huge releases – *The Sixth Sense* followed by *The Insider*. They continued the hot streak through the turn of the century with hits such as *Shanghai Noon*, *The Count of Monte Cristo* and *Keeping the Faith*. Spyglass had never produced a crime movie before, however with the rewrites by Wimmer and Glazer *The Farm* had now shifted genres. It was now a psychological thriller, which the Spyglass team did have experience with thanks to *Instinct* and *Abandon*.

Spyglass also had a five year distribution deal with Disney which would cover the release of *The Farm*. Director James Foley, well-known for *Glengarry Glen Ross*, signed on to direct. Around the same time as Foley signed on, so too did Al Pacino. He was to play the senior CIA instructor, Walter Burke. He commented: "There was a capriciousness in him, an unpredictability that I thought would be fun to get into." Irish actor Colin Farrell was cast to play James Clayton, a young recruit to the CIA. At the time, Farrell had been acting for fewer than ten years. After Farrell's breakthrough role in Joel Schumacher's wartime drama *Tigerland* in 2000, he was lauded as the next big thing and his casting opposite Pacino meant the film boasted both fresh blood and seasoned veteran. Model-turned-actor Bridget Moynahan signed on to play fellow new recruit Layla Moore and the role of a young CIA recruit called Zack was filled by actor Gabriel Macht. With casting agreed and filming set to begin, chaos rained down on the production when director James Foley dropped out for unexplained reasons. The producers quickly sourced a new director in Roger Donaldson; a New Zealander who had had success with films such as *Cocktail, Dante's Peak* and *Thirteen Days*. Gary Barber had previously produced Donaldson's 1992 crime drama *White Sands* so there was already a pre-existing working relationship.

Brandon arranged for Donaldson and the producers to visit CIA headquarters at Langley, Virginia to observe the recruitment process. "We had the opportunity to see how the operation works, and more importantly, what the people are like," Apple recalled from his time at Langley. Due to security protocols however, production was not allowed to film inside the training facilities or inside the offices of the CIA. They were also not allowed to take film footage of or photograph certain areas to aid with their set designs. Instead, this element was left to Brandon: "I measured all of the distances between the stars on the memorial wall and the size of the statues in the lobby."

Principal photography took place in Toronto, Canada (doubling as Washington and Virginia). Locations used in and around Toronto included the Art Gallery of Ontario's Tanenbaum Sculpture Atrium, the Bartending School of Ontario and the Alpha Delta Phi fraternity house. Exterior CIA office scenes were shot at the Macdonald and Mowat block on Bay and Wellesley Street. Fitness centres Florida Jack's and Epic Fitness were used for both interior and exterior shots involving Farrell. An abandoned underground platform at Bay subway station doubled as Washington D.C.'s Metro subway. The exterior scenes for The Farm recruitment compound were shot at Sunnybrook Park, Morningside Park and the former Beare Road Landfill (now part of Rouge Park walkers trail). A night time, foot-chase sequence was filmed at both the Downsview yard at the Toronto Transit Commission and Via Rail maintenance centre. The big shoot out finale was filmed east of downtown Toronto in the Gooderham-Worts distillery, primarily in front of Building 36 with its green door. One night during downtime from filming at Scotsdale Farm in Halton Hills, Farrell asked Pacino which was his favourite film out of those the actor had performed in: "He just looked at me and gave the greatest answer possible for me. He said, 'Colin, of course, it's *Scarface*.'"

During the filming of the scene in which Burke and Clayton have dinner at the Saigon Pagoda restaurant, Pacino continuously drove the car in and out of the parking lot for the establishing shot. Farrell got agitated as Pacino drove closer and closer to a metal post on the left-hand side of the car. As Pacino was reversing out, ready for the fifth take, he caught the entire left side of the car against the post. It made a long, loud crunching sound. Unable to reverse any further, Pacino leaned into Farrell and said: "I better pull it forward a bit." If you look closely at the finished film, you can see the damage done to the car.

Once filming was complete in Toronto, production shuffled around the bay of Lake Ontario to Niagara-on-the-Lake to capture some exterior shots for the kidnapping scenes. Production then uprooted to Washington D.C. to shoot exterior, interior and establishing footage. Filming took place in front of the iconic Marine Corps War Memorial (aka the Iwo Jima memorial) on Arlington Boulevard and the Jefferson Memorial at East Basin Drive SW. Union Station on Massachusetts Avenue and the Dupont Circle Metro Station on Seventh Street SW also made an appearance in the film while interior filming took place in a private luxury apartment at 3146 P Street in the Georgetown district. During post-production the title of the film changed from *The Farm* to *The Recruit* to ensure audiences realised it was a CIA thriller and not a film about a farm.

The Recruit received its first public screening at the 2003 Febiofest in Prague, Czech Republic, screening under the category of World

Cinematography News. The premiere of *The Recruit* was hosted at The Cinerama Dome in Hollywood, California on 28 January 2003. On the red carpet, most of the cameras were pointing at Colin Farrell and his new girlfriend: Britney Spears.

Critical reviews tended to praise the first two thirds of the movie, but took against the final act. *New York Daily News* said: "So much is so good about *The Recruit* that you'll wish the ending were better." *Variety* commented: "The whole picture may be hokey, but the first part is agreeably so, the second part not." Roger Ebert wrote: "It's the kind of movie you can sit back and enjoy, as long as you don't make the mistake of thinking too much." The film was released in North America on 31 January. It opened in over two thousand theatres and pulled in over $16 million during its first weekend, shooting it to the number one spot in the U.S. box office. At the end of its first week on release the film had raked in $20.5 million. After fifteen weeks in U.S. theatres, *The Recruit* finished its theatrical run having grossed $52.8 million. It also pulled in a healthy $48.3 million from other countries (Information courtesy of Box Office Mojo. Used with permission). Additional praise came from the CIA, as Brandon commented: "I must say that I appreciated the producers and directors efforts to ensure that other aspects of tactical training were realistically portrayed. Certainly, *The Recruit* shows agency life more accurately than many films in the past."

The Recruit yet again sees Pacino take up the role of a mentor/father figure to a younger actor. For the majority of this movie he plays the part in a very cool, calm manner and refrains from resorting to his trademark bellowing. This Pacino is groomed and tailored to an immaculate degree compared to many of his other roles. Here his flop-ish hair is neatly trimmed, his facial hair is equally tidy and the look is rounded off with a selection of sharp suits. Even the knot of his tie is pulled up to the top button (a rarity in Pacino's acting career). It is a more elegant version of a character type Pacino has played time and again and this is a much more straight-laced performance.

In one scene, Pacino is wrapped up in a woollen hat and a large wool coat that almost feels like a throwback to his attire while playing Frank

Serpico. Though a likely unconscious wardrobe decision, for fans of Pacino's work it's an entertaining thought that Serpico might be heading things up at Langley.

In fairness to the reviewers, the twist in this film is rather clichéd and becomes obvious early on in the story. This said, the audience is still treated to Pacino's entertaining grandstanding right at the end of the film, something we have come to expect from him. It may only last ninety seconds but it feels like the moment the entire movie has been building towards.

The relationship between Clayton and Burke is the crux of the entire film. From their first meeting, Burke calls Clayton "son" and Clayton is a character who is seeking a father figure. Pacino and Farrell bounce off each other very well. Farrell edges out Pacino in terms of aggression and violence, and his continued confusion makes him furrow his brow for almost the entire movie. Clayton is just likeable enough for the audience to hope he succeeds in his mission and findd out the truth about his father. It's easy to see why the producers chose Farrell for this role. The character could have been one-dimensional if assigned to another actor. Farrell brings his own personal aggression to the role and makes Clayton a much more interesting, if slightly disturbed, CIA recruit who takes to heart the 'Nothing is what it seems' tagline of the film.

Donaldson's direction is sharp and crisp, never overreaching what each scene calls for. Most of the movie is shot with a dark blue or grey tint. The camera work during action sequences and surprise moments is at a slight angle, known as the Dutch tilt, adding a sense of uneasiness or tension. This technique is especially effective in the metro underground chase sequence when it feels as if the viewer is looking over Clayton's shoulder. The talkative first and second acts build impressively on the initial setup and there are some moments of riveting interaction between the characters.

The director has said that the film plays better upon a second viewing; personally, it doesn't feel like it requires instant repeat viewing. It is an entertaining and thrilling movie, but not one anyone will be reaching for too often.

Actor Eugene Lipinski on *The Recruit*

What were the origins of your character, The Husky Man?

Originally he was a samurai wrestler; that's how they described it. A big Japanese man. I went along and met Roger Donaldson for the first time, a lovely man, and he is one of those guys who has an open mind. He will say, well this is the way the role is written but if someone comes along that he thinks can fill it, he will hire them. I went along for the role of the samurai wrestler and I did a great first audition. Came back for a recall and was then offered the role. It was great.

Changing the character from a Samurai wrestler to a big, brute of a man is quite a shift. What did Roger Donaldson say to you about the character?

I've played a lot of Russian characters in my career. So when I went along he seemed like one of the classic characters that just interrogates people and is a bit sadistic. He actually likes it when the person he is interrogating doesn't give him the right answers because then he can slap them more. He seems to enjoy it. So I thought, I'll take that attitude. And I knew I was beating the crap out of Colin Farrell, so I'll just pretend that when he does give me the right answer to get a bit of pleasure.

There was the scene where I had the two electrical probes and I was going to put them on each side of his head. I said to Roger: "Perhaps I should put them on his balls." He goes: "No! No! No! Eugene, stop it! That's a ridiculous idea." So, he is pretty strict. He does like a bit of improv from his actors but when they get stupid he gets very strict. There is a scene where it's revealed to Colin Farrell that this has all been a pantomime and it was just for training purposes. Originally I wasn't in that scene, and this is one of the great things about Roger Donaldson. I said: "I think my character would be in that scene, looking in so that the audience know he is part of the scam as well." Roger said: "You are absolutely right."

Was it fun to torture Colin Farrell?

Yeah it was fun. Colin Farrell is really, really lovely. He is a lovely man. He said: "Slap me harder! What kind of slap is that? My sister could slap me harder." [*Laughs*]. He is one of those actors that has to really get into it. When we were working and he was meant to be a moody guy, he would play moody music. I don't work like that. I am a classically trained actor, so I just act when I have to act. I know a lot of actors like to get things to stimulate them into the character. So when it comes time for the take they are really 100% into it. He was really nice, and really dedicated. When we were working, he was very intense. It was really fun. A really nice man.

Those scenes look agonising. I'm surprised he didn't hit you back. Did he?

No. He didn't hit me back. [*Laughs*]. He was so exhausted because he was acting like he was exhausted. I don't think he even had the strength to hit me back.

The other main actor in the film is Pacino. What was it like to work with him?

He seems a nice enough man. We just had a few interjections. I think when you get to be that stature of actor your life kind of changes so you don't have time for small talk with people. We would say pleasantries in the morning. He was friendly enough but he wasn't gush-y.

I'll tell you a funny story. At one point, when I had scenes with Colin and, I think Al Pacino had gone back to New York, I went to wardrobe and they gave me these trousers and I tried them on and said: "They seem to fit alright around the waist but look how short they are. I look like a clown." [*Laughs*]. They said: "Those are Al's trousers." [*Laughs*].

They gave me these trousers and I'm walking around going: "Look at me I'm wearing Al Pacino's pants." [*Laughs*]. He was nice enough. When we were in a couple of scenes together and he had to stay on set, he would ask me about where I went to school. I told him I went to acting school in London and he thought that was fantastic. He is a very keen Shakespearian actor as well. I liked working with him.

You've worked with some huge actors throughout your career including Harrison Ford, Dennis Hopper and Meryl Streep. How does the experience of acting alongside Pacino compare?

Whenever I work with people of that stature, I put them in one sort of... like Harvey Keitel and Meryl Steep and Harrison Ford and Clint Eastwood and Robert Duvall and when I say these names I think: 'Oh my God!' I loved the movie *Serpico*. I loved *Dog Day Afternoon*. When I would be on set and look at him, I would think: this man is so talented and so diverse and has had such a long career, I hope I have the longevity that he's having. The reason I admire people like Al Pacino is because, when you think about it, there are only one or two stars in the movie. So it's a lot more difficult to get a job. Whereas I've been a character actor all of my life, so there is always lots of characters actors in the movies. But there is really only one male or two male stars in the movie. I think the pickings are much slimmer if you are a leading man. I was talking to John Irwin, who directed *Tinker Tailor Soldier Spy*, and he said: "How you doing? and I said: "Oh, I'm not getting as many roles as I would like." And he said: "Well how do you think I feel? Lots of actors only one bloody director." [*Laughs*].

Gigli

Cast: Ben Affleck (Larry Gigli), Jennifer Lopez (Ricki), Justin Bartha (Brian), Al Pacino (Starkman), Christopher Walken (Det. Jacobellis), Missy Crider (Robin), Lenny Venito (Louis), Lainie Kazan (Gigli's Mother) **Director:** Martin Brest.

Synopsis: Hitman Gigli is looking for a big score. He is ordered to kidnap the psychologically challenged brother of a powerful federal prosecutor. When plans go awry, Gigli's boss sends in Ricki – a gorgeous free-spirited female gangster who has her own set of orders to follow. But Gigli begins to fall for the unavailable Ricki, which could be hazardous to his livelihood.

Director Martin Brest enjoyed huge box office success throughout the 1980s and early 1990s with *Beverly Hills Cop*, *Midnight Run* and *Scent of a Woman*. His next film, *Meet Joe Black* was met with mixed reviews but made a respectable $142 million at the box office. While looking for a follow up to these numerous box office wins, Brest decided to write something himself. The last time he'd penned a script was for 1979's *Going in Style* – a comedy about three pensioners who decide to rob a bank.

As Brest began the writing process, he noticed the story was thematically linked to his other movies: "Increasingly, I've found myself being pulled towards a central character who comes off mean, angry and unsympathetic." The story was a dark, edgy and rather violent look at the world of a small-time criminal called Larry Gigli. Living in Los Angeles, Gigli meets his match in Ricki: a beautiful gangster who makes it clear her sexual interests lie in women rather than men. The script follows the pair as they try to stage a kidnapping. Brest took the screenplay to his long-time friend and film executive Casey Silver who agreed to produce it through his new production company.

When casting the role of Gigli, the main character, Brest immediately approached Ben Affleck: "I thought of Ben for a couple of reasons. He has the physical presence to make Gigli intimidating, but also he possesses a wonderful vulnerability." Affleck signed on for a fee of $12.5 million and Brest knew he had to cast an A-list female for the other central role of Ricki. Very brief discussions were held in the summer of 2001 with pop star and actor Jennifer Lopez, but they never amounted to anything. It wasn't until August that Brest decided on Halle Berry as his leading lady.

An open casting call was then arranged to find someone to fill the role of Brian, the man who was to be kidnapped. Brest saw thousands of tapes from hopeful actors. Eventually, he settled on newcomer Justin Bartha. A call to his friend and *Scent of a Woman* leading actor Al Pacino ensured Brest had a larger-than-life actor to play Starkman, the big-time mobster from New York.

Pre-production ran into trouble during October however, when Halle Berry realised there was a scheduling conflict with her work on *X-Men 2* and had to drop out. Brest returned to his first choice of Jennifer Lopez, who this time agreed to star in the film for a fee of $12 million, and a small percentage of the box office profits.

Principal photography began during November 2001 in Los Angeles. The majority of filming took place on a sound stage at Culver Studios in Culver City, California. The apartment built on the sound stage, the location in which most of the film takes place, measured 60ft wide by 110ft long. Across the other side of the building, fifteen smaller apartments were built that were two storeys high and furnished with real palm trees and shrubbery. Brest also filmed at over twenty outdoor locations around the city: "I wanted to show a very particular personality of the city, a uniquely transient, depressing side." Principal photography finished without any problems, but the editing of the film was another matter. Brest put together his cut of the film that ran for one hundred and sixty minutes. The dark tone was in keeping with his original script that saw Gigli killed off at the end. When the studio screened it for test audiences they reacted negatively towards the ending. This was in part because the two leading actors – Affleck and Lopez – had become a couple off-screen during filming. The pair's love-life, or at least the tabloid version of it, was splashed all over front pages the world over everyday. The couple were dubbed 'Bennifer' and test audiences wanted to see Gigli and Ricki end up together, echoing real life. Revolution Studios, who were distributing the film, also wanted to cash in on the Bennifer bandwagon and asked Brest for re-shoots to make it into a romantic crime caper. Against his wishes, Brest was forced into re-shoots during December 2002. The big finale had to be completely re-shot to ensure Gigli and Ricki walked off into the sunset together pacifying Bennifer super-fans desperate to see the lovebirds canoodling on and off screen.

This new cut of *Gigli* had been trimmed down by forty minutes and its ending completely re-imagined. The majority of critics pounced on the uneven mess they were presented with and ripped it to shreds. *Rolling Stone* attacked Affleck and Lopez saying: "The stars display zero chemistry. They're so taken with each other they don't need an audience. Good thing, because they're not going to get one, not with this swill." *Empire Magazine* hit it even harder, stating it was: "Impossible to imagine how it could've been worse." *The New York Times* picked out one scene in which Ricki describes threatening someone by suggesting she will gouge out their eyes and remove their brain, the critic wrote: "Having seen *Gigli*, I must say that the idea has a certain appeal." A couple of upbeat reviews came from surprising names. *Variety* said it was: "An enjoyably written and performed romantic-comedy" and Roger Ebert said: "The movie tries to do something different, thoughtful, and a little daring with their relationship, and although it doesn't quite work, maybe the movie is worth seeing for some scenes that are really very good." The general public did not follow Ebert's advice and stayed away. Opening on 1 August 2003 in U.S. theatres it saw a weekend box office return of just $3.7 million from 2,215 screens. The film was dropped from theatres at the end of its third week on release. The total box office gross amounted to $6 million in the U.S. Overseas the picture fared even worse with a cumulative return of $1.1 million. It was yanked out of UK theatres after only one week. In total then, *Gigli* pulled in $7.3 million from worldwide theatrical release (Information courtesy of Box Office Mojo. Used with Permission). This was set against a budget of $75.6 million.

Further insult came in the form of nine nominations at the 24th Golden Raspberry Awards in 2004. It swept to victory in six categories including Worst Picture, Actor, Actress, Director and Screen Couple. No other film had ever wiped the board like that at the Razzies. It was an embarrassing experience from start to finish for everyone involved.

Those who say *Gigli* is the worst film ever made have clearly not seen *Battlefield Earth* or *Oversexed Rugsuckers from Mars* or Tommy Wiseau's *The Room*. Those pictures are the cinematic equivalent of fingernails raking down a chalkboard. *Gigli* is simply a huge disappointment. It's a depressing thought that a director as talented as Martin Brest could write a script and make a film that is so deeply misogynistic. The dialogue is hideously outdated and would have been an embarrassment in the 1970s, let alone the early part of the 21st century. Gigli's ceaseless dirty chat up lines have viewers wishing themselves into the shower less than thirty minutes into the film. The ideas presented aren't remotely acceptable in modern society and certainly shouldn't be seen and heard in a movie starring two A-list actors. It almost feels as though they are promoting the misogyny.

Some of the dialogue is also offensive to the LGBT community. During one "romantic" interlude Ricki explains to Gigli how women are really the alpha males when it comes to having sex and how gays are better at pleasing their lovers because they are more in-tune with each other. Ricki's speech could be viewed as an interesting examination of certain elements of homosexuality but it matters little. In the next breath, Ricki leans into Gigli and seductively whispers: "I thought you wanted to be my bitch." Undercutting everything she has just eloquently explained about same-sex lovers.

Perhaps the most infamous line in the film is Ricki's oral sex invitation: "Its turkey time," she says to Gigli before nodding downwards and adding: "gobble gobble." The word awkward doesn't quite cover the cringe-worthy nature of this moment, and there are numerous other examples throughout the film. In addition to the shameful dialogue, there are also moments in this film that simply don't make sense: the random scene with Ricki's ex; the impossibility of cutting off the thumb with a plastic knife; the Baywatch element that culminates in a kitsch ending for Brian. The new happy-ever-after ending for Larry and Ricki is eye-gougingly clichéd. Spoiler: they drive off into the sunset together.

The film does not bring out the best in Affleck, who scowls his way through most scenes and looks uncomfortable with a lot of the poor dialogue. Affleck should be thankful however, that he didn't have to go through what Lopez did. Some sort of sexual awkwardness thwarts her every scene, whether she's doing yoga in tight clothes while the moonlight shines off her backside or reading a book about peace while draped over a lounge chair in a skimpy robe. Was there a moth outbreak in the Ricki clothes wardrobe on set? Because Lopez's outfits seem to have an increasing number of holes as the runtime progresses in the most bizarre, meant to be sexy, places. The costumers also appear to have lost all of the bras assigned to Lopez's character about half way through filming.

Pacino's short, ten minute cameo see's him bellow his way through the dialogue. It's little more than Pacino being Pacino. By the time he turns up, the movie is already lost amongst a maze of chauvinistic threads but thankfully Pacino doesn't get involved in any of that. He simply turns up, delivers what you'd expect and that's the end of his scene. If only the same could be said for Justin Bartha. Bartha plays the mentally-challenged Brian like a poor man's Raymond Babbitt of *Rain Man*. You care for Hoffman's character in that film. In *Gigli*, there is no hate or love involved because Bartha's portrayal is just a plain rip off of Hoffman's. If they took the character out of the movie it wouldn't matter because, while he is the McGuffin at the centre of the storyline, he contributes nothing to the plot. If indeed you can say this film has a plot. Nothing actually happens apart from Pacino shooting somebody and Affleck and Lopez driving off into the sunset together. It's nearly one hundred and twenty minutes of nothingness, disappointment and embarrassment.

Despite how terrible this film is, the two stars involved didn't seem to suffer too much in the aftermath. Jennifer Lopez went on to star in two very profitable romantic comedies *Shall We Dance?* and *Monster-in-Law* after starring in *Gigli*. She also continued releasing multi-million selling music albums and toured relentlessly to huge sold out arenas around the world. Affleck's career as a leading man did stall after *Gigli* but he regrouped and came back stronger with his directorial debut: *Gone Baby Gone*. Since then cinema goers have seen a more intense side to Affleck through his acting in films such as *The Town*, *To the Wonder* and *Gone Girl*. He also upped his directorial game with *Argo*, which was a critical and commercial success, and received seven Academy Award nominations.

Stepping on-stage to receive the Best Picture Oscar for *Argo*, Affleck made a curious inclusion in his thank you speech – Martin Brest. Why did he thank a director who made a one of the worst films he'd ever starred in? Affleck was already a fan of Brest before *Gigli*, listing *Midnight Run* as his favourite ever film. While on-set for *Gigli*, Affleck felt he was on the same wavelength as Brest throughout the entire shoot. He asked Brest if he could be his new John Ashton a.k.a. his go-to actor for all future films (Ashton had starred in *Beverly Hills Cop* and *Midnight Run* for Brest). Upon release of Affleck's directorial debut film he included special thanks to Martin Brest in the end credits. During the press tour for *Argo*, Affleck commented: "Martin Brest is one of the really great directors. Most of what I've learnt that is good comes from Martin."

Unfortunately, Brest doesn't quite see eye-to-eye with Affleck on that score. Due to the debacle of *Gigli* he has become a virtual recluse. Leaving us in a situation where we are unlikely to see any further projects from a director who two Oscar-winners (Pacino and Affleck) happily say is one of the best directors they have ever worked for.

Actor Lainie Kazan on *Gigli*

Did you audition for the role of Larry Gigli's mother?

I did, yes I did. I had so much fun.

Did you receive the entire script? Or just your scenes?

The entire script.

What did you think to it when you first read it?

I loved it. I didn't understand that it would be changed and it would be the script it wound up to be. I was very disappointed. I never knew anything about a romance between Jennifer and Ben. There was no indication.

What was it like working with both of them?

It was great. They were great.

Was it fun to shoot the scenes between the three of you?

Yes, it was fun. Ben Affleck is a fantastic gentleman. I didn't have any on-screen scenes with Al, however I know him and I think he is a brilliant brilliant actor. But we didn't have anything to do with each other in the film.

The film is mainly shot around Ben, Jennifer and Justin Bartha. The rest of it is made up of cameo appearances – yourself, Christopher Walken, Lenny Venito and Al Pacino. Were you told why they were not reoccurring characters?

No. I just thought we were all going to be together at some point and we weren't. I was surprised that we were all in our own little worlds. They called in Christopher and Al, and they did a scene. Ben and I did a scene with Jennifer. So there was no continuity there. Which was disappointing. I had never done a film like that [*laughs*].

Was it difficult to get into the groove of your character because of that?

Not me. I had a wonderful time with Ben and Jennifer. I felt comfortable and [didn't worry] that it wasn't going to happen or that something wasn't going to be fulfilled because my scenes were fulfilled in themselves. We all did a reading together though.

What was that like?

It was fabulous. Fabulous.

Was that the original screenplay?

Yes, that was the original screenplay, which was very dark and very mysterious. When we started filming it the director had another ending, a totally different ending. Has anyone ever told you that?

I have read about it. Did you ever see the original cut?

No, I never saw the original version but they cut out a bunch of scenes that I was in and it was very sad because it was a very dark piece. All of a sudden they made it into something it wasn't and it really, really didn't work, it really didn't work.

What was it like working for Martin Brest?

Ohhhh I loved him. I felt so bad for him. I felt he did not deserve the criticism that he wound up getting. It was really awful.

His back catalogue is outstanding – *Midnight Run, Beverly Hills Cop, Scent of a Woman* – and then he received non-stop vitriol

about *Gigli* and has since become somewhat of a recluse. Which is a shame.

I know. Well it was a horrible experience for him. I feel so bad. He was so wonderful to work with and so smart. I was shocked that we had to go through that.

Do you think he will ever make any more films?

I hope so. I truly hope so. I don't know. He is so talented.

How would you describe your character in the film?

Well I think she was a lesbian [*laughs*]. I think she liked Jennifer [*laughs*]. That's the way I played it.

Do you think she knew that her son was a hitman?

I don't know because I don't know which version actually came to the screen and what the understanding was from the audience. In the original version she knew. But I don't know what happened. I was very confused by that film, very confused. He [Larry] died in the end, which version was that?

That was the original version. I heard that he died on the beach.

Yeah he died.

And then it was changed to Larry and Ricki riding off into the sunset together.

[*Laughs*] I know.

Actor Missy Crider on *Gigli*

Did you audition for the role of Robin? Or did Martin Brest contact you directly?

This was a highlight of my life. I did audition initially. Ellen Lewis [casting director] had me in. She auditioned me to play, originally, Halle Berry's girlfriend. Halle Berry had been cast in the role that eventually went to Jennifer Lopez. There was a scheduling conflict with Halle and so she had to fall out kind of at the last minute. I had secured the role of playing Halle's girlfriend, this kind of neurotic, obsessed lover of Halle's and I worked for Al Pacino['s character Starkman]. That was the deal. The first scene was this nine-page doorbell cameos that we did – Al Pacino did one, Chris Walken did one, I did one and Lainie Kazan did one. They were just nine pages each. They were just little doorbell cameos – that's what Marty called them.

So Marty, Ellen and I were really happy, and I was set to play Halle's girlfriend. Then Halle falls out. Then Ben Affleck... I guess he had just done *Reindeer Games* and *Pearl Harbor* and one other that hadn't hit opening box office weekend yet... and when she [Halle] fell out they sent me to Todd Garner's office and they wanted me to play the lead. So I was cleared and at the time Revolution [Studios] had just done *Black Hawk Down* and *Little Black Book*. So they were on a roll and I was just thrilled beyond thrilled to have a vehicle like that and to play opposite Ben Affleck. Then what happened was his reps called and said they really love and appreciate my work but they need an A-lister, like Jennifer Lopez, to shoulder responsibility for opening box office weekend. Then Marty and Ellen called me and apologised and said: "Would you please play J-Lo's girlfriend?" This was quite something for me. I was devastated and delighted at once to still be a part of this movie. So I went to the read through with the whole cast there, and Jennifer Lopez was cast, I think, about forty-eight hours before we began principal photography. So, I went through much for this movie and because Ellen and Marty believed in me for it, We just had that chemistry. It was just one of those things – magical, cool, fun things. I really respect Martin Brest – *Scent of a Woman, Meet Joe Black, Midnight Run, Beverly Hills Cop*. Ellen Lewis is amazing. I was just really thrilled.

At the table read you were working off the original script, which was much darker in tone. What was it like when you were all together taking a run through that original material?

It was pretty fun. There was a lot of anticipation in the air. There was, I feel, a kind of question mark in the air because Jennifer Lopez had just... she was incredibly lovely to me... she had just walked in at incredibly short notice. So I guess we were all just on the fly but there is an excitement with actors when you are all doing that. Look who was in the room. You've got Christopher Walken and Pacino and you've got all these amazing cast members. Also Ben Affleck and Jennifer Lopez were just hotter than hot at that moment. So I think everybody was calm but excited. It felt like we were throwing a soup together – I remember that kind of feeling.

Did you speak to Pacino and/or Walken during the table read?

Yeah. I don't remember what was said but it was just lovely. Nothing extraordinary. It was just lovely. Al Pacino's a family man. Chris Walken is so cool. I remember him lending his little readers [eye glasses] to Lainie Kazan at the table read. [They were] just really nice people.

You said "doorbell cameos" about the appearances from yourself, Walken, Venito, Kazan and Pacino. Did Martin Brest explain why they were brief appearances rather than reoccurring characters?

I feel like he did for punctuation. Martin is incredibly... well he is a perfectionist. I have never worked on a piece that felt that structured as far as the cameo roles. I know they were nine-page doorbell cameos because that is what we kept calling them.

What was Brest like to work for?

To me he is so impeccably sweet – his nature. But that is gear one. Gear five is... this is a mind that could recognise an imperfection in a quilt. He was incredibly sweet. I remember the sweet part, the gear one part. I walked up to him once and said: "Marty! I haven't heard from you much. Is everything cool?" He said something to me like: "It's perfect. If there was anything I would be talking to you," and he laughed. He made you feel so very confident. It was nice to have Marty's sweetness; there is a true strength in his sweetness. Marty gave great confidence to everyone. Fifth gear Marty is... Justin Bartha must have said the word "Hello" to me probably forty-something takes. Everybody knew Marty was a perfectionist and nobody doubted it because of his prior work. We did shoot Justin saying "Hello" a bunch of different ways and a bunch of different times.

Did you ever see the original, much darker cut of *Gigli*?

I don't think so. The first time I saw the film in its entirety was at the screening. With love I say this – I ventured a guess there are many original versions [*laughs*]. Also it took an inordinate amount of time to make and an inordinate amount of time for the reshoots. I remember prior to the final reshoots we were at $50 million [for the budget] and was like: "You gotta be kidding me! What are we making here?!" I was so nervous. I truly wish that Jennifer and Ben hadn't publicized this huge marriage and then asked the audience all over the world to believe she was meant to be gay and not want to sleep with her husband. I don't think I saw the original. I saw excerpts here and there. I saw several originals that Marty was working on for quite some time.

Brest has since disappeared from view. Do you know where he is or what he is doing?

I would not tell anybody where anybody is. I will say this though: *Gigli* really hurt... it was really painful. He worked so hard and I remember speaking to him a couple of times after it happened. He was hurt. I guess it would be difficult to ask him about *Gigli* wouldn't it? His films prior did such amazing things and then this... for political reasons, for other reasons... I bet it would hurt for him to talk about his one rotten tomato. That's how it was received. It was received like that. I don't feel that way. I feel like it was a better than good rom-com. If you look at ten romantic comedies and you look at that [*Gigli*] then I thought it was better than good. But I don't think it was a flop. But what happened is they drummed it up so bigly that if they would have just left it alone and put it out and not spent $50-60 million on it then maybe it would have had a better chance.

Angels in America

Cast: Al Pacino (Roy Cohn), Meryl Streep (Ethel Rosenberg/Hannah Pitt/The Rabbi/The Angel Australia), Emma Thompson (Nurse Emily/Homeless Woman/The Angel America), Mary-Louise Parker (Harper Pitt), Jeffrey Wright (Mr. Lies/Norman "Belize" Ariaga/Homeless Man/The Angel Europa), Justin Kirk (Prior Walter), Ben Shenkman (Louis Ironson/The Angel Oceania), Patrick Wilson (Joe Pitt). **Director:** Mike Nichols.

Synopsis: Separate but connected individuals struggle with life in mid-1980s America gripped by the AIDS crisis and a conservative Reagan administration. Prior Walter is deserted by his lover Louis after discovering he is dying of AIDS. Prior is then visited by an Angel who keeps crashing through his ceiling declaring him a Prophet. Meanwhile, conservative power monger Roy Cohn is also dying of AIDS, but he is in denial about it. While in the hospital he is continuously visited by the ghost of Ethel Rosenberg, a woman he sent to the electric chair. Roy's protégé Joe is struggling with his own sexuality and a wife that is addicted to Valium. Eventually Joe enters into a relationship with Louis, Prior's ex-lover. For each individual it is a journey through the landscape of despair and hope.

How do you film the unfilmable? This question has historically helped film industry professionals push boundaries and create new techniques. It was a question that producer Cary Brokaw wrestled with for over ten years while trying to bring playwright Tony Kushner's seminal play *Angels in America* to the screen. Kushner began writing the play in the late 1980s in part inspired by a poem he wrote and originally titled *Angels in America*. It was a dedication to a dancer in New York he'd had a crush on who had died of AIDS.

Kushner became friends with Oskar Eustis, an artistic director at the Eureka Theatre in San Francisco, who commissioned him to write a play.

The contract stipulated that it could not be longer than two hours and that it had to include singing (this condition was made at Kushner's request). The playwright then filed a request for a grant with the National Endowment for the Arts: "We had to submit a description of the play, and I said 'It's gonna have five gay men and an angel,'" Kushner recalled. $50,000 of grant money was assigned for the staging of the play. Kushner received $10,000 and the rest went towards production.

The playwright hunkered down to write and by May 1990, the first part of the play titled *Millennium Approaches* was ready to be rehearsed at the Mark Taper Forum, Los Angeles, a venue at which Eustis was also holding the reins. When Kushner delivered his one hundred and twenty page play to Eustis it didn't include the scene with the angel crashing through the ceiling, even though Kushner had initially said that scene would be included near the end. Early on in the editing process and struggling to remove large chunks of his own work so the angel scene could be included; an actor called Sigrid Wurschmidt threw Kushner a life line. He opened his notebook to show Wurschmidt a monologue that wasn't included in *Millennium Approaches*, and she turned to him and asked why it wasn't in the play. Kushner replied: "What am I gonna cut?" Wurschmidt responded: "Why don't you make it two plays?"

This was a major turning point for Kushner. He could expand the story and write two plays. After spending ten days locked away in a spider-infested cabin on the Russian River in Northern California, Kushner returned with a seven hundred page manuscript that comprised the second part of *Angels in America*. It was called: *Perestroika. Millennium Approaches* opened 7 May 1991 at San Francisco's Eureka Theatre. It was met with positive reviews and lines of theatregoers queuing around the block. *Perestroika* also premiered at the Eureka Theatre, but only as a staged reading. During the very first reading playwright and actor Ellen McLaughlin played The Angel and as she arrived on stage to announce the start of Act 5 (the first part of *Perestroika*) a woman in the front row shouted: "It's midnight. How long is this act?" McLaughlin replied: "We've never done it, so I don't know."

It was around this time that Cary Brokaw became interested in producing a cinematic version of *Angels in America*. The movie producer had read the original play in 1989 while Kushner was still working on it and one night, over dinner, Brokaw tempted Kushner into agreeing to an adaptation by offering him the option of writing the screenplay. Brokaw also asked the playwright who he would want as the director and Kushner replied: "It's going to surprise you: Robert Altman." As luck would have it, Brokaw was the producer on Altman's latest movie *The Player* starring Tim Robbins and convinced the director to watch *Millennium Approaches*. The day after Altman had watched the play he signed on to direct.

Both the director and the producer wanted the same man to play Roy Cohn; they both wanted Al Pacino. Pacino committed to playing Cohn in 1993, the same year that the entire two-part play first debuted on Broadway. It took home a Tony Award for Best Play in both 1993 and 1994. *Angels in America* achieved worldwide acknowledgement thanks to successful stage productions in North America, England and Germany. Altman continued to work on the project throughout '93 and '94, taking it to movie studios and touting it as the next feature he wanted to make.

Every studio baulked at risking $40 million on two successive one hundred and fifty minute movies, especially ones that dealt with such tough subject matter. Eventually, Altman dropped out. He was replaced with P.J. Hogan, who also dropped out soon afterwards. Neil La Bute flirted with directing the project but ultimately met the same fate. The production stagnated. Kushner kept re-writing the script during that time, and managed to edit the story into one feature film. He soon abandoned that draft, realising that there was "literally too much plot." *Angels in America* would have to be made as a mini-series or nothing else. In 2000, Brokaw was in England producing *Wit*, a TV movie starring Emma Thompson and directed by Mike Nichols, and mentioned Kushner's play to Nichols. Nichols was looking for his next project, so Brokaw gave him a couple of scripts for him to read over a weekend. When they met on the Monday morning, Nichols was in.

Brokaw told Kushner the good news: they had found a replacement director. "I put down the phone and I said to Mark [his partner] "Should I let Mike Nichols direct *Angels in America*? He's a great filmmaker, but I don't know." And Mark said, "Are you fucking kidding? Call him immediately." With Nichols onboard, another piece of the jigsaw fell into place not long after. The president of HBO Films, Colin Callender, green lit *Angels in America* as a mini-series for the premium cable network. Callender was happy to commission six chapters with a total run time of six hours. The budget was set at slightly over $37 million.

Pacino was already signed on and had been thumbing through a copy of the screenplay for months trying to discover the character of Roy Cohn. Very quickly Nichols sought out Meryl Streep for not one, not two, but three roles – Hannah Pitt, Ethel Rosenberg and The Rabbi. Streep recalls her meeting with the director: "Mike asked if I wanted to play three parts in *Angels in America*, and I said, "Yes!" And then we signed the contract, and he said "Would you play a fourth part for free?" They hadn't included the angel [Australia] in the second play. He got me for four for the price of three! He was a sly one."

Casting was swift for most of the other the roles. Mary Louise Parker signed on to play Harper Pitt and James Cromwell secured the part of Henry, Cohn's Doctor. British actors Michael Gambon and Simon Callow played Prior Walter's two ghostly ancestors. Much-like Streep, Emma Thompson signed on for multiple roles: Nurse Emily, The Angel America and a Homeless Woman. Newcomer Patrick Wilson bagged the role of Joe Pitt after Nichols saw him perform in the Broadway production of *The Full Monty*. Not to be outdone by Thompson or Streep, star of stage and screen Jeffrey Wright also took on four roles as The Angel Europa, a Homeless Man, Mr. Lies and Norman "Belize" Ariaga. Wright had previously appeared in the Broadway run of *Angels in America* and originally Nichols didn't want to use anyone from the production. Seeking out another actor for the role of Belize, Nichols went to see a play that Wright also happened to be performing in. By the end of the show, Nichols had rethought his position. Wright remembers: "I just happened to, in a Belize-like way, force my way into the door."

Actor Ben Shenkman had also appeared in two smaller productions of *Angels in America*, in which he played Louis Ironson and then Roy Cohn. Shenkman had secured small movie roles but was better known for his performances in off-Broadway plays. Shenkman heard that Nichols was looking for actors who were not household names for the characters of Louis Ironson and Prior Walter. Having previously dabbled with the character of Ironson on stage, Shenkman was a shoo-in for the role.

Finding an actor to play central character Prior Walter was tricky. Stephen Spinella had won consecutive Tony Awards for his performance as Prior Walter in the Broadway production. Brokaw and Nichols wrestled with the idea of casting Spinella in the movie but came to the conclusion he would be too old. Auditions were held and many faces were seen. One in particular stood out to Nichols, that of Justin Kirk. Predominately a stage actor, Kirk had previously met Nichols when he auditioned for a role in the director's English language version of *The Birdcage* starring Robin Williams, Gene Hackman and Nathan Lane. Kirk was young enough to play Walter and was not a household name as Nichols requested. Kirk thus signed on for his biggest screen role to date and Nichols commented to *Newsweek*: "There was no one that any part was offered to that we didn't get."

Principal photography began in May 2002. The majority of interior scenes were filmed on sound stages at Kaufman Astoria Studios in Queens, New York City. A short sequence was shot inside the Oak Room at The Plaza Hotel on 5th Avenue, featuring Pacino and Wilson. All of Pacino's scenes were shot in one large chunk as he actor was only available for a small window of time before he had to leave for another film schedule. Wilson, while filming *Angels in America*, was also playing Curly in the Broadway production of *Oklahoma!* "If you're in the middle of a scene and you've got to go to a night shoot, you don't want to be thinking about your Joe Pitt lines as you're saying Curly's." Wilson commented.

Various local New York areas were used in the making of the series. Wilson's least favourite location was probably the beach at Breezy Point at Jamaica Bay in the Port of New York and New Jersey. The shoot at that location took place on a windswept winter's day, and the scene required Wilson to strip naked in front of Shenkman and the crew. Production also used the exterior of the Riverside Memorial Chapel, a Jewish funeral home on 180 W 76th Street. There, Streep and Shenkman filmed a sequence in which Ironson talked to The Rabbi after a burial. After returning from lunch to shoot the sequence, Shenkman found Streep, Kushner and Maurice Sendak (writer of *Where the Wild Things Are*) sitting on a bench. All three of them were dressed as Rabbis and Streep was wearing layers of costume and prosthetics. Sendak leaned into Kushner and asked: "When is Meryl Streep going to show up? I thought she would be on set today?" After Nichols called "Cut" for the last time on the scene, Kushner walked away with Sendak and told him who the other Rabbi was. Sendak shouted: "I don't believe it! I don't believe it!" Apparently, Streep was "tickled" that Sendak hadn't recognised her.

Production uprooted to Italy for filming in Tivoli, a town nineteen miles north-east of Rome. Hadrian's Villa, a 2nd Century Roman structure, was used for the entire sequence in which Walter goes to Heaven to meet the angels. Returning to the United States, some seasonal shooting was completed in New York's Central Park and then on a freezing, snow-covered winter's day in January principal photography wrapped. The final scene of the entire mini-series was filmed last, right underneath the angel at the top of the Bethesda Fountain (the iconic image at the end of the opening credits to the mini-series). Emma Stebbins' sculpture, Angel of the Waters, witnessed Streep, Kirk, Shenkman and Wright deliver the final lines of dialogue. Kushner remembers that day well: "It was literally exactly the day I had written about. I wrote that last scene in *Perestroika*, sitting on the head of the fountain, on a day in January when the sun was out but it was cold at the same time, and the sky was incredibly blue. We shot it in very few takes. I'd been watching on the monitor and I thought, these people are so smart. And that last shot of them going up the stairs and everything... We sort of finished the shot at the end of the day, and the sun was going down. [It was] a lovely, lovely feeling."

A troubling aspect of production for Nichols and his team was visual effects. Richard Edlund, a visual effects wizard who had previously worked on the original *Star Wars* trilogy, was called in to help after

Nichols dismissed the previous effects supervisor because he was unhappy with his work. Edlund came into the production fold half way through filming. Just in time for the extravagant-looking first visit of the angel in Walter's bedroom. Edlund and his team created a suspended frame that featured a bicycle seat that could be winched up and down while Thompson sat on it in her costume. The team decided to add wings to Thompson's costume as they felt it would be too difficult to CG them into the shot afterwards.

In post-production the team set about creating digital shots of the scene in which Thompson and Kirk embrace in an orgasmic frenzy of fire. "We made castings of the actors and built body pans so they could lie on their sides, facing each other, and be shot in profile from above." The edited footage was then sent to R!OT visual effects studio in Santa Monica so that the additional audio and visual aesthetics to be added. Edlund also shot a sequence to be included towards the end of *Perestroika* that depicted hundreds of angels sitting at typewriters. He took inspiration from *The Trial*, a film starring Orson Welles, which included a shot very similar to the one Edlund wanted to pull off in *Angels in America*: "They got sixty desks equipped with old Olivettis and Underwoods, and a bunch of angels in gray suits with little wings. We multiplied them eight or ten times by shooting titles." Those same sequences were then copied into the background of the shot time and again to give the impression of a never-ending typing pool in Heaven. By the end of post-production Edlund commented: "*Angels in America* is one of my all-time favourite filmmaking experiences."

Following the first HBO broadcast of the show in December 2003, the production garnered great acclaim from critics and the general public alike. *Variety* felt Nichols "has brought out an elemental dimension of emotional melodrama that makes the piece compulsive screen fare without subtracting one bit from its status as great theatre." The *New York Times* claimed: "Angels is the most powerful screen adaptation of a major American play since Elia Kazan's Streetcar Named Desire more than a half-century ago." The *San Francisco Chronicle* called it the "must-see film event of the new millennium." A total of 4.2 million HBO subscribers watched *Millennium Approaches* on the first Sunday night (the two parts were split across two consecutive weekends and totalled three hours each) and with repeated performances over the following six days HBO estimated that 7.8 million viewers had seen the first part before the premiere of *Perestroika*.

The viewing figures dropped off for the second part of the mini-series with only 2.93 million watching live. Once total viewing figures had been calculated by Nielsen Media Research, HBO proclaimed the mini-series to be the most-watched, made-for-cable movie of 2003. If HBO, Nichols, Brokaw and Kushner were happy to finally see their vision on-screen with skyrocketing viewing figures, they there were going to be ecstatic when awards season rolled around in 2004. The project was nominated for seven awards at the Golden Globes, and won five. There were wins for Pacino, Streep, Parker, and Wright alongside an accolade for Best Television Limited series or Motion Picture Made for Television. Shenkman and Wilson were nominated but did not win.

Five wins was a drop in the ocean however compared to *Angels in America's* awards haul at the Emmys in September 2004. Nominated in twenty-one categories, the mini-series went on the smash the record previously held by *Roots* for most Emmys awarded to a programme in a single year by winning in eleven categories. There were individual wins for Nichols, Kushner, Pacino, Streep, Wright and Parker. Also wins in Art Direction, Make-Up, Sound Mixing and the big award: Outstanding Mini-series. Parker summed up this epic triumph while accepting her award for Best Supporting Actress by saying: "There are some roles that are so well-written, you practically start winning awards the moment you get the role." By the end of 2004, *Angels in America* also received acclaim and awards from the Directors Guild of America, the Producers Guild of America, the Grammys, the Satellite Awards, the Screen Actors Guild and the Gay & Lesbian Alliance Against Defamation (GLAAD) organization.

There is no one stand-out performance in *Angels in America* because every single actor is at the top of their game. Nichols' direction is smooth and gives all actors equal weighting. It is a testament to everyone involved that Nichols, before his passing, listed *Angels in America* as his greatest work. Kushner's long flowing monologues feel right at home coming from the mouths of every player but especially Kirk's Prior Walter who might be classed as the central character throughout proceedings. Walter's journey is epic; one of struggle and release. It is a powerful and fully emotional performance from Kirk, who spends most of the runtime in unimaginable pain. He only finds solace when he is ready to do battle with The Angel America. The titanic struggle, which has been brewing for a while, culminates in the most unlikely of wrestling matches before an ascent to heaven for a face-off with other angels.

One of those angels is played by Emma Thompson who delivers a spellbinding performance of exalted powerfulness with just a touch of humour and a hint of sex appeal. Pacino plays Cohn very similar to how he played Big Boy Caprice in *Dick Tracy* – a hunched-over, snarly man wearing clothes two sizes too big for his emasculated frame. The flamboyance of Big Boy is still there in Cohn only this time it is partnered with a lecherous, drunken attitude. While drinking with Pitt, Cohn's narrow eyes seize on his colleague. As he gets more intoxicated he leans in further, tapping Pitt's shoulder and speaking in endless double entendres. It's an uncomfortable scene to watch and one that shows Cohn at his most debauched. Digging deep into the character's physical and psychological problems, Pacino creates a performance that is utterly riveting and quite terrifying.

Cohn's battle with the ghost Ethel Rosenberg, an American convicted of spying for the Soviet Union who was executed is petrifying for the viewer. Steep's Rosenberg floats through walls but Cohn doesn't scare. She sits in a chair by his bedside all night and yet still Cohn isn't unsettled. Cohn, strapped to a hospital bed in the last throes of his life, pretends to die just so he can see a smile appear on Rosenberg's face. Cohn pops up from his bed to laugh in the spirit's face, trying to prove he will not be taken down by anyone not even a ghost. However, Rosenberg gets the last laugh by telling Cohn she watched his disbarment hearing. It's a titanic push and pull power struggle acted brilliantly by two legendary actors. Streep's performance as Pitt's worrywart mother is a much more interesting role as through a series of accidents she becomes more ingrained in the New York lifestyle than she could ever have imagined. By the end of *Perestroika* she doesn't see Pitt as her son, instead it is Walter who she pulls closest to her bosom. It's a heart-warming performance from Steep and one that shows even the hardest of cynics can change.

Steep gets a very funny third character to play – The Rabbi. Sitting on a bench mumbling to the other Rabbi's next to her, she rambles and philosophises about death to Ironson. Even under all the make-up and prosthetics you can see Steep has a glint in her eye and a cheeky smile.

Jeffrey Wright adds a certain flamboyance to the mini-series with his portrayal of Belize. A man caught up in the impending deaths of his friends, he has very little to cling to yet still finds hope within himself to help those less fortunate than himself. Parker and Wilson also give excellent performances as a couple who are seeking other, possibly not better, things in their lives. They literally have to walk through snow and ice to finally find happiness. These are pivotal performances as they not only have their own story arcs but are also accomplices of sorts in two of the main storylines. In summary, the mini-series gives a highly-impressive ensemble cast their own moments to shine without losing sight of the overall storyline. It was a phenomenal achievement for Nichols.

Angels in America explores deeply complex messages relating to life, love and tolerance. It is not easy entertainment and its social and political motives are heavy at times. The constant batting back and forth dialogue about President Reagan and his side-stepping over the AIDS virus can be grating, yet it is included in such great depth to shine a light on the President's constant failure to help those in need. Hundreds of thousands were cast out by someone who could, and should, have done more to understand and prevent an epidemic that was about to take hold and kill a large section of society. Kushner's work seems to seek accountability. Throughout all the powerful messages *Angels in America* offers, it is a simple one that is most prominent. At the end of chapter six, Walter breaks the fourth wall to directly deliver it. His last monologue includes the line: "You are fabulous each and every one."

Nichols' adaptation of Kushner's seminal works is nothing short of incredible. It is a truly remarkable achievement. HBO were brave enough to take on such a project and allow those involved to make the show they wanted to make. In return the cast and crew gave HBO a six hour piece of art disguised as a mini-series. *Angels in America* is a landmark production in the history of television.

Executive Producer Cary Brokaw on *Angels in America*

It took you thirteen years to get *Angels in America* made. What problems did you face in trying to bring it to the screen?

It was closer to between thirteen and fourteen years. I was made aware of the play when it was first in workshop at the Marquis in Los Angeles. Two friends, who didn't know each other, attended a table reading and independently over the course of a week/ten days they both touted what a brilliant play [it] was. If one of them had spoken to me then I might have ignored it however I thought there must be something here. I tracked it down and contacted Tony Kushner's agent who kindly sent me the play. Then I tracked it pretty deliberately over a number of years seeing different productions. The first production [was] at the Eureka Theatre and then I was in London and saw it in the West End. Then [I] met with Tony a few times and got to know him a little better. I should say, I thought it was beyond brilliant and of great importance and tremendous artistic integrity. I thought it was beautifully ambitious.

As I got to know him, he told me he was writing *Perestroika* [the second part of *Angels in America*] which sounded even more fantastic. We met in New York and I was really, in a gentle way, doggedly pursuing it. I appreciated how brilliant Tony was and as I got to know him and he talked about it, it was that much more exciting. We had dinner in New York one night and he had gotten to a point of trusting me I think, I don't want to speak for him but his actions suggested that, and I said: "I really would like to produce this as two movies. Would you let me do that?" And he said "Yes."

At that point we were a few weeks away from *Millennium Approaches* and *Perestroika* both being performed for the first time. At dinner I asked him: "Who, in a perfect world, would you have direct this?" and he said "Well my answer is probably going to surprise you."
"Why's that?"
"Well I sort of loosely took the structure of Angels from *Nashville* and my answer is Robert Altman." He was in post-production on *The Player*. I said: "He will be at the previews with me the week after next."

I brought Bob and Kathryn, his wife, and they were both blown away and Bob agreed to direct the movies based on the play. New Line were distributing *The Player* and we were already in discussions with them about doing *Short Cuts* next, which was either in pre-production or soon to be in pre-production. So we took *Angels* to New Line. They agreed to develop it. So Tony wrote two scripts based on the plays and, he would admit this, he was finding his way in terms of the screenplay format and the scripts were long because the play being as long as it is.

They were brilliant.

We then started to try and cast it and it was then when we approached Al initially. He had read or seen the play, I can't remember, and he was incredibly receptive right away to playing Roy Cohn and enthusiastic about it and through his agent at the time we would stay in touch as the fate of the project continued over a number of years.

Soon thereafter, although I'm a little fuzzy on this, we approached Meryl also. It may have been a bit later. Astonishingly we couldn't get the movie financed with Robert Altman, Al Pacino, I believe Meryl was attached at the time. We were proposing to make two two-hour movies of *Millennium Approaches* and *Perestroika* for $25 million. This was 1993/94 give or take. We had no takers. New Line passed twice. New Line said: "We don't want to have a sequel if the first one is not successful."

I went at least three times to each studio and independent company and couldn't get it made. By then we were making *Short Cuts* and it languished. It was incredibly frustrating. Soon thereafter I had shown it to Colin Callender and Bob Cooper, who were then running HBO's Film

& Television division, and Colin, who deserves huge credit for *Angels* coming into existence, was a champion even then. It was just too expensive for them at the time in terms of what was going on. We came close but it didn't happen. Bob Altman went off and did other things and we parted ways.

We had done *The Player* and *Short Cuts* together and developed a TV series together. He went off and did *Prêt-A Porter, Ready to Wear* and so forth. It was sort of mutual and Tony and I and he agreed he maybe wasn't the best guy to do *Angels*. It was completely amicable and respectful. We parted ways and at one point P.J. Hogan, who had done *Muriel's Wedding* and *My Best Friend's Wedding*, was attached and we were trying to get it made with him. Again – unsuccessfully. Then it languished some more.

The next significant part of the story is really when I teamed up with Mike Nichols to do *Wit*. That was 2000 I think. We developed it together and we had known each other socially but it was the first time we had worked together and we had a tremendous rapport and great partnership with *Wit*. We would drive to and from the set every day. We shot in Pinewood, in London, and we would drive to and from our hotel together. Which was one of the greatest experiences of my professional life – to share an hour in the morning and an hour in the evening with Mike Nicholls. Who is the most charming, wittiest man ever born. We would talk about everything under the sun and we got into a habit of every Friday we would start talking about what we would do next. We were having such a good time together. The second or third Friday he was asking about other things I was developing and I mentioned *Angels* and I described the history.

He said: "I always saw *Millennium Approaches* when I was in New York. I never saw *Perestroika*."

I said: "Boy you really missed it. It was brilliant. You should really see it."

"I don't know where it is going to be performed next."

"I'll get the play and give it to you because you'll appreciate it."

So I had my office send it from Los Angeles to London a few days later. It was a Friday I gave it to him and it was the bound copy signed by Tony and I gave it to him and said to him: "Whenever you get to it.

Have a read, you'll enjoy it."

There was no particular agenda. At that point Diane Sawyer was coming for the weekend, so I didn't expect him to read it for weeks. Diane ended up not coming to London for the weekend. I get in the car on Monday and Mike had this huge grin on his face.
I said: "What's going on?"
He goes: "I read *Perestroika.*"
"It's fantastic isn't it!"
"It's so fantastic. Even more brilliant than *Millennium Approaches.*"
Jokingly I said: "Well I know it's not Friday but shall we do it next?"
"Yeah, let's do it next"

He was serious.

A few days later Colin Callender, who had in the subsequent years been promoted to be the head of movies at HBO, and with whom we were making *Wit* at the time, came to visit the set and as we were having lunch the first day he was there we brought up *Angels*. He said to me: "I'll make it"
I said: "It's Meryl, its Al" and we talked about Mary-Louise Parker. We talked about Jeffrey Wright. He said: "Let's do a budget. Let's look at the scripts."

So as we were in post on *Wit* we were in pre-production on *Angels*. Everything about *Angels*... it was very hard because it is so long and it was arduous. But everything about it was a delightful process.

From rehearsals and then having to call Al. He came in so prepared, which is his way. He is, one of the reasons he is so completely brilliant as an actor is that he prepares so thoroughly. He came in for rehearsals... some people were just reading their parts and some people were giving it something. Meryl did too, and Al was fantastic from the read through.

Mike and I were pinching ourselves. We were giddy with excitement in terms of what he was going to be able to do with it. As we got further into rehearsals it was an absolute joy and, every day, just to watch the brilliance and invention and the thing that I observed with Al, and this is true, is he is so professional and prepared as an actor that when he gets there on the day he so knows every possible variation and interpretation of a line, of a moment, of an emotional key to a scene that he becomes a virtuoso... He basically can improvise with the part, within the character, and give all sorts of different colours within the scene, the moment, the line and it's just dazzling to watch. He goes to a heightened place.

The crew, without exaggeration, regularly... we would finish the take and the crew would break into applause when he was doing Roy Cohn. I'm sure you've heard this before, he would ask for additional takes. He would say: "Can I do one more? Can I do more? Can I do one more?" and then it would get to the point of absurdity and he would say to Mike: "Now let me give you a free one. Now let me give you a free one." He would do this for another four, five, even seven or eight takes and there was fifteen or twenty takes total, there were probably three or four brilliant choices. As I got to know Al, and I adore him as a person, we would finish the scene and sometimes walk back to his dressing room together and he would look at me and say: "I think seven was a little better than four don't you?" Honestly, he would never be wrong. I guarantee you that it is take seven that is in *Angels*. He would do that regularly, time after time. There was always a playful twinkle in his eye. He was just delightful. He was sweet to everyone. He is very private and has his process and his rituals. But he is a delightful presence on the set. There is something beautifully child-like about Al. He is a very generous guy.

Angels in America has such a phenomenal ensemble cast. Was it difficult to cast these actors?

It was [an] incredibly fun process. Once we had the scheduling of *Angels* we shot for... I can't remember... twenty six weeks, something like that. We broke it up. My memory's a little fuzzy but we started shooting in March. We would shoot to August. Then we had a hiatus which was probably because the crew and everyone had family vacation obligations for the month of August. So we took August off and I think we started up on the third week of September. So everybody came back refreshed and we had another eleven weeks. We probably finished a week or two before Christmas.

The scheduling was difficult because... all movies are Rubik's Cubes as far as getting actors, particularly stars, in and out on schedule and location and [with] other commitments. This was just monstrous.

Mike Haley, who is Mike Nichols' long-time first AD, and was a co-executive producer on *Angels*, was taxed to the limit trying to figure out how to do everything. Meryl would come in and work her period. Then she and Al. As far as the other actors... we went right away to Mary-Louise and Jeffrey. They were fantastic. Then we came to Justin [Kirk] and Ben [Shenkman] and Patrick [Wilson]... we tested Juliet Taylor and Ellen Lewis who were the casting directors, long-time casting partners with Mike, and as good at what they do as anybody ever, and we threw the gauntlet down to them and said: "We don't have to cast stars for these roles. Bring us the best young actors. Dazzle us."

They auditioned hundreds. Mike and I read Justin, Patrick, Ben three times and countless other actors and they just kept bubbling up to the top and surprising us in the greatest way possible. All three of them, I have nothing but fantastic things to say about them. They were just dazzling. What was exciting for Mike and I was to discover the spirit and integrity of what they brought to the persona and the voice of each of these roles. They really made it their own. Even with the dazzling precedent of Stephen Spinella as Prior on Broadway... just brilliant... and it was a difficult decision not to cast Stephen because he was so great and sort of defined the role. But we wanted to distance it just a little bit from the play. It was a joyful opportunity to cast these guys and see them do their work. They all came to work so prepared. It was something they really invested themselves in which shows on-screen.

Angels in America was nominated for many awards including the New York Drama Critics Circle, the London Drama Critics Circle, the Pulitzer Prize for Drama and a Tony Award for Best Play. Did that help alleviate the frustration of the past thirteen years of trying to get it made?

Oh yeah. That frustration disappeared when it came together with Mike and the cast. Doing what I do, if you believe in something... really believe in something you stay with it until there are too many signs that it is not going to happen. That never happened with *Angels*. I believed in it implicitly from day one and I just knew that the time would come. I can honestly say that when it came together with Mike and Al and Meryl and HBO and everyone as it did, it was the stars aligning. It happened at exactly the right time and the way it was meant to. It could not have been any better under any scenario. I think back to all those years of toiling and it feels like several lifetimes, but I feel nothing but satisfied and gratified with the result.

I imagine it makes it easier when you look at those awards sitting in your house?

Yes [*laughs*].

What feedback did you receive from the LGBT community?

It was incredibly favourable. There was not, that I can recall, one quibble anywhere. It was lauded; it was praised. They were supportive and almost activists in favour of people seeing *Angels*, for obvious reasons. I have a friend who is very big in that community and he said to me once: "There is a special door in heaven just for you because of *Angels in America*."

Who do hope will open the door? Meryl?

Any of them would be great.

What did Tony Kushner say about the production?

Tony was ecstatic. Our lives have gone different ways, being very busy. We don't see or talk that often but he is an amazing human being and a phenomenal artist. He was ecstatically happy. He has openly thanked me many times for my persistence in staying with it. I think he would agree with what I said about the stars aligning to manifest in the optimal form.

Mike Nichols described *Angels in America* as his Magnum Opus. Would you agree with that?

Mike's career, and God bless him, is so spectacular that it is one of the best... which is saying so much... his body of work is so dazzling that it is certainly one of the best three or four things he created as a director, as a filmmaker. We would talk about it and we both would feel this way about the movies we had done, they are like children – You can't pick a favourite. It's impossible because you love them for different reasons. Mike would joke: "*Angels* has got to be one of my favourite children."

Do you have a favourite scene in *Angels in America*?

Oh Boy! That's really hard. It's like the answer about children. I can't say I have a favourite scene. There are just so many. As you asked that question a kaleidoscope of about five scenes ran through my brain. I can't possibly say. I love every scene with Al. I love every scene with Meryl. Meryl as the Rabbi just blows my mind. It did on the day and it still does to this day. There are so many scenes with Jeffrey, Mary-Louise... Patrick and Al at the bar. There are so many scenes. I could never pick a favourite.

The Merchant of Venice

Cast: Al Pacino (Shylock), Jeremy Irons (Antonio), Joseph Fiennes (Bassanio), Lynn Collins (Portia), Zuleikha Robinson (Jessica), Kris Marshall (Gratiano), Charlie Cox (Lorenzo), Heather Goldenhersh (Nerissa), Mackenzie Crook (Launcelot Gobbo). **Director:** Michael Radford.

Synopsis: In sixteen century Venice, Bassanio hopes to wed Portia. But to have a chance at winning her hand in marriage, he needs to have bags of money – something he lacks. Bassanio's rich friend Antonio is unable to help, so he is forced to make a deal with the pitiless moneylender Shylock. Bassanio will get his money, and without paying interest. However, if he doesn't pay it back Shylock will be owed a pound of his flesh.

British director Michael Radford won international acclaim for films such as *Nineteen Eighty-Four* (an adaptation of the George Orwell novel) and *Il Postino* (for many years the highest grossing non-English language film ever made). Following the release of *Dancing at the Blue Iguana* in September 2000, Radford was looking for his next directorial project. During a dinner party in Los Angeles, Radford bumped into film producer Barry Navidi whose company, Barry Navidi Productions, had released the romantic drama *Big Bad Love* starring Debra Winger in 2001. Navidi suggested Radford tackle adapting Shakespeare's *The Merchant of Venice* for the big screen. Radford thought it was a great idea but hesitated because he had never directed Shakespeare before: "I read the play and said I'd be interested in doing it if we could get the right actor to play Shylock."

Navidi also broached the subject with U.S. producer Cary Brokaw who had known Radford since the late eighties. When Navidi mentioned Radford might direct the project, Brokaw jumped at the chance to work with him. The search for an actor to play Shylock began immediately and as luck would have it Brokaw was working with Al Pacino at the time on the HBO mini-series *Angels in America*. One day over lunch he suggested to Pacino that he should play Shylock. "That's really interesting," he responded, "I just started to think I was finally old enough to play Shylock." Radford was in London working on the first draft of the script, but Brokaw organised a dinner between him, Radford and Pacino in New York to discuss the project. Radford brought along the completed first draft to give to Pacino. By the end of dinner, Pacino and Radford were both on the same page when it came to approaching this adaptation.

Radford returned to England to refine the script but struggled to find a new footing for the existing work: "I sat around wondering what on earth I could do. It's all already there, and it's all theatrical." On the advice of a close friend, the director decamped to the setting of the original play: Venice. "I immediately started to get an understanding of how I was going to do this thing," he commented. During this time, producers Brokaw and Navidi spoke to other potential investors to raise the remaining finances for the feature film. Additional support came from British film financing companies Movision Entertainment and Spice Factory. Further financial aid was offered from the UK Film Council, The Film Fund of the Grand Duchy of Luxembourg and the Italian corporation Istituto Luce. Thus, the first ever cinematic version of *The Merchant of Venice* was a co-production between the UK, Italy and Luxembourg.

Casting director Sharon Howard-Field, previously head of casting at London's National Theatre cast a wide net to find other actors to appear alongside Pacino. British actor Ian McKellen, who had worked on *The Merchant of Venice* with the Royal Shakespeare Company, signed on to play Antonio. The role of Portia went to Cate Blanchett. Joseph Fiennes was cast in the role of Bassanio. British comedian Ricky Gervais turned down the role of Launcelot Gobbo. The role was instead filled by his co-star from *The Office* Mackenzie Crook. Many other roles were assigned to British actors including Charlie Cox who played Lorenzo, Kris Marshall as Gratiano, David Harewood as the Prince of Morocco and Zuleikha Robinson as Jessica. Production hit a stumbling block when some of the financing didn't arrive on time and the start of filming was pushed back from September to November. This caused two big headaches: scheduling conflicts meant Ian McKellen had to drop out. His replacement in the role of Antonio was another British thespian, Jeremy Irons.

The next production crisis came when Cate Blanchett discovered she was pregnant and had to drop out of playing Portia. Howard-Field and Radford interviewed other major movie stars including Catherine Zeta-Jones, but none of them excited the director or casting director. Radford was going through audition tapes for the role of Jessica and stopped on the tape of Lynn Collins, a relative newcomer with only a handful of small screen credits to her name. The director asked her to record herself reciting two of Portia's monologues: "Michael loved the first one and then told me that the second one was total crap [*laughing*]," recalled Collins. Radford instantly knew she was the right choice to play Portia.

The delays to the shooting schedule at least gave the actors additional time to rehearse with each other: "We sort of committed to each other and we talked to each other and engaged in a way that turned us into a troupe," said Pacino. The costume department also had more time to create the clothes for production. Designer Sammy Sheldon was given the task of creating sixteenth century stylized costumes: "Venice all through that century everything is much sexier and softer, really the proper kind of renaissance." Based on her research, Sheldon created Jewish red hats, the carnival masks for men and men's clothing designed to be worn by women disguising themselves as the opposite sex. When Sheldon flew to New York to discuss costumes with Pacino, she presented several sketches to him: "on seeing my drawings, the first thing he said was...'I'm wearing a dress?' and I was like, 'no, no it's a tunic.'"

Principal photography began on 23 November 2003 and lasted for nine weeks. The majority of the exterior shots were filmed on Luxembourg's oldest sound stage at Studio Luxembourg with some exterior scenes filmed in Luxembourg's second largest commune Esch-sur-Alzette, along the Grand Rue. During filming in Luxembourg, Pacino hired out a nightclub for the cast and crew for a well-earned night off filming where they danced and drank until the early hours. Once filming completed in Luxembourg there was a two week break for the Christmas and New Year holiday period. The cast and crew needed to be well-rested before returning to filming in early January as the second part of principal photography turned out to be brutal. Moving on to shoot film exteriors in Venice, the team found themselves at the mercy of icy weather conditions, the temperature rising to minus three degrees celcius at its highest.

Time and budget were also now against Radford and the crew started working fourteen hour days, six days a week in order to finish the project. For the first time in ten years heavy snow had fallen and settled on the city and the crew had to sweep it away for each shot. "I didn't know it was possible to be this cold and still be alive" said Marshall. The intense filming schedule meant that a full-blown riot sequence on the Rialto Bridge had to be shot in just one day. Other scenes were filmed at Doge's Palace, including shots on the large exterior balcony looking out across Venice's Grand Canal. By the end of January most of the cast and crew had caught the flu, but it didn't stop them from completing their work: "People were really concentrating and a lot of it was down to Al. He set a tone and nobody would feel comfortable if they didn't match that intensity," commented Radford. After Venice, production moved to Thiene for interior shots with the Castello di Thiene acting as Antonio's palace. The gallery on the upper floor was reconstructed by production complete with commissioned paintings that echoed the artistic stylings of the sixteenth century. The stables at the castle were used for the wedding of Bassanio and Portia and production brought in a home economist to create the perfect Venetian feast: a mix of fruits with vegetables and cooked boars and rabbits. A further notable location was the commune of Mira outside of Venice. The grand Villa Foscari (also known as La Malcontenta) was used as the home of Portia as she welcomes her suitors. Here, the cast and crew were treated to a lavish meal put on by the owners of Villa Foscari.

As *The Merchant of Venice* was shot in Italy, its premiere was scheduled at the 61st Venice Film Festival on 4 September 2004. Pacino and Collins waved to the crowds while walking the red carpet. Also on the carpet were prominent royal figures including Grand Duke Henri and The Grand Duchess Maria Teresa of Luxembourg, and Prince Emanuele Filiberto of Savoy and his wife Clotilde Courau. As the invited guests took their seats for the premiere one person was left without. Pacino's seat had been double booked, as had over two hundred other seats, including those reserved for the Bulgari family who sponsor the festival. Tempers started to rise amongst the guests and eventually riot police were called to calm the situation. The premiere finally started two hours later. Pacino was finally assigned a seat several rows behind his original seat.

No such problems occurred in the UK where it was given much more than a standard film premiere. It was a Royal London Premiere at the Odeon Leicester Square on 29 November 2004. The event was organised in association with The Prince's Trust, a charity for young people founded by Charles, Prince of Wales and Frederick John Pervin. Prince Charles and his partner Camilla Parker-Bowles walked the line of stars, stopping for an in-depth discussion with Pacino. His Royal Highness and Pacino had been friends since they met in 1997 and kept in contact by letter through the intervening years. The actor had also previously stayed at HRH's estate at Highgrove. The Royal premiere helped to raise £170,000 for The Prince's Trust.

Before the jaunt to London, Pacino and Brokaw screened the film in association with *Variety Magazine's* "screening series" at the ArcLight Theater, Hollywood. It was followed by a Q&A with both Pacino and Brokaw, moderated by film historian Pete Hammond.

A U.S. theatrical release did not happen until the final week of December 2004 and even then it was only in 4 theatres. It did manage to pull in a respectable $69,868 in its first week and then slowly the scale of the release broadened in January. While the film never troubled the U.S. box office top ten, it did spend twenty-one weeks in theatres. By the end of its run in late May 2005 it had returned $3.7 million. Even though it is a niche film *The Merchant of Venice* opened in theatres in thirty territories with total box office returns of $17.6 million (Information courtesy of

Box Office Mojo. Used with permission). Critical reviews were generally positive, with *Variety* suggesting "the polished production, prestige cast and enduring beauty of the language should make this a robust performer on the speciality stage." *The New York Times* praised the look of the production, stating: "watching the film is like seeing a gallery of Renaissance paintings come to life." The *Guardian* not only enjoyed the film: "fresh, lucid and unpretentious," they also singled out Pacino for his performance "A brilliant performance from Al Pacino.... his is a cool, considered Shylock, retaining an icy good humour." Sadly, positive reviews didn't help the film find a larger audience and it still made a loss of $9 million once the global box office returns had been accounted for. Pacino laid the blame at the promoters, saying: "For some reason the powers that be didn't promote it. The people whose job it was to do that, didn't do it."

Adapting Shakespeare for the big screen can be a tricky task. It appears director Michael Radford managed to find the magic formula by tweaking the original text just enough to make it interesting for modern-day audiences. He blends the elements of comedy, romance, politics and tragedy into one neat bundle. The fact the film was shot in Venice also gives extra gravitas to proceedings. The city comes off as a character unto itself because it is so beautifully included in the storyline. The cinematography captures the beauty of the majestic buildings and waterways. The slower pace of Radford's adaptation means that the viewer can marvel at the cinematography and also follow the story without being overwhelmed. Actors like Pacino and Irons who already know their Shakespeare make the film a much more pleasurable watch as it is very obvious they have worked hard at finding the best way to project the character for Shakespeare fans and newcomers alike. The flow to their dialogue makes it far easier to understand, even with the unfamiliar language.

One of the most thrilling moments in the film is when Pacino and Irons go toe-to-toe as they flesh out the money-lending contract. The quick-fire dialogue between them is electric. Both of them command respect from the other; challenging each other with every sentence. It's a battle of wills not just between the characters but also between the actors, both of whom are addicts of Shakespeare's work.

For long stretches of the film Pacino is absent. His Shylock looms large in other proceedings, but his presence isn't required. He shuffles around cloaked in oversized clothes and a wiry beard, with a hunched frame. It's a quiet performance from Pacino, who offers a subtle and nuanced portrayal of Shylock. The courtroom scene is utterly compelling and by the end Shylock is on his knees, emotionally pulverised by the turn of events.

Two other standout performances are delivered by Kris Marshall as Gratiano, a sarcastic joker who likes to prod and tease his mates and also enjoys wooing ladies, and Lynn Collins as Portia, a fireball of feminist spirit, one that frightens all of her male suitors in a hilarious fashion. The same cannot be said for Fiennes who seems to sulk and stare his way though most of the film, twirling and flicking his hair around. It is a performance that puts no meat on the bone of the character and is instantly forgettable. When acting alongside the Shakespearian stalwarts of Pacino and Irons, you have to bring your A game otherwise you'll be left behind.

In summary, Radford's adaptation of the bard's tale of greed, corruption, love and betrayal has real vigour. These different strands all combine into a complex storyline that is made easier to understand thanks to the contemporary direction and engrossing presentation of classic material.

Author's Note: In the summer of 2010, Pacino appeared in a stage production of *The Merchant of Venice* at the Delacorte Theater in New York's Central Park. Shortly thereafter it transferred to the Broadhurst Theatre on Broadway where it ran from October through to the following February. The production received positive reviews and strong box office returns, putting its weekly box office grosses consistently over $1 million.

Actor Kris Marshall on *The Merchant of Venice*

What was your relationship with Shakespeare's work before you appeared in this film?

I had done some Shakespeare on stage and studied at college and at school. I had done *A Midsummer Night's Dream* on stage before, but apart from that I hadn't actually performed Shakespeare before. I like to find the layman's common meaning when doing Shakespeare and I think that Al found that perfectly without honouring the time period of the piece he makes it easily understandable to a layman... to someone who isn't a studier of Shakespearian text. I always try to strive to do that myself and I think Michael Radford, the director, and Jeremy Irons they have this great ability to make Shakespearian texts come alive and make it sound like normal conversation.

What was it like acting opposite Pacino?

It's Al Pacino [*laughs*]. Not on his part, but certainly on your part there is a certain expectation and you are daunted. I remember in the first rehearsals when I first met him, my character Gratiano is a pretty awful character. He is one of Shakespeare's most nasty characters, and there is a scene in the courtroom where I have to scream in his face and the first day of rehearsals I was: "hang on this is Al Pacino. I just can't scream in his face." It was coming up and coming up and then here we go and I sort of half heartedly screamed at him and he said "What's the point in that?" He sort of chewed me up a bit. So the next time I went for it.

He is a very normal man. Every night, after we had finished shooting on location in Luxembourg and Italy, we would all go out for dinner with Al. He would sit at the head of the table. We would all have a nice bit of pasta. It was great. It was great for a young actor like me at the time to see how a statesman such as Al acts and behaves on set. His behaviour is impeccable – always. It's good for a young actor to know someone of that stature... he hasn't got anything to prove to anyone and he just a nice person. He is pleasant to everyone on the set whether they make the tea or [are] directing the film. That was a great thing to learn from him, as well as working with a master in full flow. It was a pleasure for me to be in a film with him. Lovely man.

Two for the Money

Cast: Al Pacino (Walter Abrams), Matthew McConaughey (Brandon Lang), Rene Russo (Toni Morrow), Armand Assante (C.M. Novian), Jeremy Piven (Jerry Sykes), Jamie King (Alexandria), Ralph Garman (Reggie), Kevin Chapman (Southie). **Director:** D.J. Caruso.

Synopsis: After a cruel injury rules out the prospect of a glittering football career, Brandon Lang uses his unparalleled knowledge of the professional game to get back on top, by plying his skills in the hugely lucrative sports betting industry. Lang's talent is spotted early and he's soon drafted in as a successor to Walter Abrams' extravagant sports network. Brandon's unwavering need to win takes him trailblazing into the gambling underworld where only the trust and teamwork of those closest can bring him back to normality.

Following the success of his previous films *Freejack* and *Chasers*, an action film and a comedy respectively, screenwriter/producer Dan Gilroy was looking for something a bit meatier. He had a particular interest in filming a true-to-life story that revolved around gambling.

One day, while playing a round of golf his caddy, Gilroy met a man named Brandon Lane who started talking to him about his own life. His career as a walk-on UNLV basketball player was cut short due to a knee injury and with his dream of playing pro-sports shattered, Lane ended up accepting a lowly telesales job for an audio text company. When his boss asked him to fill in for a colleague working on the sports gambling line, giving out the daily hot picks, Lane found his niche: "He discovered he had a true facility for picking games," Gilroy later said. Lane's unrelenting ability to pick the correct results caught the attentions of a New York sports advisory firm who made him an offer he couldn't refuse: join the company, they advised him, and you will become one of the top sports advisers in the gambling profession. Lane took up the offer but did eventually leave the company: "I was working under someone else's rules, dictating how I live my life and that doesn't work for me and that led to me walking away."

His subsequent meeting with Gilroy was no accident. Realising he had the basis for a film script, Lane moved across the country to Los Angeles and took a job at the prestigious Riviera Country Club as a caddy, banking on the fact that he would at some point spend four to five hours in the company of someone who would take his idea seriously. Gilroy recalls Lane saying: "Listen, do you want to hear a story for a movie? His story hooked me." For the next few hours, Lane gave Gilroy a full account of his previous working life. Lane always described himself as a salesman, a pitch-man and a closer. By the time Gilroy had made a forty five foot birdie putt, the basis for a screenplay was beginning to percolate. Rather than sticking faithfully to Lane's talent for predicting outcomes in all sports, Gilroy tweaked his screenplay to solely focus on American Football. This alteration, it was thought, offered more room for story expansion and development.

The completed screenplay found its way to director D.J. Caruso, an experienced TV director, who had worked on shows such as *Smallville*, *Dark Angel* and *Martial Law*. Caruso happened to be on the lookout for a drama that dealt with innocence being corrupted and later commented: "I was intrigued by Brandon's journey and bringing the audience into the world of sports gambling." Movie producer Jay Cohen had recently set up his own company called Light Speed Media, and came on board to produce *Two for the Money*. Cohen, an experienced producer with films such as *Boys and Girls*, *A Walk on the Moon* and *Swimming with Sharks* under his belt, brokered a finance deal with Morgan Creek Productions and a worldwide distribution agreement with Universal Pictures. Soon after, a budget of $30 million was set for the film's production.

Actor Matthew McConaughey was looking for film roles outside the rom-com genre in a bid to change the direction of his career. Gilroy's script first landed on his desk in 2001, he commented: "I was looking for a good dramatic story and this was the perfect fit." McConaughey played just about every sport possible while growing up and understood Lane's passion: "Sport means everything to Brandon. It's about the purity of the game, not the money."

The role of ex-junkie turned faithful wife, Toni Morrow was cast with ease as Gilroy had been married to Rene Russo since 1992. The part was specifically written for Russo, who also became a producer on the project: "I said Danny, [Gilroy] I don't think we should give this up this easy. We are giving up the good material because in Hollywood that's what it's all about. It's about the material. What are we? Stupid?!" Russo was also instrumental in casting the other lead role of Walter Abrams, owner of the New York sports betting network that Lane goes to work for. Russo took the script directly to Al Pacino. Inundated with offers, Pacino looked to consider the role if other projects fell through. He was deliberating official offers to star in a biopic of Salvador Dali or deciding whether to appear in an adaptation of Philip Roth's novel *The Dying Animal* instead. Rumours also swirled that he was making biopics of Napoleon and/or Enrico Ferrari. Months went by without word. Russo and Gilroy continued to pester Pacino about their movie. With other projects stalling around him, Pacino agreed to join the cast. This hugely motivated the rest of the cast and crew. Caruso called Pacino: "The template. He's the nucleus of this acting group." Russo was equally as excited to work with her fellow Sicilian descendent: "There's something about him that feels like family to me."

With the main cast in place, filming was set to commence. That was until an issue was raised with the script. Before his sports career Brandon Lane had changed his surname from Link to Lane. A New Yorker called Brandon Lane wanted payment for the use of the name. Settling a payment request like that could take months or even years to finalize before filming could commence, and the production could not afford that luxury. Gilroy resolved the issue by changing the name from Lane to Lang. Anticipating an uplifting in his sports betting work, Lane changed his surname for the third time to Lang in order to tie in with the film.

Principal photography began during September 2004. The cast had spent two weeks prior in Los Angeles rehearsing. McConaughey sat down with the real Lang several times to learn his mannerisms. The majority of the film was shot in Vancouver. Exterior locations included the Simon Fraser University, The Marine Building, BC Place stadium, a phone booth situated on the Fraser River walkway and two private homes – one located on William Street and the other in West Vancouver overlooking the shoreline. During his time in Vancouver, McConaughey refused to live in the hotel provided and instead opted for a trailer on the Musqueam Indian Reserve. "I like to do my own cooking," McConaughey commented. Sometimes, he spent hours outside cooking up meats that he would give out to passing strangers. After eight weeks in Vancouver, the production uprooted to New York for external shots. Filming in Brooklyn, the locations included: the Brooklyn Bridge, the former headquarters of the Brooklyn City Railroad company on Fulton Street, Fulton Ferry Pier, Furman Street, Cranberry Street, Columbia Heights and Brooklyn Heights Promenade. Filming continued over in Manhattan's West 52nd Street and Times Square. A couple of days were then spent filming establishing shots in Las Vegas and principal photography was completed in ten weeks.

The world premiere took place on 26 September 2005 at the Samuel Goldwyn Theater, Beverly Hills. The entire cast attended, including McConaughey who arrived on the red carpet with his family. It received its U.S. and Canadian theatrical release on 7 October. Critics were unanimous in their thoughts on *Two for the Money*, it wasn't a winner. *The New York Times* commented: "A confusion of tones, intentions and allusions, *Two for the Money* lurches from upbeat to downbeat without ever settling into a coherent groove." *Variety* found it equally disjointed, stating: "Despite nice touches, pic meanders in the middle and ends flatly." *Empire Magazine* scathed: "A preposterous, steroidal mess."

The film's box office returns were equally poor. During its opening weekend it only pulled in a lacklustre $8.7 million. By the end of its first full week in theatres, the sports drama had meekly returned only $11 million, placing it at number four in the U.S. Box Office. Its theatrical run lasted only six weeks and generated a below-average haul of $22 million (Information courtesy of Box Office Mojo. Used with permission). Universal, Morgan Creek and Light Speed Media had hedged their bets that the movie would be a big draw for sports and/or betting fans. That huge gamble turned into a huge loss.

Two for the Money is a movie about the eighties yuppie subculture which was still active in the noughties, just operating under a different guise. The underlying message? Be a winner, flash the cash and greed is good (the film's tag line was unceremoniously stolen from Gordon Gecko). Lang's rags to riches story is a common tale, but the trope is no doubt based on the fact that such a situation is one most of us have dreamt about.

McConaughey and Pacino playing Lang and Abrams respectively, establish a surrogate father-son dynamic in this film rather than a boss-employee work relationship. Both push each other to be the best and in turn reward themselves for pushing the other to the brink and, sometimes, beyond. Abrams thinks of nothing in meddling with Lang's love life and then proudly showing how his relationship with Morrow cannot be broken (in truth it's all a falsehood as Abrams passion for his wife died years ago and his only love is his sports network). The riches that Abrams reigns down on Lang is, essentially, fool's gold. Yet Lang is so caught up worshipping this surrogate father than he cannot see how he is being used. Abrams, with all the riches, creates this almost playboy atmosphere between him and Lang to show that nothing is off limits to someone as powerful as he is, and Lang can have that if he follows Abrams tutelage. It's fun while it lasts and the two actors do have natural patter between them. Pacino's Abrams is a close relation to John Milton in *Devil's Advocate*. He spouts all of the lines in the more dramatic moments with his usual zeal. Even the quieter moments, such as when Abrams aggressively whispers in Lang's ear, are delivered with intensity. There is nothing new here from Pacino, it all comes pretty easy to him as he chews up most of the scenery during the course of the performance. Ultimately, this portrayal feels a little bit like the actor is running on autopilot. This said he is experienced at creating a realistic 'buddy' relationship with younger actors after working on exactly that dynamic in films such as *The Recruit*, *Devil's Advocate* and *Donnie Brasco*.

When Anthony (Lang's alter ego) is on camera or on the phone, McConaughey plays the part with a vigour that easily matches Pacino's. McConaughey appears to be having a blast playing the character the audience loves to hate but beneath the passionate delivery of some very quotable lines from these two central performances lies very little else. Ironically given its subject matter, it's an entirely superficial movie. The family drama storyline is completely forgettable. Centring on the idea that for all his style and riches, Abrams can't hold his family together. In fact it's crumbling around him as he becomes increasingly obsessed with Lang. This choice of plotline relegates the supremely talented Russo to nothing more than a modern-day damsel in distress, which feels like a waste. The script drip-feeds titbits of Morrow's troubled family back story but these feel like mere by-products of her relationship with Abrams. It's never clear what this film is trying to say about how poor childhood experiences shape relationships in later life even though there is scope to explore this idea with Russo's character.

The problems don't stop there though as the script goes so far as to push a soccernomics ideal that could be used in sports betting. By the time the finale rolls around the script's stance has changed, implying that sports gambling is nothing more than a game of chance decided by a flip of the coin. A drastically poor final ten minutes sees redemption for Lang and Abrams both on an individual level and within the bounds of their relationship. It's a smaltzy, happy ever after, Hollywood ending that doesn't fit with the 'greed is good' message that the film preaches all the way through the runtime. The script never really makes up its mind as to what it's trying to convey about gambling and to use a betting analogy: it cashes out before the final whistle.

Actor Kevin Chapman on *Two for the Money*

Do you remember when you first started watching Pacino's films?

I'm from Boston so I was always a big John Cazale fan because John was from Boston. John played Fredo in *The Godfather* and he did *Dog Day Afternoon* with Al. He was in a number of films and John had a very short-lived career. Ultimately he was afflicted with cancer when he was doing *The Deerhunter*. That was how I got turned on to Pacino – *Dog Day Afternoon*. He did *Cruising* with Billy Friedkin, which was a dark film. The stuff he did in *Dick Tracy*. *Frankie and Johnny* I loved. *Glengarry Glen Ross... Carlito's Way...* what are some of the others? Oh... *City Hall*. *The Insider* was great. I really enjoyed him in *Any Given Sunday*. I would imagine it's tough for a guy like him to find those challenges, to keep challenging yourself. To try and find things that you can give a performance to that doesn't mirror a performance you did in the past. The *Phil Spector* movie he did for HBO and he did that Kevorkian movie too. *Angels in America* was great, he was great in that.

He has made some very brave decisions in terms of what films to make.

Oh yeah, absolutely. That was one of the things that I loved about our period of time together when we did *Two for the Money*. I would go in just to watch him work because he would do it as scripted. He would lay it out as scripted and then it wouldn't take him more than a couple of takes and he would have it. He would say to the director: "OK, now let's explore…" and they would go away from the script for a while. They would kind of improv and mine for little nuggets, little nuances that may have not been in the text or subtext of the film and then they would go back to the script. What was really great was when they went back to the script, from this improv session in the middle of it. He would bring a different subtext to some of the meanings of what was being said in the text. It was really enjoyable to watch and quite educational.

When Pacino made these changes to his acting how would you, acting opposite him, react to it?

When you're an actor in a scene you are just responding to what's being said. I remember one of the first big movies I did was *Mystic River* and I was so excited to work with Clint Eastwood. We were hanging out between takes and I said: "C'mon Clint gimme me something. Gimme something insightful. Something I can use." He just looked at me and said "Listen!" and walked away [*laughs*]. It was that simple. As an actor you can only respond to what's being said to you and you try to find the truth to what you are responding to and the truth within your response. You go along for the ride. Its Al Pacino first of all, it's not like it's the third banana on *Saved by the Bell* [*laughs*]. It's Al Pacino you're in the scene with, you know. As I said, I used to go in on my days off just to watch him work because he was amazing.

Two for the Money **has a large cast – Pacino, McConaughey, Russo, Piven, Garman, Assante. What is it like to be in that environment and watch them all act?**

For me, it wasn't like it was intimidating because I had just come off *Mystic River* working with Sean Penn, Tim Robbins, Clint Eastwood, Laurence Fishburne. My two co-stars won Academy Awards. It wasn't like it was something intimidating to me; it was enjoyable. It was like watching a play – Pacino, McConaughey, Rene Russo, Armand Assante. You had some very seasoned actors and had guys like Charles Carroll, who a lot of people aren't familiar with, who is not only a great actor but a great acting coach and has been a long-time friend of D.J. Caruso the director. It was quite enjoyable. D.J. was a fabulous director, I loved working with him. He loved to collaborate and he loved to take chances and that's all you can ask for in a director.

Your character, Southie, is one of the bullpen guys. Where did you see him fitting into the hierarchy of the whole department?

[*Laughs*]. Well, there was a little bit of subtext going on of our own you know. Al wasn't very happy with me by the time the movie ended because Al is a diehard New York Yankees fan and I'm a diehard Boston Red Sox fan and if you know anything about American Baseball then '04 was the year that the Red Sox were down three to nothing by the New York Yankees and came back to win the American League pennant. So there was quite a bit of banter between Al and I going back and forth, back and forth during the filming.

Subsequently the Red Sox went on to win the World Series, which really pissed Al off [*laughs*]. There was a moment when we were losing three nothing and Al comes up to me and goes: "You know baby, it's all over baby. It's all over." I said: "Yeah OK, we'll see Al." The Red Sox win three one and then next game he goes: "You got lucky. You got lucky kid!" Three two we win [*laughs*]. The next game it was like a big Godfather moment, he puts his hands on my shoulders – everybody refers to me as Chappie – and he says to me "Chappie! It's all over tonight baby. It's all done." Red Sox tied up three three then ultimately we go on to win the series four to three.

So the next day, I have the first scene of the day where I walk in and say something to Walter, and the whole crew had been witnessing this banter, back and forth, between Al and I about the Red Sox and the Yankees, and so instead of the delivering the line I go in and say "How about those fucking Red Sox?" Al lost his mind. He started throwing things on the set. It was pretty comical [*laughs*].

There is a small scene in the film where we see you dancing. Was that at all related to the Red Sox win?

Yeah absolutely. That fact that it was the Red Sox just drove Al insane. He was a good person about it.

Are you a big sports betting person?

I've been known to put a wager or two on a sporting event.

Were you aware of the original story behind the film?

I wasn't aware of the original story. The character Southie is from Boston, the south side of Boston. So this kid was from South Boston who I portrayed, so that's how I came about being approached to play the role.

Was there anything you took away from working with Pacino and used afterwards?

I think a lot of it, for me taking away from him, was being brave enough to take chances. To constantly explore. I noticed he doesn't judge his characters; he tries to present them as truthful as possible and then let the audience judge. I think that is something I have picked up from watching him work. He would get lost in this world and get lost in this story that is being told and try to take it to some different places to see if he has the ability to find that piece of gold somewhere.

88 Minutes

Cast: Al Pacino (Jack Gramm), Alicia Witt (Kim Cummings), Leelee Sobieski (Lauren Douglas), Amy Brenneman (Shelly Barnes), William Forsythe (Frank Parks), Deborah Kara Unger (Carol Lynn Johnson), Ben McKenzie (Mike Stempt), Neal McDonough (Jon Forster), Leah Cairns (Sara Pollard), Stephen Moyer (Guy LaForge). **Director:** Jon Avnet.

Synopsis: Jack Gramm, a forensic psychologist, receives a phone call telling him he has only 88 minutes to live. With a serial killer he helped convict awaiting execution and a copycat killer on the loose as suspects, Jack Gramm has 88 minutes to solve the biggest murder of his career... his own!

During their collaboration on *Glengarry Glen Ross* director James Foley and Al Pacino formed a strong bond. They continued working together on the small, indie film *Two Bits*, and even though the lightning of commercial success didn't strike twice for them they kept looking for projects on which they could work together. One of the projects was a real-time thriller called *88 Minutes*. Pacino first mentioned this picture during his press tour for *The Merchant of Venice* in early 2004. It was without a title at that time but Pacino commented to *indielondon.co.uk*: "He's [James Foley] developing something that I hope turns out because I really like Jimmy Foley. He's making progress for this piece, and I'm hoping it could be my next picture." Foley was collaborating with the writer Gary Scott Thompson, who previously wrote *Hollow Man* and *The Fast and the Furious*. However, only a couple of months later the project had stalled. Both the actor and director drifted away to make other films, assuming the project wouldn't happen.

Thompson continued to work on the script while also working on the story for *Hollow Man II*. It wasn't until several months after Foley and Pacino had moved on that a movie studio became interested in *88*

Minutes. "I started reading it and couldn't put it down. From the first page to the last, it moved and that's what I'm always looking for as a producer," President & co-founder Randall Emmett later commented on why Emmett/Furla Films chose to step in and make *88 Minutes*. Emmett/Furla Films had a financing deal with Nu Image/Millennium Films, an independent film company founded by Trevor Short, Danny Dimbort, Danny Lerner and Avi Lerner. It was agreed that they would all receive executive producer credit for the film, while Emmett took on the role of producer alongside Thompson, who continued his work on the script. Jon Avnet was selected as the new director. "I thought I could do something kind of compelling with it. The simplicity of the concept – a person gets a phone call telling him that he has 88 minutes to live – it's pretty easy to follow," said Avnet, after reading Thompson's script.

Avnet and Emmett set about casting the role of Dr. Gramm, and the first name on their list was Al Pacino. "We sent Al the script thinking, 'Wow, Al Pacino in this role would be magic.'" Avnet wanted actors that would shape the characters they were playing rather than just relying on what is on the page to guide them. After Pacino read the script he had a meeting with Avnet to discuss the character: "Jon went deep into the character of Dr. Jack Gramm – why he is the way he is. That's one of the reasons I wanted to do it." With Pacino signed on, Avnet began tailoring the script specifically for the actor: "Jack's inner demons are raging. Those are the kind of characters I think Pacino plays better than anybody."

While securing actors for the other roles in the film, Avnet continued to look for performers that could bring their own instincts to the parts. Alicia Witt had a laborious audition process but Avnet was impressed with how she coped with it all and thus cast her as Gramm's graduate assistant Kim. Witt spent time reading about forensic psychiatry for the role: "I wanted to get into that a little bit and just understand what it is to assess someone." Avnet also sent the script to Leelee Sobieski, having previously worked with her on the TV movie *Uprising*. She was given an afternoon to read it and then make her decision. She didn't need that long and immediately agreed to play Lauren Douglas, one of Dr. Gramm's most gifted students. Avnet offered the role of Mike Stempt, yet another of Dr Gramm's other dedicated students, to The O.C. star Benjamin McKenzie: "They said 'You know, Al Pacino is doing this movie.' You don't really say no to that opportunity." Deborah Kara Unger signed on to play the dean of the Seattle college. Pacino was also reunited with his *Dick Tracy* co-star William Forsythe, who played Dr. Gramm's colleague Frank Parks while star of TV's *Judging Amy* show Amy Brenneman agreed to play another of Gramm's colleagues: Shelley Barnes. Brenneman commented: "I wanted to be Al Pacino's sidekick. That sounded like a fun time to me."

Principal photography began on 15 October 2005. The majority of locations used for filming were in the Greater Vancouver area of Canada, including: the Vancouver Central Library, the Burrard Bridge, the Oasis Ultra Lounge, the exterior of the Hampton Court apartments on Thurlow Street, the rooftop of 417 Dunsmuir Street above the White Spot restaurant, a condo block on Homer Street and also an interchange on Hastings Street and Homer Street.. Several sites at the University of British Columbia campus were used for filming including the parking lot for the Health Sciences department, the Walter C. Koerner Library, the interior of the Life Sciences building, the exterior of the Buchanan Building and the main mall leading up to the university. The only scenes not shot in Vancouver were the exterior scenes of Dr. Gramm's office building, which were filmed at the Safeco Plaza in Seattle. Filming was completed in thirty nine days but in that time Pacino managed to twist his ankle and had to walk with the assistance of a metal cane.

Though filming *88 Minutes* took very little time, the same could not be said about finding a distribution deal. It wasn't until May 2007, fifteen months after principal photography had wrapped, that Sony Pictures paid $6 million for North American and selected international distribution rights. Due to other, local distribution deals, other countries not covered under the Sony deal got to see *88 Minutes* earlier than the territories covered by Sony. Brazil was the first country to see *88 Minutes*; it was a straight to DVD release on 14 February 2007. The picture then had a staggered release around Europe, with only a handful of countries releasing it in theatres.

The U.S. premiere took place on 16 April 2008 at the Planet Hollywood Resort and Casino. Two days later it was released into North American theatres. Upon completion of its first week in U.S. theatres *88 Minutes* had pulled in just over $9 million and entered the box office chart at number four. By the end of its second week returns had almost halved down to $4.7 million. The following three weeks saw it drop like a stone and by the end of week five it was removed from theatres. The total U.S. gross was $17.2 million. Combined with the minimal theatrical releases around the world, *88 Minutes* grossed a grand total of $32.5 million, against a budget of $30 million (Information courtesy of Box Office Mojo. Used with permission). Not exactly an impressive return and if the box office receipts weren't bad enough, the critics also stuck their claws in.

The New York Times exclaimed "Although it's often laugh-out-loud bad, *88 Minutes* is mostly just a slog." On *At the Movies* with Roger Ebert, Richard Roeper suggested: "It's quite possibly the worst movie of 2008 so far." *Variety* hit even harder, stating: "The picture easily snatches from *Revolution* the prize as Al Pacino's career worst." To add insult to injury, Pacino was nominated for a Worst Actor at the 29th Razzie Awards. He was however beaten to the Golden Raspberry statuette by Mike Myers in *The Love Guru*.

The first sign that *88 Minutes* is a film without a clear forward thrust is that the runtime is not 88 minutes, as one might expect of a film set in real-time bearing that title. Instead, this picture lumbers on for 101 minutes and thus never feels like it sits in the real-time genre as it was meant to. This further detracts from the tension as when the time remaining before a life is taken flashes up on the screen, the viewer knows this is a bluff and never invests in the premise. At the climax, the emergency services are called. If the film is still operating in real time, which it seems to be, then they are the quickest response team ever seen on film because they arrive with sixty seconds of the call being placed, and let's not forget they have to race up four flights of stairs and through two corridors before getting to the scene.

There are many other signs that *88 Minutes* is a complete duff. Scenes are played out without care or attention to how they will fit with what has gone before and what will come after. The cinematography is woeful: several scenes appear to be incorrectly framed, cutting off important elements of either the actor or action in shot. During one threatening phone call, Dr Gramm is shot at such a tight angle that we can only see his eyes and the start of his hair line. The audience don't get to see his mouth as he threatens the caller. If this was supposed to be an artistic flourish, it fails. Normally Pacino's expressive eyes could be counted upon to save the scene. But not here. Instead he stares dead ahead and doesn't move an inch. Unfortunately, this is not an isolated incident for the normally reliable actor. Pacino wanders through the film with a quizzical look upon his face. It's supposed to be because he doesn't know who the killer is and why they are targeting him, however it feels much more likely that his expression is down to the fact he has no idea why he is in this turkey of a film.

This is not a Pacino performance his fans want to remember. He is there in body, just not in mind or soul. The method actor has vanished and been replaced with someone simply trying to get through each day before he can clock off. The only interesting element of this film as far as Pacino is concerned is his large selection of hair styles. Almost every scene sees him showing off a new style. The film is little more than a conveyer belt of wigs.

Ultimately, Pacino does nothing to elevate his character and the rest of the cast are equally adrift throughout the film. Sobieski, McKenzie and Brenneman are all hung out to dry thanks to poor dialogue and a script that offers their characters nothing. Witt meanders through the film with a surprised look upon her face. How many times can you be surprised that you are the chosen target of a killer, one has to wonder?

Then there is the utterly pointless "mystery man" character played by Stephen Moyer. This film has a respectable cast, so why in the heck are they all so bad? The answer is simple: the script is shockingly poor. The majority of dialogue comes straight out of the Generic Thriller Handbook. It is all so horribly clichéd.

During the climax, Dr Gramm is summoned to the top of a building. Once there, he finds the killer with hostages. Gramm has a gun pointed at the killer who then asks: "Is that a gun Dr Gramm?" This is the level of dialogue you can expect from this film. At times it tries to bamboozle the audience with heavy dialogue about the psychology of killers, when in fact it's actually alienating everybody watching because the dialogue is utterly dumbfounding and without any merit. Another problem is the constant double, triple, and quadruple who-dun-it twists. The 'plot' is little more than a never-ending stream of red herrings and after about the third 'twist' it becomes tiresome to even think about who the real killer is because any presumption will no doubt end up being twisted again. The film is practically a parody of itself.

88 Minutes feels like a lifetime of watching Pacino et al drag their feet through this flaccid stinker.

Actor Leah Cairns on *88 Minutes*

The film set in real time, which is something of a rarity. Was that why you were interested in starring in the movie?

No, I was interested in being in the movie because Al Pacino was in it. He was the hugest selling feature. I didn't even need to read a script. As an actor, until you get to the level that Al Pacino is at, we don't have a huge say in what we audition for. We audition for things that are offered to us. But when I found out Al Pacino was in it I made a huge effort, because I was working two different shows at the time and actually couldn't make it to any of the auditions. The director was interested in seeing me specifically for it because he wanted a dancer. The audition was one of the funniest auditions I've ever been on. The short answer is: no, it had nothing to do with the script and everything to do with Al Pacino.

You have to tell the story about the audition because you just said it was the funniest one.

It's pretty funny. I was actually at a party at the weekend with the casting director from that movie and we were laughing at how bizarre it was. I was working on *Battlestar Galactica* and a Canadian show called *Godiva's*, so I missed all of the auditions but the director was hell bent on having me come in and read for the part as he knew I was a dancer and he wanted an interesting opening to the movie, but he wasn't sure what that would look like yet.

The casting director phoned my agent and asked if I would be comfortable meeting the director and her, the casting director, at the director's hotel in the evening after I got off work. Which doesn't happen often. Because the casting director is who she is and has an amazing reputation, I had no worry or issue with meeting the director at his hotel room. I went and they said: "wear some comfortable clothes because this character is supposed to be a dancer and they want to see what dancers can do." I said: "well I'm on set and I brought my jeans." So they outfitted me at work, they gave me some jogging pants to wear... to take with me and change into when I got there.

Off I went and I get there quite early and I was thinking: 'oh, they want a dancer, I guess I will be doing some stretching or some dancing so I should limber up.' So I'm in the bathroom in the restaurant that is attached to the hotel, waiting for the casting director to show up because I'm early, and I start doing some basic stretches in the bathroom and I rip the entire ass out of my jeans and I walked out and thank God I had these jogging pants. The casting director arrived and I said: "I am here and I just need to get changed. I've ripped the entire bum out of the outfit I was going to wear."

Because I still had to audition the scenes and I wanted to be dressed nicely for that part and then for the dance part my intention was to change into the jogging pants. But that's not how it worked out. I walked up and met the director looking like a schlep.

I went in and we read the scene a couple of times and then we just sat down and started talking about what he was looking for and together – Jon Avnet, myself and the casting director – came up with the opening scene where I'm standing there, stark naked doing the stretch with the electric toothbrush. The stretch was my idea and the toothbrush was the casting director's idea. I showed him what dancers can do and did some stretches and he gave me the job right then and there. Which was pretty cool and never, ever happens.

It's quite an opening scene. Were you nervous?

No, I think I was so young and naive and just excited to work... it honestly never occurred to me to be nervous. I think if I were doing something like that now I would be extraordinarily nervous. But I was young and new and excited to do it.

Did Pacino make any jokes while you were shooting that scene?

No absolutely not. He was totally professional. Funnily enough, a lot of that scene was shot without him there. I did a lot of my stuff to a mark on a camera and he was less-than-impressed when he found out I did the scene without him. I think they were just trying to save time. But once he arrived and we started shooting he was lovely and professional. My funny Al Pacino moment from shooting was: he is often always in character and I hadn't worked with such a serious method actor before, and it was a pretty light scene that opening scene, and I was having the time of my life, and he is sitting at the table between takes and I'm off chatting with the camera people. He is just 'in it' and he has his head in his hands and he is mumbling to himself and he's looking troubled and I just did what I would do with any actor who seemed like they were still trying to work through a scene. I walked up to him and said: "Oh hey Al, are you OK? If you need any help, I'm here for you." [*Laughs*]. He stopped and he looked at me and the look he gave me… I was like, oh right; I could be a boom pole for all it matters to you.

Then his face changed and I think he kind of fell in love with me in that moment because I'm pretty sure in the last thirty years nobody has said anything like that to Al Pacino. I was so wondrously naive... that's what I said. [*Laughs*].

Was he cool to work with?

A hundred percent of the time. Actually, he came up with a few ideas that he wanted to try on the spot that Jon was: "No Al," because his character is quite hung-over and he wanted to be really hung-over and silly. Jon had to shut down a few things. It was pretty funny.

The opening has a few slow-mo shots of you and Pacino dancing. Was he a good dancer?

We were doing all the stuff in the bar and the whole cast were on set and Jon came up to me and said: "Leah, are you comfortable to add an impromptu dance scene with Al?" I was: "Yeah of course. Sure." He said: "I don't know if we will have time. We will try and shoot for the end of the day." We got everything we needed that day and we had a few minutes left and Jon said: "OK OK OK, we need some music." They put a song on and said just dance. Everybody got into a big semi circle around us to watch, and Al Pacino and I just free styled for an entire song. I was so in the moment and loving every second of it, obviously I have no idea what it is looking like, and Leelee Sobieski at the end had tears in her eyes and said it was the best thing she had ever seen. I looked at her and looked at everybody else and I threw my arms in the air and said "Well... my career is never going to get better than this moment. I quit!" [*Laughs*].

It was an exciting moment. The thing is that that footage, I think, is gone. We ended up doing reshoots for *88 Minutes* a year later and Jon was lamenting about that footage because he said it was incredible footage. They used a little bit of that footage for the beginning of it, but he had wanted to get the whole thing for me and nobody knew where it was. That was a career highlight for sure – dancing with Al.

So the footage has disappeared?

I think so. If memory serves, I talked to Jon about it because he was so excited to be able to use it at the beginning of the movie. I've seen a couple of cuts of *88 Minutes*, including the release in Israel and Asia, far before it was released in North America and they ended up changing it. So I have a copy from my friends... my two friends who I used to work with were backpacking through Cambodia and found it. The kids were selling it on the street and they bought it for me. I watched it. So I've seen the original cut, and Al and I are in it a lot more than the one that was released in North America. They ended up cutting out our stuff and putting in a scene at the very beginning with two girls who were murdered.

You said you took the role because you wanted to work with Pacino. What did you see that made you think: "Wow! This is Pacino! This is the guy I wanted to work with"?

When we were in the bar, doing the bar scene, and because the whole premise of the movie is he is fighting to save his own life and save his name, and it's very high stakes, so he was in that emotional state for most of the shoot. But lucky me, I got him before all that stuff happened. I got really fun Al, and he was telling stories about filming in the seventies... he is an amazing storyteller. When we were doing this bar scene, and because he is such a method actor, I thought: is he going to come to work hammered? He didn't. He came to work stone cold sober. I watched, before my very eyes, I could see him get drunk. It literally crept through his whole body. I could see his whole body getting limper and his eyes getting droopy. I watched him get hammered in front of my eyes and by the time they called "Action!" he was sloshed. It was amazing. It was absolutely amazing. He's a pro. I've never worked with anyone like him before.

Ocean's Thirteen

Cast: George Clooney (Danny Ocean), Brad Pitt (Rusty Ryan), Matt Damon (Linus Caldwell/Lenny Pepperidge), Andy Garcia (Terry Benedict), Don Cheadle (Basher Tarr), Bernie Mac (Frank Catton), Ellen Barkin (Abigail Sponder), Al Pacino (Willy Bank). **Director:** Steven Soderbergh.

Synopsis: What are the odds of getting even? Danny Ocean and the gang are going to Vegas and this time there's only one reason to pull-off their most ambitious and risky casino heist – to defend one of their own. When ruthless casino owner Willy Bank double-crosses one of the Eleven, Danny and the gang see if they can break "The Bank."

Hollywood loves a sequel and when parts one and two of a franchise make over $813 million worldwide, the studio is highly likely to be open to a third instalment. The seeds of *Ocean's Thirteen*, the third outing of the *Ocean's* franchise, were sown even before principal photography of the second movie had finished: "I thought it would be fun to go back to Las Vegas for the next one. But it was always with the understanding that it had to be 'all in' or we were not doing it – everybody comes back or nobody comes back," said director Steven Soderbergh. Legendary producer Jerry Weintraub, who founded JW Productions for *Ocean's Eleven*, called all the main cast members individually eighteen months before filming was due to start to make sure they set aside the summer of 2006. Weintraub also ensured that Soderbergh was willing to return as well, later explaining: "For me, as a producer, there's Steven Soderbergh and then there's everybody else."

With over a year to work on a new storyline that brought the *Ocean's* gang back to Las Vegas, Weintraub and Soderbergh met with a handful of writers to hear their ideas. One duo summoned to a lunch meeting was Brian Koppelman and David Levien, who had enjoyed previous success with the gambling drama *Rounders* (which also starred Matt

Damon) in 1998. "Within minutes we were starting work on the script. It really is in their wheelhouse," said Soderbergh. Koppelman and Levien dazzled because of their intricate knowledge of the gambling lifestyle. Between them, they had read hundreds of books about con artists and were familiar with the Vegas culture. Discussions turned to why the characters would take those risks and a template was also set out as to the progression of the *Ocean's* gang since the first movie. It was decided the third movie should be about friendship and that should be the reason the characters return to Las Vegas. Weintraub and Soderbergh liked what they heard and hired the duo.

The original cast had all signed on by this stage and the only major casting decision to be made was that of villain, Willy Bank, and his right-hand woman, Abigail Sponder. Finding actors to fill these roles proved a simple task for Weintraub as he called up two long-time friends for the job. Ellen Barkin, who had shot a small scene for *Ocean's Twelve* but it was cut from the finished film, was cast as Sponder. She had known Weintraub since 1982 when he cast her in the comedy-drama *Diner* opposite Steve Guttenberg, Mickey Rourke and Kevin Bacon, and commented: "I didn't read the script. I took part over the phone. Jerry Weintraub called me up and said "How'd you like to be the girl in *Ocean's Thirteen*?" I said "You're on. Let's go," and then I read it [the script]." Weintraub received much the same reaction from Al Pacino when he spoke to him about the role of Casino boss Willy Bank. The duo's relationship dated back to 1980 when Weintraub produced *Cruising*, in which Pacino starred.

Although the bulk of the cast returned for the third outing, there were four noticeable exceptions: Peter Fonda, Bruce Willis, Julia Roberts and Catherine Zeta-Jones. Fonda, who filmed a scene for *Ocean's Twelve* but was cut from the finished film, intended to reprise the same role. Unfortunately, Fonda's schedule didn't permit time away from shooting comic book adaptation: *Ghost Rider*, so his role was cut altogether. Returning actor Bernie Mac, who plays Frank Catton, blabbed to MTV before filming had started that Willis would feature again (he appeared in the previous film) as himself. Due to Willis's heavy workload that summer (he had six films set for release during 2006), he was unable to return for his uncredited cameo. The biggest non-returnees from *Ocean's Eleven* and *Twelve* were undoubtedly Roberts and Zeta-Jones (the latter appeared in *Twelve* only). Roberts was unable to return as Beatrice Owen as she was pregnant with her third child. The absence of Zeta-Jones was down to a script issue: "Neither Soderbergh nor I would prevail on them [Zeta-Jones and Roberts] to come back and do nothing just to do it," said Weintraub.

The finance for *Ocean's Thirteen* came from three companies – JW Productions (Weintraub's own company), Section Eight Productions (a joint venture between Soderbergh and Clooney) and Village Roadshow Pictures (an Australian company that had backed many Hollywood movies including *The Matrix*, *Three Kings* and *Catwoman*. They had also been involved in the previous two *Ocean's* movies.) A budget of $85 million was set, equal to that of the first movie in the franchise.

Principal photography for *Ocean's Thirteen* began on 21 July 2006. Some exterior scenes were filmed on the Las Vegas strip. The Bellagio Hotel was used for exterior and interior filming including the corporate offices and The Fontana Bar. A section of the Venetian Hotel that was under construction was used for the Bank Casino building site scenes. The Mandalay Bay's Mix Lounge, located on the 64th floor of the hotel, played its part as one section of the Bank Casino. Filming also took place at the Southwest Airlines gate at Las Vegas' McCarran International Airport, and security closed off that area of the airport in order to shoot scenes with Clooney, Pitt and Damon. Production also trekked to the desert town of Rosamond, California to shoot scenes supposedly set in a Mexican dice factory.

For a movie set in Las Vegas, very little was actually shot on location. Taking over an entire casino for filming purposes simply wasn't viable; instead the crew used three huge sound stages at Warner Bros Burbank Studios. Stages 16, 20 and 29 were each converted into different floors of The Bank Casino and Soderbergh brought in his long-time production designer Philip Messina to create the sets. He commented: "I thought, 'This may be the only time I'll ever get to design and build something of this scale, so I'm going for it'." The multi-level gaming floor was erected on Stage 16. It is one of the largest sound stages in Los Angeles and one of the tallest in the world. It also houses a 2,000,000 gallon water tank. Production didn't require a deep water tank so structural engineers had to be assigned in order to cover up the tank with flooring that wouldn't collapse under the weight of the additional builds that Messina and his team were putting in place. Not only did the sound stage have to take the weight of the set and the constant footfall during filming, it also needed to take the additional 37,000 pound weight of the large casino elevators. The crew had to dig into the original foundations of the sound stage and erect special footings to hold them. The rest of the set featured real slot machines, a fully-equipped Asian restaurant and a check-in desk area with online computers.

The lighting rig in Stage 16 was filled with thousands of different lights and several chandeliers. Notably, a 9,000 pound hand-blown Austrian glass chandelier hung over the craps table. Supports had to be added to the roof in order to take the additional weight and it took a five-man team seven days to install it piece by piece. Another lavish chandelier, designed by Jacob Hashimoto, hung in the lobby area. The lights hanging over the entire gambling floor were designed by Messina and his wife Kristen Toscano Messina. They were painstakingly moulded using a variety of different styles to fit in with the overarching aesthetic of the movie and were strategically placed to ensure the production lights weren't seen on camera. Due to the number of lights and gaming machines needed on Stage 16 the electric bill was $60,000 per week throughout filming.

Stages 20 and 29 were not quite as full but one of them housed Bank's office and his Diamond Room. Within the Diamond Room was a chandelier called 'The Cascade,' on loan from the Swarovski Crystal Company. It was twenty feet tall and two feet wide and because of the delicate nature of the crystals they had to be hooked individually into the rigging attached to the studio's ceiling. The remaining studio space was used to build the helipad that sat atop of Bank's Casino. The five foot high platform complete with wind machines was constructed for a scene towards the end of the movie that featured a helicopter lifting a section of the Diamond Room and flying away with it.

As intricate as the sets were this wasn't the only reason the designers working overtime. Costume designer Louise Frogley spent months tailoring new looks for each of the main cast members: "They have so many characters, each of which has to have a totally distinctive quality." Clooney's outfits were clean and simple. Pitt wanted a touch of bling. Garcia adopted a 'Death in Venice' style this time. Damon had the opportunity to wear more suits as he felt Linus had grown up. Cheadle boasted the all-American look. Barkin had dresses made in a signature colour – pink. Pacino was given custom-made suits by Battaglia in a range of vivid colours.

When it came to the shooting schedule, Soderbergh orchestrated the filming of each scene so Pacino could shoot his scenes in three weeks straight. During Pacino's first day on set he said to Weintraub: "What do these guys [Clooney, Pitt, Damon etc] think of me?" Weintraub replied "It's very simple Al. What did you think of Brando when he did The Godfather? That's what they think of you." Weintraub actively discouraged the actors from retreating to their trailers during filming and came up with 'The Ocean's Club', a conference room on one of the sound stages that was redesigned to emulate the club environment. Here cast members could watch television, play foosball, try their luck at real gaming tables or just sit and read. Breakfast, lunch and dinner were also available in the club. Soderbergh liked the place so much he asked for his editing suite to be moved there.

Towards the end of filming, Soderbergh came over all emotional, stating: "Well, this is the last time I'm going to see these people in a room. There was a very strong sense of we were really lucky that these movies came about, that we got to do them and this is it." Once filming wrapped on the sound stages it was left to a skeleton crew to shoot one final scene in London which featured Damon's Linus. The scene was shot just outside Moorgate tube station and while it was a serious scene that had Linus returning back to L.A., the dialogue riffed on Damon's other film commitment at the time: *The Bourne Ultimatum*: "I've used four identities... I think I'm being followed... I have a name but I don't even know if that's right."

When principal photography wrapped, the cast and crew each received a memento in the shape of a membership card for The Ocean's Club. The club was torn down after filming finished; however it would live on thanks to the inscription on the back of the club card that read: "You are a lifetime member. But if any one of us sees any other member any place in the world and you don't have your card with you, you buy the drinks."

With a film as grandiose and stylish as *Ocean's Thirteen*, there really was only one place to hold the World Premiere: The Cannes Film Festival. On 24 May 2007, the cast walked the red carpet at the Palais des Festivals. Angelina Jolie upstaged every single one of them, including her husband Brad Pitt, as she walked into the theatre wearing a long flowing yellow dress. Two night's prior to the premiere, the charity Not on Our Watch held its launch party in Cannes. Clooney, Pitt, Damon, Weintraub, Cheadle and Human Rights Lawyer David Pressman set up the charity to help the existing relief efforts in war-torn Darfur. All the proceeds from the launch night and the premiere went to supporting the efforts in Darfur.

Back on home turf, the film had its U.S. premiere at the Grauman's Chinese Theatre, Los Angeles on 5 June. The next day the *Ocean's* gang hopped on a plane to attend another premiere of the film, this time in Las Vegas at the CineVegas Film Festival held at the Palms Casino Resort. There was also a third premiere in Chicago on 7 June. The AMC River East Theatre opened its doors to Clooney, Pitt, Damon and others.

Critical reviews were generally positive for the third film in the franchise. *The New York Times* playfully suggested: "It's lighter than air, prettier than life, a romp, a goof and an attentively oiled machine." *Rolling Stone* called it a "class act of a caper movie." *Variety* also succumbed to the movie's charm saying "*Ocean's Thirteen* continues the breezy good times of the first two series entries without missing a beat." Before the film had its U.S. release on 8 June, Warner Bros distributed the film reels to theatres under the joke-y fake title of License to Steal. With such a great buzz generated, and a nationwide release from day one, cinema goers flocked to see the movie. By the end of its first weekend on U.S. release it had generated over $36 million and the final tally at the end of its first full week was an impressive $50.7 million. In total, *Ocean's Thirteen* spent fifteen weeks in U.S. theatres with a grand total of $117 million in receipts. It faired just as well in foreign territories where its returns were $194 million. The film's final cumulative box office worldwide gross was an unbelievably healthy $311 million (Information courtesy of Box Office Mojo. Used with permission).

Much like the previous two outings, *Ocean's Thirteen* sees Clooney, Pitt and Damon command most of the screen time and have the majority of the best lines. But then, why shouldn't they? These actors are at the core of the franchise. Of the three, if anyone is sidelined, it is Damon who has to contend with goofy prosthetics while Clooney and Pitt banter their way through the movie. The script is funny by any measure and at times painfully reflects their real lives at the time of filming: Pitt tells Clooney, "Lose some weight." Clooney tells Pitt, "Have some kids." The two of them alone could have carried the film with this kind of playground-style bickering.

The main storyline zips along at great pace, swiftly establishing itself as a flashy, quick-fire narrative. Soderbergh, references to the Disco-era also adds a certain sparkle. One character who benefits from the shimmery aesthetic of the film is Willy Bank. This role gives Pacino the scope to juggle moments of deadpan comedy and ruthless drama. Bathed in gold, he stalks through his scenes like a lion on the prowl. He frequently interrupts those he is dissatisfied with and gives them a verbal thrashing: "Don't worry about it. I should have fired you a week ago." This is a Casino owner with the shortest of fuses and one that takes great care over every detail of his empire, even down to the firing (which he executes with maniacal glee).

This performance is no great stretch for Pacino but he does seem to be having an absolute blast in the role, opting to keep it low key and brutal. This is a character that in different hands could have been a grandstander, a guy who shouts and screams every time he walks into a new room. In times past Pacino would have gone down that route. In this film he is a different guy, he is a guy who commands respect through fear. He keeps his utterances concise and acerbic, even with those closest to him.

Barkin's Sponder completely worships Bank, even if he is undeserving. She knows the power he holds and that a step out of line means the end of her career. While not as obvious, it is clear that Bank also respects Sponder. He knows she is the only one who can get things done the way he wants them done. The relationship between Pacino and Barkin is not too dissimilar to their previous encounter in *Sea of Love*. This time however it is about respect rather than red hot sex. As much as it is amusing watching Pacino and Barkin reunited, their screen time is limited because, as with the previous two movies, the story revolves around Clooney, Pitt, Damon, Garcia, Cheadle and the others. There may be the odd plot hole here or there (how did they get that giant drill underground without anyone seeing it?) and there is still a dodgy accent from one actor (Cor blimey, Guv'nor), however *Ocean's Thirteen* doesn't concern itself with being in any way thought-provoking. Instead, Soderbergh and his crew are only concerned with making an entertaining popcorn blockbuster film that is slick, sexy, stylish and bags of fun.

Actor Adam Lazarre-White on *Ocean's Thirteen*

Were you aware that you would be acting alongside Pacino when you got the role?

If I remember correctly, Al Pacino was already attached to the project to play the bad guy. So I knew when I was going in as the part was called The Junior Executive, that was the title of the character and I knew that was Pacino's right hand man.

Did you have any time to rehearse with the cast?

Not really rehearse. Most TV and film jobs don't have a lot of rehearsal time like a play. There are some directors who work that way, with a rehearsal, and that also tends to be projects that need a lot of rehearsal, like musicals. There are certain directors in what you would call actor-ly movies that like to rehearse. But there isn't a lot of rehearsal, generally, in film. You show up ready to shoot. However, what I did do, because I was going to be playing Al's right hand guy, was I got permission to get in contact through his personal assistant to go over to Al's house and talk to him and spend a little time with him, and find out what he was doing in his part. Because my concept of the part, on some basic level, was: I want to be him someday [Willy Bank – Pacino's character]. That's what I'm doing, training to be him. I wanted to know if he [Pacino] had any concept or what he was doing or how he was planning to dress or present his character, and then mine would be defined by some degree by that.

When I went over to his house, his hair was slightly dyed, a lighter colour. It was a lighter brown than his hair and I said: "Oh you've dyed your hair."
He said to me: "Yeah, I think he [Banks] is very gold." [*Laughs*].

So I knew then he was already working with his concepts. So, when I got to the costumer, I said I didn't want any gold. I didn't want anything to stand up against his gold. So there was a relationship in terms of drawing my character to compliment his character. To have my hair cut perfect. My cuffs perfect. My suit perfect. My tie perfect. My shirts pressed. I had to be perfect. That was the character. There was other stuff in the script that never made it into the movie that gave me more sense of that.

As you had already met Pacino before filming began, what was your relationship like when it was time to start shooting?

My experience with Al, like a lot of people that are famous, he is more casual than the people that are with him. It's the people that are with him that are projecting the tension onto the situation. They have a casualness about them. So, if you're not tense and weird, they are not tense and weird. Al was very cool with me. I had a slight advantage in that I had met him and been around him a few times because his children, with Beverly D'Angelo, were in pre-school with my child. I had seen him at a couple of events and said hello to him. So there was another way I had met him, very casually and just a few times, where the ice had been broken already.

That all being said, your real question is: how is he on set? I would say that he is very focussed. He doesn't really walk around and chit chat with everybody. But he had worked many, many years before with Ellen Barkin on *Sea of Love,* and she was on the movie and they had a wonderful kind of old colleague dynamic that was a joy to be around. They were teasing each other, and that I was on set and being around that was fun to watch and be present around. His dynamic with me was casual, not over-played in anyway. But when he wanted to say something to me... again part of what I was doing was mimicking the relationship in real life, in the relationship in the movie. As any young actor would be, if Al Pacino wags his finger at you and tells you to come over as he wants to talk to you, you are at his side in two seconds.

When I was on set I was acutely aware of Al and yet giving him distance. I wouldn't be all over him, but I was always in view, sight, earshot, that if he wanted to say something to me about the next scene I was always there. It was [a] really nice relationship. Professional, nice, warm. There was a casual ease about it. I could talk to him. But I didn't do that that much. I didn't invade his privacy that much. I had the same relationship with Steven Soderbergh. There is a certain respect you give to the people who have reached great heights in your work. There is a respect you afford them. Al Pacino is about as high as it gets for an actor.

Did he give you any advice on how to play a scene with him?

A lot of what I did was non-verbal acting with him. It was listening, being present, taking orders. As long as I was listening and present in the scene, when I say present I mean in my soul, in my vibe with him, there was not a tremendous amount for him to direct me on. But there was one scene where I had more dialogue and he called me over and said... it wasn't so much that he gave me advice but that he let me know... I can't remember exactly what he said but he worded it: "I'm going to go... I'm going to go a little off script here. I might do something, just follow my lead." I was like: great, I get to improve with Al today [*Laughs*].

It wasn't so much about giving advice as much as... almost the unspoken advice of do as I do. If he was loose walking into a scene and prepping a little bit then I would join in. If he was very quiet sitting in his chair then I would move away and be quiet. Almost in a militaristic way – formal, standing by, ready for action when you need me. A lot of his main scenes with me, his main dialogue was with someone else and I was there. If you watch *The Godfather*, I was like Rocco [*Laughs*]. I was the body man, the guy who was always there.

That's how I looked at the character. I'm the one who knows his dirty laundry. I'm the one who knows all the secrets. I'm the one on the building with Elliott Gould when he is threatening to push him off. I know everything. So there is a level of trust that I, somehow, earned it in the back story of the movie. Even if you're not saying a lot there is a certain import to your presence because you are the one he trusts. I'm talking about the character, not Al. He was supposed to be like Steve Wynn, the most powerful guy in Vegas.

Pacino has a lot of comedic and sarcastic lines in *Ocean's Thirteen*, and most of the time you are there with him. Did you corpse at any of them?

No. I'm a professional actor. We train to be focussed in performance in the same way an athlete or a musician or a public speaker does. The whole point of seeing a trained performer is that you are able to perform under the duress of distraction whether it's the audience or a mistake or something purposeful, you are focussed on what you are doing. If he was being sarcastic in a scene, let's say working for Danny Ocean and it's causing him a problem, that's not funny to me. I work for his character and there is a problem in the casino and he is making a sarcastic remark because he is pissed off about it. Which means I'm pissed off about it too. So, it's not funny to me. It's funny to the audience, that's the way it should be. It's not a funny situation to me.

Not to mention, I'm responsible and that's some of what didn't make it into the movie. There was a whole other scene where he dresses me down because things are going wrong. I'm not laughing when things go wrong. Things don't go wrong for him [Banks] and they don't go wrong for me. I'm Mr Perfect, I don't make mistakes. That's my character. So when things go wrong it's not fun to me. It wasn't about laughing it was about doing my job; my job is to be my character in that scene. That's not to say you're never in a scene where another actor does something off the cuff and cracks you up – it can happen. That movie is written that way. He [Pacino] is making it feel improvisational and made up on the spot but it's written in the script. When you are on script and know what to expect, then you expect it. It comes in whatever form it comes but it's not going to ruin your focus to your job. My job, on some level, was to lend some severity and some danger to his presence. When you see the scene with Elliott Gould you realise he will do anything. He is that guy. He is that guy for that guy. You're talking about a guy who is inside and outside of his business whatever that might be. He's got a guy who gets his hands dirty because he [Willy Bank] doesn't get his hands dirty.

Do you have a favourite memory of working on *Ocean's Thirteen*?

I will give you one, but just to say it was such a dream-like experience, there were so many of those moments. I had an incredible several moments, even though I wasn't on camera that much with George Clooney, who is the nicest guy you've ever met. The most inclusive, funny, charming, smart guy you ever met. One of my favourite moments was eating vegetarian chilli out of a paper cup at craft service [the department responsible for on set catering] talking to George. That was a great moment.

With Al, not only is he an icon but a personal hero of mine, every single moment was a gift. That being said when we did a scene that didn't end up making the final cut of the movie... when Al calls me over and asks: "what are you going to do in this scene?" I told him, and he said: "follow my lead. I might go off a little bit here." To go on camera with Al Pacino and have him throwing new stuff at me, improvisational stuff, and being able to improv with him was a dream come true. The dialogue was maybe just four or five lines, and something terrible had happened in the casino and he was taking me to task for it. He said the first line of the scene and I said the first response and then he said: "Is this a tragedy?" I said: "Err... yes," he said: "Are you the star of this tragedy?" I said: "Err... No." I was trying to make excuses and blame somebody else and I was in this wonderful improv with Al Pacino. Talking to me, looking at me with those eyes that are size of silver dollars. It was an exciting moment I'll never forget.

Righteous Kill

Cast: Robert De Niro (Turk), Al Pacino (Rooster), Curtis Jackson (Spider), Carla Gugino (Karen Corelli), John Leguizamo (Det. Simon Perez), Donnie Wahlberg (Det. Ted Riley), Brian Dennehy (Hingis), Melissa Leo (Cheryl Brooks). **Director:** Jon Avnet.

Synopsis: Turk and Rooster are two veteran New York cops on the verge of retirement, when one last job finds them on the trail of an apparent vigilante serial killer who they thought they'd put away years before. As the net closes in on the culprit, the police force begins to suspect the murderer may be one of their own.

Hollywood studios are not normally in the business of green lighting multi-million dollar movies based on the promise of a first-time writer's script. Russell Gewirtz is one of the few who bucked that trend when his screenplay for the crime drama *Inside Man* was purchased by director Ron Howard's Imagine Entertainment. The script was to be directed by Spike Lee and Denzel Washington was to star in the picture alongside Clive Owen and Jodie Foster. *Inside Man* won favourable reviews and earned over $180 million at the box office during 2006.

After an earlier idea for a cop movie struck him, Gewirtz began writing *Righteous Kill*: "When I completed it, it took quite a while before it went anywhere. It wasn't sent out to the studios the way *Inside Man* had been," Gewirtz later commented. Once *Inside Man* became a huge success at the box office however, the studios were buzzing around Gewirtz and his *Righteous Kill* script made it into the hands of film producers Randall Emmett and Avi Lerner; the pair had been looking for a movie for Robert De Niro for some time and Emmett found that the actor "responded to" the script well. Lerner and Emmett agreed to co-produce Gewirtz's script between their studios: Millennium Films and Emmett/Furla Films and a budget of $60 million was set.

With De Niro already onboard to play Turk, the search for a director began. Emmett later commented: "The next step was backwards, because we didn't have a director. The first name that came to us was Jon Avnet." After working with Avnet on the real-time crime film *88 Minutes* starring Al Pacino, Lerner felt Avnet was the right choice: "I like his efficiency. I like the fact that he's a director and a producer from the independent world and understands the way we work." Director and star, Avnet and De Niro, had a meeting in New York to discuss the film. One of the topics was who would play the other lead detective. De Niro suggested his long time friend Al Pacino: "When I said 'what about Al?' Jon just grabbed onto that."

The idea of reuniting two legendary actors thirteen years after their first on-screen appearance together in Heat appealed to De Niro: "If you know each other as long as we've known each other, you can draw on that background." The script was sent to Pacino to see if he would be interested in taking on the role of Rooster, Turk's long time police partner. He later commented: "I felt it would be a good opportunity to work with Bob in a role I thought I could play." With Avnet directing two of the biggest actors in the world for *Righteous Kill*, word soon spread around Hollywood that Pacino and De Niro would be reteaming for a forthcoming movie "We had every agent in town calling us. But we only wanted what was right for the story, and we ended up with the perfect cast," said producer Lati Grobman.

In rounding out the cast, both fresh faces and veteran actors were brought into the mix. John Leguizamo and Donnie Wahlberg were cast as homicide detectives working alongside the characters of Pacino and De Niro. Carla Gugino was cast to play crime scene detective Karen Corelli, whose dark personal life invades her work. The role of Lieutenant Hingis, the head of the homicide squad, was filled by seasoned actor Brian Dennehy. Avnet took a chance on two non-actors for a couple of the key roles. Rambo, a skateboarding street pimp, was to be played by professional skateboarder Rob Dyrdek. For the character of Spider, a big-time drug dealer who runs a lavish nightclub, Avnet cast rapper Curtis "50 Cent" Jackson. "He read with me and then showed up at the reading with everyone and held his own." Just as filming was due to begin, a bidding war broke out for distribution rights. Both Warner Bros. Pictures and Universal Pictures put in bids of over $10 million. However they were surpassed by Overture Films. The production and distribution company had only been active since 2006 and had bid, and won, the distribution rights to *Righteous Kill* with a figure just over $12 million.

Before filming began, ex-NYPD homicide detective turned film consultant Neil Carter visited a gun range with the actors: "I showed them how to hold a gun, how to do a combat stand, exactly the way we're trained in the NYPD, and how to be prepared for a shootout."

Principal photography began on September 2007 and lasted a mere thirty-six days. The majority of filming took place around Connecticut in Bridgeport, Norwalk and Milford. Locations used in Bridgeport included White's Diner, Golden Hill United Methodist Church, The Bridgeport Hospital, the abandoned City Trust Bank vaults and the Red Cross Building. The historic Mechanics and Farmers Savings Bank building was used as the set for Spider's nightclub. The building had been vacant for several years and while production wanted to keep the layout and architecture of the interior intact they also had to spruce it up with added lights, walkways and seating areas. An upstairs room that looked out onto the main area of the bank was converted into a stylishly dark office for the club's owner, Spider. The windows were covered with either red or blue tints and the wall was littered with fake platinum music disc awards.

Avnet, his cinematographer Denis Lenoir and the camera crew watched the dailies of the nightclub office scenes on DVD each lunchtime in the director's trailer: "The first dailies were much too dark and looked underexposed by two stops, but Jon trusted me and I trusted my meter. With another director, I could have been fired! We discovered that the problem was with the DVD player in the trailer." A much more worrying problem arose during the first week of filming when a small fire broke out on the ground floor. Fire crews were called to the scene at 2:30am to extinguish the blaze. It was unclear what started the fire, however due to the quick response from the Bridgeport Fire

Department, the building escaped with only minor internal damage to the front left hand corner. Part of the set was badly damaged and required several days of repair before filming could restart.

Production then moved on to an old linen factory in Bridgeport. The abandoned offices were converted into a messy Police precinct. The downstairs workhouse still had rows of empty cylinders that once housed the rolls of linen. This area was one of three empty buildings used for the big climax between Turk and Rooster. "We called the second location the white factory. The third location was inside a big warehouse that had a little warmer look" said cinematographer Denis Lenoir. The next location on the shooting schedule was that of Milford, Connecticut where the Star Cafe was used as a double for a cop bar. The internal scenes were shot during the daytime so black sheets were wrapped around the windows to block out the daylight. A night time scene was shot outside the cafe just after 10pm so the lighting matched that of the interior shots. In Norwalk, Connecticut the local Police station, the State Superior Courthouse and the corner of Ann and Main Street were used in a variety of scenes. Production then uprooted to New York City. Exterior and interior scenes were filmed at the Criminal Courts Building on Centre Street, Manhattan. One particular filming moment took place on the baseball field in Central Park where an inter-police softball game was being filmed. Wahlberg suddenly became very nervous: "I was pitching and Jon [Avnet] told me to make sure I was throwing strikes. I said 'Don't worry, I'll throw strikes.' But then Robert De Niro steps into the batter's box, and as I'm about to pitch, it occurred to me, if this pitch is inside I'm going to hit Robert De Niro. But if it's outside I'm going to have Jon Avnet screaming at me in front of everybody. I felt like I was trying to throw the last strike at the World Series. What are you going to do? I'd rather have Jon yell at me than hit Bob De Niro in the head, so I threw the pitch about six feet outside. Then I heard Jon Avnet screaming 'Donnie, you idiot, throw a strike!'"

Once filming had wrapped and post-production was complete, a carefully-selected group of moviegoers were treated to a test screening of *Righteous Kill* in New Jersey at the tail end of February 2008. They were amongst the first people, outside of the studio, to see the movie and in exchange for this honour were required to give confidential feedback to the studio. Unfortunately, a couple of reviews appeared online the day after the screening reporting that they were more than a little disappointed with the film. The screened version ran for two hours, but was hastily re-edited down to one hundred and one minutes for its general release due to the negative feedback.

Righteous Kill received its premiere on 11 September 2008 at The Ziegfeld Theatre in Midtown, Manhattan. By the time the stars were walking the red carpet at the premiere, the critics had already released their reviews of the film and they were not pretty reading. *The New York Times* howled it was "a clutter of recycled cop-movie and serial-killer film clichés." *Rolling Stone* exclaimed: "This movie defines drag-ass." *USA Today* scathed: "Righteous Kill is an overwrought police thriller that feels like a second-rate episode of Law & Order." The film opened in North American theatres on 12 September. By the end of its first week it had pulled in $21 million and sat at number two on the U.S. box office. However, by the second week on release the box office returns had dropped by 53%, totalling a sluggish $9 million. Despite continuously declining returns, the film managed to stay in theatres for fifteen weeks but by its last week it returned a meagre $1,995 across fifteen screens. Its final North American box office tally was $40 million. Foreign returns were equally poor. Across the forty-eight countries the film generated a cumulative return of just $38 million. It lasted only two weeks in Bolivian theatres, pulling in a shocking $5,303 (Information courtesy of Box Office Mojo. Used with permission). A film starring Pacino and De Niro together had failed to recoup its budget from worldwide box office returns.

Pacino and De Niro had little screen time together in *Heat*, and thus there was always going to be demand for another collaboration. Ideally, a story that meant the pair were working together on the same side. The obvious choice would be a movie that involves, in one shape or another, a crime storyline as both actors have had massive worldwide success in that genre. In *Righteous Kill*, Avnet wastes no time in reuniting the pair on-screen. It's less than a minute in fact, as the camera pulls back to display them firing their guns at an indoor police target range. This moment sets the precedent for the rest of the film. Very rarely does the audience see one without the other; Avnet, and the producers, shove the pair together at every available opportunity. Initially, this works well as the banter between Pacino and De Niro is classic buddy cop patter, dark gallows humour punctuated with self-deprecating jokes. It's almost as if the viewer has stumbled in on a drinking session between two long-time friends.

Pacino steals the first half of the film as he sarcastically hoots and hollers his lines at De Niro, and anybody else within earshot. In one scene he larks around in the background as De Niro talks to two other detectives. It's difficult to focus on anyone but Pacino even though he's not the focus of the scene, as he plays a bit of baseball while showing off to two young ladies who are sitting on his motorcycle. It's a fun scene to watch as it's the one time in this picture that Pacino's physical comedic flair comes into the fore. Buried beneath the humour however, is a woeful script, and once the two central performers stop playfully berating each other, the film turns into a less than average cop movie that over-depends upon large chunks of clichéd dialogue and action pieces.

Was there a change of writer for the second half of *Righteous Kill*??!! Because part way through it begins to feel like a completely different movie. De Niro garners more screen time in the second half of the film as he angrily mopes around each scene spouting the same, tired lines any generic cop would when hunting a killer. When he does explode into rage, which seems to happen at the most trivial of moments, at a kids' baseball game for instance, it comes across as lacklustre. It lacks the aggression De Niro flaunted in past characters such as James Conway (*Goodfellas*), Jake La Motta (*Raging Bull*) and Max Cady (*Cape Fear*). This film offers only a diluted De Niro. Pacino for the most part lays in wait, in the background until the grand finale that offers a twist that is beyond obvious. We are left to watch on as Pacino slowly dies in an abandoned warehouse while De Niro, dressed in an oversized, grey tracksuit, leans over him. The indignation of that scene is almost too much to bear. It seems to be aiming for a *Heat*-esque finale, with the sole focus on two legendary actors playing out a scene in which one of them dies. *Righteous Kill* fudges it so catastrophically however that we are left wondering if these are the same two actors we saw holding hands in great respect of each other at the end of Michael Mann's impeccable crime thriller.

The secondary characters are of little note. They simply serve the storyline and are denied any development. Gugino's Karen Corelli is a strange character, she seems to be aiming for a deeply complex portrayal but instead comes off as a sexually submissive cop who finds eroticism in the brutal action her sexual partners endure in the field. Curtis "50 Cent" Jackson struggles with the most basic of characters – a big time musician with a drug operation. His delivery is wooden and incredibly stilted to the point that it feels like he's reading his lines off a cue card just below the camera. His kill scene is an over the top comedy slapstick death dive through a window, his body landing on the floor of his empty nightclub. It is laughably bad.

On viewing this film, one has to wonder if Pacino and De Niro only read the first few pages of the script. Blinded by the possibilities of being together again on the big screen, as a pair of grizzled cops. This was seemingly enough for them to overlook the terrible dialogue, woeful action, choppy editing, hideous direction and a twist that is obvious from minute one. If it weren't for the two legendary actors starring in the leading roles *Righteous Kill* would have been put straight to the bottom shelf of the rental store, in amongst the endless stream of cheap, modern-day action thrillers.

Writer Russell Gewirtz on *Righteous Kill*

What were the origins of writing the story?

After I wrote *Inside Man* I started on *Righteous Kill*. It was an original idea of mine and the whole concept was the basics of the film which was you start with one person, in some way, confessing to a bunch of murders and then you end with the revelations that that person wasn't the killer and that the killer was somebody else right in front of you. That was the germ of *Righteous Kill* long before anything else. That was back in 2003.

Did you alter it much after completion?

I spent a lot of time writing it. When it was done we decided not to send it out to the studios... I can't recall the reasoning why at the time but it was more about showing it here and there. There was a brief time when Edward Norton was attached to star in the film. But that version of it never moved forward. After *Inside Man* came out and was a hit I think there was more attention on me in 2006 and what happened was Bob De Niro was attached to the film first before Al. There was some sort of film that had fallen through that was going to result in some nastiness for a lot of people and they kind of needed to find another movie for Bob De Niro and *Righteous Kill* became that movie. I can't quite explain how it happened but the idea of reuniting Pacino and De Niro was in the air and that's how it happened. I don't know exactly how it happened apart from somebody wanted to put the two of them in a movie together, and they did.

What was your reaction when you first heard your script was going to star Pacino and De Niro?

I was very excited. It's strange when you write something, it's really hard... I think different writers have different perspectives but for me I don't picture specific actors in roles when I write. I've had the experience of having a major actor suggested for a role I've written and, despite the fact that this was a brilliant actor who has made a million movies and would fortunately add tremendous weight to the thing, sometimes your initial reaction will be: "No he is terrible for the role." It's always a mix of reactions. The one thing with Pacino and De Niro was that these were guys in their sixties and, generally, NYPD detectives are retired by the age of fifty. We were pushing up against the age a bit. But on the other hand it was definitely an historic casting. So there were never any doubts about it. It felt great. It felt amazing. I had one other film made in *Inside Man* and it starred two actors in it who had won Oscars. So that was quite a feather in the cap. Then when this came along you had De Niro who had two Oscars and Pacino had an Oscar. So all of a sudden I had two movies with double Oscar winners.

De Niro and Pacino both like to find their characters before starting shooting. Did you meet with them beforehand?

I met with them beforehand; in fact I was able to visit both of them at their homes beforehand. Talked about the movie and talked about the character. There is not much you can say to either of these guys about playing a New York cop [*laughs*]. There is not much I can say to either of them because they have both done it. It wasn't about me giving any advice. It was more about me talking about the movie itself. We did a couple of read throughs. Then we went and played ball. There was so much experience at the table with these guys that for the most part I sat there quietly until someone had a question.

Did they change anything from what you had written?

I don't like to get very involved in the script. There was a point early on in the filming when I was standing on the set when he [Pacino] arrived and as he was walking past he stopped and said: "Hey we should sit down and talk." I said: "Of course. Absolutely." We had a few times on set when we grabbed dinner together and talked about a scene. He had some suggestions. The scenes at the end of the movie are, to a large extent, Al's contribution.

What did he suggest?

He had suggestions as to how the end should be - the confrontation between his character and Bob's character. He and I discussed them and there was a lot of back and forth. At the end of the day it becomes a discussion between him and the director. It's not really up to me. I give my opinions but I don't have anything to do with what they end up shooting. He had a lot of input into what ended up on the screen.

When you were on set what was it like watching two legendary actors speaking your dialogue?

It's... surreal is probably the best word. I had just done it the year before with Denzel Washington, Clive Owen and Jodie Foster and that was something incredible. Here I was a year later doing it with Pacino and De Niro. It's amazing but at the same time they are regular people too. At some point you're standing there and they're standing there and we're all people just making a movie. On occasion there were moments where, as I watched the scene get done a few times, if I felt like there was something was missing or wasn't getting done right or there was a version of it I wanted to offer... once or twice I would do that. I would do it to the director though, not directly to the actors. You pick your battles. No two people will see the exact same vision of the film and that's just the way it is. Sometimes I win and sometimes I lose and that's the process. But it's a lot of fun.

There is quite a lot of humour between Pacino and De Niro's characters in the film. Did that come from you?

Most of it was written into the script. Maybe all of it. I wanted to portray two guys who had been cops forever and there is a certain jaded quality to a guy who has been a cop in New York City for twenty years where nothing surprises them. They take things in stride. I wanted to portray that. The conversations where it's the two of them on a stakeout or listening to vice, that's me. That was all in there. I feel like whenever the right opportunity, a good laugh is good.

Pacino always wanted to be a comedian when he was younger and you do see some of that in *Righteous Kill*. Were you aware of that?

I hadn't really thought about that. It's not something that came into it. My feeling is: I write the words, they say the words. We are not talking about Will Ferrell here or Zach Galifianakis. You can deliver a line with a straight face and have the audience die laughing. I don't think it necessarily depends on the actor having comedic chops.

The film received a bashing from the critics upon release. Were you disappointed with the response it got?

No, I was disappointed with the film [*laughs*]. How's that for an answer?

So were you pleased with the end product?

Absolutely not.

Where do you think it went wrong?

The script I had written was a very complex, very precise story where there were a lot of hints and clues that would lead you to the twist at the end of the movie. Many of these details were either completely deleted or not handled with the attention to detail, and the film didn't become about that. It tried to become more of a dramatic thriller and, at times, tried to create drama when none really existed.

I'll give you an example. There is a scene in the film where the three cops – I think it's Pacino's character and John Leguizamo and Donnie Wahlberg, the other two detectives – they go to the hospital where this Russian guy is in a hospital bed and he is the one guy who has been shot by this killer and survived. You don't know that there is anything afoot because De Niro is the killer and he isn't in the room so it's no big deal. But the fact of the matter is Pacino is the killer and he is standing in this guy's hospital room. For me this is supposed to be something very dramatic because the guy is supposed to be sitting there conscious but with his jaw wired shut and he sees the guy who shot him in the room and is trying to communicate this. None of that is on the screen.

How difficult is it to watch something like that? Based on your story that has all the subtle nuances and it doesn't come across. It must have been painful for you to watch it?

It's why they pay you so well. Let's put it this way: you get paid and you put the money in the bank and then you go and make the film and you go see the film and it's difficult. At that point it's not about the money. I was trying to argue these points but I failed.

So there were other points you felt were incorrect?

There were. Had it been shot the way it was written, I think it would have been reviewed better and I think people would have referenced it as one of these films that sets up and delivers a stunning twist because that's how the script itself had been received a few years earlier.

Now that time has passed, how do you feel towards the film?

Nowadays it's just one of those things. I'm still thrilled I got to work with these guys. When you get into this business you find that it's very common for people not to be happy with their finished product and to focus on the fact that: "Hey, you got to make a movie. Hey, you got to get paid on it." You have to take these things in stride. To be perfectly frank, I wasn't in love with the first time I saw *Inside Man* and that was a critical success and a box office success. I'm my own harshest critic. As time goes by it gets much much easier. *Righteous Kill* I haven't seen in quite a while. But it's a little hard for me to watch. There are some scenes I like but overall it's not my favourite film.

You Don't Know Jack:

The Life and Deaths of Jack Kevorkian

Cast: Al Pacino (Dr. Jack Kevorkian), Brenda Vaccaro (Margo Janus), John Goodman (Neal Nicol), Danny Huston (Geoffrey Fieger), Deirdre O'Connell (Linda), Todd Susman (Stan Levy), Adam Lubarsky (Brian Russell), Susan Sarandon (Janet Good). **Director:** Barry Levinson.

Synopsis: In 1990, Dr. Jack Kevorkian astonished the world as he took the end of life debate head-on with his "Mercy Machine" and performed his first assisted suicide. Kevorkian became obsessed with challenging the rules by which we live and die.

The nickname "Dr Death" is not a label that any medical doctor would want but that's exactly the label given to American pathologist Jacob "Jack" Kevorkian. It started in the 1950s, when he began to photograph the eyes of cadavers to determine the time of death. Later on, during his internship year, he became interested in euthanasia and in the 1980s he wrote a series of articles that explained his ideas about the topic. By 1987 he was advertising his "death counselling" services through the local Detroit newspapers.

Three years later, his first case of public assisted suicide took place with a woman who had, just one year earlier, been diagnosed with Alzheimer's disease: "I didn't do it to end a life" he told CNN. "I did it to end the suffering the patient's going through." He was brought to trial in 1990; however it was later dropped as there were no official guidelines as to assisted suicides in Michigan but Kevorkian did have his medical license revoked by the state and was told he could no longer work with patients.

Throughout the 1990s Kevorkian frequented local and national TV and Radio stations discussing his work. He recorded one assisted suicide and gave the video tape to the TV show 60 Minutes for broadcast. This move proved to be his undoing. He had previously fought off four different court cases relating to his assisted suicide method but the broadcast on 60 Minutes showed Kevorkian actually administering the lethal injection (something he had said the patients did themselves). It took a Michigan jury just two days to find Kevorkian guilty of second degree murder through the delivery of a controlled substance. He was sentenced to between ten and twenty-five years in prison.

Kevorkian repeatedly tried to squash the conviction but without any success and was finally released from Coldwater Prison, Michigan on 1 June 2007. Kevorkian promised not to assist in suicides anymore; instead he would work towards legalising it. The reformed "Dr Death" toured universities and medical seminars discussing his work including his infamous suicide machine (which had been built for $30 from scrap metal). While Kevorkian was in prison, two of his closest confidants and friends Neal Nicol and Harry Wylie published an authorised biography of Kevorkian called *Between the Dying and the Dead: Dr. Jack Kevorkian, the Assisted Suicide Machine and the Battle to Legalize Euthanasia*. One person who read the book before publication was Steve Lee Jones, a new movie producer in Hollywood. Jones had previously been an executive producer on several syndicated educational TV series while at 5 Star, a Florida-based production company and was itching to make the jump from local producer to international movie mogul. He'd read a range of other non-fiction books and scripts about individuals who had risen to the top that also highlighted the downside of power and wealth, but Jones felt Nicol and Wylie's forthcoming book would make a great big screen entry point for his company Bee Holder Productions. "I knew there was a big audience for it. There would be an audience of people that wanted to understand why this guy did what he did, what exactly it was that he really did and not what the media said he did," Jones commented.

After speaking with those who worked first-hand with Kevorkian and visiting him in prison several times, Jones looked for a writer who could adapt Nicol and Wylie's book into a screenplay. The title had already been changed to the shortened, punchy and powerful *You Don't Know Jack*, the first words Jones said after reading the book. Rumours circulated that Jones had snapped up film director and documentary-maker Barbara Kopple to direct and screenwriter Barbara Turner to adapt the source material. However, nothing official materialized with either party and the next official pre-production announcement was that writer Adam Mazer would be adapting the material for the big screen. Having previously written the screenplay for the 2007 true crime film *Breach*, Mazer was assigned to speak to Kevorkian upon his release from prison to gain his trust in the hope that he would open up further about his life.

Mazer visited Kevorkian's residence in Michigan several times over the course of four months to better understand the doctor's methods. Mazer also met with Nicol and Kevorkian's attorney Geoffrey Fieger. The writer was given access to some family members of the patients Kevorkian had treated. He also spoke to people who opposed Kevorkian's work. While Mazer worked on the screenplay, Jones was trying to sell the film to Hollywood studios. The rumour mill went into overdrive when it was suggested that British actor Sir Ben Kingsley was to take the lead role of Dr. Kevorkian. Sir Ben never signed on to the project. The production crept along for the next couple of years without any sign it would be green-lit by a Hollywood movie studio. Eventually, Home Box Office (HBO), who had been producing their own TV movies since the early 1980s agreed to produce *You Don't Know Jack* on the small screen.

The executives at HBO Films liked Mazer's screenplay and set about finding a director for the project. Barry Levinson, director of *Rain Man*, was sent the script by HBO. At the same time Al Pacino was also flicking through Mazer's script. He found Kevorkian's story "interesting" and signed on meaning he would finally work with Levinson (he'd written *...and justice for all* but had not directly worked with Pacino before). Levinson then sat down with Mazer, tweaking the script for filming: "You want the dialogue to feel as everyday as possible," he said. The director met with Kevorkian so he too could better understand his methods. Pacino, on the other hand, decided not to meet the real Jack Kevorkian while preparing for the role. Instead he was sent between fifty and sixty hours of recorded interviews with Kevorkian to study.

Levinson and his casting director Ellen Chenoweth set about casting the other roles in the movie. John Goodman was to play author Neal Nicol, Danny Huston picked up the role of attorney Geoffrey Fieger and Susan Sarandon signed on to play Kevorkian's fellow right-to-die advocate Janet Good. Long-time friend of Pacino, Brenda Vaccaro was hired for the role of Margo Kevorkian Janus, Jack's Sister. She videotaped four scenes from the script at the HBO office in New York and sent them off to Levinson: "I heard Barry liked the tape, and then I went and met with Al a few weeks later, and then I waited again for a few weeks, and then I heard I got the part! And I was, like, so ecstatic!" commented Vaccaro. Once the cast was in place and HBO agreed to a budget of $18 million, Levinson scheduled table readings and rehearsals for the main cast before filming started. Pacino benefited greatly from that additional time as it allowed him to truly find his Jack Kevorkian. Levinson watched him do this every single day: "He would try something and try something. And then we went through the period where we did some makeup tests and we did clothing. And slowly you start seeing him kind of absorbing all of this information and the visual aspects of it."

Principal photography kicked off during August 2009 and the majority of filming took place in New York. The cast and crew schlepped all over the city using locations as far ranging as 106th and Park Avenue and 56th St & 9th Avenue in Manhattan, and the famous Radio City Music Hall on 6th Avenue. Clinton and Pierrepoint Streets, Coyle St and Avenue U and the Fillmore Real Estate office in Brooklyn. The Clinton Diner and Bar in Maspeth (famously used in the movie *Goodfellas*) and the Wagner College and Rosebank area on Staten Island. By the beginning of October production finished shooting in New York and relocated to Michigan. The Big Boy Restaurant on East Maple Road, Troy was used for interior scenes. The Wayne County Building in Detroit was used for exterior shots. Extras lined up by the front steps with banners and placards condemning Kevorkian's actions. As Levinson shouted action they all started to chant while Pacino and Huston shot fake press interviews in the foreground.

Thereafter, production moved to Royal Oak, the home of the real Jack Kevorkian, to film some exterior scenes. During mid-October production shot in Pontiac at the Oakland County Circuit Court on N Telegraph Street. Exterior scenes of Pacino striding up to the South entrance were shot on a wet Thursday. Surrounded by extras dressed as either protesters or news crews, Levinson tried to get as much as possible shot in that one day. During the downtime, while cameras and lighting were re-shot, Pacino guided the extras into the entrance hall of the building to stay warm. County employees inside the building were requested to stay away from windows while filming took place. However, on their lunch breaks temptation got the better of them and most gathered around the windows to watch. The next day production moved inside the Court building. In a case of art directly imitating life, the filming of Kevorkian's trials, which took place in Michigan almost two decades earlier, were shot in the exact same court room. Principal photography wrapped at the end of October 2009.

In a rarity for a HBO TV movie, *You Don't Know Jack* received a theatrical premiere. The stars of the film lined the red carpet at the Ziegfeld Theatre in New York on the evening of 14 April 2010, and two people met for the first time while smiling for the cameras. Pacino came face-to-face with the real Jack Kevorkian. They shook hands for the photographers and then Pacino began to joke around with Kevorkian's hair. Laughing along with Pacino, while still shaking his hand, Kevorkian offered the actor the chance to join his poker nights in Detroit "For Jack I think I'll go do it," Pacino said.

HBO premiered *You Don't Know Jack* at 9pm on 24 April 2010 in the US. *Time Magazine* hailed it as an entertaining biopic, saying: "*You Don't Know Jack* hit the sweet spot..., filling in the story of someone I knew better as a headline than a person." *The New York Times* was also impressed by the film calling it "a compelling, at times thrilling, tale that can absorb even those with little interest or feeling for the subject." *The L.A. Times* found it to be "more interesting than affecting." *You Don't Know Jack* was slowly released in other countries after its US debut. It was shown in France, Japan and Spain during 2010. The UK, Italy, Brazil, Argentina and Sweden had to wait until the following year. German viewers finally saw it screened in 2012 and it took three years to make it onto Norwegian television sets.

By the time the film had been distributed in most countries, Pacino had received an award for his performance as Dr. Jack Kevorkian in the category of Outstanding Lead Actor in a Limited Series or Movie at the 62nd Primetime Emmy Awards. There was also a win for Adam Mazer in the Outstanding Writing for a Miniseries, Movie or Dramatic Special category. Pacino continued to pick up awards at the Screen Actors Guild Award, for Outstanding Performance by a Male Actor in a miniseries or Television Movie and at the Golden Globes, for Best Actor in a Miniseries or Television Film. As Pacino took to the stage to receive his Golden Globe statuette he thanked several people including Levinson and the rest of the cast. He also made a point about why it was important for him to take on the role: "To navigate through his [Kevorkian's] life was so much fun and interesting. It's great for actors who portray real characters, it's a special thing for the actors to get to play a real person because that relationship is so interesting and intimate and wonderful."

After stinking up the screen with *Righteous Kill* and *88 Minutes* at the tail end of the 2000s, Pacino needed to come back strong with his first movie of the new decade and *You Don't Know Jack* was perfect in this capacity. It was a role that required him to dig deep into his method acting style and demonstrate that he still knew how to create a complex character. A metamorphosis takes place in Pacino as he plays Dr. Jack Kevorkian. The person on screen is Kevorkian, it is not Pacino. The shuffling stride of a walk, the slightly hunched, stiff shoulders, the multi-coloured hair style, the baggy trouser and cardigan combinations and the large, thick, light brown glasses all combine to create the Dr. Jack Kevorkian package.

But this is not a caricature of Kevorkian, rather a full blown physical and psychological body double (even the real Kevorkian failed to pick out Pacino's Kevorkian in a photo line-up, believing the photo to be of himself rather than the actor in make-up). Pacino gives Kevorkian a tough outer shell with a mysterious centre. The character never backs down to the lawyers and is always ready for a fight in court but there is also a delicate, serene facet to Kevorkian that comes through in Pacino's performance. We see him calmly explain what will happen when the patients administer the death drip. These should be harrowing scenes; instead Pacino relaxes the moment. This is achieved through Pacino's reserved yet spirited performance and also Levinson's direction which is never heavy-handed or aggressive. Keeping an easy tone ensures the film never becomes overwrought with emotion. Levinson also includes a lot of humour, especially focussing on Kevorkian's natural wit with his friends: "Shall we celebrate with some water?" Kevorkian asks his long-time friend Neal Nicol. Later on he growls at his lawyer Fieger that "Decaf [coffee] is for cowards." The interactions between Pacino and Goodman are most entertaining. After their stellar work together in *Sea of Love* three decades earlier they appear to have picked up where they left off in that film. Watching those two bicker is a delight and doesn't feel forced. Pacino also bounces off the other leads very well too. There is an evident respect between him and Sarandon that conveys a loving friendship to the bitter end. Pacino and Vaccaro seem like real-life brother and sister. There are no airs and graces between them, they love and hate each other in equal measure like most siblings. Danny Huston should get a special mention for embodying the nineties version of Pacino by chewing up the scenery in spectacular fashion. He happily blasts anyone who, even slightly, goes against him. It is an impeccable homage to his co-star.

Levinson and Pacino allow us just brief glimpses behind the Kevorkian "Dr Death" mask to see what truly went on in his private life. These little titbits create an air of mysticism about Kevorkian. We never really get to understand his personal life, echoing the title – *You Don't Know Jack*. This is a theatrical movie slumming it on TV. But it's not TV, it's HBO. *You Don't Know Jack* should not be put into the TV Movie genre to sit alongside feature films made by the Hallmark or Lifetime channels. It should be sat on the same shelf as some of the most powerful and moving biopics ever produced. It is a movie that takes a very tough subject and does not offer a stance on right or wrong. Instead it invites the viewer to make up their own mind on Kevorkian and assisted suicide.

Actor Adam Lubarsky on *You Don't Know Jack*

Were you aware of the real-life Jack Kevorkian and his work before becoming involved in the film?

Most certainly. I am an advocate of what Jack Kevorkian attempted to do and spearheaded for euthanasia.

In the film you play Brian Russell, who is Jack Kevorkian's long time friend. Did you meet the real life Brian Russell beforehand?

I did not meet him but I did have conversations through emails with Brian. He made some jokes about he was so more much handsome than I was [*laughs*]. It makes me smile to this day that he reached out. He actually reached out to me.

You share several scenes with Pacino. What was he like to work with?

He is the most generous man. I had an absolute blast. The combination of Al Pacino and Barry Levinson... that was the very first time I had done principal work and I couldn't have been more comfortable. Al being generous on leaving openings and Barry, he doesn't stop the film. It's not one take and then two, his cameras keep on rolling and you go back to your first mark and go again and improve a little along the way. Barry then picks and chooses. That afforded Al being very generous.

Is it difficult as an actor to keep up with Pacino when he changes his performance from take to take?

No. It felt very comfortable. It really did. Knowing where we were to be... he very much made it comfortable. There wasn't any expectations waiting for lines it was just give and take. I was in the museum scene, the art gallery scene and also playing poker. John Goodman was another one, he was sitting off to my right and Al was to my left. John's another one... a very funny man when the film isn't running and when the film is running but... both of them are very generous actors. When you have pro's like I was around... the museum scene was Susan Sarandon and a bunch of other people besides Al, it was like everybody was at the art show and you felt the liveliness of that group of people just bouncing off each other as lines would come out.

It is a very reserved performance from Pacino. Did you expect that?

Yes, because of the character he was playing. In one of the scenes I was in there is a touch of the lunacy underlined in that... he is explaining in that he is going into the assisted suicide business. The scene where he announces his intentions to his best friends over a game of cards.

What was Pacino like when the cameras had stopped rolling?

He pretty much stayed in character while we were still on set. He would be very quiet. At least, that's what I experienced.

You mentioned that you are an advocate of Kevorkian's work. Did you think the finished film did him justice?

I thought the depiction of Jack was great. If hearts went out they went out to Jack for what he went through and the cause he was championing.

The Son of No One

Cast: Al Pacino (Detective Charles Stanford), Channing Tatum (Jonathan 'Milk' White), James Ransone (Officer Thomas Prudenti), Ray Liotta (Captain Marion Mathers), Katie Holmes (Kerry White), Tracy Morgan (Vincent Carter (adult)), Brian Gilbert (Vincent Carter (child)), Juliette Binoche (Loren Bridges). **Director:** Dito Montiel.

Synopsis: As a youth growing up in New York's Queensborough projects, Jonathan 'Milk' White killed a couple of junkies. His dead father's former police partner, Detective Stanford got him off the hook for the crime. Now a rookie police officer himself, Jonathan remains haunted by the incident. When a local newspaper reporter receives anonymous tips regarding the crime, the implications for both White and Stanford are far reaching.

Writer/director/musician/painter Dito Montiel announced his arrival in the U.S. film industry with the deeply personal and semi-autobiographical film: *A Guide to Recognizing Your Saints* starring Robert Downey Jr., Shia LeBeouf and Channing Tatum. His next film also starred Channing Tatum; it was about the underground world of street fighting and thus aptly titled: *Fighting*. The genesis of his third film, *The Son of No One* was rooted in an incident that happened in Montiel's teenage years when he lived out his days in the Ravenswood projects, New York. "We were 14, and my friend and I used to hang out in his apartment. A lot of older people would hang out there, drinking all day and smoking crack. There was this guy, Hanky, that used to show up a lot, and he used to really scare us because he was 18 or 19 and he was always cracked out. One day, somebody killed him. They killed him when he was in the hallway, and I remember the police were taking him away while they were smoking and eating sandwiches and laughing. My friend Vinny looked over at me and said, "Nobody cares. Nobody cares about any of this. It doesn't matter.""

Montiel used that real-life incident as the basis for a book he had started to write called The Story of Milk. It revolved around a kid called Jonathan who witnessed a murder at a young age and grew up to become a police officer in his local, New York neighbourhood. As he approached the halfway stage of the book, Montiel realised that The Story of Milk would work better as a movie: "So, I started writing it more as a movie, and seeing the scenes." Following this change in format, Montiel set about casting his movie. For the lead role of Jonathan 'Milk' White there was only one person Montiel wanted and it was his go-to actor: Channing Tatum. Once Tatum signed on the other major roles were filled quickly and easily. Katie Holmes joined the production to play White's wife Kerry. *The Sopranos* actor James Gandolfini bagged the role of White's police Captain, Marion Mathers. Robert De Niro was hired to play ageing Detective Charles Stanford. French actor Juliette Binoche agreed to play newspaper reporter Loren Bridges (the part was originally written as Larry Bridges and when Binoche joined the cast she requested that the dialogue stayed the same rather than be doctored to reflect the character's change in sex).

Terence Howard was cast in the adult Vincent Carter role. For the role of young Vincent Carter, Montiel found his actor by chance. A teacher at a school in Harlem, who was in possession of Montiel's business card and knew he was searching for child actors, put in a phone call to the director. Montiel arrived at the school and the teacher showcased seven boys. Thirteen year-old Brian Gilbert stood out and Montiel asked him to do a rehearsed piece: "he says 'Well I have this monologue...' So he did it, and it just blew me away." For the other two younger roles, Montiel went with known child actor Jake Cherry, from *Night at the Museum 1 & 2*, and first-time actor Simone Joy Jones as the young Jonathan White and young Vicky respectively. The cast was in place and finance to the tune of $15 million was provided by Avi Lerner's production companies Nu Image and Millennium Films but production hit the skids when some cast members had to drop out of filming due to scheduling conflicts. Ultimately, De Niro and Gandolfini were replaced with Al Pacino and Ray Liotta. Finding a replacement for Howard proved trickier until Montiel spoke to his long-time associate editor Jake

Pushinsky. After watching *Jimmy Kimmel Live!* the night before, Pushinsky suggested to Montiel that comedian Tracy Morgan could take on the role of the adult Vincent Carter. "I said 'Are you crazy?' and then he [Pushinsky] sent me this interview and Tracy was talking about his father. He was pretty serious and I thought, 'Wow, how cool would that be? That would be really fun,' Montiel later recalled. A meeting between Montiel and Morgan took place in New York shortly after and resulted in the comedian taking on his first ever straight acting role.

In keeping with the storyline and Montiel's upbringing, principal photography took place in and around the Queens and Bronx boroughs of New York City. Starting in February 2010, production used the Queensboro Bridge that links Manhattan and Queens. Further scenes were shot underneath the bridge in Queensbridge Park and other locations used in Queens included: The Douglaston Parkway and Northern Boulevard, 31st and Ditmars Boulevard and the street level of 21st St and 41st Ave. The rooftop of 34 Vernon Boulevard and 41st Ave was used for the big finale involving Tatum, Morgan, Liotta and Pacino while some of the street scenes were filmed along the main strip of Metropolitan Avenue. Production then moved from Queens into the Bronx with filming on 151 Street and all along the Grand Concourse. Filming was wrapped up swiftly by the end of April.

The Son of No One received its world premiere at the 2011 Sundance Film Festival in Utah. It was scheduled as the closing film of the festival. Most of the cast and the director attended the premiere and they all stepped up to the microphone to answer questions after the public screening. However, a private press screening earlier in the day did not go so well. In a room filled with critics and studio heads, *The Hollywood Reporter* claimed that there had been an exodus of people well before the credits and that only one person started to applaud at the end. The real reason behind the walk out later proved to be a problem with the editing of the movie. During the big finale two gun shots ring out, in between them the film fades to white and the credits roll. Most of the audience took that as a sign the film had finished including the theatre manager who switched on the house lights. The theatre manager noticed the film was still playing minutes later and dimmed the lights, but by that time most of the attendees had left the room.

Critics who saw the film at Sundance were scathing in their assessment of it. *Indiewire* said: "A career low for director Dito Montiel." *The Wrap* pulled no punches, saying the film was "a narrative mess predicated on a fairly predictable central mystery." *The Hollywood Reporter* called it "atmospheric and intriguing but not wholly satisfying." They also heavily critiqued the fade to white at the end suggesting that it was "a tactic that here looks suspiciously like cover-up for a finale that didn't play well as originally shot." After the disastrous screenings at Sundance, Montiel went back and re-cut the ending, removing the fade to white.

The Son of No One opened in only ten U.S. theatres on its release on 4 November. It pulled in a feeble $26,000 by the end of its first week and by the end of its second week, when it generated a return of just $4,000, it was removed from U.S. theatres (Information courtesy of Box Office Mojo. Used with permission). By the time it came to DVD in North America it had already been snuck out on DVD in many foreign territories without any great fanfare. The only positive to come from *The Son of No One*'s release was a nomination for Brian Gilbert at the Young Artist Awards under the category of Best Performance in a Feature Film – Leading Young Actor. Gilbert lost out to Dakota Goyo from Disney's science fiction sports film: *Real Steel.*

Most picture goers understand that a big name cast doesn't necessarily equate to a good film, and such is the case with *The Son of No One.* Anybody picking up the DVD of this film and noting the six big actors on the front cover could easily be left wondering why they have never seen this film. The reason is simple: it's not very good. It's not that *The Son of No One* is a bad film, but it is a dull and uninteresting one. Even the acting talent involved can't lift the basic and rather insipid material they are working with. It's a typical police procedural drama with added who-dun-it twist. Unfortunately, the supposed twist is telegraphed far in advance due to the recognisable tones of the rather unique voice making the threatening telephone calls.

The constant jumping around to different time frames also creates a very confusing structure. It never settles on one time period long enough for us to get to grips with the characters and their troubles. It possibly would have worked better with a linear narrative rather than using non-linear films such as *The Godfather Part II*, *Reservoir Dogs* or *The Usual Suspects* as a template. The claim from director Montiel is that this movie is from an unpublished work called 'The Story of Milk' and the chances are that it reads impressively as a page-turning crime thriller. The transition to screen however seems to have somewhat let the material down.

Not one member of the main cast looks particularly inspired to be in this film. Tatum plays the majority of the film with his head down looking at the floor, making it difficult for the audience to engage with his portrayal. It's a distracting performance and made worse by Tatum's terrible, wafer-thin moustache. Binoche is hideously miscast, but thankfully she is spared too many blushes in the film because her screen time is minimal. The same too can be said for Holmes, who fulfils every 'long-suffering cop's wife' cliché ever seen on screen – the lone parent, the tears, the wondering where her husband is. It's all been done so many times before. Liotta chews up the scenery in his usual entertaining style. He barks and bites his way through the clichéd police captain dialogue and makes it more entertaining than it has any right to be. The problem is that Liotta is better than this; the material is holding him back, and does the same to Pacino.

This is a role Pacino has played many times – a cop with a troubled past – but it feels below him here. The film never lets Pacino off the leash, and it so desperately needs to. Instead all the audience witnesses is a subdued actor with below par dialogue. There is also a question as to why a director would cast Pacino and use him so minimally. He might as well have been given the 'and' credit, he is on-screen so little. Essentially, the storyline never gives any of them, but especially Pacino and Liotta, anything to work with other than hideously undercooked, one-dimensional characters.

The one actor who escapes with a little bit of credibility intact is Tracy Morgan. A comedian through and through, this performance is a transformation into a dramatic actor, and that shift has powerful results. There is a sense that his demons are incredibly real every minute of every day. Much like the performance Robin Williams offered in Christopher Nolan's *Insomnia*, Morgan stepping out of his comfort zone is the one shining light throughout the entire film.

The Son of No One doesn't even start with a bang and go out with a whimper. It limps its way through ninety-something minutes of tired, clichéd and dull dialogue with equally uninspiring direction that offered no hope to the star-studded cast of creating an entertaining and dramatic police procedural movie.

Director Dito Montiel on *The Son of No One*

You had originally envisaged *The Son of No One* as being a novel. Why did you change your mind and make it into a film?

I grew up right around the projects and someone told me the story of Cabrini Green, which was in Chicago, and they were these projects that were torn down for gentrification reasons. It got really interesting for a moment. So when I had the opportunity I thought maybe I could make a movie out of this, why not?

The story is part autobiographical, isn't it?

Yeah. I grew up with these guys and, basically, they would say we were inseparable. We were so close when we were kids and I don't see much of them anymore. I ran into one randomly one day in New York and it's almost word for word how he would talk to me is how Tracy Morgan's character speaks to Channing in the film. He would just compliment me because he wanted to get away as quick as possible: "Good to see you. Glad you're doing good. I'm gonna go." That was so haunting to me.

***The Son of No One* has a large and well-known ensemble cast. As a director, what approach did you take to managing them all?**

These guys are really talented and I've been lucky to work with some really good ones, so life is easier when you have them. Robin Williams, Al Pacino - they know where the light is, they know where the camera is. They know exactly what to do. You just give them your words and they give their feedback. It's not so much managing them; it's trying to not find yourself sitting in awe. It's like being on a team with LeBron James, try not to stare at him too much, you know?! [*Laughs*]. That's kind of the way I think it is.

Pacino and Liotta have made numerous crime films over the decades. Did you worry about giving them direction in a genre that they are already established in? Or were they open to what you suggested?

It's intimidating until it's happening. It's not really difficult but only because they are actors and I'm coming from a place of respect. I'm actually listening more than I'm suggesting. You know... what are you going to tell Al Pacino about holding a gun? I think he's done it before. You want Ray Liotta to seem a little off the cuff? Maybe he's done that before [*laughs*]. You're talking more about this scene here, now, on this spot as opposed to this incredible legacy.

What was it like working with Pacino?

The most incredible thing... there were many incredible things. The idea you get to meet him. Once again you have to try not to stare. I want to ask him ten thousand questions but will limit it to about twenty. The thing that is still remarkable about him is he came the first day and he had this long scene where he was talking to a little boy sitting outside. It was about seven pages of dialogue. It was way overwritten but I was enjoying sitting there watching Al Pacino say all these words. He said to me: "Can we rehearse this one time?" I said: "Of course." He said: "Maybe you want to roll the camera." So we roll the camera and he does all seven pages and I swear to God he says every word. Then at the end he looks at me and says: "I think I may have missed two words." I'm thinking Wow! That is even crazier, that you know you have missed two words. That night he was going to do Shakespeare in the Park and he had just turned seventy. It really touched me that I was lucky enough to be working with him.

Directors who have worked with Pacino have said that he slightly changes each take he does but they don't notice until they are in the editing room. Did that happen to you?

I was really lucky because when I was going to make *A Guide to Recognizing Your Saints* I got into Sundance Labs and in the labs they pick twelve writers a year and they bring you in and they assign writers to you and one of the people assigned to me was Frank Pierson, who had written *Dog Day Afternoon*. He told me this story; he said when he worked on *Dog Day Afternoon* that there was a scene that he had written where Al Pacino makes out with his lover. Not his wife, his lover. Al Pacino said: "I'm not doing that." He [Pierson] said: "You gotta do it." Pacino said: "I'm not gonna do it." He [Pierson] got all upset and they were thinking of recasting it. He didn't speak to Al Pacino, and Frank was a pretty tough guy. Then Al Pacino calls him a couple of weeks later and says: "What's going on? You gonna cast somebody else? Listen... you didn't ask me why." He [Pierson] said: "I just thought it was because you didn't want to kiss a man." He [Pacino] said: "No. If I kiss that guy in that scene that's all everyone is going to talk about and the movie is so much more than that." He [Pacino] felt that scene would be exploitative. Not because he cared less about a man kissing a man... Frank would tell me: "Man, that guy was so smart. He saw through that exploitative kiss that I put in there just to sort of shock the audience." I don't know how much that answered your question, but yes he would change things and had very interesting ideas on why or why not he should do things. You don't have these actors on set very long and he was on our set for maybe three days. So in three days he had like ten different instances like that with me. He would just discuss why: "Why would I be that mean to the kid's mother?" As far as the takes, yeah I would notice certain things in it. But it was more about the discussions as to why. And it wasn't one of these annoying ones either: "Why am I eating?" "Well... because you're hungry." He wanted to know why and he had very, very interesting reasons for it.

So there was always give and take? And it never got argumentative?

Oh no, we never got to that point for sure. It wasn't just out of respect. He was happy to have discussions about things. Give and take might sound like a compromise but it certainly wasn't a compromise.

Tracy Morgan is in the film and in it he plays a very serious role. This is against type for him. Were you surprised he decided to take on the role?

No, not really. I'm a fan of comedians acting and acting is talent and dealing with fear, getting up on stage and telling jokes. I can't think of anything more terrifying you know. I remember thinking: "Gosh you know who would be really good in this role – Tracy Morgan." Then I got to meet him. I love him as a person and I'm a big fan of Tracy. So I wasn't surprised.

Given the huge cast, do you feel like this film was your most ambitious project to-date?

Everything is ambitious. It's all ambitious. It's supposed to be ambitious. I'm happy with the films and that makes me feel good. When the people involved feel good about the film they got to make then hopefully you get to make more.

Actor Brian Gilbert on *The Son of No One*

***The Son of No One* was only your third on-screen role and your first as a main character. How did you land the role of young Vinnie Carter?**

I started acting when I was really young and the place where I trained was a place called The Harlem School of the Arts and I had been there periodically, and one of the people I knew had been teaching the class and I said: "I'll take the class." Dito [Montiel] came [to the school] because he was looking for talent. I had an agent and headshots and I went to the audition. Dito liked my performance; I did a monologue in front of him when he first came. Then the casting director came and then we did stuff from the movie.

Your character, Vinnie acts as one of the catalysts for what happens to older versions of the characters in the subsequent decade. Were you surprised to find your character so heavily involved?

I was. There was a couple of other scenes... me and Jake [Cherry] always joke about this to the other kid in the movie that it was its own self-contained movie. I got those scenes early because I was auditioning with them and that was their story arc. Then I got the script and read more scenes that were in it and I was excited. Then when I knew who was going to be in it, like Channing Tatum, and I saw one of Dito's movie's - *Fighting*. I went to see Bruno but it was too much, I walked in and then out again [*laughs*] it was too much. I watched it later on television and thought this is funny, it's offensive. Back then it was too much. [I] bought tickets for *Fighting* anyway and got in before it started and I really, really liked it. I liked Channing Tatum's performance. I had never seen *Step Up*, I had known of it, and I saw *G.I. Joe* and liked him in that. I knew he was in a couple of other things I had seen so I was a fan of his and I liked *Fighting*. It was unlike any fighting movie I had seen. I liked the performances and I liked it took place in New York because I'm from there. I was familiar that Dito had worked with Channing twice before and then I saw *A Guide to Recognizing Your Saints* and loved it. I got an idea of how *The Son of No One* would be. It would be dark and dealing with a bunch of different themes. It was exciting.

You were already a fan of Montiel and Tatum. What was your reaction when they told you that Ray Liotta, Tracy Morgan and Al Pacino would also appear in the film?

I saw *Scarface* when I was ten years old and I loved it [*laughs*]. I loved *Scarface*. *Scarface* was one of my favourite movies and then I got into *Dog Day Afternoon* and *...and justice for all*. I loved every performance he [Pacino] did, so I was excited that Al Pacino was a part of it. *Goodfellas* is one of my favourite movies and Ray Liotta is just funny [*laughs*]. I remembered him in the Michael Cera movie *Youth in Revolt* and he was just hilarious. I was excited. Then Katie Holmes and Tracy Morgan... In that year Tracy Morgan had two movies come out – *Cop Out* and *Death at a Funeral*. I saw both of them before we started filming. I knew that Dito always got great cast members for his movies. This is the first time you see Al Pacino and Ray Liotta in a movie together and I like *The Son of No One* a lot for that. I love the scene they have together. That's my favourite scene of the movie. They are top-notch actors and bring one hundred percent to everything they do, so I knew I would have to as well. This cast was full of people that were just pure, pure talent.

You and Jake [Cherry] have a scene with Pacino. What was he like to act with?

He was relaxed. He was so relaxed and he was talking to everybody on set. He was talking to people who lived in the projects. I can't tell you anything specific... I can't remember anything specific he said in terms of the craft of acting. I just remember him being very mellow and cool and calm and bringing the performance. Having been in that moment... he's so powerful and he doesn't even say anything [*laughs*]. He has... how do you say it?... when he is there you feel it. It elevates everyone and everything. He was extremely nice.

What was it like for you, as a young actor just starting out, acting opposite Pacino and Liotta? Given that they are still at the top of their acting game.

It made me want to work hard and achieve what they had achieved because I was always a fan of theirs. I would watch their work on the movie and then afterwards went back and got into it more so I understood it more than I ever had before. I ended up watching everything... everything. What it did for me... after that is when I started to write my own film. Dito inspired me to do that. Being on set those days seeing everyone inspired... it was the nicest cast, the nicest cast. I met Tracy Morgan because he was there that day we were filming the roof scene. The scene with Tracy Morgan and Channing Tatum, they were shooting that after the scene we shot on the roof and I saw him that day. It was an honour to be part of that movie and meet everyone involved. The film meant a lot to Dito. This one was very, very personal to him as he grew up in Queens. It was great to be in a film that was connected to him.

It sounds like you had a fun time on set.

It was. It was a fun shoot. Emotional scenes but it was a fun shoot. It was pleasant.

Jack and Jill

Cast: Adam Sandler (Jack/Jill Sadelstein), Al Pacino (Al Pacino), Katie Holmes (Erin Sadelstein), Elodie Tougne (Sofia), Rohan Chand (Gary), Eugenio Derbez (Felipe/Felipe's Grandma), David Spade (Monica), Nick Swardson (Todd), Tim Meadows (Ted). **Director:** Dennis Dugan.

Synopsis: Jack Sadelstein is a successful advertising executive in Los Angeles. He dreads one event each year: the holiday visit of his identical twin sister Jill. Her neediness and passive-aggressiveness drive Jack crazy and turn his normally tranquil life upside down. Things spin even more out of control when Jack needs Jill to date Al Pacino and tempt the actor into starring in a commercial he is producing.

Many of Hollywood's film scripts go through one or two rewrites before filming begins. *Castaway* starring Tom Hanks took five years and over two hundred and fifty rewrites before it was ready to go in front of the cameras. So it is not unusual for a film script written by one person to have extensive rewrites from other script writers. This happened to actor/writer/producer Ben Zook who sold his script for a comedy called *Jack and Jill* to Happy Madison Productions run by comedy megastar Adam Sandler. Zook had sold scripts before but only two had made it into production. *I Hate Valentine's Day* was made into a feature film starring Nia Vardalos. Before that he had co-written and co-directed his own comedy dance film called *Can't Stop Dancing*.

The sale of *Jack and Jill* was a big one for Zook. However it did mean relinquishing control of the script to Happy Madison Productions. As with any film produced through Sandler's company and starring the actor, it was given a rewrite by Sandler himself and Steve Koren - an old *Saturday Night Live* writer from the days when Sandler was on the New York-based satire comedy show. Koren had also been a script editor on episodes of *Seinfeld*. The script received a further re-write from Sandler's friends and comedy writers Robert Smigel and Allen Covert. A second rewrite was completed by Covert before it went back to Sandler and Koren to finish. One of the big plot points in the finished script was having a world-renowned and legendary actor play an over-the-top version of themselves. The actor's name written into that part was Al Pacino.

Not knowing if it was ever to be a reality, Sandler sent the script to Pacino, whom he had occasionally bumped into in L.A., expecting it to be returned with a "No thanks" reply. However Pacino had been made aware of Sandler's work through his young children, twins Anton and Olivia. He liked the idea of playing a crazy, heightened version of himself falling in love and he signed on. At the same time as Pacino was in talks to star in the film so too was actor Katie Holmes. Holmes had been a fan of Sandler's for many years and was excited to finally get to work with him. When Sandler first arrived at Holmes's house to discuss coming onto the film he thought she was joking until she gushed about how much she enjoyed his work. It was only when he saw a poster of one of his films on a wall that he took her seriously.

Sandler was set to play both Jack and Jill and fleshed out the rest of the cast with some of his comedy buddies. David Spade, Nick Swardson, Norm MacDonald and Gary Valentine all secured roles in the film. Sandler also managed to convince Dana Carvey to take a small role in the film as a crazy puppeteer who is making a TV advertisement with TV presenter Regis Philbin. It was to be Carvey's first feature film appearance in nine years. Legendary Mexican comedian Eugenio Derbez bagged a male and a female role in the film as the Sadelstein's gardener Felipe and also Felipe's Grandma. Further famous cameos included comedian Drew Carey, supermodel Christie Brinkley, ex-tennis player John McEnroe, ex-American football player Bill Romanowski, Sportscaster Dan Patrick, ex-Basketball stars Shaquille O'Neal, Lamar Odom and "ShamWow" pitchman Vince Offer. Sandler hired his go-to director Dennis Dugan for the project. It was the eighth time the pair had worked together. Happy Madison Productions secured a distribution deal with Sony's Columbia Pictures for *Jack and Jill*, along with a budget of $79 million.

Principal photography began during the first week of October 2010. Nearly all of the interior scenes were shot on sets built on a sound stage at Sony Pictures Studios in Culver City, California including the Sadelstein's home, a Dunkin' Donuts restaurant and a Majorcan castle. Numerous exterior scenes were shot within Los Angeles. Production was caught shooting scenes near the Staples Center on S Figueroa Street. The interior of the Staples Center appeared on camera when filming took place during a real L.A. Lakers game. The scene involved Sandler (as both Jack and Jill), Pacino and a cameo from Johnny Depp who was sitting courtside during the game.

By the end of November production had finished in L.A. and moved to Fort Lauderdale, Florida to film on one of the largest cruise ships in the world – The Allure of the Seas. The ship was still being built as Dugan and his team were in pre-production which gave the team chance to send a couple of electricians to Norway, where the ship was being finished, to lay cabling and figure out how and where to film onboard. When the ship docked in Florida it had not opened to the first public guests. Production had ten days to film before real guests arrived. A restaurant was built in the bow of the ship for interior filming to take place. As the film was to be set at Christmas, production bought thousands of Christmas decorations and covered the ship with them.

The toughest job throughout filming fell to director of photography Dean Cundey and visual effects supervisor Dan DeLeeuw. Both had to ensure that the filming of Sandler as Jack and then as Jill matched correctly on screen. "Sometimes, it's a fairly simple process, as simple as a split. You film it twice, with the actor playing one character on one side of the frame, and then again, playing the other character on the other side of the frame. Then you go into the computer and put them together," Cundey explained. For the trickier shots, when Jack and Jill had to touch each other, it meant Sandler being given an in-ear headphone so he could hear the dialogue from Jack and react to it. A monitor was also set-up showing the original movements of Jack so Sandler could see where to move as Jill. "The motion control technicians made sure we were getting the exact camera movement over and over again. Finally, the on-set compositor could put it together as we did it and show us how it's going together so we could evaluate it and judge it," said Cundey. Creating the illusion of Jack and Jill on screen together fell to DeLeeuw: "For many shots, we'd shoot Adam with a body double as Jill. The body double would wear a green hood over his head, which we could remove later and replace with Adam, as Jill."

Most of filming on the ship took place on the bow and because of the natural sunlight moving throughout the day, it caused a problem when trying to combine the Jack and Jill scenes. With no paying guests onboard, an ingenious plan was hatched: "We were able just to have them turn the ship, so the sun would stay the same all day for us," commented Dugan. "The Captain did one very long, slow turn. One degree every six minutes, so the sun stayed in exactly the same spot with reference to the ship," explained Cundey. Dugan took a secondary film unit for a brief sojourn to Majorca to film exterior shots of a castle. While there Dugan stepped in as Pacino's body double for a long shot of "Pacino" chasing Jill through the battlements under cover of night. This wasn't the first time Dugan had played a role previously acted by Pacino. During 1983 Dugan starred in a TV pilot called *Full House*. It was to be a TV spin-off of the film *Author! Author!* that Pacino had starred in the previous year. Dugan played the lead character Ivan Travalian, the same character Pacino played in the original film but the TV pilot was not made into a series.

Shooting on *Jack and Jill* finished up back where it started, in Los Angeles, with shooting taking place on Wilshire Boulevard, Flower Street and Grand Avenue. The final day of filming was the day in which the Al Pacino/Dunkaccino advert was shot. The set had been designed exactly like a Dunkin' Donuts shop. Production used real signs, counters and donuts from the company. Principal photography completed by the end of January 2011 and post-production wizardry was completed at Method Studios in Vancouver, Atomic Fiction and Colorworks in Los Angeles.

Jack and Jill received its premiere on Sunday 6 November 2011 at the Regency Village Theatre in Westwood, Los Angeles. The stars of the film, including Pacino, walked the small red carpet while giving interviews to the press. The film was not screened for critics before release so on 11 November 2011 Adam Sandler fans and professional critics paid to see *Jack and Jill*. The divide between the two groups was huge. The critics poured scorn on it in every review. *Rolling Stone* gave it zero stars and said: "On a scale of 1 to 10 on the laugh meter, *Jack and Jill* is a negative 10." *Time Magazine* hissed: "More than 24 hours has passed since I watched the new Adam Sandler movie *Jack and Jill* and I am still dead inside. It made me feel as if comedy itself were a dirty thing." *The Hollywood Reporter* sneered: "*Jack and Jill* is witless and sloppily constructed, getting by on fart gags, homeless jokes, Latino stereotypes and that old favourite, explosive chimichanga diarrhoea." That review finished with the line: "Maybe there's an audience for it, but they should be embarrassed."

The audience referred to here was not embarrassed at all and arrived at theatres en masse to watch the new Sandler comedy. Its opening week on release in the United States saw it haul in nearly $30 million. By the end of its sixteen weeks in U.S. theatres, closing at the end of February 2012, it had amassed a crowd-pleasing $74.1 million. Bad critical reviews in other countries could not stop *Jack and Jill* raking in over $75 million in total from the other countries it opened in (Information courtesy of Box Office Mojo. Used with permission). In terms of Sandler/Dugan movies it still sat someway behind their biggest collaboration *I Now Pronounce You Chuck and Larry* which had a worldwide gross of $186 million compared to *Jack and Jill*'s $149 million. Despite the huge box office returns, many critics still list this picture as one of, if not the, worst film of 2011. It also swept the board at the 32nd Golden Raspberry Awards. It was nominated in ten different Razzie categories with Sandler being nominated twice for Worst Actor. It won in all ten categories making it the new record holder for most wins by one film.

In her book, *Anatomy of an Actor: Al Pacino*, film critic and journalist Karina Longworth suggests that *Jack and Jill* was: "a go-for-broke gamble that didn't pay off" for Pacino. She is correct. Not only was it Pacino's shot at returning to big mainstream movies (His last leading role in a successful mainstream movie was 2003's The Recruit), it was also an opportunity for Pacino to participate in a comedy film. But Pacino's comedy stylings simply don't work in the Sandler comedy world of fart jokes and fat suits, no matter how much money they make at the box office. Pacino's screen time is limited to less than thirty minutes and he is thus saved from complete humiliation. Even an actor of Pacino's stature has bills to pay, but his appearance in this film does leave one wondering what type of bills he had to pay. They must have been very large ones, because this is a complete misstep for him.

The most interesting moments of Pacino's performance are when he is allowed carte blanche to include lines from Shakespeare's *Richard III* and Cervantes's *El Ingenioso Hidalgo Don Quijote de la Mancha* aka *Don Quixote*. These scenes allow him the opportunity to inject something of worth into proceedings but are still in keeping with the film's tone as they end with a comedic finish: Pacino answering his phone during a performance of *Richard III* or battling a ceiling fan dressed as Don Quixote. Pacino does also seem to be having over the top fun in the Dunkaccino commercial at the end. It may be difficult to believe what is happening on screen but there is an almost crazy, self-referential comedy going on throughout.

Pacino spoofing himself is something that would never have happened in previous decades. The older and more self-assured Pacino is happy to play along. His best comedic line comes at forty-seven minutes in and it is the only funny joke in the entire film. Jill, playing swingball in Pacino's house, hits the ball into his *Scent of a Woman* Oscar statuette. She cries out "Oh I'm so sorry. I'm sure you have plenty more though." To which Pacino replies: "You would think." A funny and very poignant line about his lack of Oscar success. For the rest of his screen time Pacino is involved in an embarrassing love story with Jill. This plotline is the one driving the film essentially and Pacino and Sandler (dressed as Jill) cosying up together is too much to bear even for the strongest of stomachs.

The supposed main story about sibling love is meant to suggest that through all the hatred twins still love each other, and still come through for their sibling in times of great need. That doesn't come across in the film however so it relies on short prologue and epilogue clips with real twins talking about each other to convey this message. Those moments are undeniably interesting and heart-warming. The "relationship" between Jack and Jill is not. Sandler plays Jack as a business-savvy film-maker (basically himself) who feels put upon at every turn by his overbearing sister. That performance by Sandler is actually OK for most of the film. There are no feelings of hatred towards the character because it does feel like he, at times, is being passive-aggressively bullied by his sister. Sadly that is all lost once Sandler decides that Jack needs to become Jill in order to win over Pacino (it all sounds so bonkers... and it is). Sandler throws away all of the audience's good will away for the sake of making the story more bizarre. Jack is the straight man of the film and Sandler knows this. So why change him into a character that loses his mind for just one scene? It does not play out well at all. All this, however, is eclipsed by Sandler as Jill who is possibly one of the worst screen characters of all time. A nasty, scathing, manipulative woman who doesn't talk, but screeches. Every time Sandler does Jill's voice it is fingernails down a chalkboard painful. There is parody and then there is going far beyond that and missing the entire point of who the character is. She should be someone who is a little lost in life but comes to her brother to re-discover herself. Instead Jill hawks and hollers her way through scene after scene of awfulness. The slapstick antics are dreadful and the desperate-for-a-man story is truly demeaning to all women. Jill's dialogue also includes casual sexism and racism and several anti-Semitic jokes that only Mel Gibson would laugh at. Sandler includes his standard fat and flatulence jokes as well (it wouldn't be a Sandler film without them clogging up the script, would it?).

The tagline for *Jack and Jill* is "His twin sister is coming to visit... And it ain't pretty." Ain't pretty is an apt description of this film. It is a hideous monstrosity of a comedy. Sandler, whether you like him or not, is one of the most prolific and highest grossing comedians of all time and Pacino is one of the greatest movie stars of all time. Putting them together possibly seemed like a golden idea but sometimes, and this is one of those times, opposites do not attract. Instead Sandler appears on autopilot (in both roles), Pacino bumbles his way through it and the entire movie is filled with unfunny, and at times offensive, dialogue. *Jack and Jill* is a lazy drag show of a so-called comedy that was hated by the critics, swept the board at the Razzies, and yet still made nearly $150 million at the box office.

Director Dennis Dugan on *Jack and Jill*

You've worked with Adam Sandler before. What do you say when he calls you up and says: I'm going to make a film where I dress as a woman and seduce Al Pacino?

At that time I think we had done seven or eight movies in a row. This was one of them. I started to prepare for *Jack and Jill*. I had gone to New York, New Jersey, Queens to start looking at locations. Just taking photographs of possible locations. When I got back from that trip they said: we are going to push *Jack and Jill*, we are still going to shoot it this year. We are going to push *Jack and Jill* to the second part of the year and do *Just Go with It* with Jennifer Aniston in the first half of the year, and you are going to do both of them. I said: I'm directing two movies in a year? And they say: Yep! We are doing it. And we did!

So I had known about *Jack and Jill* as it had been drifting back and forth in the conversations and I knew the character, and I knew they were working on it. When Adam came up with the idea of using Pacino I said: "Oh my god! That's a genius idea." But we are all asking will we get Pacino? He's a very thoughtful guy in terms of what he is going to do and he takes quite a while... he wants to know what you are doing, what the script is going to be like and how you see it. So you have a lot of meetings with him just to make him comfortable if he is going to commit to a project. Finally he said: "Yes I'm doing it." The thing about him is, when he commits he is committed. As far as he is concerned everything is *Macbeth* or *Hamlet*. He is doing our comedy where he is falling in love with Adam Sandler as a woman and he completely believes in it. He's such an amazing artist that when he says: "I'm going to be there," then he is there. There is not a question for him about what he is doing. He is an actor and he is fully committed to this piece of art. It was spectacular. I was thrilled when Al said: "Yeah I'm doing it."

Sandler and Pacino are not two actors you would expect to see on screen together. How did they bond with each other?

Adam is as committed to making a good piece of work as Al is. It was no surprise to me at all... Sandler and I will have conversations once in a while and I'll ask: "Who works harder? You or me?" and Adam will go: "Well, you work really really hard" and I will say: "Well, you work really really hard." Eventually I say: "Oh Adam you work harder than I do," because it's better for me [*laughs*]. Nobody works harder. It's not an accident that he is as successful as he is because he works really hard. He works really hard on making it funny and also true and making a real world. So it's completely logical that these two guys would get along together. Adam works like crazy on the script and then once we've done it and got a couple of takes with the script the way it was written then it's a free for all. Anybody can throw in lines and Al loved that.

Al likes being funny and he likes saying funny things. The first day when Adam and I were outside the sound stage and somebody came out and said: "Al's just come in" We look at each other and go: "Holy shit! Al Pacino is in there and we are going to go work with him." We do the rehearsal and get everything set and then we do a number of takes, we do a lot of takes, and Adam wants to get comfortable with what he is doing and I want to get comfortable with what I'm doing. We finish twelve or thirteen or fourteen takes of the first master and I said: "Adam, you got what you want?" and he goes: "yeah," I say: "I got what I want. OK, we are going to move on." Pacino said: "WAIT!" everybody gets real quiet and he goes: "WE DO ONE MORE FOR FREE!" and I go: "Great let's do one more for free. There might be something. Let's do one more as there might be something more." He would always do that [*laughs*] and we would do one more for free.

When Pacino was a teenager he experimented with stand-up comedy but now nobody associates him with comedy. Did he have good comic timing and styling while you were directing him?

He's a comedic actor. He has a really great sense of comedy and he has perfect timing. Look at his films, he gets the joke. He is a funny, funny man. There was no time when I had to say: "Hey Al, make it better."

What was he like away from the set?

He is a very, very sweet guy. Just a really nice guy.

I imagine the day when you filmed the Dunkaccino commercial was completely bonkers.

I wouldn't say bonkers is the word. The choreographer was a really good guy and we worked and Pacino would go over in-between takes and do the choreography because he is a song and dance man. The choreographer and Al would go over to a different stage and work on the dance. It was just keep on dancing and dancing and dancing. We did take after take after take and I finally said: "We got it. Stop." Al isn't the youngest guy on the Earth so I had to say stop. He loved dancing, just loved it.

How many takes did you shoot?

That was an all-day shoot. There was a ton of stuff. Cranes, choreography, comedy and dialogue and girls swinging on donuts [*laughs*]. It was a full day. Into the night that was. It was the last day of filming. It was a big production number and went into the night. We probably went till eleven or twelve o'clock.

During the film Pacino's character plays Richard III on stage, which in real life he has done several times and made a docu-film about it. Was that a conscious decision by Adam and yourself? To include something so personal to him.

Yes. That happened without me. That went on in one of the script conferences. It was great because he is such a huge Shakespearean actor. I played his understudy in the movie and we hadn't rehearsed that scene at all before that day and I was directing and when we were getting lit, getting ready, I just popped into the dressing room and put on the costume that made me look exactly like Al. I was an actor for a long time before I started directing, but we hadn't rehearsed it with me in the costume so here I am standing off-stage and he is doing the thing and somebody else shouts: "Action!" and I get my cue and step on stage and say: "Mr Pacino, would..." he looks up at me and here is this guy, now I'm actually in a scene with Al Pacino and on stage in a scene in a movie... I'm in a play in a movie with Al Pacino [*laughs*]. He looks up at me and, because we had known each for a while by now, he just burst out laughing [*laughs*]. Oh man, the last thing I thought I would be, Al Pacino breaking in a scene together [*laughs*] so we had to do it again.

What did the role of Al Pacino's understudy entail?

In theatre everybody in a play knows another role in case someone gets sick. If Michael Caine is doing a play on the West End and he gets ill there is still a group of people coming to the theatre that night so his understudy will go on. That's what I played in the movie. Played his understudy in case anything happened.

Pacino always alters something in every take, whether it is dialogue or movement, and I imagine Adam does that too to keep the comedy fresh. When it comes to editing, how do you decide which version to include?

It's a process. Having done ten movies with Adam, everybody knows everybody. In a normal situation, you make the movie and the editor does an assembly and then the director works about a couple of months and then presents his director's cut and then everybody starts working together. But in the Sandler world we worked together so long that we are looking at scenes being edited as we go. Which also helps because you can say "Hey we are missing this. Let's get it while we are still here." By the time we are done with the movie, about three days after we have a cut Adam and I work on it together because we are making the cut. Then whenever we have a version that we think is good we put it in front of some people and they laugh or they don't laugh. Where they don't laugh we change that. Our preview process is quite complicated in that we show it a lot of times because it's all about the comedy. Like I say, if they laugh – that's good. If they don't laugh – that's not good. So if they don't laugh we either try to fix it or cut it. Sometimes they will laugh over the next joke so you have to make it a little longer so they can hear the next joke. There pretty much isn't a joke that we have tried on stage that we don't put in front of people at some point because we want to find the funniest version of the movie.

On release, *Jack and Jill* made $140 million in North America alone. Yet it received negative reviews. Does that affect you?

If you think about $140 million that is a lot of people going to the movie. If I got negative reviews and nobody went to the movie I'd go: "Oh boy, that was not a good movie." But if I get negative reviews and it makes $140 million I go: "Well, I like those reviews." Why take one person's opinion when I have fifty million other people who think differently. Negative reviews have never stopped any of our movies from making money. I don't think critics necessarily like comedy anyway. It doesn't bother me at all. Truthfully, the person who should be bothered is the person who says... let's say *Grown Ups*... the reviewer says: "*Grown Ups* is a terrible movie and it's not funny and it's stupid" and then it makes a gazillion dollars. Who should feel worse? Me? Or the guy who tried to sink it? Because I succeeded and he failed. God Bless those reviewers, it's nice that they have a job and, truthfully, they wouldn't have a job if people didn't make movies.

You've directed a lot of comedy films. Where does *Jack and Jill* rate for you?

Every film is a different experience and to me it's all about the work, who you worked with, what were you trying to accomplish and did you accomplish it? If we say we went to make a movie where Adam plays twins and we got to work with Al Pacino and Katie Holmes and Eugenio Derbez. Suddenly you go: "That was a great experience." It was something we had not done before in terms of the camera work and trickery with Adam playing with Adam. We solved that problem really well. I got to work with Al Pacino, and there aren't a lot of comedy directors who get to work with Al Pacino. I rate that as a huge win for me, and my career. I had a spectacular time.

Stand Up Guys

Cast: Al Pacino (Val), Christopher Walken (Doc), Alan Arkin (Hirsch), Julianna Margulies (Nina Hirsch), Mark Margolis (Claphands), Lucy Punch (Wendy), Addison Timlin (Alex), Vanessa Ferlito (Sylvia), Katheryn Winnick (Oxana), Bill Burr (Larry), Courtney Galiano (Lisa). **Director:** Fisher Stevens.

Synopsis: After serving 28 years in prison for refusing to give up information on one of his close criminal associates, Val is released and picked up by his best friend Doc. They soon reteam with their old getaway driver Hirsch, and the three embark on what turns into their last crazy night together. As the sun rises, a dangerous secret comes to light, and the trio are forced to confront their past once and for all.

Playwright Noah Haidle had never written a feature film screenplay before 2010. His stage work had been heavily praised and he had written two pieces that were turned into short films. The idea to write a full-length screenplay came to Haidle after he had been sitting on the Brighton Beach Boardwalk in Brooklyn, New York watching an old man paint a sunrise. Sitting there, Haidle imagined what the man's life was like after he walked away from painting on the Boardwalk. This person, unbeknownst to him, became the seed of inspiration for the *Stand Up Guys* screenplay (originally titled "Old Timers"). Haidle's completed manuscript found its way to Jim Tauber, the COO and President of Sidney Kimmel Entertainment. As is the way in Hollywood, the script was passed around producers until Tom Rosenberg and Gary Lucchesi of Lakeshore Entertainment happened across it. The pair felt that Haidle's script would the perfect fit for their next project and signed it for production.

The script was then sent out to directors and agents to gauge interest in the three leading roles and also to see if anyone was particularly enthusiastic about sitting in the director's chair. Initial word came back that Oscar-winners Christopher Walken and Al Pacino would both be interested in making the movie. Finding a director proved tougher and the project began to stall. Walken and Pacino had no choice but to drop out and make other movies but *Stand Up Guys* was reawakened in 2012 when Rosenberg watched a PBS documentary about Woody Allen. One of the producers on the credit list was familiar to him and Rosenberg decided that maybe this was the guy to direct the stalled project.

Fisher Stevens was probably best known for his role as Ben Jabituya, the computer geek in *Short Circuit*. While still acting, Stevens started to forge a successful career as a producer of documentaries. He had also ventured into directing and his first feature film was the romantic comedy *Just a Kiss* starring Marisa Tomei and Taye Diggs. Rosenberg said of Stevens: "Fisher is very intelligent. He really understands actors. I thought he would be good for the project." Stevens was enamoured with Haidle's screenplay and signed on to direct: "I really related to the story's take on friendships" the director commented.

Once he'd officially taken directorial control, Stevens called Walken, who had previously been set to play Val, and asked his opinion as to who he should look to hire for the other two roles. The producers had given Stevens a list of five possible actors to play Doc, but Pacino wasn't one of them as he was working on other projects. Once again the production began to stall because Stevens couldn't find desirable actors to fill the roles. Then, three days before Christmas, a shining opportunity came to Stevens. The telephone rang and Pacino was at the end of the line. He had just watched the Woody Allen documentary and was calling to see if Stevens would be interested in working with him on another project. Stevens declined the offer as he was working on a feature film. It was one that Pacino had previously been attached to but was no longer interested. The reply came: "I'm not interested? You're directing it? Let me look at it again." Within four weeks of that phone call Stevens had assembled his team of actors. Walken and Pacino were signed. Veteran actor Alan Arkin was cast for the third leading role of Hirsch: "If I'm not a hundred percent excited about the script, then that hundred percent has got to be made up by the people I'm working with and the director, so in some way everything has go to add up to a hundred percent," said Arkin.

Stevens tapped up Julianna Margulies, an old friend from his Naked Angels theatre company, to play Nina (an ER nurse and Hirsch's daughter) who said: "No brainer! I mean you can't pass up a chance to work with Al Pacino and Christopher Walken." There were also secondary character roles for Mark Margolis (who, thirty years earlier, had starred opposite Pacino in *Scarface*) as mobster Claphands, British actor Lucy Punch as Wendy the brothel madam, comedian Bill Burr as a mob heavy called Larry and *So You Think You Can Dance* professional dancer Courtney Galiano as Lisa, a young lady who Val tries to seduce in a club. As late as a month before filming was due to start there were still ongoing auditions for the role of Alex, Doc's granddaughter. The role eventually went to Addison Timlin, who had previously been seen in the hit TV show *Californication* with David Duchovny.

With cameras set to roll shortly, Walken spoke to Fisher about his character Val. He didn't feel he was the right person to play that role and that he would be more comfortable playing the Doc character. Pacino was playing the Doc role; however, after a discussion with the director and producers, he was happy to make the switch. A modest budget of $15 million was set.

Principal photography began in April 2012 in and around the greater Los Angeles area. The only interior studio set, used for the interior of Doc's apartment, was an apartment at Lacy Street Production Center. It was a set previously used in *Catch Me If You Can* and the TV series *Cagney & Lacey* but naturally it was redesigned for the film. Exterior and interior shots were filmed at the St Louis Pharmacy in Boyle Heights. A private residence close to the University of Southern California was transformed into a whorehouse. The dark wood interior of Three Clubs on Vine Street was used for a sequence that featured Pacino slow-dancing with Galiano. The Brite Spot Diner closed its doors for a couple of days to allow interior filming to take place. A suit store in The Garment District was also used for a scene in which Doc and Val are buying new outfits.

Hundreds of clothing stores line the streets in that district, but Stevens chose the store that was most in keeping with the style of his movie.

Exterior Los Angeles street filming locations, where most of the shots were taken through the night, included W 24th Street and S Western Avenue, W Avenue 33 and Humboldt St, Glendale Boulevard and Park Avenue, E 2nd St and S Garey Avenue, Mesquit St/6th St access road, Santa Fe Avenue and Banning St and 1335 Willow St. 544 Mateo St was also used, best known as the exterior of the bar in the hit TV show *It's Always Sunny in Philadelphia*. The car chase sequence was filmed across the iconic 6th Street Bridge over two nights and the big shoot-out finale took place at 949 E 2nd Street on the junction with S Vignes Street.

Principal photography was completed in just over thirty days but during that time Pacino had medical attention after a foreign object became lodged in his eye while he and Walken were filming a shoot out. Also during that time musician Jon Bon Jovi had written a song to be featured in the film. He had originally received the script from his acting agent before the shoot began. Within two days he'd written 'Old Habits Die Hard.' Rosenberg told Stevens that Bon Jovi wanted to write a song for the film. Stevens, while a fan, wasn't sure it would be the right fit. Bon Jovi sent the director 'Old Habits Die Hard' Stevens liked it and asked Bon Jovi to visit the set for a couple of days. Bon Jovi went back to his hotel room after one of his days on set and wrote another song called: 'Not Running Anymore.' He recorded a rough demo on his iPhone and sent it to Stevens who felt it would perfectly sync with the closing scene of the movie, Bon Jovi asked to sing it live in the editing room as the film played out and Stevens later said: "Jon came up with some great stuff. His songs are great and he's a nice dude, too."

Stand Up Guys opened with its world premiere at the 48th Chicago International Film Festival on 11 October 2012. This was followed two days later with a screening at the Mill Valley Film Festival in San Rafael, California. However, the film had to wait a further four months to make its grand entrance in U.S. theatres. This was Pacino and Walken's first time acting on-screen together and the critics gave both their performances and the film itself the thumbs up. Roger Ebert stated:

"These men move through the monuments of sad lives. They have not lost the gift of bitter amusement." *Rolling Stone* suggested that "Al Pacino, Christopher Walken and Alan Arkin turn the insubstantial *Stand Up Guys* into solid entertainment." *The Hollywood Reporter* commented: "Stand-out performances from Pacino, Walken and Arkin as old-timers prove that losing a step can't keep you off your feet."

With high praise such as this, it's shocking to think that *Stand Up Guys* failed to connect with U.S. audiences upon release on 1 February 2013. Opening in nearly seven hundred theatres, the movie pulled in a poor return of $2.1 million. By the end of week two this figure had dropped by more than half again, with a pitiful haul of just $935,000. By the end of the fifth week the movie was removed from U.S. theatres, grossing just $3.3 million. It fared even worse in the foreign territories where it had a theatrical run. Not one of the nineteen countries managed to hit the $1 million mark in box office returns (Information courtesy of Box Office Mojo. Used with permission). The only bright spark came when Bon Jovi's 'Not Running Anymore' was nominated at the 70th Golden Globe Awards for Best Original Song. It lost out to 'Skyfall' by Adele from the James Bond film of the same name.

Fun is the word most easily assigned to *Stand Up Guys*. Pure 70s gangster fun. Pacino, Walken and the supporting cast are visibly enjoying themselves and the film doesn't bow to taking itself seriously until the final few frames. At its core, this picture is a comedy revenge movie with a senior citizen discount card. Pacino and Walken establish the bromance between their characters with witty, sarcastic banter. Exchanges such as: "You look like shit!" "You look worse" and "So, what'll it be? Chew gum or kick ass?" "I'm all outta gum" trip off the tongues of these two veteran actors so naturally it almost feels like the viewer is watching authentic patter that just happens to have been caught on camera. Given this chemistry, it's a wonder that nobody ever thought to put these two actors in a film together before.

Pacino gets all of the over-confident dialogue, leaving the audience wondering if he is still holding onto the macho persona he had before he was banged up. This barrier of bravado soon comes down however to reveal a man filled with regret. Someone who knows he has done wrong for many many years and knows it is too late to fix any of it. He is ready to meet his maker. Pacino leans on his subtle yet amusing brand of comedy acting in this performance while Walken portrays his character as the quiet assassin. He doesn't instigate the comedy but finishes most of the lines with his now critically lauded deadpan demeanour. In short, Walken and Pacino are a match made in gangster heaven, their complementary styles of delivery work like a treat in the comedy genre. Arkin, though only featured briefly, manages to keep up with Pacino and Walken in the comedy stakes between wow-ing ladies of the night and speed racing a top of the line car through the L.A. streets at three in the morning. Live fast, die...er... old.

The emotional heart of the movie is rooted in the characters of Margulies and Timlin who become accidentally caught up in the fray. They are happy to give a little help, but not too much. It's only when it's too late do we see what their older family members (fathers/grandfathers) truly meant to them. These small supporting roles instigate a respectable sized emotional punch towards the end of the film. The finale does feel like a bit of a tonal misfire given the mood of the rest of the movie. It simply isn't in keeping with the previous ninety-three minutes of comedy. It is almost as if this scene was cut from a completely different movie and tacked onto the end of this one to resolve the main storyline within a two-minute window.

Stand Up Guys is a pleasurable watch that straddles a couple of movie genres. Maybe Fisher, Pacino, Walken et al have created a new one?! The senior citizen revenge comedy.

Contemporary dancer and actor Courtney Galiano on *Stand Up Guys*

Most people will know you from *So You Think You Can Dance* and/or *Glee*. So how did you end up in a comedy gangster movie with Al Pacino, Christopher Walken and Alan Arkin?

My agency has a theatrical department as well as a dance department, so they called me for the audition and of course I was excited to attend. Before *Stand Up Guys*, I already had worked with Mr. Pacino when I danced in Adam Sandler's *Jack and Jill*. The audition process was actually really fun… while I was walking in the room, the casting director said: "The director [Fisher Stevens] is going to keep going at the end of the scene so just improv." I ended up making everyone in the room laugh, including the producer Tom Rosenberg!

In the film, when Val first comes over to you, alongside the other ladies, Pacino has a terrible chat up line. Was that the only one Pacino said in each take? Or did he change it each time?

I would say he changed it a little every time but the gist of what he was saying was the same.

Would you say your character, Lisa, is nice or nasty? Because when Val first walks over she gives him quite a frosty look. But she soon melts and dances with him.

I would said say at first, she has a typical reaction any girl out with her girlfriends would have… some older man hitting on a group of girls and she gives him the: "you can't be serious look," especially after he makes his crude comment. When he comes over and apologizes, I do think she feels a little empathy for what he's been through. I think all in all, she's a nice person and finds him to be endearing.

What was it like to act with Pacino?

I had the opportunity to go to his house with the choreographer Marlyn Ortiz. I remember he asked me if I would like some French pressed coffee and I just said to myself: "Am I really sitting in Al Pacino's house drinking a French pressed coffee?" We talked about a bunch of things, acting, life, his kids, where he grew up. He was very down to earth. When we talked about life he said: "You have to always be present. Life is too good to be missed." I knew who Al Pacino was my whole entire life. My father's favorite movie of all time is *The Godfather*... the theme song is his ringtone and if you want to find him on Thanksgiving.... he's watching the 24-hour marathon on AMC.

He grew up in East New York where my grandfather grew up. I come from a very New York Italian family so Al Pacino was never a stranger in my house. At first, of course I was nervous! That was the first movie gig I have ever had with a speaking role. Even though it was only a few lines, I made sure I was prepared and ready for anything. After the first take, I felt very comfortable. Al made me feel comfortable from the beginning. I think the nervousness was just me saying to myself: "What the hell is my life right now?!" He really has a powerful presence with a very kind spirit. He reminded me of my family. I have never asked anyone for a picture when I work with them ever, I think it's unprofessional but Father's Day was coming and I wanted to get something made for my Dad. I shared that with Al and without hesitation he took a picture with me and signed it. I had it professionally framed and now it hangs in my Dad's office. We danced so much more than they showed in the film. After the slow song, they played an upbeat song and I remember having the most fun during that time! I took off his jacket and we were pretending it was a bullfighting cape. It was hilarious. Getting to do a scene with Al Pacino was something I'll never forget.

Pacino has danced in movies before. Disco dancing in *Cruising*, the Tango in *Scent of a Woman* and in *Stand Up Guys* he slow-dances with you. Is he a good dancer? Or did he keep stepping on your toes?

He didn't step on my toes at all! He was a wonderful dancer, a great leader, which I think is something that translates into his life. After I got the job, I watched the powerful dance scene in *Scent of a Woman* over and over. I asked him what that was like. He said it was a lot of practice having to keep his eyes open the whole time and not make any eye contact. He was a great dance partner!

Did it take him long to learn the steps?

Not at all! They definitely wanted him to spin me at some point which we did but we really freestyled a bunch. I just followed his lead!

What were Pacino and Walken like together once cameras had stopped rolling?

They seemed to like each other a lot. I loved watching some of the other scenes with just the two of them.

I get the feeling it was quite a fun set to be on. Is that correct?

It was a blast. Everyone made each other laugh and it felt very East Coast. I can't explain it. Everyone seemed to be from New York or Chicago. I never felt out of place not even once and these some huge names! Fisher Stevens and Tom Rosenberg were incredible to work with. I took my mom to the premiere and they all came over to her and introduced themselves. It was really such an awesome experience. Even writing all this down now and remembering those few days makes me smile ear-to-ear. Everyone was so welcoming but extremely professional and got things done. I'll never forget it!

Phil Spector

Cast: Al Pacino (Phil Spector), Helen Mirren (Linda Kenney Baden), Jeffrey Tambor (Bruce Cutler), Chiwetel Ejiofor (Mock Prosecutor), Rebecca Pidgeon (Dr. Fallon), John Pirruccello (Nick Stavros), James Tolkan (Judge Fidler). **Director:** David Mamet.

Synopsis: Lawyer Linda Kenney Baden helps defend music producer Phil Spector, on trial for the murder of actress Lana Clarkson. As Baden engages with Spector in preparation for the trial, she begins to believe he might actually be telling the truth.

The U.S. TV network Home Box Office, known as HBO, cornered the market on subscription television by the early 2000s. It produced award-winning shows such as *The Sopranos, Sex and the City* and *Six Feet Under*. The ongoing aim was to establish the network as the home of intelligent storytelling without being at the mercy of advertisers. HBO also produces its own movies. In fact, movies is what they started with in terms of self-produced content. It was the first U.S. cable channel to take this leap and generated movies like *The Hitcher, Amistad* and *My Big Fat Greek Wedding*. The peak of its film-making power has been during the 2010s when HBO released movies starring A-list actors such as *Sex and the City 2, The Sunset Limited* and *Behind the Candelabra*. Thus, when legendary playwright, screenwriter and film director David Mamet wanted to make a movie about the murder trial of music producer Phil Spector, HBO seemed like the perfect company to turn to. Mamet wanted space to create a piece that didn't so much as examine whether Spector was guilty or not, but explored whether Spector's celebrity influenced his trial.

Mamet first became interested in the real Phil Spector trial when watching the BBC documentary, *The Agony and the Ecstasy of Phil Spector*. Vikram Jayanti's documentary premiered in the U.S. on 30 June 30 2010. Mamet's agent called him and told him should be watching it. The playwright was addicted to all things Phil Spector from then on. He saw the music mogul as "a mythological character: this is a man avowed by all to be a monster. He is the Minotaur." Keen to use a different angle than that of Jayanti's documentary, Mamet decided to challenge the audience by seeing if he could "take an irrefutable proposition – the guy's obviously guilty – and see if I could refute it." After completing the screenplay, Mamet tracked down Spector's real-life defense attorney Linda Kenney Baden. He spoke with her on her cell phone while she was at the Golden Door spa resort in California. The screenplay was sent to Baden and shortly after she became the film's go-to person for checking the legal jargon was correct.

For the role of the music pioneer on trial, Phil Spector, Mamet turned to an actor he had worked with twice before: Al Pacino. The pair worked together on the stage production of *American Buffalo* in the early 1980s and then on the film adaptation of Mamet's *Glengarry Glen Ross* in 1992, and had formed a friendly bond. Pacino commented to the *Hollywood Reporter*: "For me, over the years, the relationship and the collaboration with David Mamet has been one of the richest and most rewarding." In contrast to Pacino's usual approach to preparing for a performance, he chose not to meet the real Phil Spector before filming began. He cited the need to find the earlier, pre-trial Spector: "This person I'm playing is the guy who was there before he was convicted. He hadn't even gone through the first trial yet. So, I wanted to follow another route."

Instead Pacino sat for hours watching archival footage of Spector, trying to understand the man he was to portray. Meanwhile, Bette Midler signed on to play the troubled music producer's defense attorney Linda Kenney Baden. It was an interesting casting choice from Mamet as at this point Midler had been last seen on US TV at the start of the noughties in her poorly-received sitcom *Bette*. The show only ran for sixteen of the eighteen scheduled episodes. At the same time as Midler's appointment was announced, it also came to light that Jeffrey Tambor had agreed to play Baden's defense attorney colleague Bruce Cutler, a trial attorney who had represented Italian American mobster John Gotti several times. Chiwetel Ejiofor was also cast as a mock prosecutor alongside James Tolkan as Judge Fidler and John Pirruccello as Nick

Stavros, a former LAPD officer turned P.I. and right-hand man to Baden and Cutler. HBO merrily paid for all this talent without even blinking; the company turned over $4 billion in 2010.

Principal photography began during the first week of July 2011 in New York City. Manhattan's 7th Avenue and 10th street were closed off so that Mamet could film scenes depicting Spector in his youth, including a reconstruction of an incident in which he fired a gun in a studio during a recording session with John Lennon. Not a week into filming however, Midler was carried off the set due to a herniated disc. She had filmed for only three days. Mamet addressed the cast and crew on set, explaining they'd have to recast the part. Filming was then suspended while the team searched for a replacement for Midler. The following day, Midler released a statement: "I am heartbroken to be forced to leave this terrific project, working with David Mamet and Al Pacino was a dream of mine; but the pain I am in has made my participation impossible."

Only a week later, the role of Baden was recast with British actress Dame Helen Mirren stepping into the vacant role at short notice. When they told the real Baden of the recasting choice she said: "That's really great. Really cool. Yes! Helen fuckin' Mirren!" Filming restarted on the final week of July 2011. For the first couple of days in August the cast and crew worked out of New York's Nassau County Courthouse for external courthouse shots, shooting scenes that involved picketers yelling and screaming, and palm trees were installed to achieve the Los Angeles aesthetic. Filming had moved to the Brooklyn Courts on Court Street, Brooklyn by 4 August.

The shoot was brief and principal photography finished within thirty days of the recasting of Mirren. It was left to Mamet and his editor Barbara Tulliver to put together a rough cut in time to show HBO, and for HBO to figure out where to include it in their schedule. Tulliver had previously worked with Mamet on *House of Games*, *Things Change* and *Homicide*. She was cutting the movie while Mamet was still shooting, and presented the director with a very early cut of the film a week after he had finished filming, she commented: "HBO likes to see things early, so David had his initial cut done after five weeks, instead of the typical ten-week frame." Notes from HBO executives were returned to Mamet, and on that basis the director felt a couple of additional days of shooting were required. Post-production was put on hold until HBO sanctioned the additional costs. "That took awhile until HBO approved it," said Tulliver. Once those extra shooting days were completed, the additional footage was incorporated into the existing cut.

Songs from Spector's back catalogue were also required to create the finished product. Even though Spector's businesses (run by his wife Rachelle) owned most of the masters to his work, Universal Music and EMI Records still had to license use of some of his most famous recordings including Unchained Melody, You've Lost That Loving Feeling and Be My Baby amongst others. One song Mamet wanted to include was John Lennon's Imagine, he had spoken to John's wife Yoko Ono who was open to the idea of including it. However, she and the director couldn't agree on a way to integrate it organically. Eventually the idea to include the song was dropped.

The completed film sat on the shelf for several months without news of an on air date. Finally, at the Television Critics Association meeting on Friday 4 January 2013, a date was announced: it was to debut on HBO on 24 March 2013. A press screening was arranged for 14 March at the Los Angeles County Museum of Art. The screening was picketed by over fifty members of the Friends of Lana Clarkson protest group; led by Clarkson's former publicist Edward Lozzi who had tried to stop the movie from being made. When the project went into production, they changed tack and tried to thwart Pacino's chances of receiving award nominations. Placards read: "HBO's Phil Spector murders the truth," and "No Emmy for the film that hurts people alive today."

The protest didn't stop the screening going ahead however. Critical reviews were fairly positive. The L.A. Times called it: "better than most films of its kind, even if it remains unsatisfying as historical recreation." Time Magazine said it was: "Mamet's strongest drama in ages, and a seductive, devious essay on the tortured celebrity soul." Variety were not so enamoured with it, stating the film was "watchable [but] the cinematic equivalent of a bad hair day." The Independent felt Mamet's drama was being "dishonest, pretending to a candour that it doesn't actually possess." One person who spoke out venomously against it was Spector's third and current wife Rachelle Spector. Criticizing it for the way they portrayed her husband as a gun nut into "wacky stuff" and she further stated that it was a "cheesy portrayal of my husband." She even slammed the on-screen relationship between Pacino and Mirren, saying it was "disturbing" and the "relationship was not that close. So that was kind of a fail." The movie went on to receive eleven Primetime Emmy Award nominations, two Golden Globe and Screen Actors Guild Award nominations. It only won once and that was at the 20th Screen Actors Guild Awards in the category of Outstanding Performance by a Female Actor in a Miniseries or Television Movie. Dame Helen called the award "sexy" and thanked Mamet and also her co-star Pacino by saying: "To work with Al and to watch him at close hand was an incredible lesson for me."

Phil Spector is a courtroom drama without the courtroom. Billed as "an exploration of the client-attorney relationship" Mamet's desire to get under the skin of the two most important people associated with the trail is both intriguing and beguiling. To understand the man on trial we have to understand the man himself. Pacino portrays Spector as a curious creature. Both pitiful and egotistical. Mamet is evidently keen to suggest there is a frightened person underneath all the bravado and hair. Pacino plays his part with gusto for the majority of the film and conveys a man who is on edge through the constant twitching of the hands, the darting eyes and the loud slapping of the lips. Yet, it's the quieter times in which Pacino manages to paint a portrait of a murderer who is both frail and fragile. Spector, in this depiction, is doddery and his thought processes bordering on schizophrenic.

Pacino watched a lot of video footage of Spector in preparation for the role but rather than mimicking every little eccentricity, he takes a few trademark idiosyncrasies and emphasizes them in his own unique way. Though it's a pleasant surprise to see Pacino reign in the showmanship for the majority of the film, the real star of the movie is Dame Helen Mirren. Dropped into the middle of a media circus, Dame Helen's Baden glides effortlessly through the piece without once resort to the usual shouting and banging of desks normally seen in a courtroom drama. It's a very unassuming role and one that is difficult to imagine Midler portraying in the same light. Mirren knows how to keep Baden's demeanour relaxed within the confines of the hectic drama that surrounds her. Keeping her peace and surveying the landscape is her greatest power. Mirren and Pacino bounce off each other like an old married couple, and the pairing of these two impressive actors is the film's masterstroke.

Through his alternative courtroom drama, Mamet has created a piece of cinema that refuses to deal in over-simplistic, black and white terms. Unfortunately, his idea of "trial by celebrity" never really pays off. Mamet's alternate take on proceedings doesn't captivate in the same way some of his previous works have. His insistence on sitting on the fence on the issue of Spector's guilt will also prove infuriating for some audience members. If a TV movie this high profile appeared on the Lifetime channel, it would be spoken about as an almost masterpiece. But this is not standard TV, it's HBO, and given the finance and the talent behind it the finished piece should have been that much better.

Actor John Pirruccello on *Phil Spector*

Is your character, Nick Stavros, based on a real life police detective or an amalgamation of people?

He is absolutely an amalgamation. He was a way to accomplish something in the script. So he is not based on a real person. He is a combination of a bunch of people, I think.

Do you remember your first audition?

I auditioned... oh man... when did we even make the movie? Was it 2011?

Yes, the film was made in 2011 but not shown until 2013.

Oh man that was a trip. You go on with your life and do other work but in the back of your mind you go: hey, that movie hasn't come out yet. What's going on with that?! We all speculated as to what was going on. So, we were thinking it's a scheduling thing because Al did the Kevorkian movie in-between, we were thinking maybe... he did that before but it hadn't aired yet so maybe there was a scheduling thing with HBO. We were speculating that maybe there was some other... who knows what HBO was doing in terms of rolling out their stuff? I believe I auditioned for it in the summer of '10.

How big a gap was there between auditioning and the start of filming?

David told me about this part. He sort of mentioned it in passing because we had done a couple of other things and he mentioned it in passing like: "I'm writing this role in this movie I'm doing and it's this reporter and he follows the action around."

When I read the script the reporter has one line and [*laughs*] God bless David Mamet for even thinking of me at all. If he had me as a rock in the background I would do it [*laughs*]. I gave the script back to him and said: "Which role am I?" And he looks at me and says: "You're Nick Stavros." At that point it dawned on me what a big deal it was. It was a large part of the story and [I] did work on the movie for almost three months in New York.

Were you concerned about the film leaning too far one way or the other. For or against the real Phil Spector?

As an actor that doesn't even enter my head. I learn my lines and show up and David tells me how to say them and where to stand when saying them and that's the beginning, middle and end of my job. Whether he is guilty or not has no effect on my work. My character is suspicious. He has his doubts, he has questions and there are things that don't make sense to him. He is going to bring those up because my character was completely in support of Helen's character. That is what drove me. I would show up to work every day and support Helen.

Alongside Pacino, the movie has a great cast including Dame Helen Mirren, Jeffrey Tambor, Chiwetel Ejiofor. What was it like working with these actors?

They couldn't have been greater. They couldn't have been more generous. There was no egos involved. It really felt like an ensemble, like how it is when you do theatre. Everybody is supportive of each other.

I remember my first day shooting the car scenes and we are getting dragged around a parking lot and it was hundred and eight degrees Fahrenheit and I'm, understandably, a little nervous. I had dinner with her [Mirren] the night before and we chatted to break the ice a little bit and then we went and saw... David's wife Rebecca is an accomplished musician so we went and saw one of her shows. That was cool. But then to show up to work and be sitting in this town car and be cramped in there with a camera and a focus puller and a DP and Helen and me in this hot car, it was daunting.

I had one or two lines and I had my script down on the floor and I picked it up to look at it to make sure I didn't screw her up and I went to throw it back down and she said: "Let me look at that a moment," and she looked and then put it down. It was very comforting to me that she... it felt like she was saying: 'I'm an actor too.' Whether she was saying that or not... but it's how it felt.

I do remember there was one moment where David changed something, where Helen and I... I don't even think it's in the movie, but when we are first walking into the court room and we have to walk and talk and hit a mark and turn a corner and head for the end. David decides at the last minute there is a bunch of business he wants me to do that involves badges and paperwork that he wants me to hand to her. He is very precise about when he wants things to happen and how, he really is an artist in that way. I had all this brand new stuff to think about and do the lines, and we are doing it and there was a moment where she [Mirren] looked back at me and I thought: "That's Helen Mirren," [*laughs*] and it had never happened before and I got completely discombobulated for a second and flubbed it up. So we have to go back and start again. I don't know what compelled me to do this but I said to her: "Man, I'm really all up in my head right now. I'm definitely self conscious in my head. I gotta just jump. I gotta jump off the cliff here." And she looks at me, and goes: "Yeah, yeah, jump, jump," and she is this tiny, beautiful creature and she is going: "yeah jump" like a wood nymph or something. It was magical.

I jumped and we did the scene. She is something special.

Most of your scenes with Pacino are in confined spaces. What was that like?

It was unbelievable. It was beyond words. At one point there is a scene in the mock court room where he blows up and they wheel out the tape of his ex-wife accusing him of things and the whole idea of the scene was to show the character, this is what it would be like if he had to go to court. They were making it really rough on him and Al stands up and blows up and is basically fighting for his life. "They kill people" he yells

"I know how this works. I'm not an idiot." They did a rehearsal of it before cameras came up so I'm sitting there in a chair, and this is during a rehearsal, and he [Pacino] is three feet away from me and all I could see was this guy fighting for his life. This is a guy with the whole weight of the world on his shoulders fighting for his innocence and a tear just rolled down the side of my face. I was stunned, absolutely stunned. That was a rehearsal. He went on to do that take after take. There really isn't a better actor than him as far as I can tell and I've watched him three feet away and he's the real deal.

Did he stay in character off camera?

No. He was all business on-set but he would see you each morning and smile and say: "Good morning." From where I'm sitting he's got this whole thing on his shoulders. Al is the main character. He has a lot of lines. The whole thing is turning on him, just as if you were a line cook you aren't going to chat with the chef because he has a lot to do. I'm still going to take my cues from him [Pacino]. So no, he wasn't in character but he was tremendously focussed on what he was doing

What did you think when he turned up with a different hairstyle each time?

[*Laughs*] I heard something about that. Those wigs were a character unto themselves weren't they! I heard that the actual hair that Phil had was so big that when they did a wig that was accurate it was too unbelievable. So they made it smaller and it was still too unbelievable. The wig that he is in in court was significantly smaller than the actual wig that Phil Spector wore in court. The first thing I saw when I showed up in New York to do my fitting, I saw all of Al's costumes at Deb McGuire's shop. She was the costumer, and that was cool. That was like, this is going to be what's coming: all of this.

Earlier you briefly mentioned working for David Mamet. Could you elaborate more?

He is without a doubt... there is no one better. I guarantee you that any actor that has ever worked with him will tell you that it was the best experience of their life. He is absolutely warm and funny and brilliant and efficient and when he tells you what he wants, you understand it and it's simple and actionable. The whole tone on the set was fun. We would play Bingo at lunch. There was a lot of laughing. He is a really, really brilliant, kind, thoughtful man and it's a privilege to even be in the same room with him. Much less help him make something.

What did you think of the film?

I loved the film. I thought the film was fantastic and it just looked great, and the music was great. It came together great. It was funny, smart... I loved the movie. We had a hurricane... we had an earthquake during the shooting of it. It definitely felt like survival at times. There was a moment when we were out on Long Island and a hail storm happened and then when it broke I got word that David and Helen wanted to have a rehearsal of a scene. So I jumped up out of my trailer and ran over and met up with Dave. He said "Let's go over to your trailer." It might seem like nothing but I was thinking if I had straightened up [*laughs*]. Oh gosh, they are coming over to my trailer. Next thing I know Dame Helen and David Mamet... David is on the floor sitting in the stairwell and Helen is on the couch in my trailer. For a moment I just thought: "is this really happening?" It was like a dream. It doesn't sound very interesting but it was incredible to me.

Salomé &

Wilde Salomé

Cast: Al Pacino (King Herod/Himself), Jessica Chastain (Salome/Herself), Kevin Anderson (John the Baptist/Himself), Roxanne Hart (Herodias/Herself), Estelle Parsons (Herself), Barry Navidi (Himself), Richard Cox (Robert Ross). **Director:** Al Pacino.

Synopsis: Based on Oscar Wilde's controversial play, Salomé is a filmed version of the play starring Jessica Chastain in the title role (and her debut film role) and Al Pacino as Herod. The documentary Wilde Salomé delves into Pacino's passion for Oscar Wilde and tracks the challenges he faces in putting on the play while simultaneously directing these two features.

"I went a little mad during the year and a half of doing this," Pacino commented when asked about making the films *Salomé & Wilde Salomé*. The actor / director first saw Oscar Wilde's play staged in London during 1988 with actor, author and playwright Steven Berkoff in the role of King Herod. Pacino's desire to fully understand Wilde's most controversial work simmered for almost two decades after that.

His first production of the play was a staged reading at New York's Circle in the Square theatre during December 1990 and January 1991. It was by selected-invite only and ran for just four performances. Brat Pack sweetheart Molly Ringwald played Salomé during this short run. Fifteen months later Pacino staged a full production of *Salomé* (rotated alongside his production of Ira Lewis's *Chinese Coffee*) at the same venue. Playing the infamous Salomé was *Twin Peak*'s star Sheryl Lee and the production ran from 25 May to 29 July 1992.

Variety called it: "an explosion of Biblical Kitsch." *The New York Times* suggested Pacino's performance: "flirts dangerously with camp but stays strictly with character." It would be a further ten years until Pacino had the opportunity to play Herod again. Directed by Estelle Parsons of The

Actors Studio, this production was titled *Salomé by Oscar Wilde: The Reading* and ran from the 12th of November to the 22nd of December 2002 at the tiny St. Anne's Warehouse in Brooklyn, New York. Oscar-winning actor Marisa Tomei starred as Salomé.

The New York Times review commented: "They find both a scary emotional intensity and a pitch-black sense of humour." *Variety* saw something different in the production by claiming: "It's nothing – merely silly," before questioning at the end of the review why Pacino and Parsons would stage it as a reading: "Have they lost their heads?" Almost three years to the date after Pacino opened *Salomé* in New York, he staged a month-long production at the Wadsworth Theatre in Los Angeles. The twenty-six performances ran from 14 April through to 14 May 2006.

Direction under Parsons continued and Pacino reprised the role of King Herod. However, in this production *Salomé* was played by newcomer Jessica Chastain. The actor had been brought to the attention of Parsons in 2004 by Richard Nelson the writer/director of *Rodney's Wife*, a play Chastain was appearing in. Parsons suggested to Pacino that Chastain would be perfect for the role of the flame-haired seductress. Another version of events is that Pacino was alerted to Chastain via his *Bobby Deerfield* co-star Marthe Keller. Whichever story is to be believed, it resulted in Chastain bagging the role of Salomé.

Soon after, the madness took hold of Pacino. He decided, not only would he star in the play, but would also film it to be made into a movie and include behind the scenes footage of how he put the play together. This all-in-one film and documentary was to be called *Salomaybé* and would be financed and produced by Pacino's company Chal Productions, alongside Navidi Productions: a company managed by Pacino's long-time friend and business partner, Barry Navidi. Robert Fox Productions also played a part in producing this picture. An entity managed by English theatre and film producer, Robert Fox.

The first time the cameras rolled specifically to film footage for the documentary was in March 2006 while Pacino prepped for the play.

Navidi took charge of the camera and would, on occasions, continue to film Pacino on a small digital camera. The filmed section of the play was shot during afternoons on Stage 6 of GTS Studios in Culver City before the cast went off to give their live performances each evening. The filming of the documentary was to be an erratic experience. Before and during the play and the film shoot, the documentary cameras followed Pacino around as he hustled the productions into shape. Interviews with Pacino and the cast took place ad hoc in the stalls and dressing rooms of the Wadsworth Theatre. Footage was also shot that captured the cast rehearsing on stage before the play opened. In mid-November, Pacino, the film crew and a host of actors drove to the El Mirage Dry Lake Bed close to the Angeles National Forest. They were a different set of actors to those performing in the play, and together they worked together to stage and enact the piece in the searing heat so the segment could be filmed. Pacino wandered around shooting behind-the-scenes bits and pieces just in case they were required. The actor also brought a camel in for filming and wound up wandering around aimlessly with the animal on its lead.

During late November, Pacino accepted an honorary patronage from the Philosophical Society at Dublin's Trinity College. Pacino, Navidi and journalist/biographer Lawrence Grobel flew into London on 19 November and were immediately ushered to the Eurostar for a train ride to Paris. Footage of Pacino reading from Wilde's work was shot on the Eurostar train from London to Paris and once the production arrived in the City of Light, filming began at L'Hotel on the Left bank of the Seine. Here, Pacino, Navidi and Grobel were treated to a tour of Wilde's bedroom. Further filming took place in front of the Eiffel Tower. The crew were then flown over to Dublin in a private jet where Pacino received the honorary patronage and where more filming took place.

While at the college, Pacino was shown around the Old Library and the Long Room, places Wilde used as a study area when he was an undergraduate. Further footage was shot by the documentary crew as Pacino visited other Dublin locations such as the National Gallery of Ireland, The Gate Theatre, The Oscar Wilde House and the statue of Wilde located in Merrion Square Park. From there, the production team made the short hop over the Irish Sea to London in order to visit Wilde's London home on Tite Street and The Cadogan Hotel where Wilde stayed. During this whirlwind Wilde tour, the crew visited three countries over five days.

The never-ending filming continued back in the U.S. as footage was filmed at Pacino's Chal Productions office in New York and also at the Oscar Wilde Memorial Bookshop in Greenwich Village before Pacino returned to L.A. in March 2007. There Pacino dressed as Oscar Wilde and filmed scenes alongside actors Richard Cox and Jack Huston. Pacino and Navidi flew to New York again in the July of 2007 to interview Merlin Holland, the only grandchild of Oscar Wilde, at the Algonquin Hotel.

Despite all this progress, it was clear the film wasn't going to be released in 2007 and Pacino moved on to other projects while Navidi tried to whip the documentary into shape. The hope was to screen the film to studios and distributors who might buy it. During production, the filming crew amassed talking head interviews with writer Gore Vidal, British playwright Tom Stoppard and pop star Bono from the band U2. They also tried to interview singer-songwriter Anthony Kiedis from the Red Hot Chili Peppers, however that idea had to be dropped as Kiedis' schedule didn't allow for the time needed to film.

If the filming of *Salomaybé* appeared chaotic, it was nothing compared to the editing. The first cut of the movie was three hours and forty five minutes long and the first screening for friends and family on 14 September 2006 included a dinner break in the middle. Editing continued at pace as nearly a hundred different cuts were shown to invited audiences over the course of five years. Even then, Pacino continued to film new segments to be included. Pacino employed four editors – Roberto Silvi, David Leonard, Pasquale Buba and Stan Salfas over the course of filming because he couldn't decide how he wanted the film to look and would argue against decisions each of the editors made. He also sought advice on how to cut the film from actor Danny Huston and his *Sea of Love* director Harold Becker.

Eventually Pacino had to sign off on a finished version, now called *Wilde Salomé* rather than *Salomaybé*, in January 2011. His hand was forced due to pressure from outside investors and also because he, personally, could not raise any further money for the project due to his accountant embezzling money from him. Nearly five years in the making and *Wilde Salomé* was finally finished at a cost of $4.2 million. Navidi had originally envisaged that the production cost would be slightly over $1 million. However, due to the ongoing filming and editing, the budget spiralled beyond anything Navidi, Fox or Pacino could afford which meant Navidi had to seek outside investment. The additional costs were covered by a host of private investors from countries including The United States, Italy and Iran.

On 4 September 2011, *Wilde Salomé* received its world premiere at the 68th Venice Film Festival. Chastain and Pacino were both in attendance, and the actor/director received the Jaeger-LeCoultre Glory to the Filmmaker award. This prize is awarded to those who have made a significant contribution to contemporary cinema. Past winners included Takeshi Kitano, Agnés Varda and Sylvester Stallone. Pacino was also presented with the Queer Lion trophy, an award for the best movie with GLBT Themse & Queer Culture.

Wilde Salome was also screened at the 2012 Jameson Dublin International Film Festival. The screening took place on 20 February at Dublin's oldest working cinema: The Savoy. Pacino was in attendance to introduce the film on the night. A U.S. premiere was held on 21 March 2012 at the Castro Theatre, San Francisco. That date marked the 130th anniversary of Oscar Wilde's visit to San Francisco and the premiere served as a fundraiser for San Francisco's LGBT Historical Society. The audience included fashion designer Jean Paul Gaultier, burlesque performer Dita Von Teese and playwright Tony Kushner. A new cut of the film was shown at Aero Theatre, Santa Monica on Sunday 4 August 2013. *Wilde Salomé* was screened alongside *Salomé*, a full length film version of the recorded sound stage production running for eighty-one minutes (*Wilde Salomé* ran for ninety-six minutes). Pacino was on hand for a discussion after the screening.

A screening of *Salomé & Wilde Salomé* occurred at London's BFI Southbank cinema on 21 September 2014 and both Pacino and Jessica Chastain were in attendance. This double screening was also broadcast via satellite to cinemas around the UK and Ireland. Pacino and Chastain stayed for a Q&A afterwards, hosted by English comedian, writer and presenter Stephen Fry (who played Oscar Wilde in the 1997 movie *Wilde*).

Reviews of *Wilde Salomé* were a mixed bag. *The Guardian* suggested that: "Too much chaos ultimately prevails." *The Hollywood Reporter* commented: "For all its esotericism, the film can count on the star appeal of veteran Pacino and rising star Jessica Chastain." *Empire Magazine* said: "It delivers in fits and starts but mostly baffles." A DVD release of *Salomé & Wilde Salomé* appeared in the UK and Ireland on 24 November 2014. The box set carried one DVD for the film and another for the documentary. It included introductions and interviews from the screening at London's BFI Southbank. Also included is the on-stage Q&A between Fry, Pacino and Chastain.

This double bill of Pacino's pursuit to discover the true meaning of Oscar Wilde's play is filled with both triumphs and tribulations. *Salomé* is a filmed staged production that is small in scale with an equally small cast and a set minimised to several chairs, a stool and two sets of lighting: blue hues and deep reds. The majority of the production is bathed in dark blue light generating a cold atmosphere. It's not until Chastain performs a very sexual dance that the lights alter into a sensual yet dangerous red. This effect emphasises Chastain's red hair, lipstick and billowing red scarf. This was Chastain's first film performance but it's obvious she was destined for stardom based on her acting in *Salomé*.

Initially Chastain's character is portrayed as a woman who has fallen for the wrong man, but her attitude soon changes as the temptress uses her wiles to get what she wants. At one point in the production she hisses vengefully at Pacino's King Herod. Her turn in this picture wouldn't be out of place in a horror movie. Her dance is every bit as seductive as the words Wilde used to describe it. The fast-paced editing makes it seem like we are watching an MTV-style music video from a pop star such as

Madonna or Rihanna. Sex doesn't ooze but rather gushes from the screen as the dance gets more sexual and approaches its climax. When Chastain finishes with her back arched and her breasts on display the camera cuts to Pacino's Herod who sits there on the edge of his seat panting heavily at what he has just witnessed. In that two minute sequence Chastain brought Salomé to life and delivered a thrilling, breakout performance.

Pacino, on the other hand, hoots and hollers his way through the majority of the dialogue. It's clear he has an understanding of what Wilde was addressing in the play. The problem is that the late-90s bellowing Pacino makes a return which doesn't sit well with some of the more serene moments of the play. He is still magnetic to watch but maybe dialling it back slightly would have helped the performance. *Salomé* was shot simply and Pacino has to be praised for making the material easily accessible. It's an engaging merging of play and film that showcases the depth of Wilde's work in an easy to understand format.

Wilde Salomé allows us to peek behind the curtain and learn what it takes to stage not only a reading of the material but also a play, a film and a documentary. The documentary opens with the words: "This is a story about an obsession." Six words fade away and the word "obsession" is left to burn on the screen in deep red. This echoes Pacino's approach to directorial work. He doesn't like to let anything go instead he works on projects for years and years and years. He wants it to be perfect, he wants the vision he can see in his mind to be transposed onto the stage and into the film. He is an obsessive and, in this case, traversed the world in the search for a deeper understanding of Wilde's work.

While in Ireland, he paid a visit to the statue of the famous playwright asking him for inspiration. It's Pacino's own version of kissing The Blarney Stone. *Wilde Salomé* showcases the many different sides to Pacino's personality. We know he is the method actor who wants to understand every single facet of the character he is about to play and that comes across in great detail as he seeks out knowledge from famous fans of Wilde while also discovering the root of Wilde's troubled life and the tragic circumstances around his death. We also see Pacino the comedian as he jokes about his age, the way he puts on his King Herod outfit and as he pretends to play *Scarface* to entertain a group of teenagers. These funny moments keep the documentary enjoyably light. But dark shadows do appear and we also see Pacino the aggressor as he becomes bad-tempered and frustrated in the face of the problems he endured during production and post-production.

This film depicts a man trying to realise his vision and being cut off at almost every turn. His grievances over the editing, however, are well-founded because if you view *Salomé* before *Wilde Salomé* (which is the correct order) then the scenes from the film are played out for far too long in the documentary. Why include, at great length, the same scenes all over again in the documentary? It makes the documentary feel padded out which is odd considering how much behind-the-scenes footage they must have recorded and could have used instead.

As a double feature, *Salomé & Wilde Salomé* showcases Pacino's obsessive desire not only to understand but also adapt a deeply controversial work from a literary giant.

Biographer Lawrence Grobel on *Salomé & Wilde Salomé*

You have known Al Pacino for many years. You have written the <u>only</u> authorized biography about him, which includes many of the interviews you conducted with the actor. As a tie-in with the release of *Salomé & Wilde Salomé* you published a book called: *"I Want You in My Movie!" My Acting Debut and Other Misadventures Filming Al Pacino's Wilde Salomé*. Where did that project start for you?

I had a contract for *"I Want You in My Movie!"* book, powerHouse Books wanted it. Al didn't want me to put it out until the movie came out. I said: "That's not a problem" but the movie, at that time, I thought was ninety five percent finished and I said: "Al, they need a year to put it out anyway so I'll make an agreement with them to not put it out until the movie comes out. At least they will have it ready." That's when we had our big fight/falling out over this. I cancelled the contract. Then when it [the film] didn't come out and it still didn't come out, I said: "You know what, I'm putting it out [the book]." I put it out in 2014. I could have put it out in 2007 or 2008. I waited six years.

How many times did you re-edit the book because of the delay with the film?

Because I kept it on a daily basis I didn't have to edit it up until publish, it was only towards the end you started to see the entries are a year later rather than every three days. There was a lot more about me in it, in the first version. I took myself out more and more just as it happened in the movie. In the movie I was in it thirty-five times. I counted every time you saw me in the movie. The first few versions I was hardly in it. Al says: "I got to get you in there more," and then the next thing I'm in there a lot and Harold Becker [*Sea of Love* director] was joking "The movie gets better the less you are in it" [*laughs*].

There is a scene in the documentary where you are talking to Pacino in the stalls of the theatre that was being used to stage the play. He snapped at you and walked away. Was that him acting? Or was that for real?

Probably did. I got to remember the scene. The funniest one was right in the beginning when, the very first day of filming I go there and I don't know how I'm supposed to be. I had no instructions. He [Pacino] doesn't give me: "I want you to do this. I want you to do that." He says: "Just be yourself. Interrupt me. You can ask me questions any time. If I'm talking to somebody interrupt." Well that's an interesting instruction if you're an actor or a director, like Estelle Parsons who was directing the play, that is kind of obnoxious to see. She doesn't know who I am so I went up and introduced myself. I said: "You know who I am?" she said "You're an actor right?" I said "No, no. I'm Al's friend but he wants me to interrupt him while he is talking to you. So I'm apologising in advance."

He didn't even want me to do that. I brought a tape recorder with me because I figured this is a movie about a play and the making of the play and I'm not in the play. So the only thing I am is a reporter and I'm going to write about it. So I have to act like a reporter which meant taking my tape recorder right?! I figured this out by myself, not by talking to Al. The first day we were in the back of the theatre sitting down, he's sitting down, and I come up to him and I take my tape recorder out and I sit down and he says: "What are you doing with that?" I said: "I'm taping you." He said: "No, you don't need to do that." I said: "I do" and we are getting into an argument about this tape recorder. He said: "We don't need that because we got that," and he points at the camera. That makes sense to me but are we allowing the camera that much into it that we are acknowledging the camera and that we are play acting?! I ignored him and kept trying to tape. He took my tape recorder. He just took it, turned it off and put it in his pocket. I guess he really didn't want me to tape [*laughs*]. Who knew?!

There were moments where things would happen and sometimes if I would ask him a question, and he would walk away. With him you don't know. He's a good actor. You don't know if it's real or him acting. That scene with the tape recorder I still, to this day, do not know if he was acting or if that was real. I don't know [*laughs*]. I'm real the whole time; I'm not acting because I was just being who I was. I was asking questions. I was walking around. You see me in a stupid overcoat... I was wearing this overcoat and my wife and kids hated this coat and they said: "Don't wear the coat," but I liked it because it could hold my tape recorder and hold my notes. It was a big old jacket but when I see it on camera I say: "Holy cow! I look like I weigh three hundred pounds" [*laughs*] it was ridiculous.

Most of the scenes with you wearing the coat were filmed while you and Pacino were in the UK. What was it like being with Pacino during that trip?

When we went to Trinity [college], he is very popular in Ireland, and we would be walking around and there would sometimes be lines of people if they had heard about it, or they would gather. One woman got next to him and I think it was in the newspaper the next day with a picture, and we saw her the next day and she screamed: "I'M FAMOUS! I'M FAMOUS." It was like she had gone crazy. The funniest one is the one I included in the book which was when we were in an elevator in Dublin and someone said to Al: "You going to hit some pubs?" and he says: "No. I don't drink" and she just looked at him like: 'you're a bit of a pussy aren't you' and I think she called him something [laughs] it was funny. One kid comes up and wanted his father to meet him, and he [the father] said to him: "Oh you're not as tall as I thought you were."

People generally insult him without realising it. I don't know if it was in Paris or in London but there was a piano player and we walked in and he starts playing *The Godfather* theme. We try to be inconspicuous and all of a sudden DA-DA-DA-DA-DA-DA-DUM and everybody starts turning around [*laughs*]. It happened but it wasn't as much as I've seen here in the [United] States. The most I've ever seen here is when we would take walks into Beverly Hills, I think I describe that in the book, and we are crossing the street – and he lived only two blocks away from the main Rodeo Drive area – and for some reason [they] would go crazy and traffic would come to a halt because we were walking and cameras would be pulled out. I would say: "Why don't we call you a driver to come get us?" and he would say "No. Once we cross the next street we will be OK." It was like animals in a cage in a way. Don't cross that street and go up into that neighbourhood. And he was right. Very few people would stop by. The crowds stopped once we got out of Beverly Hills proper. I've seen a lot of that stuff.

In the Beverly Wilshire Hotel we would be having tea or a sandwich and a woman would come up and wouldn't leave him alone. He tried to be nice but after a while it would be: "excuse me I'm talking to a friend." It's not fun being recognised all the time. They get used to it. That kind of fame, I never craved because I had been around it and seen that it is uncomfortable. You really do feel trapped. You can't do certain things. One time we were walking down the street and a woman must have jumped out of a car, I think she wanted to give him a DVD or something, and she was wearing very soft shoes because we didn't hear her coming and she just came from behind and tapped him on the shoulder. He jumped. He really got scared. The woman was like: "Oh I'm sorry. You're my favourite actor." She wants to give him this thing, so I took it and said: "Thank you very much." You have to be a little scared about those things.

You saw the New York and Los Angeles stage productions of *Salomé*. Did they differ at all?

He did two things in New York. One was a reading, which he also did at the Wadsworth [Theatre, Los Angeles] as well. A reading is basically where the actors, although they mostly know the material, they have stands where they can place the script in front of them so the play is there and they are not in costume. But they are acting. They are reading the play in their voices. That's an interesting idea to see but it's not as fulfilling as to see an actual play with people in costume, moving around and stuff. It's like being an insider. In a sense you are paying a lot of money to just to see how actors prepare. Also at the reading you can stop in the middle... you can direct a little too. You are watching a behind the scenes kind of thing, but in public. Then he did it in costume in New York and that was good. I think it was Marisa Tomei in New York...

Yes, it was.

They were different. When he [Pacino] found Jessica [Chastain], and it was Marthe Keller who was the one who recommended Jessica, he really felt she had something and he was right because look what happened to her career. But where his mistake was, he didn't get this out first so he could have actually claimed to have discovered her. It still hasn't come out in the States. Nobody has seen Jessica in this thing. When he did it here [in Los Angeles] and it was a reading and then they got more into costume and it became more of the play. When we went to the desert and started doing it there, he hired other people to be Herod and Salomé. That was all part of his vision. I've seen it in different versions. It's hard to say one is better than another. I've seen like thirty-five different versions of the movie. What is the best version?

Well there were certain versions where the talking heads were put into black and white. I didn't like that. I felt it was distracting – I'm watching it in colour and there here is Gore Vidal or here is Tom Stoppard in black and white. I didn't like that. All along the way I got to give my two cents. I always told him what I thought. We argued a lot about stuff. The thing about *Salome* is just that he loved the words. He saw Berkoff [in the play] and he loved the language of it. He wanted to be able to play with those words himself. That's what I always liked most about Al. He loved Shakespeare. He loved Heathcote Williams. He loved Bertolt Brecht and Mamet. These were the people whose writings that he enjoyed saying the words. Remember he is not an educated man, so I think this thrilled him. That he could present difficult concepts, words that weren't always easy to say and say them in such a way as to make you believe in them and it gave him pleasure. That's what I respect the most about Al – the artistry. It wasn't ever about money for him.

The film is split into two parts: the play and the documentary. Do you remember when you first saw it in two parts?

I never saw it in two parts. The split happened in England. You tell me, what you saw is it the play and then the full documentary?

It is the play on one DVD and then the documentary on another DVD.

I have never seen it. I've seen thirty-five versions and it's always been the documentary – the docu-drama. The play I never saw it on disc as one play and I never understood why he would do that. Does it work more? I don't know. The docu-drama, I think, ended up running at eighty-nine to ninety minutes. That was what was to be released here. So, this [split] was a last minute decision about putting it out as a two disc. That's his ego, that's the actor's ego in there. Do you feel you could sit through both being a huge Pacino fan? Or would just the docu-drama suffice? Or would you rather just see the play?

I have watched both. But I would happily watch the docu-drama again. The play, not so much.

Not having seen it because the DVD is not available here, there should be outtakes. There were some great scenes in there and it's in my book. So when he is doing Spartacus as Kirk Douglas, he loved those scenes. I thought they were ridiculous but I thought they would be good outtakes. Our time in Las Vegas... there were some great outtakes in Las Vegas. On the aeroplane where I'm wearing the [*Scarface*] shirt and he goes: "What the fuck are you doing?" There are funny outtakes in there. I always thought that would be the way to go, you show the docu-drama and then you have about thirty minutes of outtakes that people would enjoy seeing. I don't know what happened with it. Barry [Navidi] keeps telling me it is going to be released here but it has never been released. It's ridiculous, I'm in a movie and I've never seen it [*laughs*].

Do you think Pacino is still tinkering with it now and that's why it hasn't had a U.S. release?

I don't think so. I just think it's a distribution thing. Originally Arclight was going to be doing it and then Sony Classics had it for a bit. I'd write to Barry about it and he would say: "Oh yeah, it's going to be in December or this or that." I think he doesn't want to be reminded of it anymore. He raised about a million and half dollars himself and then Al put in another million/million and a half. I think the total of that film was like four million dollars. It is a lot of money for a vanity project basically. He is an interesting character is Al. You look at *The Local Stigmatic*, you look at *Chinese Coffee* and *Looking for Richard* and all of them took four years, five years and this thing is now taking... well you have it but it's not been released here. But until it's had some kind of viewing... he showed it up at San Francisco at an event. It's bizarre.

I love the ending of the docu-drama where you are all in the screening room and Al just walks out because he has no idea what to make of it. I think it should have ended there with Al walking out and the door closing behind him. However it continues onto the desert where he is walking around with a camel while looking confused. Do you think the desert scenes work?

Norton was the name of the camel in that [*laughs*]. I think I took a great shot of him walking with that camel. It's on the front of the book. Just that whole ending scene... the day he wanted to shoot the idea of sitting in that little screening room, he said: "I want everyone to compliment the movie. Larry, you tell me what you think. Just say something like it needs work." That's all he said. He has cameras set up and we watch a quick clip of the movie and then they are saying: "Gold! Gold!" and I said: "It may be Gold Al but its fool's gold" [*laughs*]. He jumped up... he screamed: "GOD DAMN IT! WHO THE FUCK DO YOU THINK YOU ARE?" It was really shocking. None of us knew what he was going to do. He jumped up and stormed out.

He yelled at all of us and then said: "Let's go to the desert" [*laughs*]. That was the first take and then he came back and said: "Got you guys didn't

I?" [*Laughs*]. I never did it twice. I always came up with a different line. Then I would lean forward and say: "It doesn't work Al. The play works but movie doesn't" and then he would go: "I know." Each time he did something different and I did something different. The other guys all did the same thing "Looks like gold, Al." The same thing over and over. One time I made him laugh, I said something that cracked him up. We did about eight or ten takes. I don't even know what one he used and I don't know if you can even hear what I said.

No, it does not have your line in it. It shows you leaning forward and it is pretty obvious you have said something to him, but the cut is between you leaning forward and him getting out of his chair.

There are a number of things missing, like the time in the train. I went to Harrods because he wanted to get a hold of *The Ballad of Reading Gaol*. We, Barry and I, went to the bookstore upstairs at Harrods and we got the collected works of Oscar Wilde and we meet Al back in the car and we go off to the train. We get the train and he says: "Read it to me." I'd never read it before, it's not an easy thing to read, but I started to read it and Barry started to film it. No rehearsals and no indication that Barry was going to film and it was crazy. It was totally crazy. I really got into reading it, I read the whole thing. Then we got to Paris, he said: "That's the best part of the movie. You reading it and me listening." He never read the poem, I did. We get back and we can't wait to see it and we watch it. You would think you would hear my voice and then sort of see me start reading so you would know who it was and then it would go to him. But by the time the movie is ready he is doing the whole reading. He is looking out the window and he is reading the whole thing. [In one version] you hear me reading it and then it goes into his voice. Is that how it is in the movie?

No. I would not have known you were on the train unless I'd have read your book beforehand.

Right... right... I read the whole thing. It was so funny [*laughs*]. I got thrown out of more and more scenes, but scenes I should have been in.

The same thing with the ending where you don't hear what I say. You should hear something like: "It's not working" but by this time he was pissed off with me about the book so probably took as much out as he could [*laughs*]. He couldn't get me out of the whole movie because I'm in too many scenes but I think he tried to remove a lot of it. That's just what happened. But yes, when he storms off it could easily have been the end of the movie. But I need to see the cut you have. I thought I saw it. I went to see a screening of it. He was there and I was sitting at the back and he came over and we talked for a while about it. As far as I was aware that was it.

But the desert... it cost a lot of money to go there and have all those people. He had that in his mind the whole way and that was part of his vision, just like he had Las Vegas. He originally thought the ending would have Tom Jones singing 'It's Not Unusual.' He saw that as the ending of the movie. We were in Vegas and he saw that as the end of the movie [*laughs*]. That didn't happen. I also remember the ending that I liked and I don't think it's in the movie either. We are standing in the desert and he is facing us... he had us lined up, I was in one corner then there was Barry two or three people further down. There were a lot of the extras about but we had to be upfront and we had about four or five of us, the main characters from behind the scenes, and the camera went from one of us to the other. So you saw all of our faces. Then it turned around and went back to Al. He is looking at us. That was how it was ending and it was going to be a fade out. I liked the idea of going back to the Thames in London and you have Oscar Wilde's words from one of his poems... it was very moving piece... and Al read that and I thought that was the way it was ended. It was quite powerful.

Also, the way I wanted to end it was I wanted to go to Oscar Wilde's grave. We were there, we should have done it. I wanted it to end with a shot of the grave with him talking over it. But we never shot that. [The film is] about a frustration trying to get this right and it is never getting right in his mind and he will go to this extreme with the camel and he is still trying to figure it out. In the end he doesn't figure it out. I think that is what he was trying to say.

The Humbling

Cast: Al Pacino (Simon Axler), Greta Gerwig (Pegeen Stapleford), Nina Arianda (Sybil), Dylan Baker (Dr. Farr), Charles Grodin (Jerry), Dan Hedaya (Asa), Dianne Wiest (Carol), Billy Porter (Prince), Kyra Sedgwick (Louise Trenner), Lance Roberts (Walter). **Director:** Barry Levinson.

Synopsis: Ageing, suicidal stage actor Simon Axler struggles to find a passion for life again. Near his breaking point, he finds motivation in the form of a young and lustful lesbian, Pegeen Stapleford, who has had a crush on Simon since childhood. As their relationship heats up, Simon has a hard time keeping up with the exuberant Pegeen. He feels more alive than ever before but with many disapproving people protesting their relationship, Simon must decide where his true passion lies.

By the time Philip Roth released his novel *The Humbling* in 2009 he had previously published twenty-nine other fictional works. He had also received numerous literary awards including three PEN/Faulkner Awards, two National Book Awards for Fiction and a Pulitzer Prize.

When *The Humbling* was released in the autumn it was met with indifferent reviews. Some of which suggested it was a badly misjudged piece from the award-winning novelist. One person who disagreed with the critics was actor Al Pacino, who had been given the book by his agent. Pacino immediately identified with the character of Simon Axler: "A book about an actor going downhill and losing it and getting older and falling apart seemed very appropriate for me. I thought 'this is going to work.'"

Pacino optioned the book to be made into a movie and around the same time was invited, as a guest, to the Rome Film Fest in New York. Wandering the rooms at a party he came into contact with Roth and decided to talk to him about his decision to purchase the movie rights. Pacino recalls: "I didn't know what to do so I just said: 'I'm a real admirer and my name is Al Pacino,' and he stood up and said 'I know who you are.' I said 'I just love the book, and it's funny too.' WOAH! I went too far. He just looked at me and said: 'It's not funny.'"

When looking for someone to direct the project, Pacino turned to a director he trusted: Barry Levinson. Who knew Pacino through co-writing the movie *...and justice for all*, and more recently through shooting with the star on the HBO TV movie *You Don't Know Jack*. Levinson recalls why he accepted the job as director: "Al Pacino asked me to read it. In talking we discovered that we shared the same interest in the book, and the tone of the film came to us very naturally." Pacino and Levinson felt the movie needed more humour than Roth had included in his book and needed a script writer who could inject just the right level of humour, without making it a full-blown comedy. A suggestion from Pacino's agent led him to Buck Henry, legendary screenwriter of *The Graduate*, *What's Up, Doc?* and *Get Smart* the TV series. "Buck can't help himself. That wit runs right through him," commented Pacino.

Henry, along with screenwriting newcomer Michal Zebede, adapted Roth's novel into a screenplay for Pacino and Levinson that included more humour and less hardcore eroticism. It was a long process for Henry and Zebede as they sought a happy medium that stayed true to the novel, yet removed the more meandering thoughts of the character. Levinson explained: "A book and a film are very different works and the difficulty is to successfully maintain the essence of the first in the second." Finance for the film came from Levinson's Baltimore Pictures and Dubinmedia, a U.S. based production company. Pacino and Levinson wanted to keep the budget very low in order to give it the look and style of a small indie movie. CEO of Dubinmedia Kristina Dubin commented: "We made sure that the budget is sufficient to make a film of this quality while remaining reasonable." A budget of just $2 million was set. All that was left was to find somebody to play opposite Pacino in the role of Pegeen. Levinson chose Greta Gerwig, commenting: "We were not looking for a glamorous actress. We did not want a classic love story. Greta is a kind of chameleon, which works well for the character." Gerwig received an email from her agent about the project. Thinking she had hallucinated the email Gerwig read it again and noted the cast. She immediately wanted to read for the part and was summoned to Levinson's office where she read a couple of scenes. Without hesitation Levinson offered her the role and she signed on. Four days later Gerwig was on set acting opposite Pacino.

Principal photography was a guerrilla shoot over the course of twenty non-consecutive days starting in October 2013 and finishing during December. Scenes had to be shot around Pacino's schedule so Levinson and his crew had to be ready to film at a day's notice. Fortunately, production was confined to only a handful of locations. Most notably in the director's real house in Redding, Connecticut, where most of the film was shot. It had everything production needed including the outdoor swimming pool at the rear. One other location used for numerous scenes was the St. George Theatre on New York's Staten Island. Filming took place throughout most of the theatre and Wayne Miller, the theatre's executive director, watched some of the scenes being filmed including a big on-stage confrontation involving Pacino. He said: "I don't think the guy knows how to blink. It was as if he had lasers in his eyes." Filming wrapped before the end of the 2013, and the director was particularly impressed with the chemistry between his two leading actors: "They had never worked together before, but they had no trouble finding their rhythm on set because they stimulate one another."

At the start of February 2014 an announcement was made that Millennium Films had purchased the worldwide rights to *The Humbling* but no release date was set. It did however receive its world premiere at the 71st Venice Film Festival on the evening of 30 August. The film was then screened at several film festivals around the globe including Toronto, Rio de Janeiro and Stockholm. It also appeared on home turf at the Savannah, Virginia and Palm Springs film festivals. The critical consensus veered wildly. *Rolling Stone* thought it was Pacino's finest performance in years: "He's a daredevil going full throttle. To watch him do it is a master class." *Variety* were also taken with the performances but not so much the film saying: "Fronted by a vibrant, deeply committed Al Pacino performance and very fine support from Greta Gerwig, this uneven but captivating film deserves to find its own audience." Rex Reed in the *New York Observer* simply stated: "Be forewarned: It is dreadful."

A full nationwide theatrical release never materialized. Instead it received a limited release in a handful of U.S. and Canadian theatres for just a few days to make it eligible for Oscar season. Not that it bothered The Academy; the film was thrown out via U.S. video on demand streaming services on 23 January 2015 and a DVD release followed on 3 March. *The Humbling* only saw a full theatrical release in nine countries and the box office returns were abysmal. The two highest totals came from Spain ($223,000) and Turkey ($53,919) (Information courtesy of Box Office Mojo. Used with permission). In the UK it received a DVD release on 4 May, and the title was changed to *The Last Act* (a reference to the finale in the book which was also called The Last Act). Robbie Collins from *The Telegraph* summed up its release schedule as well as the film itself: "*The Humbling* is such inept, shuffling nonsense that an apter title might have been The Bumbling."

Arguably, Axler, Pacino's role in the movie is the character that most resembles the behind-the-scenes, real-life Pacino. The character struggles to understand the role he is playing on and off stage even at this late stage of his life. He questions everything and doesn't truly trust anybody, especially his agent. As he tries to stay motivated about acting in his play he looks out into the audience to see a man using his phone, a woman reading the programme while nonchalantly looking at him over the top of it. All of this and more has happened to Pacino when he has been on stage performing (famously he was on stage in London during the 1980s and a woman walked up to the front and asked him: "Got a light?" for her cigarette). Axler's tired attitude to all things acting is juxtaposed with his enthusiastic demeanour when he's in the company of Pegeen. There is life in the old dog yet it seems.

However, even this opportunity comes with its own complications as Axler struggles to understand modern-day sexuality. One thing Axler hasn't lost is his sense of sarcasm. His dead pan replies to some of Pegeen's outlandish statements are brutally funny. One such moment is when a back injury leaves Axler slowly shuffling around the house bent over in pain. He brings two champagne glasses on a tray to the bedroom and Pegeen asks: "Oh dear! Is your back still hurting?" To which he sarcastically replies: "No dear, no.... it is going to pass." She fires back with: "Is this how you play Richard III?" His responds: "No this is Igor in Old Frankenstein."

Levinson's direction reins Pacino in throughout, allowing him just the briefest moment right at the end of the film to let loose at full volume. For the rest of the time, his performance is subdued as he portrays a man who is consumed by the dizziness of the fast-paced modern-day. He shuffles around in ill-fitting clothes and with wild, bushy hair while Gerwig gives a rousing performance as Pegeen. Dominating Axler like a true alpha, she barks commands and knows once that first kiss has sunk in that she has Axler wrapped around her little finger. Her sexuality and promiscuousness is what, at first, turns Axler on but as their relationship progresses it soon becomes a metaphoric noose around his neck, tightening the more she demands of him even though he isn't physically able to perform. Gerwig doesn't instantly ooze sex appeal in the role but over time becomes an alluring beauty due to her bravado. It is a performance that demands authority from the character and Gerwig brings that throughout.

It is also a pleasure to see Charles Grodin in a dry comedic role as Axler's agent. His sharp tongue combines wonderfully with some very sarcastic comments, the best being the moment in which Axler is trying to kill himself on stage during a performance of King Lear, and Grodin turns to the sound guy, proclaiming: "This is genius!"

Overall, *The Humbling* is a darkly comedic tale about sexuality and acting in the modern age.

Actor Lance Roberts on *The Humbling*

What was your audition process like?

Interestingly enough, I auditioned for another role in the film, but they cast me as Walter, the orderly. My first day on the picture, I was added to a scene as Simon was being released by his doctor, played by Dylan Baker. I looked at the pages that day to see if there was any stage business that I needed to be familiar [with]. While filming, I noticed that Mr. Pacino was saying everything that was on the page, but also adding some other interesting bits. They were all things that his character would say. My one-on-one scene with him was to be filmed on another day, so I decided to find out as much information as I could about this Walter. I found the initial email from my agents which had a description of Walter. The main thing that jumped out at me was that he was described as Simon's #1 fan! That fueled me with so much back story. It was easy for me to play that as I am also a big fan of Al Pacino's dating back to *Dog Day Afternoon* and *Serpico*.

Did discovering the back story to Walter help when filming your scenes?

I only had about 3 or 4 lines in the scene as written, but just like the scene with Dylan Baker, Al Pacino started adding lines. For a second, I panicked and then in the next second, I just reminded myself that I was Simon's #1 fan and I started improvising with Al Pacino. For every ball he threw, I was there and ready to catch. I ended up with like 10 lines!

What was it like working with Pacino?

The genius of Al is that he said all of the written lines, so cues could be picked up, but he made the scene so much more alive and immediate by adding the additional dialogue. When our director, Barry Levinson yelled: "Cut. Print", I was on cloud nine! We shot the scene in one take!!!! I wanted to chat Al up after the scene, but I had to do a couple of close-ups of my hand knocking on the door and by the time I was done, he was already in a deep conversation with Barry about his next scene and they released me for the night.

What did you think to the finished film?

I got to see a screening of the film where Al did a talk back after. I still couldn't get to him. When I watched my scene on the big screen, I was waiting to hear all of the new dialogue that we had added, but the way it was edited, it ended up being almost exactly what was on the page from the beginning. It was still a thrill as I watched my face magnified in a two shot with an Academy Award winning legend.

As an actor yourself, do you identify with what Simon Axler is going through in the movie?

As an actor, I am faced with many dilemmas, very much like Simon's, but on a smaller scale. Each role, you wonder whether you will succeed. When the role, or even the audition, is getting the best of you, wonder if you should just stop, disappear and look at your posters, playbills and residual checks. But then you try and figure out what else would you do and none of the options fills your soul as much as being a performer, so you stay. Sometimes you win and sometimes you fail, but you try your best, so that if you fail, you fail gloriously and look to the next challenge. You think about how long a career people like Al Pacino have had and yet they are still hungry. You want to be like that.

Manglehorn

Cast: Al Pacino (A.J. Manglehorn), Holly Hunter (Dawn), Harmony Korine (Gary), Chris Messina (Jacob), Skylar Gasper (Kylie), Brian Mays (Carl), Herc Trevino (Robbie), Angela Woods (Steve), Marisa Varela (Patricia). **Director:** David Gordon Green.

Synopsis: A.J. Manglehorn is an ageing, ex-con locksmith who has loved, lost and has disconnected from his life for good. Bitterly disenchanted and alone, he stubbornly refuses to let go of the past, even once he meets Dawn and has the opportunity for a new beginning. But while he might be finished with life he soon finds out life hasn't finished with him just yet.

Every year billions of people around the world tune in to watch the American Football final. The 2012 final – New York Giants vs New England Patriots - was the most-watched programme in American television history with an average audience of 111.3 million US viewers. It is not just the sports teams that viewers tune in to watch. The halftime show featuring legendary music acts has now become almost essential viewing.

During the commercial breaks, taking advantage of the huge audience, big companies often launch their new products. A thirty second advert during the half time of Super Bowl XLVI cost $3.5 million but that price tag didn't deter Fiat Chrysler Automobiles buying a two minute time slot to air their "Halftime in America" advertisement. It was narrated by and featured Clint Eastwood, who growls his way through the sparse dialogue about how America gets back up again after being knocked down and "the world's going to hear the roar of our engines." It delivered a powerful message to the millions watching. The advert was orchestrated by Wieden+Kennedy advertising agency and American director David Gordon Green but Eastwood wasn't Green's first choice for the commercial. His first choice was Al Pacino.

Sitting across a boardroom table from each other months earlier, Green and his team tried to persuade Pacino, and his agents, that making this commercial would be a good move. As the minutes ticked by the agents, mangers and hangers-on started to leave the room. Eventually the only people left were Green and Pacino. Pacing around the boardroom trying to find the character in the advert, Pacino began to mutter under his breath as he struggled with the decision. In those moments something sparked Green's imagination: "I just started seeing this character I wanted him to play that pulled from elements of Al's life and characters of his that I loved growing up." Green told Pacino not to do the commercial; instead he wanted to make a movie with him. Pacino replied: "I love it!" Hence why Eastwood was cast in the Chrysler Super Bowl commercial instead.

On the plane ride home, Green started to write down notes for his untitled Al Pacino movie. He recalled being enthralled by Pacino's early work such as *The Panic in Needle Park*, *Scarecrow*, *Serpico* and *The Godfather*, and began to write what was almost a love-letter to the many versions of Pacino he'd witnessed on screen. He also remembered a conversation he had with a man in his seventies at the Nantucket Film Festival a few years previously: "Here was this man talking about the regrets of his life and having left the love of his life. He became extremely successful, but was never happy. So I took that to heart and blended the two ideas," (this was the official line, however it turned out to be an actor friend of Green's who shared that story with him). Green had also thought of a title for the movie – *Manglehorn*. The title was inspired by a discussion he had with a friend several months earlier while fleeing a hurricane during the filming of the TV series *Eastbound and Down*. Finding himself lost in Teachey, North Carolina Green called up his friend and told him where he was. When his buddy came to pick him up, Green asked him: "Who's Mangle Horn?" His friend explained: "Some guy that used to live down that street a long time ago. Crazy Old Mangle Horn."

Back home in Austin, Texas David Gordon Green spoke to his next door neighbour, Paul Logan, about his Manglehorn idea. Logan had been trying to break into screenwriting for a couple of years after previously writing a ten minute short to accompany a music video. He had also been the talent driver on Green's movie *Prince Avalanche* starring Paul Rudd and Emile Hirsch. Green knew Logan was a massive Pacino fan and so offered the first-time scriptwriter a job: "I said, 'Why don't you take a stab at this for Al?'" Logan produced an eighty-five page script in two weeks while on a European tour with the band Explosions in the Sky. He mailed it back to Green who held off sending it to Pacino, believing it wasn't quite ready. Over the course of several months, the writer and director tinkered with the script. It was only when Green was in post-production on his movie *Joe* that he felt the script for *Manglehorn* was ready to send to Pacino. Summoned to Los Angeles, Pacino said to Green: "I read it and thought, 'What the hell did he see in that boardroom to think of me for this?'" They sat and talked about the film and Pacino liked the idea of doing a character piece that was based on his own life and work: "It was literally the quickest I've ever had an actor read a script and say yes. Ever."

After Pacino agreed to star in the film he wanted to workshop the script before going into pre-production. Consequently, Green flew from Texas to L.A. every four to six weeks for a few months to watch Pacino, and a group of his friends, read it out loud and make notes. Green would then take the notes back to Logan so he could tweak the script accordingly. With a Pacino-approved script in place and a budget of $4 million rolling in from Worldview Entertainment (who had previously financed *Joe*) Green could focus on casting the roles of the main characters. Holly Hunter signed on to play Dawn, Manglehorn's friend-cum-love interest. Chris Messina bagged the role of A.J.'s son, Jacob Manglehorn. Messina's time at the Actors Studio brought him into close contact with Pacino through the productions of *Salome* and *Oedipus*: "I used to have posters of him on my wall when I was a kid – he was my hero. There were a couple of times I had to stop and go: 'That's Al Pacino.'"

Provocative actor/writer/director Harmony Korine joined the cast as Gary, an ex-student of Manglehorn's. Green was in touch with Korine via email and wrote: "Answer this question, would you be interested in acting in a movie with Al Pacino?" Korine came back with "sounds dope." The most important casting, after Pacino, was that of A.J. Manglehorn's cat: Fanny. Amazing Animal Productions brought in two fluffy, white, doll-face Persian cats called Prince and Cinderella to play the role.

Principal photography began on 4 November 2013 in Austin, Texas. The majority of the filming locations were around the neighbourhood in which Green lived so he could walk to work each day. Green and his location manager Richard A Wright decided on a location for Manglehorn's house that was just a block away from Green's home: "We were looking for that retirement house that you would never notice on the street. When we found the house we said: 'Yeah, that's exactly where he [Manglehorn] lives.'" The private residence was transformed into Manglehorn's dark, dusty house. Pacino visited the house before production, set foot in it and offered some suggestions as to how the setting might reflect the character.

Production placed a mailbox outside the residence for the scene featuring Manglehorn removing letters from a bee covered mailbox. Local Texas beekeepers spent a week collecting over a thousand male drone bees because they have no stingers. On the day of the shoot the neighbourhood bees all swarmed over the hive along with the drones. Green asked Pacino's stand-in Ted Ferguson to film the scene as it was only going to show Manglehorn's hands. The first take went off without Ferguson getting stung however Green felt it wasn't quite right and asked for another take. Cinematographer Tim Orr recalls what happened next: "You feel bad asking him to do it again, but we really had to have it, and of course that's when he definitely got stung."

Another private residence was used for Dawn's apartment. Hunter visited the premise before set decorators added their props: "I wanted it to have life – things are alive. It's a place that someone who loves and enjoys spending time there and throws open the shades in the morning." The crew filled the apartment with plants, fish, pictures, and a dog. They tiled the bathroom in yellow and black tiles giving it a "bumblebee" theme. The Tan Man Salon was also a private residence, a house that had a layout like a race circuit that production transformed into a Day-Glo Salon-cum-Brothel. Production moved on to the Sharp Brothers Locksmith premise at 507 W Mary St. This location would serve as

Manglehorn's key-cutting business. Phil Sharp, one of the owners, gave Pacino a tutorial to on how to cut keys. Production painted over the Sharp Brothers exterior signage with their own sign designed by Green's father, who used to be a sign painter. After shooting had finished at the Sharp Brothers Locksmith, they kept the stylings the film crew had put in place and created a brand new logo that closely resembled that of Green Sr.'s work for the film.

Each day, come quitting time Green and the main cast would eat out at a local restaurant. There, they would discuss the next day's scripted pages. Talk always turned to Pacino and his life in films: "We'd talk about *Serpico* and *Dog Day [Afternoon]*, and he'd tell amazing stories about when he first met Brando on the set of *The Godfather*," said Messina.

Exterior filming took place in the Hyde Park, North Shoal Creek and Bouldin Creek areas and on Weir Ranch Road in Georgetown. Further street locations included in front of Burnet Middle School, the old 2205 Hair Salon on Ohlen Road and on El Paso Street. During exterior filming Pacino was often found sitting in a chair on the street, happily reading the local newspaper or chatting to anybody who walked by. He would also work on some of the letters that Manglehorn was sending to Clara, sometimes going as far as writing whole letters. When finished he would collar one of the sound guys and go off to record voice overs: "The more I learned about who I was in that part, the more the letters just came out," said Pacino.

Numerous other locations were used such as the Austin Animal Clinic where Fanny's operation was filmed and Luby's Cafeteria in East Oltorf in which the big date scene between Manglehorn and Dawn was shot. A former Elks Lodge was also transformed into a dark casino with working slot machines and Paul Logan was invited to be a background artist in the scene. Sitting around, waiting for Green to call them to their markers, Logan and some of the other actors were chatting: "We were talking about Al Pacino, and Al was doing a scene with him [an extra], and the guy said, 'oh I don't know if I'd be able to do a line around Al Pacino.' One of the guys in the crew went up and told him: 'You know, you've been sitting next to Al Pacino'" Logan recalled. Principal photography wrapped in mid-December.

Green and his long-time editor Colin Patton then had to find the right cut of the film. They assembled over eighty different versions. Eventually they settled on one with an ending that wasn't scripted. One that Green had decided to shoot during an afternoon's downtime on set while waiting for the sun to drop for evening filming. It turned out to be the perfect fit for the finale. Other footage shot but ultimately cut from Green's final version included a massacre at the Bank and an earthquake that spurred Clara to return to Manglehorn. The soundtrack turned out to be an easy box to tick as Logan had been on tour with Explosions in the Sky and that made it easy for Green to ask the band, and David Wingo, to score *Manglehorn*.

The film received its world premiere on 30 August 2014 at the 71st Venice International Film Festival. The film played In Competition but lost out to the Swedish movie *A Pigeon Sat on a Branch Reflecting on Existence*. *Manglehorn* then went on to the festival circuit playing at world renowned festivals such as Toronto, Zurich, Stockholm, Istanbul, Beijing, Edinburgh and many others. It also played at South by Southwest Film Festival in Green's home town of Austin, Texas. It wasn't until late October 2014 however, that IFC Films picked up the film for distribution. A limited U.S. theatrical and full VOD release was announced for 19 June 2015.

Critics found very little to rave about in their reviews. *The New York Times* saw a "peculiar brand of soulful jive" to Pacino's performance. *Variety* said: "this pic feels as scruffy and dishevelled as its subject." *The Hollywood Reporter* called Logan's script "ham-fisted" and suggested the film was a "wrong turn" for Green. In its first week on release, it only played in three theatres and grossed a paltry $17,887. The next three weeks did see it play on nineteen, twenty-seven and twenty-six screens respectively. But by the end of its four-week U.S. theatrical run it had only pulled in $12,930 (Information courtesy of Box Office Mojo. Used with permission). And didn't fare much better in other territories. *Manglehorn* was never, realistically, going to trouble the box office and

Green knew this when he first set out to make it: "It's pretty difficult to sell it [a movie] to an audience, these days, to come to the theatre."

Manglehorn was the first truly art-house movie Pacino had been involved since *Bobby Deerfield* but the film doesn't particularly gel with Pacino's method acting. The storyline has many different beats going on for A.J. Manglehorn. All of them intertwine and then separate over and over again. Clara's story is probably the most intriguing, and at times feels like it could develop into a horror movie. This is where Pacino is at his best in the film, wandering around with a long-lost love percolating in his mind. He mentally flogs himself everyday with images and memories of this person from his past. Slowly growling his way through scenes, with Manglehorn Pacino conveys a character who might as well be a ghost. He drifts in and out without anybody remembering he had been there. He awkwardly peers over the top of his small hexagonal glasses. Never looking anyone in the eyes until his final sentence when he's walking away.

Manglehorn is a character who has something to hide and there are stories to tell behind those weary eyes. Yet on the surface, he trudges on, cutting keys, taking care of his cat and depositing cheques. Pacino gives a subtle performance that is pivotal to the character. There is also some sterling work between Pacino and Messina as father and son. Despite the resentment between the pair there is an understanding and a love for each other deep down. Even though times have moved on for both of them and they no longer relate as well as they used to. Messina boldly takes on the challenge of acting alongside Pacino with an aggressive performance, conveying a less than likeable character. It is only with their final meeting that we begin to understand the baggage Manglehorn Jr. is carrying because of his father.

The later life romance story between Pacino and Hunter is sweet and would warm the heart of even the most cynical of people. Dawn quietly watches Manglehorn as he twists himself into knots trying to express his true feelings. The scene in the dining hall is a perfect example of two great actors taking scripted dialogue and making it feel very personal.

The film struggles, and so too does Pacino, when the picture veers too far into art-house territory - the car crash, the bee nest and the dual-voiced scene in the tanning salon, grate against the storyline. At first they come across as bizarre, nonsensical little segments but pretty quickly these obvious metaphors are slapping the camera so hard they are in danger of breaking through the screen at any moment. Subtlety is not a strong suit in the movie. Green directs with a woozy, wandering camera that at times becomes frustrating to watch. Pacino occasionally struggles to convey the inner turmoil that Manglehorn clutches on to. He is holding on to that pain too long and very rarely releases his twisted feelings.

This film may well be billed as a cautionary tale of one man's lost obsession but actually the most resounding message is that Manglehorn is simply a crazy cat man. There are usually fascinating stories behind these oddball characters, but Green opts to keep everyone guessing as to what the mystery is with the title character and as such said character is never fully realised.

Manglehorn strives to create a snapshot of a life already lived, yet the dots are not fully connected between the script, the direction and the acting. This leaves the viewer in search of something more than just a piece written about Pacino, for Pacino.

Actor Ted Ferguson on *Manglehorn*

How did you go from being a radio programme manager to acting opposite Al Pacino?

This is a journey just like everything else is. Naturally, radio is a base for acting. Particularly if you're allowed to do a bit of improv because you click a mic and roll. The nemesis of being in radio is that radio is the theatre of the mind. So you have a tendency to over-pronounce, to be more dramatic because you don't have the benefit of pictures. What you wind up doing is, what we call, face acting with a lot of eyebrow crap and stuff like that. What you want at the back of your mind when you are overacting is you want them to get it. Do you get that I'm happy? Do you get that I'm sad? With a camera on you all the time they are going to get it. So you have to learn to back off.

What's been a nemesis for me for forever is overacting. It's not necessarily overacting, it's what the casting director perceives as overacting because a lot of these guys... when I am in front of certain casting directors I know that they are known for being real sticklers for that. So you back it way up and really underplay it to get cast. There are times when you do a particular read for an audition and you feel like you did a good enough read for the role and you still don't get the role.

What I did, I was in radio for all those years and then I retired from radio in 1999 and I went back to school at Louisiana State University in 2005 just for kicks. I moved down from Baton Rouge to Shreveport. Lived in the college housing. Took a full-time load for two semesters and got into an improv class, which I had always wanted to do anyway. They were shooting a film on campus and I saw the extras standing around and thought: well I could do that just for fun, just to see how it went.

After Katrina all the stuff that was shooting in New Orleans came to Shreveport. Consequently what happened was I found out who was casting extras, called them up and said I'd like to do it. They put me in one of the Kevin Costner movies [*Mr. Brooks*] and then they put me in *Blonde Ambition* with Jessica Simpson. By then I had already gone to an agent in Shreveport and at that time, eleven years ago, it was real easy to pick up an agent. There wasn't everybody and his brother wanting to be an actor. Now you can't do that, they won't accept people with no experience because there is too many people wanting to do it.

They cast me as a priest in *Blonde Ambition*, there were four priests and Jessica Simpson was there and Luke Wilson was there. So the way I did it was... they were Norwegian priests and I knew that Norwegian and Swedish were the same language so I called the Swedish embassy and got the whole scene translated into Swedish. So when I got on set there were two priests that were going to be speaking and two that weren't. I told the extras casting director that I could do the dialogue in Norwegian if need be. That impressed the director so I got the other speaking role. That's how I got into acting.

How did you get the part in *Manglehorn*? Did you audition?

It was weird because I saw the avail. They have something called actors access, and sometimes they post avails, meaning casting roles. I saw it and thought: boy that would be fun to be his [Pacino's] photo double. I happen to be in Austin Texas with John Williams and the casting station, they were the ones casting. They asked me to come down for a Toyota commercial. It was a Monday and I said to the lady who was doing the session for the Toyota commercial: "Well don't you think I look like Al Pacino? I'd like to do that Al Pacino role." She looked at me and said "No. You don't look like Al Pacino." I laughed and she laughed. She fiddled around a bit and then said "Well, what the hell. Go up against the wall and I'll take a picture. I'll send it over and see what they think." So she did, and they sent a note back saying: no his hair is too short. Then, fifteen minutes later, they sent another note saying: send him over.

I went over there and they looked at me and sent me to the hair lady, and the hair lady said: "I can put extensions in the back." Then they sent me to wardrobe and I was the exact same size as him. They let me try on one of his deals. Then they said: "You got it." Right then and there. Whenever I got on set it was learn how to walk like him because he has this funny, floppy walk and that was no problem. All that stuff is easy for me. Then we did the basic photo double stuff. After we had finished all that and we were getting ready at the end, the director and the first AD came over to me. The director is David Gordon Green who is a seasoned director, he's a young guy but he's done some movies. They said to me with a smile, they said: "You don't have to do this. But we would very much appreciate it if you would very much consider doing the bee thing." Meaning grabbing this beehive barehanded.

I never hesitated because I wasn't doing the stunt double or the photo double stuff to be a photo double. I was doing it to get in front of David Gordon Green, so he would consider me for another movie, and in addition to the fact it was an experience to work with an icon of the industry. Al Pacino is a respected icon and somebody that I like. I like him on-screen. He has done some excellent roles. It was intimidating a bit but for some reason I was not afraid at all. It never struck me as being 'oh shit what am I going to do?' I just did. I knew I was going to do it. My mind is set and I'm going to do it.

It was Holy Saturday – I promise you, I prayed [*Laughs*]. I said: "Lord please protect me on this one. Please don't let those bees be after me." I did three takes with the bees and I did two takes with a kind of dummy nest that didn't have too many bees on it. I did three takes with full on bees. These were neighbourhood bees, they all could have stung me. I got popped once and that was it.

Did you spend time with Pacino while on set?

You cut those guys a lot of slack because he's not there to shoot the bull with me. You stand back and stay away from them because that's what they want you to do. He is focussed on doing what he is doing. Some of those old boys are pretty chatty but, most of the time, everybody on set is really focussed on getting the deal done! A couple of times he and I chit-chatted a little bit. He would make a joke about my wardrobe, that mine was better than his.

He'd say: "Yours looks a little better than mine"

I'd say: "If you want I'll just strip off right here and give them to you."

I told David and the first AD, Atilla is his name, I told them: "the deal is I'll do it but I have to have a picture with you and Pacino."

They agreed. David went over to ask him about taking the picture with me, I could see in his face he didn't really want to do it. But he did. I got the picture with us mugging.

Was he nice when you had the picture taken?

He's always nice. He's got no reason to be not nice to anybody. He's a smart cat. He gets it. He understands. He's always nice. I could see in his face that he was a little surprised that David would ask him to take a picture right there on the set. I could see that. But it didn't deter me because I wanted a picture with the guy.

Do you think the bee scene had a deeper significance in the film?

I didn't get it. Why he did the bee thing, I don't know. Maybe it was just a bizarre thing. They held it till the end. It was near the very end of the movie, if I recall correctly. But I didn't get the watermelon thing either. They had some watermelon truck that had gotten into a wreck with watermelons everywhere and maybe it was just for bizarreness in the movie. Maybe they just did that for effect. Maybe that's what he was doing and the bee thing was the same kind of thing. I didn't get it. I think the bee thing played. The cat [Pacino] was there and you could see that because he was doing his mouth thing. You would never know that it wasn't him doing the hand thing.

What are your thoughts on the finished film?

Personally, it was an opportunity for him to do some acting. He wasn't running. He wasn't shooting. He wasn't doing anything. He was doing heart thing [romance] with Holly. I thought there were times in the movie where it did get a little slow. But it's a slow movie, it's a heart movie. It's about him wanting to reach out and have a relationship with a woman. As far as my work: it was what it was. I knew what to expect and that was exactly what it was. I wish they had put a little tattoo on my hand that read: this is Ted Ferguson [*Laughs*].

Location Manager Robbie Friedmann on *Manglehorn*

How did you become involved with this film?

It was a fun project. I've known David [Gordon Green], the director, for many years and I really like working with him. He is really focussed and knows what he wants from his department heads. In this case he knew what he wanted for his locations. I read the script and consult with him and the production designer. David really knows [what he wants] and at the same token he is really good about giving me some creative liberties to find something unusual or different that we can incorporate into the film. One location in particular – at the end there is a boat graveyard – and most people have never seen where boats go to die, it was pretty neat. Once he saw that he said: "We have to put that in the movie somehow."

It is always fun working with him, and working with Pacino... he is a pro. He was really fun to watch. Every single take of the movie he could bring something different. David likes to cast a lot of local people and real people and so they may have been intimidated by Pacino, but Pacino makes them really comfortable very quickly. He is really deep and sincere... I think if you were to meet him for the first time you would be really nervous but then he is easy to talk to and a real person. It was really fun to watch him work his magic. It was the chance of a lifetime.

There are stories that Pacino was sat in a chair on the street, waving to people and reading the local paper while waiting for his next scene.

He was doing that. It was amazing. He wasn't afraid for someone to come up and talk to him. He was putting himself out there. He was enjoying his time here [in Austin, Texas]. I love when actors do that. A lot of them like to be sheltered from the public and don't like to do autographs. It always helps me because I'm going into neighbourhoods and businesses and we are trying to hold people back. He wasn't worried about anything, which is pretty great.

How long did you spend finding the locations?

We usually have a couple of months of preparation. The first thing I do is read the script and I'll make a list of all the locations and then I'll sit down with David and the production designer and say: "What type of direction do we want to go here?" Sometimes it's vague and I have creative liberty to find something unusual or different. I read it one way and then find out they had a different idea. It's a collaborative effort. The locations can help define the characters on what lifestyle they lead and live and their social status. In this case we wanted just a modest, simple house for Pacino. It was tiny house to film in and a lot of us were concerned it was going to be too small for our lights and cameras and equipment and crew, but David said: "This fits his character and I want this house." So we made it work and I thought it worked out really well.

Was it a private residence?

Yeah. It sure was. It happened to be a gentleman who happened to be in the sheetrock business and travelled a lot. It worked out quite nicely because we had the house for, I think, about six weeks where he was on the road and we paid him for the use of his house. We went in and removed all of his things and redecorated and then we restored it at the end. One of the stories I wanted to tell you about is: when we were restoring the property, we are painting things and we are doing our thing and we have about a week to get out of the house before he comes back and I get a call from someone doing work at the home saying a kind of limousine/town car just pulled up and a beautiful woman gets out and the driver gets out and pops open the trunk and gets out a shovel and a big Cyprus tree and they walk around the yard a little bit. The next thing the driver starts digging a hole and proceeds to plant the tree. I had one of my crew members go over and talk to them. They called me back and said: "This woman has been following Al around ever since *The Godfather*, and every film since *The Godfather* has a tree planted at its location." I couldn't believe it.

Did anyone know who she was?

To be honest I don't know, but I had seen her around a little bit and I think Al definitely knows her and they have a friendship of some sort. It turned out she was in town for weeks. She put herself up, I think she was in a nice hotel in town and she had a driver for the whole time she was in town. We were filming at a hotel and I remember her sitting... we were filming in the restaurant and I would see her sitting in the bar area. I went up to her and said: "Can I help you with anything?" she said: "No, I'm just here and maybe wanted to talk to Al if he had a few minutes." I guess they had known each other in forever. But I thought it was an amazing story. I had never heard anything like it. I thought it was unusual but also very cool at the same time. I called the property owner and told him the story and he was blown away by it. I asked: "Would you mind if they planted a Cyprus tree in your yard? Because it's actually already planted" [*laughs*]. He goes: "No. That sounds great." It was kind of a memento for him. Unfortunately the house got torn down and they built a new modern home in its place.

Have you seen the finished film?

I have.

What did you think to it?

I really enjoyed it. When I read it, I see it as one way and when I see the actors and their performances it takes me down a whole 'nother road. I loved Pacino's character. He had such a simple life and he was content and his son with the issues he has. We all, as we grow older, have these quirky things we do and his [Pacino's character] was to go to the cafeteria and eat liver and onions on a certain day of the week. It was so awkward when he went on his date. He goes to her house to pick her up... who would have the time to go to the bathroom? I mean like number two going to the bathroom [*laughs*] prior to picking up the woman on a date. That is what is great about David because he could quite as easily not put that scene in there but it was character development that he insisted be there. David does a lot of things like that where he really wants to go down this road which may not be necessary but it makes a statement. Pacino went along with it, he thought it was funny [*laughs*] and agreed to it. I always like talking to David after and saying: "Well, how did you tell Pacino that you wanted him to go to the bathroom?" David always has a funny way of telling the story, he would say: "OK, you go in there and you're going to meet her and tell her she looks nice and you are going to rush off to the bathroom" [*laughs*]. I loved it.

Danny Collins

Cast: Al Pacino (Danny Collins), Annette Bening (Mary Sinclair), Jennifer Garner (Samantha Leigh Donnelly), Bobby Cannavale (Tom Donnelly), Christopher Plummer (Frank Grubman), Katarina Cas (Sophie), Giselle Eisenberg (Hope Donnelly), Melissa Benoist (Jamie). **Director:** Dan Fogelman.

Synopsis: Danny Collins, an ageing 1970s rocker, can't give up his hard-living ways. But when his manager uncovers a 40-year-old undelivered letter written to him by John Lennon, he decides to change course and embark on a heartfelt journey to rediscover his family, find true love and begin a second act.

English folk singer/songwriter Steve Tilston had a friend and fan in John Lennon. Sadly, Tilston didn't know this until decades after Lennon was shot dead. Lennon's interest in the singer came about due to an interview given to British underground rock music magazine *ZigZag*, a twenty-one-year-old Tilston was asked by journalist Richard Howell if he thought being rich beyond his wildest dreams would change him. Tilston responded that he thought it would change him and the experiences he would have: "Yes, it would have a very detrimental effect." The interview was published in *ZigZag* during the summer of 1971. A copy of the magazine found its way to Lennon's Tittenhurst Park country house. After reading it and disagreeing with the new singer/songwriter's comments, Lennon penned a letter to Tilston and Howell courtesy of the magazine. In the letter, written in black inked scrawls, Lennon said: "Being rich <u>doesn't</u> change your experience in the way you <u>think</u>," and went to explain how experiences, emotions and relationships are all the same no matter if you are rich or poor. He signed it off with "So whadya think of that?" and included his home phone number so Tilston could call him to discuss it further.

Lennon didn't know Tilston's home address so mailed it to ZigZag's office in London, but the letter disappeared. It is said to have arrived at the office but some shameless employee had noted where the letter had come from and promptly kept it for themselves. Neither Howell nor Tilston knew of the existence of the letter at that time. Then in 2005, Tilston received a phone call from an American collector of music memorabilia who wanted to verify that the John Lennon letter he had purchased was genuine and as it was addressed to Tilston who better than to confirm its authenticity. "My first reaction, after the bemusement, was to laugh," recalls Tilston. He confirmed that he had given an interview around that time to *ZigZag Magazine* so the letter could be from Lennon. The collector hung up and over the next few days Tilston told the story to his friends and family. Five years later and with the impending release of Tilston's first novel; *All for Poor Jack,* a bout of press interviews were arranged with different outlets and publications. During the interview with *The Daily Telegraph*'s Laura Roberts the final question asked was: "Tell us something we don't know about Steve Tilston?" He then began to tell the incredible story of Lennon's letter to him.

Tilston thought no more of the interview until the day of publication. Monday 16 August 2010 was the day Tilston's world exploded, thanks to the interview with *The Daily Telegraph*. His story went viral around the world. One of the millions, possibly billions, who read Tilston's astonishing story, was American producer and screenwriter Dan Fogelman. After receiving writing acclaim for his script of the romantic comedy film *Crazy, Stupid, Love* starring Steve Carell and Julianne Moore, Fogelman was looking for his next story: "I was just completely stumped and procrastinating and sitting in front of the blank computer for months on end and looking at the internet as you do when you are procrastinating and I came across this musician who receives a letter from John Lennon forty years too late." Immediately Fogelman was on the phone to Tilston about his Lennon letter story. As Tilston told him more Fogelman started to believe that his story could be the starting point for his latest film script. Over the next few months Fogelman beavered away on the script. While the Lennon letter was imperative to the storyline, Fogelman wanted to make sure the story was geared more towards the idea of family reconnecting after years of estrangement.

When writing the script Fogelman had only Al Pacino in mind for the title role. Pacino was currently starring in the Broadway production of Shakespeare's *The Merchant of Venice*. Luckily, Fogelman managed to get backstage during one of the performances in late 2010. He spoke to Pacino about his script and asked if the actor would be interested in portraying the flamboyant one-hit wonder Danny Collins: "I was asking him to trust me to direct even though I'd never directed anything before. I knew I had to do right by him, which was very stressful." Pacino was excited by the idea of playing a character in a world he had not entered into during his previous film roles. After receiving praise for his turn in *Crazy, Stupid, Love,* comedian Steve Carell was approached by Fogelman to play Danny Collins' estranged son: Tom Donnelly. Carell's production company – Carousel – had a distribution and financing deal with Warner Bros, which made it easier for the studio to green light the production.

The finance and lead actors were in place, and a title had been decided on: *Imagine,* after Lennon's most famous solo song release so it looked as though it'd be safe to start filming. However, the production hit difficulty at Warner Bros and shortly afterwards Carell dropped out which in turn meant that Carousel and Warner Bros pulled out of the deal to finance and distribute. Fogelman, not willing to give up his directorial debut, continued to seek financing for the project while his other scripted works such as *Tangled* and *Cars 2* raked in money for the house of mouse. Still he was struggling to get *Imagine* made until the American talent agency William Morris Endeavor Entertainment stepped in and brokered a deal under their WME Global department with Inimitable Pictures and Mister Smith Entertainment. A $10 million budget came from film producer Nimitt Mankad and also Inimitable Pictures which ran a film fund backed by Manoj Bhargava, the inventor of the 5-hour Energy drink. Around the same time finance was confirmed, a couple of new cast members were announced. Jeremy Renner joined the production to play Tom Donnelly, the role vacated by Carell, and Julianne Moore signed on to play Mary Sinclair the manager of a local Hilton Hotel.

Principal photography was scheduled to begin in the spring of 2013 but, once again, production hit the skids. This time due to the conflicting filming schedules of Moore and Renner. Neither could make it work and consequently both actors dropped out. Fortunately, Fogelman and the producers acted swiftly and tied up Bobby Cannavale (after a recommendation from Pacino) and Annette Bening for the vacant roles. Fogelman convinced Christopher Plummer to sign on for the role of Frank Grubman, Danny Collins' manager and best friend, after Michael Caine had to drop out because of scheduling conflicts. "There is a delicious relationship [between Collins and Grubman], but never cute or sentimental," said Plummer. Jennifer Garner bagged the role of Samantha Leigh Donnelly, Tom's wife, "This gets to the heart of what makes us all love one another and why it is so complicated to love someone else," she later commented.

During pre-production Fogelman and his producers managed to secure the licensing from Lennon's estate for use of the original master recordings of nine songs including 'Working Class Hero,' 'Beautiful Boy,' and 'Imagine.' These songs reflected the tone of the entire film. Two original compositions were needed for the film. 'Hey Baby Doll,' the smash hit that launched Danny Collins' career, was written for the film by Australian singer/songwriter Greg Agar and his Northern Irish singer/songwriter friend Ciaran Gribbin, who had previously worked with Madonna, Paul McCartney and been a lead singer with INXS. The song itself is an earworm that bears an uncanny resemblance to Neil Diamond's 'Sweet Caroline.' For the moody ballad 'Don't Look Down,' Fogelman enlisted American musicians Don Was and Ryan Adams to write something that was the opposite of the upbeat 'Hey Baby Doll' and when Fogelman turned up at the studio to hear the finished track he knew it would be the perfect accompaniment to Collins' introspective moments during the film: "Once Ryan played it for me, I knew it was our song. It's just as important as the first song in setting up who Al's character is." Aware that he had to sing in the film, Pacino spent time with singer/songwriter/pianist and music teacher Gerald White who taught the actor the basics of singing and also how to play the piano. One last production change occurred. The film's title *Imagine* had to be changed because of competing projects that also used the works of Lennon. It could also have been to ensure the film wasn't confused with the 1988 documentary of the same name by Andrew Solt. Fogelman's film was retitled as *Danny Collins*.

Principal photography began in Los Angeles during July 2013. The legendary Chateau Marmont hotel on Sunset Boulevard was used for exterior filming and the sequence in which Pacino drives down Sunset Strip was filmed as dawn was breaking and the streets were empty. A private, two-storey open-plan house with an elevator and a pool was used as Collins' L.A. residence. As the film required concert footage of Collins singing, Fogelman organised a fifteen minute shooting schedule in the middle of a real concert by the band Chicago. On the night of 2 August at the Greek Theatre in Los Angeles, just as the real band broke for their interval, various recording technology was wheeled on stage in preparation for a fake band to arrive. The crowd looked bemused until one of the crew grabbed the microphone and explained that they were about to film a sequence for an upcoming movie and the audience would be involved. Little did they know the performer set to arrive on stage was Al Pacino as Danny Collins. Production flashed up chants on the big screens by the side of the stage so the audience knew what to chant. As Pacino ran out on the stage the crowd leapt to their feet with an almighty roar and started to cheer. "We ran the song seven times. He was actually performing and totally connected to the real audience. It was chaos. It was Pandemonium," recalls Fogelman. As Pacino side-slided his way around the stage, high-fiving those lucky enough to be on the front row, Chicago stood at the back of the stage watching and singing along. The real concert started up shortly afterwards but Pacino was not finished on stage and returned during Chicago's encore of their hit song '25 or 6 to 4' to dance and sing. As the band finished Pacino walked up to the standing microphone and thanked everyone: "This has been so great for a shy guy from the South Bronx."

After filming completed in Los Angeles production jumped to the east coast. A street in leafy New Jersey was used as the lead up to the Donnelly's home, which was a private residence where filming took place outside and in. The majority of filming took place in one New

Jersey location – The Hilton Woodcliff Lake hotel on Tice Boulevard. It was used so much that over 70% of the finished film was shot there. All the exterior footage at the hotel was shot on location. The interior was filmed on a sound stage in Los Angeles. The design team visited the hotel before filming began to take detailed photographs and measurements so they could recreate the exact layout of each room. Fogelman chose that hotel because he had a personal history with it: "I went to every eighth grade party [there]. I was actually a best man four different times in that hotel." It was also chosen because Fogelman wanted the most bizarre hotel that someone of Collins stature would check into: "I pictured the Woodcliff Lake Hilton" he said. Production did such a fantastic job of recreating the interiors that when the film was screened in New Jersey locals thought they had actually filmed inside. Hilton Worldwide were ecstatic that one of their hotels was heavily featured in a new Pacino film and put out a statement that also included the historical, and hugely appropriate, fact that "John Lennon wrote the lyrics to *Imagine* at Hilton New York Midtown."

Even though principal photography had wrapped by the end of summer 2013 *Danny Collins* did not receive its premiere until eighteen months later on the night of 18 March 2015 at the AMC Lincoln Square Theater, New York City. However, this was not the first time the film was screened for an invited audience. Three days earlier a very special preview screening was organised by the Hilton Woodcliff Lake Hotel at the Ramsey Theater in New Jersey. It was followed by a Q&A with Fogelman. To tie in with the U.S. theatrical release, Hilton Hotels placed Steinway Grand Pianos in the lobbies of three of their most high profile locations including the New York Hilton Midtown. Custom notepads were placed in seventy-nine Hilton Hotels in which guests were asked to write down what inspires them and then take a picture and share it on Twitter. Every U.S. Hilton Hotel offered *Danny Collins*-inspired cocktails during March and April.

The film was released in selected U.S. theatres on 20 March 2015. It garnered glowing reviews from the critics with the praise mainly aimed at Pacino. *Rolling Stone* said: "Al Pacino is the life of the party as Danny Collins." *The Washington Post* thought Pacino was "channelling equal parts

Tom Jones and Barry Manilow" and that he "delivers an impressive performance." *The New York Times* wrote: "Al Pacino injects a zany charge of adrenaline into the title role." For all the positive reviews that were flying around for *Danny Collins* the slow release schedule did not help ticket sales. It opened in only five theatres during its first week of U.S. release generating a minimal return of just $96,000. By week four it had expanded into seven hundred and thirty-nine cinemas and took a respectable $2 million during that week alone. That was as good as it got for *Danny Collins*. The film slowly started to be pulled from theatres the following week. It eventually made it to eleven weeks before disappearing completely. In that time it had returned $5.6 million (Information courtesy of Box Office Mojo. Used with permission). Even though it was an independent release, a total U.S. theatrical receipt of $5.6 million against a budget of $10 million was not the type of return anyone would have wanted. It also struggled in other territories upon release. It didn't make over $1million in even one of the other thirty-one countries it was released in. Pacino did pick up a Golden Globe nomination for his performance, but lost out to Matt Damon in *The Martian*. 'Hey Baby Doll' and 'Don't Look Down' were also long-listed for Best Original Song at the 2015 Academy Awards but were cut from the final shortlist. By the middle of the year nearly everyone had forgotten about *Danny Collins* except *Entertainment Weekly's* Chris Nashawaty who suggested it was one of 2015's most overlooked movies in his "Ask the Critic" column. He was puzzled as to the "lack of love" it received and that it contained Pacino's "best performance since 1997's *Donnie Brasco.*"

Finally, it clicks. Finally, Pacino gets to perform in a comedy that is actually funny. That offers him the chance to not only be wacky but also to use his method acting and it all culminates in a delightful and heartfelt performance. At times he hams up the part in spectacular fashion; this is not a criticism rather a belief that this approach best fits the character of Collins and the storyline. The opening scene in which Pacino sings in front of thousands sees him skip and hoot around the stage with a great big smile on his face and there are many other moments in which he revels in the comedic side of Collins. Some of the finest moments in the film come from the interaction between Pacino and Bening as they playfully bicker about going on a date or what Collins is wearing i.e. "How do I look?" asks Collins. "You look slightly ridiculous," replies Sinclair. To which Collins beam a wide smile and says "Nahhhhh, I look sharp!"

Bening is especially on top form when playfully teasing. She keeps Collins at arm's length, tantalizing him enough to keep coming back with the same dinner request in the hope that she will say "Yes." There could be a whole other film made about those two characters simply interacting with each other. Pacino's method acting comes into play as a lot of what Collins has been through in the previous decades – drink, drugs, and women – mirrors Pacino's life during the 1970s. It is one of the few times in his career in which he could dig into his own life to find the character. Arguably Pacino wasn't able to so personally relate to a character he was playing since *Scarface*. The actor perfectly captures the male tendency of not opening up until it's too late.

The story then offers a chance for Pacino and Cannavale to bounce off each other with the inclusion of some tender moments. The casting of Pacino and Cannavale as father and son is inspired. Not only do they look alike but they also are very similar in terms of acting styles. Both are reserved but showcase the occasional touches of flamboyance. There is great respect, compassion and depth between the two actors and their characters. They could, genuinely, pass as father and son if you saw them on the street together.

It isn't just Pacino, Cannavale and Bening who connect so well however, even the secondary characters play off one another like they are real family and/or friends. From Christopher Plummer's deadpan one liners to Jennifer Garner's loveable yet exhausted mother all the way through to Josh Peck's wet behind the ears hotel valet. It is a menagerie of different characters who fit together like a complex jigsaw.

Danny Collins was Fogelman's feature film directorial debut (he had been a writer for a while, so it's no surprise he can create great characters) and with it he has created a film that explores the most universal of human needs – love. The film proudly wears its heart on its sleeve for all to see. It doesn't do anything different to what has been done many, many times before but the journey through the rippling waters of comedy, drama and romance makes the film enjoyable viewing. It helps that the writer/director knows how to end a film with a tear or two of joy. The final two minutes of *Danny Collins* pack one heck of an emotional gut punch.

As adorable and funny as *Danny Collins* can be, the emotional core of the film focuses on the idea of a man trying to find himself and, hopefully, start over again.

Actor Katarina Cas on *Danny Collins*

What did you think to the script when you first read it?

I thought it's a beautiful story about redemption and values, and I liked the fact that Sophie (the character I am portraying) serves as a kind of comic relief to the story, which is really a story about reconnecting with one's self and family.

Do you think Sophie was only ever after Danny's money? Or was there a more loving side to her we didn't see?

I think Sophie and Danny love each other, maybe just not in a traditional way. Danny is like a father figure to her, he takes care of her, and in return she represents the youth and spontaneity that is fleeing from him. If she was just another blonde, he would've just had fun with her and then ditched her, yet he made her his fiancée, so there must to be something more here that made him feel it could work. I think Sophie is sweet and genuinely likes him and respects him in return, but she's also young and beautiful and she likes to have spontaneous fun, so maybe that's the reason she has a younger lover on the side, besides the obvious, gaping age difference between them. I see Sophie and Danny remaining friends, even after Danny realizes they are seeking different lifestyles and takes on a new path in life.

Sophie is quite bold with her body and how much she shows of it in this film. Did you find that a daunting prospect?

Sophie is such a funny character. The nude scene was written just for comic relief really and I didn't find it sexy or sexual, just funny. I think the scene really shows her character beautifully, she's careless, young and free, so why would she be embarrassed before her fiancée's eyes?

***Danny Collins* showcases the comedic side of Pacino. What was he like to act opposite?**

Pacino is genuinely a funny and sweet guy, so this makes it very easy to act opposite him, he really makes you feel at ease. He's witty, calm and willing to talk about all sorts of stuff. I had lots of fun on-set with him and Christopher Plummer, who is also very sharp and witty and he was over 80 when we shot *Danny Collins*! Pacino and Plummer were so cute together, they laughed a lot doing their scenes. Adorable.

Did he give you any advice or tips on the way to play a scene with him?

He more or less just let me do my thing. Of course we talked about the scenes and the motivation of the characters and I felt very relaxed playing scenes with him... Even during auditions, when I had to play opposite him for the first time, I was surprised that I wasn't feeling nervous around him at all. He was just so cool, it felt like we knew each other for ages. He even improvised in that scene, and I went along and had loads of fun! Auditions aren't always fun, they can be very stressful, but not with Pacino in the room. I think his relaxed mode and his natural way of acting drives an actor opposite him in the same direction. Everything feels natural, even the shower scene we did, haha.

Is there a difference between Pacino on and off camera?

Well, of course. Privately I didn't feel like I was talking to Tony Montana from *Scarface*, in reality he's a really sweet guy. We talked about all kinds of stuff and we also discussed theatre a lot, which we found we are both really fond of. I really enjoyed listening to all his stories. How he and Bobby Cannavale met, how he discovered Jessica Chastain and what a great experience it was working on his film *Salomé* with her. We talked a lot about Scorsese as well, since we've both worked with him etc. It's hard to explain what an honour it was for me that I can talk about all this stuff with a legend like he is. Oh, and yeah... he has a golden retriever like I do. And I like people who like dogs.

Dan Fogelman is a well known comedic actor/writer/producer. *Danny Collins* is his feature film directorial debut. How did you find him as a director?

Dan was very sweet and funny and it was great working with him. We talked a lot about the scenes and he was modest and open to suggestions from us actors, so it really felt like a collaborative process, which I liked. I like directors who focus on the story first. And he really is funny, no wonder he writes so many funny stuff. He is a cool fun man, and I wish him all the best.

The movie certainly makes it appear that everyone involved had an enjoyable time making it. Was that the case for you?

Your feelings are correct. There was a really nice energy from everyone on the set - from the producers to all the actors and the crew and it made the whole experience really enjoyable for everyone, it was really a beautiful bunch of people.

Final question, did you get to taste the _Danny Collins_ cake that is served at the birthday party?

Haha, no I didn't. There was so many good stuff in the catering cart, they really spoiled us on-set, so in the end I didn't even crave the cake.

Misconduct

Cast: Josh Duhamel (Ben Cahill), Anthony Hopkins (Arthur Denning), Al Pacino (Charles Abrams), Alice Eve (Charlotte Cahill), Malin Akerman (Emily Hynes), Byung-hun Lee (The Accountant), Julia Stiles (Jane Clemente), Glen Powell (Doug Fields). **Director:** Shintaro Shimosawa.

Synopsis: When an ambitious young lawyer takes on an important case against the ruthless executive of a large pharmaceutical company, he becomes embroiled in a world of blackmail and corruption.

Many films released in Hollywood come from spec scripts: non-commissioned unsolicited screenplays that writers produce hoping to sell to a studio or production company. If the script is overwhelmingly impressive it can end up on The Black List, a website that lists the most promising motion picture screenplays yet to be produced. Previous Black List entries include Oscar winners such as *The Fighter*, *Life of Pi* and *The Wolf of Wall Street*. The majority of spec scripts don't make it onto The Black List yet still manage to be picked up for production thanks to agents who are keen to flog their client's works to studios at any price. Some writers even take a fee of $1 simply to get their films made and bolster their script writing credentials.

Adam Mason and Simon Boyes began writing movies in 2006. The first script the pair ever had produced was a horror film called *Broken*. In addition to penning the screenplay the duo also took responsibility for the direction. They followed that project up with more horror films: *The Devil's Chair*, *Luster* and *Blood River*, a comedy: *Junkie* and a thriller: *Not Safe for Work*. Their next script: *Beyond Deceit* was picked up by Skydance Productions. The success of films such as *Mission Impossible- Ghost Protocol*, *Jack Reacher* and *Star Trek Into Darkness* meant Skydance Media were actively seeking screenplays, and Mason and Boyes's thriller was next on their list. However, the production stalled very early in development and was put on hold. Two of the executive producers on the film – Barry Brooker and Stan Wertlieb – took the screenplay to their colleagues at Lionsgate Films, who immediately jumped at the chance of taking the project on.

Following the switch from Skydance to Lionsgate, *Beyond Deceit* was swiftly put into pre-production under the studio's subsidiary company Mandate Pictures. Shintaro Shimosawa was brought in for his directorial debut and due to his writing & producing experience on TV shows such as *Ringer*, *The Following* and *Intelligence* (and due to his writing experience on the movie *Repentance* starring Forest Whitaker and Anthony Mackie), Shimosawa did a rewrite on Mason and Boyes's script: "I love thrillers with smartly drawn characters. There's nothing more compelling than watching people make horrible mistakes who can't live with themselves," commented Shimosawa. By early February 2015 a full cast had been assembled including Malin Akerman as Emily Hynes, Julia Stiles as Jane Clemente, Byung Hun Lee as The Accountant and Dan Stevens as Ben Cahill. Also, for the first time ever, veteran actors Al Pacino and Sir Anthony Hopkins would come face-to-face on camera as they played Charles Abrams and Arthur Denning respectively. The shoot was due to start in New Orleans around late March, but production hit a problem just a month beforehand. Stevens had to drop out due to scheduling conflicts with the filming of Disney's live action retelling of *Beauty and the Beast*. Shortly after the setback, production replaced Stevens with American actor Josh Duhamel and also signed up British actor Alice Eve to play Ben's wife Charlotte. A budget of $11 million was set by Mandate Pictures and Mike and Marty Productions, a new production company based in New Orleans.

Principal photography began in New Orleans on 20 March 2015. Pacino had been working with FBI profiler Jim Clemente on the psychology of his character, Abrams. Not that he needed that much background information when he was on-set for less than five days. Sir Anthony also managed to film his scenes in less than a week. It was left to Duhamel, Eve, Akerman, Stiles and Lee to complete their scenes by the end of scheduled filming on 17 April. Lee later said of his scene with Pacino: "I memorized all of my lines perfectly, but forgot everything when I stood in front of the camera. I had to stop filming in the middle, and Al Pacino came up to me to say "It's OK. Just keep going, and do it again" It was an amazing experience to work with Al Pacino."

Several private residences and an office building overlooking the famous U.S. Route 90 that snakes through New Orleans were used as shooting locations. Three days were spent filming in the residential area of St. Charles Avenue and Valence Street. The Octavia Art Gallery on Julia Street and the legendary Palace Cafe on New Orleans famous Canal Street were also included in the schedule. Production shut down the restaurant for interior filming and closed off the street to film the inside action from the outside. Once principal photography wrapped, Lionsgate quickly acquired the US distribution for *Beyond Deceit* (thanks in part to their subsidiary Mandate Pictures producing the film) and set a vague, early 2016 release date. Film Bridge International, a US financing and distribution company, were hoping to sell the film internationally at the Cannes Film Festival later that month.

The first trailer appeared online on 16 December 2015. However, the film had been re-titled to *Misconduct* as executives felt that *Beyond Deceit* could be misheard and misconstrued as Beyond Da Sea. Reviews started to appear from early February 2016. *The New York Times* said: "Except for Anthony Hopkins and Al Pacino, going through their familiar paces, incompetent is the word." *The New York Daily News* hit harder: "The title doesn't but should, refer to the filmmaker's professionalism." Its short U.S. theatrical run returned just $24,000. If that blow wasn't bad enough, the knockout punch came when it was released in the UK. Only the Reel Cinemas chain agreed to screen the film upon its release on 3 June (it did also receive a VOD release at the same time). Even then, it was only programmed at five of Reel's fifteen cinemas and all of those screenings took place outside London, at the likes of Kidderminster and Burnley – small provincial towns.

By the end of its first full weekend on UK release the film had earned a grand total of £97 ($188.41). Websites and newspapers were rife with stories of Hopkins and Pacino's latest film bombing spectacularly. *The Telegraph's* Tim Robey called *Misconduct*: "The worst film Anthony

Hopkins and Al Pacino have ever made." The film did manage respectable returns in South Korea, where it raked in over $900,000, and Italy, where it made just shy of $700,000 (Information courtesy of Box Office Mojo. Used with permission). In Sweden, France and Germany it snuck out on DVD and Japan had to wait until January 2017 before being able to watch what Wendy Ide of *The Guardian* called: "World-class levels of dreadfulness."

Two of the three actors listed above the film's title have "Academy Award Winner" next to their names but *Scent of a Woman* and *The Silence of the Lambs* are distant relatives to this terrible piece of trash. *Misconduct* wants to play out like a neo-noir thriller with more twists and turns than a helter skelter. When actually it's an under-cooked movie that is trying way too hard and lacks any intrigue. Its main focus is pharmaceutical corruption but numerous other elements are thrown in, in the hope that something will be of interest to the viewer. None of it is. The director should have got to grips with the plot right from the start; instead it appears as if Shimosawa directed individual scenes without any thought as to what preceded it or was to follow. Sloppy direction, when present, normally leaks into other areas of a film, and that is certainly the case here. The continuity is all over the place in terms of character stylings and set design. The cinematography includes some of the strangest decisions ever committed to celluloid, including shooting a conversation between Duhamel and Powell in which we only ever see Powell and a scene in which Pacino walks down a hall-way completely consumed in darkness, even though the hallway is bathed in strip lighting. One final case in point, is towards the end of the film, when Duhamel, Eve and Lee's characters are seen in a disused church, the final shot is slowly revolved 180 degrees. These are just a few of the many many bizarre directing decisions in this film.

Misconduct is a film written by men, directed by a man, the main stars are men and, evidently from the treatment and portrayal of the female characters, the movie is aimed at men. Stiles' private bodyguard cum detective is little more than a mouth piece to inform Denning what his next moves should be. It is a complete waste of a secondary, yet influential character. Meanwhile, Eve has been directed to play her character Charlotte Cahill as moody, self absorbed and distant. As soon as she appears on screen the audience take an instant dislike to her. She seems to be away with the fairies for half the runtime, and the other half is spent bitching to her husband. The worst female character in the film however is undoubtedly Akerman's Hynes: a sexual predator who sheds her clothes the second she is through her apartment door. Her character is the catalyst for the entire plot (or, at least, what plot there is), yet she is treated despicably by the writers as she seduces and is then abused by a variety of men. If that wasn't enough, Akerman has to suffer the indignity of standing at the apartment window topless for no reason whatsoever other than affording the target audience the luxury of seeing her breasts glistening in the moonlight.

All this said, the male characters are given mere fragments more, in terms of character. Duhamel prods and pokes his way through what is a central role. He could be an interesting character but with poor writing, a lack of clear direction and some below-par acting it is a lead character that nobody cares about. Those coming to this film to see Hopkins and Pacino face-off against each other shouldn't bother. Both of them have minimal screen time and are phoning it in throughout. Hopkins cocks his head back and delivers his lines as if he's still secretly playing Dr Hannibal Lecter, completely grating against the tone of the movie. He creates a character without sympathy or empathy and it makes for awkward viewing. The script is incredibly weak but Hopkins could have offered more than a watered down Lecter.

Pacino, with a bouffant of hair and chiselled goatee, ducks in and out of the film at irregular intervals. Struggling to capture a southern accent. Abrams could, and should, have been an interesting character in the hands of an actor of Pacino's calibre. Instead we are presented with a one-dimensional lawyer who is less interesting than the pen he writes with. Pacino and Hopkins are two of the greatest scene-chewers in cinema history. So why hold them back? This film was crying out for them to bark at each other during the one scene they have together but both spend more time talking to Duhamel. The tension and thrill of watching Hopkins and Pacino go toe-to-toe in *Misconduct* should have been akin to the diner scene in *Heat* between Pacino and De Niro.

Instead Pacino and Hopkins lazily huff and puff their way through three minutes of wasted opportunity. The one saving grace for Pacino, and the entire movie, is the finale where he gets to spout Shakespearean dialogue (probably a direct request from Pacino) to Duhamel and waves a gun around frantically. It is the one lively moment in the entire narrative but the audience is made to sit through ninety-something minutes of utter bilge to witness two minutes of quality acting.

During one scene, Pacino snarls the line: "What are we doing here?" A question a little too close to home for viewers of *Misconduct*.

Actor Skye P. Marshall on *Misconduct*

When you signed on to star in *Misconduct*, were you nervous about acting opposite two legendary movie stars?

I was more excited than nervous to be working with Al Pacino and Sir Anthony Hopkins. Like most, I am a huge fan of both actors, and have been since I was a teenager. I knew this experience would be an opportunity of a lifetime. I just wanted to appreciate every moment and remain grateful.

Your character Hatty appears to be quite an aggressive lawyer, do you think she would have eventually become CEO at the law firm?

I loved playing Hatty! She was all about the business. A straight shooter. Hatty was surely working her way up the ladder full of hungry wolves at that law firm. CEO would've definitely been on her vision board.

There is a boardroom scene between Pacino and Hopkins. What was it like to be part of that?

At first, I wasn't supposed to be in the boardroom scene. But then the director, Shintaro Shimosawa approached me and said: "We're putting you in the scene and sitting you next to Pacino." I actually fell to my knees while tightly hugging Shintaro's legs yelling: "Thank you, thank you!" Being an actor, sitting in that boardroom was definitely a master-class. Pacino and Hopkins have two very different acting techniques, respectfully. While absorbing their every move, I couldn't help but to think: "I'm watching Tony Montana have a face-off with Hannibal Lecter!!!" It was the only scene in the movie, and in their careers, where they performed together. It is definitely one of the most unbelievable moments of my life that I will cherish.

What was it like to act alongside Al Pacino?

I first met Al Pacino during a rehearsal with Josh Duhamel at the beautiful Saenger Theatre in the French Quarter [New Orleans]. I was in awe of him. Just his presence alone was captivating. When he introduced himself to me, he had a way of really connecting with his eyes accompanied by his warm smile. During the boardroom scene, we would joke and laugh between takes which for me, took the pressure off. Pacino is great at improvising. You never know what he might say. The cast would have to stay true to the moment and just go with his flow. He was incredible.

Did you get to spend much time with him off-camera?

The night before our first day of filming, Pacino invited a few cast and crew members to dinner at Brennan's Restaurant in the French Quarter. As I walked into the restaurant, Pacino and one of the producers, Chris Brown, were already seated. I decided to take the seat next to Pacino. I probably didn't breathe for the first ten minutes. But then Pacino turned to me and asked: "So where are you from?" From that moment we were instant friends (in my head), chatting away about our experiences living in NYC and LA for a good twenty minutes. Then Josh Duhamel, who was sitting at the end of the table asks: "So Skye, is it true you served in the military?" I froze, as all eyes were now on me when they should've been on Pacino! It was an incredible night hearing his stories about *The Godfather*, *Scarface* and dating Diane Keaton. I also learned that Pacino has quite the sweet tooth. We had another dinner together the night before he wrapped. This dinner was more relaxing for me because I had been stalking him around set for the past two weeks. It was as lovely as the first time.

What was the off-camera interaction between Sir Anthony and Al like? Were they always laughing and joking? Or did they behave like serious actors discussing their craft?

The one day of production when Pacino and Hopkins worked together, I can tell they were both very happy to have finally had the opportunity to share a camera frame. They looked to be more serious in conversation than joking (while I hid behind a nearby hallway plant in attempt to eavesdrop).

What is it that makes Al Pacino one of the greatest actors ever?

What makes Al Pacino one of the greatest actors ever, is his majestic ability to captivate an audience in suspension of disbelief. He pours his heart and soul into every character he plays, while fully embodying their pain and pleasure. He is a magician on the screen and stage with a thousand masks. He is the definition of hard work, gumption and dedication. Al Pacino is a true legend in the world of performing arts.

Acknowledgements

Thank you to Alfredo James Pacino for producing such a rich and varied acting career.

Thank you to all the interviewees who feature in this book. Your time and willingness to talk to me is hugely appreciated.

Also thanks to all the managers, agents and lawyers who said "Yes" and scheduled time with their client(s).

My personal thanks go to the following people who aided me with this book: Lawrence Grobel, Nigel Floyd, Jason Palmer, Joff Hopkins, David Inger, Cat Park @ Ten Letter PR, Maryann O'Connor, Daniel Hatton, Harry Lin, Leonard Sultana, Simon Thompson and Sam, Damian, Mark & Michael at Copyright Repro Ltd.

This book would not have been possible without the love and support of the following three people:

Helen Cox. A brilliant editor who made me a better writer during the process. Every writer needs an editor and I'm proud that Helen agreed to be mine. You were a delight to work with and never stopped pushing me. Also Helen is 50% responsible for me writing this book when she planted the seed of an idea in my mind one drunken day in a London boozer. Thank you Helen.

My Mum, Denise. Thank you for everything you have ever done for me. You are a true inspiration and an amazing mum. My mum is 50% responsible for this book when, years ago, she would rent the Scent of a Woman VHS tape for me on a near weekly basis because I was underage. Thank you (I think?!).

My partner, Samantha. Firstly an apology – Sorry for talking about Al Pacino far too much over the past two years. I imagine it got quite boring. I'll try to stop now. In all seriousness, thank you for putting up with me while writing this book and thank you for your unconditional love through the years.

About the Author

Mark Searby is a film critic and broadcaster. He is the resident film critic on the Anglian Radio Station network in the UK and has written for numerous media outlets including: Heat Magazine, MTV, New Empress Magazine, Entertainment Focus, Flicks And The City, Screenjabber and An Englishman in San Diego. Mark has written and presented video retrospectives on movies such as *Serpico*, *Scarecrow* and *The 'Burbs*. He is also a seasoned interviewer and has conversed with film industry figures such as Mark Millar, Ben Wheatley, Michel Gondry and many more.

Before becoming obsessed with movies, Mark was a DJ for many years. He travelled around the UK appearing at numerous bars and nightclubs including Ministry Of Sound, The Dogstar and Sugar Hut Brentwood.

Mark can be found following, and being regularly disappointed by, his favourite football team Nottingham Forest. He is huge addict of the TV show The Wire and will tell anyone & everyone that it is the greatest TV show of all time. He is also an avid collector of limited edition movie memorabilia.

More information about Mark can be found on his website: www.marksearby.com

He can be found on Twitter: @Mark_Searby

Bibliography

Books

Aiello, Danny. *I Only Know Who I Am When I Am Somebody Else*. New York: Gallery Books, 2014.

Baxter, John. *De Niro: A Biography*. London: HarperCollins UK, 2003.

Cowie, Peter. *The Godfather Treasures: The Official Motion Pictures Archives*. London: Carlton Publishing, 2012.

Gilvey, John Anthony. *Jerry Orbach, Prince of the City: His Way from the Fantasticks to Law & Order*. Milwaukee, Wisconsin: Applause Theatre & Cinema Book Publishers, 2011.

Grobel, Lawrence. *Al Pacino The Authorized Biography*. Great Britain: Simon & Schuster, 2006.

Grobel, Lawrence. *"I Want You In My Movie!" My Acting Debut and Other Misadventures Filming Al Pacino's Wilde Salome*. New York: HMH Press, 2014

Heard, Christopher. *Depp*. Toronto, Canada: ECW Press, 2001.

Hunter, Allan. *Gene Hackman*. New York: St. Martin's Press, 1987.

Jenkins, Tricia. *CIA in Hollywood: How the Agency Shapes Film and Television*. Austin, Texas: University of Texas Press, 2012.

Keaton, Diane. *Then Again*. London: Fourth Estate, 2011.

Kendrick, James. *Hollywood Bloodshed: Violence in 1980s American Cinema*. Carbondale, Illinois: Southern Illinois University Press, 2009.

Kondazian, Karen. *The Actor's Encyclopedia of Casting Directors*. Los Angeles, California: Lone Eagle Publishing Company, 2000.

Longworth, Karina. *Anatomy of an Actor Al Pacino*. Paris: Phaidon Press Limited, 2013.

Lumet, Sidney. *Making Movies*. New York: Vintage Books, 1996.

McNally, Terrence (Edited by Silverman Zinman, Toby). *Terrence McNally: A Casebook*. New York: Routledge, 2013

Meyer, Janet L. *Sydney Pollack: A Critical Filmography*. Jefferson, North Carolina: McFarland & Company, 1998.

Munn, Michael. *Gene Hackman*. London: Robert Hale Limited, 1997.

Perkins, Murray."Case Study: The Panic in Needle Park (1971)." *Behind The Scenes at the BBFC*, edited by Edward Lamberti, 87. London: Palgrave Macmillan, 2012.

Schoell, William. *The Films of Al Pacino*. New York: Citadel Press, 1995.

Sheldon, David & McCall, Joan. *When I Knew Al*. Augusta, Georgia: Harbor House, 2005.

Sylbert, Richard. *Designing Movies: Portrait of a Hollywood Artist*. Westport, Connecticut: Praeger Publishers, 2006.

Taylor, David. *The Making of Scarface*. London: Unanimous Ltd, 2005.

Yule, Andrew. *Al Pacino A Life On The Wire*. Great Britain: Warner Books, 1992.

Magazines

Collins, Andrew. "The Boys and the Black Stuff." *Empire* 104 February 1998: 60-64.

De Semlyen, Nick. "Cuban Fury." *Empire* 296 February 2014: 120-123.

Fussman, Cal. "The Actor." *Esquire* Vol 12 No. 10 October 2002: 178-184.

Gray, Marianne. "Speak of the Devil." *Film Review* February 1998: 48-51.

Gray, Marianne. "Talk of the Devil." *Flicks* Vol 11 January 1998: 26.

Mottram, James. "The Total Film interview: Al Pacino." *Total Film* 230 April 2015: 118-121.

Nathan, Ian. "Pacino." *Empire* 181 July 2004: 120-126.

Websites

American Film Institute. *afi.com* 29 September 1967. 25 March 2016.
<http://www.afi.com/>

Box Office Mojo. *IMDB.com, Inc* July 2008. 14 March 2017.
<http://www.boxofficemojo.com/>

Cinema Review. *Cinema Review* n.d. 20 December 2016.
<http://www.cinemareview.com/themain.asp>

Filmography – Al Pacino's Loft. *Susan Duckett* September 1997. 11 May 2017.
<http://velvet_peach.tripod.com/apacinofilmography.html>

The Internet Movie Database. *IMDB.com, Inc* 17 October 1990. 7 May 2017.
<http://www.imdb.com/>

Playbill. *Playbill Inc* n.d. 25 January 2017. <http://www.playbill.com/>

Webpages

Abrams, Simon. "Inessential Essentials: Re-considering Christopher Nolan's Insomnia." *Movieline* 3 July 2012. 5 January 2017.
<http://movieline.com/2012/07/03/christopher-nolan-insomnia-al-pacino-robin-williams/>

 "Al Pacino injures eye during gunfight scene on Stand Up Guys set." *Ace Showbiz* 26 April 2012. 14 October 2016.
<http://www.aceshowbiz.com/news/view/00050009.html>

"Al Pacino plays Dr. Kevorkian in HBO's You Don't Know Jack." *Tiny Swot* 17 April 2010. 15 November 2016. http://tinyswot.com/al-pacino-plays-dr-kevorkian-in-hbos-you-dont-know-jack/

"And the Oscar for best scenery..." *USA Today* 20 March 2003. 6 January 2017.
<http://usatoday30.usatoday.com/travel/news/2003/2003-03-20-movie-wanderlust.htm>

Andrew, Geoff. "Christopher Nolan." *The Guardian* 27 August 2002. 5 January 2017. <https://www.theguardian.com/film/2002/aug/27/features>

Arbeiter, Michael. "Interview: David Gordon Green on making Manglehorn."
Indiewire 17 June 2015. 20 November 2016.
<http://www.indiewire.com/2015/06/interview-david-gordon-green-on-making-manglehorn-an-homage-to-al-pacino-working-with-harmony-korine-and-more-262873/>

B, Brian. "Jeremy Irons replaces Ian McKellen in The Merchant Of Venice."
Movieweb n.d. 4 September 2016. <http://movieweb.com/jeremy-irons-replaces-ian-mckellen-in-the-merchant-of-venice/>

Badertscher, Vera Marie. "Alaska: Movie-Insomnia-Drop Dead Gorgeous." *A Traveler's Library* 26 January 2011. 6 January 2017.
<http://atravelerslibrary.com/2011/01/26/alaska-movie-insomnia-drop-dead-gorgeous/>

Bamigboye, Baz. "Another film flop for Katie Holmes? Reports of audience walking out exaggerated." *Daily Mail* 26 January 2011. 1 November 2016.
<http://www.dailymail.co.uk/tvshowbiz/article-1350556/Katie-Holmes-film-flop-Reports-audience-walking-exaggerated.html>

Bennetts, Leslie. "Author! Author! shoots in N.Y., N.Y." *New York Times* 24 January 1982. 20 April 2016
<http://www.nytimes.com/1982/01/24/movies/author-author-shoots-in-ny-ny.html?pagewanted=all&_r=0>

Bernstein, Richard. "Despite the Odds, Glengarry is being filmed." *The New York Times* 15 August 1991. 16 April 2016.
<http://www.nytimes.com/1991/08/15/movies/despite-the-odds-glengarry-is-being-filmed.html>

"Beyond Deceit miscellaneous notes." *TCM* n.d. 8 November 2016.
<http://www.tcm.com/tcmdb/title/2057029/Beyond-Deceit/misc-notes.html>

"Beyond Deceit: film prject announced in Berlin." That Dan Stevens 8 February 2015. 7 November 2016. <http://www.dan-stevens.co.uk/content/beyond-deceit-film-project-announced-berlin>

Bhanoo, Sindya N. "Dr: Death Jack Kevorkian dies at age 83." *The Washington Post* 3 June 2011. 14 November 2016.
<https://www.washingtonpost.com/local/obituaries/dr-death-jack-kevorkian-dies-at-age-83/2010/12/03/AGhktuHH_story.html>

Blackwelder, Rob. "Memento recognition landed Christopher Nolan in the director's chair for big-budget Insomnia." *Spliced Wire* 6 May 2002. 5 January 2017. <http://www.splicedwire.com/02features/cnolan.html>

Brown, Mick. "David Mamet on Phil Spector: I Don't Give A Damn About The Facts." *The Telegraph* 29 June 2013. 10 March 2016. <http://www.telegraph.co.uk/culture/tvandradio/10148042/David-Mamet-on-Phil-Spector-I-dont-give-a-damn-about-the-facts.html>

Butko, Brian. "Tunnel Diner in Jersey City slated for demolition." Brian Butko 26 March 2008. 26 April 2016. <https://brianbutko.wordpress.com/2008/03/26/tunnel-diner-in-jersey-city-slated-for-demolition/>

Butler, Isaac and Kois, Dan. "Angels in America: The complete oral history." *Slate* 28 June 2016. 20 October 2016. <http://www.slate.com/articles/arts/cover_story/2016/06/oral_history_of_tony_kushner_s_play_angels_in_america.html>

Byron, Shaun. "You Don't Know Jack shooting of HBO film takes place in Pontiac." *Oakland Express* 16 October 2009. 14 November 2016. <http://www.theoaklandpress.com/article/OP/20091016/NEWS/310169990>

Caffeinated Clint. "Interview: Ellen Barkin." *Moviehole* 14 June 2007. 30 September 2016. <http://moviehole.net/200711151interview-ellen-barkin>

"Cannes: See Al Pacino, Anthony Hopkins in first Beyond Deceit photo." *Yahoo Movies* 6 May 2015. 7 November 2016. <https://www.yahoo.com/movies/cannes-see-al-pacino-anthony-hopkins-first-beyond-180132736.html>

Carroll, Larry. "Movie file: Sylvester Stallone, Jack Black, Fantastic Four 2, Claire Danes & More." *MTV* 26 October 2005. 15 November 2016. <http://www.mtv.com/news/1512325/movie-file-sylvester-stallone-jack-black-fantastic-four-2-claire-danes-more/>

Castillo, Monica. "Manglehorn director David Gordon Green talks working with Al Pacino and growing up at any age." *International Business Times* 19 June 2015. 20 November 2016. <http://www.ibtimes.com/manglehorn-director-david-gordon-green-talks-working-al-pacino-growing-any-age-1975652>

"Casting Call: New York City auditions for Channing Tatum's Son of No One." *Channing Tatum unwrapped* 4 March 2010. 30 October 2016. <http://channingtatumunwrapped.com/2010/03/casting-call-new-york-city-auditions-for-channing-tatums-son-of-no-one/>

Cerone, Daniel. "Exorcising His Dark Side." *L.A. Times* 13 August 1994. 28 April 2016. <http://articles.latimes.com/1994-08-13/entertainment/ca-26620_1_paul-schrader>

Clark, Ashley. "Revolution in the head? – Al Pacino and the 1980s." *BFI* 28 January 2014. 19 April 2016. <http://www.bfi.org.uk/news-opinion/news-bfi/features/revolution-head-al-pacino-1980s>

Collin, Robbie. "Heat: how Michael Mann made his coolest film." *The Telegraph* 19 February 2015. 16 June 2016. <http://www.telegraph.co.uk/film/blackhat/pacino-deniro-making-of-heat/>

Collins, Glenn. "Back in the Maelstrom; Filming Resumes." *The New York Times* 23 May 1991. 31 March 2016. <http://www.nytimes.com/1991/05/23/movies/back-in-the-maelstrom-filming-resumes.html>

Connecticut Bob. "Pacino, De Niro filming in Milford." *Future DV* 16 September 2007. 4 August 2016. <http://futuredv.blogspot.co.uk/2007/09/pacino-de-niro-filming-in-milford.html>

Culpepper, Andy. "The Insider goes public." *CNN* 5 November 1999. 30 June 2016. <http://edition.cnn.com/SHOWBIZ/Movies/9911/05/insider.culpepper/>

"Danny Collins." *History vs Hollywood* n.d. 5 December 2016. <http://www.historyvshollywood.com/reelfaces/danny-collins/>

David. "Daily Film locations." *Before The Trailer* 27 January 2011. 11 December 2016. <http://www.beforethetrailer.com/2011/01/jan-28-through-30-filming-locations-in-los-angeles-chicago-new-york-and-other-locations-including-shameless-now-and-jack-and-jill/>

David. "Filming locations for movie Win Win in New York." *Before The Trailer* 15 April 2010. 1 November 2016.

<http://www.beforethetrailer.com/tag/filming-locations-for-movie-win-win-in-new-york/>

"Donnie Brasco 15th Anniversary: 25 Things You Didn't Know About Johnny Depp's Classic Mob Movie." *Moviefone* 27 February 2012. 10 April 2016. <http://www.moviefone.com/2012/02/27/donnie-brasco-15th-anniversary/>

"Donnie Brasco True Story – Real Joseph D. Pistone, Lefty Ruggerio." *Chasing The Frog.* 9 April 2016. <http://www.chasingthefrog.com/reelfaces/donniebrasco.php>

Doty, Meriah. "On 20th Anniversary of Heat, Henry Rollins recalls getting punched in the face by Al Pacino." 14 December 2015. 16 June 2016. <https://uk.movies.yahoo.com/on-20th-anniversary-of-heat-henry-rollins-170722830.html>

Easton, Nina J. "Paramount's Epic Godfather III Struggle." *L.A. Times* 25 December 1990. 5 March 2016. <http://articles.latimes.com/1990-12-25/entertainment/ca-7119_1_godfather-iii/3>

Ebiri, Bilge. "Barry Levinson on Kevorkian, Pacino and his enduring love of Baltimore." *Vulture* 23 April 2010. 14 November 2016. <http://www.vulture.com/2010/04/barry_levinson_on_kevorkian_pa.html>

Eder, Richard. "Film: Gassman in Scent of a Woman." *New York Times* 26 January 1976. 27 May 2016. <http://www.nytimes.com/movie/review?res=9D02E1DB123DE532A25755C2A9679C946790D6CF>

Fagerholm, Matt. "Pacino, Lennon and Danny Collins: A Chat with Dan Fogelman." *Roger Ebert* 16 March 2015. 4 December 2016. <http://www.rogerebert.com/interviews/pacino-lennon-and-danny-collins-a-chat-with-dan-fogelman>

Feldberg, Isaac. "Josh Duhamel, Alice Eve go Beyond Deceit." *We Got This Covered* n.d. 6 November 2016. <http://wegotthiscovered.com/movies/josh-duhamel-alice-eve-deceit/>

Ferenczi, Aurélien. "What was Truffaut going to do with Spielberg?" *Télérama* 26 October 2014. 10 January 2016. <http://www.telerama.fr/cinema/qu-allait-donc-faire-truffaut-chez-spielberg,118402.php>

"15 things you (probably) didn't know about Carlito's Way." *Shortlist* 14 July 2014. 6 April 2016. <http://www.shortlist.com/entertainment/films/15-things-you-(probably)-didnt-know-about-carlitos-way>

Figueroa, Daniel. "Everything You Ever Wanted To Know About The Al Pacino – Robert De Niro Scene In Heat." Uproxx 17 January 2015. 17 June 2016. <http://uproxx.com/movies/the-diner-scene-in-heat/>

"Finding the true story: Producer Steve Lee Jones." *Variety 411* n.d. 16 November 2016. <http://variety411.com/article/finding-the-true-story-producer-steve-lee-jones-3941954/>

Fisher, Bob. "Packing Heat." *International Cinematographers Guild* 1 September 2008. 4 August 2016. <http://www.icgmagazine.com/web/september-cover-story-righteous-kill/>

Fleischer, David. "Reel Toronto: The Recruit." *Torontoist* 12 August 2008. 6 July 2016. <http://torontoist.com/2008/08/reel_toronto_the_recruit/>

Fleming, Michael. "Minutes helmer clocks in." *Deadline Hollywood* 18 July 2005. 8 August 2016. <http://variety.com/2005/film/markets-festivals/minutes-helmer-clocks-in-1117926172/>

Foley, Jack. "Ocean's Thirteen – Al Pacino interview." *Indie London* n.d. 30 September 2016. <http://www.indielondon.co.uk/Film-Review/oceans-thirteen-al-pacino-interview>

Foley, Jack. "The Merchant Of Venice – Al Pacino talks Shakespeare." *Indie London* n.d. 5 September 2016. <http://www.indielondon.co.uk/film/merchant_venice_pacinoQ&A.html>

Foley, Jack. "The Recruit – Roger Donaldson Q&A." *Indie London* n.d. 5 July 2016. <http://www.indielondon.co.uk/film/recruit_donaldsonq&A.html>

Fordham, Joe. "Cinefex Vault #1: Angels in America." *Cinefex* 19 April 2016. 18 October 2016. <http://cinefex.com/blog/angels-in-america/>

Fox, Chloe. "Rialto Bites." *Telegraph Magazine* n.d. 4 September 2016. <http://www.movision.co.uk/nonflash/documents/DailyTelegraphMoVenicespread.pdf>

Frederik. "Move of the Week: Angels In America." *Simply Streep* 9 January 2012. 18 October 2016. <http://www.simplystreep.com/2012/01/09/movie-of-the-week-angels-in-america/>

French, Philip. "Glengarry Glen Ross review." *The Guardian* 14 September 2014. 17 April 2016. <http://www.theguardian.com/culture/2014/sep/14/glengarry-glen-ross-classic-dvd-philip-french-review?utm_source=twitterfeed&utm_medium=twitter>

Friedkin, William. "William Friedkin pens Tribute to Jerry Weintraub." *Hollywood Reporter* 15 July 2015. 23 March 2016. <http://www.hollywoodreporter.com/news/william-friedkin-pens-tribute-jerry-808558>

Frook, John Evan. "Miramax buys U.S. rights to Two Bits." *Variety* 12 January 1994. 6 May 2016. <http://variety.com/1994/film/news/miramax-buys-u-s-rights-to-two-bits-117386/>

"Gainesville's own little slice of Hollywood." *The Gainesville Sun* 3 March 2006. 24 May 2016. <http://www.gainesville.com/article/20060303/entertainment/60302008>

Golianopoulos, Thomas. "The unhinged madness behind the making of Any Given Sunday." *Complex* 21 December 2015. 30 May 2016. http://uk.complex.com/sports/2015/12/any-given-sunday-revisited

Gordon Bette & Sussler, Betsy. "Al Pacino" *Bomb Magazine 1990*. 15 February 2016. <http://bombmagazine.org/article/1363/al-pacino>

Green, Jessica. "Al Pacino on Elliot Morton: A Mafioso Richard III?" *Open Vault* 15 July 2011. 12 May 2016. <https://blog.openvault.wgbh.org/2011/07/15/cataloging-elliot-norton-a-mafioso-richard-iii/>

Harris, Will. "Zeljko Ivanek on Damages, Lost, and playing the good guy for a change." *AV Club* 17 September 2012. 8 April 2016. <http://www.avclub.com/article/zeljko-ivanek-on-idamagesi-ilosti-and-playing-the--84984>

Hartlaub, Peter. "Andrew Niccol's present tense/director takes current technology to the next level in comedy Simone." *SF Gate* 22 August 2002. 12

September 2016. http://www.sfgate.com/entertainment/article/Andrew-Niccol-s-present-tense-Director-takes-2807796.php

Henry, Katie. "Adam Sandler says he did Shirtless things to get Katie Holmes on board for Jack and Jill." *Popsugar* 10 November 2011. 12 December 2016. <http://www.popsugar.com/entertainment/Adam-Sandler-Katie-Holmes-Jack-Jill-Video-Interview-20333030>

Heron, Christopher. "Art vs. Commerce: David Gordon Green interview (Manglehorn)." *The Seventh Art* 6 September 2016. 20 November 2016. <http://theseventhart.org/david-gordon-green-interview-manglehorn/>

"Hilton Hotels & Resorts sets the stage for a story about love, inspiration and second chances." *Hilton* 13 March 2015. 3 December 2016. <http://news.hilton.com/index.cfm/news/hilton-hotels-resorts-sets-the-stage-for-a-story-about-love-inspiration-and-second-chances?tl=fr>

Howard, Becky. "Film Flash!" *This Is London* 13 May 2004. 8 August 2016. <http://www.standard.co.uk/goingout/film/film-flash-6966871.html>

Humphreys, Justin. "Out of order: Norman Jewison dishes on Justice." *Read The Hook* 5 November 2009. 17 March 2016. <http://www.readthehook.com/83878/film-out-order-norman-jewison-dishes-ijusticei>

"In brief: Pacino gets 88 Minutes to save his life." *The Guardian* 19 July 2005. 9 August 2016. <https://www.theguardian.com/film/2005/jul/19/news2>

"In Pictures – Merchant of Venice Premiere." *BBC* 30 November 2004. 4 September 2016. <http://news.bbc.co.uk/1/hi/in_pictures/4054601.stm>

"Insomnia filming locations." *Chris Nolan Wikia* n.d. 5 January 2017. <http://chrisnolan.wikia.com/wiki/Insomnia_filming_locations>

"Insomnia." *Film In America* n.d. 6 January 2017. <http://www.filminamerica.com/Movies/Insomnia/>

"Insomnia: Christopher Nolan." *SBS* 6 September 2002. 6 January 2017. <http://www.sbs.com.au/ondemand/video/11693123634/insomnia-christopher-nolan>

"Insomnia: Steven Soderbergh on choosing Christopher Nolan." *Movieweb* n.d. 6 January 2017. <http://movieweb.com/movie/insomnia/steven-soderbergh-on-choosing-christopher-nolan/>

"Interview with Jerry Schatzberg for Scarecrow." *Fresques* n.d. 4 June 2016. <http://fresques.ina.fr/festival-de-cannes-en/fiche-media/Cannes00418/interview-with-jerry-schatzberg-for-scarecrow.html>

"Interview with Tony Kushner." *HBO* n.d. 17 October 2016. <http://www.hbo.com/movies/angels-in-america/interview/tony-kushner.html>

Jacobs, Alexandra. "Television; When it comes to TV Angels, He's batting .500." *The New York Times* 7 December 2003. 17 October 2016. <http://www.nytimes.com/2003/12/07/arts/television-when-it-comes-to-tv-angels-he-s-batting-.500.html?_r=0>

Jacobs, Susan. "Hilton rolls out the red carpet for Danny Collins film release." *Smart Meetings* 20 March 2015. 5 December 2016. <http://www.smartmeetings.com/trends/3451/hilton-rolls-out-red-carpet-for-danny-collins>

Jacques, Ian and Shoults, Tim "Williams wows 'em." *The Chief* 29 May 2001. 6 January 2017. <https://web.archive.org/web/20141223231057/http://squamishlibrary.digital collections.ca/uploads/r/squamish-public-library/2/2/22816/20010529_The_Chief.pdf>

James, Caryn. "Al Pacino reins himself in for Danny Collins." *The Wall Street Journal* 12 March 2015. 5 December 2016. <http://www.wsj.com/articles/al-pacino-reins-himself-in-for-danny-collins-1426175789>

Jay Cohen." *Show Me The F#ck!ng Money* n.d. 15 May 2016. <http://showmethefkingmoney.tv/jay-cohen/>

Jobson, Robert and Sanchez, Matheus. "Charles and Camilla meet pal Pacino." *Evening Standard* 30 November 2004. 4 September 2016. <http://www.standard.co.uk/showbiz/charles-and-camilla-meet-pal-pacino-7198384.html>

Kaplan, James. "Why Keanu won't sell his soul." *Whoa is (not) me* n.d. 25 May 2016. <http://www.whoaisnotme.net/articles/1997_09xx_why.htm>

Kelly, Laurent. "Al Pacino movie The Son of No One prompts walk-outs at Sundance." *What Culture* 25 January 2011. 1 November 2016. <http://whatculture.com/film/al-pacino-movie-the-son-of-no-one-prompts-walk-outs-at-sundance>

King, Susan. "Catching the Scent of a Rising Star." *L.A. Times* 26 December 1992. 26 May 2016. <http://articles.latimes.com/1992-12-26/entertainment/ca-2363_1_gabrielle-anwar>

Kish, Dean. "Interview: Christopher Nolan talks about Insomnia and other future projects." *Showbiz Monkeys* 7 May 2002. 6 January 2017. <http://www.showbizmonkeys.com/features.php?id=1268>

Kit, Boris. "Lionsgate picks up Al Pacino-Anthony Hopkins thriller Beyond Deceit." *Hollywood Reporter* 1 April 2015. 6 November 2016. <http://www.hollywoodreporter.com/news/lionsgate-picks-up-al-pacino-785773>

Knowles, Harry. "Harrison Ford and Jonathan Demme to team up on their next film... Insomnia." *Ain't It Cool News* 8 September 2000. 5 January 2016. <http://www.aintitcool.com/node/6875>

Ktgriswell. "Rhodes Theatre." *Cinema Treasures* 26 June 2007. 14 February 2016. <http://cinematreasures.org/comments?page=2&theater_id=11660>

Lafrance, J.D. "Glengarry Glen Ross." *Radiator Heaven* 2 March 2012. 16 April 2016. http://rheaven.blogspot.co.uk/2012/03/glengarry-glen-ross.html

Lamble, Ryan. "Michael Mann's Heat: how research created a classic thriller." *Den of Geek* 8 May 2013. 14 June 2016. <http://www.denofgeek.com/movies/heat/25530/michael-manns-heat-how-research-created-a-classic-thriller>

Lang, Brandon. "About Me." *About Me* n.d. 15 May 2016. https://about.me/brandonlang

Lang, Brent. "Lowell Bergamn on why Mike Wallace really hated The Insider." *The Wrap* 14 May 2012. 30 June 2016. <http://www.thewrap.com/lowell-bergman-why-mike-wallace-really-hated-insider-39206/>

"Larry King goes one-on-one with Gene Hackman." *CNN* 7 July 2004. 5 June 2016. <http://edition.cnn.com/TRANSCRIPTS/0407/07/lkl.01.html>

Lawrence, Malcolm. "Interview with James Foley." *Tower of Babel* December 1995. 6 May 2016.
<http://www.towerofbabel.com/sections/film/cinemastardust/foley.htm>

Lee, Alana. "The Recruit: Al Pacino interview." *BBC* n.d. 5 July 2016.
<http://www.bbc.co.uk/films/2003/02/19/al_pacino_the_recruit_interview.s
html>

Leins, Jeff. "Al Pacino, Katie Holmes join Jack and Jill." *News In Film* 26 August 2010. 14 December 2016.
<https://web.archive.org/web/20100830025744/http://www.newsinfilm.com
/2010/08/26/al-pacino-katie-holmes-join-jack-and-jill/>

"Letter from Lennon: The Leicester folk singer and the true story behind the film Danny Collins." *Leicester Mercury* 18 July 2015. 5 December 2016.
<http://www.leicestermercury.co.uk/letter-lennon-leicester-folk-singer-s-true-
story/story-26931933-detail/story.html>

Levine, Debra. "Scarecrow cinematographer Vilmos Zsigmond @ LACMA."
Arts Meme 23 January 2011. 5 June 2016.
<http://artsmeme.com/2011/01/23/vilmos-zsigmond-scarecrow-
cinematographer-lacma/>

Lindsay. "The Jack and Jill House." *I am not a stalker* 24 April 2012. 11 December 2016. <http://www.iamnotastalker.com/2012/04/24/the-jack-and-
jill-house/>

"Looking Through Richard: Al Pacino and his call to Shakespeare." *American Popular Culture* December 2001. 12 May 2016.
<http://www.americanpopularculture.com/archive/film/pacino_shakespeare.h
tm>

"Lopez and Affleck ordered to reshoot Gigli." *Killer Movies* 13 December 2002. 27 September 2016.
<http://www.killermovies.com/g/gigli/articles/2606.html>

Lowe, Alexander. "Exclusive interview: David Gordon Green talks Manglehorn." *We Got This Covered* n.d. 19 November 2016.
<http://wegotthiscovered.com/movies/exclusive-interview-david-gordon-
green-talks-manglehorn/>

Lublow, Arthur. "Travolta and Stallone" *People Magazine* 7 March 1983. 6 March 2016. <http://www.people.com/people/archive/article/0,,20084435,00.html>

Lucca, Violet. "Interview: Bill Pankow" *Filmcomment* 26 March 2015. 4 April 2016. http://www.filmcomment.com/blog/interview-bill-pankow/

Luck, Richard. Always Be Closing: The Making of Glengarry Glen Ross." *Sabotage Times* 14 August 2014. 16 April 2016. <http://sabotagetimes.com/tv-film/always-closing-making-glengarry-glen-ross>

"Mangelhorn." *Cinema Cats* n.d. 20 November 2016. <http://www.cinemacats.com/?p=7598>

Martin Donovan." *Oocities* 15 May 2003. 6 January 2017. <http://www.oocities.org/hollywood/makeup/1432/insomnia.html>

McClintock, Pamela. "AFM 2012: Jeremy Renner, Julianne Moore join Al Pacino starrer Imagine." *Hollywood Reporter* 23 October 2012. 5 December 2016. <http://www.hollywoodreporter.com/news/afm-2012-jeremy-renner-julianne-381971>

McNamara, Melissa. "Clooney Dives into Ocean's 13." *CBS News* 28 March 2008. 1 October 2016. <http://www.cbsnews.com/news/clooney-dives-into-oceans-13/>

McNary, Dave. "Al Pacino-Anthony Hopkins thriller Beyond Deceit gets financing." *Variety* 13 May 2015. 7 November 2016. <http://variety.com/2015/film/news/al-pacino-anthony-hopkins-thriller-beyond-deceit-financed-1201494760/>

Miller, Julie. "Al Pacino did not want Michelle Pfeiffer for Scarface and 8 other revelations about the gangster classic." *Moveline* 24 August 2011. 13 April 2016. <http://movieline.com/2011/08/24/al-pacino-did-not-want-michelle-pfeiffer-for-scarface-and-8-other-revelations-about-the-gangster-cla/>

Minow, Neil. "Interview: Dan Fogelman writer/director of Danny Collins." *Movie Mom* n.d. 5 December 2016. <http://www.beliefnet.com/columnists/moviemom/2015/03/interview-dan-fogelman-writerdirector-of-danny-collins.html>

Mobarak, Jared. "Interview: David Gordon Green, director of Manglehorn." *Jared Mobarak* 19 June 2015. 19 November 2016.

<http://www.jaredmobarak.com/2015/06/19/interview-david-gordon-green/>

"Mobile Home For Sale." *Fireline* n.d. 24 May 2016.
<http://www.fireline.org/kb4mhh/forsale/location.html>

Morris, Gary. "William Friedkin's Cruising." *Bright Lights Film Journal* 1 April 1996. 23 March 2016. <http://brightlightsfilm.com/william-friedkins-cruising/#.VmayUtKLR48>

Mulcahey, Matt. "Maybe the mechanic would be good for this: DP Tim Orr on Manglehorn." *Filmmaker* 25 June 2015. 20 November 2016.
<http://filmmakermagazine.com/94686-maybe-the-mechanic-would-be-good-for-this-tim-orr-on-manglehorn/#.WCLmzNSLR48>

Myers, Wayne. "A wretched Richard III and a splendid Richard III." *Oneida Daily Dispatch* 26 February 2006. 11 May 2016.
<http://www.oneidadispatch.com/article/OD/20060216/NEWS/302169995>

Neibuhr, Gustav. "Sculpture in a Movie Leads to Suit." *The New York Times* 5 December 1997. 26 May 2016.
<http://www.nytimes.com/1997/12/05/us/sculpture-in-a-movie-leads-to-suit.html>

"No seat for Al Pacino in Venice." *Rediff* 8 September 2004. 4 September 2016.
<http://www.rediff.com/movies/2004/sep/08pacino.htm>

Nunez, Jessica. "You Don't Know Jack brings Al Pacino and other big stars to Detroit." MLive 15 October 2009. 14 November 2016.
<http://www.mlive.com/entertainment/detroit/index.ssf/2009/10/you_dont_know_jack_brings_al_p.html>

O'Farrell, Stephen. "Al Pacino Wilde Salome Premiere." *Click TV* n.d. 29 January 2016. <https://vimeo.com/37427927>

Olivieri, Christopher. "Al Pacino comedy The Humbling was filmed at St. George Theater." *This Way On Bay* 4 February 2015. 24 October 2016.
<http://thiswayonbay.com/al-pacino-comedy-humbling-filmed-st-george-theater/#>

"Pacino first heard about Carlito Brigante in a YMCA gym in New York in 1973." *Liquisearch.* 6 April 2016.
http://www.liquisearch.com/carlitos_way/production

Patches, Matt. "Martin Brest directed Beverly Hills Cop, Midnight Run and, Yes, Gigli. Then He vanished. Why?" *Playboy* 19 December 2014. 26 September 2016. <http://www.playboy.com/articles/what-happened-to-director-martin-brest>

"People I Know." *Myriad Pictures* 2 March 2001. 10 October 2016. <https://web.archive.org/web/20010302055319/http://myriadpictures.com/PeopleIKnow.html>

"People I Know." *On The Set Of New York* n.d. 10 October 2016. <http://onthesetofnewyork.com/peopleiknow.html>

Perry, Amanda. "Young actor bonds with Pacino in Two Bits." *The Daily Cougar* Vol 61 Summer 1996. 5 May 2016. <http://archive.thedailycougar.com/vol61/87fubar3/8a.html>

"Photo Flash: Al Pacino, et all attend Wilde Salome premiere." *Broadway World* 4 September 2011. 30 January 2017. <http://www.broadwayworld.com/article/Photo-Flash-Al-Pacino-et-al-Attend-Wilde-Salome-Premiere-20110904>

Pierrette, Maximilien. "The cinema (visionary) by Andrew Niccol." *Allocine* 17 April 2013. 12 September 2016. <http://www.allocine.fr/article/dossiers/cinema/dossier-18591758/?page=4&tab=0>

R, Nathaniel. "Not much divergence in these box office grosses." *The Film Experience* 22 March 2015. 26 October 2016. <http://thefilmexperience.net/blog/2015/3/22/not-much-divergence-in-these-box-office-grosses.html>

Radish, Christina. "Writer/Director Dito Montiel The Son of No One interview." *Collider* 4 November 2011. 1 November 2016. <http://collider.com/dito-montiel-the-son-of-no-one-interview/>

"Rahway On Film." *Rahway Rising* 10 March 2008. 26 April 2016. <http://www.rahwayrising.com/rahway-on-film/>

Reeves, Tony. "The Recruit film locations." *Movie Locations* 7 September 2014. 6 July 2016. <http://www.movie-locations.com/movies/r/Recruit.html#.V2zmA9QrJ49>

Reid, Michael D. "Robin Williams endeared himself during Port Alberni shoot." *Times Colonist* 11 August 2014. 5 January 2017. <http://www.timescolonist.com/news/local/robin-williams-endeared-himself-during-port-alberni-shoot-1.1308498>

"Remembering the film Revolution." *King's Lynn Forum* 22 June 2015. 1 May 2016 <http://www.kingslynn-forums.co.uk/viewtopic.php?f=14&t=352>

Reynolds, Dave. "You Don't Know Jack – Or, Kevorkian: The Movie." *Ragged Edge Online* 1 November 2005. 14 November 2016. <http://www.raggededgemagazine.com/departments/mediacircusblog/000581.html>

Reysen, Jamie. "The Secrets of Kaufman Astoria Studios." *AM New York* 13 January 2016. 6 April 2016. <http://www.amny.com/lifestyle/secrets-of-new-york/secrets-of-kaufman-astoria-studios-1.11310255>

Rigoulot, Leslie. "Looking For Richard." *Film Scouts* 28 January 1996. 12 May 2016. <http://www.filmscouts.com/scripts/interview.cfm?File=al-paci>

Robert. "Jack and Jill (2011)" *Movie locations and more* 12 April 2014. 11 December 2016. <http://movielocationsandmore.blogspot.co.uk/2014/04/jack-and-jill-2011.html>

Roberts, Sheila. "Danny Collins interview: Al Pacino." *Collider* 17 March 2015. 5 December 2016. <http://collider.com/al-pacino-danny-collins-interview/>

Rogers, Jude. "How a letter from John Lennon to foilk singer Steve Tilston inspired the new Al Pacino movie." *The Guardian* 21 May 2015. 5 December 2016. <https://www.theguardian.com/music/2015/may/21/letter-john-lennon-singer-steve-tilston-al-pacino-film-danny-collins>

S, Paul. "Heat" *Then & Now Movie Locations* n.d. 16 June 2016. <http://thennowmovielocations.blogspot.co.uk/2013/12/heat.html>

"S1m0ne." *Box Office Prophets* n.d. 11 September 2016.
<http://www.boxofficeprophets.com/tickermaster/listing.cfm?TMID=624:S1
m0ne>

Saenger, Diana. "Screenwriter conquers Insomnia." *Reeltalk* n.d. 5 January 2017.
<http://www.reeltalkreviews.com/browse/viewitem.asp?type=feature&id=20>

Sampson, Mike. "Interview: Christopher Nolan." *Joblo* 22 May 2002. 4 January
2017. <http://www.joblo.com/movie-news/interview-chris-nolan>

Savlov, Marc. "Psych analysis: An interview with screenwriter Joseph Stefano."
The Austin Chronicle 15 October 1999. 5 May 2016.
<http://www.austinchronicle.com/screens/1999-10-15/74285/>

"Scarecrow filming locations." *The Movie District* n.d. 6 June 2016.
<http://www.themoviedistrict.com/scarecrow/>

Scott, Mike. "Legal thriller Beyond Deceit starring Al Pacino and Anthony
Hopkins, begins filming in new Orleans." *New Orleans Times-Picayune* 1 April
2015. 6 November 2016.
<http://www.nola.com/movies/index.ssf/2015/04/al_pacino_new_orleans.ht
ml>

Shone, Tom "Ben Affleck talks about his new film Argo." *The Telegraph* 6
November 2012. 27 September 2016.
<http://www.telegraph.co.uk/culture/film/9646122/Ben-Affleck-talks-about-
his-new-film-Argo.html>

Simon, Alex. "Cruising With Billy." *The Hollywood Interview* 12 February 2013. 22
March 2016. <http://thehollywoodinterview.blogspot.co.uk/2008/01/cruising-
with-billy.html>

Simon, Alex. "Mike Newell: Cinema of the Common Man." *The Hollywood
Interview* 11 November 2012. 10 April 2016.
http://thehollywoodinterview.blogspot.co.uk/2008/03/mike-newell-
hollywood-interview.html

Smith, Anne. "The Recruit: Roger Donaldson interview." *BBC* n.d. 5 July 2016.
<http://www.bbc.co.uk/films/2003/02/19/roger_donaldson_the_recruit_inte
rview.shtml>

Smith, Scott W. "Writing Scent of a Woman." *Screenwriting from Iowa* 30 March 2010. 26 May 2016. <https://screenwritingfromiowa.wordpress.com/2010/03/30/writing-scent-of-a-woman/>

Smith, Scott. "Andrew Neiderman." *Complete V.C. Andrews* n.d. 25 May 2016. <http://www.completevca.com/art_palmsprings.shtml>

Snider, Eric D. "12 Fascinating Facts About Dog Day Afternoon." *Mentalfloss* 21 September 2015. 4 January 2016 <http://mentalfloss.com/article/68565/13-fascinating-facts-about-dog-day-afternoon>

Snider, Mike. "Scarecrow: Hackman at his best." *USA Today* 11 July 2005. 5 June 2016. <http://usatoday30.usatoday.com/life/movies/reviews/2005-07-11-hackman-dvds_x.htm>

Solomons, Jason. "Director Hugh Hudson on the shooting of Revolution with Al Pacino." *The Observer 21* March 2009. 5 May 16. <http://www.theguardian.com/film/2009/mar/22/revolution-al-pacino-hugh-hudson?CMP=share_btn_tw>

Stern, Christopher. "Settlement reached in Devil's Advocate case." *Variety* 16 February 1998. 26 May 2016. <http://variety.com/1998/film/news/settlement-reached-in-devil-s-advocate-case-1117467814/>

Steven Soderbergh's state of cinema talk." *Deadline* 30 April 2013. 1 October 2016. <http://deadline.com/2013/04/steven-soderbergh-state-of-cinema-address-486368/>

Stivers, Cyndi. "Sunny-Side Up." 1 October 1991. *Premiere Magazine* 30 March 2016. <http://www.gorgeouspfeiffer.com/blog/?p=1357>

"Story Notes for Donnie Brasco." *AMC* August 2011. 10 April 2016. <http://www.amc.com/talk/2011/08/story-notes-trivia-donnie-brasco>

Swanson, Tim and Fleming, Michael. "Lopez is getting Gigli." *Variety* 29 October 2001. 28 September 2016. <http://variety.com/2001/film/news/lopez-is-getting-gigli-1117855030/>

"The Insider." *Jeffrey Wigand* n.d. 28 June 2016. <http://www.jeffreywigand.com/theinsider.php>

"The Son of No One." *On The Set Of New York* n.d. 1 November 2016.
<http://onthesetofnewyork.com/thesonofnoone.html>

"13 Questions with Brandon Lang." *Askmen* n.d. 17 May 2016.
<http://uk.askmen.com/celebs/interview_200/215_brandon_lang_interview.h
tml>

"Through the smoke: An in-depth analysis of The Insider." *Team The Mass* n.d.
28 June 2016. <http://teamthemass3.blogspot.co.uk/p/wigand-reality-vs.html>

Tobias, Scott. "Christopher Nolan." *AV Club* 5 June 2002. 7 January 2017.
<http://www.avclub.com/article/christopher-nolan-13769>

Topel, Fred. "Soderbergh emotional over Ocean's Thirteen." *Rotten Tomatoes* 12
December 2006. 1 October 2016.
<https://editorial.rottentomatoes.com/article/soderbergh-emotional-over-
oceans-thirteen/>

Topel, Fred. "Two for the Money: An interview with Matthew McConaughey."
Black Film October 2005. 18 May 2016.
<http://www.blackfilm.com/20050930/features/matthewmcconaughey.shtml
>

Tuner, Matthew. "Interview: David Gordon Green (Director of Manglehorn)."
Vodzilla 5 August 2015. 20 November 2016.
<http://vodzilla.co/interviews/interview-david-gordon-green-director-of-
manglehorn/>

"U.S. Premiere of Al Pacino's Wilde Salome." *Esse PR* 10 May 2012. 29 January
2017. <https://www.behance.net/gallery/3887993/US-Premiere-of-Al-
Pacinos-Wilde-Salome>

Valdez, Joe. "Glengarry Glen Ross." *The Distracted Globe* 17 July 2008. 16 April
2016. <http://thisdistractedglobe.com/2008/07/17/glengarry-glen-ross-
1992/>

Van Maanen, James. "Dito Montiel's The Son of No One opens: Q&A with the
talented, energetic filmmaker." *Trust Movies* 5 November 2011. 29 October 2016.
<http://trustmovies.blogspot.co.uk/2011/11/dito-montiels-son-of-no-one-
opens-q.html>

Walsh, David. "Hysteria never helped anyone." *World Socialist Web Site* 12 February 2000. 31 May 2016. <https://www.wsws.org/en/articles/2000/02/anyg-f12.html?view=article_mobile>

Wayne, Gary. "Dexter filming locations season 8." *Seeing Stars* n.d. 11 December 2016. <http://www.seeing-stars.com/Dexter/ItalianRestaurant.shtml>

Wayne, Gary. "Filming locations of the movie Heat." *Seeing Stars* n.d. 16 June 2016. <http://www.seeing-stars.com/Locations/Heat1.shtml>

Weinraub, Bernard. "Real-life Drama." *Chicago Tribune* 15 October 1992. 15 April 2016. <http://articles.chicagotribune.com/1992-10-15/features/9204030557_1_pacino-and-lemmon-glengarry-glen-ross-jerry-tokofsky>

"'The Winning Streak' When Terrence Winter was producing The Sopranos ten years ago." *The Economist* 20 August 2011. 12 March 2016. <http://www.economist.com/node/21526314>

Wood, Jennifer. "Heat at 20." *Rolling Stone* 15 December 2015. 15 June 2016. <http://www.rollingstone.com/movies/news/heat-at-20-michael-mann-on-making-a-crime-drama-classic-20151215?page=6>

Zurawik, David. "In winning 11 Emmys, Angels is part of history." *Baltimore Sun* 20 September 2004. 19 October 2016. <http://articles.baltimoresun.com/2004-09-20/news/0409200257_1_hbo-mini-eleanor-and-franklin>

Image Credits

All photos courtesy of Alamy.com except

"Al Pacino & Courtney Galiano" © Courtney Galiano

"Jessica Chastain & Al Pacino at Salome & Wilde Salome premiere" © Mark Searby